Educational I

Steven M. Mininger

MW01277766

Educational Psychology
An Introduction

Gary S. Belkin
Long Island University

Jerry L. Gray
University of Iowa

Wm. C. Brown Company Publishers
Dubuque, Iowa

Book Team

Ed Bowers, Jr. Publisher
David Corona Designer
Marilyn Phelps Design Layout Assistant
Mary Heller Visual Research
Ruth Richard Manager, Production-Editorial Department
Joyce Oberhausen Production Editor

Wm. C. Brown Company Publishers

Wm. C. Brown President
Larry W. Brown Executive Vice-President
Ann Bradley Director of Marketing Strategy
Jim Buell Director of Information Management
John Carlisle Assistant Vice-President, Production Division
Robert Chesterman Comptroller
David Corona Design Director
Lawrence E. Cremer Vice-President, Product Development
Richard C. Crews Publisher
John Graham National Marketing Manager
Chuck Grantham National College Sales Manager
Linda Judge Director of Personnel/Public Relations
Roger Meyer Assistant Plant Superintendent
Paul Miller Vice-President/Director, University Services
Roy Mills Assistant Vice-President/Plant Superintendent
Ed O'Neill Vice-President, Manufacturing
Dennis Powers Director of Information Services

Contents

Part 1   The Life of the Learner

vii

Part 2 The Psychology of Learning

Contents

7 Conditions and Processes of Affective Learning 243

8 Conditions and Processes of Cognitive Learning 301

9   Conditions and Processes of Psychomotor Learning   341

Part **3** **Teaching: Art and Science**

10   The Teacher as a Person   367

11   Theories and Processes of Teaching   409

12   Approaches to Classroom Management   445

13   Elements of Instruction: A Survey and Synthesis   475

14   Teaching the Exceptional Learner   511

15 Group Processes in the Classroom   561

16 Evaluation of Learning and Teaching   591

We asked ourselves at the beginning of this venture two questions: What is the value of an educational psychology textbook? and, Is there a need for another text in this area? These are, we soon realized, not independent questions, but two halves of the same question. In our attempts to find answers, we raised new questions, and from these blossomed still other questions. Finally, through persistent questioning and challenging of answers, we arrived at the format for this book.

We recognized at the outset that education, and particularly educational psychology, always begins with the learner. The learner is the central focus of every educator's efforts. We decided, therefore, to investigate the life of the learner in all of its psychological, intellectual, and sociocultural complexity. This led us into the areas of developmental psychology and child development research, where we found a wealth of information that helped us to appreciate better how the learner comes to be what he or she is.

Throughout these months of research, we were troubled by a number of questions. Should an educational psychology book emphasize developmental psychology? If so, which areas should be highlighted? How can the findings from these areas be translated into insights valuable to the teacher? What principles of organization should guide our choice and arrangement of material?

From these questions, the structure of Part One, "The Life of the Learner," began to emerge. At the same time, we began to recognize that a new introductory educational psychology textbook could have important value in showing the student the breadth and depth of developmental processes from an educational perspective: that is, focusing on those findings most germane to the concerns of teachers and educators.

As we approached the crucial subject of learning—the sine qua non of educational psychology—new problems and questions began to crop up. Which theories of learning are most applicable to the classroom situation? How can some of the more complicated theories be presented clearly, yet comprehensively? Which types of learning should be stressed? How should the areas be organized?

The task was formidable, but we knew that our efforts to organize the vast resources of research would directly affect the student's ability to learn the material. We divided between us the theories and domains of learning: Jerry Gray took on the challenges of explicating the theories of learning and motivation and of examining the conditions and processes of cognitive and psychomotor learning; Gary Belkin focused on the affective domain and moral learning. As we worked, we sought out each other's ideas in making these sometimes confusing, sometimes difficult theories into practical, usable ideas to which students could refer when they became teachers. Again, we wanted the text to serve as a tool in later teaching endeavors.

The structure of Part Two, "The Psychology of Learning," reflects what we considered to be the major contributions of learning theory. Chapter 6 outlines the basic principles of learning and motivation— including transfer, conditioning, and retention—setting forth the prominent theories, and synthesizing their myriad insights into practical implications. The next three chapters examine, with more attention to detail, the three domains of human learning: the affective, the cognitive, and the psychomotor. For each, the conditions and processes for successful learning are presented, with examples that we hope will be useful for the classroom teacher.

Finally, the greatest challenge was at hand: the analysis and discussion of teaching. Teaching is so complex a subject that volumes and volumes of literature and research could barely touch the surface. We decided, again, to work in the areas each of us knew best: Gray assumed the almost impossible task of making statistics, evaluation, and measurement palatable to students; Belkin toiled with the other areas. Recognizing that we could not cover even a fraction of what we wanted to cover, we used as our guiding principle the question, Of how much value will this information be to the future teacher when he or she walks into the classroom? While we did not avoid theory, we again stressed the practical implications.

Part Three, "Teaching: Art and Science," attempts to portray a realistic view of teaching—including all the frustrations, rewards, doubts, and achievements that teachers are heir to. We began, in chapter 10, with a candid look at the teacher as a person, examining how the teacher's personality and problems affect the teaching experience. The qualities of an effective teacher are delineated so that the reader can openly assess his or her strengths or weaknesses as a potential teacher. Each of the next six chapters examines, in some depth, major strategies of effective teaching: basic processes and theories; approaches to classroom management; instructional techniques; ways of working with the exceptional learner; group processes; and evaluation. Teaching, throughout Part Three, is approached as a multimodal interaction between one person functioning as teacher and one person functioning as learner. The qualities that con-tribute to teaching effectiveness, the organization of behaviors for successful implementation of teaching goals, and the special problems the teacher invariably encounters are each given their proper attention.

Throughout the text, three perspectives of development, learning, and teaching are presented: the psychodynamic, behavioral, and humanistic. We have tried, through balance and criticism, to maintain an integrative perspective that draws freely from each position and combines their strongest insights. Again, turning back to our opening question, we recognized that a valid purpose for a new text in educational psychology could be found in the integration and synthesis of the principal factions that characterize the thinking in the field today.

Several learning aids that we considered to be helpful are used throughout the text. Each of the three parts of the book is introduced by a short essay that organizes the material of the chapters included in that part. Each chapter is then introduced by a brief outline of its major points. Important insights are highlighted throughout the text by large-type displays at the tops of the pages. Key terms appear in boldface to indicate that they are included in the glossary. For students who wish to pursue a topic in depth, selected annotated bibliographies, with representative quotations, appear at the end of each chapter.

We have tried throughout this book to present men and women, girls and boys equally—both as teachers and as learners. Since the English language is deficient in providing a neutral pronoun, we have opted to balance out, as much as possible, our use of *he* and *she* in their neutral usage. In some cases, for the convenience of the reader, we have allowed the ubiquitous *he* its traditional priority; but we wish to point out that in such instances it is not our insensitivity to sexism in language but our consideration for the smooth flow of prose that has governed that decision.

While authors' names appear on the cover of a book, a book of this magnitude is always a cooperative effort between many individuals, each sharing his or her own area of expertise. Our editors at Wm. C. Brown Company Publishers encouraged us from the beginning and offered many valuable suggestions throughout the development of the manuscript. Joyce Oberhausen's creative editing of the manuscript deserves our deepest indebtedness, for she gave a polish and precision to the writing as well as offering many important contributions in other areas. The reviewers, whose perceptiveness, knowledge, and guidance resulted in a more balanced, accurate, and comprehensive book, deserve special mention. We would like to thank wholeheartedly Dr. Lola Doane, Chairperson, Department of Educational Psychology, Eastern Kentucky University; Dr. James W. Hall, professor of education and psychology, Northwestern University; Dr. Mina Berkowitz, Long Island University; and Dr. Charles West, Department of Educational Psychology, University of Illinois. We owe a special debt of gratitude to Dr. Henry Angelino, Department of Psychology, The Ohio State University, who bore with us throughout this project, providing insights, suggestions, research, and criticism, along with warm encouragement.

We would like to express appreciation to our students in educational psychology—Richard Boulton, Debbie Sidwell, and Andrew Searle, in particular—for their helpful critique of the manuscript prepared for this book. We would also like to acknowledge the encouragement, support, and insights shared with us by our wives, Melanie Belkin and Tania Gray, throughout this endeavor.

Gary S. Belkin
Jerry L. Gray

This text, *Educational Psychology: An Introduction,* is accompanied by the following learning aid:

Instructor's Manual for Educational Psychology: An Introduction

Educational Psychology

Education and Psychology: Definitions

Operational definitions of these two terms are compatible to allow us to relate the goals and methods of one to the other. We look at both disciplines in terms of areas of study, processes, and products.

A Day at Public School 321

We attend a faculty-staff meeting at a "typical" elementary school to examine the interaction of school personnel.

The School Team

The school team consists of the teacher, administrators, school psychologist, and the school counselor. The educational psychologist is called the "invisible" member of the team. The respective roles of each member—and possible role conflicts—are considered.

The Roots of Educational Psychology

Educational psychology was not born at a single time with a single purpose. Rather, it combined a number of different influences. John Dewey, Edward L. Thorndike, and the testing movement created the initial impetus. Developmental psychology, psychoanalysis, and behaviorism made further contributions.

Educational Psychology Today

The three basic factors central to the discipline are the learner, the teacher, and the process. The interrelationships between the three, and the different perspectives from which each can be studied, can be organized into a holistic study.

Educational Psychology in Perspective

Several different perspectives for studying the processes and products of education are considered: experimental, psychodynamic, humanistic, and behavioral. An argument is presented that these can be synthesized into making psychology a human science.

1 What Is Educational Psychology?

What is educational psychology? This entire book, actually, will be concerned with answering this single question. The lengthy answer is necessary not only because the question is so complex but because the discipline that we call educational psychology has so many sides; covers so many different topics; includes so many different positions; brings together, in a single inquiry, the tools and perceptions of so many different disciplines. We will use this chapter, therefore, not simply to answer this question, which gives the chapter its name, but also to flesh out a general outline of the discipline and to chart the terrain that the remainder of the book will explore in depth.

What is educational psychology? Included in this question are the two words that lead us to an answer: *education* and *psychology*. We might first attempt to answer the questions, What is education? and What is psychology? before attempting to answer the broader, more challenging question.

Education and Psychology: Definitions

The dictionary (*Webster's New World Dictionary*, 1970) defines education as "the process of training and developing the knowledge, skill, mind, character, etc., especially by formal schooling; teaching; training."[1] We see, then, that education is a process that contributes to individual development in several different areas—knowledge and mind (**cognitive** development), skills (**psychomotor** *and* cognitive development combined), and character (**affective** development). Moreover, we see that the specific developmental processes include schooling, teaching, and training.

All of these different areas of development, of course, are embodied in a single organism—the learner—and they are interrelated to each other within the context of the learner's world. It would be impossible to understand fully any of these concepts—knowledge, skill, mind, or character—without first understanding the learner as a total, functioning human being.

The *education* half of our initial question leads, then, to some insights, if not answers:

1. Educational psychology helps us account for different areas of the learner's development: specifically, cognitive development (in which knowledge and depth of mind are attained), psychomotor development (through which we achieve motor skills), and affective development (in which strength of character comes into being).
2. Educational psychology relates these areas of development to the

---

1. With permission. From *Webster's New World Dictionary of the American Language,* Second College Edition. Copyright © 1970 by the World Publishing Co.

EDUCATION: The process of training and developing knowledge, skill, mind, and character and so forth, especially by formal schooling; teaching; training.		PSYCHOLOGY: The discipline that describes, explains, and may attempt to change the behavior and conscious life of the person.
Cognitive skills Affective skills Psychomotor skills	**AREAS OF STUDY**	Conscious life Behavior
Schooling Teaching Training	**PROCESSES**	Description through observation Experimentation Explanation through theory
Fully functioning individual (learner) Effective teaching Accurate assessment of the processes	**PRODUCTS**	Holistic theories that account for different aspects of human behavior and conscious life Ability to predict the most successful course of action from a number of alternatives Multiple perspectives of the individual that are mutually compatible

Figure 1.1 The Elements of Educational Psychology

processes that facilitate them: schooling, teaching, and training (or **instruction,** as we shall call it).

3. Educational psychology helps relate the means to the ends; helps us understand how *process* is related to *product* within the contexts of the definition.

Now, let us see what a definition of psychology can contribute to our understanding of educational psychology.

Silverman (1974) offers a simple definition of psychology: "Psychology is the science that seeks to describe and explain and, on occasion, to change the behavior of man and other animals." This definition can be expanded, as Drever (1969) suggests, to include studies of "the phenomena of conscious life and behavior, in their origin, development, and manifestations," in which case we can view psychology as a more comprehensive discipline, examining not only behavior but conscious processes as well.

Putting together these two definitions, we emerge with a picture of psychology as a discipline that *describes, explains, and may attempt to change the behavior and conscious life of the person* (see figure 1.1). When we relate this back to our earlier definition of education, the areas of **conscious** life and behavior that are described, explained, and changed (cognitive, affective, and psychomotor) and the processes of change (teaching, training, and schooling) become related, and a more inclusive picture of educational psychology begins to emerge. Figure 1.1 relates the elements of these definitions into a whole picture that offers us our first clue toward answering the initial question, What is educational psychology?

We have at this point a general model, as shown in figure 1.1, from which we can begin working. Before filling in some of the details, which will give this model its practical applicability, let us turn our attention to a day in the life of some people at Public School 321—the William Penn School.

A Day at Public School 321

Miss Ciletti teaches the third-grade Junior Guidance class, which is a euphemism for the classes for emotionally disturbed children. Next door to her room is Mrs. Calhoun, who teaches the IGC classes for intellectually gifted children. And next to Mrs. Calhoun is Mr. O'Hara, who teaches the "typical" fourth-grade class, **heterogeneously** grouped. The three teachers are friends, and exchange shop talk during coffee breaks and lunch periods. Much of their conversation is about their students, and much concerns the school personnel who work with them: Dr. Novack, the school psychologist; Mrs. Porter, the guidance counselor; Dr. Black-Miller, the psychiatric-resource person (as she is called); Mrs. Kalmar, the school social worker. Together, these people comprise the educational team, and they, along with the other faculty and staff, are responsible for the education of the seven hundred children at P.S. 321.

However, this team, which works together and knows each other well, works along with another team—the administrative team, although there is not always smooth sailing when the two teams meet. The administrative team includes the principal and assistant principal, the curriculum coordinator, the top administrators at the board office, the immediate supervisor and a number of middle-management functionaries along the way. While in theory the two teams are at functionally different levels, in practice—despite occasional frictions—they work together toward fulfilling the goals of the educational process as they are defined by mutual consent and understanding.

Today there is a staff meeting, and both Miss Ciletti and Mr. O'Hara are to present a progress report on one of their students. Miss Ciletti discusses the problems and progress of Calvin, one of her more difficult students. She points out how she, Mrs. Kalmar (the social worker), and Mrs. Porter (the guidance counselor) decided to send Calvin to Dr. Black-Miller for a psychiatric examination, considering that there was some evidence of brain damage. The neurological results were negative, but the psychiatrist suggested that Calvin take **Ritalin** to help him control his untoward behavior. Mrs.

Kalmar added that she and the classroom teacher worked out a curriculum that would be more practical for the short attention span of Miss Ciletti's students, and that Calvin had been responding well for the past two weeks. They did not know whether to attribute it to the drug treatment or to the curricular changes.

Mrs. Calhoun, who was not scheduled to present a case today, interjected a few thoughts. "You know," she said, "just because I teach the IGC, it's always assumed that I don't have the kind of disciplinary problems you people do. But that's not so, although I wish it were. My class has been acting up *terribly* lately, maybe because of the spring weather. I consulted with Dr. Novack, the school psychologist, and he suggested that I set up a behavior mod program for the class. 'They're a bright group,' he told me, 'but a little out of control.' He gave me a little pamphlet on how to set up a program, and when I had questions, I called him, and he was *really* very helpful. That's why I think it's good to have a school psychologist aboard; and he can probably help you with your children, too."

"I've spoken with him," Miss Ciletti answered, "and he was helpful. But he told me to contact Dr. Black-Miller since he thought a neurological exam was indicated and that drug therapy might be useful."

The principal, listening carefully, interrupted. "I like the idea of teamwork. You teachers seem to make use of our team. Mrs. Porter, how do you as the guidance counselor fit into the team effort?"

Mrs. Porter answered unhesitatingly. "I act primarily as a referral person. If Miss Ciletti or Mrs. Calhoun came to me with a problem, I might first try to deal with it directly, but if I'm not able to, then I'll suggest that they see Dr. Novack, Dr. Black-Miller, or someone else whose expertise I think is appropriate. I also work with the teachers to set up new curricula." She looked around to the teachers who nodded in support of her efforts.

The curriculum coordinator, Mrs. Dern, spoke up. "Yes, I've had several consultations with the teachers and with Mrs. Porter. We're always willing to modify the curriculum to meet the special needs of the classes. Why, we all know well that what will work in Joe's class"—pointing to Mr. O'Hara—"is not going to work in Melanie's"—pointing to Miss Ciletti.

The principal nodded in approval. "Well, Joe, what do you have to present today?"

Joe thought for a moment before speaking. He was never one to waste words and disliked talk-for-talk's-sake, as he referred to it. When he began, he had the full attention of the others in the room.

"My class has been running pretty smoothly lately, and I think we all have to take some credit for this. I, as the teacher, am willing to take credit for the day-to-day responsibilities of managing the class, but, as we all know, there is much more to teaching, to education for that matter, than day-to-day classroom activities. The leadership of the school is important, and for that we can thank our principal and A.P. (assistant principal). Mrs. Dern has done a remarkable job this year as C.C. (curriculum coordinator), and the whole administrative staff has supported my individual efforts to teach as best I can."

He paused for a moment. The administrators were beaming, and the others looked around, waiting for their kudos.

"Whenever a problem arose in the class—whether it was a behavioral problem, a learning problem, or even a personal problem in one case, I always felt comfortable dropping by Mrs. Porter's office. She is willing to give of herself, and when she recognizes a specific problem is beyond her scope, she has proven capable in referring me to the right person. I've had several consultations with Dr. Novack and Dr. Black-Miller, and these have usually borne fruit.

"In short, what I'm trying to say is that our team effort has enabled me to have a successful term with my class, and for that I want to thank all of you."

There was a moment of silence and then a slight wave of hesitant applause. Joe had made each member of the school team feel his or her individual importance and had helped the group as a whole recognize its important interactive element.

You may note that never once did anyone mention an educational psychologist, nor did an educational psychologist play any part in ostensibly helping anyone in the school setting. What, then, does an educational psychologist do; what is the purpose of educational psychology; and, why does it remain hidden from view when we look into the goings-on of our average school? These are the questions we will attempt to answer in the next section.

The School Team

We saw how the school team functioned at typical P.S. 321. Let's review the role of each member of the team, and then we can appreciate where the educational psychologist stands within the context of this team's efforts.

First, we have the teacher. We all are intimately acquainted with what the teacher does, and this will be the subject matter of much of this book. For now, we can simply say *that the teacher is the person in immediate contact with the student; the person through whom the curriculum is presented and by way of whom educational decisions, made at all levels, reach the student.* In short, the teacher is the direct embodiment of the educational system as it is presented to the learner in the classroom.

This is a brief definition, barely inclusive of the myriad subtleties of the teacher's role. But it is our purpose at this point to sketch the role of the teacher in contrast to the other members of the school team.

Administratively above the teacher, but functionally equal as team members, are varied personnel, including the principal, assistant principal, supervisor, and curriculum coordinator. These personnel not only handle routine administrative matters but also make decisions that affect specific teaching activities: decisions involving who will be taught by whom; how much time is devoted to what; the subject matter itself; general managerial principles that have classroom ramifications; teacher evaluations (which reflect, directly or indirectly, administrative value orientations). An effective administration not only works cooperatively with teachers but makes decisions using teacher input and teacher feedback.

So far, our team looks something like the structure illustrated in the figure below.

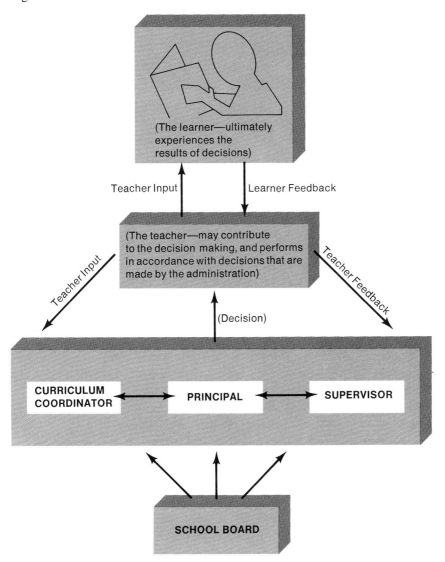

Figure 1.2 The Teacher and the Administration: Decision-Making Interactions

(The learner—ultimately experiences the results of decisions)

Teacher Input   Learner Feedback

(The teacher—may contribute to the decision making, and performs in accordance with decisions that are made by the administration)

Teacher Input   Teacher Feedback

(Decision)

| CURRICULUM COORDINATOR | PRINCIPAL | SUPERVISOR |

SCHOOL BOARD

Now we come to the school personnel that are usually called in for problematic situations, although they may be involved at all levels of decision making and practice. The school counselor and school psychologist (or, in some cases, school social worker and school psychiatrist) are members of the teaching team, but function for the most part in an adjunctive capacity. There is much confusion about the relative roles of the school psychologist (often erroneously confused with an educational psychologist) and the school counselor, and they each deserve their due in these pages. We will briefly survey their respective roles.

The School Psychologist
As a broad definition, we can say that *the school psychologist is a specialist who is concerned with applied psychology in the school setting*. This means, in effect, that all of the areas of applied psychology are under the school psychologist's purview, but that their special application to the school is of paramount importance.

More specifically, Perkins (1964) cites five "areas of functioning" that are of special importance to the school psychologist:

1. *Child study*—essentially a clinical approach to learning difficulties for which intellectual and personality evaluations are needed.
2. *Consultation*—occurring in two major areas: (a) pupil-oriented problems, similar to child study, but the pupil is not seen by the psychologists, (b) school-oriented problems relating to grading, curriculum, instruction, and so forth.
3. *In-service training*—seminar type of teaching, application of psychological and mental health principles to the school setting.
4. *Research*—experimental psychology with a very practical approach to school problems.
5. *Community services*—drawing upon sociological factors relating to broad needs of families and the functions of community agencies. (p. 8)

These, again, are broad areas, and in all likelihood the specific work of a school psychologist will depend more upon the school in which he works than on an operational definition of the role itself.

While the work itself is relative, the skills of the effective school psychologist are uniform. "It is now generally accepted," Holt and Kicklighter (1971, p. 2) point out, "that the school psychologist is a dually trained specialist. He must have competency in child development, **psychopathology,** learning, and in behavioral management and change. In addition to his psychological background, he must have a thorough understanding of the educational process, of instructional techniques, of group management and social development."

We see from this compendium of skills the broad background in psychology and education required for the school psychologist. In terms of role, Reinert (1976, p. 161) has summed it up aptly:

The school psychologist may serve as a consultant to teachers or other staff, may do individual psychological evaluations, and may work with individual children or small groups. In addition, the school psychologist acts as a liaison to families and community agencies and lends support to in-service activities for the school staff. In states that require individual intelligence testing the psychologist is generally responsible for providing this service.

Now, let us turn our attention to the role of the school counselor, after which we will try to piece together the teacher-psychologist-counselor team.

Within the context of the particular school in which he works, the school **The School Counselor** counselor is a specialist who is asked to perform a variety of specialized services, ranging from intensive counseling to implementing extra-curricular programs. As a specialist, he is expected not only to have know-how but to communicate to his colleagues and clients a professional attitude and a maturity that reflect his competency as well as his personal achievements. Carmical and Calvin (1970) tried to determine how school counselors "viewed their job functions and what their role in these functions should be." They found that the top five functions as rated by counselors were:

1. Providing the student an opportunity to "talk through his problems."
2. Counseling with potential dropouts.
3. Counseling with students concerning academic failures.
4. Counseling with students in evaluating personal assets and limitations.
5. Counseling with students concerning learning difficulties. (p. 282)

We see from these vocational activities that the work of the school counselor is not radically different from the role of the school psychologist. In fact, in many areas the boundaries of duties overlap. This may, as we can imagine, cause some role conflicts between the counselor and psychologist in a school.

Unfortunately, many instances of conflict between the counselor and school psychologist have prevented these two related specialists from achieving the harmony and concordance they need so much in order to work effectively. Sources of conflict between the counselor and the school psychologist usually are a result of failure to define adequately their roles or the relationships between their respective roles, or a failure of communication, which invariably leads to misunderstandings. Where the two are able to work together—as is sometimes the case—the consequences are most advantageous to the students.

A number of writers have scrutinized the coordination between the counseling and school psychologist functions (Johnson et al., 1961; Mathewson, 1962; Patterson, 1962; Byrne, 1963; Gray & Noble, 1965). Gray and Noble (1965), who have reviewed the literature, point out that "working together always demands some compromises and some giving up of cherished functions," and they argue that both the school psychologist and the school counselor must recognize this in order to work together effectively. Perhaps the simplest solution to the difficulties that divide these professions is for the school counselors and school psychologists to engage in mutual consultation, in which each utilizes his particular expertise for the benefit of the student. The school psychologist may be more adept at psychological testing and clinical diagnosis, while the counselor may prove to be a more skillful interviewer. The school psychologist may be better able to detect developmental disabilities, including learning problems, while the counselor may be more proficient in designing treatment activities. The point is that each should concentrate on his respective areas of strength.

The Educational Psychologist

The educational psychologist is the invisible member of the teaching team. He or she is not present in the school, nor in the administration. Yet, the work done by educational psychologists bears directly on the activities of the teacher, the administration, the school counselor, and the school psychologist.

Educational psychologists pursue different types of studies in different areas of education and psychology with a single goal in mind: understanding the processes of education and working to make these processes more effective. In training, the educational psychologist is primarily a psychologist, but his specialization is applied to the educational process. The educational psychologist's particular area of expertise may be developmental psychology, learning theory, experimental methodology, clinical psychology, social psychology, and so forth, or an amalgam of these subspecialties. In either case, what makes a psychologist an *educational* psychologist is the emphasis on the educational process that permeates all of his work.

This definition, unfortunately, does not tell us, in the type of detail we would like, what educational psychology actually is; nor does it explain adequately what you will be discovering in this book and why this material has been included. To answer these questions better, let us take a brief journey in time and examine the forces that shaped the discipline of educational psychology as we know it today.

The Roots of Educational Psychology

In many ways, the roots of educational psychology illuminate its current areas of study. There was no single point in the history of psychology at which someone had the idea to apply psychological principles systematically to education. On the contrary, long before psychology arose as a discipline, thinkers in different areas were passionately concerned with the problems of education, and they applied whatever tools they had to answering the basic questions that concern educators. It was through a number of fortuitous circumstances that, near the beginning of this century, educational psychology started to come into its own. But before we can focus on that period, we must turn our attention far back into history to understand the historical progression that ultimately led to the beginnings of educational psychology.

Long before psychology emerged as a separate discipline, philosophers put their efforts into trying to understand how we learn about our world, how we acquire information, how we process it, and how we act on the environment to change it. For example, Aristotle discovered that a person learns to know things through contiguity, comparison, and contrast. Such contemplations are known as a theory of knowledge, or epistemology. Until relatively recently in our history, learning was not separated from knowledge.

If we are engaged in studying learning for the purpose of finding ways of making learning more efficient and effective, then it becomes essential to separate the processes of **learning** from the results of **knowing.** That is, to isolate the specific processes by which the individual learns. The failure to make this distinction proved to be a serious deficiency in philosophy as a practical system. Psychology in general and educational psychology in particular have been directed to the processes of learning in separation from what is learned, and these efforts have been invaluable in devising ways of improving learning and, consequently, in making teaching more effective.

Nevertheless, recurrent throughout more recent efforts are historical overtones of philosophical ideas. In this brief section, we will point out some of the major influences of philosophy in order to understand better the historical continuity of the development of learning theories.

Plato's Theory of Recollection

Plato's theory of learning and knowledge, known as *Platonic Idealism,* is somewhat difficult for a contemporary reader to understand because its assumptions are so far removed from our modern perspective. We think of knowledge as a product of experience, usually acquired through the senses and through a variety of interactions with the environment. Plato's position, on the other hand, assumes the existence of *forms*. Forms are perfect ideas that exist independent of our perception and judgment. For example, forms include such things as circularity, justice, space, time, virtue, beauty, and truth. While our own learning produces copies of these forms, the resulting knowledge is never as perfect as the true forms themselves. Thus, when we draw a circle, or contemplate beauty, or measure space and time, or strive toward justice, we are approximating the forms of these things without perfectly reproducing them in our system.

The second aspect of Plato's theory is equally as incongruous to people with a contemporary perspective. Plato does not argue that we learn by studying things that in some way or another resemble the forms, but, rather, he proposes that all knowledge—all forms—are in our deepest memory, and we learn by remembering, or as he calls it, by recollecting, what is already inside us. Plato demonstrates this in some of his Socratic dialogues by showing how a person can arrive at a right answer, such as the answer to a mathematical problem, without knowing the specific rules involved. This is done through recollections; that is, through the process of learning what is already there, but which is not directly accessible through the reasoning process.

Plato's theory of knowledge is much more complicated than this, of course, but the ideas of form and recollection are the predominant motifs. Applications of these ideas have found acceptance in many modern classrooms. For example, a teacher may recognize that there are no absolutely right answers to questions, but rather answers that approximate more and more the "truth." Such a teacher might emphasize **divergent** rather than **convergent** thinking. Methods of teaching have also been influenced by the Platonic theory of recollection. Although most teachers roundly reject the notion of recollection, the method Plato used in his dialogues has been widely used in teaching. It is commonly known as the **dialectical method.** It consists of questioning and then questioning again the answers to the previous question in a circular manner. Its purpose is to bring the learner closer and closer to the truth, with the recognition that the truth itself—the pure form— can never be reached. "Socrates' discovery that teaching must begin in the accepted challenge to inquire is one of his lasting contributions to modern educational thought" (Brumbaugh & Lawrence, 1963, pp. 34–35).

Locke's Empirical Position

We now skip two thousand years of history to the mid-seventeenth century, when the empirical position, established in England by John Locke, David Hume, and George Berkeley, became an enduring philosophical outlook. The empiricists began their ventures into epistemology with the senses. "All ideas," Locke argued, "come from sensation or reflection. Sensation is the great source of most of the ideas we have." Sensory information is transformed into reasonable thinking when the mind, reflecting on the products of sensation, comes up with new ideas and insights.

Sensation and *reflection* are the two critical concepts to the empiricist. We take in the world through sensation and process the information through reflection. Consider the following passage from Locke's *An Essay Concerning Human Understanding:*

. . . The better to conceive the ideas we received from sensation, it may not be amiss for us to consider the . . . different ways whereby they make their approaches to our minds, and make themselves perceivable by us:

First, there are some which come into our minds *by one sense only.*

Secondly, there are others that convey themselves into the mind by *more senses than one.*

Thirdly, others are had from *reflection only.*

Fourthly, there are some that make themselves a way, and are suggested to the mind by all the ways of sensation and reflection. (p. 17)

It is through these limited categories that Locke and the other empiricists analyzed all of the processes of learning and the components of knowledge.

There are valuable premises from the empirical position that can be applied to learning theory and that have direct relevance to teaching as well. Three major points sum up the translation of empiricism to more contemporary positions:

1. Learning occurs only through experiences. The basis of all our learning is the information provided by the senses. Therefore, the learner should be encouraged to explore the world through the senses—to feel, see, and experience in all ways the world around us.
2. What is learned is continually tested against our experiences. Truth and falsity are, for the most part, tentative concepts that must be refuted or reaffirmed by our continuing experiences. Thus, while the child learns a simplified mathematics, the greater complexities are revealed in advanced courses in high school, where the answers that were sufficient during the earlier stages are no longer satisfactory.
3. Finally, Scheffler (1965, p. 3) sums up the last major contribution of the empirical position:

In the empiricist tradition, natural science is taken as the basic model. Natural phenomena are revealed by experience; they are not disclosed by intuition, nor are their interrelationships derivable from self-evident axioms. . . . The mind, in Locke's phrase, is a *tabula rasa* (a blank slate) at birth, and it is dependent upon experience both for the content of its elementary ideas and for their interrelationships.

Kant's Transcendental Epistemology

Immanuel Kant's epistemology, most clearly stated in his *Critique of Pure Reason*, is a direct challenge to empiricism. Kant argues that not all knowledge is derived from the senses, but rather that—

Experience is by no means the only field to which our understanding can be confined. Experience tells us what is, but not that it must be necessarily what is and not otherwise. It therefore never gives us any really general truths; and our reason, which is particularly anxious for the class of knowledge, is roused by it rather than satisfied. General truths, which at the same time bear the character of inward necessity, must be independent of experience—clear and certain in themselves. (*Critique*, p. 1)

Kant's major argument is that there are certain processes of mind through which we derive knowledge, and these processes are independent of sense experience. Such processes would include the ability to perceive relationships between hypothetical constructs ("Beauty is truth, truth beauty. . . .") and to reason accurately where we have not directly learned such reasoning ability.

A teacher who uses the Kantian model believes that the learner is natively equipped with mental processes that are integral to reasoning, and he or she would work to develop these processes. For instance, in the area of moral development, a Kantian would begin by teaching the learner strict rules, and then progress to justifying the rules according to principles in ascending order of complexity.

The Emergence of a Psychology of Education

The beginnings of modern experimental psychology is usually traced to 1879, when Wilhelm Wundt set up a laboratory in Leipzig, Germany. The introspective method used by Wundt for his experiments would probably be considered the first distinctly psychological method. This approach consisted simply of analyzing the contents of consciousness by paying attention to whatever crossed the subjects' minds. From this early beginning, departments of psychology sprang up throughout the Western world, and, in the United States, a number of these departments led, directly or indirectly, to the birth of educational psychology as a discipline.

In most cases the emergence of educational psychology was inadvertent. At the University of Chicago, for example, John Dewey, known primarily as a great American philosopher and educator, headed a joint department of psychology, philosophy, and pedagogy. The rationale behind such a department was not only the overlapping concerns of the three disciplines but Dewey's own interest in applying psychological research to educational problems. Dewey's research in psychology was used to support his practical educational proposals, and he must be credited as the first person to use educational psychology as a viable social and political instrument.

Many scholars minimize Dewey's role as a psychologist and applaud his philosophical works. Roback (1952, p. 214), in his classic work on the history of American psychology, for instance, states that "Dewey had only taken on psychology as an avocation." Nevertheless, he did produce substantial works on the thinking process and, more importantly, influenced hundreds of young psychology students in the field of education. While Dewey is not truly the "father" of educational psychology, he is certainly its major early inspiration.

The "father" of educational psychology, if we are to speak of one, is the American psychologist, Edward L. Thorndike. Thorndike did pioneering work in intelligence and associative learning, setting down much of the foundation for later behavioral research. "Thorndike was concerned,"

Edward L. Thorndike

Arnold Gesell

Edward L. Thorndike and Arnold Gesell contributed much to the foundations of later-day educational psychology. Thorndike's work in intelligence, measurement, and laboratory psychology set the stage for empirical research and advances in mental testing. Gesell's longitudinal studies became the prototype for some of the major developmental studies of the twentieth century.

Edwards (1971) points out, "about the application of psychology as a science to human behavior." This interest, combined with his work setting at Columbia University's Teachers College, led to his development of the three-volume landmark work, *Educational Psychology,* the first textbook on this subject. The subject matter covered in these volumes is still representative of the concerns of contemporary educational psychology: intelligence, testing, a theory of learning, evaluation and measurement, and so forth.

One of the major influences on the shaping of educational psychology during this time was the testing movement, which began in France under the leadership of Alfred Binet. As intelligence tests were developed and **standardized,** educators lost no time recognizing the enormous potential of this tool. Now, for the first time, objective measures could be used to assess the learner's capabilities and to design a curriculum that would be appropriate to his abilities. Academic departments of tests and measurements turned out a spate of freshly trained personnel that were, in present-day terms, educational psychologists.

The influence of Dewey, Thorndike, and the testing movement are indicative of the experimental part of educational psychology. But other influences were being brought to bear as well. At Yale University, Arnold Gesell conducted longitudinal studies of child growth and development, setting the stage for wide-scale research into child psychology and developmental patterns. Much of Gesell's work was applied to education, since the learner is in the very midst of this growth during the formative school years. In Vienna, Sigmund Freud was developing the study of psychoanalysis, which focused on the person's unconscious thought processes and their relation to behavior. While Freud's theory generated great controversy, many of his ideas were either adopted or transformed by psychologists into coherent developmental positions. Murphy (1959), in his history of psychology, places Freud's work in context:

Even more important for the history of psychology was the merging of psychoanalytic ways of thinking with other approaches to the study of childhood growth, particularly the study of emotions, dreams, and fantasies of children, whether such studies were pursued as parts of a clinical concern for the mental-hygiene needs of children or as integral parts of research projects. More and more one finds the literature of child psychology peppered with investigations of unconscious dynamics, in which the child rather than the adult is the center of interest. *It is hard today to imagine a child psychology devoid of psychoanalytic coloring, for even the most objective of behavior analysis is heavily indebted to psychoanalytic conceptions.* (p. 398)

In more recent years, yet another force (in addition to experimental and developmental psychology) has begun to make an impact on educational psychology. The burgeoning psychotherapy movement has found numerous translations into educational ideology. Many of the well-known therapists have written books on education, applying their therapeutic insights to the teaching-learning process. Carl Rogers, the founder of **client-centered therapy;** William Glasser, the founder of **reality therapy;** and Anna Freud (Sigmund's daughter), among others, have been notable in this effort.

Finally, the rise of behavioral psychology has had a widespread impact on education. Because **behaviorism** is concerned with the person's actions, and because it specifies ways of changing these actions, it is an ideal psychology for education. It would be fair to say that, during the past decade, behavioral psychology has held the single leading position in the educational psychology discipline.

There are other influences as well, but these are the major ones—the ones felt most profoundly today. We see from these bits and pieces that educational psychology did not arise as a single discipline but, from its very roots, embraced a number of different psychological positions in a common concern for applying psychology to better human life.

Educational Psychology Today

We have looked at educational psychology as a part of the total effort to provide maximum learning and effective teaching in the schools. The educational psychologist, we have suggested, is an "invisible" but important member of the educational team. Now, after examining the origins of educational psychology as a discipline, we are better able to discuss the role of educational psychology today.

Central to the discipline are three basic factors: the learner, the teacher, and the process that transpires between them. All of the concerns of educational psychology are derivatives of these three fundamental, underlying factors. Each deserves individual attention.

The learner is a person. This simple statement has major ramifications that, although obvious, bear many important subtleties. The learner, as a person, is the product of certain developmental stages and is in the process of continuing growth. The learner is never at a state of rest; on the contrary, he or she is always in motion, in the throes of change, heading in new directions. Trying to pinpoint the learner as a static object at a determined place in space is like trying to seize an electron in orbit. It is futile.

The Learner

But for the educational process to succeed, we must deal with the reality of the learner. This entails two separate but related efforts. First, we have to understand how the learner came to be the way he is today. If we understand the path that the learner travelled to reach his level of proficiency at the time we meet him, we are in a better position to understand ways of remediating deficiencies developed along that path. Moreover, understanding the basic principles of development helps us design educational programs that recapitulate, when appropriate, the logical stages of sequential developmental growth.

Second, we have to know how to assess the learner's capabilities at the time we are teaching him, and to understand the ways of using our assessment to design better programs. Just as our studies of developmental processes will enable us to understand *how* the learner got to where he is, the study of assessment and measurement will tell us *where* the learner is.

These two aspects of the learner's presence—his background and his level of ability at the present—will constitute an important part of our study. But we must keep in mind that, within the contexts of educational psychology, the learner is never studied in vacuo; but rather, as he is involved in the teaching-learning process.

The teacher, like the learner, has a background that accounts for where he is and who he is today. The developmental psychology that concerns educational psychologists, therefore, is just as applicable to understanding the teacher as it is to understanding the learner. In addition, the personality of

The Teacher

the teacher, both in its superficial and deeper sense, is relevant to his or her performance in the classroom. Thus, the educational psychologist attempts to pinpoint those variables of the teacher that prove effective or detrimental to the teaching process.

The Process   It is the teaching process itself that has earned most attention in the field of educational psychology, and rightly so. For it is within the contexts of this process that the learner and teacher meet, face-to-face, and that education actually takes place. An analysis of the teaching process requires two distinct but related studies: the analysis of learning, and the analysis of instruction.

When we speak of learning, we are including under a single rubric a multitude of processes that produce different kinds of outcomes. For simplicity, we generally divide learning into three domains: the cognitive, affective, and psychomotor. Cognitive learning is factual, intellectual learning; affective learning is more subjective, emotional, value laden; psychomotor learning is the learning of voluntary movements of the body. At any given point, the person's behavior reflects all three types of learning.

For example, let us say that John is studying for a math test and gets hungry. He goes to the refrigerator and opens a package of cheese and eats it. This simple act reflects cognitive, affective, and psychomotor learning. His knowledge of where to find food and how to get there is a cognitive skill. His preference for cheese over other foods in the refrigerator is affective. His ability to navigate through the house and to position himself correctly at the refrigerator is reflective of psychomotor learning. Just as this simple behavior includes all three, many of our complex behaviors also embrace the three types of learning.

Although there are different types of learning, each with its own individual components and idiosyncracies, there are, of course, common elements that underlie all the learning processes. Educational psychology has directed specific attention to these processes of **motivation, readiness, retention,** and so forth, to understand better the principles that serve as the foundations of learning.

Just as there are different types of learning, there are also different types of teaching—different approaches to facilitate learning. In part, the type of teaching used depends on learning goals: Is affective learning the goal? Are cognitive skills the goal? Is psychomotor proficiency the goal? But there are other variables, too, that affect the type of teaching that is used: the personality of the teacher, the status of the learner, the setting where learning takes place, and so on.

Teaching can also take place in both the individual and group setting, and the setting does have an important influence on the process and the outcomes. We shall, in the course of our examination of teaching, consider the group setting that is typical of most school encounters as an important part of the teaching-learning process.

Let us consider all of the variables we have mentioned that contribute to the teaching-learning process: developmental processes, cognitive learning processes, affective learning processes, psychomotor learning processes, different methods of teaching, the personality of the teacher, the teaching setting. As we probe more deeply, we will find even more variables that directly or indirectly affect teaching. It is difficult, therefore, to conceive of the study of educational psychology as a unified discipline when it treats so many different variables in so much detail.

Toward an Organized Study

To help organize the variables and make them useful for study, psychologists assume different *perspectives* of education and of psychology. Let us say three friends make a trip to a foreign country for a week during their vacation. One is an economist, one a sociologist, and the third a medical doctor. They travel together and do the same things, and when they return, a fourth friend, who did not go with them, asks them what they observed on their trip. Certainly, there will be many common experiences and shared perceptions between them. "We saw the Arc de Triomphe, ate at a fine restaurant, met nice people, saw the Folies-Bergère." But each one will also have had individual experiences because of the perspective that he brought with him on the trip. "I noticed how inflation has affected food prices," the economist might say, "but that clothing prices are still fairly stable." The sociologist might indicate that certain customs and mores were strikingly different than at home. The medical doctor comments on the hygiene of the people and the availability of health services. The point is this: Even though they spent their time together and observed the same things at the same time, each came back with different perceptions and conclusions as a result of their "frame of reference," their perspectives, that they brought with them.

So, too, do educational psychologists approach the very serious matters of education, personality, and human nature in general in very different ways; from different vantage points—different perspectives. This is not to suggest that the discrepancies between their vantage points indicate gross contradictions and inconsistencies, although this is sometimes the case. Rather, it suggests that there are many different ways of looking at the same thing, and the attitude with which we enter the venture will, to some extent, determine what we get out of it.

So here we are! Confronted by a multitude of variables, a number of perspectives, a variety of issues—we are asked to engage in the study of educational psychology. In Part One, we will consider how to go about this effort in a relatively unbiased, objective way, refusing to bend inordinately to any of the single vantage points, and maintaining instead a perspective of all the perspectives—an objective detachment.

Educational Psychology in Perspective

Although there are many different perspectives that have characterized efforts in the psychology of education, it is reasonably fair to cite four major ones that account for almost all of the important insights. The primary perspective—the one that has characterized the discipline from its beginnings—is experimentalism. This perspective yields to the position that to learn about anything we have to set up an experimental design based on the scientific model. This is exactly what Thorndike did in his pioneering efforts and to this very day most educational research is conducted along these lines.

The *experimental* perspective has several important implications. First, since it relies on scientific methodology, it differentiates between hypothesis and conclusion. It's fine to say that the person is influenced by situations during the first four years of life, but can we prove it? We can surely suggest that people naturally tend to productive activities, but can this hypothesis be demonstrated? The experimental perspective does not exclude any hypothesis but demands that it be tested and statistically analyzed to determine the significance of the results.

Secondly, the experimental perspective does not restrict itself to any one area of inquiry. We can study development, learning, methods of teaching, and other areas by the same methods. In fact, all of these variables can be combined in sophisticated experimental procedures. One advantage of the experimental perspective is that it combines many of the variables of the educational process and from the different perspectives into well-designed experiments that test out the hypotheses.

Another perspective, quite different from the experimental, is derived from the work of Sigmund Freud and his colleagues around the turn of the century. Psychoanalysis, which has undergone many drastic revisions and modifications since its inception, still holds a powerful sway over psychological thought, especially in the areas of clinical psychology and child development. While classical Freudian psychoanalysis is not widely accepted nowadays because of its lack of empirical evidence, the works of Erikson, among others, has assured that **psychodynamic** approaches to understanding the individual remains extant.

The psychodynamic perspective does not place any importance on the experimental testing of **hypotheses.** Rather, it uses the clinical setting ("the couch," as it is often called) to determine the validity of its assumptions. While this is viewed as a weakness by the experimentalists, the partisans of the psychodynamic perspective argue that the methods of experimental psychology are not relevant for understanding the unique makeup of the individual.

Along with this psychodynamic perspective, the **humanistic** perspective, derived from the philosophy of humanism, tends to disregard the value of empirical investigation in the understanding of human personality, motivation, and behavior. Unlike the psychodynamic psychologists, however, the humanistic psychologists do not see the unconscious (the hidden mind) as a major force underlying behavior. Rather, they place stress on the person's growth potential and emphasize the positive, healthy aspects of the individual.

The conflict between the experimental approach and the psychodynamic-humanistic approach has caused a rift in psychology over many years. Giorgi (1970), in a lengthy essay that addresses itself to this conflict, tackles the perennial argument that has raged between those who demand scientific methods in psychology and those who are partisans of the more human aspects of the discipline. He distinguishes between psychology as a *natural science* and psychology as a *human science*. As a natural science, psychology draws its methods from the scientific laboratories of the nineteenth and twentieth centuries, utilizing the statistical and experimental methods of scientists to test and verify hypotheses. As a human science, psychology attempts to understand the total person, in all of his complexity, and this cannot be limited to strictly scientific methods. Giorgi finally suggests a synthesis of the two positions.

> . . . far from being a contradiction, the project of establishing psychology as an empirical human science is distinctly feasible. . . . To be scientific psychology must deal with the experiential-behavioral relationships of man in a detailed way. . . . To be objective, the psychologist must be able to arrive at intersubjectively valid knowledge. . . . To be empirical, psychology must be based upon phenomena that are given in experience. To be human, it must have as its subject-matter the human person and he must be approached within the frame of reference that is also human, i.e., one that does not do violence to the phenomenon of man as a person. (pp. 224–225)

Unfortunately, this integrative perspective has not yet been fully achieved, and there is still a great deal of factionalism in psychology and in educational psychology.

A fourth perspective, one that fairly dominates the field today, is the **behavioral** perspective. This is derived from the experimental position, but has a few basic differences. The behavioral perspective, in its broadest definition, looks at the person in totality as a result of what he has learned. While behaviorists recognize different kinds of learning, they generally believe that man is the sum of what he has learned. Minimizing the importance of natural tendencies and hidden meanings, the behavioral psychologist concentrates on the different processes of learning, so that behavioral psychology is, in short, learning theory.

Implications in Education

Each of these four perspectives has something to offer us in our attempts to understand the educational experience and the variables involved. Throughout this book we will attempt to understand the variables of the teaching-learning process by focusing our attention through the lenses of psychodynamic psychology, humanistic psychology, and behavioral psychology. Moreover, the rich harvest of experimental research will be illuminated throughout the text to support or to question the insights from the other perspectives.

A perspective is always a perspective of something. In our hypothetical story of the three friends who traveled to Paris, their visit was perceived through their personal perspectives. The subject matter of this book includes the many different variables we have pointed out in this chapter, as well as other variables. To organize this myriad of variables into coherent units, we have chosen to use the concept of the **total person** as the framework of our efforts.

The total person—what does this mean? In short, it reflects that the many variables of living are embodied within the organism. The teaching-learning process, despite its complexities, boils down to this: How does one person change another person? When we stand back from the particulars of our scrutiny and look at the person as a fully functioning organism—with cognitive, affective, and physical dimensions—the organization of our findings becomes evident without further effort.

Part One, "The Life of the Learner," will show the stages of growth and development that lead the learner to the day he enters the classroom. Life is full of many pitfalls, as we know, and it is often deviations from the normal course that have the greatest implications in our future life. Thus, we will look not only at the normal patterns of development, paying particular attention to their relationship to later performance in school, but also at exceptional problems, such as the abused child, the child from the single-parent family, and so on, to consider their effects. This first part of the book, in which the four perspectives we have mentioned will be explicated, will serve the purpose of focusing our attention on the learner as a total person whose developmental and growth processes can be understood.

Part Two, "The Psychology of Learning," will maintain this total person emphasis. Instead of looking at learning as something that happens to animals in experimental laboratories, we will look at learning as it really happens to people—in the three domains: cognitive, affective, and psychomotor. Each of the chapters devoted to one of the domains will offer a cross-sectional view of the total learning experience.

Finally, in Part Three, the longest section of the book, we will examine teaching both as an art and as a science. Here, again, we focus on the total person—this time the person of the teacher. We will not only look at the personality of the teacher and at his or her problems, but we will examine how the teacher's perspective, like that of the educational psychologist, influences the course of teaching.

We shall begin now by examining the life of the learner, keeping in mind that you, the reader, are a learner and that this book is about you.

Summary

In this chapter, we have attempted to answer the fundamental question, What is educational psychology? In answering this question, we examined the history of the discipline, its major concerns today, and the role that educational psychology plays in school practice.

The source material for educational psychology is found in both education and psychology—related but separate disciplines. In studying the origins, too, we find contributions from both disciplines. Moreover, if we examine the uses to which educational research is put, it helps us clarify the concerns of the discipline as well as its methodology.

The school team—which includes the teacher, administrators, the school psychologist and school counselor, among others—draws practical applications from different areas of educational and psychological research. The synthesis of these research areas and their organization (into coherent, workable wholes) characterizes educational psychology as a discipline.

The variables that are inevitably used are the learner, the teacher, and the process. It is the interrelationships between these variables, and the perspectives from which they can be examined, that constitute the primary subject matter of educational psychology.

Suggested Additional Readings

Education and the Good Life by Bertrand Russell (*New York: Liveright, 1970*)

It is interesting to see that one of the most perceptive books ever written in educational psychology was written not by a psychologist, but by a philosopher, writing as a concerned parent. Russell's concerns about his children's education resulted in his forming a school from which he developed an interesting, very perceptive view of what education is all about.

Although both older and younger children are important, contemporaries are far more so, at any rate from the age of four onwards. Behavior to equals is what most needs to be learnt.

from *Education and the Good Life*

History of Psychology, edited by William S. Sahakian (*Itasca, Ill.: F. E. Peacock, 1968*)

An excellent collection of original source material that traces, in detail, the evolution of psychology as a discipline. Moreover, many of the seminal contributions to educational psychology, such as the papers of Thorndike, Gesell, Cattell, Allport, Rogers, Maslow—and others—are included.

The variety of men and subjects herein treated spans more than merely two milennia of time; it covers 133 different men, and schools as diverse as behaviorism and existentialism.

from the preface, *History of Psychology*

Education and Ecstasy by George B. Leonard (*New York: Dell Publishing Co. paperback, 1969*)

An inspiring, beautifully written prophetic essay on what education *should* and *could* be. For the student of educational psychology, the main value of this book is in its goals for a better educational system—goals that can be reached through further application of insights already tested and verified.

All environment has the capacity to educate. We are rapidly becoming capable of controlling all environment we can perceive. It may someday turn out that what we can be *will be limited only by what we can* perceive.

from *Education and Ecstasy*

Urban, Social and Educational Issues (2d ed.) edited by Leonard Golubchick and Barry Persky (*Dubuque, Iowa: Kendall/Hunt Publishing Company, 1976*)

This anthology touches all of the important topics that are of concern to educators today. In some ways, it outlines the scope of educational psychology by outlining the practical problems to which educational psychologists must address themselves.

Are the schools relevant? Is education, as traditionally structured, a legitimate means for the exploited to escape their deprivation or an institution which the Establishment manipulates to control the masses? Is our faith in education justified, or are schools reinforcing a rigid status quo in which blacks exist as a permanent underclass?

Bayard Rustin, "Irrelevant Schools or Irrelevant Critics?"

Part 1

We are all one—born into this
rich earth, into the human
experience. We carry a dream,
a special vision inside, and
when the load gets heavy we
can reach for that dream.
Through it life unfolds and we
find strength, faith, love.

Yvonne Rankin

The Life of the Learner

Long before the child enters school, years of development and maturation have resulted in the creation of an individual who is different from all other individuals in the world. No two people are alike, and so great are the differences between any two people that it would take volumes and volumes just to list the types of dissimilarities that exist, let alone to measure and classify them. Yet, while each person is distinct and different from all other persons, there are certain similarities that underlie human nature; similarities so striking that they often suggest to us that all people are really alike, their differences slight, the uniqueness merely idiosyncracies. In fact, however, even if two people were born with the exact same genetic makeup and at the exact moment in time, since they cannot occupy the same space and cannot have the exact same experience each second, by the time they are one year old, they each have had 31,536,000 different experiences! And that is assuming they are born with identical genes, which only occurs in rare instances of monozygotic twins.

What we are suggesting is that people are more different than they are alike. As we get to know people intimately—whether it be friends, lovers, students, teachers, colleagues—we see how distinct these differences really are.

When we speak in Part One about the life of the learner, we are not really speaking about a particular learner but rather about those general principles that can help us better understand an individual learner—the person. When we teach, we try, as best we can, to understand the person in his or her totality: as a uniquely functioning, individually perceiving and responding organism. But this requires great effort—there is so much to learn in so little time. The insights of developmental psychology are valuable in facilitating this process in which we gain understanding about an individual. We must be cautious, however, not to use the psychological insights in lieu of attempting to understand the person himself.

There are certain recurrent themes that the reader will note throughout the following four chapters, which are organized chronologically. First, we will explore at every junction the theme of freedom versus determinism. In chapter 2, which provides a general overview of issues and principles, we will see how the bonds of heredity are loosened as the person begins to learn to function as an individual. In the fifth chapter, on adolescence, this theme of freedom versus determinism will appear in the tension that exists between the high school student's individual needs and the constraints of society and the school. Throughout the rest of these four chapters, this theme will continue to be explored in various contexts relevant to the age level under discussion.

A second theme, referred to time and again, is the interactive influence of the school and the home on the individual's development. One of the important ways that educational psychologists differ from developmental psychologists in approaching a given question is that the educational psychologist will pay special attention to ways in which the school does influence or *can* influence the course of development. We will make every effort to point out in Part One how experiences in the school situation can modify, positively or negatively, the course of a person's development. Likewise, we will take pains to point out to the teacher the implications of what it means in terms of the child's education when the influence of the home is prominent.

A third theme, implicit rather than explicit, is that although there is an abundance of theories to explain how the personality develops, how the mind begins to grasp the world around, there are enough parallels between the common points in all these theories to allow us some access into the mysteries of the human psyche. To understand the theories and lose sight of the person is to miss the point entirely. Rather, we should draw freely at any time from any theory to help us better understand the specific situation of a particular student.

The organizing principle behind the chapters in Part One is to acquaint the reader with the basic processes and conditions of growth and development that bear a direct relevance to the education of the person. "Growth," Cardinal Newman said, "is the only evidence of life," and the ways in which we grow determine, more than anything else, the course of our life. When we speak of growth we are speaking of change, and any change can be for better or worse. What makes some changes for the better and some for the worse? What influences mold our growth and how do these different influences interact? More important to our interests, how can the schools affect for the better the growth of the learner? These, as we shall see, are not easy questions to answer.

There are a number of alternative ways of looking at the growth of the person. We can examine it topically, according to various accepted categories of developmental psychology. Or, we can examine it chronologically, studying the life of the learner year by year. Each of these approaches has some advantages and some disadvantages. By combining the two approaches, however, we find that we not only better understand the interacting forces that shape the individual's destiny but, at the same time, gain a better perspective of the way each of these forces helps shape a part of the total person's developmental progress.

We must be specific when we speak about *interacting forces* and *developmental categories*. The most cited interacting forces are the individual's genetic endowment; the early maternal environment; the family as a unit; the peer group; cultural influences; and, the school. The developmental categories most frequently discussed are physical growth; cognitive development; socialization; emotional maturity; and personality development (which synthesizes some of these developmental categories into a coherent pattern). The respective importance of each of these varies from age level to age level, and the attention directed to each depends to a large extent on the reasons for the study. An educator, for example, is more interested in the development of cognitive skills than in patterns of physical growth because the educative task has more concern with cognitive skills. Nevertheless, we are all aware that none of these forces and none of these categories exists independent of and in isolation from the others.

The purpose of this part of the book, then, is to understand the life of the learner as a developmental process that amalgamates many different forces. We shall see that some of the processes of growth are beyond the individual's control, or beyond anyone's control—genetic factors, for instance; some are directly attributable to the parents, some are dictated by the society, and some can be influenced directly by teachers. We shall attempt to sort out those processes of growth that can be influenced by the teachers and by the school and to explore ways in which they can be positively influenced. In short, we will look at human development with a view toward improving it to the extent to which the teacher is realistically able.

Chapter 2, "The Foundations of Growth and Development," will direct attention to major topical perspectives of the developmental process. We will examine the influence of heredity on development and study some of the controversy that surrounds this elusive issue. This is no easy task and it is beset by challenges from the outset. At this point in time, we do not fully understand the limitations placed on our growth by genetic factors. While strides in genetic sciences have allowed us to measure the heritability of many traits, those traits most directly relevant to the educative process are those that are least clearly understood in terms of genetics. Ascribed human characteristics such as intelligence, social interactions, motivation, and psychopathology are the centers of continued debate between **environmentalists** and **nativists.** We will not attempt to resolve these complex issues in this book; that is far beyond our modest scope. Rather, we will examine the main points of the different positions and extract from the theories and research, ideas that can be useful to the teacher.

Chapter 3, "The Preschool Years," will examine the development of the preschool child as a de facto antecedent to formal education. When the teacher first comes into contact with the student—say, at about five or six years old—the child is already deeply molded by other forces. The foundations of personality have been set; language, at least in its rudimentary form, has been acquired; basic cognitive processes have been established; preliminary socialization skills have been developed. But the child is not yet fully acculturated, not yet fully in tune with the social order. It is this process of **acculturation,** in its fullest sense of intellectual, affective, behavioral, social action, that is deeply influenced by the educational process. Acculturation has important precursors that we shall examine in this chapter, with the view of better understanding what education *can* do to help facilitate appropriate social growth and individual development.

We shall continue to explore the development of the child in chapter 4, "The Elementary School Years." Since the foundations of the developmental processes have already been discussed in detail in the first three chapters, we shall use this chapter to explore special problems and situations of the child's life during these years: the battered child who is the victim of family abuse; the child from a single-parent family; the bilingual and culturally different child. We shall also continue to study the "normal" lines of development and gain some further understanding of how language skills and socialization continue to progress through these years. But our essential interest in this chapter is the child's personal experience in the elementary school years, including specialized areas that are outside the purview of traditional developmental studies.

Chapter 5, "The Secondary School Years," will focus with some detail on the adolescent experience. The traditional periods and stages of adolescence will be presented, but with a special focus on issues of particular concern to the secondary school teacher. The chapter begins with an exploration of early adolescent experiences, focusing on physical and intellectual development, and continues with other normal growth patterns of adolescence. But special problematic topics are also considered: adolescent drug and alcohol abuse; sexual development; the adolescent and the world of work. The theme throughout this chapter is that the teacher can make a positive change in the adolescent's life, and ways in which this can be done are considered.

The reason we have chosen to include this comprehensive material on developmental psychology is because we believe that education is a continuous process that combines a host of different forces with which the teacher should be familiar. The life of the learner, which begins at conception and ends with death, should be viewed in its full complexity in order that the teacher can more realistically understand his or her role in the learner's development. With this in mind, let us begin our study by looking at the foundations, or basic principles, of human growth and development.

Nature and Nurture: The Crucial Interaction

Genetic and environmental factors interact to produce individual characteristics. It is not clear at the present time to what extent genetics and to what extent environment are responsible for those traits with which educators are most concerned.

Developmental Theories

A developmental theory of personality helps us understand how, through the life cycle, a person becomes what he or she is.

The Psychoanalytic Position

This position views man as an instinctual creature, driven by unconscious forces. The dynamics of the mind are explained by the concepts id (primitive energy), ego (reality principle), and superego (conscience). Adler and Erikson add an important social dimension to Freud's original model.

The Behavioral (Learning Theory) Position

This position relies on the concepts of stimulus and response to explain the processes of learning. According to the behavioral position, the individual is a product of his conditioning. All of what we are, the behavioral psychologist argues, is what we have learned to be.

The Humanistic Position: Toward Growth and Self-Actualization

This position stresses the "healthy" aspects of the person. It comprises several different psychologies that share the common belief that the person, in the stages of growth, is always in the process of becoming. Major embodiments of the humanistic stance are found in Maslow's self-actualizing psychology, Rogers's client-centered approach, and in the existential psychologies.

Continued

2 The Foundations of Growth and Development

**Three Positions on Cognitive Development:
An Overview**

The behavioral position breaks down learning into
stimuli and responses that are associated with them. The
cognitivist's position focuses on the thinking and
perception of the person. Piaget's genetic psychology
studies the stage-by-stage development of the child,
indicating four major periods of development: the
sensorimotor period, the preoperational period, the
period of concrete operations, and the period of formal
operations.

From the moment that the male and female reproductive cells merge at conception, there is a certain inherent order and logic at work that determine, to some extent, the individual's future life. Molecular-chemical codes, deeply hidden within the nuclei of cells, specify the prenatal developmental patterns of the growing organism. The interactions between these biological "designs" and the prenatal environment provided by the mother result in birth differences that generate, as the person grows and matures, into more profound differences in many areas of development. At birth, the **neonate** is helpless and incapable of independent survival, not yet fully an individual. "The biological birth of the human infant and the psychological birth of the individual," Mahler, Pine, and Bergman (1975) point out, "are not coincident in time. The former is a dramatic, observable, and well-circumscribed event; the latter a slowly unfolding intrapsychic process."

The caretaker—or **"mothering one"**—nurtures the newborn child, feeding and loving, stimulating with touch and sound, protecting from the often nefarious forces in the environment that threaten the helpless neonate's well-being and survival. The infant, however, is busy at work from the beginning, "taking-in" and trying to make sense of the things around him. The infant, through experimentation and exploration, begins to learn the "tricks" of living; tricks of mastering the environment, of carving out an individual destiny, of surviving. The moment at which the organism breaks free of its genetic bondage and begins to *individuate* through the processes of sensation, perception, behavior, and affective experience—all the precursors of reasonable living—marks the beginnings of the educational process.

We, as teachers or teachers-in-training, can do little about the "innate circumstances" of the person. True, we can and should understand the implications of genetic differences and the crucial components of the so-called nature-nurture interaction: the interaction between **heredity** and **environment.** Nor can we do much but hope to understand the profound implications of parental care and familial response during the preschool years. In fact, it has been suggested (and will be explored in chapter 3) that most important developmental foundations have been laid before the child reaches school age. Yet if we recognize that education begins as the child separates himself or herself from the genetic bond, and continues somewhat smoothly through the preschool years and the postschool years until death, then we can deal more effectively with the learner and develop programs that will be both realistic and profitable for the people whom we teach.

To understand the complex processes that characterize **individuation**— that is, the learned deviation from our basic nature to creatures of free will and learned behavior—requires that we study the growth patterns of the person in a number of different areas. How does the instinctual reflexive response behavior of the infant transform into individual, idiosyncratic behavior patterns that differ so greatly from person to person? How does the primitive **sensorimotor** intelligence of the newborn become the logical, complex thinking of the older child or adult? Are there universal patterns to intellectual development, consistent from culture to culture, from subculture to subculture? How are the myriad complexities of language skills mastered in so short a period of time, and what, if any, is the relationship between **cognitive** skills, emotional development, and language acquisition? These are just a few of the questions we will attempt to answer in this chapter.

We will begin by examining the genetic foundations of development, paying particular attention to the interaction between heredity and environment. Then, we shall turn our attention to the most significant developmental theories that have been offered to explain patterns of development that seem to be stable and universal. These will include both cognitive and emotional (affective) theories.

Nature and Nurture: The Crucial Interaction

When we look at the total person, we see the results of millions of interactions between nature and the environment; between the genetic endowment of the individual and the living forces that have modified that genetic potential. Since Gregor Johann Mendel laid the foundations of genetic studies a hundred years ago, we have continually struggled with the question, How much of what we are is the product of genetic interactions? The question becomes even more important in the light of Charles Darwin's (1859) concept of evolutionary development that states, in effect, that genetically determined abilities (both physical and social) and disabilities are in part responsible for our survival and our progress as creatures on this earth. Darwin's concept of *survival of the fittest,* which states that those with most favorable genetic characteristics tend to surpass those with less favorable characteristics, also has profound implications, socially and educationally, for our children. There are two ways of looking at this issue. One way emphasizes the importance of genetic endowment over environmental factors. A person might say, for instance, "In a society, those who are born with greater genetic potential will do better at surviving and succeeding in

> "While the nativists acknowledge the importance of environment, and the environmentalists acknowledge the importance of heredity, each position emphasizes the importance of one over the other."

Regardless of the child's inherited predispositions, the environment in which the child grows up plays a signal role in what the child ultimately becomes. The father of these children not only endowed them with specific inherited traits but now, through his interactions with them, helps create the environment that will prove influential throughout their lives.

life than those born with less potential." Such a position, characteristic of *social Darwinists,* implies that the weaker, less capable members of society will "die off," or in some unspecified way, fail to survive the challenges of life. But one can take the opposite position as well. If we say, as many do, "Although heredity provides some foundation for growth, it is the environment and nourishment provided to the person that determines what growth takes place," then we hold a totally different point of view.

The first position is called **nativism** and the second **environmentalism.** While the nativists certainly acknowledge the importance of environment, and the environmentalists are quick to acknowledge the importance of heredity, each position emphasizes the importance of one over the other. Figure 2.1 shows how nativists and environmentalists deal with certain human traits.

How the Nativist Sees It	Trait	How the Environmentalist Sees It
Primarily an inherited trait that is influenced by the environment. Jensen assesses the relationship 80% heredity, 20% environment.	INTELLIGENCE	Primarily a result of the care given to us early in life and the environment in school and at home as we grow up. Cultural deprivation, such as that which burdens the poor, is a powerful influence on IQ
Genetically determined, although modified by custom and learning. The genetic basis of social behavior is survival of the species, according to Charles Darwin.	SOCIAL BEHAVIOR	Not at all genetic—rather, a result of what we learn by modeling our behavior on others around us. While it is inherited in animals, it is not in humans—which distinguishes us from lower animals.
Much mental illness is genetic in basis. Studies of twins have shown the likelihood that the psychoses particularly are inherited, although they are worsened by a poor environment.	MENTAL ILLNESS	A social problem in which the adaptation of an individual is not in accord with social norms. R. D. Laing advocates this environmental position. Change the person himself (or the individual's perception of himself) *or* change the environment, and the so-called mental illness ceases to exist.
Adler, among others, argued that people are born with "constitutional weaknesses" or "inferior organs" that are inherited. This is the basis of many physical diseases.	PHYSICAL ILLNESS	A result of environmental problems, exposure to pathogens, etc. Has little, if anything, to do with genetics (except for clearly inherited disorders, which can be demonstrated scientifically and predicted before birth).
There is an innate, inherited mechanism for learning. Chomsky, a partisan of this position, argues that we inherit the ability to learn language; the mechanisms of grammar are in our genes.	LEARNING	We learn by our exposure to situations. S-R model, which is independent of genetics, explains most of our learning.

Note: Most psychologists represent a middle ground between these extremes.

Figure 2.1 Understanding Human Traits: Two Extreme Positions

The controversy over the relative influences of **heredity** and environment still rages heatedly. Later in this section we will look at some of the important implications of this debate for teachers, educators, parents, and students. Charlesworth (1972, p. 11) points out that "biology and culture do not work separately at separate times during development. The two sources of influence on human behavior are inextricably merged together throughout the organism's whole existence. And a major job of the developmentalist is to disentangle such influences with the best analytic techniques available." But such tools are not yet available; at the present time, "working out the equation of the interaction of genetic and experiential factors is like deriving an equation without constants but with several variables of unknown, changing values" (Anandalakshmy & Grinder, 1972, p. 31). Before we look at the social and educational implications of this issue, let us examine the genetic principles that underlie the controversy.

The human organism is made up of cells. There are different kinds of cells, each with specialized functions and individual characteristics. For example, there are red-blood cells and white-blood cells, visual cells, bone cells, nerve cells, liver cells, and many others. Each performs a different function in the perpetuation of life. All cells contain twenty-three matched pairs of **chromosomes,** or forty-six chromosomes altogether. A chromosome is made up of a chain of smaller units called **genes.** These genes are linked together through molecular interactions forming the long strands that are the chromosomes.

A Genetics Primer

Genes

The gene is the chemical message unit that encodes our genetic information through its molecular structure. The chemical responsible for this coding is *deoxyribonucleic acid* (DNA), which has been called the "building block of life." This chemical is found in the nucleus of the cell, and plays an important part not only in heredity but in life itself. For example, if we cut our finger, new cells will appear when the finger heals, cells just like the ones that were destroyed in the cutting. Why don't liver cells or hair cells grow in their place? Because the **DNA** in the adjacent cells carries the message that these cells have certain distinct characteristics—that is, that they are skin cells. Likewise, as the cells in our body die off and are replaced by fresh cells, it is the DNA that communicates, through its coded molecule, what types of cells should be built to replace the old cells.

There is one type of cell in the human body that does not contain the full forty-six chromosomes, but only half, twenty-three chromosomes. This type is the reproductive cell, which is called a **gamete.** The gamete contains only one chromosome instead of the matched pair of chromosomes that we find in other cells of the body. When the male's gamete (sperm cell) combines with the female's gamete (ovum or egg cell), the resulting cell (zygote) contains forty-six chromosomes: half from the male, or father, and half from the female, or mother. Thus, the fertilized egg, the beginning of life, has a genetic code within it that is half the mother's and half the father's.

The information contained in this **zygote**—information that is stored in the forty-six chromosomes, half from the mother and half from the father—is the basis of *all* inherited characteristics. The millions of strands of molecules of DNA that contain this code are in a process of reproduction, governed according to the coded messages in this single cell.

Phenotype and Genotype

Certain characteristics of the person are determined the day that the mother's egg is fertilized, and these are totally independent of the environment or any other extraneous factors. Eye color is a clear example of this; so is blood type, skin texture, and certain genetically transmitted diseases such as hemophilia and sickle-cell anemia. We cannot necessarily tell what the underlying scheme of the genes is when we look at a human characteristic. For example, if we study twenty-five people with brown eyes, it is likely we will find that they have different genetic makeup in regard to eye color. The expression of a genetic trait (such as the person's eye color) is called the **phenotype.** But the potential for traits, the underlying genetic makeup, is called a **genotype.**

The relationship between genotype and phenotype is most interesting. One possibility is that an observed trait is a compromise between several genetic codes. This would be true for such traits as skin color, height, and certain skeletal characteristics. In such cases, the genes are much like the ingredients in a recipe: none are discernible in themselves, but all are present in the final product. Another possibility is that different genes are present, but some of them are much more dominant than others and therefore outweigh the others in determining the phenotype. Eye color is often cited as a typical example of this phenomenon. The gene that encodes brown eye color is more dominant than the gene that encodes blue eye color. Thus, if the person has one gene for brown eyes (from one of the parents) and another gene for blue eyes (from the other parent), the phenotype will be brown eyes.

Where characteristics of a less dominant or recessive gene appear in the phenotype, such as in a person's blue eyes, it indicates that the person has inherited the recessive genes from both parents and therefore has no dominant genes to cancel out or dominate over the recessive traits. But in cases where the phenotypical characteristic has been identified as dominant, we cannot determine from the phenotype alone what the genotype is since it may well conceal some recessive characteristics.

There is a third important factor in the relationship between phenotype and genotype that is not illustrated in such examples as eye color or disease symptoms. Many genotypes are less specific and exact than the ones cited. Take, for example, the genes that determine the body's propensity to put on weight. These can never be looked at entirely independently of what the person is eating. In other words, at times environmental factors contribute much to the phenotype and obscure the true nature of the genotype, which could only be determined by examining the family history and the observed traits of all the genetically related members of the family. But this is, as you can imagine, extremely difficult. While "geneticists working with plants or animals can answer this question easily by controlled breeding" as Rosenthal (1971) points out, when we wish to study the problem in people, "we have no control over breeding but must find where we can cases that represent the kind of breeding and rearing environment we would have deliberately planned if we wanted to study the genetics of a disorder in a controlled way (p. 56)." As you see, the difficulties are enormous.

Heritability

Heritability is the degree to which certain traits or tendencies are determined by genetics, as opposed to environmental determinations. The degree of heritability is supposed to answer the question, How much of the difference or variation among individuals in the population is attributable to (i.e., caused by) genetic differences and how much to environmental differences? (Jensen, 1973, p. 43). In other words, heritability is a measure that supposedly separates the amount of genetic and environmental interaction in the production of phenotypes and allows us to see the relative importance of each.

Research Methods

In understanding the problem of resolving the nature-nurture controversy, we should be familiar with the various research methods used in heritability studies, and particularly the practical and theoretical limitations of these studies. Rosenthal (1971) cites the basic methods that have been used in the genetic studies of behavioral disorders, which are closest to the genetic questions that confront educators (heritability of intelligence, creativity, learning disabilities, etc.). Although we cannot explore any of these methods in detail, each will be described briefly.

Pedigree analysis is the method previously referred to in which each lineal (parent, child) relative and collateral relative (sibling, aunt, uncle, etc.) is examined. Rosenthal points out that "at least two generations are neces-

> "At the present time, it is not certain to what degree heritability influences the traits that we, as educators, would be most concerned with."

sary for the analysis to be meaningful; more are preferable," and this restriction is, indeed, one of the major obstacles to conducting effective pedigree analyses. *Consanguinity studies* compare the incidence of a disorder (or behavior) among the general population, close relatives, and further-removed relatives, with the assumption that if incidence increases with the closeness of the relationship, then it is likely genetic. Probably the single most important class of studies are *twin studies*. These may use identical twins (**MZ** for **monozygotic**—one fertilized cell) or fraternal twins (**DZ** for **dizygotic**—or having two different fertilized cells). Since MZ twins have the exact same genetic endowment, differences between them can be attributed to environmental factors. For this reason, the most compelling studies are those in which MZ twins have been reared in separate environments since we are able to observe how the identical genetic makeup materializes into traits under different environmental conditions.

What is even more important than understanding the specific details of these methods (and other methods as well) is understanding their limitations, which have a direct bearing on the credence we give to their conclusions. None of these methods are exact insofar as human populations are concerned, and each is open to a number of stringent criticisms. For example, even where we have accurate data about the correlation of intelligence with heredity it does not necessarily imply the causality. Also, it has been pointed out in studies of racial differences that there is no way to establish a "racial" gene pool; that is, to sequester those genes that are supposed to be indigenous to one race only. Most importantly, since there is no practical way of separating the respective influences of heredity and environment, and since even those methods that examine the heritability are not precise enough, the entire issue becomes obscured in the controversy it generates. At the present time, therefore, *it is not certain to what degree heritability influences the traits that we, as educators, would be most concerned with.* While we can venture educated guesses, we cannot be certain enough to tamper with the lives and futures of the children who are our charges.

Implications for Teachers In one sense, our genetic endowments limit each of us. Genes, as potentials of maximum development, are the seeds of the blooming individual. The nurture and care of the person in stages of growth play just as crucial a part. During the preschool years, the early genetic-environmental interaction matrix determines what the child will be like when he or she enters the school

44   The Life of the Learner

setting. By the time the teacher first comes into contact with the child, the results of this interaction are already evident.

In the **nature-nurture interaction,** the teacher becomes a significant part of the nurture element, nature already having done its work. Recognizing the quality of this interaction, the teacher can do all in his or her power to provide an enriching environment that will fully help the genetic potential develop. To believe that the child is totally limited, incomplete, or nonfunctional because of genetic limitations (with the exception of disabilities whose description follows), belies the purpose of the teacher's role. In other words, the teacher provides most favorable environment so that the genetic potential can approach actuality.

Certain developmental abnormalities evident during the preschool years are determined genetically, with no environmental influence. We might consider each of these briefly. Since they do not involve the environment, the teacher (or parent) can do little to ameliorate their debilitating symptoms. By recognizing the genetic flaws in the individual, the teacher can then provide a compensatory environment to improve a child's development.

Congenital Physical Defects

Many children with **congenital** (present at birth) physical defects attend regular classes, although those with more severe symptoms may be sent to special schools or special classes within the regular school. Some common congenital defects include limb deformations, skeletal anomalies that result in failure to walk or poor coordination, heart defects (restricted activities), or disfigurations. Although disfigurations do not interfere directly with locomotion or motor functioning, they can make the child an outcast. Most of these congenital defects are genetic, although some may be the result of birth trauma or prenatal difficulties.

Down's Syndrome

Commonly known as *mongolism,* Down's syndrome is a genetic disorder with a variety of common characteristics, including mental retardation and such physical signs as the following: "(1) flattened skull which is shorter than it is wide, (2) abnormally up-turned nostrils caused by undeveloped nasal bones, (3) abnormal toe spacing (increased space particularly between the first and second toes), (4) disproportionate shortness of the fifth finger, (5) fifth finger which curves inward, (6) fifth finger which has only one crease instead of the usual two, (7) short, squared hands, (8) epicanthic fold at the inner corners of the eyes, (9) large, fissured tongue, (10) single crease across the palm of the hand (simian crease), (11) abnormally simplified ear, (12) adherent ear lobe, and (13) abnormal heart" (L'Abate & Curtis, 1975, after Gibson et al. 1964, pp. 52–53).

Mongolism is always a genetic disorder and there is no cure nor treatment for it, although children suffering from the disorder can be trained to function. The age of the mother has been shown to have a direct relationship to the likelihood of having a mongoloid child: the older the mother the greater is the likelihood that **mongolism** will occur.

Turner's Syndrome

A chromosomal abnormality in which the child is born with forty-five instead of forty-six **chromosomes** is known as Turner's syndrome. The person suffering from this disorder lacks one sex chromosome and has the appearance of a female, although genetically the child is not a female. Intellectual level is not affected directly by this disorder.

Mental Retardation

This is a broad term for many disorders whose symptom is intellectual impairment. The full topic will be considered in more depth in chapter 13, but we should mention at this point that many forms of mental retardation are caused entirely by genetic factors. The most common cause of the mental retardation that is caused by genetic factors is a metabolic disorder, carried by a recessive gene, which is called *phenylketonuria* or PKU. This disorder prevents the proper metabolism of certain proteins, and may be identified soon after birth through blood analysis, which is now a mandatory test in many states. Examination of the amniotic fluid during the mother's pregnancy can also reveal the presence of PKU.

Of the many topics regarding the nature-nurture interaction, **intelligence** *is probably the topic of greatest interest to those in the field of education. How much of a person's intelligence is genetically determined and how much is attributable to the environment? While the question is still highly controversial, there is a wealth of research on the subject, and the implications of this research are important for teachers. Nearly all researchers are in agreement that intelligence results from action between genetic potential and environmental interactions. No one has suggested that either one or the other is solely responsible for intelligence. The major* *questions are, To what extent is intelligence hereditary? and, Can we, through environmental improvement, significantly improve a person's intellectual capacity? And it is in answer to these important questions that we find the greatest controversy. Let us look at the major issues regarding the relative roles of nature and nurture in the development of intelligence.*

Probably the most solid research in this area has been done by Arthur R. Jensen, a professor of educational psychology at the University of California at Berkeley. Jensen, through a mathematical analysis of many studies of intelligence, concludes that "the **heritability** of IQ as estimated from the average of all published studies of the subject is .80, which means that on the average the studies show that 80% of the population variance in IQ is attributable to genetic variation, and 20% to nongenetic factors" (Jensen, 1971, p. 13). This is a high heritability value for intelligence (although it would not be considered high for height), and it has been criticized on many fronts.

One area of criticism points out that there is not sufficient empirical proof to support such high heritability figures. Alland (1971) cites studies that challenge Jensen's use of Sir Cyril Burt's studies of monozygotic twins and the meager samples in much of the research Jensen relies on.

A second attack against Jensen's position questions the relevance of large population data (as is inherent in such genetic studies) when we are concerned about individuals within the population. Confusion results when we want to know about an individual's intelligence and we study a population. "Their question about intelligence is, in fact, being asked about the development of a single individual," Hirsh (1970) points out, referring to nativists such as Jensen, ". . . however, they do not study development in single individuals. Usually they test groups of individuals at a single time of life. The proportions being assigned to heredity and environment refer to the relative amounts of the variance between individuals comprising a population, not how much of whatever enters into the development of the observed expression of a **trait** in a particular individual has been contributed by heredity and by environment respectively. They want to know how instinctive is intelligence in the development of a certain individual, but instead they measure differences between large numbers of fully, or partially, developed individuals" (p. 101). The implications of this position are that (1) educators cannot predict the individual's intellectual limitations through population studies that offer heritability figures, and (2) such studies do not adequately explain how the environment or the genetic makeup affects any given individual's intelligence.

A third important renunciation has been well articulated by Dr. Edmund W. Gordon, a man who describes himself as "a humanist, an edu-

> "Jensen concludes that 80 percent of the variation among individuals is due to heredity; 20 percent to environmental factors."

cator, and a twentieth-century black man." Gordon typifies the position that is critical of the entire nature-nurture interactive **paradigm,** and he questions whether it is really meaningful to reduce such complex issues as intelligence to the question of how much is nature and how much is nurture.

The confusion between the two concepts "genetic" and "determined" underlies much of the problem. That is, while all aspects of an organism may be thought of as 100 percent genetic, they are not 100 percent determined. Rather, phenotypic expressions are the result of a continuous biochemical and physiological interaction of the gene complex, cytoplasm, internal milieu, and external environment throughout the life of the organism. (Gordon, 1971, p. 242)

This argument is probably the strongest against Jensen's and the nativist's position. Stated in terms that are relevant to the teacher, we can say that a student's genotype (or genetic endowment) cannot be a direct limiter of the student's intellectual abilities, nor can it be strictly isolated from the physical, cultural, familial, and social environment in which the student functions. In other words, when we look at the total person as an interactive, living, growing, dynamic organism, we must also consider his or her intelligence as something which is not fixed at 20 percent, 30 percent, 50 percent, or 80 percent by genes and by genes alone; but rather, as something that can be changed, influenced, and affected by the environment provided by the teacher and the school, even though we cannot agree with certainty to what extent this change is possible.

It should be pointed out that Jensen in no way disagrees with the position that we must educate the **total person.** Only the misinformed critics persist in charging Jensen with arbitrarily categorizing the person by his or her race. In fact, Jensen (1971) argues:

Individuals should be treated in terms of their individual characteristics and not in terms of their group membership. This is the way of a democratic society, and educationally it is the only procedure that makes any sense. Individual variations within any large socially defined group are always much greater than the average differences between groups. There is overlap between groups in the distributions of all psychological characteristics that we know anything about.

He goes on to suggest that "group racial and social class differences are first of all individual differences, but the causes of the *group* differences may not be the same as of the *individual* differences. This is what we must find out, because the prescription of remedies for our educational ills could depend on the answer" (Jensen, 1971, p. 28). This is Jensen's rationale for his research.

> " 'Individuals should be treated in terms of their individual characteristics and not in terms of their group membership. This is the way of a democratic society.' "

What we have considered here is only a preliminary view of the complex issue of human intelligence and its roots and influences. The study of intelligence will be a recurring theme throughout this book. What is more important is the crucial interaction between heredity and environment in much of our development. What we must do before we can begin to appreciate the quality and quantity of this interaction is understand the paths of individual development, and there is no better way to do this than to examine the general theories that have been offered to explain how the person becomes what he or she ultimately does become.

There are two classes of theories we will consider: personality theories and **cognitive-developmental** theories. Personality theories are, on the whole, more comprehensive. They try to account not only for the emotional development of the person but for social and cognitive development as well. The cognitive theories focus more directly on how we learn and process information and are particularly useful to us as teachers and educators. In this chapter, we are going to look at an overview of these positions, which will be examined in more depth (by age-level) in the following three chapters.

Developmental Theories

Now that we have examined, in some detail, the genetic basis of human development, we return to the question raised at the beginning of our inquiry. In what ways does the individual break free of his or her genetic bondage and begin to develop as a person of free will and individual destiny? This question comprises many smaller questions: How do we learn to perceive the world around us and to deal with it? How do we master the cognitive tasks necessary for processing information and dealing with problems and obstacles that we encounter? How do we grow emotionally—in which direction and because of which factors? These and allied questions have been tackled by several theorists, of both compatible and contradictory positions, and throughout the following chapters, we will be examining some of their viewpoints in some detail. In this section we shall take a sweeping panorama of the positions that in later chapters we shall examine in depth, and then compare these positions with respect to developmental constructs that influence educational practices (see table 2.1, p. 63).

A theory of **personality** is more than the term implies. In its most useful sense, it is not simply a technical description of the structure and development of the individual's personality but a comprehensive view of man, an understanding of the motivations behind behavior, a systematic philosophy of life-style and behavior. A theory of personality explains, through its own terminology and concepts, how the person becomes what he or she is. While theories of personality concentrate, for the most part, on the emotional (or **affective**) dimensions of the individual, they are, in varying degrees, also related to cognitive development, although separate cognitive development theories have evolved over the years and these have gained increasing recognition as independent theories.

As we grow, we establish our individual identities. Note how these identical twins use different hair styles and wear different styles of shoes.

> "While no given individual can be fully explained by *any one* personality theory, bits and pieces drawn from different theories enable the teacher to account for *patterns* of behavior and to link together different aspects of the learner's behaviors and feelings into workable constructs."

A theory of personality, despite its theoretical nature and psychological aim, is of enormous importance to teachers and educators. *It helps us to better understand the individual in all of his or her complexity.* Specifically, it helps us organize our many disjointed perceptions and insights about the person into meaningful wholes that can be used pedagogically, therapeutically, or in other ways for the learner's benefit. While no given individual can be fully explained by *any one* personality theory, bits and pieces drawn from different theories enable the teacher to account for *patterns* of behavior and to link together different aspects of the learner's behaviors and feelings into workable constructs.

In the following chapters, three major personality perspectives will be examined: the psychoanalytic, the behavioral, and the humanistic. At this point, we will provide a brief overview of each.

The Psychoanalytic Position

The psychoanalytic position is derived from the writings of Sigmund Freud (1856–1939), mainly from his work with neurotic patients. Although Freud acknowledged that the sources of his theory were his neurotic patients, he argued that the implications applied equally to "normal" and well-adjusted individuals as well. He assembled around him a group of brilliant followers who at first agreed fully with his ideas but in time broke away slowly, rejecting one point or another, and each started his or her own neo-Freudian movement. At the present time, when we speak of the psychoanalytic position, we include not only Freud but also later exponents of derivative positions: namely Carl Gustav Jung (1875–1961), Alfred Adler (1870–1937), Karen Horney (1885–1952), Harry Stack Sullivan (1892–1949), and Erik Erikson (1902–   ). Erikson's position, more than any of the others, has had a profound influence on education and will be given equal attention to Freud's seminal position from which it was derived.

Freud viewed man as an inherently instinctual creature, driven by his strivings for infantile gratification. Throughout his life, the individual is strongly motivated to seek out satisfaction of his primitive instinctual drives, sex and aggression, often beclouding in the process his perceptual and emotional awareness of self and others. He distorts the reality of the world around him by utilizing **defense mechanisms** (see chapter 7) that protect his ego by allowing him to block out and subjectively redefine that which he cannot accept. While this does protect the ego, and consequently his sanity and stability, it alters his conception of the world and his relationships with others significantly so that what he sees, thinks, and feels consciously is only a fraction of the wide range of possibilities that are within him. Man's vision of life, according to Freud, is obscured by his unconscious fears and wishes, by his persevering and often unmet needs of childhood, by his maturational limitations—all of which are rooted in the first five years of life. He is basically selfish and self-satisfying except insofar as he is able to sacrifice his gratification "of the primitive impulses . . . for the common good."

To explain specifically the dynamics of the mind, Freud postulated the concepts of **id, ego,** and **superego.** The *id* is the primitive, unorganized mass of energy behind the unconscious mind. It is the part of the mind from which all psychic energy springs, but it is undirected, unorganized, and in total obedience to the pleasure principle—the striving for gratification. The *ego* is the executive of personality, the part of the mind that mediates between the id and the real world. The function of the ego is to satisfy the instinctual demands of the id by carrying out transactions with the external world. The *superego* is the part of the psyche in which parental introjections are located. It is roughly equivalent to conscience, and includes all the things the parents taught the child he "should" or "should not" do or think.

Freud's view of man is deeply influenced by his notion of the unconscious. Our personality and actions, he argues, are in a large part determined by the thoughts and feelings contained in the unconscious. These thoughts and feelings are not always directly accessible to consciousness, cannot be readily recalled, and are consequently outside the person's field of awareness, observation, and self-reflection. To Freud, the individual's life and behavior is simply the revelation of the **unconscious,** outside the person's control and awareness. This idea rests firmly on the notion of man as a creature of emotion for whom reason is a secondary influence on behavior.

The followers who broke away from Freud's point of view cited his dogmatism and his lack of "faith" in the nature of man. Each of these followers, in his or her own way, viewed man as more of a *social* creature who, although influenced by unconscious remains of childhood, also adapted quite consciously to the social world around him. Alfred Adler developed his Individual Psychology, which views the person within a social context. De-emphasizing Freud's emphasis on sexuality, Adler developed in its place a comprehensive view of man and his actions, dominated by alternative social and psychological motivations, feelings, intuitions, and strivings. The child is born with deep, imbedded feelings of **inferiority,** Adler argued, and strives throughout life to gain **superiority** over the environment and over others. One reason that Adler's position has gained such prominence in education is that it views the person within a social context and as a social animal. Since the school provides such a context for the learner, Adler's theory can help the teacher better understand how the personality is molded within the classroom setting, as well as in the home.

Scarth (1969) summarizes the main assumptions of the Adlerian position as follows:

1. Personality is the individual's unique and self-consistent unity.
2. Behavior is purposive and goal-directed. All things an individual does serve a purpose for him.
3. There is one basic dynamic force behind all human activity, a striving from a felt minus situation toward a plus situation, from a feeling of inferiority toward a superiority, perfection, totality.
4. The individual is striving for success in the solution of his problems, this striving being anchored in the very structure of his life.
5. Man is socially embedded. He becomes what he is in interaction with other people. *The individual should be perceived in a social context if he is to be understood. . . .*
6. Social interest, i.e., a concern for others and its expression in cooperation, is necessary for the solution of life's problems. . . .
7. Each individual creates his own unique life style based on his subjective perception of himself and his environment, and what appears to him as success.
8. In the healthy individual social interest, as the ultimate form of mankind . . . a normative ideal, gives direction to the striving. In mental disturbance, where social interest is lacking, striving is on the socially useless side.
9. *Inferiority feelings are present in all individuals.* The minus situation gives the impetus to action.
10. People approach life with different degrees of activity. (Scarth, 1969, pp. 146–147)

Clearly, the psychoanalytic position that dominates educational thinking today is Erik Erikson's. Erikson began his career as an artist, but soon became interested in child psychology and travelled to Vienna where he studied with leaders of the psychoanalytic movement. He became a child analyst, and many of his views are a result of his intensive work with children. Deeply influenced by the work of Henry Murray, a personality theorist, and by anthropologists such as Ruth Benedict and Margaret Mead, Erikson's theory integrates insights from many different disciplines to explain the development of the child. While he is in essence a psychoanalytic thinker, in his emphasis on childhood and psychosexual development, he also incorporates socio-psychological insights into his work that result in a significant difference from the Freudian position.

Two major points in Erikson's position differentiate it from Freud's. First, Erikson views the course of development throughout the person's *entire* life, noting that the adolescent period is particularly important in forming a sense of *identity*. Whereas Freud was not much concerned with psychological development after the age of six, Erikson views the adolescent period as critical. Second, while Freud looks only at the parent-child interaction, Erikson also examines the play of social forces that make themselves felt in the child's mind during various stages of development. "Cultures," Erikson (1963, p. 108) points out, ". . . elaborate upon the biologically given and strive for a division of function between the sexes, which is, simultaneously, workable within the body's scheme, meaningful to the particular society, and manageable for the individual ego." Since the individual interacts with the culture throughout his entire life, the results of this interaction continue to foster psychological growth. Erikson's "Eight Ages of Man," which summarize his views of developmental stages, in some ways are parallel and in some ways are different from Freud's. Figure 2.2 compares their stages.

Throughout the following three chapters, insights from these three psychoanalytic positions—Freud's, Adler's, and Erikson's—will be used to clarify some of the psychodynamic processes of growth and development. Moreover, table 2.1 (p. 63) shows how the implications of the psychodynamic perspective influence our understanding of learning processes, classroom techniques for correcting inappropriate behavior, learner motivation, self-perception, and related areas of interest to the classroom teacher.

Figure 2.2 Psychoanalytic Stages of Development: Freud and Erikson

Approximate chronological age	Freudian stage	Erikson's stage
0	Oral	Basic trust vs. basic mistrust
1	Oral	Basic trust vs. basic mistrust
2	Anal	Autonomy vs. shame and doubt
3	Anal	Autonomy vs. shame and doubt
4	Phallic	Initiative vs. guilt
5	Phallic	Initiative vs. guilt
6	Oedipal stage	Initiative vs. guilt
7	Oedipal stage	
8	Latency	Industry vs. inferiority
9	Latency	Industry vs. inferiority
10	Latency	Industry vs. inferiority
11	Latency	Industry vs. inferiority
12	Genital stage	
13	Genital stage	Identity vs. role confusion
14	Genital stage	Identity vs. role confusion
15	Genital stage	Identity vs. role confusion
16	Genital stage	Identity vs. role confusion
17	Genital stage	Identity vs. role confusion
18		Intimacy vs. isolation
19		Intimacy vs. isolation
20		Intimacy vs. isolation
Adult		Generativity vs. stagnation
		Ego integrity vs. despair

The Behavioral (Learning Theory) Position

Whereas the psychoanalytic position relies heavily on instinct theory and innate motivating forces, the behavioral theory of personality development relies on the insights from learning theory. Personality, if indeed there is such a thing, is the result of learning, not of nature, behaviorists argue. Although there are wide differences within this position, as there are within the psychoanalytic school, there is less contradiction and conflict between the different positions. Rather, each attempts to explain different aspects of growth and development, and most are compatible with each other.

The roots of contemporary behavioral psychology are found in the work of John B. Watson (1878–1958), an American psychologist who founded behaviorism. Watson's argument, used by behaviorists to the present day, is that the proper study of psychology is the person's observable behavior. This is a direct refutation to the introspectionist psychology—a psychology that had gained popularity in Europe—but applies equally as well to the psychoanalytic position, which also tries to take into account the inner workings of consciousness. "As a science," Watson points out (1924), "psychology puts before herself the task of unraveling the complex factors involved in the development of human behavior." The purpose of doing this—and to educators this is of special importance—is not only to understand the person but to control the person's behavior as well.

The interest of the behaviorist in man's doing is more than the interest of the spectator—he wants to control man's reactions as physical scientists want to control and manipulate other natural phenomena. It is the business of behavioristic psychology to be able to predict and control human activity. To do this it must gather scientific data by experimental methods. Only then can the trained behaviorist predict, given the stimulus, what reaction will take place; or, given the reaction, state what the situation or stimulus is that has caused the reaction. (Watson, 1924, p. 11)

In order to develop uniform laws that will help explain and predict as well as control human behavior, Watson explicates the concepts of **stimulus** and **response**—terms that have become integral to the behaviorist's vocabulary. A stimulus may be defined as any change in the organism's internal or external environment. For example, hunger is a change in the *internal* environment, and a sudden loud noise is a change in the organism's *external* environment. A response is a behavior by the organism in relation to the stimulus. Thus, seeking out food or holding one's ears would be responses to the stimuli listed above. The critical principle—*that each stimulus is linked up to a response*—has become the basic rule of behavioral psychology.

From this central axiom, a number of different positions have developed, sometimes along different lines and usually with different purposes in mind. But in all cases, to the behaviorist *the individual is a product of his conditioning*. The behaviorists speak of the S-R paradigm (stimulus-response) as the basic pattern of all human learning. Each person reacts in a predictable way to any given stimulus, depending upon what his training has taught him. People are no different than animals except that their responses to stimuli are more complex and on a higher level of organization.

Conditioning need not take place only in the laboratory setting, where it was originally discovered. In the home, the mother and siblings condition the child through reinforcement of certain responses over others.

The key word underlying the behavioral view of man is **conditioning.** Although there are several types of conditioning, there are two basic classes that are usually discussed: **classical (respondent) conditioning** and **operant (instrumental) conditioning.** Classical conditioning "is the process whereby an originally neutral stimulus, through continuous pairing with an unconditioned stimulus, acquires the ability to elicit a response originally given to the unconditioned stimulus" (Price, 1972). This is the type of conditioning illustrated in Pavlov's famous experiment with the dog. As you may recall, Pavlov discovered, while studying digestion in animals, that if a bell rang immediately before a dog was fed, after a time the ringing of the bell itself would cause the dog to salivate. The pairing of the ringing bell (*conditioned* stimulus) with the feeding (*unconditioned* stimulus) caused the dog to respond to the bell by salivating.

The second major type of conditioning is operant or instrumental conditioning. This is the type of conditioning generally associated with the work of B. F. Skinner. "In operant conditioning, voluntarily or spontaneously emitted (operant) behavior is strengthened (or discouraged) by positive reinforcement (reward) or by negative reinforcement, which is a **stimulus** whose removal increases the probability of the behavior it follows, by lack of reinforcement . . . or by punishment" (Patterson, 1973, p. 80). Figure 2.3 compares classical and operant conditioning.

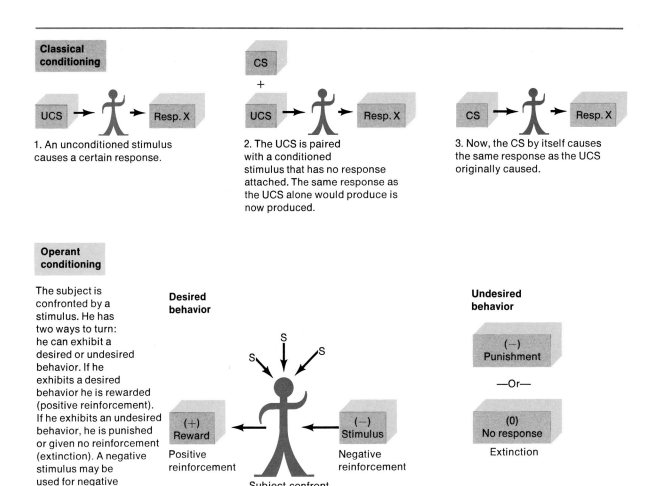

Classical conditioning

UCS → 🧍 → Resp. X

1. An unconditioned stimulus causes a certain response.

CS
+
UCS → 🧍 → Resp. X

2. The UCS is paired with a conditioned stimulus that has no response attached. The same response as the UCS alone would produce is now produced.

CS → 🧍 → Resp. X

3. Now, the CS by itself causes the same response as the UCS originally caused.

Operant conditioning

The subject is confronted by a stimulus. He has two ways to turn: he can exhibit a desired or undesired behavior. If he exhibits a desired behavior he is rewarded (positive reinforcement). If he exhibits an undesired behavior, he is punished or given no reinforcement (extinction). A negative stimulus may be used for negative reinforcement.

Desired behavior

(+) Reward
Positive reinforcement

(−) Stimulus
Negative reinforcement

Subject confront stimulus S

Undesired behavior

(−) Punishment

—Or—

(0) No response
Extinction

Figure 2.3 Classical (Respondent) and Operant (Instrumental) Conditioning

Consider, for example, what happens in a simple Skinner box. In this contraption, an animal is taught to push a lever and is rewarded with food *(positive reinforcement)*. This pattern of behavior eventually becomes learned. The learning principle behind operant conditioning is that *new learning occurs as a result of positive reinforcement, and old patterns are abandoned as a result of negative reinforcement.*

In addition to these conditioning paradigms, **modeling** is an important process in behavioral psychology. Modeling occurs when the behavior of a subject is changed by observing the behavior of another person—a model—after whose behavior the subject models himself or herself. Much of our early behavior in life, according to this position, is modeled after the behavior of our parents and significant others in our environment.

The behavioral psychologist accounts for most of our early learning through the use of these paradigms. Certain behaviors, arrived at by trial and

> "Maslow began with the assumption that psychology should start by studying the normal, healthy personality rather than the 'pathological,' unadapted personality, which serves as the basis of Freudian psychology."

error, are rewarded (by food, praise, or a toy, for example) repeatedly, and these behaviors tend to become strengthened. Other behaviors continue because the child observes similar behaviors on the part of adults. Some behaviors are extinguished by the lack of either positive or negative reinforcement. **Extinction** occurs whenever a behavior is ignored; that is, neither reinforced nor punished.

The difference between punishment and negative reinforcement should be emphasized since this is often confused. A **negative reinforcer** is an unpleasant stimulus that elicits a behavior intended to avoid the stimulus. "If a stimulus can be used to strengthen behaviors which escape or avoid it, we can call that stimulus by its functional designation—a negative reinforcer" (Bijou & Baer, 1965, p. 98). An example of the use of negative reinforcement is commonly found when a parent applies a bitter substance to a child's fingers to discourage thumb sucking. It is to avoid this bitter taste that the child gives up the "bad" habit.

Punishment, on the other hand, occurs after behavior has been observed. If the parent scolds the child every time he is caught sucking his thumb, this would be a form of punishment. In many cases, negative reinforcement and punishment are used in tandem to increase the probability of eliminating undesirable behaviors.

The Humanistic Position: Toward Growth and Self-Actualization

This view of personality development comprises a number of related positions that share a common foundation. Embracing the **client-centered** psychology of Carl Rogers, the existential philosophy and psychology that originated in Europe, and the "third force" humanism of Abraham Maslow and Gordon Allport that has had an enormous impact in the United States, the humanistic approach is truly a synthetic position. We shall try in this section to examine briefly some of the common principles that underlie this position.

Maslow began with the assumption that psychology should start by studying the normal, healthy personality rather than the "pathological," unadapted personality that serves as the basis of Freudian psychology. "If one is preoccupied with the insane, the neurotic, the psychopath, the criminal, the delin-

The Healthy Individual

quent, the feeble-minded," Maslow (1954) argues, "one's hopes for the human species become perforce more and more modest, more and more 'realistic,' more and more scaled down, one expects less and less from people. . . ." But Maslow expected a lot from people, and he worked toward developing a psychology of **self-actualization** that would account for the health-giving characteristics of the person: the growing, changing, flexible, fulfilled individual. To break away from the traditional Freudian and behavioristic approaches, he abandoned in part the cool, scientific approach and used in its place a subjective, personal perspective. As Goble (1970) points out:

> Maslow was convinced that we can learn a great deal more about human nature through consideration of the subjective as well as the objective. . . . Maslow felt that a comprehensive theory of behavior must include the internal or intrinsic determinants of behavior as well as extrinsic or external and environmental determinants. Freud had concentrated on the first, the Behaviorists on the second. Both points of view needed to be combined. An objective study of human behavior was not enough; for complete understanding, the subjective must be considered as well. We must consider people's feelings, desires, hopes, aspirations in order to understand their behavior. (p. 87)

This is precisely what Maslow has attempted to do in his study of human development and personality formation. The basic framework within which Maslow proposes to do this includes the concepts of growth, **self-actualization,** and a **hierarchy** of needs. Self-actualization as described by Maslow (1954) is "the full use and exploitation of talent, capacities, potentialities, etc. Such people seem to be fulfilling themselves and doing the best that they are capable of doing." The self-actualizing individual is continually in the process of becoming, of finding his true self among the myriad of his possibilities. He is usually a talented, creative, responsive individual; one who is in touch with reality and able to accept it as it is, and to accept his place within the world. His perception is clear, he is confident yet not grandiose, sure of himself and sensitive to all his limitations. He is committed to some meaningful project, some plan, which holds much of his interest. He is spontaneous and less inhibited than the person who is not self-actualizing.

Carl Rogers's view of man follows a similar course, but with some modifications. Rogers sees man as essentially good, with a natural inclination toward growth. One of his clearest and most direct statements on the subject is found in his response to those writers who have discussed his view of man.

> My views of man's most basic characteristics have been formed by my experience in psychotherapy. They include certain observations as to what man is not, as well as some description of what, in my experience, he is. Let me state these very briefly, and then endeavor to clarify my meanings.
>
> I do not discover man to be well characterized in his basic nature by such terms as fundamentally hostile, antisocial, destructive, evil.
>
> I do not discover man to be, in his basic nature, completely without a nature, a *tabula rasa* on which anything may be written. . . .

I do not discover man to be essentially a perfect being, sadly warped and corrupted by society.

In my experience I have discovered man to have characteristics which seem inherent in his species, and the terms which have at different times seemed to me descriptive of these characteristics are such terms as positive, forward-moving, constructive, realistic, trustworthy. (Rogers, 1957, p. 199)

This view of man is integral to Rogers's personality theory—which is best called a theory of individual development, of "self." While it is not a developmentally based theory, it attempts to account for the ways that the person develops a set of perceptions and insights—an individuality—in the same way that developmental theories usually do, and thus it can be grouped in the class of personality theories.

Rogers looks at man in his continual interaction with the environment. The environment, argues Rogers, is not an objective reality, mutually perceived by all the people in the world, but a subjective, personal reality, dependent upon the individual's feelings, perceptions, and abilities. This reality, as it is perceived, is called the **phenomenological field.** As a person's experiences and feelings change, so too does the individual's environment, which is a product of these feelings and experiences. Thus, his interaction with the environment is one in which both the individual and his environment change in relation to each other.

The individual's sense of self emerges from this interaction with his phenomenal field. Rogers defines the self as "an organized, fluid, but consistent conceptual pattern of perceptions of characteristics and relationships of the 'I' or 'me,' together with values attached to these concepts . . . which emerge as a result of interaction with the environment, and particularly as a result of evaluational interactions with others" (Rogers, 1951, p. 498). The ways in which the individual behaves and the ways he adapts to situations are always consistent with his self-concept. His actions are reflections of his perceptions. Rogers's general rule is that the experiences that the individual undergoes are either (1) organized into self-structure, (2) ignored because they are inconsistent with the sense of self, or (3) perceived distortedly because they are not harmonious with self-perceptions. Consequently, the individual is said to be well-adjusted when he is able to assimilate on a symbolic level all of his experiences into a consistent relationship with the concept of self. In this respect, Rogers's thinking is similar to Freud's concept of the **integrated personality.**

Rogers's view of man differs most markedly from Freud's in its emphasis on the changing, protean, evolving nature of man. In opposition to Freud's deterministic viewpoint, Rogers sees man as a creature of changing destinies, capable of dealing with his own problems, of reorganizing his perceptions, and of learning to understand people who are different.

> " 'For the existentialist, the self is devoid of character or coloration before action is undertaken. When the individual begins devising projects and purposes, he begins creating an identity.' "

The Existential Positions
The humanistic positions of Rogers and Maslow can be said to be existential positions in the sense that they deal with the realities of man's existence as a living, dynamic, changing organism in interaction with others and with the environment. There is a more clearly defined existential position, however, that underlies the theories of other thinkers. While this position is not so much a theory of personality, it is a view of man that infuses all of the existentialists' efforts to understand any of the individual's problems or situations. Thus, from the point of view of the teacher, or educator, existentialism is a perspective that helps us better understand the unique individuality of the learner.

Maxine Greene (1973), the foremost existential educator in the United States, points out the implications of existentialism not only for better understanding the learner but for the teacher's own decisions as well:

For the existentialist, the self is devoid of character or coloration before action is undertaken. When the individual begins devising projects and purposes, he begins creating an identity. No outside factor or force, no science or set of rules or moral law, can make decisions for him. The only significant choices are those that involve him totally and project his existence into the future still unknown. The only meaningful choices are those for which he takes full responsibility. If he sits back and makes abstract judgments ("Yes, racism really should be abolished"; "Teachers are justified in joining the union"; "Classes here ought to be individualized") he is in danger of "bad faith." His chances of authentication are diminished, because his authenticity depends on his capacity (or his courage) to cope with the anxiety of the human condition. The ability to confront the threat of nothingness, to acknowledge mortality, moves a person to act. He *knows* the only meanings that exist are the ones he achieves, the only values that exist are the ones he creates; he knows that if he does not act, nothingness will overtake him and his world. (p. 256)

Existential psychology, like the existential philosophies from which it comes, has no single unified theory, but is beset by rifts and factions representing some serious points of disagreement. However, concerning the fundamental nature of man, the existentialist position can be summed up in five basic tenets that translate into specific educational and psychological practice and theory:

1. "Existence precedes essence"—What we do determines who we are. The individual's innate capacities are secondary to the acts of volition that characterize his behavior. To say, "I am what I am because this is how I

was born, or because this is how my parents made me, or because social forces have conspired against me" is contrary to the existential position.

2. Man is free to choose and is responsible for the consequences of his choices—behavior can never be viewed in isolation from the other options not chosen, which were available to the individual.

3. Man's life is always lived with a view-toward-death. His authenticity derives from his ability to be aware of this the ability to recognize death as a fact of life, and to accept it as such, is a part of emotional maturity and mental health.

4. Man's existence is never completely separate from the existence of others —as we grow, we learn to live in the world with others. While, in part, we define our own "being" through our interactions with others, we are also able to differentiate our existence from the existence of others.

5. Perception is more valid when it is free from subjective preconceptions and perceptual biases—an important part of learning is learning to see things as they really are, in their objective naturalness.

Table 2.1   Three Theories of Personality Development: Comparisons and Implications

	Psychoanalytic	Behavioral	Humanistic
The Origins of Behavior	Instinctual—innate in the person	Conditioning—all behavior is learned	Within the interactions between the total person and the environment
Processes of Learning	Identification Introjection	Respondent conditioning Instrumental conditioning Modeling	Interactions between the organism and environment, cohered by the "self"
Method of Correcting Deficiencies or Problems	Returning to the past and reliving psychological trauma	Learning new response patterns to old stimuli	Allowing for the full potential of the person's growth
How We Perceive the World Around Us	Obscured by the defense mechanisms	As stimuli to be responded to in an automatic way	Through individual perceptions that reconstruct reality phenomenologically
Motivation	The id—the instinctual energy striving for gratification; the "pleasure principle"	Internal or external changes in the environment; *stimuli*	Satisfaction of a hierarchy of needs, striving toward self-actualization
Developmental Sequence	Oral Anal Phallic Oedipal Latency Genital Stage	No developmental sequence. Personality develops in stages of learning, each building upon the other	Self-actualizing—tending toward higher levels as basic needs are met

The three positions of personality development characterized in table 2.1—the psychoanalytic, the behavioral, and the humanistic—will be referred to time and again throughout this book. While each position includes several theories, which are sometimes at odds with each other, they represent the three major views of man that characterize Western psychological thought in the twentieth century. Their influences and implications are staggering: they affect the way we perceive people, the way we treat them therapeutically, the way we help them learn and grow, the way we formulate and crystallize our ideas about teaching.

In the chapters that comprise Part One, "The Life of the Learner," we will use these three personality perspectives to better understand the development of the learner. We will note how the psychoanalysts, the behaviorists, and the humanists each go about explaining how the person becomes what he or she is. In Part Two, "The Psychology of Learning," we will study ways in which these positions translate into learning theories. The behavioral position, we shall see, is strongest in this area; the psychoanalytic position, the weakest. The humanistic view of man has many implications for learning in the affective domain, which will be discussed fully in chapter 7. In Part Three, "Teaching: Art and Science," we will consider what each of these three positions means to the teacher, particularly how they influence the teacher's attitudes, behaviors, perceptions, and goals in the classroom.

Now, we will turn our attention to a brief overview of learning positions —theories of cognitive development—that help explain how the learner develops the cognitive capacities to function effectively in the school setting and to master the intricacies of learning.

Three Positions on Cognitive Development: An Overview

One of the mysteries that has continually challenged psychologists (and long before them, philosophers of the mind) is how the individual develops the capacities to learn, what processes are involved in learning, and how the information from the "senses" is translated into meaningful learning. As we study the life and development of the learner in this part of the book, we will attempt to understand the stage-by-stage, age-level development of cognitive functioning. First, we should look briefly at some major positions that attempt to sum up and explain how the individual learns about the world and learns to make sense of the things around him.

The Behavioral Positions   The behavioral theory of development, discussed previously in terms of personality development, is predominantly a **learning theory;** that is, it suggests that the personality develops as the individual learns, and then goes on to explain how that learning takes place, according to the relationship between *stimuli* and *responses*. Since we have already discussed this position, at this point we will sum up its four main implications for understanding cognitive development:

1. Associations occur between stimuli and responses. These associations are *learned* through interactions between the organism and its environment.
2. Some behaviors are strengthened and others weakened; this depends upon whether the behavior is reinforced positively or negatively, or not reinforced at all.
3. Motivation is a consequence of the situation that the person is in. Environments can be manipulated to be more or less motivating to the learner.
4. The person also learns by watching and modeling himself after the behavior of others. This may be especially important in accounting for such early learning tasks as language acquisition.

We shall see, in the following chapters, several instances in which the behavioral position is used to explain how the learner masters, at different stages of development, the tasks that are necessary for survival.

The cognitivist, in contrast to the behaviorist, is more interested in the thinking of the person than in the behavior. Different cognitive theories attempt to explain how the person integrates new perceptual awareness into experience. Studies attempt to determine the subtle processes of thought in the hope of illustrating the patterns of growth through explaining the development of more sophisticated thinking.

The Cognitivist's Position

Studies of infant perception, such as the work of Robert Fantz discussed in the following chapter, are examples of cognitivist studies. In this type of research, sophisticated experimental designs are used to delve inside the infant's psyche and better understand how the infant is processing information, what the infant is doing with the information, and what the information means to the infant.

Cognitivism derives from the perceptual psychology known as Gestalt psychology. This psychology differentiates the myriad perceptions that lay before the person, at any given time, into *figure* and *ground*. We select, from the things available to us, some to be dominant and some to be less pronounced; those which dominate are the figure and the others remain in the background. As the child develops, he or she acquires increased capability at differentiating things in the environment. One reason children enjoy such games as Find the Hidden Figure in This Picture, or What's Wrong in

This Picture? is that it sharpens and tests their increased perceptual awareness.

One specific type of cognitive position has gained prominence in the twentieth century: the position of Jean Piaget, a Swiss psychologist. We shall be examining Piaget's stages of cognitive development in some detail in the following chapters, but at this point we will take a brief overview of his position.

Piaget's Position: Equilibrium Through Adaptation

It is impossible to study the cognitive development of the child without referring to the work of Jean Piaget, whose research on children's cognition has been a major influence on twentieth-century thinking. While Piaget is primarily noted for the stages of cognitive development, a discussion of which will follow, the theory that underlies his work—its organizing principle—is of signal value in understanding not only *how* the person achieves full cognitive functioning but *why* he does.

Two key terms that are integral to the theory are **equilibrium** and **adaptation.** While the usage of these terms by Piaget does not differ from their dictionary definitions, they do have special application to cognitive functioning. Equilibrium, Piaget (1967) points out, has always had a major role in psychology in explaining behavior, but "what is important for psychological explication is not equilibrium as a state but, rather, the actual process of equilibration" (p. 101), that is, the process whereby the organism brings about a state of equilibrium. Piaget attempts to examine this process of equilibration, first by comparing concepts of equilibrium in different natural settings (physics, physiology, etc.) and then by applying the results to cognitive functioning:

> Generally speaking, the equilibrium of cognitive structures can be conceived as a compensation for external intrusion by means of the activities of the subject which are responses to these intrusions. The latter may be presented in two different ways.
>
> In the case of the lower, unstable . . . forms of equilibrium, the intrusion consists of real and actual modifications of the environment, to which the compensatory activities of the subject respond as best they can without a permanent operational system. . . .
>
> In the case of the higher or operational structures, on the other hand, the intrusion to which the subject responds may consist of virtual modifications; i.e., in optimum cases they can be imagined and anticipated by the subject in the form of the direct operations of a system (operations expressing transformations in some initial sense). . . .
>
> *In short, the compensations start by being effectuated by degrees but can end by consisting of pure representations of the transformations with the intrusions, like the compensations, being reduced to certain operations of the system.* Between these two extremes, there are, of course, all kinds of intervening steps. . . . (Piaget, 1967, p. 113)

This is a difficult selection which requires some clarification. What Piaget is saying in effect is that the child's cognitive structure responds to new objects in the environment that are presented *(intrusions)* by changing in different ways and in different degrees. The changes (compensations) constitute the equilibrating process. "Human action consists," he points out in another part of the book, "of a continuous and perpetual mechanism of readjustment or equilibration" (p. 7).

In studying the ways that the individual progresses in his or her compensatory activities, Piaget discovered different developmental stages, each of which is more sophisticated than the preceding one. Figure 2.4 shows the sequence of stages, which will be considered in the following chapters by age level.

Figure 2.4 Piaget's Stages of Cognitive Development

Stage	General description	Age level
SENSORIMOTOR PERIOD	The child progresses from instinctual reflexive action at birth to symbolic activities, to the ability to separate self from object in the environment. He develops limited capabilities for anticipating the consequences of actions.	0 ½ 1 1½ 2
PREOPERATIONAL PERIOD	The child's ability to think becomes refined during this period. First, he develops what Piaget calls preconceptual thinking, in which he deals with each thing individually but is not able to group objects. The child is able to use symbols, such as words, to deal with problems. During the latter half of this period, the child develops better reasoning abilities but is still bound to the here-and-now.	2½ 3 3½ 4 4½ 5 5½ 6 6½ 7
CONCRETE OPERATIONS	At this stage, the child develops the ability to perform intellectual operations — such as reversibility, conservation, ordering of things by number, size, or class, etc. His ability to relate time and space is also matured during this period.	7½ 8 8½ 9 9½ 10 10½
PERIOD OF FORMAL OPERATIONS	This is the period in which the person learns hypothetical reasoning. He is able to function purely on a symbolic, abstract level. His conceptualization capacities are matured.	11 11½ 12 12½ 13 13½ 14 14½ 15

The Foundations of Growth and Development

> "What Piaget is saying in effect is that the child's cognitive structure responds to new objects in the environment by changing in different ways and in different degrees."

So, we see at this point that the person's cognitive structure is always governed by the force of equilibrium; it must maintain balance when "upset" by intrusions—new objects from the environment. This process of changing —either the cognitive structure or the environment—to preserve balance is the organism's ability to adapt. Hence, it is called **adaptation.** Adaptation consists of two kinds of processes: **assimilation** and **accommodation.** These processes extend to all age levels and infuse all the cognitive developmental processes. "Before examining the details of development," Piaget (1967, p. 7) suggests, "we must try to find that which is common to the needs and interests present at all ages. One can say, in regard to this, that *all needs tend first of all to incorporate things and people into the subject's own activity, i.e., to 'assimilate' the external world into the structures that have already been constructed, and secondly to readjust these structures as a function of subtle transformation, i.e., to 'accommodate' them to external objects"* (p. 8, italics ours).

Phillips (1975) provides good examples of these processes:

Assimilation occurs whenever an organism utilizes something from its environment and incorporates it. A biological example would be the ingestion of food. The food is changed in the process, and so is the organism. Psychological processes are similar in that the pattern in the stimulation is changed and, again, so is the organism. But at the same time that the input is being changed by the structures, the mediating processes are being changed by the input. For example, object constancy . . . can be used to illustrate this. Each "correction" that is applied by the brain to a retinal image had to be learned—i.e., the structures that act upon the input have themselves been shaped by that input. . . . The mechanism by which those changes occur Piaget calls "accommodation." (pp. 10–11)

As we examine the Piagetian theory in the following chapters, concentrating on the types of functioning that are characteristic of different age levels, we will note how adaptation of the organism's cognitive structure comprises both assimilation and accommodation in attempts to maintain equilibrium.

An understanding of Piaget's theory is essential for the teacher. The reason its influence in educational thought has been so extensive is twofold. First, it allows us to better understand the capabilities of the learner at a given age. We know that the seven-year-old child, for instance, is not capable of hypothetical reasoning because he has not yet reached the necessary level of abstraction. Second, it allows us to present material to the learner in a way that the learner can understand. Recognizing that the processes of assimilation and accommodation are the key processes underlying all learning (at

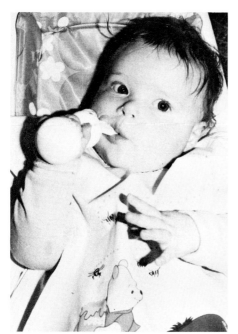

During the sensorimotor stage, the child's physical explorations of the world lead to the formation of new cognitive structures.

least, in the sense of "meaningful" learning), we can structure curriculum—subject-matter— in such a way that the learner will be able to reconstruct it in his or her own cognitive faculty. In the following chapters, we will examine its specific applicability at the preschool, elementary, and secondary school levels.

Summary

In this chapter, we have attempted a broad overview of the course of human development as it is seen in different perspectives, from different theoretical points of view. We began by examining the genetic basis of human development, considering the interactive influences between the genes and the environment. Heredity is a potential, we have pointed out, which is actualized as we live, as we interact with the environment. Next, we looked at some theories which try to explain how the person develops and breaks free from the genetic bondage. First, we considered three basic types of personality theories: the psychoanalytic, the behavioral, and the humanistic. Next, we examined three theories of cognitive growth: the behavioral, Piaget's position, and the cognitivist's position.

In the following three chapters we will examine specific areas of growth and development that are age-related: first, to the preschool years; then to the elementary school years; finally, to the secondary school years.

Suggested Additional Readings

Genetic Diversity and Human Equality by Theodosius Dobzhansky (*New York: Basic Books, 1973*)

In a book written for the lay person, one of the world's foremost geneticists discusses the moral issues involved in theories of genetic determinism. Combining philosophical and scientific insights, this work addresses itself directly to many of the central issues in the nature-nurture controversy, particularly as these issues relate to education.

Human equality is an ethical precept, not a biological phenomenon. A society can grant or withhold it from its members.

from *Genetic Diversity and Human Equality*

Genetics and Education by Arthur R. Jensen (*New York: Harper & Row, 1973*)

Unfortunately, many people condemn Jensen without ever having read him. If you want to get into Jensen's basic theory, this is the book to read. It includes his famous (infamous?) essay, "How Much Can We Boost IQ and Scholastic Achievement?" and several of his more recent papers on the subject of heredity, intelligence, and education. His writing is clear and tight—but, be warned, somewhat technical at times.

To a psychologist observing all these phenomena, the question naturally arises as to why so many otherwise objective and dispassionate intellectuals display such vehement moral indignation and even zealous combativeness toward any explanation of human behavioral differences, especially social class and racial differences. . . .

from *Genetics and Education*

Piaget Sampler: An Introduction to Jean Piaget Through His Own Words, edited by Sarah F. Campbell (*New York: John Wiley & Sons, 1976*)

This is a fine, representative selection of Piaget's writings. It is particularly useful for the beginning student who wants to get the "feel" of Piaget without plunging into the more difficult works. Campbell asked students to pick out the most accessible portions of some of Piaget's major works, and these constitute the bulk selections in this sampler.

This book is intended for anyone who comes into contact with children, teachers, parents, and parents-to-be. . . .

from *Piaget Sampler*

Psychosocial Development of Children by Irene M. Josselyn (*New York: Family Service Association of America, 1948*)

This short, clearly written book gives an excellent overview of the psychodynamic position on development. It has been reprinted eighteen times over the past twenty years, attesting to its popularity and appeal. The person's development through adolescence is covered.

The primary function of knowledge concerning asocial behavior is its use in correcting that behavior if possible, so that the individual is able not only to live within the limits imposed by the social group but to do so constructively.

from *Psychosocial Development of Children*

Toward a Psychology of Being (2d ed.) by Abraham H. Maslow (*New York: D. Van Nostrand, 1968*)

This is the best introduction to the humanistic perspective of growth and development. Maslow analyzes all areas of human growth: cognitive, affective, social, and emotional. Whoever wishes to understand how the concepts of self-actualization and peak experiences became of such importance in psychology must read this book.

In the normal development of the healthy child, it is now believed that, much of the time, if he is given a really free choice, he will choose what is good for his growth. This he does because it tastes good, feels good, gives pleasure or delight. . . .

from *Toward a Psychology of Being*

Childhood and Society (2d ed.) by Erik H. Erikson (*New York: W. W. Norton & Co. 1964*)

This is the work that placed Erikson at the forefront of psychoanalysis. While there are many chapters that are difficult to read, the effort put in is always worthwhile because the author brilliantly combines his learning from many different disciplines into a unified psychoanalytic theory.

I came to psychology from art, which may explain, if not justify, the fact that at times the reader will find me painting contexts and backgrounds where he would rather have me point to facts and concepts. . . .

from *Childhood and Society*

The Growth of Intellect During the Preschool Years

At birth, the infant has little ability to put his perceptions together into meaningful wholes. He responds primarily through reflexive actions. Piaget's description of the sensorimotor period explains how the infant begins to differentiate the world around him and to organize his perceptions.

From Babbling to Speech

The early random babbling sounds of the infant become the foundations of later language learning. Language is broken down into small units called morphemes and phonemes, and it is the appropriate arrangement of these units that constitutes the grammar of a language.

The Acquisition of Language: Two Positions

The behavioral position argues that operant conditioning and modeling play a primary role in language acquisition. The main spokesman for this position is B. F. Skinner. The opposing position, articulated by Noam Chomsky, argues that there is an innate mechanism for generating grammars, independent of the learner's specific language. The acquisition of language has important implications for thinking and expression.

Personality Development

The Freudian theory of personality development divides the child's early life into four psychosexual stages: oral, anal, phallic, and Oedipal. Erikson's "Eight Ages of Man" integrate social functions into the developmental scheme. His first three stages are basic trust vs. basic mistrust, autonomy vs. shame and doubt, and initiative vs. guilt. The behavioral position places primary emphasis on the child's conditioning.

The Beginnings of Socialization

The environment provided by the mother is the prototype for later social development. Much of the child's early social learning occurs through play activity and through interactions with peers. The foundations of sex-role identification are set during the preschool years. Montessori, among others, suggests ways that the teacher can facilitate early socialization.

Continued

3 The Preschool Years

The Preschool Years: Conclusions and Implications

The development of the child before he enters school results in the raw material with which the teacher will work. The teacher's understanding of preschool developmental patterns will contribute to an understanding of the child.

> "Although the infant's eyes are capable of sensing light stimuli, the infant has little ability to put together the sensations into patterns."

Having now examined some of the basic processes and theories of growth and development, we will turn our attention to the specific developmental epoch that extends from birth to the time the child enters school. We have selected, from the wealth of research on this critical period, those areas that are most relevant for the teacher who is trying to understand the young learner. This chapter will pay particular attention to the following topics: cognitive growth, the development of language skills, personality development, and early patterns of socialization. We will examine the implications for the teacher for each topic, and attempt to point out how early developmental patterns play a significant role in the child's later school performance.

The Growth of Intellect During the Preschool Years

At birth, the neonate can hardly be said to be a creature of anything but the most basic intelligence. Regardless of how we define intelligence, narrowly or liberally, the fact that the **neonate** is incapable of survival, unaware of the reality around, and cannot respond individually to stimuli from the environment, places it in the class of "creature of instinct" rather than "creature of intelligence." What is present at birth, however, are many of the sensory and perceptual requisites that, in later months and years, become the foundations for intelligent actions.

In a comprehensive investigation of the development of sensation and perception in early life, three Soviet child development specialists (Yendovitskaya, Zinchenki, & Rizskaya, 1971) outline our knowledge to date regarding what the infant is capable of sensing and perceiving during the period of infancy. The following conclusions, drawn from their investigations sponsored by the APN-RSFSR (Academy of Pedagogical Sciences, Russian Soviet Federated Socialist Republic), are in agreement with the findings of American researchers during the past thirty years.

"The visual apparatus of the newborn," they point out, ". . . begins to function at birth." Although the infant's eyes are capable of sensing light stimuli, the infant has little ability to put together the sensations into patterns, and the response to stimuli takes such gross forms as visual pursuit, in which the infant turns its head to follow the source of light. While the newborn appears to have the ability to discriminate colors, "the newborn does not yet possess the mechanism that would provide for the ability to distinguish between spatial relations of objects." An American researcher, Robert L. Fantz, who has done extensive work in this area, has found, in a series of studies, that infants do have some perceptual ability; that they can distinguish between various shapes and forms, giving priority to some over others. In his early studies, Fantz (1958, 1963) showed that newborns could discriminate between different types of patterns, and showed preferences for certain types over others, particularly for patterns that resembled a human head. In a more recent study (Fantz & Miranda, 1975), it was found that infants chose to fix their gazes on curved contours rather than straight contours when various forms were presented to them. Again, since curved contours are more characteristic of the human head, it appears that infants, even prior to any training, prefer to view things that look like the human head.

In regard to **auditory sensation,** the Soviet scientists (Yendovitskya et al.) point out that there is abundant evidence that the newborn can respond to sounds, although the infant's ability to differentiate between sounds is still not well established. By the fourth month of life, they point out, it is easy to demonstrate the child's ability to differentiate visually and auditorily.

In addition to taking in the world through the eyes and ears, the child also responds to tactile stimuli—through the receptors in the skin. "Tactual sensitivity," they point out (p. 7), "is highly developed in the newborn. . . . It emerges during the prenatal period in the area of the mouth-nose cavity and spreads throughout the entire surface of the body in the early postnatal period. In the first few days of life, a touch on the infant's cheek evokes exploratory responses—opening of the mouth, wrinkling of the lips, and sucking movements. . . ." Also, there is much research to support that the infant is sensitive to changes in temperature, also conveyed through the skin receptors.

The sense of smell, they have found, is almost nonexistent, and the sense of taste is limited to sweet, sour, and salty and it is not exceptionally discrete even in those areas.

What are the implications of these findings? First, that the infant's intelligence is limited to its sensory capacities. It relies primarily on touch, visual perception, and audition—approximately in this order (although touch and vision may each dominate at different times). Secondly, that since the parameters by which the infant's intelligence is measured are so limited, knowledge of the nature of the infant's intelligence is also severely limited, although recent efforts have been intensified to measure infant intelligence, using such measures as the Cattell Infant Intelligence Scale and the Piaget Object Scale. Third, that when we speak of infant intelligence, we are speaking of a type of intelligence vastly different from other types of intelligence; more specifically, it is a nonverbal intelligence that cannot be fully differentiated from sensory abilities or motor responses. For this reason, infant intelligence is often referred to as "sensorimotor intelligence," a term that reflects Jean Piaget's analysis of the infant's intellectual growth.

Piaget's contribution to the understanding of cognitive development is immense, and will be discussed in other chapters. His conception of the *sensorimotor period,* the first two years of life, accurately describes the type of intellectual growth during this crucial time. Flavell (1963) tersely summarizes Piaget's major findings:

> During this important first period, the infant moves from a neonatal reflex level of complete self-world undifferentiation to a relatively coherent organization of sensory-motor actions, vis-a-vis his immediate environment. The organization is an entirely "practical" one, however, in the sense that it involves simple perceptual and motor adjustments to things rather than symbolic manipulations of them. (p. 86)

A more detailed analysis reveals the subtle patterns of intellectual growth during this period. Piaget (Piaget & Inhelder, 1969) divides this period into six stages, which reveal the growth of **sensorimotor intelligence:**

Stage 1: During this stage the child is a creature of reflex. Although these reflexive actions are modified through experience, "the stage is primarily characterized by the absence of genuine intelligent behavior" (Flavell, p. 89).

Stage 2: This is the stage of "habits." Piaget is careful to point out that "even if we use 'habits'—for lack of a better word—to refer to acquired behavior while it is being formed as well as after it has become automatized, habit is still not the same as intelligence" (Piaget & Inhelder, p. 9). By habits, he is referring to conditioned responses to stimuli.

Stage 3: This stage "introduces the next transitions after the beginning of coordination between vision and prehension. . . . The baby starts grasping and manipulating everything he sees in his immediate vicinity. For example, a subject of this age catches hold of a cord hanging from the top of his cradle; which has the effect of shaking all the rattles suspended above him. He immediately repeats the gesture a number of times. Each time the interesting result motivates the repetition. This constitutes a 'circular reaction' . . . where the result to be obtained is not differentiated from the means employed" (p. 10).

Stage 4: "In a fourth stage, we observe more complete acts of practical intelligence. The subject sets out to obtain a certain result, independent of the means he is going to employ; for example, obtaining an object that is out of reach or has just disappeared under a piece of cloth or a cushion" (p. 10).

Stage 5: "In the course of a fifth stage, which makes its appearance around eleven or twelve months, a new ingredient is added to the foregoing behavior: the search for new means by differentiation from schemes already known. An example of this is what we call the 'behavior pattern of the support.' An object has been placed on a rug out of the child's reach. The child, after trying in vain to reach the object directly, may eventually grasp one corner of the rug (by chance or as a substitute), and then, observing a relationship between the movements of the rug and those of the object, gradually comes to pull the rug in order to reach the object" (p. 11).

Stage 6: In this stage, which represents the highest level of sensorimotor intelligence and growth, the child "becomes capable of finding new means not only by external or physical groping but also by internalized combinations that culminate in sudden comprehension or *insight*" (pp. 11–12).

Table 3.1 (Phillips, 1975) traces the development of intelligence from simple reflexive behavior to insightful thinking-out of situations. While the early stages can hardly have been considered examples of intelligence, they are the foundations of the intelligence on which subsequent refinements depend.

This ten-month-old girl learns about the world through basic sensorimotor processes. This simple type of behavior is the foundation of intelligence.

The Life of the Learner

Table 3.1   Multidimensional View of Development During the Sensorimotor Period

Stage	Developmental Unit	Intention and Means-end Relations	Meaning	Object Permanence
1	Exercising the ready-made sensorimotor schemes (0–1 mo.)			
2	Primary circular reactions (1–4 mo.)		Different responses to different objects	
3	Secondary circular reactions (4–8 mo.)	Acts upon objects	"Motor meaning"	Brief single-modality search for absent object
4	Coordination of secondary schemes (8–12 mo.)	Attacks barrier to reach goal	Symbolic meaning	Prolonged, multi-modality search
5	Tertiary circular reactions (12–18 mo.)	"Experiments in order to see"; discovery of new means through "groping ac-commodation"	Elaboration through action and feedback	Follows sequential displacements if object in sight
6	Invention of new means through mental combinations (18–24 mo.)	Invention of new means through reciprocal assimilation of schemes	Further elaboration; symbols increasingly covert	Follows sequential displacement with object hidden; symbolic representation of object, mostly internal

From *The Origins of Intellect: Piaget's Theory*, Second Edition, by John L. Phillips, Jr. W. H. Freeman and Company. Copyright © 1975.

Space	Time	Causality	Imitation	Play
			Pseudo-imitation begins	Apparent functional autonomy of some acts
All modalities focus on single object	Brief search for absent object	Acts; then waits for effect to occur	Pseudo-imitation quicker, more precise. True imitation of acts already in repertoire and visible on own body	More acts done for their own sake
Turns bottle to reach nipple	Prolonged search for absent object	Attacks barrier to reach goal; waits for adults to serve him	True imitation of novel acts not visible on own body	Means often become ends; ritualization begins
Follows sequential displacements if object in sight	Follows sequential displacements if object in sight	Discovers new means; solicits help from adults	True imitation quicker, more precise	Quicker conversion of means to end; elaboration of ritualization
Solves detour problem; symbolic representation of spatial relationships, mostly internal	Both anticipation and memory	Infers causes from observing effects; predicts effects from observing causes	Imitates (1) complex, (2) non-human, (3) absent models	Treats inadequate stimuli as if adequate to imitate an enactment —i.e., symbolic ritualization or "pretending"

> " 'The essential difference between a child in the sensorimotor period and one in the preoperational period is that the former is relatively restricted to *direct interactions* with the environment, whereas the latter is capable of manipulating the symbols that represent the environment.' "

The Preoperational Period

Following the sensorimotor period, according to Piaget, the child enters the period referred to as **preoperational.** It is at this time that the child begins to use words and images to deal with his environment and can employ some basic mediating processes in his thinking. "The essential difference between a child in the sensorimotor period and one in the preoperational period," Phillips (1975) points out, "is that the former is relatively restricted to *direct interactions* with the environment, whereas the latter is capable of manipulating symbols that represent the environment" (p. 62).

During this period the child is still unable to process information in a sophisticated way (as he will be able to do during the next period, called "concrete operations.") However, he is able to deal with future and past events and to recognize basic causative factors that link events in time. The primary mode of doing so is through the use of language, with which the child is able to differentiate between the object itself and the sound that signifies the object symbolically.

Studies of Infant Intelligence

In one important study, Birns and Golden (1972) investigated the prediction of intellectual performance at three years old from infant intelligence tests and personality measures. They wanted to determine the correlation between the measures obtained in infancy with later development in order to assess how valid a predictor are measures of infant intelligence. "The most significant new finding of the present study," they conclude, "is that the amount of pleasure manifested by 18- and 24-month-old infants on the Cattell and Piaget Object Scales was predictive of their later intellectual performance on the Stanford-Binet at three years of age." Although there is "discontinuity between perceptual-motor development and later problem-solving ability on the verbal level . . . there may be continuity in terms of certain personality traits related to both preverbal and verbal intelligence" (p. 57).

In another important study by the same researchers (Golden & Birns, 1971), the question under scrutiny is whether there are sensorimotor intelligence differences during the late **infancy** period, eighteen to twenty-four months old. The conclusion was "that social class differences in intellectual development or cognitive style are probably not present during the sensorimotor period, and the Socioeconomic Status (social class) differences emerge somewhere between 18 and 36 months of age, when language enters the picture" (p. 2116).

These studies reaffirm that although individual differences in the intellectual development of infants certainly do exist, they cannot be characterized by the same guidelines that are applicable to preadolescence and adolescence. Also, since the child at this age is both preverbal and preconceptual, it is necessary to alter radically the meaning of intelligence when we use the term with respect to children of this age.

Case (1973), in reviewing Piaget's findings and their implications, points out:

Conclusions and Implications

In constructing his world, the small child seems to follow a definite series of steps, or successive approximations, to the world we know. When he is just beginning to toddle, one can hide his favorite toy under a bright red handkerchief (in his full view) and he will remove the handkerchief with great glee. Aha, you say, he has learned that an inanimate object continues to stay where it was put. But has he? After you have played this game a few times, place the favorite toy again in full sight, under a yellow handkerchief. Then watch as he looks under the red one again and appears baffled that the toy is not there. What he appears to have learned is only a first approximation. . . . How does the child acquire . . . knowledge? If you watch an infant, you will note that he is continually exploring things with his mouth, his hands, his eyes, and so on. At first these explorations occur independently of each other; later they are coordinated; and finally they are extended to include shaking, throwing, other actions. Such exploration and testing may not be too easy on the parents, but the indications are that it is universal. (p. 21)

As we mentioned previously, it is generally agreed that intelligence has a genetic basis, although to what extent the genes and environment intermix is still not clear. The universality of the sensorimotor stages, as well as the general predictability of intellectual growth, supports the genetic foundation. But what role do the parents (and particularly the care of the mothering one) play in the infant's and child's intellectual growth? The subject has been much explored, and Freeberg and Payne (1967), in a detailed review of the literature, conclude that "despite increasing interest in this area, systematic research concerned with specific rearing practices as they affect particular cognitive skills is only beginning to become available" (p. 65). In spite of the paucity of concrete findings, what is important, they point out, is the tendency to more specific types of studies that avoid such vague concepts as "enriched experience," and so on, and test in their place specific qualities of the parent.

One area, closely linked to the questions of intellectual growth in childhood and infant potential, is the learning of language. How is language learned? What processes are involved? And what is the relationship between language learning, general communication skills, and intelligence? We will consider some of these issues in the next section.

The child's innate curiosity motivates cognitive growth.

The Life of the Learner

> "The baby is eminently capable of emitting sounds, but they are unstructured sounds, spontaneous expressions that lack any meaning to outsiders."

From Babbling to Speech

The remarkable facility with which the infant learns to speak during the first two years of life has been a source of great fascination and perplexity for specialists in child development from the beginning of systematic study. How, in such a short period of time, can a creature who can do so few other intellectual things learn to master a language? Despite the many difficulties in investigating this question, a great deal of progress has been made in recent years in attempts to answer it.

The baby, as we all know, is eminently capable of emitting sounds, but they **Early Sounds** are unstructured sounds, spontaneous expressions that lack any meaning to outsiders. Some sounds the baby makes may attract more attention than others. For instance, if the baby accidently stumbles upon the sound "ma"— or, better yet, a "maamaa" sound—eager parents are likely to gather round the crib in praise and admiration. The baby will tend, after only a few months, to repeat these sounds in rhythmic patterns, such as *ah-la-ah*. This babbling, as it is called, is the precursor of formal speech.

Fawcus (1968) discusses the importance of babbling behavior, using an analysis of baby's early vocalization by M. M. Lewis (1957):

In the early stages of babbling—what has been called the prelinguistic phase of babbling—the stimulus for the repetition of such sounds is obviously the pleasure the baby gains from "the complex stimulus," as Lewis puts it, "of motor and auditory sensations." The importance of babbling in the development of language lies, as Lewis says, "in that it is a means by which a child, through repeated practice, acquires skill in making sounds. *As other forms of play give a child the rudimentary skills upon which his later complex skills are based, so babbling gives him the beginnings of the highly complex skills that go to the production of the sounds of speech.*"

The child is developing an awareness of his own body and of separateness from his mother—and at the same time a growing awareness of parental approval and consciousness of his ability to gain attention and win approval. It is at this stage that the parent, who has hitherto satisfied the child's material needs . . . gives the stimulus of social approval. . . . She reinforces his babbling by showing obvious signs of pleasure at his vocal attempts, develops his imitative faculties and further reinforces the process by imitating the babbling of the child. (pp. 448–449)

There are several key points that emerge in this short analysis. First, that babbling as an activity gives the baby pleasure; that there is an innate enjoyment in babbling itself. Second, that the baby begins to learn from its babbling through the maternal and environmental responses. Finally, that babbling is a part of the vast individuating process that helps the baby achieve an identity separate from the parents.

While the infant is thus engaged in exercising its vocal cords and delighting in the resultant sonority, adults in the immediate environment are communicating to the infant at the same time. "Look here at daddy"; or "What a cute little baby you are"; or "What does baby want?" are some typical examples. Probably these sounds are at first as meaningless to the infant as the infant's sounds are to us. But gradually the infant begins to see the sense behind the sounds, to discern meanings and reference points where there was only sound before. At about nine months old the infant begins to develop *word recognition,* the ability to separate certain sounds from others. This important differentiation ability precedes the infant's capacity to use sounds as meaningful communications.

"The child must learn," Carroll (1971) points out, "to perceive the various instances of a given sound or word as similar, and eventually to differentiate the several contexts in which a given sound or sound pattern is used" (p. 242). For example, the child will have to recognize the difference between such homonyms as *no* and *know,* or *hours* and *ours.* The child learns to differentiate by listening attentively to the sounds that adults make and by repeating, randomly sometimes and selectively and intentionally at other times, certain sounds that elicit or evoke specific, desirable responses. In short, the child begins to learn words and to acquire a working vocabulary.

The beginnings of language learning then comprises the learning of sounds and the learning of sound patterns—words. The relationship between the acquisition of these abilities and psychological individuation, discussed above, is further emphasized by Smart and Smart (1973), who point out:

Language supplements the tactile link between the young child and other people and supplants that link in many of the child's relationships with others. Language is a vital tie between past, present, and future, both for the individual and for groups of people. *The rapid acquisition of language by the preschool child, shown by increase in vocabulary and development of grammatical structures, is intimately related to the development of autonomy and initiative, to the growth from egocentric thought to objectivity, and social relationships.* (pp. 97–98, italics ours)

So much for the social purpose and precursory elements in speech. Let us now turn our attention to the processes by which sounds become language.

Units of Language   When we look at a written language on paper, we think of the primary unit as the letter and the secondary unit as the word, with subsequent units in sentences, paragraphs, and so forth. This, of course, does not express the units in spoken language, which is a more basic form of language than is written language. In the spoken language, the primary units are the **phoneme** and **morpheme.**

A phoneme is the smallest unit of sound that makes up a language. It may be a *k,* a *uh,* and an *ee* sound. Most phonemes have no intrinsic meaning, but combine with other phonemes to form *morphemes*—the smallest, *meaningful* units of sound. A morpheme may be a word, such as *man, the, it,* or a meaningful unit that is not a word, such as *-ed,* the past tense ending that is attached to words, or *s* the plural ending of words.

When phonemes are placed together in such a way as to form morphemes that have meanings to others, they are words (or qualities of words, such as tense or plural). For example, the *-ing* morpheme, when attached to certain verb morphemes such as *walk,* indicates a participle: *walk, walking.* The child learns all of these things naturally long before he learns the rules for them.

It is much easier to understand how the child learns sound, whether they are phonemes, morphemes, or words, than it is to comprehend how the child learns to put all these sounds together in a grammatical or syntactical order so that they make sense to others. Miller and Ervin (1964), in attempting to explain this process, conducted a research project using twenty-five children in a longitudinal study. Although the children "began forming primitive sentences of two or more words before their second birthday" (p. 13), these sentences were far removed from the model of adult grammar that was used as a standard. Further collection of data and a careful linguistic analysis revealed some patterns of language (grammatical) development. They found that the child does not learn grammar in the same way he or she learns phonemes. Some grammatical categories are more open to generalization than others; some, such as singular/plural, can be generalized into the making of possessives, and there are many cases of **transfer.** Where the preliminary grammatical processes are applied to new language situations, more complex—such as the formation of passive sentences—transfer can be demonstrated.

"A child's mastery of the grammatical structure of the language," Elkonin (1971) points out, "includes not only acquisition of the grammatical forms, but also of the verbal composition of speech" (p. 154). This means, in effect, that the child is able to use language to express ideas and to communicate effectively; the words and grammatical structures work hand-in-hand.

Psychologist B. F. Skinner argues that the acquisition of language can be explained by the behavioral model of conditioning.

Having now considered these preliminary issues, let us consider the two main positions on how children learn **syntax,** grammar, and communication skills.

The Acquisition of Language: Two Positions

We see now that there is an important difference between learning words and learning to use a language. A person might say, "It house for was be over to when a mouse if," using all correct English words, but making no sense. The child first learns some words and then starts using the words "grammatically," by placing them in a recognizable order that is meaningful to others; that is, which *communicates.* The progression might look like this, over a period of thirty months:

blanket (or a babbling equivalent, such as "blalah")

me blanket

me want blanket

I want blanket

I want the blanket.

This is a very simple sentence, and we see in it some of the stages of its linguistic development. But how the child progresses from one linguistic level to another still remains a point of contention.

One position developed to explain the learning of language is the behavioral position, exemplified by B. F. Skinner. Skinner argues that the principles of **operant conditioning** play an important part in the learning of language. As certain of the child's sounds and patterns of sounds are reinforced, they become stronger and the child begins to use them more readily. Skinner explains these processes through the behavioral model, which relies on stimulus and response, which he feels adequate for describing language *as a behavior.* His position runs like this: The baby associates "da-da" with a positive response from the environment (people make a fuss), and then as the baby begins to place words in their appropriate order, he or she is further rewarded. The behavioral principle of **modeling** is also important; the child models his speech on the speech of those around him.

The behavioral position has come under much criticism, most notably by world-famous linguist Noam Chomsky. Chomsky (1959), in his important review of Skinner's book, *Verbal Behavior* (1953), argues that the behavioral model cannot fully account for all the complexities of language learning. He criticizes, one by one, most of Skinner's major arguments, pointing to the weaknesses both in its theory and in its research support. He states, most unequivocally, that "if we take his terms in their literal meaning, the description covers almost no aspect of verbal behavior, and if we take them metaphorically, the description offers no improvement over various traditional formulations" (p. 574). Chomsky argues instead that there is an innate ability for language acquisition, which is independent (for the most part) of the child's conditioning. "It is not easy," he says, "to accept the view that a child is capable of constructing an extremely complex mechanism for generating a set of sentences, some of which he has heard, or that an adult can instantaneously determine whether (and if so, how) a particular item is generated by this mechanism, which has many of the properties of an abstract deductive theory. Yet this appears to be a fair description of the performance of the speaker, listener, and learner" (p. 577).

Linguist Noam Chomsky argues that there are innate mechanisms involved in the child's ability to acquire a language.

Since the research on this debate has still failed to resolve the basic issues, we are not yet entirely clear about the importance of learning mechanisms (such as conditioning) and innate structures in the acquisition of language. Some of the recent experimentation in this area has been quite interesting, if not entirely revealing. In one experiment, Love and Parker-Robinson (1972) investigated children's ability to imitate grammatical and ungrammatical sentences, and their ability to recall sentences according to whether or not they were constructed grammatically, regardless of the words involved —which could be nonsense words. Their findings are:

To summarize the main results, for both age levels grammatical sentences were easier to imitate than ungrammatical ones only when function words were included in the sentence; with function words absent, there was no significant difference.... When normal relationships among words (even unfamiliar or nonsense words) are violated in an adult's speech, it becomes very difficult for the child to repeat the unusual sequence of words, and the present results suggest that the context provided by function words is more important than inflection.... (p. 318)

While there is no specific theory to explain these results, they would seem to indicate the importance of *context* in the acquisition of language; that is, the importance of the surrounding sounds in learning the use and meaning of a specific sound. This study indicates that the function words, more than the inflections used, are responsible for providing the necessary contextual cues, and this might be used as further support for Chomsky's position.

The Preschooler's Use of Language

In one of the most comprehensive studies of the preschooler's linguistic abilities and the uses to which language is put, Bloom (1970) studied in detail the language development of three children, from their earliest utterances to speech competency. "A young child's success in learning to talk," she points out, "depends on his ability to perceive and organize his environment, the language that is a part of that environment, and the relation between the two.

Thus, *the acquisition of language is a complex process that is crucially related to the child's cognitive-perceptual growth and his interaction in an environment of objects, events, and relations*" (p. 1).

The detailed analyses of how these three children mastered the complexities of grammar and reached linguistic competency included a recognition of behaviors that accompanied all utterances. In this way, the researchers were better able to understand the psycholinguistics of language development. "Overt behavior and features of context and situation," she argues, "signal the meanings of what children say in a way that is not true for what adults say" (p. 9). She goes on to expand this point:

> . . . Generally, it is not possible to understand what adults mean by observing context or behavior; adults transmit information, and the exchange is essentially linguistic. If an adult or an older child mounts a bicycle, there is no need for him to inform anyone who has seen him do it that he has done it. But a young child who mounts a tricycle will often "announce" the fact: "I ride trike." (p. 9)

The implications of this and other points in the study is that the language of the preschool child, if we accept the broadest possible usage of the term *language,* includes verbal and nonverbal behaviors. It is only as the child grows older that more complex and more emotional thoughts can be expressed through words, and through words alone. Early language experiences combine physical expressions with verbal expressions. The greater the young child's language proficiency, the less the need to accompany behaviors with redundant words, and the less the need to emphasize and clarify words with physical behaviors.

Consider, for example, how adjectives and intensifiers "color" language and give words a dimension that compensates for early physical gestures. If the teacher sees the child stretch his arms out to emphasize a point, the teacher can repeat the child's statement, using the intensifier *very* to help the child develop a word to replace the physical gesture.

This is not to suggest that as we develop a more competent language of expression, other nonverbal forms of expression disappear. Psycholinguistics, the study of the relationship between different parts of the communicative processes, focuses on ways in which our communication includes different types of expression. "Communication," Frostig and Maslow (1973) point out, "involves both verbal and nonverbal forms, because people express ideas and feelings not only through words, but also through vocal intonations, facial expressions, and body movements. Information is thus received both by hearing the spoken word and by observation" (p. 217). If we watch a preschooler tell a story, we observe dramatic movements of the body which parallel the subject-matter of the story. An adult speaker is more capable of relating the story through words alone. As the transformations of the gram-

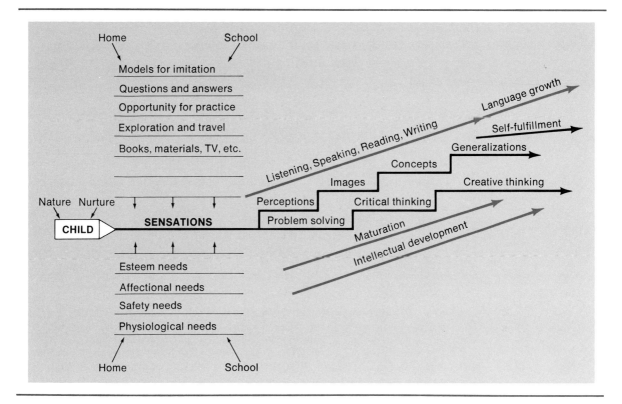

Figure 3.1 A Schema for
Language Development. From
*Guiding Children's Language
Learning* by Pose Lamb
(Dubuque, Iowa: Wm. C. Brown
Company Publishers, 1967),
p. 24. Reprinted by permission.

mar become more sophisticated, and as the vocabulary increases, the need for
the body to add to the expression diminishes.

Lamb (1967) has provided a schema for language development (figure 3.1) that represents a holistic approach to understanding language development. The child "comes to school with a unique set of learnings and potentialities that have been shaped by nature and nurture. The school environment continues to be influential in further language growth which is shaped largely by the quality of experiences offered by the home prior to school entrance" (Lamb, 1967, p. 23). We see from this figure the interrelationship between the many factors that go into language competency and the way that language is used. We also see how many variables are included in the process of language acquisition and how these variables interact in a cumulative manner.

Now that we have examined some of the cognitive development of the preschool years—development that serves as the foundation for learning in the elementary grades—we will turn our attention to the other side of the coin: the development of personality and socialization, the foundations of affective growth and learning.

> "The Freudian theory of personality is a deterministic one, which proposes that by the time the child is five years old the basic foundation of his personality is already well established."

Personality Development

Although there is a perennial struggle to adequately define the term *personality,* we will avoid the issue in this section since it is our intention to look at some theories of personality development that might be of help to the teacher in understanding the student rather than to present a comprehensive overview of personality theory, assessment, and research. In the manner we will approach this, we will rely on a synthetic definition of personality, much like the one used by Lucy Rau Ferguson in her fine little book on the subject. Ferguson (1970), also eager to avoid technical haggling, says that:

> ... In this text it [personality] will refer primarily to patterns of social behavior and interpersonal relations. An individual's personality, then, is the sum total of the ways in which he characteristically reacts to and interacts with others. "Personality" will include such overt patterns of social behavior as aggression, or attention-seeking, as well as such behaviors and motives as achievement striving. .... Personality also involves the more subjective aspects of emotions and perceptions of others, which may often be expressed in fantasy rather than in direct social behavior. *A person's conceptions and feelings about himself also hold a central position in his social world; thus self-concepts and self-evaluations are important in our definition of personality.* (pp. 2–3)

Using this definition as our parameter of interest, we will now look at some of the major personality theories and consider their relevance for the educational setting. Since our primary concern, as teachers and teachers-to-be, is to facilitate the processes of learning and growth by providing an optimal educational environment, we shall pay special attention to ways in which these theories reveal optimal learning conditions.

Freud's Psychosexual Stages of Development

The Freudian theory of personality is a **deterministic one,** which proposes that by the time the child is five years old the basic foundation of his personality is already well-established, and that experiences of the later years are relatively unimportant in effecting changes on the deeper, dynamic level of the mind. Freud divides the early years of development into five stages, each of which has its unique characteristics and problems. Each of the first three stages is named after the part of the body that is most sexually stimulating to the child during that stage—the primary **erogenous zone.** These are the oral, anal, and phallic stages.

The Oral Stage

This is the first stage, extending from birth to about the middle of the second year of life. It is a crucial period during which the child's awareness of reality (his *ego*) begins to develop. During this period the mouth is the primary erogenous zone, thus giving the stage its name. The skin serves as another erogenous zone, and the child exhibits **tactile eroticism** in its pleasurable responses to touch.

The main source of gratification during this period is eating—the taking in of nourishment, accomplished through the processes of swallowing and spitting out. When the teeth develop, pleasure is obtained through biting. If, as the child passes through this stage, he does not receive *enough* oral gratification, or if he receives *too much* gratification (that is, if the mother is overstimulating!), he may become **fixated** at this stage, maintaining in later years characteristics that are more appropriate to the infant. For example, such disorders as psychosis, severe depression, obesity, and addiction—as well as withdrawal from reality—are associated with fixation at the oral stage. Because during this stage the child is completely dependent upon the mother for nourishment and security, deprivations may result in lifelong feelings of inadequacy, overdependency, and worthlessness.

The Anal Stage

At approximately eighteen months of age, there is a shift of erotic activity from the mouth to the anus, and the **anal stage** begins. During this period, the child receives erotic pleasure through the act of defecation, and he expresses his will through the retention or expulsion of feces. Society, in general, and parents, in particular, reinforce anal behavior in many ways. At this age, much attention is focused on toilet training activity and the child learns that he can exert control over his parents through the manipulation of this bodily function. If the parent is overly strict in toilet training, the child may hold back his feces and become constipated. This might show itself later in such adult traits as hoarding, stinginess, excessive neatness, or obstinacy. He might also show rage by expelling feces at inappropriate times. This could be the prototype for later inappropriate behavior patterns in the school and home settings: temper tantrums, extreme messiness, cruel and destructive "play" behavior, and so forth. Since the toilet training experience is our first learning experience with another person (the parent), Freudians view many of our later attitudes toward learning as derivatives of this stage. For example, the person who views learning tasks as inherently frustrating and who is not able to cope with the required discipline may, according to this theory, be reacting to early anal-stage situations.

The Phallic Stage

At about the beginning of the third year, the genital area becomes the primary erogenous zone. During this stage, genital masturbation is not uncommon, nor is an intense interest in the genitals of the opposite sex. This stage is important for the introduction of two important dynamic concepts—**castration anxiety** and **penis envy,** both of which are the subject of heavy debates in recent years.

According to Freud, when the boy first becomes sensitive to the differences between the male and female genitalia, he cannot accommodate the fact that women do not have penises and therefore fantasizes that women must have lost the penises they once had. He develops, from this false premise, an anxiety about the loss of his own penis, and may express this fear in the forms of play, dreams, or other symbolic communication. When the girl, at the same age, recognizes the difference in the male and female genitalia, she attributes this absence of a penis to some loss from the past; that is, that she once had a penis and that it has been taken away from her. As she attempts to compensate for this loss and to get the penis back, she develops *penis envy,* which too can take many social forms, in home and at school.

While this aspect of Freud's theory of the psychosexual stages is central to much of his thinking, it has been roundly rejected in recent years by psychologists, feminists, and social scientists. At the present time, there is certainly inconclusive "proof" to support or refute this position, but it still stands as a central concept in the Freudian schema.

The Oedipal Period (Oedipus Complex)

This stage derives its name from the famous Greek legend of Oedipus, the king of Thebes, who unwittingly killed his father and married his mother. When he discovered what he had done, he blinded himself in an agony of remorse. Freud says that during this Oedipal conflict the child falls in love with the parent of the opposite sex and develops feelings of rivalry and hostility toward the parent of the same sex, who is the "rival parent." The boy wants to possess his mother, although he does not have full-formed ideas of sexuality. He views the father as the prime competitor and wishes to remove him. The girl, likewise, desires her father and wishes to remove the mother.

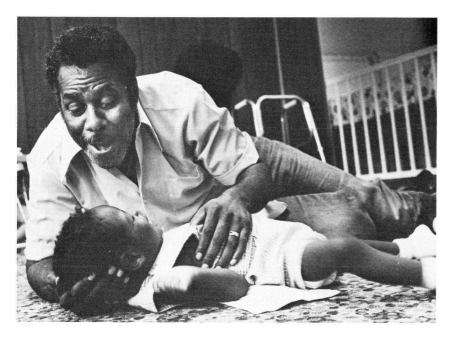

According to Freud, as the child enters the Oedipal period, the relationship with the father is of great importance in future emotional development. The boy may see the father as a "rival" for the mother's affection; the girl may view the father as her "ideal" man.

The resolution of the conflict differs for the two sexes and from person to person. The boy's growing hostility toward the father causes him to fear retaliation. His *castration anxiety* grows stronger as his fear of the father castrating him becomes more pervasive. The dissolution of the girl's Oedipus complex is somewhat more complicated. To begin with, the little girl originally loved her mother, just as the boy does, because it is the mother who nurtured and cared for her as an infant. She exchanges her original love object, the mother, for the new love object, the father, when she discovers that a boy possesses a penis and she does not. She blames the mother for the castrated condition and transfers her love to the father because he possesses the valued sex organ.

How can such a complex situation be satisfactorily resolved? Irene Josselyn (1948), an interpreter of Freud's position noted for her practical applications of Freud's somewhat technical positions, explains the resolution of the boy's and girl's conflicts this way:

Faced with this conflict, the young boy may find a solution that will make him more comfortable in his environment. One of the motivating factors in the choice of solution he makes is his wish to have the love of the mother. . . . The healthy solution is to identify with the father and incorporate the father's goals and standards into his own pattern of behavior. . . . In order to retain the love of the father and avoid the danger of his retaliation, the boy strives to be like his father but renounces his mother as a sexual love object. This identification with the father gives him new security. The father is gratified to see his male child become a real boy. The mother responds positively to the masculinity of the male child. The child has gained his goal, even though it is a less intensively gratifying victory than he had originally sought. . . .

> "One of the truly important contributions of the Freudian approach is to emphasize the vital, dynamic influence of childhood sexuality, often obscured in the myths and presuppositions of childhood innocence that permeate our cultural outlook."

Ultimately, if the little girl is to advance toward healthy emotional maturation, she must find gratification and security in a feminine role. To do this she identifies with her mother but represses the sexual aspect of the identification. She, like the boy, incorporates the pattern of the rival parent, and in the process establishes her superego. She too then turns to outside contacts in order to lessen the intensity of her tie to the parent figures and diverts her energies into non-sexual channels. (p. 58)

The successful resolution of the Oedipus complex leads into the latency period: a time when the sexual strivings remain dormant and the child concentrates primarily on socialization. It is in this period that the child enters the elementary school, and characteristics of this stage will be dealt with more fully in the next chapter.

Implications of Freud's Theory of the Psychosexual Stages

Although the Freudian position is controversial and not directly supported by empirical evidence, many of its insights have proven useful to teachers, educators, and parents in understanding and dealing with children (Anna Freud, 1935). While a totally Freudian perspective may be an exaggeration of the child's complex functional reality, no doubt many children's interests, inclinations, fantasies, and pathologies are amenable to a Freudian explanation. Moreover, one of the truly important contributions of this approach is to emphasize the vital, dynamic influence of **childhood sexuality,** often obscured in the myths and presuppositions of childhood innocence that permeate our cultural outlook. Freud may be extreme in one direction, but many of his insights have nevertheless served his opponents well by counterbalancing their opposite positions.

Erikson's "Eight Ages of Man": Stages I–III

Freud's position, as we see, pays little attention to social and cultural influences on the child's development and regards personality development as more or less complete by the time the child is six years old. Erikson, as we pointed out in chapter 2, looks at development as a lifelong process and has been instrumental in proposing a theory of adolescent development (which is discussed in chapter 5). His "Eight Ages of Man" describes the stages of life-long development, presented in his major work, *Childhood and Society* (1963). These stages integrate the social and psychological perspectives of the growing person. In this chapter, we shall examine the first three stages, which are relevant to the preschool years.

I. Basic Trust vs. Basic Mistrust

In the earliest pattern of development, the baby, through its relationship with the mother, develops its feelings of **basic trust** or basic mistrust, depending upon the care afforded the child by the mother. "The firm establishment of enduring patterns for the solution of the nuclear conflict of basic trust versus basic mistrust in mere existence is the first task of the ego, and thus first of all a task for maternal care. But let it be said here that *the amount of trust derived from earliest infantile experience does not seem to depend on absolute quantities of food or demonstrations of love, but rather on the quality of the maternal relationship. Mothers create a sense of trust in their children by that kind of administration which in its quality combines sensitive care of the baby's individual needs and a firm sense of personal trustworthiness. . . ."* (p. 49, italics ours).

II. Autonomy vs. Shame and Doubt

The existence of the child as an autonomous creature, capable of choosing from options within the environment, is crucial for the child's individual survival and psychological maturation. While the child may, in reality, require some external control and parental restraint during these early years, the child must, at the same time, be allowed outlets to grow as an independent, autonomous creature. "For if denied the gradual and well-guided experience of the autonomy of free choice," Erikson argues (p. 252), ". . . the child will turn against himself all his urge to discriminate and to manipulate." Shame and doubt ("doubt is the brother of shame") are consequences of stifling the child's striving for autonomy, and can be avoided when the parents allow the child the appropriate outlets to develop autonomously: "A sense of rightful dignity and lawful independence on the part of adults around him," Erikson (p. 254) points out, "gives to the child of good will the confident expectation that the kind of autonomy fostered in childhood will not lead to undue doubt or shame in later life."

III. Initiative vs. Guilt

During this stage, which extends from about the time the child is three years old to the end of the kindergarten year, the child extends the autonomy of the second stage into initiative, the willingness to contemplate and execute new actions on his own, the emergence of an individual identity, derived from but also differentiated from the parents' identities. With this new direction toward *initiative,* many changes come into the child's life. Most importantly, the child begins to develop his or her sexual identity; the sense of *maleness* or *femaleness.* The child transforms his infantile sexual behavior and feelings, growing from a "pregenital attachment to his parents, to the slow process of becoming a parent, a carrier of tradition" (p. 256). The boy's identification with the father and the girl's identification with the mother, both characteristics of this stage, become the basis for later sexual identification, and during the stage itself motivate the child to activities that help differentiate its identity. When the child is thwarted in its efforts toward initiating behaviors, it may experience guilt from the reactions of the parents.

The implications of this developmental stage are especially relevant for the educator. "The child is at no time more ready to learn quickly and avidly," Erikson points out, "to become bigger in the sense of sharing obligation and performance than during this period of development" (p. 258). He goes on to discuss the implications:

He is eager and able to make things cooperatively, to combine with other children for the purpose of constructing and planning, and he is willing to profit from teachers and to emulate ideal prototypes. He remains, of course, identified with the parent of the same sex, but for the present he looks for opportunities where work-identification seems to promise a field of initiative without too much infantile conflict or oedipal guilt and a more realistic identification based on a spirit of equality experienced in doing things together. At any rate, the "Oedipal" stage results not only in the oppressive establishment of a moral sense of restricting the horizon of the permissible; it also sets the direction toward the possible and the tangible which permits the dreams of early childhood to be attached to the goals of an active adult life. *Social institutions, therefore, offer children of this age an economic ethos, in the form of ideal adults recognizable by their uniforms and their functions, and fascinating enough to replace, the heroes of picture books and fairy tale.* (italics ours)

We see then that this final stage of the preschool period is crucial not only for the personal development of the child but for preparing the child for the tasks and demands of the school environment as well.

The Behavioral Position Behavioral psychologists view the personality development of the child during the preschool years quite differently. Rather than examining the "dynamic" components of psychological growth, they concentrate on how new behaviors are learned. They do not deny feeling states—emotions—but view these as entwined with behaviors that are learned by the behavioral processes described in chapter 2.

The most striking example of the discrepancy between the Freudian and the behavioral positions is found in their theories on the roots of aggression. Whereas belief in the innate basis of aggression is central to the Freudian position, behaviorists argue that exposure to aggressive behavior is the

> "While there is no *single* behavioral position, there is general consensus that much of the infant's learning can be accounted for by the behavioral models, and this learning includes attachment, love, and other factors generally associated with personality."

foundation of aggression, and that the resulting behavior is learned. The child observes the parents' aggression and models himself after this. But this explanation of familial exposure was weak, and behaviorists have extended their theory to include other aggressive forces after which the child models himself. Bandura (1973), a leading spokesman for this position, argues:

Within a modern society, three major sources of aggressive behavior are drawn upon to varying degrees. One is the aggression modeled and reinforced by family members. Though familial influences play a major role in setting the direction of social development, the family is embedded in a network of other social systems. The subculture in which a person resides and with which he has repeated contact provides a second source of aggression. The types of behaviors that are exemplified and valued in community subsystems may support or counteract familial influences. The third source of aggressive behavior is the symbolic modeling provided by the mass media, especially television. . . . (Bandura, 1973, p. 93)

This passage reflects the tendency among behavioral psychologists in recent years to extend the *sources of influence*—both in modeling and in conditioning that affect the development of the personality. Krumboltz and Krumboltz (1972), for instance, point out the many interacting forces and processes that help change a child's behavior as he grows. Still, to some extent, the behaviorists, like other child development specialists, recognize the immense importance of the home environment and attempt to explain development in the home in terms of the conditioning paradigm.

Gewirtz (1961) has discussed the ways the infant forms attachment to its mother in terms of operant conditioning. Corter (1974), in looking at this and other literature on the subject, concludes that "the mother's talking, smiling and cuddling her infant may be as important, even more important, than her filling his stomach with food" (p. 176). Millar (1974) has examined in some detail conditioning and learning in early infancy and provides an exhaustive review of the literature to date. He suggests a model that takes into account not only operant and classical conditioning but other learning processes (such as habituation) also.

While there is no *single* behavioral position, there is general consensus that much of the infant's learning, if not all of it, can be accounted for by the behavioral models, and this learning includes attachment, love, and other factors generally associated with personality.

Table 3.2   Developmental Tasks in Ten Categories of Behavior

Behavior Category	Infancy (Birth to 1 or 2)	Early Childhood (2–3 to 5–7)
1. Achieving an appropriate dependence-independence pattern	Establishing one's self as a very dependent being Beginning the establishment of self-awareness	Adjusting to less private attention; becoming independent physically (while remaining strongly dependent emotionally)
2. Achieving an appropriate giving-receiving pattern of affection	Developing a feeling for affection	Developing the ability to give affection Learning to share affection
3. Relating to changing social groups	Becoming aware of the alive as against the inanimate, and the familiar as against the unfamiliar Developing rudimentary social interaction	Beginning to develop the ability to interact with age-mates Adjusting in the family to expectations it has for the child as a member of the social unit
4. Developing a conscience	Beginning to adjust to the expectations of others	Developing the ability to take directions and to be obedient in the presence of authority Developing the ability to be obedient in the absence of authority where conscience substitutes for authority
5. Learning one's psycho-socio-biological sex role		Learning to identify with male and female roles
6. Accepting and adjusting to a changing body	Adjusting to adult feeding demands Adjusting to adult cleanliness demands Adjusting to adult attitudes toward genital manipulation	Adjusting to expectations resulting from one's improving muscular abilities Developing sex modesty
7. Managing a changing body and learning new motor patterns	Developing physiological equilibrium Developing eye-hand coordination Establishing satisfactory rhythms of rest and activity	Developing large-muscle control; learning to coordinate large muscles and small muscles
8. Learning to understand and control the physical world	Exploring the physical world	Meeting adult expectations for restrictive exploration and manipulation of an expanding environment
9. Developing an appropriate symbol system and conceptual abilities	Developing preverbal communication Developing verbal communication Rudimentary concept formation	Improving one's use of the symbol system Enormous elaboration of the concept pattern
10. Relating one's self to the cosmos		Developing a genuine, though uncritical, notion about one's place in the cosmos

B. E. Todd and H. Heffernan, "Developmental Tasks in Ten Categories of Behavior," *The Years Before School: Guiding Preschool Children*, 2nd ed. (New York: Macmillan Publishing Co., 1970), pp. 45–46. Used with permission.

Many researchers eschew any theoretical orientation and attempt to understand the development of the child in terms of the tasks learned and the levels of **maturation** accomplished. Muller (1969), for example, has written extensively about childhood in terms of what he calls its "tasks," referring to, but not depending on, a number of different theories. Table 3.2 (from Todd & Heffernan, 1970) shows the major developmental tasks of this period of early childhood, the preschool years.

One of the most important developmental tasks of the preschool years is socialization. We will now turn our attention to examine in some detail the processes of socialization.

The Beginnings of Socialization

Socialization is a process that begins at birth and continues until death. During the early years, the mother (and to some extent, the other family members) provide the avenues to socialization for the child. Although the more evident progress in socialization occurs during later years—from the time the child enters school until early adulthood—the foundations for these steps in social development are laid during the preschool years. In this section, we will look at some of the influences on early social development, paying particular attention to the ways in which early patterns blossom into fully developed characteristics by the time the child enters school.

It is generally acknowledged by specialists in developmental psychology that the emotional, physical, and nurturing environment provided by the mother —or as Harry Stack Sullivan calls the child's primary caretaker, the "mothering one"—is the most significant factor in early development. The mother is, after all, the first important person in the child's social learning. Through the relationship with the mother, the child not only learns about the world but develops sufficient ego strength to deal with many of the contingencies of living. Klatskin, Jackson and Wilkin (1956) investigated the effects of child-rearing practices and maternal care on the child's early behavior. They conclude that ". . . child behavior during the first three years is more consistently influenced by maternal handling than by other environmental factors." However, they point out, the significance of this relationship is not clearly demonstrated during the first year of life but rather during the subsequent two years, and they are not able to explain this phenomenon. In any case, they are convinced that this period in the rearing of the child does have a significant influence on the child's behavior.

The mother is primarily responsible for protecting the child from dangers, for providing nourishment, and for stimulating the child in order

> "The mother is primarily responsible for protecting the child from dangers, for providing nourishment, and for stimulating the child in order to help the child develop from a creature of inherent passivity to a more mature child capable of social activity, of reaching out to others."

to help the child develop from a creature of inherent passivity to a more mature child capable of social activity, of reaching out to others. One of the most important things provided by the mother to the child is her *touch*—the catalyst for early stimulation and the precursor to later social involvements. "To be deprived of enough touch," Arthur Janov (1973), the founder of primal scream therapy argues, "is not to be loved, no matter how loudly parents protest to the contrary." He goes on to explain the deep significance of touch to subsequent development:

> Not only must infants be touched very often, but for it to be effective there are critical times when it must take place. An institutional child adopted at eighteen months into a warm family may have already been traumatized for a lifetime. No touch during the first eight months of life when the nervous system is most receptive and when other sensory modalities are yet not completely developed may cause lifelong damage. . . . (p. 119)

Some of the most important research in this area has been conducted by Harry F. Harlow, whose pioneering studies with infant monkeys over a forty-year period have expanded our awareness of the human infant's needs.

In Harlow's famous series of experiments, baby monkeys were separated at birth from their natural mothers and were provided instead with surrogate mothers. The monkeys were divided into two groups, each of which was provided with a different type of mother: one made of wire mesh, with a wooden block at the head position; the other of the same size and shape, but covered with a soft terry cloth, backed by sponge rubber, with its head painted and glued with false features. Both mothers contained a hole through which the nipple of a nursing bottle protruded at feeding time. Each mother was a source of food for the monkeys assigned to it, but Harlow found that between feedings all the monkeys preferred to cuddle up to the cloth mother, even those who were fed by the wire mother. And when a fearful object was placed near them, all the monkeys clung only to the cloth mother as a security base. The wire mother was never used in this way. This led Harlow to conclude that the warmth and comfort of the mother is more important than the fact that she is a source of food.

The implications of this behavior in terms of social development have also been examined. In a follow-up study of the monkeys, Harlow found that

Harry F. Harlow's pioneering research with primates has shed light on the importance of early maternal attachment.

as adults these monkeys showed no interest in normal sexual behavior and when the females were mated involuntarily and became mothers, they failed to show any maternal behavior. However, if they were given an opportunity to interact with other young monkeys during childhood, they showed more normal heterosexual adjustment.

In a similar type of study, Ruppenthal et al. (1974) studied the development of firstborn infant monkeys who, unlike most laboratory monkeys, were reared in a nuclear family setting for the first three years of their lives. They found that these monkeys, who were allowed close proximity to the family, developed "sophisticated patterns of social behavior seldom observed in laboratory-reared monkeys and maintained levels of interactive play longer chronologically than has been reported for feral-raised (in the wilds) monkeys" (p. 670). These results again support the thesis that the nuclear family situation facilitates socialization and that premature separation from the parents may be a factor that impedes appropriate socialization.

Other studies, using human subjects, have also attempted to investigate the relationship between family intactness and different aspects of socialization. Bowlby (1958, 1960, 1969), in an impressive series of studies, has concluded, like Harlow, that close physical contact between child and mother are essential for the well-being of the infant and for its subsequent development and normal adjustment in later childhood, adolescence, and adulthood. A number of studies have directed attention toward the working mother. Does the working mother provide a less adequate maternal environment for her child? Do children of working mothers perform less well in school? Although there have been a number of conflicting findings over the years, Black (1974), in a recent paper that summarizes much of the literature of the past ten years, concludes:

The attachment needs of young monkeys are strikingly similar to the human baby's need for warm, loving maternal contact. As Harlow's experiments show, infant monkeys prefer physical contact with a cloth mother even when they are fed by a wire mother.

... how a child does in school is not in any major way affected by whether or no the mother works. . . . There has also been concern over the possible adverse effects of maternal employment upon the personality or behavioral problems. Decades of research supports the statement that employment is not related, overall, to emotional or behavioral problems. However, such a statement represents a finding about averages; it appears that sometimes family situations and children's reactions become worse when the mother works, sometimes there is no change, and sometimes things become better. . . . Two major factors determining a child's reaction are the age of the child when the employment begins and the nature of the child care arrangements made. . . . (p. 51)

The last sentence is particularly important, for it is generally agreed that during the first year of life (at least) the mother should *not* be working in order that she can provide the moment-to-moment tactile care that the child so desperately needs.

> "In addition to the influences of maternal care on the child's socialization, the child also learns to adjust to the social reality from his or her play experiences and, particularly during the three-year-old to six-year-old period, from his or her peers."

Children's Play and the Influence of Peers

In addition to the profound and pervasive influence of maternal care on the child's socialization, the child also learns to adjust to the social reality from his or her play experiences and, particularly during the three-year-old to six-year-old period, from his or her peers.

Play is an integral part of the child's development as a social animal. While play, to the child and perhaps to the parents, is a diverting, pleasurable, hardly serious activity, psychologists have long recognized the importance of play in socialization and in cognitive development. Erik Erikson (1963) argues that play is one of the major functions of the ego, and he studied children's play in order to better understand the child's sense of reality, of ego development. He noted that children's play is not the equivalent of adult's play—it is not *simply* recreation. Rather, he believes that through play the child is enabled to advance to new developmental stages and to deal with life experiences, which the child attempts to repeat, to master, or to negate. Play, he argues, *involves self-teaching and self-healing; for in the play situation, the child can make up for frustrations and defeats in the real world.* The child who fails at a task in the outer world can retreat into the "safe island" that play provides and can overcome the feelings of failure within his or her own set of boundaries. Erikson describes the different stages of children's play from its original focus on the self until the child can reach out and play with others, demonstrating its crucial role as a socializing factor.

"Play," Smart and Smart (1973) conclude after a thorough summary of the research, "the main occupation of the young child, is his mode of learning new patterns of thought, feeling, and action and of integrating them. While sensorimotor play persists throughout life, social and imaginative play become increasingly influential upon the preschool child's development" (p. 176). They go on to describe the development of modes of play and their importance:

Early social play involves exploration of other children as objects and as persons. Parallel play, typical of two-year-olds, means engaging in the same activity with little interaction other than watching and imitating. Interactions between young children are temporary and fleeting, increasing as children mature. The earliest group play is loosely structured, permitting children to shift in and out of activity easily. Sympathetic and cooperative behavior occur in young children. . . . As children grow older, they tend to quarrel less frequently but more aggressively. Positive, friendly behavior increases with age, occurring very often in well-liked children. . . . Immature children are likely to elicit aggression from children the same age who are more mature. (p. 176)

Through play, the child develops a "social style."

105

> "Much evidence indicates that extensive sex-role learning occurs during the preschool years. By the time the child reaches school age, many of his or her ideas of male and female roles are already established."

The developmental sequence of play has been studied in much detail since it reveals, step by step, how the child socializes and, more importantly, how the child's social development is related to other areas of growth such as cognitive growth, psychomotor development, and so on. Neale (1969) points out that "maturation of the individual allows an increase in the breadth of play. The infant, if indeed he does play, is limited to activity with his body and the nipple of the breast that feeds him. As the child develops, play may come to involve other objects, feelings, and thoughts. Although it begins as a private activity, it may become 'parallel' play, and then group play with 'social rules' " (p. 83). Jersild (1947) too found that the earliest forms of play involve only motor activities, while around the second year, language (even in the form of babbling) becomes an integral part of play. Almy (1966) and Sutton-Smith (1967) agree that play is also a crucial part of the child's intellectual development.

Children's playfulness tends to bring them into contact with their peers, and the peers begin to exert pressures on the child; pressures that, in the long run, facilitate socialization. The peer group influences primarily by its pressure to *conform;* that is, the child is overtly or covertly pressured into behaving in a way that is acceptable to the peer group. Costanzo and Shaw (1966), in a study of conformity as a function of age level, found that "from the preadolescent to the adolescent period of development, the amount of conformity to external social pressure increases" (p. 973). In another study, Charlesworth and Hartup (1967) found in an observational study of preschool children that "the older groups reinforced their peers at a significantly higher rate than those in the younger groups," confirming earlier findings that four-year-olds responded more dramatically to peer group pressures than did three-year-olds.

Sex-Role Learning Much evidence indicates that extensive sex-role learning occurs during the preschool years. By the time the child reaches school age, many of his or her ideas of male and female roles are already established. During these years, many pressures come to bear on the child to conform to certain explicit and implicit sex-role expectations. Hetherington (1970) points out that the assignment of sex roles begins very early in life: "males are expected to be powerful, independent, aggressive, and competent in manipulating the environment, in achievement situations and in decision making. . . . Females are expected to be more dependent, socially sensitive, and nurturant, but to suppress aggressive and sexual impulses" (pp. 193–194). By the time the child is five or six years old, there is already a concept of sex identification at work in the socializing process. Nadelman (1974) found, for instance, in testing five-year-old and eight-year-old boys and girls from all socioeconomic groups, that the children preferred and were better able to recall and learn "opposite-sex" items. In other words, their sense of sexual identity had already been fairly well set and was influencing their cognitive as well as their social growth.

But where do children learn this sex-role identification? It is generally agreed that the parents are primarily responsible for this, although there is some disagreement on the relative importance of the mother and father, for either the boy or girl child. Rosenberg (1973), echoing what is the generally held belief, states that there is no biological basis for sex-role identification: that "children's gender identity was that which their parents had brought them up to have" (p. 383).

Although parents are the primary influence on our sex-role development, the educational system also serves to reinforce sex-role stereotypes. Weitzman and Rizzo (1974) analyzed the contents of the most widely used textbooks in the country and concluded that children are being warped by the latent messages in the books. For example, they found that females (who represent 51% of the population) are shown in only one-third of the illustrations in second-grade books, and that this drops to one-fifth of the total number of illustrations on the sixth-grade level. In other words, as textbooks increase in sophistication, women become less numerous and, by implication, less significant as role models. Covertly then, a young girl is told that she, a female, is less important as the textbook world shifts to the world of adults. In addition, the study revealed that in the textbooks, boys are shown as active, skilled, and adventuresome; girls as passive, watching and waiting for the boys. Adult men are shown in over one-hundred-fifty different occupational roles, while almost all adult women are depicted as housewives. In science books, boys are shown looking through microscopes and pouring chemicals, while girls stand and watch them; in arithmetic books, men are shown earning money, while women are pictured slicing pies. These textbook stereotypes are reinforced by all the media; by popular music, by books, by movies and television (Chafetz, 1974).

With so many children entering school at an early age now, whether it be nursery school, day-care center, or some type of "head-start" program, teachers are finding more and more opportunities to influence the child's early de-

Implications for Teachers

> "While some might argue that the teacher has to provide the children with a desirable role model, this does not mean that the teacher has to directly intervene in the children's exploratory social situations."

velopment. There are a number of important insights that the teacher may apply in dealing with the young child, particularly in attempts to facilitate the child's socialization.

One of the pioneers in progressive methods for helping young children develop social skills is Maria Montessori, whose teaching ideology has become one of the most widely practiced in the world today. Some of her principles are particularly applicable at the age level in question. In *The Absorbent Mind,* which concerns the first six years of the child's life, she makes the following comments on the role of the school in the child's social development:

> We started by equipping the child's environment with a little of everything, and left the children to choose those things they preferred. Seeing that they only took certain things and that the others remain unused, we eliminated the latter. . . . So we may truly say that these things have been chosen by the children. . . . A child chooses what helps him to construct himself.
>
> There is only one specimen of each object, and if a piece is in use when another child wants it, the latter—if he is normalized—will wait for it to be released. Important social qualities derive from this. The child comes to see that he must respect the work of others, not because someone has said he must, but because this is a reality that he meets in his daily experience. There is only one between many children, so there is nothing for it but to wait (*sic!*). And since this happens every hour of the day for years, the idea of respecting others, and of waiting one's turn, becomes an habitual part of life which always grows more mature.
>
> Out of this comes a change, an adaptation, which is nothing if not the birth of social life itself. Society does not rest on personal wishes, but on a combination of activities which have to be harmonized. From their experiences another virtue develops in children: the virtue of patience, which is a kind of denial of impulses by means of inhibition. So the character traits that we call virtues spring up spontaneously. We cannot teach this kind of morality to children of three, but experience can. . . .
>
> When adults interfere in this first stage of preparation for social life, they nearly always make mistakes. . . . Teachers who use direct methods cannot understand how social behavior is fostered in a Montessori school. They think it offers scholastic material but not social material. They say, "If the child does everything on his own, what becomes of social life?" But what is social life if not the solving of social problems, behaving properly and pursuing aims acceptable to all? (Montessori, 1967, pp. 223–224)

Montessori aptly points out the tendency of many teachers to "interfere" in the child's tentative experimental forays into social interaction. While some might argue (particularly proponents of modeling theory) that the teacher has to provide the children with a desirable role model, this does not mean that the teacher has to directly intervene in the children's exploratory social situations. In fact, the teacher might serve as an even more powerful role model by allowing the children to make and then recognize their own mistakes; by not intruding in their worlds; by providing opportunities (such as the one Montessori describes) for the children to deal with real-life social situations instead of unnecessarily overprotecting them.

Todd and Heffernan (1970), in discussing how teachers of preschool children (and the same would apply to parents) can help them learn to participate in the culture, argue that—

although the individual teacher must decide about activities especially appropriate for the children in her group, all preschool teachers should provide experiences that help the children "learn" the following:

—The role of a child, as distinct from that of adults
—The role of a boy, or of a girl
—Family roles, including those of mother and father
—The artifacts of the society and how each is used
—Roles of different community helpers
—Differences between city and country
—The nature of school
—Relationships of people in the world
—Basic concepts of the society as exemplified in special days
—Activities associated with special holidays
—Costumes appropriate for a particular activity or occasion, as well as for the weather (p. 264)

These are viewed as the preliminary learning tasks that are prerequisites for successful socialization. They can be "taught" either through carefully constructed lessons or simply by responding to the questions raised by preschool children, questions born from their natural curiosity and interest in the world around them.

In today's rapidly changing social milieu, where traditional values, assumptions, and precepts are openly questioned and challenged, the teacher is bound to wonder what responsibility he or she has for helping young children develop a "contemporary" social awareness. Two particular areas pose difficult questions for the preschool teacher: ethnic perceptions and sex-role stereotyping. Both of these, according to the bulk of research, are heavily influenced during the preschool years, and the preschool teacher is in an excellent position to act as an ameliorative influence. Let us consider each of these socializing aims briefly.

Ethnic awareness and racial sensitivity have two basic dimensions: helping the minority group student perceive himself in a positive light, and helping every student understand the fundamental equality of all people, regardless of racial differences. A number of studies have clearly indicated that children's racial attitudes are influenced by the school environment and can be changed through the teacher's behavior and curriculum refinement. In a classic experiment, Trager and Yarrow (1952) compared the racial attitudes of two groups of young children. One group was exposed to a democratic curriculum and the other group to an ethnocentric curriculum. They found "that children learn prejudices not only from the larger environment but from the content of the curriculum and its values. *If democratic attitudes are to be learned they must be specifically taught and experienced."* In reviewing this and other studies, Banks (1972) arrives at the following conclusions regarding changing children's racial attitudes in the school:

> ... *The research suggests rather conclusively that children's racial attitudes can be modified by experiences in the school designed specifically for that purpose.* However, specific instructional objectives must be deliberately formulated; incidental teaching of racial relations is apparently ineffective. Also, clearly defined teaching strategies must be structured to attain the objectives. Attitude changes induced by experimental intervention will persist through time, although there is a tendency for modified attitudes to revert back to the pre-experimental ones. However, the effects of the experimental treatment do not completely diminish.... (p. 21)

The minority group child, particularly at this early, sensitive age, must be allowed to experience a feeling of pride in his racial heritage. One area in which many teachers inadvertently attack the child's heritage is in correcting children's idiosyncratic use of language—particularly the dialects of black students. Abrahams (1970), among others, admonishes teachers that they must recognize the legitimacy and value of the so-called substandard English spoken by many black children. "The fact is," he argues, "that most of the lower-class black children who come into the classroom have a well-developed sense of language and its power to pass on information and to control interpersonal relationships." The problem, he goes on to state, is not with the children, but with the teachers who do not recognize the legitimacy of the children's tongue:

> ... Negro children find, when they go to school, that the language skills they have learned are in a tongue that is despised as substandard and performed in a manner that is regarded as hostile, obscene, or arrogant. They learn very quickly that the easiest way of getting by in the classroom is to be quiet—and so they are accused of being nonverbal. This derogation of language and language skills, furthermore, does little for the development of self-confidence. (pp. 16–17)

Although many of the problems of dealing with racial sensitivity are inherent in the elementary school level, the preschool years are the foundations for that level, and racial perceptions are often fairly well-established during the kindergarten and first-grade years.

Sex-role identification, although mostly a result of family training, is also influenced in the day-care, nursery, and kindergarten environments.

"Through identification of sex role, the child not only comes to understand himself or herself better but develops a more appropriate social attitude toward members of the opposite sex."

Sex roles are learned early in life, not only through conscious educational efforts but by the inherent sex-role stereotypes the child is exposed to.

Through identification of sex role, the child not only comes to understand himself or herself better but develops a more appropriate social attitude toward members of the opposite sex. "The establishment and acceptance of his sex role contributes to the concept of self. Male and female roles are outlined by the culture and defined in detail by the family. The family teaches by direct instruction and prohibition, by sex-typing the environment, and by differential treatment of boys and girls. Children respond by identifying with one role or another, by their preference for either role, and by the concepts of family members which they build" (Smart & Smart, 1973, p. 242). The teacher supplements this training by not reinforcing stereotyped sex-role behaviors and by providing materials that can enrich the student's perception of male-female similarities and differences.

The Preschool Years: Conclusions and Implications

We have seen in this chapter how the years before formal schooling begins are important in developing the prerequisites necessary for success in later educational tasks. In the introduction to this section, we mentioned how education begins at the moment the person breaks free of the genetic bondage, at a moment near birth. In this chapter, we examined some of the specific occurrences of early education, from the suckling babe deriving nourishment at the mother's nipple, to the toddler learning his first sentences, to the four-year-old playing with other children and learning through play. What are the implications of these insights about child development?

For the teacher who encounters the child after the completion of this period, the key questions are, What is the raw material I have to work with? and, What can be done to improve the potential of this raw material? To answer the first question, the teacher can assess the child by systematically evaluating the child's capacities in each of the important categories we have covered: How bright does the child appear? How verbal, how interested in language is the child? Does the child show an inclination toward others or is he withdrawn and isolated from those around him? Are there any signs of abnormal personality development? Is therapy indicated? Are there physical or other abnormalities that might be genetic and is treatment available? Does the child require special placement?

Many times these are difficult questions that yield painful answers. But if the teacher can answer these questions properly during the early years—in the preschool or the kindergarten—then interventions can prevent further damage and perhaps correct the difficulties before they become unmanageable; before they stigmatize the child and alienate him from the school altogether.

In regard to the second question—What can be done to increase the child's potential?—there are many answers available. For specialized problems, such as serious learning disabilities, physical and perceptual impairment, emotional conflicts, and so forth, the use of specialists is highly recommended. Fortunately, if these types of disorders are diagnosed early enough, the treatment prognosis is highly favorable, much more so than if they are diagnosed in the upper grades. The teacher can also provide enrichment in each of the areas covered: Language skills can be easily developed, first through the spoken language and then through reading, as the teacher helps the child feel comfortable speaking, expressing ideas, communicating verbally; socialization skills are also developed in the classroom, especially where the teacher recognizes the social aspect of the child as a significant part of the total educative process. Creative play and role-playing are both useful tools in helping the child develop social skills. Personality problems, if they are not severe enough to require specialized treatment, can also be handled in the classroom. When the teacher observes the child functioning on a level significantly below that indicated for his or her age, appropriate interventions (discussed under "Emotional Education" in chapter 11) can help the child reach maturity more quickly. Finally, as the teacher recognizes the crucial interaction between home and school life during the early preschool years (which include nursery, day care, and kindergarten), he or she will show a willingness to work along with the parents to assure that the developmental processes of intelligence, language skills, personality, and social growth are facilitated as much as possible.

Summary

In this chapter we examined the developmental processes that precede the years of formal schooling. We considered the ways in which the infant acquires cognitive and emotional characteristics from interactions with the maternal, family, and social environments.

Special attention was directed toward understanding how the child acquires language. The child's early socialization efforts, particularly through play, were related to subsequent social development. Intellectual growth during the preschool years, we noted, is staggering, and Piaget's concepts of the sensorimotor stage and the period of preoperational thinking were examined.

Suggested Additional Readings

One Little Boy by Dorothy W. Baruch (*New York: Delta Books, paperback, 1964*)

> A touching, readable true story of Kenneth, an eight-year-old boy experiencing emotional problems. In the course of learning about Kenneth's inner world of turmoil, the author opens up to us the experience of growing up, how the child's feelings are shaped, what influences play the greatest part in emotional and social development.

He knew from the beginning that his father and mother were having trouble. It came to him at night from their room across the hall.
"In bed they keep thinking dark thoughts."
He would lie rigid. His legs tight, his chest tight, his breathing tight in his body. . . .

from *One Little Boy*

The Conditions of Human Growth by Jane Pearce and Saul Newton (*Secaucus, N.J.: Citadel Press, paperback, 1969*)

Based on the writings of Harry Stack Sullivan, this excitingly written book not only outlines a detailed theory of personality and growth but also shows how the individual combats the many terrifying forces in the environment. Although heavily psychoanalytic, many of the insights are so universal that even partisans of nonpsychoanalytic positions will find themselves impressed.

Beginning with adolescence, the new dimension that appears as the major challenge in life is the assumption of the responsibility for one's growth. One is from this time on the architect for his own patterns of living.

from *The Conditions of Human Growth*

Colin: A Normal Child by Lois Barclay Murphy and associates. (*New York: Basic Books, paperback, 1965*)

Unlike many clinical books about children, this one traces the growth of a normal American child. "Implicit through all of the volume is our effort to see Colin concretely, to understand what he was going through, and what his behavior meant to him as well as to the children and adults around him. . . ." The book succeeds in providing a representative portrait of how a child develops into what he or she is.

In the middle of this winter Colin's mother was concerned about the amount of attention he wanted from her at home; he expected a great deal of help in dressing himself, and wanted to be fed. . . .

from *Colin: A Normal Child*

A Child's Mind by Muriel Beadle (*New York: Jason Aronson, 1971*)

This book provides a detailed treatment of how children learn during the first five years of life. Covering such important topics as perception, motivation, concept formation, the family constellation, and social class, the author does a deft job of pointing out interrelationships between all of the forces that contribute to learning and growth. Particularly valuable are the insights about the nature-nurture interaction.

As living creatures ascend the evolutionary ladder, the amount of their behavior that is controlled by fixed—that is, inherited and unmodifiable—action patterns is broken down into smaller and smaller units. This allows the organism . . . an increasing amount of freedom to modify its behavior as a result of learning.

from *A Child's Mind*

Aggression: A Social Learning Analysis by Albert Bandura (*Englewood Cliffs, N.J.: Prentice-Hall, 1973*)

This is the most comprehensive treatment of the behavioral position on how children learn aggression. The study goes beyond developmental psychology in its attempts to explain aggressive social actions through the concepts of social learning theory. Many of the book's insights are directly applicable to the school setting.

Many interventions intended as punishments actually serve as positive reinforcers that maintain troublesome behavior. . . .

from *Aggression: A Social Learning Analysis*

Overview of the Elementary School Years

These years, which comprise the periods of middle and late childhood, see many profound changes in the child. Intellectually, the child learns to read, write, and compute arithmetically. Emotionally, the child becomes more extroverted and autonomous. Two of Erikson's stages are characteristic of this period: "industry vs. inferiority" and "identity vs. role confusion."

The Child's Intellectual Development

Language becomes a major factor in the child's understanding of the world. Piaget's period of "concrete operations" describes the child's cognitive processes during this period.

Growth and Change During the Elementary School Years: A Matrix of Interacting Forces

The home, school, and peer influences combine during the elementary school years to shape the child's mind, character, and personality. The family, particularly, can provide strong incentive for positive or negative development.

The Battered-Child Syndrome

Children may be physically abused or severely neglected. There are specific guidelines for recognizing the signs of child abuse in the school. Generally, a parent of the abused child was abused himself as a child. It is suggested that the school coordinate efforts with community agencies to develop comprehensive programs for dealing with this pervasive social problem.

The Single-Parent Family

Although the child of the single-parent family may have certain difficulties, there is no evidence that blanket generalizations can be made about such children. The teacher's sensitivity to the family situation, however, will help him understand the child better. The situation is true, too, for the family with a working mother.

Continued

4 The Elementary School Years

Birth Order and Relationships with Siblings

There is some evidence to indicate that the child's position within the family structure as a result of birth order bears some influence on the child's overall development and subsequent personality. Several different theories on the relationship have been explicated.

The Influence of the School

The influence of the school works in conjunction with the family influence: Where the school and home experiences are congruent, the impact on the children is reinforced.

The School as a Socializing Institution

The child's functioning in the classroom is directly relevant to his socialization within the school. The bilingual child may encounter special difficulties in the school setting. The teacher's sensitivity to the special needs of the culturally disadvantaged child is critical to effective socialization. In the classroom, all children learn behavior patterns from observing and interacting with the teacher and with the peer group.

In early September, the Taylors watch proudly as their daughter Janet dresses for her first day of school. There is a mixture of pride and nervousness in the air; pride on the part of the parents and nervousness on the part of the child. "Mommy, will you stay there with me," Janet asks plaintively, knowing full well that her mother will *not* be staying with her for the day. "Mommy will stay with you for awhile," her father assures her, knotting his tie and looking into the mirror. "Won't you, honey?" he asks his wife as an afterthought.

"I'll stay with you for awhile," Mrs. Taylor assures her daughter, "but your teacher, Miss Gold, will take good care of you. You'll like school. And I know you'll like Miss Gold."

Janet Taylor is a normal, well-adjusted five-year-old. Although she speaks her native language, English, fluently, she is still not able to express complex thoughts. Her thinking, especially her reasoning about things which are not tangible, is naive. She is unable to deduce conclusions from propositions, unable to formulate hypotheses that can be used as a guide for action. She does what she is told, and if she doesn't, she knows she is being "naughty." Her primary social reference is the family, although she is influenced to varying degrees by her friends on the block with whom she plays. Together, family and friends exert a major influence on her life. She can visually recognize a few words her parents have taught her, but she still cannot read. While her motor skills are normal in all respects, she is unable to coordinate her muscles as quickly as would be necessary, say, to type on a typewriter. Janet Taylor, in short, is a normal, or "average," five-year-old child.

In the month of June, the Taylors proudly attend their daughter's graduation from sixth grade. Six long years have passed since that nervous first day of school when Mr. and Mrs. Taylor had to calm their anxious daughter, and Janet will be attending the intermediate school next September. The Taylors are quite pleased with their daughter, for Janet is one of the better students in the class. She is a bright girl and exhibits many of the sophistications of thinking and reasoning that are normally associated with the teenage years. True, the Taylors are somewhat troubled and confused by what they call Janet's "rebellious behavior," which started just a few months ago. It seems that lately Janet has started experimenting with her mother's makeup and has been picking out her own glittery clothing, which Mrs. Taylor says is "tawdry," a word Janet despises. She is no longer satisfied with the functional, tailored clothing that her mother brings home for her. Mr. Taylor too is irritated by what he calls his daughter's "manner": a word whose meaning has never been made quite clear. But on the whole, their daughter's intellectual promise and social grace make the Taylors very happy parents.

The elementary school years, which encompass the latter years of middle childhood and all of the late childhood period, bear witness to the important and profound changes during which the helpless "babe-in-arms" grows and develops into a functioning, basically independent, rational human being. So much happens during these six years—emotionally, intellectually, socially, physically, and culturally—that it is almost impossible to describe all the changes. Ironically, Freud called these years the period of **latency** because the "sexual striving" of the earlier developmental epochs remain dormant, or quiet. But these are hardly quiet years; rather, they are years where remarkable changes take place, although they may slip by, often barely noticed.

Consider this: The child learns not only to read a language but to understand subtleties of meaning; the child forms significant attachments in addition to the primary family, many of which are as influential in his or her life as the family formerly was; the child learns the basic skills of mathematical reasoning and logic; the child's value structure becomes systematic (although still not integrated—see chapter 7); the child begins to develop a sense of the past and its relationship to the present—a sense of history, of cultural awareness, a sense of place and time.

In this chapter, we will examine the basic influences that are exerted on the child's growth and development during the years that he or she is in attendance at the elementary school. After a brief overview of the period, we shall look at the psychological and social development of the child, the influence of the family, the influence of the school, and finally arrive at some conclusions that can be helpful to the teacher in trying to understand and work with the elementary school child.

Overview of the Elementary School Years

Developmental psychologists generally divide childhood (which extends from birth to puberty) into three phases: early, middle, and late. All of the years of early childhood have passed by before the child enters school. As a general criterion, early childhood ends when the child learns to speak. The middle childhood period, from about two to seven years, is almost completed by the time the child enters the elementary school. The late childhood period, from about seven years to the onset of puberty, comprises the main period of the elementary school years.

When the child enters the kindergarten or first grade, he or she is approaching the end of middle childhood, and the developmental hallmarks of this period are still highlighted as the child comes to school. George Cruchon (1969) in his remarkably perceptive book, *The Transformations of Childhood,* outlines some characteristics of middle childhood:

> "We see that the first two years of school are particularly important as a transitional period during which the child develops more autonomously than he or she did during the previous period."

> The first period, spent in the family . . . or in the nursery school or kindergarten, is still full of creative fantasy and imaginative games; the child tries to express and assert himself according to his own manner of being, impelled by a very rich interior life, which were it not the normal thing, would seem to be introverted thought of the autistic type, with little regard for the real; in any case there is little progress in mastery of the exterior world. . . . (p. 49)

But then the child moves on to the school years, and,

> In the second period the child generally goes on to kindergarten from nursery school or enters primary school; his thought emerges of its own accord, and proceeds to orientate itself upon the pole of exterior reality. The child begins to subject himself or herself to the requirements of group life outside of the family and also to the little directed scholastic efforts which are set before him. In this way the following phase is gradually prepared in which attitudes of objective interest appear (the school age properly so-called); the father becomes a hero worthy of admiration after having been held in defiance for some time and regarded as a rival. . . . (pp. 49–50)

So, we see that the first two years of school are particularly important as a transitional period during which the child develops more autonomously than he or she did during the previous periods.

Intellectually, this period serves two important functions. First, the child makes the transition from a predominantly oral culture, in which the primary emphasis is on speaking, to one in which reading and writing become of importance. Just a few years earlier, the child was rewarded for making certain sounds; for learning to speak the language of his parents. Now, as the child is exposed to the beginning of formal schooling, he is expected to learn the alphabet, to learn to write, and to learn the beginnings of reading skills. At times, confusion may occur when appropriate connections are not made between the written and spoken languages. This must be taken into account by the teacher of the first-grade and second-grade child. "Since speaking precedes writing and reading," Strang and Hocker (1965) point out, "it may be less effective to teach children a vocabulary comprising only words that occur with the most frequency in printed material than to teach them to read words that they themselves know and use. There is evidence that children find it easier to read the stories that they write than stories that are written for them by adults" (p. 250).

A second important intellectual development during this period is the child's transition from what Piaget calls the "preoperational period" to the period of "concrete operations." This means that the child is able to master more abstract processes, such as classifying a number of common elements into a group, or performing a process that can be reversed (adding and then taking away, for example). This will be discussed in more detail in the section on intellectual development.

Late Childhood

As we mentioned earlier, late childhood is generally synonymous with the elementary school years. Cruchon (1969) has also provided a descriptive overview of late childhood:

> This is a period of marked extraversion, in contrast with the preceding period; the child has practical and positive interests, and through them he gets out of himself, his dreams, and his troubles of conscience, and turns to both the things and persons who are about him. Therefore, it is a time in which he moves toward new conquests over things and in which *homo faber* (Man the Maker) reappears industrious and active. All kinds of play activities are deployed, not only to exercise the inward imagination . . . but also to discharge great quantities of muscular energy in the open air; there is relative skill with instruments and tools and good organization and an awareness of spatial relationships. It is a time of socialization; unless he is held back by too tender or too watchful affection from his parents, the child adapts himself and attaches himself enthusiastically to groups of children of his own age, both within the family . . . and above all at school. Egocentricity is replaced by fellowship, comradeship, mateship, and cooperation; this change may have its awkward side, but it is not to be less approved of for all that. (p. 130)

We see that as a general tendency the child moves during this period from a basically inner-directed person to a more outer-directed person. This process, which encompasses emotional, intellectual, and social components, is facilitated or retarded by factors from the home and from the school that will be described in later sections of this chapter. Erikson, whose early stages are discussed in the previous chapter, provides a stage-by-stage description of this period.

Erikson's Stages of Development

Erikson's (1950) stages reflect, in somewhat more detail, the overview position provided by Cruchon. Stage four of the "Eight Ages of Man" is called *industry vs. inferiority*. This age coincides with the beginning of formal schooling. "The child must forget past hopes and wishes," Erikson (p. 258) writes, "while his exuberant imagination is tamed and harnessed to the laws of impersonal things—even the three R's." Erikson relates the child's personal development to social aims through the concept of *industry*. In one sense, industry is the logical extension of play, only with industry as opposed to play, there is a tendency toward completing a project with a productive end. "To bring a productive situation to completion is an aim which gradually supersedes the whims and wishes of play" (Erikson, p. 259). The industriousness of the early school-age child is reflected in his or her ability to master educational goals, including all types of projects from reading to crafts.

Industriousness serves an important social purpose in channelling the child's energy into socially productive tasks and in enabling him to work cooperatively with others. It also serves an important psychological function in allowing the child to compensate for feelings of inferiority. Although this is an integral part of Erikson's conception, it is also promulgated by and associated with the work of Alfred Adler, whose phrase "striving toward superiority" describes the tendency of children to try to overcome their basic feelings of inferiority. A cognitive psychologist, Robert White (1959), has suggested a similar idea, which he calls "competence motivation" or "effectance" and which also acts as a motivating, yet stabilizing, force in the personality. Although Erikson, Adler, and White use their ideas somewhat differently, they all emphasize that the child develops competence to gain mastery over his or her environment to become more the master of circumstances rather than the helpless victim of the environment.

Erikson's fifth stage is called *identity vs. role confusion*. Although this stage has been traditionally viewed as the first stage of the adolescent period, there is evidence that children are maturing earlier. By the middle of the sixth grade, there is already a strong tendency toward finding "one's identity," particularly through attachments to groups, such as the "youth culture" (Coleman, 1968, 1971). Certain social conditions, such as television, pop records, and teenage magazines make this culture accessible to children at an earlier age. As the identification with this "outer culture" begins early, attachments to the family decrease proportionately.

In the following section, we will look at the major intellectual changes during the elementary school years.

The Child's Intellectual Development

The intellectual tasks of the elementary school years serve as the foundations for all later learning. Without the ability to read printed matter, more advanced learning (at least in our culture) is implicitly precluded; without mastery of the elements of arithmetic reasoning, future development of quantitative skills is not to be expected. Without the rudimentary social skills of cooperation and appropriate deference, it is very unlikely that the more ad-

> "The order in which the curriculum is structured . . . is determined—at least to the extent that it is successful—by what we know of children's abilities at different stages of development."

vanced conceptions of citizenship, democracy, and group function will evolve. So, the ability to master the learning necessary for success in elementary school is also a prerequisite to all future learning.

An important concept in understanding the variables involved in each child's quest for mastery is called *developmental readiness*. This means that the child is intellectually and psychologically ripe at the time he or she approaches a certain subject matter. The order in which the school curriculum is structured is neither arbitrary nor culturally-biased; rather, it is determined —at least to the extent that it is successful—by what we know of children's abilities at different stages of development. Reading skills always follow speaking skills and always precede writing skills; ability to perform arithmetic operations must precede the more deductive challenges of algebra. Simple logical reasoning (such as use of the syllogism) must be mastered before the child can understand such abstract concepts as justice and democracy.

Piaget (1970), who has done much to make explicit the reasons for this orderliness in intellectual development, argues that the structure of knowledge itself parallels the child's ability to learn knowledge: "Genetic epistemology," he says, "attempts to explain knowledge, and in particular scientific knowledge, on the basis of its history, its sociogenesis, and especially the psychological origins of the notions and operations upon which it is based. . . . genetic epistemology also takes into account . . . social formalizations applied to equilibrated thought structures and in certain cases to transformations from one level to another in the development of thought" (Piaget, 1970, p. 1). In other words, his attempts to understand the entire structure of knowledge—that is, objective knowledge—requires that he understand the development of mental operations in the child.

This principle shows itself clearly in the elementary school child's continuing mastery of language skills. Although the child is fluent in language when he or she enters schools, the vocabulary and syntactic structure is restricted, thus limiting not only expression but also the ability to fully understand one's experience. Until the child develops more sophisticated language skills, he or she is not ready developmentally for more advanced learning. In fact, *our perception and understanding of the world around us are in many ways dictated by our language, including not only the vocabulary but the grammar and syntax as well.* This is known as the Sapir-Whorf hypothesis, named after Edward Sapir and Benjamin Lee Whorf. Whorf (1952) argued,

"Our perception and understanding of the world around us is in many ways dictated by our language, including not only the vocabulary but the grammar and syntax as well."

"We cut up and organize the spread and flow of events as we do largely because, through our mother tongue, we are parties to an agreement to do so, not because nature itself is segmented in exactly that way for all to see. Languages differ not only in how they build their sentences but in how they break down nature to secure the elements to put in those sentences. . . ." One aspect of developmental readiness, then, is that the child have the language ability to perceive, differentiate, and act upon his or her environment.

In addition to language readiness, the child must have the capacity to process the perceived information in a way that will be useful and productive. Piaget's description of the elementary-level child's group grasp of concrete operations helps explain this ability. Let us turn our attention to a brief summary of his ideas.

Piaget refers to the period of intellectual development from seven to eleven years old—the elementary school years—as the period of concrete operations. During these years, the child develops several related abilities that enable him to process information in a more sophisticated way than was possible during the preceding period of "preoperational" thought. For example, the child develops the ability to *classify;* an important process that enables the child to organize separate things into classes which have at least one common element. Classification can be demonstrated in the following example:

Piaget's Period of "Concrete Operations"

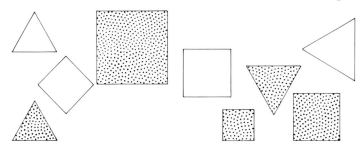

How many triangles are there? How many dotted objects? How many squares? To answer each of these, the various objects have to be classified into categories, such as (triangles; triangles with dots; squares; squares with dots), and the answer to How many dotted objects? is the sum of two of these classes—triangles with dots and squares with dots).

Conservation is generally considered the most crucial elementary concrete operation developed during this period. Conservation can be defined as the recognition of continuity and sameness as a thing changes form, shape, or appearance. In the famous beaker experiment, a constant amount of liquid is poured from a tall, thin beaker into a short, wide beaker, and the child is asked which beaker holds the greatest amount of the liquid. When the child has the knowledge of conservation, he recognizes that the liquid content has remained the same even though the shape of the container has changed. Conservation can also be demonstrated in these examples:

Does one row have more *X*'s than the other or do they have the same amount?

Which line is longer or are they the same length?

Lefrancois (1972) describes some of the other logical processes that the child develops during these years:

1. *Closure*—the child realizes that the sequential application of two operations forms a third operation. In a mathematical sense adding two and three yields a third number, five.
2. *Reversibility*—for any operation there exists an inverse cancelling operation. For example, adding three to two yields five, but subtracting three from five cancels the first operation and the result is again two.
3. *Associativity*—if any three or more operations are combined it makes no difference what the order of the combination is. For example, two plus three plus four is equal to four plus three plus two.
4. *Identity*—this implies the awareness that there are operations that leave objects unchanged. For example, two plus zero is equal to two.
5. (a) *Tautology*—the repetition of a relation or a class does not change it. For example, the class of all men plus the class of all men, etc. is equal to the class of all men. (b) *Reiteration*—repetition of a number produces a new number. Three plus three plus three is equal to nine. (pp. 304–305)

The importance of this period is that it enables the child to finally master equilibrium. "With the appearance of concrete thought," Piaget (1958) points out, "the system of regulations, though maintained in an unstable state until this point, attains an elementary form of stable equilibrium." He goes on to explain this as follows:

As it reaches the level of complete reversibility, the concrete operations issued from the earlier regulations are coordinated into definite structures (classifications, serial orders, correspondences, etc.) which will be conserved for the remainder of the life span. Of course this is no bar to the organization of higher systems; but even when higher systems emerge, the present system remains active in the limited area of the organization of immediately given data. . . . (Piaget, 1958, p. 248)

Although the child still does not have the capabilities necessary for abstract and hypothetical thought (which will develop in the following stage, the period of formal operations), he or she is able to process information sufficiently to maintain a balance—an "equilibrium" in Piaget's terminology.

Growth and Change During the Elementary School Years: A Matrix of Interacting Forces

Having now examined some of the basic developmental principles associated with this period, we shall turn our attention to the more specific influences that play a part in shaping the child's life and carving his destiny. The childhood years are a period of rapid, turbulent growth and change. We cannot be sure exactly what proportion of this growth and change is directly attributable to any given factor since there are so many factors interacting in so many different ways simultaneously. But it is generally agreed that there are two major categories of influence in the child's life during these years: the home and the school (including peer influences).

The genetic reality, discussed in the previous chapter, is a constant that stands firm regardless of the environmental influences. For the most part, however, this genetic constant is *potential* rather than *actual*. It is always subject to change and modification. This genetic constant is the crucial influence of the child's primary environment that determines to what extent this potential, when positive, will be maximized; and, when negative, to what extent it will be minimized. If the child is born with a strong tendency toward high intelligence, it is the richness of the environment that nurtures this predisposition into an active, productive intellect. If, likewise, the child is born with an organic predisposition toward bodily frailty—a "constitutional weakness" —then a healthy, nutritious diet and preventive health care, also provided by persons in the child's environment, can forestall or prevent entirely the illness and poor health cast in the genes (such as in PKU).

> "The school environment and the family environment cannot be viewed as two independent settings; rather what the child takes out of the home, he or she brings into the school setting."

We will examine this environment, which shapes the course of the child's development, in terms of its two basic contexts—the home and the school—through which the child is exposed to most of his or her learning. While it can be argued that social influences, such as television, peer pressure, and the popular motifs of the youth culture, exert pressure upon the person, these are secondary as developmental factors. Traditionally, texts in development cover the physical, intellectual, emotional, and social trends. We shall pass by the physical aspect, since this is not a text on developmental psychology, and limit our discussion of the other topics to that material that is particularly relevant to the teacher as he or she tries to understand the learner and to act as a positive influence in the learner's development. One important topic, the moral development of the person, will be left to a later chapter—chapter 7, "The Affective Domain"—in order to provide continuity in that important area.

In the following sections, we shall try to come to grips with the following questions, problems, and challenges: What special family circumstances are likely to cause havoc upon the education of the child? What are ways the teacher and other personnel in the school can act to mitigate unfavorable family circumstance? Is the school an important influence in the child's development? How can the school experience be modified to act maximally upon the child?

The Influence of the Family

In the previous chapter, we examined how the family—and particularly the maternal environment—provides an important influence on the child's preschool development. This influence extends into the elementary school years, during which the child's social judgments and psychological soundness are more influenced by the family environment than by any other single factor. The school environment and the family environment cannot be viewed as two independent settings; rather, what the child takes out of the home, he or she brings into the school setting. In other words, the home environment shapes the raw material with which the teacher will work. In this sense, the family is the foundation of the educational experience.

There are many ways in which the family can provide a positive, growth-producing environment for the child. The demonstration of love and care in the family instills in the child a sense of confidence and self-awareness that impels him or her to strive toward successful goals. The security and stability provided by a sound family structure enable the child to take upon himself challenges that might otherwise go unmet because of diffidence and fear. Social skills are developed when the child has an opportunity to model appropriate behaviors after the examples set by the parents in their relationship with the child himself, with the child's siblings, and with adults to which the child is exposed. Moreover, the family also provides an important source of intellectual stimulation that encourages the child's innate curiosity to pursue productive goals. The language used in the family becomes an important factor in the child's language development. The richness of intellectual endeavors is directly related to the rewards and stimulation provided in the family setting.

On the other hand, there are many problems during these years which can be traced directly or indirectly to the family situation. The conflicts within the family milieu inevitably bring their results into the classroom. These conflicts can range from mild deprivations and lack of concern to severe mistreatment and neglect of the child. In many situations, the teacher is powerless to correct the inequities observed; but in some situations the teacher can provide a palliative, if not curative, environment to undo some of the harm done in the home. Let us examine briefly two of the more common problems that may be brought to the teacher's attention and consider how the teacher can deal with these problems, both from an educational and from a mental health point of view. First, we shall look at the abused child; then at the child from the single-parent family.

The Battered-Child Syndrome

Throughout history, there have been recorded cases of mistreatment and abuse of children. These range from the extremes of infanticide, in which parents murder their children, to the training of children into the criminal professions (à la Oliver Twist), to the unprovoked torture and mistreatment of the child. Only in recent years, however, has the term **battered-child syndrome** been advanced by psychologists and other social and mental health professionals to account for the entire pattern of child abuse, usually at the hands of the parents.

The first comprehensive efforts to view child abuse as a syndrome (dubbed the battered-child syndrome) is credited to C. Henry Kempe, a pioneer in this field, who published a seminal article on this problem in 1962 (Kempe et al., 1962), setting the stage for further study. Six years later, Helfer and Kempe (1968) edited a major work on the battered-child syndrome, and in the years since the publication of this book, hundreds of articles—many case histories, some research studies—have appeared in the professional journals. The subject is multidisciplinary, of equal concern to psychologists, pediatricians, social workers, nurses, teachers, and specialists in the mental health professions.

The recognition of this problem as a specific syndrome enables professionals to become more cognizant of its frequency. In recent years, *reported* cases of child abuse have trebled, although this clearly does not indicate that the syndrome itself is on the rise. Rather, it indicates that there is a consciousness and concern about the problem today that was not present years ago when a battered child could more easily be passed off by the parents as the victim of an unfortunate accident. Let us consider some of the major issues involved in the study of the abused child and the abusing parent.

What Is Child Abuse? There is no clear-cut, universally accepted definition of a battered child. Generally, however, care is taken to distinguish between the physically abused, or battered, child and the child who is psychologically neglected, but not assaulted, by the parents. A number of definitions have been established for research purposes. In one study (Lauer, Ten Broeck, & Grossman, 1974), a narrow definition was used: "A 'battered' or 'abused' child was defined as any child under ten years of age hospitalized because of physical injuries believed to have been caused intentionally by a parent, other household member or a regular caretaker. In screening charts we excluded uninjured children even though they may have been neglected or otherwise maltreated and we accepted the staff's decisions that the children's injuries were nonaccidental" (p. 67). In many studies, however, child abuse is defined more broadly to include severe neglect as well as assault (Burland, Andrews & Headsten, 1973). Although this poses a certain problem, inasmuch as the evidence against the abusive parent usually emphasizes the violent physical assault in which the parent loses control as a result of experiencing rage, the broader definition is more helpful in our efforts to help the abused child in the school setting. It is the child who is the victim of severe parental neglect that makes it to the school, while the physically beaten child lies in the hospital or clinic recovering from his "accident."

Systematic studies and analyses of child abuse are relatively recent, and there are many different points of view in the profession about the causes, prevention, and treatment. The Day Care Council of New York (205 East 42nd Street, New York, N.Y. 10017) publishes an informative booklet, *Children at Risk,* that discusses ways in which the professional mental health worker or teacher can recognize child abuse before it leads to death (see display 4.1). Using a definition of child abuse that includes both physical abuse and neglect, a series of guidelines are put forth to help the child-care worker recognize early signs of abuse.

The study goes on to say, "Unless you pick this child up and do something about him, unless you see how the family can be helped, this is a child

Let's talk for a moment about some factors associated with child abuse. A composite picture of families studied on a community-wide basis shows that in New York City abusing families have these characteristics:

- Social and mental problems are common, including drug addiction.
- Rates of out-of-wedlock births among the abused children are high.
- There is frequent family disunity.
- The majority of the families live in poor, over-crowded housing.
- There is little pre-natal care.
- There are high infant mortality rates.
- There are high tuberculosis and venereal disease rates.
- There are high crime rates.

Knowing that a common background of abuse often exists, let us now look at some of the characteristics of the abused child and of the abusing parent as an aid in identifying possible cases. **We have to prevent a child's death by knowing how to pick out children *before* they are battered.**

The "battered baby syndrome" brought the problem of its prevention to the attention of medical, legal, and social disciplines of our country and led us to define the "maltreatment syndrome."

The outward symptoms of the maltreatment syndrome which a teacher, physician, nurse, clinic, or dispensary should recognize are:

- Failure to thrive
- Poor skin hygiene
- Dirty fingernails
- Diaper rash
- Dirty, torn, or inadequate clothing
- Repressed, irritable, or aggressive personality
- Bruises, burns, scars, or abrasions and parent's reluctance to answer questions about them.

So you may be on the lookout for the child who is aggressive, disruptive or destructive, the habitual truant, or the child who is chronically late. He will be inadequately dressed for the weather and his clothes will be dirty or torn. He is under-nourished and sleeps in class or the day care center. He is in need of medical care and seems anemic. And, if you see that he also has welts and bruises or a black eye, you can surely suspect abuse.

This child is crying out for help. If he is an older child he will be hostile, tardy or often absent from school. When he does show up he may have a black eye or fractured or dislocated arm. And his clothes are dirty, he is not properly bathed, and he smells.

From a study by Dr. Herbert H. Frazier, Jr., Columbia College of Physicians and Surgeons, in *Children at Risk*, pp. 10–11. Published by the Day Care Council of New York, 205 East 42nd Street, New York, N.Y., 10017. Used with permission.

that is eventually going to be brought to the emergency room—and then it may be too late. The battered child is the last phase of the spectrum. It doesn't take any diagnostic ability to recognize him. He is bleeding from the mouth and parents have brought him to the hospital because they have panicked" (p. 12).

Using some of the guidelines suggested in this booklet, as well as plain intuition, the teacher will be able to spot the abused child—hopefully before the abuse reaches the point of severe battering, requiring hospitalization. But once the teacher recognizes this, what can be done? This depends in part on the attitude of the school district, the principal, and other professionals that work with the teacher. *"Schools can make a significant difference,"* argues Martin (1973), "by reporting child abuse to the appropriate authorities. To

Figure 4.1 The Traditional Cycle of Child Abuse as Compared to the Cycle of Prevention, Which Includes Education of Occurrence Avoidance As Well As Treatment. Eric Brettschneider, Queensboro Society for the Prevention of Cruelty to Children. Prepared for study funded by The New York Community Trust.

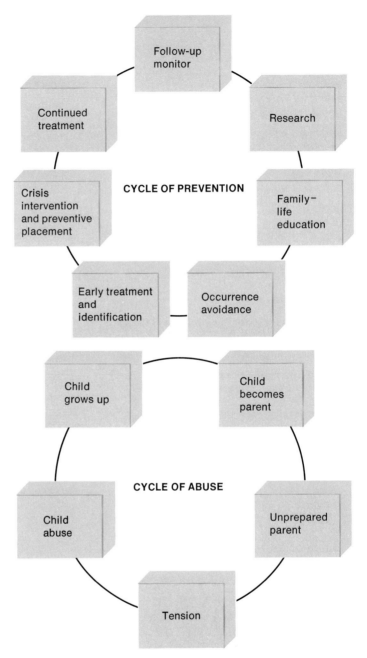

this end, *specific school board policies and reporting procedures are absolutely necessary"* (p. 53). The nature of these procedures should assure that (a) the child is placed in a safe environment, or at least made to feel that he can tell the teacher of further instances of abuse, and (b) that the parents are made to understand that treatment is imperative, (c) records are maintained that will inform subsequent teachers to keep an eye on this child.

> "Child abuse is a self-perpetuating disorder in which the abused child grows up to be an abusing parent."

It might also be helpful if the teacher had some understanding of the psychological profile of the abusing parent. This subject has been studied in some depth and a great deal is now known about parents who abuse their children. They are often highly disturbed individuals who themselves were severely abused in childhood. *Child abuse is a self-perpetuating disorder in which the abused child grows up to be an abusing parent.* Moreover, the abusing parent is usually insecure, violent and unable to control anger, and has a tendency to project his or her own inadequacies onto the child. In a comprehensive review of the literature on the child-abusing parent, Spinetta and Rigler (1972) analyze the results of over sixty-five studies on the subject. A number of compelling points emerge. First, there is much evidence that in abusing families there is "a high incidence of divorce, separation, and unstable marriages, as well as minor criminal offenses." Second, they point out that "one basic factor in the etiology of child abuse draws unanimity: Abusing parents were themselves abused or neglected, physically or emotionally, as children." These parents also "share common misunderstandings with regard to the nature of child rearing, and look to the child for satisfaction of their own parental emotional needs." Nurse (1964), in a classic study of familial patterns of parents who abuse their children, found, in conclusion:

In summary, these data were consistent with previous formulations of parental abuse in that almost without exception a single child was selected as the victim, some tendency was noted for the parents to protect each other and to resist outside influence. Prevalent was isolation and generally a passive orientation to community resources. In a third of the familes, the passive parent was also abused. Striking was the evidence that parental abuse expresses overdetermined needs of the parent rather than a reality based reaction to a provocative child. The picture emerged of a primitive parent from an emotionally and economically deprived background whose aggression seemed unmodified by maturation. In more than half the cases, the birth of the child victim was unwelcomed and in most families the victim was devalued in relation to other children. In some cases, close parallels were noted between the childhood experience of the abusing parent and his aggressive behavior toward his own child. A high incidence of emotional disorder was found when the parents were psychiatrically examined. Half of the aggressors had court records for assault or theft. (p. 304)

These two studies reflect what is generally called the *psychopathological position,* which explains child abuse as a result of an "emotional sickness" of the parents. While this is still the majority position, a recent critique by Gelles (1973) has gained some attention. Gelles provides a sociological critique and reformulation of the child-abusing parent, responding to this predominantly psychopathological model. He argues that the psychopatho-

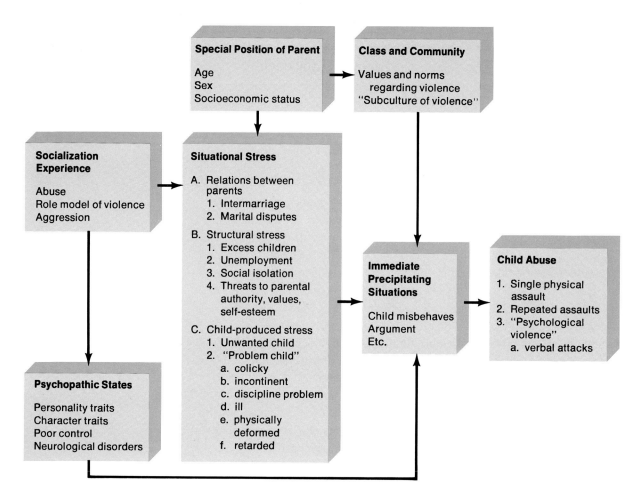

Special Position of Parent

Age
Sex
Socioeconomic status

Class and Community

Values and norms
  regarding violence
"Subculture of violence"

Socialization Experience

Abuse
Role model of violence
Aggression

Situational Stress

A. Relations between parents
  1. Intermarriage
  2. Marital disputes

B. Structural stress
  1. Excess children
  2. Unemployment
  3. Social isolation
  4. Threats to parental authority, values, self-esteem

C. Child-produced stress
  1. Unwanted child
  2. "Problem child"
    a. colicky
    b. incontinent
    c. discipline problem
    d. ill
    e. physically deformed
    f. retarded

Immediate Precipitating Situations

Child misbehaves
Argument
Etc.

Child Abuse

1. Single physical assault
2. Repeated assaults
3. "Psychological violence"
  a. verbal attacks

Psychopathic States

Personality traits
Character traits
Poor control
Neurological disorders

Figure 4.2 A Social Psychological Model of the Causes of Child Abuse. From "Child Abuse as a Psychopathology: A Sociological Critique and Reformation" by R. J. Gelles, *American Journal of Orthopsychiatry,* 1973, *43*, 611–21. Copyright © The American Orthopsychiatric Association, Inc. Reproduced by permission.

logical theory is inconsistent and that the literature on child abuse is not based on hard-core empirical research that meets the rigorous standards of social science. Instead, Gelles uses a sociocultural analysis of the situation. His model (figure 4.2, above) combines the processes of socialization with psychopathological insights to provide a synthesis of the two. At this writing, empirical research has not yet established the validity of either model; but Gelles's model is a strong contender, based on his multidisciplinary orientation.

Whatever the specific causes, it is universally agreed that the abusing parent is in need of help. Quite often the parent knows this, but for fear of legal and social retaliation is unable to seek the help needed. But when the child is referred to the appropriate authorities—and this may be through the school—then the possibility of obtaining help may become more likely.

What kind of help is available to the battered child and to his parents? This varies greatly from state to state, from district to district within states.

> " 'The biggest barrier to aiding the abused child is the unwillingness of those who notice the child's distress to report the abuse.' "

In recent years, most of the states have enacted specific laws for the reporting of child abuse, and many school districts have issued guidelines for teachers and administrators who observe instances or suspect the existence of child abuse, including severe neglect (although it has been argued that the extremely neglectful parent fails to send the child to school altogether!)

Nagi (1975) has conducted a national survey to evaluate the variety of services available. One troubling finding of his survey is that about one-third of the estimated cases are never reported to the appropriate agencies, and this may in part be the fault of the school personnel who are reluctant to report cases for fear of social or legal repercussions or through apathy and unwillingness to "get involved." On a more encouraging note, Nordstrom (1974) shows how a school system in Colorado set up an effective program for the reporting and treatment of abuse and neglect. This model, if studied, can be applied to almost any school system. But as Sanders, Kibby, Creaghan and Tyrrel (1975) point out, "the biggest barrier to aiding the abused child is the unwillingness of those who notice the child's distress to report the abuse," and no matter how well-intentioned is the school system, this remains a refractory barrier that only education can overcome. Teacher workshops can help teachers recognize the signs of child abuse, learn the standard reporting procedure, and, most importantly, find out that reporting instances of suspected abuse and neglect is crucial. Such workshops are being conducted throughout the country and offer a promise that the problem may be mitigated during the next decade. With the cooperation of the school counselor or school psychologists, such programs can prove effective and inexpensive to operate (Forrer, 1975).

The Single-Parent Family

Most children have a mother and father in the home, and teachers often assume in discussing children's homelife with them that both parents are present. But statistics show that increasingly more and more children from single-parent families (usually with the father absent) are enrolled in the schools. Although this is more prevalent among the lower socioeconomic groups, it is not uncommon among any class or among any race. A number of reasons have been cited for this increase, but certainly the most common cause is the high rate of divorce among couples having young, school-age children.

In this section, we shall examine some of the effects coming from a single-parent family has upon the child.

Herzog and Sudia (1973) provide the most comprehensive review and analysis of the literature, although their work is unfortunately limited to the children of fatherless families. Moreover, the studies examined concern the effects of father absence on boys, which reflects the general trend of the research. In this area particularly, girls have been sorely neglected. In summarizing the findings of over 120 studies, Herzog and Sudia (1973) conclude:

Three subject areas have been discussed in some detail: juvenile delinquency, school achievement, and masculine identity. Evidence concerning each . . . is neither clear enough nor firm enough to demonstrate beyond doubt whether fatherless boys are or are not overrepresented among those characterized by the problems commonly attributed to them. (A possible exception here is school achievement, about which the finding "no difference" seems solid.)

Despite the ambiguity of the results, the review does provide sufficient basis for some firm conclusions that apply to all three areas, and probably to any research on the effects of father's absence.

1. However inconclusive present evidence may be, there is firm basis for rejecting blanket generalizations about the consequences of father's absence. Its behavioral and psychological effects are probably much less uniform and much less uniformly handicapping than is widely assumed.
2. The impact of father's absence on a boy is conditioned and to a large extent mediated by a complex of interacting variables and probably cannot be explored fruitfully as a discrete, critical variable in itself.
   More specifically,
3. The impact on a boy growing up in a fatherless home is strongly affected by elements that were present before the father's absence.
4. The number of parents in the home is likely to be less crucial to the child's development than the family functioning of the present members—which is far harder to assess. Family functioning would include the mother's role and coping ability as well as the general family climate.
5. Family functioning is determined not only by individual characteristics and the interactions of its members but also by the circumstances and environment of the family unit. (p. 214)

These are broad conclusions, drawn from a wide range of studies conducted over many years, using different methodologies, different assumptions, and attempting to answer different types of questions. Such studies rarely touch upon the child's deeper feelings, which may include feeling "different from other children," anger at the absent parent, or, as some studies have shown (Baker et al., 1967), the child may develop an image of the father based on information and attitudes from the mother.

Studies often prove inadequate in answering questions about the child from the single-parent family, because the absence of a parent is only one of the many different factors affecting the child, and "absence of parent" per se tells us little about the family condition. Recognizing this problem, Nass and Nass (1976) pinpoint seven "variables which contribute to the differences

The Life of the Learner

> "Studies are often inadequate in answering questions about the child from the single-parent family, because the absence of a parent is only one of the many different factors affecting the child."

in the children of split and intact families," and these might be carefully considered by the teacher in assessing the child's situation: (1) the age at which a child is deprived of a parent; (2) the sex of the single parent who rears the child; (3) the family attitudes and social values of the parent in charge of the household; (4) the economic consequences of the split household; (5) the circumstances which deprive a child of either parent (i.e., death, divorce, separation, illegitimacy, military leave, etc.); (6) the race and cultural norms of any particular one-parent household; and, (7) the sibling composition of a one-parent family. Most of these variables are just as relevant in assessing any child, which may imply that the same factors that influence all children's behaviors should be considered in viewing the child from the single-parent family.

It is extremely important, however, that the teacher be aware of which students are from single-parent families. This not only enables the teacher to be especially sensitive to any problems that may arise because of this situation

For the child in a single-parent family, contact with sympathetic adults is an important influence in appropriate socialization.

but also assures that the teacher will not place the child in an embarrassing situation that could easily have been avoided.

Illustration: Ms. Darby gave Alonzo a note to bring home to his mother and told him, "If you don't bring this note back, signed by your mother, I'm going to report you to the principal. Alonzo failed to show up at school for the rest of the week, and Ms. Darby contacted the school social worker. It turned out that Alonzo's mother was dead—he lived with his aunt and, off and on, with his father—and he was emotionally shaken when told to give a note to his "mother." Had the teacher known that Alonzo didn't live with his mother, she would have avoided such a damaging faux pas.

In cases of father absence, either temporary or permanent, the special needs of the single mother may have to be taken into account by the teacher, or counselor, for these special needs often place an obligation on the child or affect the child in a more secondary way. "The single mother," Ruma (1976) points out, "has to deal with her own feelings of loss as well as these feelings in her children. Frequently children increase demands and expression of aggression toward the person with whom they have most frequent contact, which usually is the mother." A considerate teacher will realize this, and will try to work out day-to-day problems with the child without unnecessarily calling in the mother.

The Working Mother

Children of two-parent families may experience some parallels to the child of the single-parent family if the child's mother works outside the home. While years ago it was relatively rare for the mother to be working, modern perspectives on womanhood as well as changing financial realities have made the working mother a common phenomenon in all schools. It is no longer unusual for the teacher to find that a large number of students in her class have mothers who work either full time or part time.

Why should the working mother be of particular concern to the teacher? If we examine the research on this subject, we find that although many years ago certain antisocial behaviors and **psychopathologies,** as well as lower school performance, were associated with children of working mothers, this is no longer the case. In a 1960 study, Stolz found that teachers rated the children of working mothers as lower in intellectual achievement than children of nonworking mothers. Hoffman (1961), in a paper written around the same time, points out that the working mother might tend to overprotect the child out of a sense of guilt and this may have an adverse effect on the child's performance in school. Times have changed, however, and recent research shows different conclusions.

Williamson (1970), for instance, found no differences in IQ between students of working and nonworking mothers. Black, whom we quoted earlier, reviews the literature to date and concludes:

> "There is some evidence to indicate that the child's position within the family structure as a result of birth order, which is called *ordinal position,* bears some influence on the child's development and subsequent personality."

. . . how a child does in school is not in any major way affected by whether or not the mother works. . . . There has also been concern over the possible adverse effects of maternal employment upon the personality or behavioral problems. Decades of research supports the statement that employment is not related, overall, to emotional or behavioral problems. However, such a statement represents a finding about averages; it appears that sometimes family situations and children's reactions become worse when the mother works, sometimes there is no change, and sometimes things become better. . . . *Two major factors determining a child's reaction are the age of the child when the employment begins and the nature of the child care arrangements made.* (p. 51)

Apparently, then, factors other than working or nonworking mothers in themselves are relevant to the child's adjustment and performance in school.

There are certain practical difficulties the teacher of the child whose mother works may encounter. The mother may not be able to visit the school as much as necessary (especially where parental intervention can be helpful) if she is unable to leave the work situation. There may be difficulties in sending the child home early because of sickness or inclement weather, and communication with the mother may be limited because of her working. At times, the mother's cooperation in helping the child with his or her homework may be stifled by work commitments. But on the whole, the teacher should not assume that the mother's working necessarily has any influence —positive or negative—on the child's development or performance in school. It may be important, however, as a factor in better understanding the child's life situation as a whole, which is always relevant to his life in school.

Birth Order and Relationships with Siblings

There is some evidence to indicate that the child's position within the family structure as a result of birth order, which is called **ordinal position,** bears some influence on the child's development and subsequent personality, although the evidence at this time is still confusing and far from conclusive on any given factor. But since sibling relationships and birth order variables are likely to influence the child's classroom behavior—where, after all, the other children in the class are surrogate brothers and sisters—it is helpful for the teacher to understand the impact of birth order and sibling relationships on development and maturity.

The first important theory on birth order and personality was put forth by Alfred Adler, who made ordinal position an integral part of his personality theory. Adler argued that the position the child occupies in his family influences various facets of his personality. He noted, for example, that the oldest child is likely to develop leadership qualities later in life, but, because he has been dethroned as a child by the arrival of the second born, he is also likely to feel insecure and develop problems relating to this later on. The second, or middle, child "may resist the authority asserted by the older child and develop a rebellious nature. He may become uncooperative in the presence of authority. Such oversensitivity to authority may retard adjustment to group life" (Garfinkle, Massey & Mendel, 1976). Because the youngest child never experiences being replaced by another sibling, he is most likely to become the "spoiled" child and to present a problem later on in life.

Adler's work, although sustaining a pervasive influence, was more speculative than scientific. In the years since his ideas appeared, however, many studies have been conducted, some of which support his theory, some of which are quite different, and some of which refute his main points. Stanley Schachter (1959), investigating factors related to gregariousness and conformity, serendipitously produced one of the definitive studies of the effects of birth order on development. He found that the firstborn child tends toward group values and is more likely to be a conformer than the later-born child (p. 87). Firstborn children also tend to have higher IQ scores than children born later. This seems to be due to the fact that parents pay less attention to any one child when there are many and to later-born children in general. Although a number of studies have persuasively argued that the firstborn is more adult oriented than later-born children (Bradley, 1968; Bragg & Allen, 1970), it has been pointed out that while there may be some truth to this assumption, other factors besides birth order are primarily responsible for the differences (Sinver, 1971). Some of the "other" factors commonly cited are: sex of the child, sex of the siblings, social class, maternal attitude and expectation, and size of the family.

Although firstborns have been more extensively studied than later-borns, there is also some research on the latter. McGurk and Lewis (1972) found, for instance, that second-borns sought more adult help and more adult approval than did either firstborns or later-borns. Moreover, second-borns, they point out, "also spent more time in individual activity . . . were generally more talkative . . . and expressed more negative affect than other subjects" (p. 366). One of the important conclusions of this study, in regard to the middle child, is that "the effects for birth order are more revealing and highlight the second-born as different from his firstborn or later-born siblings.

Second-borns, for example, showed more dependency behavior (seeking help, approval, and affection from adults) than subjects from the other two ordinal positions."

An advantage of being the youngest child that is often cited in the literature is that having older siblings increases opportunities for early socialization. Having an opportunity to "model" himself or herself after the interactions of older siblings offers the youngest child opportunities to explore avenues of social interaction in the home environment that were not available to the oldest child. In one interesting study, Collard (1968) investigated firstborn and later-born infants' responses in unfamiliar situations. The purpose of this study was to determine if later-born infants, who had opportunities to interact with older brothers and sisters, as opposed to firstborns, whose interactions were limited to the parents (and usually to the mother), would be less fearful of strangers. An experimenter, with whom the infant was not familiar, placed a toy on a table in front of the infant, who sat on the mother's lap; and the time it took the infant to pick up the toy was judged to be directly related to the infant's anxiety over the presence of the "strange" experimenter. On the average, firstborns took about fifty-five seconds to pick up the toy; later-borns, on the average, took about eight seconds—a significant difference. Moreover, in analyzing the data, it was also found that not only ordinal position was important but so too was the degree of age difference between the later-born and his or her older sibling. Infants with widely spaced birth orders, whose older sib was considerably farther removed than the norm, responded similarly to the way firstborns did, confirming that they lacked the opportunities to socialize that are available to more closely spaced later-borns. "The first-born and widely spaced infants made significantly fewer responses to the toy than did the later-borns matched to them. . . . Firstborn and widely spaced infants made significantly more negative social responses such as fussing and crying than later-born infants did" (p. 172).

There are several important implications from this study that transcend the birth order question itself. Collard concludes, in part:

. . . infants receiving social stimulation from few persons will tend to show more fear of strangers than will infants receiving stimulation from a variety of persons. Compared to later-borns with preschool siblings, first-born and widely spaced infants tended to make fewer exploratory and play responses to a novel toy and to respond more slowly to the strange person and toy. . . .

"The child's exposure to others during the early years facilitates socialization; later-born children, who have an older brother or sister close in age, will tend to be the most social children, the most comfortable in the school situation."

Variability among infants in degree of acceptance of strangers is probably determined by a number of factors, including (a) the number of persons the infant is exposed to and their variety in terms of appearance and behavior, (b) the frequency and duration of exposure to different person, and (c) the infant's developmental level at the time of exposure to others. . . . (p. 173)

The implications of these findings are particularly relevant to the teacher, who bears witness to the child's level of socialization in the classroom. Without overemphasizing the causative and predictive validity of ordinal position as a factor in personality, we can say that the *child's exposure to others during the early years facilitates socialization; later-born children, who have an older brother or sister close in age, will tend to be the most social children, the most comfortable in the school situation.*

During the past few years, Robert Zajonc has done important research concerning the relationship between intelligence and birth order. With his colleague, Gregory Markus, Zajonc (1975) has proposed a direct relationship between intelligence and ordinal position. Display 4.2 describes their theory.

Display 4.2

Intelligence and Ordinal Position: A New Approach

According to Robert Zajonc and his colleague at the University of Michigan, political scientist Gregory Markus, intelligence, while influenced to some extent by heredity, styles of child rearing and quality of education, is more a product of birth order and family size. Zajonc has for years been alternately fascinated by birth order effects and frustrated by the abundance of contradictory research findings in this area. In 1975 he and Markus published an article in *Psychological Review* in which they developed a theory, called the confluence model, to explain the effects of the immediate intellectual environment on intellectual growth. It is based on the mutual intellectual influences among children as they develop in the family context.

The basic idea is that intelligence declines with family size: the fewer children in a family the smarter they are likely to be. Intelligence also declines with birth order, older children being generally brighter than their younger siblings. This model defines a family's intellectual environment as an average of the absolute intellectual levels of all members. Each contributes to the total intellectual atmosphere, which is subject to continual changes as childen develop, the most dramatic changes occurring when someone joins the family or leaves it.

To illustrate these relationships, Zajonc and Markus arbitrarily set the absolute intellectual level of each parent at 30 units, and that of a newborn child at zero. The first child is thus born into an intellectual environment of 20 units [(30 + 30 + 0) ÷ 3]. If a second child is born when the first is two years old and has reached an intellectual level of four units, the family intellect drops again [(30 + 30 + 4 + 0) ÷ 4 = 16]. Should a third child come along when the intellectual level of the first is at, say, 7 and that of the second is at three, the family's pool of intellectual capacity would be reduced to 14, and so on.

With each additional child, the family's

intellectual environment thus depreciates. Which means that children in large families, who tend to be heavily influenced by their intellectually pint-sized siblings, are likely to develop more slowly and attain lower IQs than children in small families, who have more contact with adult minds.

This model of intellectual environment and sibling influence does not, however, assert that intelligence necessarily declines with birth order. Another critically important variable affecting intelligence is the spacing between children. For a family of two children, for example, the larger the age separation between children, the longer the older child can remain in an environment "undiluted" by another childish mind. Long birth intervals, says Zajonc, give older children the benefits of being in a small family for a longer time and during an early phase of growth, when they are most sensitive to environmental effects. The younger child also has the advantage of being born into an intellectually more mature environment. In other words, the negative effects of birth order can be nullified or even reversed, given sufficient spacing between children.

While their theory disregards much that social scientists have contributed to the controversial study of intelligence, it does have the advantage of parsimony. It makes rather specific predictions that can be verified in a straight-forward manner. And indeed, Zajonc has gathered impressive evidence from several large-scale studies to corroborate his theory.

In one, psychologist Hunter M. Breland studied 800,000 students who took the National Merit Scholarship Qualification Test and compared their scores on the basis of family size and birth order. Similar studies have been carried out in Scotland, France and the Netherlands on 70,000. 100,000 and 400,000 individuals respectively.

The results of all four studies indicate that intellectual level generally declines with family size. In all of them, first-borns and children from small families did better than later-borns and children from large families. This held true regardless of race, class or income level and despite the fact that these studies represent four different tests of intellectual performance, four different age groups and four different countries.

Moreover, the data from these huge samples, together with evidence provided by still other researchers, support Zajonc's theory with regard to a number of predictable differences among individuals and groups.

- Twins, who represent the closest possible interval between successive siblings, score consistently and substantially lower on intelligence and other tests of intellectual performance than do non-twins.
- According to the confluence model, a one-parent household constitutes an inferior intellectual environment and the children so reared should show intellectual deficits. Most studies in this area have examined the effects of father absence (due to death or divorce) on intellectual performance, and virtually all of them support Zajonc's theory. Differences in intellectual performances between children from fatherless and intact homes increases the longer the parent is away and the earlier the parental loss occurred.
- The theory can also account for group differences in intelligence. Blacks, for example, who score lower, tend to have more children and to have them closer together than the average white family. And more black families are headed by a single parent, typically the mother. Conversely, Jews, who as a group do well on IQ tests, generally have smaller families with both parents present.

The one possible kink in the confluence model is that only children who, mathematically speaking, would be expected to be the smartest of all, are not. But Zajonc has an explanation for this apparent theoretical flaw. Only children, he suggests, are at a distinct disadvantage in that they don't have an opportunity to be "teachers." Children with siblings, he notes, "show their younger brothers and sisters how to hold a bat or skip rope, help them tie their shoes, explain the meanings of new words, and the rules of new games, warn them about what may get them into trouble, divulge what they may get away with, are quick to spot errors and ineptitude and are ready to offer critiques."

Zajonc is quick to point out that family configuration is not the sole determinant of intellectual prowess. He notes that economic resources, educational opportunities, linguistic habits, literacy rates and so forth all contribute to regional, ethnic, national and racial differences in intellectual test performance scores.

From Sharland Trotter, "Zajonc Defuses IQ Debate: Birth Order Work Wins Prize." *APA Monitor,* May 1976, pp. 1 and 10. Reprinted by permission of the American Psychological Association.

Still, the bulk of evidence on ordinal position does not strongly support any single theory or point of view. One of the main difficulties in drawing firm conclusions is the fact that other variables interact with birth order and it is difficult, if not impossible, to separate them in research studies. To say, "The firstborn child is. . . ." or "The middle child is. . . ." or "The youngest child is. . . ." must always be at best a reasoned guess rather than a valid statement. Variables such as sex of the child, sex of the siblings, number of years' difference in age, maternal environmental variables, socioeconomic class, and so forth, are all vital factors that interact with ordinal position in the normal course of development. Perhaps the best capsule summary of the research status to date is provided by Helmreich (1968), who says: "It seems that the most parsimonious explanations for widely observed birth order phenomena are based on different experiences in childhood. Greater motivation for achievement and more pressing needs for social comparison seem to account for many of the observed differences between first- or only-borns and later-borns. *At present, though, any theories concerning these phenomena must be evaluated as not proved"* (p. 168, italics ours).

Some Conclusions on the Influence of the Family

In this section we have emphasized some of the negative influences that the family can have on the child as he goes through the elementary school experience. This is not because we believe the family is a negative influence in the preponderance of cases. On the contrary, the large majority of children in our schools benefit from a healthful, loving, growth-enhancing family relationship that instills in them a zest for living. Children learn appropriate social skills from their families. They are motivated to learn to read from the family environment. Yet, it is the children who lack this family environment—the battered child, the child from a fragmented family, the culturally disadvantaged child—who are most in need of guidance and special assistance in the classroom. The child whose family provides a backbone of support can survive minimal teaching competency. The child who lacks the family's support desperately needs excellence in teaching.

In the following section, we will examine the influence of the school on the child's development, noting how the family and school interact cumulatively to produce a major force in the child's development. In the concluding section, we will examine strong and weak family influences on the progress of development, including learning and mastery of school tasks.

The Influence of the School

Now that we have examined some of the patterns of overall growth and development during these years, we must ask ourselves what type of influence is exerted by the school on development in general as well as on specific areas of

> " 'Where the school and home experiences were congruent, the impact on the children was reinforced.' "

development. Is the school an important factor in the child's growth or is it more or less extraneous to the developmental progress? What can the teacher do to facilitate the child's intellectual, social, and emotional development? Is the family a far more significant factor than the educational community, and if so what can the school setting provide to compensate for possible deficiencies? These are some of the questions we will try to answer in this section.

Two important book-length studies have appeared in recent years that **Two Studies** measure, with some cogency, the influence of the elementary school upon the child's development. In 1969, *The Psychological Impact of School Experience* (Minuchin, Biber, Shapiro, & Zimiles) was published. The study centers on the basic question of How do different kinds of education affect the learning and development of children? (p. 3). Using nine-year-old and ten-year-old children as the subjects, the study compared these fourth graders in four urban schools that ranged in methodology and philosophy from traditional to highly innovative. In this way, the results can be broken down into categories to see if they are attributable to a specific methodology or to the school experience itself.

Although the thrust of the findings were designed to compare the different schools, the overall findings—of the school experience in general—are more germane to our interests at this point. A condensation of some of the authors' findings follows:

First, it seems clear that the schools affected the lives and functioning of the children in ways that were pervasive and perhaps profound.
Second, it was evident from the data that the potency of the school's orientation in affecting the children was a function of two conditions: the orientation of the home and its interaction with the school influence; and the extent to which the school operated as a total integrated environment.

This second conclusion is particularly important, and we should look at some of the details of this finding, for it emphasizes the importance of the *interaction* between home and school as a critical variable. The authors go on to point out:

(*a*) The school appeared as the most likely prevailing force in some areas, such as intellectual functioning, while the home was apparently dominant in others, such as role orientations among girls.
(*b*) Where the school and home experiences were congruent, the impact on the children was reinforced.
(*c*) By virtue of the new context it provided, the school might extend or modify

the attitudes established in the family. The child's understanding of authority and his concept of the rules and principles that govern human interaction provide an example of this. In the school context, the child's experience was extended beyond the family; he was exposed to another vision of society, how it works and what it expects of him, and in this context he was somewhat free of the intricacies and deep relationships that are part of family life. . . .

(d) Under some conditions, the uniqueness and power of schooling is such that its impact may be strong even in areas that are usually shaped by the home and even if home and school orientations are not congruent. (pp. 391–392)

Let us take these conclusions and examine their implications for the elementary school teacher. In earlier sections of this chapter, we have examined two broad influences on development: the epistemo-genetic (Piagetian), in which there are predictable sequences, and the more variable influences, the environmental, in which values and attitudes are shaped by significant people (real and symbolic) in the child's environment. We see now that the school can be a synthesizing agent between these forces; that it both combines and modifies the forces of the home and the pressures from the child's peer environment.

Putting this another way, the child brings *into the school* the products of other processes and they are *transformed* in the school setting, for better or worse, into measurable behavior and performance. Figure 4.3 shows the nature of this interaction by illustrating the learner as the product of transformations of different influences that may work in harmony or discord.

In the second study, Kraus (1973) conducted a longitudinal investigation of children from kindergarten to the adult years, analyzing specifically

Figure 4.3 How Influences Interact in the Learner's Development

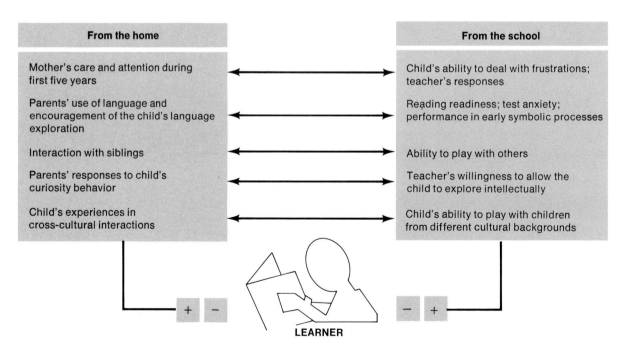

From the home	From the school
Mother's care and attention during first five years	Child's ability to deal with frustrations; teacher's responses
Parents' use of language and encouragement of the child's language exploration	Reading readiness; test anxiety; performance in early symbolic processes
Interaction with siblings	Ability to play with others
Parents' responses to child's curiosity behavior	Teacher's willingness to allow the child to explore intellectually
Child's experiences in cross-cultural interactions	Child's ability to play with children from different cultural backgrounds

LEARNER

Children learn early patterns of socialization from their siblings as well as from their parents.

> "The influence of the school may be directly proportionate to the level of the child as he functions in the classroom: the more normal the child, the greater the influence."

the influences of the school on the child's overall development. Five New York City schools were used in the study, which was conducted over a period of twenty years. Several of the conclusions of this study are particularly worthy of our attention. First, we have the somewhat disheartening finding that, "Most of the children reported as having adjustment problems in any one of the early grades remained problems and were subsequently reported by two or more teachers. Furthermore, all but three of those reported in the sixth grade had displayed their difficulties before the end of the third grade and continued to have problems in the junior high schools and well beyond" (p. 144). What this says, in effect, is that the schools have failed to resolve behavioral difficulties that become apparent early in the elementary school years and persist with a stubborn continuity. Perhaps the teachers of these students were overburdened; perhaps the problems were not sufficiently diagnosed and consequently no treatment provided; or, perhaps we don't have the tools available today to treat such problems. In any case, we can say that the difficulties that appear in the school setting, and are clearly related to the child's home environment, are not likely to be resolved as the child progresses up the educational ladder.

A second finding of this study is equally as troublesome:

Special gifts and talents were discovered, for the most part, either by teachers who possessed these gifts themselves or who provided programs of such depth and variety that children had opportunities to demonstrate special talents. Where programs of instruction were narrow and limited, few children were identified as being gifted. (p. 144)

This implies that just as the difficult child is not given the needed special attention during the elementary school years, the gifted child is neglected as well. The implications of these findings might be restated as follows: The school experience is directed toward the "normal" child—the child who is average in most respects. Those at either of the extremes of the distribution— the gifted, the maladjusted, the slow child—rarely receive the specific attention they require within the confines of the normal classroom. Thus, the influence of the school may be directly proportionate to the level of the child as he functions in the classroom: the more normal the child, the greater the influence.

Generally, it is in the area of "special education" that attention is directed toward the students at the extremes of the distribution. But many of the insights from this specialized field are applicable to all of the children.

In an excellent little book called *Special Education in the Regular Classroom,* Ernest Siegel (1969) discusses the teacher's role in dealing with nine basic classroom problems, and these problems are common for all kinds of students: (1) poor self-concept; (2) anxiety; (3) difficulty in paying attention; (4) difficulty in organizing; (5) difficulty in copying written material; (6) poor coordination; (7) difficulty in abstract thinking; (8) behavioral problems, (9) social immaturity. Siegel shows that all of these can be adequately dealt with in the regular heterogeneous classroom with students of all levels, needs, and abilities.

The School as a Socializing Institution

One important way that the school influences the child's development is in providing an area for socialization. The preschool experience centers around the family, and the child is likely to learn all of his or her social behavior within the family context. But once the child enters the school, he or she learns cooperative behavior with other children as well as methods of responding to the authority figure of the teacher. Much socialization is the result of *modeling:* the process where the child learns by imitation of behaviors. The child models himself not only after the other children but after the teacher as well. Socialization may also be facilitated through the curriculum. Lessons in the social studies can be particularly helpful in instilling in the children the attitudes that can make them more successful students and better citizens later in life.

In one interesting study designed "to investigate children's ability to describe and make inferences about feelings, thoughts and intentions that occur in interpersonal relationships," which is an important basis for socialization, Flapan (1968) showed to six-, nine-, and twelve-year-old school children movies depicting various social situations and then asked them questions to determine how they perceived the social interactions. The children's method of perceiving social situations showed some marked developmental trends.

. . . With increase in age there were more children who gave causal explanations. Also, with age there was an increase in the number of children who made interpretations of feelings or who inferred thoughts and intentions not obviously expressed or specifically labeled. Development seemed to progress from describing a situation and/or reporting the overt action and dialogue to attempting to account for what had taken place in the social interaction by giving an explanation and then to inferring thoughts, intentions, and feelings that were not obviously expressed or interpreting what was expressed on some "deeper" level.

There was shift in the kinds of explanations given. At the six-year level explanations were primarily in terms of the situation in which the interaction took place, whereas with age there were more explanations in psychological

The peer group is an important source of the child's socialization.

> "Socialization is a *learned* process, and the child's general ability to learn is intricately related to his or her socializing skills."

terms; that is, in terms of a person's feelings or motives or thoughts and more explanations in terms of one actor responding to his perception of a co-actor's feelings or thoughts.... (p. 62)

These findings, which are consistent with conclusions reached in the area of intellectual development and moral development, indicate that there is an important relationship between the child's cognitive abilities and social skills. After all, socialization is a *learned* process, and the child's general ability to learn is intricately related to his or her socializing skills. Other studies have also shown that retardation in mental abilities is highly correlated with social retardation.

Certain cultural and social barriers may also act to retard the socialization process. Cultural deprivations, poverty, and bilinguilism are three prominent examples. Each of these has in one way or another been shown to have some influence upon performance in school, upon social competency, or upon the development and mastery of those skills that are requisites for social mastery. Let us examine each of these briefly, although many of the issues touched upon will be taken into account in other chapters.

In one of the earliest studies in this area, Arsenian (1937) investigated the effects of bilingualism on the mental development of children of Jewish and Italian immigrants in New York City in the 1930s. He concluded from this study that bilingualism offers advantages as well as disadvantages:

Bilingualism

The acquisition of two language systems of the bilinguist ... does not seem from the data of the present study to have a detrimental influence on mental ability and development. Bilingualism may be advantageous in providing an extension in one's experiences and contacts with the achievements of other cultures; it may on the other hand involve certain difficulties in the mastery of any language, in facility and accuracy of expression, in rapidity and comprehension of reading, in pronunciation, and may even have certain emotional consequences not altogether desirable. There is a dearth of experimental data on all these problems. At the present time, at least, no detailed and definite conclusions are available to be applied to all cases of bilingualism. (pp. 153–154)

In the forty years since that study was published, despite the fact that there is no longer a dearth of data because there have been many studies published in the interim, Arsenian's conclusion still holds—that is, that we cannot form any conclusions at all. Let's look at some of these studies.

In 1949, Leopold published a three-volume longitudinal study of an infant raised by parents who spoke both English and German. Leopold concluded that bilingualism provides a richer, more complex world view;

that it "trains the child to think instead of merely speaking half mechanically" (volume III, p. 188). But Leopold goes on to add that bilingualism "will lead to conflicts which can wreck a weak personality, but will improve the mettle of a strong one, who can overcome the difficulties" (p. 188). In a more recent study along similar lines, Burling (1959) studied his son's simultaneous acquisition of two languages. He noticed that in many instances his son "simultaneously learned English and Garo words with approximately the same meanings, as though once his understanding reached the point of being able to grasp a concept he was able to use the appropriate words in both languages." For instance, he learned the color words in both languages simultaneously.

Lambert and Peal (1972), in a still more recent study, used a group of monolingual and bilingual children from a French-Canadian school to study the effects of bilingualism on intelligence. Their findings contradict some previous studies:

> ... this study found that bilinguals performed significantly better than monolinguals on both verbal and nonverbal intelligence tests. Several explanations are suggested as to why bilinguals have this general intellectual advantage. It is argued that they have a language asset, are more facile at concept formation, and have greater mental flexibility. . . . The bilinguals appear to have a more diversified set of mental abilities than monolinguals. (pp. 154–55)

With the swelling Spanish-speaking population in the United States (particularly, Cubans in the southern states; Puerto Ricans in the large urban areas; Chicanos in the western states), there has been much interest in the effects of bilingualism upon this group. One such study was undertaken by Anastasi and Cordova (1953) among Puerto Rican children in New York City schools. They noted that when a child speaks one language at home and another in school so that his or her knowledge of each language is limited to certain types of situations, inadequate facility with the language of the school interferes with the acquisition of basic concepts, intellectual skills, and information. The frustration resulting from these scholastic difficulties may in turn lead to discouragement and general dislike of school. "Unfortunately," the authors point out, "an ill-advised policy with regard to the way in which English was introduced in the Puerto Rican schools has served only to make Puerto Ricans illiterate in two languages and has prejudiced them against English which they blame for their educational difficulties and confusion" (p. 3). This conclusion, written over twenty years ago, is still fairly accurate today despite the recent efforts to introduce bilingual teaching.

The Culturally Disadvantaged Child

So much has been written on the culturally deprived child in the school in recent years that at times we're not able to see the forest for the trees. One area that has gained increasing attention is the deprived child's attitudes toward achievement—that is, how motivated to achieve is the child. In one important study, Child, Davidson, Gerra and Greenberg (1965) investigated the attitudes of black children from badly deprived home environments toward a number of concepts presumed to be important for success in school learning. Results indicated that "while black subjects may score high in value orientation, that is, expressing adherence to prevailing values of society, they score low in personal achievement motivation" (p. 60). Conclusions drawn from the data suggest that "poor achievement might result from the greater defensive needs of the poor achievers" (p. 61). On the other hand, good achievers seem to possess or demonstrate self-confidence that may help them to succeed in school.

Another way in which the culturally deprived child suffers a disadvantage in the socializing process is through language limitations. Since the child learns much of his language skills in the home and brings these into the school, we see again how the influence of the home directly translates into school performance. For the culturally disadvantaged child, J. McV. Hunt (1962) points out, "the variety of linguistic patterns available for imitation in the models provided by lower class adults is both highly limited and wrong for the standards of later schooling" (p. 28). Indeed, not only formal language per se but also the rudimentary skills of effective education may be lacking. As Amos and Grambs (1968) point out:

The deprived child frequently does not know how to ask and answer questions. He does not know how to study; taking tests is very difficult. His style is apt to be slow and cautious; hence, he encounters still another unfamiliar attitude of society, emphasis on the importance of speed. Since he cannot quickly grasp problems, especially in the abstract, he is apt to make a poor showing when the criterion is speed. (p. 20)

Certain specific patterns of social development have also been noted that are indigenous to culturally deprived groups, particularly blacks, who have been studied in the most depth. Baumrind (1972), in a study of black-white comparisons of child socialization, found that black daughters of authoritarian parents, when compared with white girls, were significantly more domineering and independent, and somehow more resistant and dominant. The fact is that when "black families were viewed by white norms they appeared authoritarian, but . . . unlike their white counterparts, the most authoritarian of these families produced the most self-assertive and independent girls" (p. 261).

We could go on and on, citing cultural differences between blacks and whites, between the culturally disadvantaged and the culturally advantaged, but these have been covered so well and so repeatedly in the literature that there is no need for this. The main question with which we have to concern ourselves is What can the teacher do to help the culturally disadvantaged

> " 'Teaching deprived children does not consist of gimmicks or tricks. Much more decisive are certain basic attitudes.' "

child? The research is also rich in insights in helping to answer this fundamental question.

Riessman (1962), in writing about effective teaching for this group of children, points out:

> Teaching deprived children does not consist of gimmicks or tricks. Much more decisive are certain basic attitudes. . . . Perhaps the best overall principle is to be *consistent*. These children want a teacher on whom they can depend. If she tells them to stop chewing gum one day, she cannot permit them to do it the next.
>
> . . . The teacher should be straight-forward, direct, and should clearly define what is to be done as much as possible. At the same time she should be informal, warm, down-to-earth. Snobbishness and indirection are major pitfalls. So is cynicism, although naivete is equally dangerous. . . .
>
> The teacher should recognize the special "value problem" she faces in a culturally deprived setting. Her own values are likely to be different from those of her pupils. . . . Even if the teacher herself comes from a deprived background, her present situation in life has undoubtedly produced a new frame of reference. . . . (pp. 81–82)

The teacher's attitudes toward the culturally disadvantaged learner is always of prime importance. Grambs (1972), who has written extensively on this topic, points out how significant the teacher's attitudes are in communicating expectations to the students. If the teacher views these students as "stupid, vapid, and intellectually incompetent," this is certainly to influence the student's behavior through the *self-fulfilling prophecy*—the compulsion to act out one's self-expectations, either positive or negative.

Although there is much disagreement about who is more to blame for the abysmal failure of the culturally disadvantaged student to "make it" in the educational system, it seems pretty clear that both the home and the school must shoulder a part of the responsibility. Lincoln (1974), in a recent paper, argues that it is his "considered judgment that low achievement in the inner-city school is attributable to practices in the school more often than to conditions in the home. . . . The home is used as scapegoat in far too many instances . . . and unless educational methods are upgraded substantially, achievement may continue to remain appallingly low" (p. 82). Boyer and Boyer (1974), also acknowledging the responsibility of the school, argue for curriculum changes: "The curriculum has not assumed the levels of diversity possible to meet adequately the needs of the urban poor and economically disadvantaged learner" (p. 624). They suggest that subject matter be made relevant to the special needs and interests of the disadvantaged learner:

In teaching the disadvantaged, the principles of concreteness through meaningful examples cannot be overemphasized. Teachers committed to curriculum diversity will need to experiment with many examples in order to find the most vivid and most functional. Examples can be concrete, however, without being meaningful. To present concrete examples that have no meaning for disadvantaged pupils, urban or rural, is also an exercise in futility. Meaning comes from values attached by the student to concrete experiences in his environment. Therefore, the effective teacher must select and use *current, contemporary* examples related to the daily experiences of the disadvantaged pupils. (p. 626)

We see from the sum of these various positions that the socialization and in-tellectual growth of the culturally disadvantaged learner are intricately en-twined. This is not surprising inasmuch as a certain level of social skill is re-quired to maintain the attention and perseverance necessary for school success. The teacher, recognizing the special problems of teaching this child, will make every effort to assure that method and curriculum are structured to maximize learning efficiency.

> "Children learn aggressive social behavior by watching others act aggressively—others, including their peers and the teacher."

The School as a Socializing Agent: Some Conclusions

In this section, we have examined some of the areas in which the child's social development intersects with the school environment. While again we have concentrated on problematic areas—which may be a minority of the cases, but which provide a majority of the difficulties—we must emphasize that socialization is often a smooth, healthy, natural process in the school, beset by few if any difficulties. Some general remarks about the smooth normal process of socialization might be in order at this time, especially to end the chapter on a positive note.

In the classroom, the child learns much from observing and interacting with his or her peers. Costanzo and Shaw (1966), whom we've discussed earlier, point out how peer pressure induces conformity, especially during these elementary school years. Albert Bandura, the behavioral psychologist who promulgates the importance of *modeling,* has also shown how much of the child's social behavior is the result of modeling himself or herself after others. In one experiment, Bandura, Ross and Ross (1961) examined the transmission of aggression through imitation of aggressive models. "Children were exposed to aggressive and nonaggressive adult models and were then tested for amount of imitative learning in a new situation. . . . The prediction that exposure of subjects to aggressive models increased the probability of aggressive behavior is truly confirmed" (pp. 575–576). The implications of this study, which have been replicated several times over, are important: Children learn aggressive social behavior by watching others act aggressively —others, including their peers and the teacher. The teacher may not realize how his or her own aggressiveness is communicated to the students.

Behavioral problems in general, but aggressiveness in particular, are attributable to inadequate or incomplete socialization. Laurel N. Tanner (1974), has pointed out, "Behavior problems are on the rise because increasing numbers of children are growing up without adequate socialization. These children function on impulse. They do what they want when they want, regardless of its effect on others. . . ." She goes on to show how important it is that the teacher intervene to encourage appropriate socialization in such cases:

As teachers, we concern ourselves with the socialization of children because knowing how to act and how not to act is the sign of caring about the consequences of one's action for oneself and others. As teachers, we try, above all, to develop self-direction in children and socialization is inherent in self-direction.

Defects in the socialization of the child must be overcome if he is to become a responsible person who contributes to the well-being of others rather than exploiting them.

In this sense, socialization is as important as individuation. . . . Social values can be an invaluable aid to the self-expression of the individual. And it is time for a new synthesis of individual and social values in education. Effective class control depends on it as does the balanced development of the individual. (p. 32)

Margaret Mead (1973), the noted anthropologist, emphasizes the importance of continuity between the home and the school in providing adequate socialization. She suggests that teachers visit the home and that parents visit the school to increase the likelihood of this kind of socialization.

Thus, we see that, in the end, socialization is a process that involves the interaction of the home and school, of the teacher and parent, for better or worse, in the child's development.

Summary

The elementary school years represent a major period of growth in the learner's life. During these six years, the person develops the fundamental skills necessary for all future learning endeavors. Emotional growth is rapid, and the child develops a sense of industriousness, competency, and identity. While the acquisition of a spoken language is generally well along its way by the time the child enters the elementary school, it is during the elementary school years that this oral language is translated into cognitive structures that serve as the foundation for more complex learning. Through reading and through the written language, the child has the world of learning at his fingertips.

Many children suffer severe personal traumas during these years. We paid special attention to the battered child, who is either physically abused or sorely neglected by the parents. The child from the single-parent family, while not necessarily deficient in maturation and growth, may require special attention. We also examined how ordinal position—the position within the family unit in terms of birth—is believed to have an effect upon personality and academic performance.

Finally, we considered the role of the school as a socializing institution. We noted that much of the child's social development takes place in the school, and when the school and home experiences are congruent, this tends to reinforce children's behaviors. We considered some special problems of socialization for the culturally disadvantaged and the bilingual student. Finally, we considered the teacher's influence on the child's socialization.

Suggested Additional Readings

Latency by Charles Sarnoff (*New York: Jason Aronson, 1976*)

This is the most comprehensive treatment of the latency period ever written. Covering psychological, social, sexual, cognitive, and other areas of personal development, the author draws from a rich and diverse literature to present a unified, consistent picture of the child's growth during the elementary school years.

Both girls and boys of latency age find a ready escape from painful situations and disappointments by entering a world of fantasy which is believed in as firmly as the baseball games and ballet lessons. . . .

from *Latency*

JR by William Gaddis (*New York: Alfred A. Knopf, 1975*)

Nowhere is the turmoil of the interaction between the student, the teacher, and the school system depicted more cleverly than in this brilliant, often-outrageous novel about a sixth-grade boy who becomes a multimillionaire through fast business dealings. Inept educators, textbook salesmen, frustrated teachers, and students directed down the wrong corridors pass through this school in symbolic movement through the entire educational process.

. . . help motivate the elementary youngster's potential carwise that is to say, potentiate them for a real meaningful driving experience when they're big enough to get out and hit the, hit our nation's highways. . .

from *JR*

The World of the Child, edited by Tony Talbot (*Garden City: Anchor, 1974*)

A rich, wide-ranging anthology of the basic literature in child psychology. Covering such topics as "the nature of childhood," "patterns of growth," "child education," and "the child's reactions to pain," the editor has wisely selected from the writings of partisans of different viewpoints, giving balance and equal perspective to the experiences of childhood.

Childhood, with its lightning changes of mood, its gratifications and deprivations, its fantasies and yearnings, its helplessness and power, is a purgatory to be traversed, and a paradise to be lost, as well as a key to the adult's psychic life.

from the introduction to *The World of the Child*

Black Self-Concept, edited by James A. Banks and Jean Dresden Grambs (*New York: McGraw-Hill, 1972*)

An unusual collection of essays that describe what it feels like to be black in America and how these feelings relate to the development of self-concept. Throughout the book, implications for education are considered. Special attention is directed toward improving black children's self-concepts.

❧

While recent research is inconclusive and somewhat contradictory, the bulk of it indicates that the black revolt has not significantly changed the self-concepts and self-evaluations of most black children and youth.

from the introduction to *Black Self-Concept*

Children in Conflict: A Casebook by Anthony Davids (*New York: John Wiley & Sons, paperback, 1974*)

In fifteen cases, most of which are quite exciting, the author presents a range of problems children may encounter, including behavioral, psychosomatic, learning disorders, and emotional difficulties. Specific approaches for treating all of these problems are presented, and the elementary school teacher will certainly find much of value in this book.

❧

Our information about this black male child begins at the time he was found in the basement of a rooming house in a large mid-Western city. He was wrapped in a sopping wet towel with a bottle of curdled milk lying beside him. . . .

from "The Case of Roy" in *Children in Conflict*

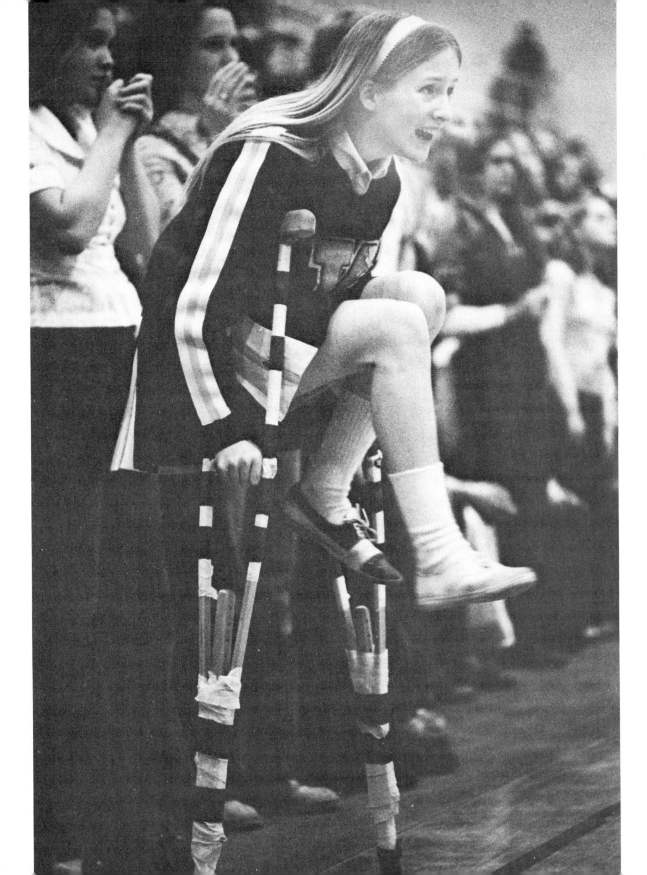

Puberty (Early Adolescence)

This is the period that links childhood with adolescence. The pubescent develops secondary sex characteristics, and a number of psychological conflicts often come to the fore. Several common stresses of puberty have been identified: dealing with biological changes; adjusting to the secondary school setting, rising sexual feelings, and new role status.

Middle Adolescence: Two Views

This period may be viewed as a time of "storm and stress" or as a period of stabilizing, goal-directed readjustment. The teacher can be extremely helpful in assisting the adolescent to come to grips with new values and insights to deal with the changing realities of his life.

The Adolescent's Values

The adolescent's values are influenced by peer pressure and by significant other individuals. The teacher, who falls into the latter group, can help the adolescent learn values within the classroom context.

Dating Behavior: Sex and the Adolescent

Dating and courtship are important areas of the adolescent's socialization. Much of this activity is manifested in the school. One of the chief purposes of this period is to help define, clarify, and strengthen sex-role identification. The adolescent may need enlightened sex education during this time, and the teacher's own knowledge and attitudes will be a critical variable in the success of such programs.

Cognitive Growth in Adolescence

Adolescents develop the capacity for "formal operational thought," which involves hypothetical, abstract, deductive reasoning. Adolescents are able to plan out their future and reason the consequences of actions.

Continued

5 The Secondary School Years

Adolescent Drug Abuse

Drug abuse involves the dependency upon drugs. One of the prevalent problems in the schools today is adolescent alcohol abuse. The teacher can be a mitigating force by providing useful drug education and prevention programs. This requires that the teacher be familiar with the language and mores of the adolescent drug culture.

The World of Work

The secondary school years are important in the formation of career decisions. Several theories account for the way career choices are made. Schools can provide the adolescent with necessary skills for finding employment; and counseling, in and out of the classroom, can help the student make appropriate vocational choices.

Studies of the Adolescent

Several developmental studies have shed light on some of the complexities of this period. Although adolescence is conceptualized in different ways, John E. Horrocks has summarized some of the major consistent findings over the years.

Current Perspectives: The Adolescent in the 1970s

Recent youth surveys have indicated that adolescents are becoming increasingly concerned with their own economic success. The use of alcohol has become the number-one drug abuse problem in the schools. Other attitudes have remained fairly constant over the past decade.

Conclusions and Implications

The teacher can provide the adolescent with the intellectual and emotional tools necessary to deal with the complications of this period.

162

The "teenage years," which include the periods of **puberty** and **adolescence,** comprise an important, transitional period of development that may prove critical to the ultimate success or failure of the individual's socialization, adjustment, and later achievements in life. Like other important transitions in life, this one requires a number of important readjustments: It requires learning to act in a new, different, and presumably more mature way that is constantly reinforced by society-at-large and in particular by those around us. For some this is a difficult, tumultuous time of life, while others enjoy a smooth, natural, healthy transition. Many factors influence the course of development, and we shall pay particular attention to those that are relevant to the school setting.

During these terribly important years, marked differences in development, attitude, and social style are apparent between boys and girls, between one social class and another, between culture and culture, between generation and generation; and some of these differences have a direct effect upon performance in school. Many of the principles of adolescent development are universal and constant—geographically and temporally. But so much of what actually happens during these years—so much of the real core experience of being an adolescent—is the product of direct and indirect social and cultural influences that the task of accurately and vividly describing the global qualities of adolescence, the teenage experience itself, is challenged with obstacles at the outset.

The massive differences in environment and opportunity between the "haves" and "have-nots," between those who glide gracefully into the mainstream of society and those who hover precariously on its borders, make the task of capturing the experience of adolescence and evaluating its implications for teachers and educators all the more difficult. Nevertheless, since this is such an important period in the life of the learner, and since the teacher may play an important role in the adolescent's social and psychological as well as intellectual development, the teacher wants to be able to understand the many complexities of meaning and perception that characterize the world of the adolescent.

We shall begin with the period known as puberty.

Puberty (Early Adolescence)

Puberty is the period of life that links childhood and adolescence. While it occurs simultaneously with the early period of adolescence, and the two terms are used interchangeably with some degree of freedom, puberty describes more the physical period of development while adolescence is used more to describe a psychological period (Aubrey, 1975).

"In many subcultures within our culture, it is at this age that the child breaks away from the control of the parent and fends for himself."

Puberty derives from the Latin word for adult, *pubertas*. In many cultures, the attainment of puberty, often marked by inveterate rites and rituals, signals the beginnings of adulthood. Jewish boys, for example, celebrate the puberty rite of bar mitzvah, in which the rights of adulthood are conferred on the thirteen-year-old boy. Other cultures initiate the boy or girl into adulthood with their own rituals.

Although our society does not generally accord to the pubescent the rights of adulthood, the biological reality of puberty indicates that from the physiological point of view the pubescent is capable of all the activities of the adult. Moreover, in many of the subcultures within our culture, it is at this age that the child breaks away from the control of the parents and fends for himself. Black lower-class youngsters use the term *ready* as an adjective to describe the early adolescent who "knows the street and how to operate in it, how to appreciate what is to be appreciated there, how to defend himself against its dangers, and how to win the rewards that are available there" (Rainwater, 1970, p. 281). This "readiness" usually occurs during puberty.

> "It is important . . . that the junior high school teacher be sensitive to the subtle relationships between the student's physical maturity, social standing, and the resultant behavior and performance in the school setting."

There is no specific age that clearly marks the beginning of puberty, although some general norms have been established. For boys, the onset of puberty has traditionally been considered to be between the ages of twelve and fourteen-and-a-half, while girls are generally thought to enter puberty slightly earlier, say between ten and thirteen years old. If we consider the hallmark of puberty sexual fullness, then these figures are basically accurate. Menarche—the first menstruation—signals the girl's entrance into puberty; sexual potency—the presence of sperm in the semen—signals the boy's entrance. Even more important, in terms of social and psychological development, is the appearance of **secondary sex characteristics.**

These are the characteristics that differentiate boys from girls but that are not directly related to the procreative (reproductive) process. Stiller (1966) cites the male characteristics as pubic hair, facial hair, deepening of the voice, heavy muscular development, and angular body build. For the female, the secondary sex characteristics are breasts, triangular pubic hair patterns, more subcutaneous fat giving a rounded body contour. These changes in the body are the clearest signs of the onset of puberty and, more importantly, are signs that are readily visible to the teacher.

The physical changes of puberty are accompanied by changes in attitude and interests, which are either the direct or indirect result of the rapid sexual maturity. Many of the responses from the peer group are responses to the manifestations of these secondary sex characteristics. The size of a girl's breasts may help or hinder her popularity with boys; may make her a butt of jokes, a pariah, or an object of lust pursued by the socially prestigious older boys. Likewise, a boy's lack of facial hair may place him at a disadvantage in comparison with his more hirsute peers who equate facial hair with virility. It is important, therefore, that the junior high school teacher be sensitive to the subtle relationships between the student's physical maturity, social standing, and the resultant behavior and performance in the school setting. While we would not suggest that it is only the physical reality of this period that exerts a profound influence, it is a highly significant part of the early adolescent experience and must be recognized as such.

McCary (1973) points out some of the psychological components of this period:

Psychological Conflicts in Puberty

This is a period of "sexual awakening" which is met with ambivalent reactions by both sexes. Attitudes, emotions, and interest change. Experimentation and new physical gratifications, such as masturbation, begin to occur or increase in frequency. Possessing a positive attitude toward the biological sexual urge and condition, as well as an understanding of society's expectations of the newly emerging self, is essential to the emotional well-being of both sexes at this time. (p. 31)

A number of factors have been identified as important forces during puberty (Adams, 1976). Social constraints, which check and stifle the burgeoning forces of sexuality, may become objects of rebellion or disdain. The family, which until now had served as the nexus of social interactions, may now be viewed as an alien institution; may, in fact, become a symbolic Goliath to be slain by an enraged and confused David, striving to come into his own. Similarly, in the school situation, where the **pubescent** spends a large portion of his time, teachers and other personnel may be viewed as the oppressors, encouraging, by their mere presence, rebellion and rage.

Hamburg (1974), in an analysis of the stresses of puberty, has pinpointed the three following challenges as primary to the pubescent's consciousness:

First, there are the challenges posed by the biological changes of puberty. The individual must cope with the flagrant and undeniable impact of change in body configuration. He perceives, at times erroneously, his emerging size and shape as the physique that will characterize him throughout his adult life. This concern over body image is pervasive, and there are deep concerns about physical attractiveness. . . .

Second, there are the challenges that are posed by the entry into a new social system, the junior high school. With this transition, the student relinquishes the former security of membership in one stable classroom and is faced with the task of negotiating six or seven changes of teacher and classes each day. . . .

The third set of challenges derive from the sudden entry into a new role status. The admission into junior high school has become a convenient marker for the conferring of adolescent status and the badge of entry into the "teen culture." In a dimly perceived way, the early adolescent urgently feels himself in need of a new set of "adolescent" behaviors, values, and reference persons. (pp. 105–106)

These challenges pose a host of problems to the junior high school teacher. The early adolescent student may act out many of his conflicts within the school setting. Or, he or she may perform poorly in school because of the conflicts that are besetting him on the outside. Macomber (1968) has suggested that the school act as an integrative agent for the adolescent. To accomplish this, he says, it is necessary to take into account the adolescent's basic needs during this period; that is, the needs which underlie the ostensible problems. These include among other needs learning to communicate effectively, understanding the elements of reproduction, knowing how to appreciate the beautiful things in the world. When these needs are taken into account, "we may conclude that the aims of education should be formulated in terms of the kind of behavior patterns required for the individual living in society"

(Macomber, 1968, p. 240). When the teacher is able to identify for the student the social and psychological benefits derived from particular learning tasks, the process of learning becomes more meaningful and relevant to the student. This is particularly true for the pubescent student, whose needs may be somewhat overpowering during this period.

Middle Adolescence: Two Views

One view of **middle adolescence,** developed during the 1950s and early 1960s, views this period as a time of painful growing in which the individual is beset by numerous conflicts, doubts, and difficulties in adjustment. Another view, developed more recently, deemphasizes this "storm and stress" conception of adolescence. In this section, we will consider both positions and examine their implications for teaching and learning.

Ausubel (1954), in his classic study of adolescence, sees the conflicts of this time caused by two inexorable forces: the need for independence and the **psychosexual conflict.** "Adolescent emotional instability in our culture," he argues, "is chiefly attributable to culturally determined frustration of physiological sex drives . . . the possession of sex desires is normal and proper, but their satisfaction is morally unallowable" (p. 17). Blum (1953), looking at adolescence from the psychoanalytic point of view, expresses essentially the same point, describing it as a battle between the ego and id, brought about by the newly blossoming sexual desires. Lidz (1968) too views the adolescent as a person "beset by conflicting emotions, struggling to maintain self-control and to achieve self-expression under the impact of sensations and impulses that are scarcely understood but insistently demand attention. It is a time of physical and emotional metamorphosis during which the youth feels estranged from the self the child had known" (p. 298).

Some of the more contemporary writers emphasize the stabilizing, goal-directed aspects of adolescence rather than this turbulent perspective. Lipsett (1974), for example, points out that the youth of the 1970s have returned to the patterns of hard work and goal-directed behavior that characterized youth of the 1940s. Recent surveys have confirmed that young people today are job-oriented, less active politically, and more ambitious than their contemporaries of ten years ago. Sabine (1971) interviewed sixteen-hundred secondary school students about their attitudes toward parents, schools, society, and peers, and his findings suggest that contemporary youth are more moderate and more in the mainstream of society than youth of ten years ago. But they are still "hurting," according to Sabine, and many of their fundamental needs still go unmet. Display 5.1 presents the conclusions of this *youth poll,* along with many implications for secondary school teachers.

What did the students say? Perhaps different things to different persons, but this is what I heard:

1. **Our youth are hurting.** Very much, in many different ways. Hurting for a chance to be themselves, to express themselves, to be respected for having some sense and some principles of their own, to be understood by their parents and the other important adults in their lives. To be listened to, instead of being told to shut up. To be heard as well as seen.

2. **For the most part, their comments are valid.** I believe them. Surely, there are exaggerations and some statements written in anger, but by and large, there simply is too much evidence to ignore. In public protests, much of what students demand may be for shock value, so they'll be listened to, but it would not be right to dismiss what they privately told YOUTH-POLL by an "Oh, that's just the spouting off of a radical minority few." It's much more than that.

3. **We made them the way they are.** Boys and girls don't just sit down and consciously decide "Today I am going to be critical of my parents." Or dissatisfied with school. Or approving of protest. These opinions and feelings well up from their experiences, from the attitudes and affluence we plant and provide.

4. **Teen-agers need to be needed more**. They do not have enough to do. Most are not needed to contribute to the family economically. They mature earlier physically. They are taught more to think and question. They really do know more than most of their parents did at the same age. And the adult response of "You stay in your place" (which is what we say when we refuse to listen) just makes matters worse.

5. **We are wasting good time and energy.** The youngsters spend it just to be taken seriously and listened to. Adults waste it by not harnessing teen-age energy and ability to help lick our problems.

6. **Students are finicky about protest.** The great majority approve, but not blindly. They pick and choose. "Just" causes, yes; just "any" cause, no. Nonviolently, yes. Violently, no.

7. **The really far-out "hopheads" are few.** For example, the only 1% who approved of taking (or had taken or would take) "hard" drugs. The number who reported having participated in violent demonstrations (3 had, 1,600 had not). The very small number insisting that students completely take over the administration of their colleges. The very few (5) who said they will "drop out" of productive life after college.

8. **Most of what they want, most adults would like, too.** The end of the Vietnam war. [This poll was taken in 1971.] Cleaner air. Less superficiality and more meaning in life. Not so much population that babies starve. Racial harmony. It's a little hard to argue against such goals.

9. **The trouble begins at home.** Students who have happy home lives are less likely to be critical of their schools or to support protest. Where the youth does not relate to either parent, has had no direction from his parents, and feels rejected by them, little wonder he brings a rebellious, frustrated attitude to school. Then his teachers have less chance to "get through" either on a personal or a subject matter basis. And he sees school as a "bad trip," leading most often to protest and beyond. Of students who reported using soft drugs: 67% more had been rejected by their families than supported by their families; 77% more received direction from neither parent than were in a family where the father was boss; 93% more related to neither parent than related closely to both parents.

10. **Adults are important to youths.** Otherwise, why would they bother to criticize us so much? If we were unimportant, they would ignore us (as they feel adults ignore them and in so doing, appear to indicate how little—to them —youth count).

11. **Parents are particularly important.** We all want to please the ones we love. Despite all their critical and negative comments about their parents, these youths still would be most pleased and rewarded if they could do something to make their mothers and fathers notice them, and openly love them.

12. **Students want to be stretched more intellectually in school.** As things now stand, they have higher expectations of their courses and teachers than do those teachers, their parents, school administrators or members of the school board. The students may not know all the ingredients of a good education, but they surely know when they're being short changed (which many think they now are being). Consistently, they report their best teacher as the one who worked them hardest; that person may have taught any subject—accounting, driver education, one of the basic "solids," or anything else. A great human being is recognized as such, regardless of subject matter.

13. **The more able the youth, the more severe his criticism and protest.** The evidence is that the higher on the ability scale, the more sensitive the student to the ills of the society and the world. The college-bound group in YOUTHPOLL will have more than its numerical share of the future leaders, the actives who are going to take from adults, later or perhaps sooner, their decision-making power. They won't be the only leaders, of course, but they'll be over-represented at the top in the future. And these are the ones who now criticize and protest most.

14. **There is too much of an "adversary" relationship between youths and adults.** A competitive relationship between generations is easy to understand; we always have had it. But today there is too much of parent *versus* child, teacher *versus* student, police *versus* protected, lawmaker *versus* citizen. It has become bitter, and it won't get better until communication improves.

15. **It is the adults' turn to take the first step to improve understanding of youth.** We need to listen harder, and respect more. This does *not* mean we have to agree—to run schools or country exactly and entirely the way students think they should be run, for example. But it does mean we must have and display more respect. It will cost time. It will cost a more open mind. It will require that we judge more by what youths say, less by how they look. And the payoff can be great, for by listening better and more sincerely, we can turn much of the unrest into something more productive.

16. **There are many ways to take that first step.** Any principal could conduct a "YOUTHPOLL" in his own high school. Any school could sponsor parent-student sit-downs-for-better-understanding (and lessen its own problems by improving family relationships). Any legislator could tune in to soon-to-become voters by systematically seeking their attitudes and opinions. Any parent or teacher could use the private "self-rating charts" in chapter 4 to gauge how close he is to what students describe as "best." [chap. 4 is not included in this excerpt]

It is hard to read all the student comments and not be chagrined, discouraged, anguished.

Chagrined because the students are right more often than they are wrong in the reasons they give for protest.

Discouraged because so many of them have had such defeating experiences in high school (which ought to be a great place and a great time in life).

Anguished by the detailed report of what takes place (and does not take place) inside the home and the family.

You know there is substance beneath the outcry, and you wish some very precious boys and girls did not have to go through all this pain as part of the move from childhood to teen-age to almost-adult years.

You don't condemn all teachers, or all schools, or all parents, or all lawmakers. That would be as wrong as lumping all youths into one generalized glob, or visiting upon the many the excesses of the few.

But you hear youths saying that they, too, should be able to dream dreams, and one of theirs is that all America and all Americans would be as good and great and perfect as some of our history books suggest.

Youths grasp for this perfection. They yearn for beauty and joy in life.

Instead, what they feel they get is adult indifference. They feel they are ignored.

One writes, "Look at me. I'm real, I walk, I talk, I hurt"—and you know so much is missing from his life that he feels like a nothing, a cipher, a zero.

What is more natural for him than to try to become a someone—even if a disliked or feared or possibly hated someone?

Can a teen-ager who does not find love at home next look to a teacher to help him hold together emotionally? That's the kind of responsibility you can safely bet is not mentioned in any teaching contract; you have to be the go-the-extra-mile kind of great human being if you are to supply it in your classroom. And if the teacher cannot deliver, what is more natural for the student than to turn to peers having the same kind of problems, and thus cement his alienation?

Having the chance to be heard was for YOUTHPOLL respondents something of a catharsis. They wrote and wrote and wrote (the quotations in this book include fewer than half the words the students penned and penciled). They became convinced—correctly—that they would be taken seriously. They liked that.

What our sons and daughters and students ask for is firmness, both from their parents and their teachers.

They want leadership.

They want to have idols and ideals they can respect.

They want to be proud.

From those adults they consider important, they want more understanding "*you*-thoughts" instead of merely so many old-style "youth-oughts."

Gordon Sabine, "This Is What We Heard" from *How Students Rate Their Schools and Teachers.* National Association of Secondary School Principals, 1971. Used with permission.

> "Through subject matter and through personal anecdotes of the teacher's experiences, the teacher can communicate to the adolescent ways of dealing with some of the more common problems of this period."

A synthesis of the positions shown in display 5.1 might explain this period in terms of the individual's struggle between freedom and the demands made upon him. Irene Josselyn, in her sensitive book, *The Adolescent and His World* (1969), describes some aspects of this conflict. "In our culture," she points out, "society not only makes heavy demands upon the adolescent, but it fails to provide him with a preconceived and carefully outlined pattern to help him meet these demands" (p. 26). One of the jobs of the school, as Macomber (1968) suggested, might be to define behaviors and competencies that are necessary for the adolescent to deal with his problems.

For instance, the teacher might help the adolescent discover the artist within himself. By encouraging expression through creativity in all the artistic media, the adolescent may well find an outlet for expression that was closed off before. Artistic expression can be encouraged in all the disciplines through writing, painting, crafts, music, creative drama, dance, and the like.

Through subject matter and through personal anecdotes of the teacher's experiences, the teacher may communicate to the adolescent ways of dealing

A coach, or teacher, can help students discover the athlete or the artist in themselves.

with some of the more common problems of this period. The teacher's flexibility is an important factor in this process. Friedenberg (1965) has cautioned us about the school's tendency to function as an "instrument through which society acculturates people into consensus before they become old enough to resist it as effectively as they could later" (p. 170). To avoid this tendency, the teacher might be open to styles of behavior and expression that are different than his own, and which allow the adolescent student to express feelings and perceptions—basic needs—in the most comfortable ways.

Finally, the teacher attempts to understand the values of the adolescent and to appreciate the factors that influence value change. We shall explore this in the following section.

The Adolescent's Values

A major factor in the person's development during puberty and adolescence is the refinement and reshaping of value orientations. Value change is an integral part of human growth, and during this period there is active or potential growth in every area of life.

Factors in Value Change The adolescent's values and the reshaping of these values are centered around two basic forces: the peer group and significant older individuals—authority figures and parents—with whom the adolescent identifies. Endler and Marino (1972), in a recent study, examined the effects of the peer group in shaping values and behavior. Using the global term *conformity,* which covers both values and behavior, they found that prior experience with peers strengthened the probability of conformity, while those whose prior experience was with authority figures were less likely to conform because of peer group pressures. Moreover, girls were more likely to conform to peer group demands than were boys. "For males," they assert, "the emphasis is more on independence, assertion, and achievement" (p. 26). One of the important conclusions of this study is that for adolescents in general, peers are a more potent reference group for value orientation than are authority figures.

Munns (1972), in another recent study, also found that adolescents conformed more to the peer group values than to the parental values, and that they saw themselves and their friends as holding values that differed from the parents, except for certain social, religious, and political values. Cooper and Blair (1959), in an earlier study, shed some light on what specific factors determine the areas in which the adolescent agrees most closely with parents' values. They found that subjects who felt very positively about their parents tended to express relatively close ideological similarity to the parent. It may well be, then, that negative or positive feelings about one's parents are important indicators of ideological, or cognitive, agreement. We can say, then,

> "Under certain conditions the parents are a powerful reference group, while under other conditions the peers hold great sway over the adolescents' values."

that under certain conditions the parents are a powerful reference group, while under other conditions the peers hold great sway over the adolescent's values.

Many of these insights are used by Cooper (1971) in his lengthy, articulate paper that attempts to examine the complex of questions brought out in the adolescent's world. Cooper argues that "parents, particularly the father, could be viewed with considerable justification as the adult society's resident ambassador in the family court. As such, parents derive their authority and wisdom, implied or real, from their position as representatives of the adult power structure. . . ." (p. 1109). Cooper disagrees about the importance of the so-called generation gap, arguing that the majority of adolescents do, in fact, get along well with their parents.

Values in the Classroom

Belkin (1974) has put forth the argument that values are inevitably communicated between teacher and student in their classroom interactions:

In the typical classroom, the teacher does not set aside a period of time each day for the teaching of values. . . . On the contrary, he busies himself with the subject-matter at hand, complacently convinced that his duties and performance are guided by such noble goals as the presentation of facts and theories, the endowment of knowledge, the objective unraveling of Truth.

. . . Yet, because we know that values permeate all areas of our thoughts and actions, the neutral stance is difficult to swallow. A critical analysis of class time will reveal that values are implicit in all teaching: so much so, that rarely can a moment of teaching be isolated where the teacher's values are not the primary shaping force in the teaching activity. . . . (pp. 176–177)

This has several important implications in regard to teaching the adolescent student. Since values are implicit in the teacher's classroom activities, it is the responsibility of the teacher to see that in whatever areas value clashes between the teacher and students occur, they should be brought to the surface and discussed. For example, there may be a conflict between the teacher's values that hold that certain behavior is acceptable in class and the student's values that maintain that other types of behavior (perhaps some version of courting) should be permitted. Instead of arbitrarily enforcing his own standards of behavior, the teacher might do well to allow students to verbalize their criteria for appropriate classroom behavior, and it is likely that an acceptable compromise can be worked out. Students will often be surprised to hear a teacher express such flexibility. At first, they may not know how to deal with it. But, given time and shown patience, they will inevitably come to respect the teacher and to recognize that there are no absolutely *right*

The peer group provides not only companionship but also a subtle shaping and reinforcement of values, beliefs, and behaviors.

values and no absolutely *wrong* values, but that values and their accompanying expression in behavior can be discussed, reconsidered, and modified to meet the demands of the occasion. This not only helps the student learn more appropriate social behavior but encourages the student to think critically about the values that underlie his behavior as well.

An important principle for the teacher to remember is this: *Since the peer group exerts an inordinate amount of influence on the student's value formulations, the teacher should try to be sensitive to the value orientations of the peer group.*

Research has also shown that a number of significant barriers exist between teachers and students of different ethnic and socioeconomic groups (Vontress, 1968; 1973). Some of the barriers cited include ignorance of the student's background, language barriers, reciprocal racial orientations. While these barriers are applicable to all levels, they become particularly pronounced in dealing with the adolescent student since this student's quest for identity is likely to be tied up with his search for values. As Sebald (1968) points out, in discussing the black youth's quest for identity, the black youth "carries with him the legacy of his slave forefathers. . . . His self-image is highly influenced by the awareness of his racial background and is beset with deprecatory connotations from which he finds it difficult to escape" (p. 287). As part of his way of coping with this, the black adolescent may establish a value structure strongly determined by ethnic considerations (Guthrie, 1970), and the teacher might take this into account.

> "At the very point in life where sexuality becomes a compelling, object-directed force, social rules and regulations place great burdens upon the individual to control, or even repress, these desires."

One area in which values, behavior, and biology mix thoroughly is in adolescent sexuality. In the following section, we shall examine the adolescent sexual experience, particularly as it relates to problems that can carry over to the school setting.

Dating Behavior: Sex and the Adolescent

Nowhere is the male-female and social class differences between young people more striking than in their sexual attitudes and experiences. In this section, we will look at some general views of the adolescent's sexual awakening and at some specific differences between the boy's sexual experiences and the girl's experiences; between the middle-class youth's confrontation with sex and the lower-class youth's. Then, we will examine the implications that these insights have for the classroom teacher.

At the very point in life where sexuality becomes a compelling, object-directed force, social rules and regulations place great burdens upon the individual to control, or even repress, these desires. The adolescent must learn to function within the constraints of these rules and regulations. He may circumvent them, rebel against them, or deny and ignore the passions that rage within him. The consequences of any course of action is staggering.

Haley (1973) argues that one of the most important learning tasks of this period is successful "courtship behavior." This behavior, which becomes the basis for later, permanent attachments, often pits the adolescent against the adult world, creating conflicts where there are really no need for them. Let us look at some aspects of courtship behavior, cutting across class and gender differences when necessary.

Dating behavior is primarily defined by the culture. It consists of conventions that allow the individual to attract, interact with, and possibly maintain sexual relations with persons of the opposite sex. For the middle-class youngster, this is likely to be a slow process, proceeding from the onset of puberty to the end of adolescence. In a thorough study of adolescent boys' sexual behavior, Daniel Offer (1971) found that promiscuity and early sexual experiences are not as common among middle-class, suburban youth as is commonly believed. Some of his findings are:

Dating

1. A significant number of our subjects (45%) had not gone out with girls by the end of the Freshman year of high school. The number . . . who dated increased slowly in the next two years. . . .
2. Most teenagers date irregularly and did not seem to either relish the experience or think that it is important for teenagers to date.
3. According to our subjects, if anyone felt that 'teenagers should date,' it was the parents and especially the mothers.
4. In the beginning, a major reason for dating was a social one. They shared their experiences with their peers almost immediately after they brought the girl home. The minute dissection that goes on among the boys telling each other what they did, right or wrong, is extremely helpful and suggestive. They try to do better next time, not so much because they enjoy kissing or petting, but so they can tell their friends.
5. As their anxiety diminishes in their relations with girls, they begin to enjoy the encounter more. . . .
6. Too much sexual closeness was frightening. "We are just not ready for it," was repeated over and over.
7. Almost all the subjects . . . said that they daydreamed about girls, but only a small group stated that it included girls they knew personally. In the latter case, it was often an older woman.
8. The cardinal findings are that the normal middle-class adolescent does not experiment much with sexuality. He is slow in getting involved sexually with a girl, and fantasy plays as significant a role as the actual deed. (pp. 40–46)

While these findings are likely to fluctuate from community to community and from year to year, they are, in general, a reasonable but limited estimate of middle-class adolescent male sexuality.

The black, lower-class adolescent, on the other hand, is likely to have more precocious sexual experiences than his middle-class counterpart (Guthrie, 1970). Rainwater (1970), in a detailed study of black families living in a housing project in St. Louis, describes the various opportunities the black adolescent (and pubescent) is likely to have in learning about sex, both vicariously—through tales and stories—and through direct participation. Many of the youngsters express their sexual fantasies and fears in the form of rhymed jokes, or *joans* as they are called. Precocious sexual behavior is also more common among white lower-class youth than it is among the middle class and, in general, seems to be more a characteristic of socioeconomic class than race.

One of the chief purposes of the dating period, and of dating behavior in general, is to define, clarify, and strengthen one's sexual-gender identity. Boys and girls find their gender identities and begin to assume adult social roles through dating But because these roles are often narrowly and inequitably distributed between boys and girls, this can pose a number of problems for the junior high school teacher and other school personnel. For example, girls are not generally allowed the outlets to express aggression that are opened up more readily to boys. "The problem for the girl," Konopka (1966) points out in her study of the delinquent teenage girl, "is the fact that since aggression in itself is considered bad, it is forbidden to her." She goes on to examine the consequences of this double standard.

When a boy fights, he may be considered delinquent . . . but his role in society does not prohibit fighting per se. On the contrary, the prevailing mores consider fighting part of the accepted male role.

Girls handle this problem by subtle disguise of the aggressive act. Unconsciously many protect themselves against harsh self-censure by avoiding open aggression (p. 111). . . . The ideal image of the girl is still 'sugar and spice.' The natural adolescent drive for adventure may be satisfied through activities not accepted by society or through provisions of it by boys, who have easier access to the tools for it, e.g., cars. (p. 121)

These sanctions against feminine aggression may account for the fact that delinquency rates among boys are considerably higher than among girls. Although the cited rates vary from five to one (Sexton, 1961) to three-and-one-half to one, the fact remains that boys traditionally exhibit more antisocial behavior than do girls, although the latter's rate is on the rise.

The process of sexual-gender identification for the lower-class boy may lead to conflicts in the classroom. Boys, especially boys of the lower class, express their masculinity through rebellious classroom behavior. Sebald (1968) describes this phenomenon:

In the school setting, the "masculine" values of the lower-class youngster lead him to reject the "eager-beaver" and "apple-polishing" style that conforms to the middle-class norms of respecting the teacher, being neat, and accepting the middle-class orientation. Since the teacher is most likely a female, conformity to and compliance with her demands and wishes would be a surrender and degradation of masculinity and toughness. (p. 330)

There are a number of important points implicit in these views. As the teacher recognizes the dynamics of dating behavior, as he or she perceives its importance in the life space of the adolescent student, the teacher becomes eminently capable of helping students through the difficulties that dating behavior inevitably entails. If the teacher and school administration are willing to allow appropriate socialization activities in the school, this may help the adolescent channel much of his or her sexual energy into constructive, school-related activities. There are also lessons to be learned, social tasks to be introduced and discussed. Boys have to learn how to treat girls properly, and vice versa; each must also learn to expect proper treatment from the opposite sex. Books, films, songs, television shows, plays, and role-playing in the classroom can all be used to this end. The teacher should also recognize how much of disruptive classroom behavior is the natural consequence of dating activities. This recognition might make it easier for the teacher to accept some types of behavior that he or she would not otherwise be so willing to accept.

> "The adolescent first learns that sex is beautiful through the stimulation of his or her own body."

Having now looked at some general ideas of adolescent dating, we will turn our attention to some of the specific problems of adolescent sexuality.

Masturbation Although many young people are troubled about masturbation, often plagued by feelings of guilt and confusion, it is generally agreed by experts in psychology and education that masturbation is a normal, healthy, constructive part of the adolescent sexual experience. According to definitive studies (Kinsey et al., 1948), approximately 95 percent of adolescent boys and 50 percent to 80 percent of adolescent girls practice masturbation. Despite this rate of practice, masturbation may cause the adolescent—particularly the early adolescent—to experience guilt, self-disgust, and remorse.

One particularly constructive use of masturbation is learning to experience heightened sexual pleasure (Ford, 1966). At this period of life, with its limitations and taboos on sexual activity, it is through autoerotic activity that the healthy boy or girl learns to appreciate sexual response. The appreciation takes two forms: fantasy and bodily stimulation (Ford, 1966). Through fantasy, the young person is able to appreciate the diversity and creativity of the sexual experience. Through bodily stimulation, he or she learns about the areas of the body that are most sensitive to stimulation and stroking. It is through these two activities that the adolescent forms his feelings about sex. Through fantasy, for example, he or she may bring into sexual consciousness those others who will ultimately become sexual objects. Ironically, the adolescent first learns that sex is beautiful through the stimulation of his or her own body.

Petting The earliest type of overt sexual activity occurring between young people of the opposite sex is usually petting. Broadly speaking, petting is sexual activity that does not culminate in sexual intercourse. It may include kissing, touching parts of the body, oral stimulation of the erogenous zones, and mutual masturbation. Because petting arouses heightened sexual interest—because it is very pleasurable and very stimulating—but does not at the same time provide for sexual release, it is often the basis of anxiety and confusion resulting from increased pressure without the opportunity for discharge.

Petting may also be the subject of much moral confusion for the adolescent, especially for the adolescent girl. Questions regarding the propriety and morality of petting are not unusual in informal classroom discussion, especially if the teacher invites students to speak about their feelings. Girls, victims of an insidious double standard that permeates all our sexual mores, may risk the loss of their social esteem, the possibility of a defamed reputation, and complete ostracism as punishment for sexual activities. Boys, on the other hand, acquire a new social status, the respect of their peers, and a better self-image as a consequence of their sexual exploits. Part of the teacher's role as a facilitator of emotional growth might be to help the adolescent boy and girl gain a more appropriate, fulfilling perspective of the reality of the sexual situation.

It is most important that contraceptive information be made available to those adolescents who are having sexual intercourse. While this is usually more the responsibility of the family or family physician than of the teacher, there are many instances where the teacher, in the school setting, might have occasion to advise students about appropriate contraceptive measures. The teacher should recognize that contraception is a touchy matter and can provoke unnecessary controversy; but he or she should also realize that contraceptive information is an appropriate part of the learner's total health program. **Contraception**

It is helpful, then, if the teacher is familiar with the various methods of contraception. He or she should be able to intelligently and accurately answer students' questions regarding contraception, although care must be taken not to overstep professional bounds. An excellent source for the teacher is J. L. McCary's *Human Sexuality* (New York: Van Nostrand Reinhold, 1974), which has a comprehensive chapter on this subject. The teacher may also wish to organize sex education groups that, among other things, would cover this topic in sufficient detail.

Policies of the school system regarding the dissemination of contraceptive information should be of interest to the teacher. The teacher would also want to be familiar with the state laws regarding the subject; these laws vary widely from state to state. The teacher can often obtain legal information either from the counsel to the school board or from the attorney for the teachers' union, where there is one. Usually, the teacher can do more good, working entirely within the framework of the law rather than side-stepping it, even when he feels this might be for the benefit of the students. Also, religious convictions must always be respected.

The schools have been most negligent in dealing with the problem of venereal disease, a problem that has finally reached epidemic proportions among young people during the 1970s. Although during the past decade the schools have taken on an ever-increasing interest in preventive health care, they have shown little or no interest in detecting the presence of venereal disease and in educating students about the prevention and recognition of these diseases. Yet both of these are simple procedures, and the teacher, counselor, and school medical personnel might well find themselves involved in a program to **Venereal Diseases** deal with this problem. This may be a part of the total sex education program, or it may be directly under the auspices of the school counselor or school physician (where there is one). In either case, if the teacher is well informed about the nature and prognosis of different venereal diseases, he or she will be in a unique position to help students and to work effectively with other school personnel.

Pregnancy and Abortion   The pregnant teenage girl has always been a subject of controversy, a source of embarrassment, a victim of confused mores in the school setting. Yet, there are still many girls who become pregnant, and there shall continue to be girls who become pregnant. The schools, therefore, are being forced to adapt their policies accordingly.

While teenage pregnancy occurs in all social and economic classes, it is far more prevalent in the lower classes. Schulz (1969) explains the reasons for this in terms of the black ghetto youth:

> The most common dilemma faced by the high school girl is posed by the conflict over "career" versus motherhood. In the ghetto, however, this has much more of an ominous overtone than in the world of the middle class. The problem is accentuated by the fact that many girls have had sexual relations by the time they enter high school. It is considered the normal thing to do to "please" your boyfriend. They are, however, largely ignorant of effective contraceptive techniques, fearful of using them, or conduct their sexual activities in situations where several contraceptive devices would be useless because they require that lovemaking be planned in advance. (p. 48)

It is not only the failure to use contraception that causes pregnancy, however. Many girls, to fill an emptiness in their lives choose, consciously or unconsciously, to become pregnant. Appropriate counseling is helpful in such cases to help the young girl to decide what course of action to take. While the large majority of pregnancies are dealt with outside the school setting, it is not unlikely that the teacher may at some point or another have occasion to counsel a pregnant teenager. *Since teachers are often important figures in the life of the adolescent, the pregnant girl may turn to the teacher for help and guidance in times of doubt and confusion.*

Homosexuality   The comments about pregnancy and abortion are equally as true in dealing with another very sensitive subject that is likely to crop up in the school setting: what to do about the homosexual student.

An area of increasing interest, brought about in part by an increasing willingness of homosexuals to "come out of the closet" and to acknowledge their homosexuality, is the plight of the homosexual student in the secondary school. At a period in life when acceptance by peers and conformity to images are of paramount importance, it is indeed difficult, if not impossible, for the adolescent homosexual to express himself to his peers and to engage in the type of sexual activity and courtship that is available to his heterosexual counterpart. The main question that has hung threateningly over the head of the homosexual adolescent is whether or not homosexuality is a sickness. Professionals in the fields of psychology, psychiatry, and education disagree vehemently on this question, but recent sentiments are that homosexuality may be an alternative life-style rather than an emotional illness (Jones, 1974).

Even so, homosexuality may become a problem for the teacher if it is expressed overtly and aggressively in the school setting. Just as heterosexual behavior can become disruptive if it is not appropriately expressed, homosexual behavior can upset the majority of students. In such cases, the teacher might attempt to relate to the homosexual student, without the overt value judgments and condemnations that may be responsible for the student's provocative actions in the first place. The teacher can make the student feel that it is not his homosexuality that is being attacked, but only his inappropriate behavior. Often disruptive behavior is the student's reaction against his fears about his homosexuality. An understanding and sympathetic teacher, who is comfortable and secure about his or her own sexual orientation, can do much to help such a student learn appropriate social behavior within the context of his sexual preferences.

The homosexual student may, on the other hand, be exposed to ridicule and contempt by his peers. The class "fag" or "queer" must bear the burden of other students' homosexual fears. One way the teacher can be helpful in such cases is to protect the student, to teach the other class members the virtue of tolerance, and at the same time to educate students about the diversity of human preferences—in sexuality and in other sensitive areas.

Since the homosexual student is likely to experience more pressures than the heterosexual student and, at the same time, to find less social reinforcement, it is advisable that the student be exposed to some type of counseling, either inside the school setting or from without. The teacher can ascertain if the school counselor is capable of dealing with a homosexual student. If not, the teacher may inquire about community services, which may be provided by homosexual groups, by churches, by hospitals, or by the board of education.

Sex Education in the Secondary School

One of the most helpful ways in dealing with all of these problems and conflicts of adolescence is to establish a sex education program in the secondary schools. McCary (1967) discusses the "why" of sex education at some length. He points out:

The only way our society is going to achieve proper sexual stability and mental health, which are undisputed requirements for maturity, is to instigate and persevere with a sound sex education for everyone. This goal means that those who are in a position to instruct must freely admit to what they do not know, at

> "Typically, a sex education program geared to the adolescent will include three phases: informational, group counseling, and individual counseling."

the same time teaching that which they know to be the truth. They must educate, not indoctrinate; teach fact, not fallacies; formulate a code of ethics, not asceticism; be objective, not subjective; be democratic, not autocratic; and seek knowledge, not emotionally biased constructs. This will be difficult because most people have grown up in a culture which produces and espouses most or all of the negative agents in sexual ignorance and maladjustment. (p. 17)

McCary's remarks illustrate what may be one of the more important considerations about sex education in the secondary schools. Such a program would be beneficial not only to the individual student but to the entire society as well.

Typically, a sex education program geared to the adolescent will include three phases: informational, group counseling, and individual counseling. The informational phase may include films, books, magazine articles, demonstration devices, and lectures. Many publishing companies now offer sex education kits, which are multimedia packages that cover one or more of the topics relating to adolescent sexuality. In some school districts, sex education specialists visit the classroom to conduct lessons, while in other districts a team of teachers, counselors, and other school personnel coordinate a team to develop and implement a sex education program.

Group counseling can be provided in the classroom itself. It can be integrated into lessons, or set off separately. Some feasible goals of group counseling might be to help the adolescent understand the complexity of the sexual drive, to facilitate expression of sexual feelings, to clarify what the informational aspect failed to clarify, and to assure that each adolescent has the basic intellectual and emotional tools necessary for dealing with the conundrums of his or her sexual reality.

When required, individual counseling may also be provided. In fact, one of the important purposes of the group experiences is to identify those students who could benefit from individual counseling (Gazda, 1972). As we indicated earlier, the homosexual student might be such a case. Also, it might be discovered through the group counseling experience that related school problems might be rooted in sexual confusion or dysfunctioning.

Cognitive Growth in Adolescence

In addition to the social and psychological changes we have been discussing, adolescence proves to be a critical period in the intellectual development of the person. In fact, it is during the years of adolescence that the full capacities

> " 'In thinking about the future . . . the adolescent is paving the way to finding out where he belongs in a world whose complexities he has just begun to ponder.' "

of human intellect—its ability to deal with abstractions and complex relationships—come to fruition. In this section, we shall look at some views of cognitive growth in adolescence and examine the implications of these positions for the junior high school and high school teacher.

Piaget and Inhelder (1958) provide the most detailed description of cognitive growth in adolescence, but unfortunately they do so in a language that is so technical and cumbersome that it is comprehensible only to the most dedicated and persistent reader. In essence, they argue that "the thinking of the adolescent differs radically from that of the child" (p. 335) because the adolescent is capable of **"hypothetico-deductive reasoning"**—that is, abstract reasoning in which the adolescent is able to use logic and hypothesis testing in his mind. Lefrancois (1972) describes this stage more clearly:

Piaget's Position

What this means, in effect, is that the adolescent can now think hypothetically in a logical manner. He has become freed from the necessity of considering only the real and concrete. His thinking has become potentially completely logical and is characterized by rules which, unlike those of the period of concrete operations, apply to the system as a whole. (p. 306)

Elkind (1970) also explains clearly how the "formal operations" of adolescent thinking work:

Formal operations not only permit the young person to construct all the possibilities in a system and construct contrary-to-fact propositions; they also enable him to conceptualize his own thought, to take his mental constructions as objects and reason about them. (p. 66)

What this means, in effect, is that the adolescent is capable of the same sophisticated type of thinking we associate with the mature adult.

The consequences of this cognitive growth during adolescence are myriad. Birns (1967) explains how this Piagetian position affects the world of the adolescent:

To Inhelder and Piaget, it is neither sexuality nor rebellion against parents that is most characteristic of adolescence. For them the major transitions consist of the assumption of adult roles and the transformation of thought. Due to changes in cognitive structures the adolescent not only thinks of what he is now, but begins to plan for the future. He not only thinks of how he himself wants to evolve but also plans to change society. Whereas the young child does not really reflect, the adolescent is reflective, and thinks critically of his own thought. In thinking about the future, about all of the possible ways of being, and of the ordering of one's life, the adolescent is paving the way to finding out where he belongs in a world whose complexities he has just begun to ponder.

We see here how much of the social awareness and concern that is typical of the adolescent is the end product of his cognitive growth. His new cognitive abilities create numerous possibilities of social development and growth. "The new cognitive capacities," Lidz (1968) argues, ". . . enable youths to embrace ideologies, to challenge status quo, to envision a better world, to gain gratification through fantasy while waiting to become able to achieve [it] in reality, and in general to soar above the prosaic world with its plodding inhabitants. . . ." (p. 317)

In the classroom, these new cognitive capacities pose many challenges to the teacher. What can the teacher do to stimulate the growing, ever-increasing comprehension and curiosity of the adolescent student? How can the teacher make the subject matter, and the teaching itself, relevant to the adolescent's increasing ideological and goal-directed interests? As the teacher confronts these questions, he or she will become increasingly aware of the developing cognitive styles of the adolescents in his or her classroom.

It should be emphasized that these delineations of adolescent cognitive development are not always attained in reality. Many students in the high school are not yet capable of formal operational thought; that is, they do not yet possess the ability to deal abstractly and hypothetically with problems but are, instead, restricted to the concrete operational thought of the earlier period. It is up to the teacher to determine the student's level of reasoning ability and to present subject matter in such a way that the student's cognitive faculties will be able to deal with it.

Adolescent Drug Abuse

One of the more serious and pervasive problems facing the educator is the widespread misuse of mind-altering drugs and alcohol by school-age youth, particularly by the adolescent student. Much has been written about this problem, much research conducted, and large sums of money have been spent by the government to combat drug abuse; yet the problem persists. One of the more tragic aspects of this problem is the way in which drug abuse patterns have spread cancerously during the past few years: from relative confinement in a few inner-city schools to the entire range of schools in city and suburb; from high schools to junior high schools to elementary schools; from a few social or economic classes or delinquent cliques in each school to the general school population. While the particular drugs most likely to be abused change from season to season—whether it is glue, or pot, or uppers or downers, or alcohol—the problem remains essentially the same.

In this section, we shall examine some of the causes and symptoms of drug abuse, noting particularly what the teacher can do preventively and remedially, in the classroom and on the outside, to help alleviate this very difficult problem.

Although there may be nothing intrinsically dangerous or destructive about a certain drug, it can be abused in a number of ways. Overusing drugs, using them at an inappropriate time, taking a drug when it is not required, or forming a psychological addiction are all forms of drug abuse. If the drug in itself is not specifically dangerous, then the problem arises as a result of the uses to which the drug is put. Alcohol, for example, is sipped graciously at teachers' conventions with no discernible harm to anyone. But when a seventh-grade boy comes to school drunk each day, or when the parents of a high school girl cannot give her appropriate supervision because of their dependence upon alcohol, these clearly are drug abuse problems. Marijuana, a drug with no proven danger to the user, produces pleasant, relaxed feelings, with heightened sensual awareness. When a high school youth, however, becomes unable to study because of excessive use of this substance, or when a student loses his ability to function except when using the drug, then we are dealing with a serious drug problem.

What Is Drug Abuse?

Some drugs, on the other hand, are inherently dangerous and may always be considered instances of drug abuse if they are not taken under the direction of a physician. Heroin, a synthetic derivative of morphine, is a highly addictive substance with no legitimate medical uses. Most heroin-related deaths are a result of overdosage or of toxic agents mixed with the heroin to dilute it. The hallucinogenic (psychedelic) drugs—LSD, DMT, mescaline, and psilocybin—give the user the illusion of expanded consciousness, of awareness and sensitivity that is lacking without the drug. In fact, however, these drugs produce gross distortions of reality, hallucinations, and erratic behavior and thinking. They are extremely unpredictable and very dangerous. Barbiturates and other depressant drugs produce in the user a feeling of relaxation and blissfulness that enables the user to forget all of the problems that he faces in life. These are highly addictive drugs that may result in fatality upon withdrawal. Continued use of barbiturates may also produce psychotic or violent behavior. Cases of suicide under the influence of barbiturates are not uncommon. Amphetamines are stimulant drugs that result in great feelings of optimism and mania. They are used by adolescents as sleep inhibitors, appetite suppressants, and for relief of depression. Prolonged use of amphetamines may result in hallucinations, psychosis, and violent behavior. Table 5.1 offers some useful information on drugs that are subject to abuse. Display 5.2 enumerates some of the common symptoms of drug abuse, and display 5.3 lists terms used by a narcotic addict. The teacher who is likely to encounter drug abuse problems in the school setting should familiarize himself with this material.

Table 5.1   Useful Information on Drugs Subject to Abuse

Name	Heroin	Codeine	Morphine	Methadone	Cocaine	Marijuana
Slang Name	H, Horse, Skag, Junk, Snow, Stuff, Harry, Joy Powder, Smack	Schoolboy	White Stuff, Miss Emma, M, Dreamer	Dolly	Speedball, Gold Dust, Coke, Bernice, Corine, Flake, Star Dust	Texas Tea, Nezz, Weed, Pot, Grass, Locoweed, Mary Jane, Hashish, Reefer, Hemp, plus local slang names
Pharmacologic Classification	Depressant	Depressant	Depressant	Depressant	Stimulant	Stimulant, depressant, or hallucinogen
Medical Uses	None	Ease pains and coughing	Pain relief	Pain relief, detoxification of drug addicts, maintenance of drug addicts	Local anesthesia	None in U.S.
How Taken	Injected or sniffed	Swallowed	Swallowed or injected	Swallowed or injected	Swallowed	Smoked or swallowed
Usual Dose	Varies	30 milligrams	15 milligrams	Varies depending on use or abuse	Varies	1 or 2 cigarettes
Duration of Effect	4 hours	4 hours	6 hours	Varies depending on use or abuse	Varies	4 hours
Initial Symptoms	Euphoria, drowsiness	Drowsiness	Euphoria, drowsiness	Less acute than opiates	Excitation, talkativeness, tremors	Relaxation, euphoria, alteration of perception, judgment
Long-term Symptoms	Addiction, constipation, loss of appetite, convulsions in overdose	Addiction	Addiction, impairment of breathing	Addiction	Depression, convulsions	?
Physical Dependence Potential	Yes	Yes	Yes	Yes	No	No
Mental Dependence Potential	Yes	Yes	Yes	Yes	No	?
Note	Usually found as white crystalline powder in paper or glassine envelopes or capsules		Usually found as a white powder		Usually found as a white crystalline powder	Usually found as dried, pulverized flowering tops, seeds and leaves

Barbiturates	Amphetamines	LSD	DMT	Mescaline	Psilocybin
Barbs, Candy, Goofballs, Sleeping Pills, Peanuts, also: (1) Yellows, Yellow Jackets, Nimby, Nimble, (2) Reds, Pinks, Red Devils, Seggy, Seccy, (3) Reds and Blues, Double Trouble	Bennies, Dexies, Co-Pilots, Wake-ups, Truck Drivers, Hearts, Pep Pills, Proppers	Acid, Sugar, Big D, Cubes, Trips	Business-man's High	Cactus, Peyote	Mushrooms
Depressant	Stimulant	Halluci-nogen	Hallucinogen	Hallucinogen	Hallucinogen
Sedation, relieve high blood pressure, hyper-thyroidism, epilepsy	Relieve mild depression, control appetite, narcolepsy	Experi-mental study of mental function, alcoholism	None	None	None
Swallowed or injected	Swallowed or injected	Swallowed	Swallowed	Swallowed	Swallowed
50 to 100 milligrams	2.5 to 5 milligrams	100 micro-grams	1 milligram	350 micrograms	25 milligrams
4 hours	4 hours	10 hours	4 to 6 hours	12 hours	6 to 8 hours
Drowsiness, muscle relaxation	Alertness, activeness	Exhilar-ation, excitation, rambling speech	Exhilaration	Exhilaration, anxiety, gastric distress	Nausea, vomiting, headaches
Addiction with severe withdrawal symptoms, possible convulsions	Delusions, hallucinations	May in-tensify existing psychosis, panic reactions	?	?	?
Yes	Yes	Yes	No	No	No
Yes	Yes	?	?	?	?

(1) Pentobarbital Sodium (Nembutal)
(2) Seconbarbital (Seconal)
(3) Amobarbital (Tuinal)

Prepared for the Addiction Services Agency of the City of New York by Lenox Hill Hospital with funds made available by its Woman's Auxiliary.

1. Changes in school attendance, homework quality, discipline or grades.
2. Poor physical appearance.
3. Sudden and unusual emotional outbreaks or flare-ups.
4. Furtive behavior regarding drugs or possessions.
5. Sudden change of associations and social patterns.
6. Borrowing money from students to buy drugs.
7. Wearing sunglasses at inappropriate times to hide pupils of eyes.
8. Stealing small items from school or home.
9. Finding student in odd places during school day, such as closets or storage rooms, to take drugs.

Specific Drug Symptoms

Glue
1. Excessive nasal secretions, plus watering of eyes.
2. Odor of substance inhaled on breath and clothing.
3. Slurred speech, very slow response.
4. Poor muscular control, drowsiness or unconsciousness.
5. Presence of plastic or paper bags or rags containing dry plastic cement.

Stimulants (Amphetamines, Bennies)
1. Excessive activity, restlessness.
2. Acute irritability, argumentative, nervous, difficulty in sitting still.
3. Dilated pupils.
4. Chain smoking during recess.
5. Dry mouth and nose with licking of lips and rubbing or scratching of nose.
6. Sudden exhaustion or sleep from long periods without eating or sleeping.

Depressants (Barbiturates, Goofballs)
1. Falling asleep or lack of interest in class.
2. Symptoms of alcohol intoxication without odor of alcohol on breath.
3. Staggering or stumbling walk.
4. Drowsy or disoriented behavior.

Marijuana (symptoms will appear only when person is "on" the drug.)
1. Animated and hysterical behavior with rapid, loud speech and bursts of laughter.
2. In later stages, sleepy or stuporous appearance.
3. Indications of distorted depth and color perception.

Hallucinogens (LSD)
1. Fearful or panicky behavior or paranoid reaction to group.
2. Dreamy, trance-like state.
3. Indications of distorted sight, hearing, touch and/or time.
4. Changes of mood or behavior.
5. Widely dilated pupils requiring dark glasses to protect eyes from light.

Narcotics (Heroin)
1. Hidden syringes, burned spoons, cotton and needles.
2. Traces of white powder around nostrils if user is inhaling (snorting) heroin.
3. Scars (track marks) on inner arms from injections (mainlining).
4. Constant wearing of long sleeve shirts to hide scars.
5. Constricted pupils which do not respond to light.
6. Lethargic behavior.

Prepared by The City of New York, Addiction Services Agency, 71 Worth Street, New York, N.Y., 10012.

1. Heroin is known as stuff, junk, dope, goods, merchandise, a taste of sugar.
2. A five-dollar purchase of narcotics is known as a "nickle bag." A ten-dollar purchase is a "dime bag."
3. Poor quality narcotics are known as flea powder, lemon, lemonade, Lipton tea, dummy, blanks, turkey.
4. A supplier of drugs is known as dealer, connection, big man, peddler, pusher, mule, bagman, bingle, swingman, cap man.
5. To purchase drugs is known as to score, to hit, to connect, to make a meet, domino.
6. A container of drugs is known as deck, cap, bindle, paper bag, piece.
7. To withdraw from drugs is known as kicking, turned off, fold up, hang up, make the turn, catch up, wasted up, to be off, cleared up.
8. To inject drugs is known as jab, pop, bang, shoot up, a geezer, mainlining, bingo.
9. To be under the influence of drugs is known as high, lit up, blasted, wasted, shot down, coasting, floating, on the nod, banging, a boot, fixed, flying, leaping, belted, stinking, hitting the stuff.
10. A narcotic addict is known as a junkie, hype, glow head, hophead, junker.
11. The equipment for injecting drugs is known as works, biz, tools, machinery, factory, layout, artillery, gun, gimmick, needle (spike or nail), eyedropper (dipper or gun).
12. A non-addict is known as square, do-righters, apple, johns, out of it.
13. A small, irregular drug habit is known as joy popping, play round, ice-cream habit, chipping, weekend habit, dabble.
14. To be arrested is known as busted, clipped, fall, glued, batted, out, dropped, nailed, canned, jugged.
15. A policeman is known as fuzz, heat, bull, the man, pig, big john, harness bull, fuzzy fail.
16. A Federal narcotics agent is known as fed, narc, sam, T man, whiskers, Uncle Sam, gazer, narcotic bull.
17. A gun is known as a rod, cannon, heater.
18. A knife is known as a shiv, blade.

Prepared by The City of New York, Addiction Services Agency, 71 Worth Street, New York, N.Y., 10012.

One of the more unfortunate aspects of the drug abuse problem is the student's inability to distinguish between the relative dangers of different drugs. Often a student experiments with LSD or a barbiturate as readily as he would with marijuana or hashish, far less dangerous drugs. Thomas Thompson (1973), in his poignant account of the short life of Richard Diener, tells how young Richie's experimentation with "downs" led to such a state of mental deterioration and social malfunctioning that he finally ended up in a face-to-face duel-to-death with his father. What is interesting in Thompson's account is the amalgam of social, familial, and psychological forces that play a part in the drug activity of the young person.

Perhaps the single most accurate criterion of what determines drug abuse is the attitude the individual has toward the drugs. If the drug experiences serve as an occasional social meeting ground, this is a far different situation from the one in which the drug has become a panacea that the young person cannot live without. If the addictive or nonaddictive substance becomes the central focus of the adolescent's existence—his raison d'être— the individual may clearly be said to be exhibiting signs of drug abuse.

> "The problem-drinking adolescent is likely to have a high absentee rate, may appear intoxicated in class, and will invariably fall behind in schoolwork."

Adolescent Alcohol Abuse

Beginning about 1972, alcohol began to emerge as the single most abused drug in the secondary schools. Several factors have been identified as responsible for this, including vigorous law enforcement efforts against marijuana use, easy accessibility of alcohol, and a subtle glorification of alcohol consumption by such charismatic musical celebrities as Alice Cooper and Janis Joplin, who were accompanied in public by their beer and Southern Comfort respectively. The same addictive personality traits that presage drug addiction resulted in the rise of alcohol addiction among high school youth as they nonchalantly experimented with "alcohol highs."

Although alcohol is legal and marijuana is not, one interesting study revealed parallels between antisocial patterns in abusers of alcohol and drugs. Globetti (1972) investigated problem high school drinkers in two small towns where alcohol was prohibited. He found that the alcohol abuser, like drug abusers, tended to have generally antisocial and mildly criminal characteristics, although this result may not be valid for communities where there are no restrictions on the sale and use of alcohol. Widseth (1972), in another study of high school abusers of alcohol, found that delinquent girls with drinking problems were dependent on their mothers and had not matured enough to break the powerful maternal bond.

The manifest symptoms of alcohol abuse among teenagers is as clear or more clear than the symptoms of drug abuse, which at times may be obscure. The problem-drinking adolescent is likely to have a high absentee rate, may appear intoxicated in class, and will invariably fall behind in schoolwork. It is not uncommon to find a flask of alcohol concealed on the person, and the student may even imbibe during the class itself—so strong is the drive, so weak the control The teacher, rather than responding punitively, might recognize the serious medical-psychological nature of this problem and should encourage the student to seek help.

Films and other presentations designed to lessen alcohol abuse among adolescents are available from The National Council on Alcoholism, Washington, D.C. Local school boards, particularly in enlightened areas, have also acquired resources for preventive education in this area. But most importantly, as in the case of drug abuse, the teacher's own awareness of and sensitivity to the existence of this problem is a critical factor in all preventive efforts.

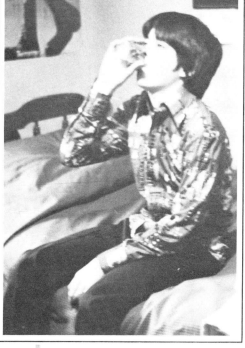

Drug and alcohol abuse can be public or private. Just as it is not uncommon to find drugs peddled in the school lunchroom or on the streets, it is not uncommon to find a junior high school student sneaking drinks in his room. Well-known youth culture personalities glorify drug and alcohol consumption.

The teacher might begin by exploring honestly his or her own feelings about drug use, about alcohol consumption, and about the adolescent "drug culture" in general. An empathic understanding of why many adolescents have the need to abuse drugs may then follow reflection and study. Kelly (1969) has referred to adolescents as a "suppressed minority group," which places them in the same untenable position as other minority groups—but without advocate spokesmen and without the sanctions of the larger, adult society.

A person undergoing such stresses as these is more likely than a mature person to rely on drugs for escape, for fantasy, for peer group approval and recognition. The escape value of these drugs lies in their potential for allowing one to forget one's problems and to seek refuge temporarily from the real world, and who needs this more than the conflict-torn, changing, disequilibrated adolescent. A fantasy world is set up, a world where the individual is freed of all responsibilities and where nothing is important, where there is no way to get hurt by others. It is a false, unrealistic world, but a world where the fragile young person is safe from the hurt and rejection he encounters in his daily living. It is imperative that the teacher—possibly from a different world and hopefully more mature, more "settled" than the adolescent student—understand the full, frightening, dynamic complexity and tumultuousness of this world.

For a time the drug problem was ignored because it was believed to be indigenous to the lower classes alone. The results of our tardy recognition are tragic. Gottlieb and Heinsohn (1971), in the introduction to their book on growing up poor in America, point out:

Long before middle-class youth showed signs of alienation and discontent there were, and still are, the White, Black, Chicano, Puerto Rican, Indian, rural, urban and poor youth who were angry, cold, sick, and hungry. Long before marijuana came to the suburbs, heroin was killing youth in the ghetto, yet we—those in power, those with the resources—gave these poor youth only passing consideration. . . . One result was that, when the opportunity arose to bring about some change in the status of poor youth, we were far from prepared. (p. vii)

We are still "far from prepared" to fully help youth who are abusing drugs. While it is generally agreed that the schools can assume a large burden of the drug education and addiction prevention programs, it is unclear what roles the teachers, counselors, administrators, and others should be specifically expected to play in this vital effort. Logically, there should be a coordination and integration between their functions that will enable the student to utilize maximally the range of resources available to him. Directing himself to how teachers and counselors can be helpful, Demos (1968) suggests:

Become more familiar with the subject matter . . . Be aware of the differences between narcotics and other drugs. Too frequently the terms are used interchangeably. There is no quicker way to lose a knowledgeable audience than

> "If the teacher was not brought up in a culture that exposed him to drug usage, it can be helpful for him to first embark on a program of drug education for himself."

to refer to LSD or marijuana as a narcotic. *Provide avenues for drug users and potential users to level with you with impunity.* Is there a place well-known to young people in your school and community where talk about drugs and drug usage is privileged communication? *Strive to be a better model.* Young people are searching for authentic models. . . . Let us influence the young by being authentic, open, trusting, and honest. . . . *Listen to the young.* What are they saying? Is there any validity to their charges? How viable are their dreams and aspirations? . . . *Offer youth accurate information.* . . . Inaccurate information widens the credibility gap between youth and the adult society.

If the teacher was not brought up in a culture that exposed him to drug usage, it can be helpful for him to first embark conscientiously and open-mindedly on a program of drug education for himself. Table 5.1 and displays 5.2 and 5.3 provide some information, for example. He might also attempt to understand the drug world from the students' own points of view—to see how they perceive different drugs and what these drugs mean to them in their world.

This understanding will be counterbalanced by the teacher's own rational understanding of the situation, based on research and experience—not on myths and wishful thinking, nor on social values and school-dictated sentiments. It is important, for example, that the teacher be able to approach sources of information objectively as well as know the law.

One effective gesture the teacher can make in dealing with this problem is to create a facilitative, joyous environment—what George B. Leonard (1968) calls a "climate of delight"—within the school. In many ways, widespread alienation and drug abuse may be signs of deficiencies within the school environment. "If the educator is to learn anything from the current striving for drug-induced perceptual, emotional, and cognitive changes," Cohen (1969) argues, "it is that important areas of human experience have been neglected by our child-rearing and child-teaching practices." Perhaps the teacher can do more to correct this problem, and to lessen the evils of drug abuse, than is generally realized.

The World of Work

An important area in the life of the adolescent, an area entwined with his life goals and plans for the future, is the world of work—and the possibilities and challenges that it offers. As the adolescent, particularly the late adolescent, looks ahead surveying the future of his life, work is likely to have a large place in it. While, traditionally, work and career were more associated with the boy's future plans, changing social roles and family expectations now give girls the same set of opportunities and expectations as well. In this section we shall examine aspects of the world of work that are relevant to the life of all adolescent students.

Career Choice Much has been written about what factors determine our career choices and which stages of life are critical to these choices. Many investigators (Roe, 1956, 1957) view the early childhood period and the relationship in the home as decisive factors. Other researchers (Holland, 1966) discuss broad personality characteristics as paramount factors in vocational choices. Ginzberg (1952, 1972), on the other hand, sees puberty and adolescence as critical times in career development. Let us look briefly at Ginzberg's theory.

Ginzberg divides this period into three stages. At about eleven years of age, the individual enters the *fantasy period*. During this stage, the pubescent translates his needs and impulses into occupational fantasies and expectations, without regard to a realistic assessment of capabilities and opportunities. Following this brief stage, between the ages of eleven and seventeen, is the *tentative period*. In this period, interests and capacities become relevant factors in selecting an occupation, although neither the interests nor the capacities are yet fully formulated. At about fifteen years, values become prime factors in specifying a tentative occupational choice. Finally, at about seventeen years, the adolescent enters what Ginzberg calls the *realistic period*. It is during this crucial period that choices are more critically and realistically arrived at.

This final stage—the realistic stage—comprises three parts: exploration, crystallization, and specification. In the explorative part, all of the job opportunities are investigated. Crystallization is the period in which the individual makes a general choice—such as, I want to go into the health professions. Finally, during the period of specification, the choice becomes specific—I want to become a physician, a nurse, an X-ray technician, and so forth.

Two important points emerge from Ginzberg's work. First, that the process of occupational choice occurs most dominantly during the periods of puberty and adolescence. While some theories emphasize early childhood determinants, Ginzberg places the greater emphasis on these critical years of puberty and adolescence. Second, that the process is not smooth and continuous; but it is a result of compromises, reverses, and self-reflection. It is a process that leads the individual from fantasied, unrealistic expectations of work to well-thought-out, realistic job choices. "Occupational choice," Ginzberg (1972) argues, "is a lifelong process of decision making in which the individual seeks to find the optimal fit between his career preparation and goals and the realities of the world of work." Much of this process occurs when the individual is a student in the junior or senior high school.

While Ginzberg's theory is generally helpful and relevant, it does not account for the special problems that are faced by the poor, the minorities, the culturally and socially disadvantaged. To many of the students in our schools there is no choice—because there are no jobs!

A Special Problem

The problem of unemployment among these youths is staggering. "Young people," Perella and Bogan (1968) point out, "are faced with the paradox of comparative prosperity overall and increasing difficulties for themselves in a labor market progressively and rapidly more selective under the impact of technological change. Jobs of the types which served as entering wedges for young workers are not increasing in proportion to the growing numbers competing for them" (p. 243). In some areas, unemployment rates for the young—and particularly, the minorities—are ten times the national average.

Part of the problem is in the environment in which the poor and disenfranchised grow up. They are not exposed during their formative years to the types of vocational role models that the middle-class youth is likely to see. Claude Brown, in *Manchild in the Promised Land* (1971), vividly describes the experience of growing up poor in Harlem. While social and economic factors do play a vital role in the exclusion of black youth from the labor market, psychological factors play an equally important part. In this area, the school can be of help.

Traditionally, the role of occupational counseling and facilitating career choice has been left to the school guidance counselor, and properly so. The counselor is equipped to deal with the myriad of problems that converge in efforts to help people make the appropriate choices and find the right job. Nevertheless, the teacher too can play a part in the total process.

What the School Can Do

The teacher can be facilitative in a number of ways. First, recognizing the importance of these years to ultimate vocational success or failure, to satisfaction or disenchantment, the teacher might attempt to integrate into the subject matter material that will prove relevant to the students' choices and that will prove helpful in decision making. For example, the teacher might do well to raise the aspirational level of girls and minority students, who suffer the most from poor role-modeling (Schlossberg & Pietrofesa, 1972). Utilizing Ginzberg's levels, the teacher will recognize the different needs of the eleven-year-old, the middle-adolescent, and the late-adolescent. The fantasies of the pubescent can be explored in the classroom, and the informational needs of the middle-adolescent can be provided for in the high schools. The school counselor is usually happy to provide the concerned teacher with technical assistance and other support services.

Second, and more importantly, the schools must provide the adolescent with the skills necessary for "making it" in this world. Perrone, Ryan, and Zeran (1970) discuss some of the responsibilities of the school in this area:

Vocational training in the secondary school may provide the foundations for adult vocational skills.

What effect does the school now have on the individual's career development? While the school helps the individual learn to use and develop the basic tools of communication and learn basic concepts which eventually may become relevant in on-the-job behavior, the public elementary and secondary schools have not been given the responsibility to prepare individuals for specific jobs. . . . The school does accept responsibility for helping each individual develop as far as possible various behaviors such as reading, writing, computation, verbalizing, and even interpersonal relations. Quite unintentionally the school accomplishes some unwanted outcomes. Individuals learn, after competing and losing, that some are better than others and that some cannot function in the school setting— as it exists. Those who learn this latter lesson must also accept the realization that their vocational aspirations must be curtailed by their educational expectations. . . . The school in effect serves as a funnel, but with the individual unfortunately coming out of the small end. (pp. 177–178)

It is this disastrous funneling effect that the teacher can help to prevent. By assuring that each student develops the skills, attitudes, and other requisites for functioning effectively in life, the teacher can reverse the flow in the funnel, pouring out more quality and substance than he was given at the beginning of the school year.

Finally, the teacher can familiarize students—particularly poor students who might have no other way of obtaining the information—with the full range of vocational opportunities. Recognizing that students cannot aspire to what they do not know exists, the teacher can acquaint them with the opportunities available so that they can not only hope for but strive for them as well.

The Life of the Learner

Studies of the Adolescent

Over the years, a number of psychologists, sociologists, and educators have directed attention to the adolescent period, attempting to make some order out of the many elements that are common to this stage. John E. Horrocks has written extensively on this subject since the early 1950s, synthesizing the results of many different studies in his textbooks on adolescent development and psychology. In the most recent edition, he cites six points of reference for viewing the adolescent:

1. Adolescence is a time when an individual becomes increasingly aware of self, endeavors to test his ramifying conceptions of self against reality, and gradually works toward the self-stabilization that will characterize his adult years. . . .

2. Adolescence is a time of seeking status as an individual. There is a tendency to attempt emancipation from childish submission to parental authority, and usually a struggle against relationships with adults in which the adolescent is subordinated. . . .

3. Adolescence is a time when group relationships become of major importance. . . . He tends to desire intensely to conform to the actions and standards of his peers. . . .

4. Adolescence is a time of physical development and growth that forms a continuous pattern common to the species, but idiosyncratic to the individual. . . . During this time physical maturity is attained.

5. Adolescence is a time of intellectual expansion and development, and academic experience. . . . He is asked to acquire many skills and concepts useful at some future time but often lacks immediate motivation. . . .

6. Adolescence tends to be a time of development and evaluation of values. The quest for the controlling values around which the individual may integrate his life is accompanied by the development of self-ideals and acceptance of self in harmony with those ideals. It is a time of conflict between youthful idealism and reality. (Horrocks, 1976, pp. 4–5)

These points are comprehensive enough to cover the range of studies on this subject. Moreover, they reflect the six key areas of investigation that have been of special interest to researchers in the area of adolescent psychology.

Studies of the adolescent fall into two general categories. One type of study is the empirical study, in which the researcher tests out some hypothesis on a sample of adolescents. The results of this kind of study are reported in their appropriate places throughout this chapter. The second type of study is a more in-depth, psychological study, usually of a psychoanalytic, or psychodynamic, nature. The chief studies of this second type will be presented in this section. We will examine some of the insights about adolescents found in the writings of Hall, Freud, Erikson, and Blos. It must be emphasized, however, that these studies reflect one particular perspective of the adolescent experience, and to some extent, adolescence is colored by the "lens" of the researcher.

G. Stanley Hall

One of the earliest and most comprehensive studies of the adolescent was conducted by G. Stanley Hall during the first decade of this century. Hall, who pioneered the child study movement in this country, believed that the objective, scientific study of the adolescent was a prerequisite to implementing meaningful curricula and to finding appropriate methodologies for the burgeoning public high schools across the country.

Hall's theory of individual development is based on Darwin's theories of evolution. He suggests in his writings that the development of the individual parallels in many ways the development of the entire species through its evolutionary history. The adolescent period, he argues, is distinct from childhood, paralleling the evolutionary period when man became a fully thinking creature.

Hall views adolescence as a period of rebirth, intellectually and socially, characterized by turmoil, confusion, and extreme stress. He describes in great detail the thinking and emotional make-up of adolescence. Hall's most important contribution to education is his principle that the adolescent should be treated more like an adult than a child, since he is more the adult of the future than the child of the past. Although this principle is hardly startling, it was somewhat revolutionary for his time.

Sigmund Freud

Freudian psychoanalysis, although it places primary emphasis on earlier periods of development (see chapters 1 to 3), offers some insights into the adolescent experience. In his paper, "The Development of the Libido and Sexual Organizations" (1935), Freud deals with the recrudescence of the Oedipal conflict during puberty. The purpose of this reappearance, Freud argues, is to help the person to free himself from the constraints of childhood.

From the time of puberty onward, the human individual must devote himself to the great task of *freeing himself from the parents;* and only after this detachment is accomplished can he cease to be a child, and so become a member of the social community. (p. 295)

Freud describes the psychosexual stage associated with puberty as the *genital stage.* It is during this period of life that adult heterosexuality ("primacy of the genital zones," in Freud's language) reaches full development.

But aside from these few comments, Freud's writings are not rich with insights about the adolescent.

Erikson, on the other hand, provides a rich and detailed description of the adolescent experience, viewing the search for identity as the major motivating and organizing principle. "It is in adolescence," Erikson (1968) argues, ". . . that the ideological structure of the environment becomes essential for the ego, because without an ideological simplification of the universe the adolescent ego cannot organize experience according to its specific capacities and its expanding involvement." The various components of this search for identity are explored throughout his writings, with specific emphasis placed on the relationship between identity, feelings of personal worth, and ego development. Whereas Freud looked at the development of the ego in terms of the early childhood relationship with the mother, Erikson takes a broader view, assessing the social forces at work during the adolescent years as significant factors.

Erik Erikson

In *Childhood and Society,* Erikson looks at adolescence as a period of identity versus role confusion and vividly describes some of the conflicts and characteristics of this period:

In their search for a new sense of continuity and sameness, adolescents have to refight many of the battles of earlier years, even though to do so they must artificially appoint perfectly well-meaning people to play the roles of adversaries; and they are ever ready to install lasting idols and ideals as guardians of a final identity. . . . The sense of ego identity, then, is the accrued confidence that the inner sameness and continuity prepared in the past are matched by the sameness and continuity of one's meaning for others, as evidenced in the tangible promise of a "career." (pp. 261–62)

He goes on, in this book and in his other writing, to explain how the adolescent embraces ideologies as a means of completing the development of his ego. "It is the ideological potential of a society," Erikson (1968) argues, "which speaks most clearly to the adolescent who is so eager to be affirmed by peers, to be confirmed by teachers, and to be inspired by worthwhile 'ways of life' " (p. 130).

Erikson's writings, perhaps more so than that of any other thinker, have a direct relevance for the classroom teacher. As the curriculum, subject matter, and classroom atmosphere become more conducive to the processes of identity formation, the adolescent student will be more inclined to find meanings in his life through the school situation. The relevance of the school, therefore, depends to a large part upon its ability to accommodate itself to the specific ego-forming needs of the adolescent.

Blos, another psychoanalytically oriented writer, sees adolescence as the second major effort in life to develop individuality. Blos (1967) explains his theory this way:

Peter Blos

I propose to view adolescence in its totality as the second individuation process, the first one having been completed toward the end of the third year of life with the attainment of object constancy. Both periods have in common a heightened vulnerability of the personality organization. Both periods have in common the urgency for changes in psychic structure in consonance with the maturational forward surge. Last but not least, both periods—should they miscarry—are followed by a specific deviant development. . . . What is in infancy a "hatching from the symbiotic membrane to become an individualized toddler" (Mahler 1963), becomes in adolescence the shedding of family dependencies, the loosening of infantile object ties in order to become a member of society at large, or simply, the adult world. . . . (p. 163)

As a second rebirth, adolescence offers both opportunities and dangers. The trauma of our first birth must necessarily be repeated; but so too will be the valuable periods—surges—of growth and change. All of this, the achievements and the obstacles, will be apparent in the classroom where the teacher must deal with them.

Current Perspectives: The Adolescent in the 1970s

Recent research, while it has not radically altered any of the more traditional approaches to adolescence, keeps us abreast of the changing values and perceptions of the youth culture. While some of these changes are superficial and others more fundamental, they are all relevant to the "here-and-now" reality of the classroom.

A number of recent youth surveys, beginning with Sabine's (1971) YOUTHPOLL, indicate that adolescents are becoming increasingly concerned about their own economic success. This produces a more personal goal-oriented type of thinking, somewhat away from the political-social emphasis of the 1960s youth. Moreover, while premarital cohabitation is gaining wider acceptance among young people, the tendency to plan to marry and to envision a family as a part of one's future is on the rise with adolescents (Sabine, 1971).

The widespread drug use of the 1960s has led to a spate of research findings in the 1970s. Pittel et al. (1971), in an in-depth study of the Haight-Ashbury hippies of the 60s, found that drug abusers were likely to come from environments where "they have been subjected to a series of familial or other pressures, often of a traumatic nature, which have created for them a world of chaos and confusion from which they could find no respite. The psychological consequences of these childhood events frequently become intensified in early adolescence, and it is then that many of them suffer most acutely from their isolation and sense of separateness" (p. 655). While the social manifestations of such conflicts change from season to season, the underlying conflict of isolation and loneliness remains a constant part of many adolescents' experiences.

"The invisible children"—those who are not enrolled in schools and never appear in educational data—have become a source of study recently (Children's Defense Fund, 1974). It is estimated that 20 percent of the adolescent population throughout the country are not enrolled in schools. It is often difficult to locate this invisible segment of society and therefore difficult to study them, but efforts are currently underway to examine the factors that lead to a person either dropping out of, or not enrolling in, secondary school.

Adolescent alcoholism is on the rise in the 1970s as the use of other drugs declines. Programs have been instituted in a number of large cities to curb this spreading problem, and the National Science Foundation has sponsored a number of research projects to determine the causes and appropriate treatment of adolescent alcoholism. At a recent meeting of the National Education Association (1974), a number of prominent educators agreed that the schools would soon be taking an active role in alcohol prevention programs.

Conclusions and Implications

Several questions now come to mind. Does the period of adolescence really have innate characteristics, or is it, like adulthood, a period so different for all people that it cannot be described through generalizations? Probably the answer is between yes and no, and each teacher will come to his or her own conclusions. As the teacher does so, he will inevitably formulate his own theory of adolescence.

Another question of importance is, What can the teacher—and the school—do to facilitate growth during the adolescent years? This question breaks down into several parts. First, we want to know how influential the teacher is in the adolescent's life. This will certainly vary from teacher to teacher, and from student to student. Each teacher might want to consider how he or she can become a positive influence in the student's life. Second, in what areas can this influence make itself felt? In the preventive area, the teacher will want to see that the student has available all the tools—intellectual, social, and emotional—to deal with common problems, such as drug abuse and early dating and socialization patterns. The teacher may be helpful too in assisting the adolescent to learn to accept his or her sex role and, at the same time, to gain acceptance and respect from the opposite sex. Emotional education can also take place in the classroom as the teacher endeavors to allow the adolescent to express troubling—(or confusing)—feelings.

In short, the quest for independence and individuality, so much a part of the adolescent experience, can be helped immensely by a teacher who is willing to provide the cognitive tools through subject matter and method and the emotional tools through class discussion and personal involvement.

Summary

In this chapter we have looked at some of the difficulties and developmental variables of the adolescent period. We have examined ways in which the value structure of the adolescent is developed and modified, and considered some particular values, such as those relating to dating and sexual behavior. We have also looked briefly at the drug problem, so prevalent in the schools today, and considered the adolescent as he confronts the world of work. Finally, we saw a representative sample of theories of adolescence and some modern perspectives.

Suggested Additional Readings

The Therapeutic Classroom by Monica Holmes, Douglas Holmes and Judith Field (*New York: Jason Aronson, 1974*)

An unusual book that describes a therapeutic classroom environment that was used to help six angry, practically illiterate ninth graders. The authors show how to combine therapy with teaching, particularly in dealing with the underprivileged adolescent youngster. An in-classroom mental health team, in conjunction with a teacher, can, as the book demonstrates, make remarkable gains with seemingly intransigent adolescents.

Developing relationships was a day-to-day, minute-to-minute process that went on continuously throughout the year on the several fronts where we were meeting the students' needs.

from *The Therapeutic Classroom*

Scoring by Dan Greenburg (*New York: Dell Publishing Co., 1973*)

Times have changed—to be sure—but many of the sexual hang-ups that the adolescent boy has to conquer have not, and this memoir is a riotously funny recollection of the adolescent period, with all of its confusion. The title refers to "making points" with girls.

If I had been a really good-looking kid, I would have been popular with my classmates, I would have been smooth with the girls, I would have started scoring at about age fourteen, I would have been a big fraternity guy in college, and I would have wound up selling Oldsmobiles...

from *Scoring*

Counseling for Career Development by E. L. Tolbert (*Boston: Houghton Mifflin, Co., 1974*)

This is a comprehensive overview of theories of career development and ways of helping adolescents make career choices. All of the major theories are covered, along with some interesting research on decision making. The book will be especially helpful for the secondary school teacher who recognizes the importance of the world in the life of the adolescent.

The choice of work is one of the most important decisions one makes. It determines, to a large extent, how time will be spent, who will be chosen as friends, what attitudes and values will be adopted, where one will reside, and what pattern of family living will be adopted. The job provides an identity for the individual.

from *Counseling for Career Development*

Richie: The Ultimate Tragedy Between One Decent Man and the Son He Loved by Thomas Thompson (*Bantam Books, paperback, 1975*)

A touching, poignant account of Richard Diener, a high school student who was killed by his father—a "decent man." The breakdown of the family structure, because of drug abuse and other adolescent problems, is shown in painful detail. This book is powerful!

"Richard's New Year's Eve 'Pot Party' fell through," wrote George in his December 30, 1971, entry of the log. In celebration of Christmas, perhaps, he had taken the tap off the telephone. . . .

from *Richie*

Part 2

Hear my words that I might
    teach you,
Take my arms that I might
    reach you.

Paul Simon, ''The Sounds
of Silence''

The Psychology of Learning

It is not possible to speak of education, or of teaching, without understanding the processes of learning. When we think of learning we tend to think of one type of learning—cognitive learning—but actually there are many different types. Not only are there different types of learning, but the term itself has many different definitions, reflecting the diversity of approaches. All types of learning, all approaches, all theories, all processes come together in a single physical organism—that of the learner—and we know from the preceding section how complex an organism the learner is. It will be the purpose of Part Two of this book to examine learning in its totality so that we can come to grips with such issues as: How and why does the person learn? What types of things are learned? What are the relationships between different types of learning? How can learning be most successful? While we will direct attention to the specifics of these questions, our approach will be holistic, and by the completion of Part Two, the reader should have a pretty clear idea about the relationship of learning to teaching and a good understanding of the processes of learning in human activity.

Before we can understand the processes of learning, we should consider *why* people learn. Theories that attempt to answer this "why" question are called motivational theories. An understanding of the organism's incentive to learn is integral to understanding the processes of learning. **Motivation** cannot be considered in vacuo, for, in practice, motivation is intricately entwined with the processes of learning. A theory of learning is designed to account for the relationships between motivation and learning processes and to provide an integrative perspective in all the mechanics of learning. In chapter 6, "Theories of Learning and Motivation," we will explore the purposes of a learning theory and then look in some detail at the major contemporary theories. Since the purpose of a learning theory, at least to us, is to help us understand ways in which learning can be facilitated, the implications of these theories for teaching will be considered throughout.

As we mentioned earlier, learning is not limited to cognitive learning but includes many different types of learning. In fact, each of the psychological positions we have been using throughout this book— psychoanalysis, humanism, behavioral psychology—has direct and indirect applications to learning theories. Moreover, since the growth of the learner, as it was presented in Part One, consists mostly of learned behavior, we will certainly be interested in how the learner acquires these growth patterns, how he develops new behaviors. We have used the traditional trichotomy of learning domains—the *affective, cognitive,* and *psychomotor* domains— to break down and analyze the totality of processes. In this way, we can understand how the learner learns his subjective, personal, emotional world (the affective domain), how he learns objective, factual, subject matter (the cognitive domain), and how he learns to navigate the world physically (the psychomotor domain).

It should be emphasized that these domains of learning are not independent of each other but are connected in a number of ways at several different points. The implications of the psychological positions infuse all the domains, but psychoanalysis and humanism are especially germane to the affective domain. In chapter 7, "Conditions and Processes of Affective Learning," we will explore ways in which the learner masters emotional, interpersonal, moral, and other subjective types of learning. In chapter 8, "Conditions and Processes of Cognitive Learning," we will concentrate more on factual, subject-matter types of learning. In chapter 9, "Conditions and Processes of Psychomotor Learning," we will focus almost exclusively on physical learning tasks. In all three chapters, however, we will attempt to keep our perspective of the learner as a total person, whose integral, synthetic point of reference toward the world combines subjective, objective, and physical perceptions and behaviors.

One last point deserves mention. We use the word *conditions* in the title of each chapter, in addition to the word *processes*. This reflects our bias toward the educational perspective. For when we speak of the *conditions of learning,* we refer to the environmental, physical, intellectual, social, and related variables that affect directly or indirectly the processes of learning. It is the ability to control these conditions that makes effective teaching possible. While we will restrict our discussion in this part of the book to an overview of the conditions of learning, in Part Three, "Teaching: Art and Science," we will explore in detail the ways in which conditions are designed to affect learning output maximally.

With these ideas in mind, let us begin our venture into understanding the theories of learning and motivation.

What Is Learning?

Several definitions of learning are offered. Learning can be defined as "the process by which an activity originates or is changed through reacting to an encountered situation, provided that the characteristics of the change in activity cannot be explained on the basis of native response tendencies, maturation, or temporary states of the organism" (Hilgard & Bower, 1966). This is one broad definition, but other definitions, both narrow and broad in scope, are also offered.

What Is a Theory?

The purpose of a learning theory is to predict and explain the relationship between learning conditions and learning outcomes.

Contemporary Theories of Learning

Five basic theories are presented. From the traditional orientation, the learner is endowed with natural tendencies to relate actively to the environment. Behaviorism and neobehaviorism are closely related theories based on the assumption that one's behavior results from one's experiences or situational conditions. The cognitive-field theory relates behavior to thought processes, and defines learning in terms of changes that occur in one's organization of knowledge and uses of problem-solving strategies. The humanistic theories emphasize the learner's innate mechanisms of self-development and self-actualization.

Implications of Theories for Teaching-Learning Processes

From a traditional viewpoint, readiness is an undesirable characteristic of the learner. The behaviorist and neobehaviorist view readiness as any other behavior. From a cognitive viewpoint, the task and method must be adapted to the readiness of the learner. Basic assumptions of the humanistic positions are that the learner is the best judge of what his developmental and momentary needs are.

Continued

6 Theories of Learning and Motivation

Answers to Teachers' Questions

The following questions are answered in accordance with the five positions: Why is a particular topic so difficult for students to learn? Why do some students learn better under one method than another? Why aren't the students interested in learning the goals of a unit that the teacher considers important?

What Is Instructional Theory?

The goal of instructional theory is to identify the most effective conditions of learning for particular kinds of educational goals for particular kinds of learners. Instructional theory is a broad generic term that includes all important aspects of the classroom learning environment.

Instructional Objectives

Instructional objectives are statements of educational goals. Essentially, the question is, What instructional procedures are most likely to optimally develop student learning for particular objectives and for particular learners in relation to performance outcomes?

Entry Behavior

Entry behavior refers to the readiness of the learner for educational experiences. Learner readiness includes affective, cognitive, and psychomotor characteristics.

Instructional Procedures

Instructional procedures are the methods used by teachers. They include lecture, demonstration, discussion, audiovisuals, and so on.

Performance Assessment

Performance assessment refers to the evaluation of learning outcomes after instructional objectives, entry behavior, and instructional procedures have all been investigated.

"There are two critical conditions of learning: characteristics of the learner and characteristics of the situation in which learning occurs."

The learner is the most important part of education. While the teacher and the student are mutually responsible for achieving the goals of the school curriculum, it is the student who must do the learning. Consequently, educational psychologists through the years have shown vast interest in understanding how **learning** occurs and in studying the effects of different **conditions** of learning on student achievement.

There are two critical conditions of learning: characteristics of the learner and characteristics of the situation in which learning occurs. These conditions make it either easier or more difficult to attain goals from learning experiences. Since the primary function of teachers is to arrange situational conditions—which include teachers themselves—to help students learn, it is not surprising that they frequently seek answers to questions about learning. Why is a particular topic so difficult for students to learn? Why do some students learn better under one method than under another? Why aren't the students interested in achieving the goals of a unit that the teacher considers important? You can find explanations to these and many other such questions through a study of learning theories. An understanding of learning theories can also enable you to find solutions to problems related to the effectiveness and ineffectiveness of learning conditions on student achievement outcomes.

What Is Learning?

We usually think of learning as the **acquisition** of new knowledge. But this is a very limited definition because a person also acquires new attitudes, new skills, and new ways to use previously learned attitudes, knowledge, and skills. Unless learning is more adequately defined, it can be easily confused with other phenomena such as **maturation** and **performance.** It will be necessary, then, for us to define what learning is and what learning is not if we are to understand this concept.

There are several factors that must be considered in defining and measuring learning. First, a distinction must be made between learning, maturation, and performance. Learning implies a change in the individual as a result of some intervention. It may be viewed as an outcome or as a process. When we view learning as an outcome, we pay attention to its external

> "A definition of learning referring to knowledge acquisition would be of narrow scope while one referring to the acquisition of knowledge, attitudes, and skills would be of broad scope."

manifestations. "John has *learned* to speak French," or "Mary has *learned* to drive a car." On the other hand, when learning is viewed as a process, as an internal change within the learner, we infer what is learned by translating process into performance—an outcome. When the teacher administers an exam that requires the students to think out problems—to "use their minds" —what the teacher is doing is making the students translate what they have learned into a measurable performance.

All performance, however, is not a result of learning. Some is the result of growth, or maturation. In reality, it may not be possible to separate the parts of an outcome into what is the result of learning and what is the result of maturation. For example, a certain maturational level is necessary before the child can learn a language, but once that maturational level is reached, it is necessary to teach the language to the child. Thus, the readiness to learn may be more determined by maturation as are the capacities for learning (processes), but the contents of learning (outcomes) are entirely dependent upon the uses to which these processes are put.

Second, the definer's basic orientation as to the relationship between the learner and the situation must be considered. These basic orientations are that the learner is the critical condition, the situation is the critical condition, and an interaction between the learner and the situation is the critical condition. If it is assumed that the learner is the critical condition in learning processes and outcomes, it is necessary to give only limited consideration to situational conditions. On the other hand, if situational conditions are perceived to play a paramount role in learning processes and outcomes, primary consideration should be placed on the situation.

Third, the scope of the outcomes must be considered. If learning were the acquisition of knowledge only, acquisition of attitudes and skills could be excluded. A definition of learning referring to knowledge acquisition only would be of narrow scope while one referring to the acquisition of knowledge, attitudes, and skills would be of broad scope.

Finally, the nature of the processes must be considered. If learning were the acquisition of outcomes only, the **retention** and **transfer** of previously learned outcomes could be excluded. A definition of learning referring to the acquisition process only would be a simple view of learning while one referring to acquisition, retention, and transfer processes would be a complex view of learning.

Table 6.1 *Processes, Conditions, and Outcomes of Learning*

Processes	Conditions		Outcomes
	Learner	*Situation*	
Learning	Abilities	Goals	Affective
Acquisition	Motivation	Sequence	
Retention	Learning style	Structure	Cognitive
Transfer		Practice	
		Reinforcement	Psychomotor
Maturation		Cognitive feedback	
Performance			

A summary of the factors that must be dealt with in defining learning is presented in table 6.1. Examples of the various factors of learning are given so that you may effectively conceptualize the diverse ways in which theorists have defined learning. Definitions of learning reflect the orientation of the theorist. Let us look at definitions of learning from several alternative viewpoints.

Hilgard and Bower (1966, p. 4) define learning as "the process by which an activity originates or is changed through reacting to an encountered situation, provided that the characteristics of the change in activity cannot be explained on the basis of native response tendencies, maturation, or temporary states of the organism." This definition, broad in scope, has a complex view of learning, has a situational condition orientation, and makes distinctions between learning, performance, and maturation. The term *organism,* used in this definition, is often used by theorists to refer to the learner.

Travers (1972, p. 8) states that "learning occurs when a response shows relatively permanent modification as a result of conditions in the environment." Whereas Hilgard and Bower make a distinction between learning as a process and performance as an outcome, Travers considers learning to be an outcome only. That is, change in the activity of the learner is exactly equal to what has been learned. This definition emphasizes situational conditions.

Garry and Kingsley (1970, p. 8) define learning as "the process by which an organism in satisfying its motivation adapts or adjusts its behavior in order to reach a goal." The learner condition is emphasized in this definition. The definition considers learning to be a process rather than an outcome.

The final definition has been given by Ausubel (1968, p. 24). Ausubel states, "learning is the long term acquisition of stable bodies of knowledge and of the capacity needed for acquiring such knowledge." This definition is of narrow scope but does provide for complex processes. The primary emphasis is on the learner condition.

> "The purpose of learning theory is to predict and explain the relationship between learning conditions and learning outcomes."

Since our purpose in this chapter is to consider diverse theoretical views of learning and to consider alternative conditions for many kinds of learning, we will regard each of these definitions as meaningful statements and will not attempt to define learning in still another way. As these definitions were selected on the basis of their being consistent with one of the learning theories to be considered later in this chapter, we shall return to them again.

What Is a Theory?

We sometimes think of a **theory** as a hunch that has no factual basis. In the area of learning, however, this is not at all how a theory is defined. Rather, a learning theory is defined as a set of interrelated principles that present a systematic view of learning based on empirical relations among variables. The purpose of a learning theory is to predict and explain the relationship between learning conditions and learning outcomes. Learning conditions are referred to as **independent variables** and learning outcomes as **dependent variables.** We alter an independent variable to see what the effect is on a dependent variable.

The relationship between theory and fact is given schematically in figure 6.1. Learning phenomena are studied either through direct observation or through instrumentation, such as an exam. The degree of relationship between independent and dependent variables is determined. The relationship that is found is called a fact regardless of the probability of the variables occurring together. The results of any one test of the relationship between independent

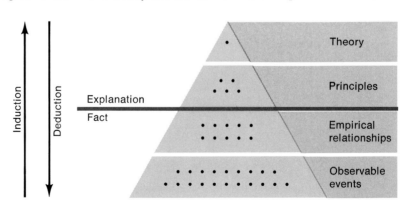

Figure 6.1 The Relationship Between Explanation and Fact. From *Child Psychology, Growth Trends in Psychological Adjustment* by George Thompson (Boston: Houghton Mifflin, 1962). Adapted from display on p. 10, with permission.

The Psychology of Learning

and dependent variables would be accepted as a fact, but not as truth—or Fact with a capital F. Truth, or high probability of certain relationships, is based on replication of results. Replication of results is important in two ways. First, it is important to be able to replicate the relationships under similar conditions again. Second, it is important to determine the range of situations in which the relationships hold up.

A principle is an explanation of a replicated empirical relationship between two concepts that best fits the data. An integrated explanation of two or more principles is called a theory.

There are two systematic approaches to the explanation of facts. In the first approach, one can hypothesize relationships that might be expected among observable events, based on an understanding of previous explanations and facts, and then test the hypothesis by studying the degree of relationship between the variables of concern. This is called a **deductive approach** in that the logic of the approach proceeds from the general to the specific.

The second approach is to raise a hypothesis about observable events and after studying the empirical data, explain the relationships. This is called an **inductive approach** in that its logic proceeds from the specific to the general.

While systematic learning theorists favor one approach or the other, the combination of approaches favored by many theorists has resulted in a vast accumulation of knowledge related to the relationships between learning conditions and learning outcomes. Just as science is based on replication, however, it is also based on the spirit of inquiry. Hence, explanations of learning phenomena are subject to modification as new facts are gathered.

There are two other orientations to the study of learning besides the systematic approaches. One approach, **functionalism,** is concerned with the usefulness of the empirical facts rather than with the explanation of them. The second approach, **eclecticism,** is concerned with the utility of the explanations given from different theoretical orientations rather than being restricted to just one systematic theory.

When the complexity of conditions, processes, and outcomes of learning experiences are considered, it is not surprising that most users of the knowledge of learning tend to adopt either eclecticism or functionalism. However, there are some cautions that should be observed. First, it is important for the eclecticist to understand each of the systematic positions so that alternative explanations are available. Second, the eclecticist or functionalist has to weigh and evaluate the many facts that have accumulated about learning phenomena if his approach is to be practical and useful, rather than confusing. Finally, both the eclecticist and the functionalist must be willing to view the learner in his totality, as a unique individual rather than as a predictable respondent to clearly defined laws and principles.

Table 6.2 Basic Orientations and Implications of Learning Theories for Education

Theory of Learning	Learner-Situation Emphasis		Nature of Learning Process and Conditions		
	Notation	Direction	Acquisition	Retention	Transfer
Traditionalism	O-R-s$_p$	Active	Rote memory of facts	None	Formal discipline
Behaviorism	s-R-S$_r$	Passive	New behavior through contingency of R-S associations	Reinforcement and extinction of R-S associations	Identical elements
Neobehaviorism	S-o-R-s$_r$	Reactive	New behavior through contiguity of S-R associations	Overlearning and interference of S-R associations	Similar elements
Cognitivism	s-O-s$_f$-r	Interactive	Restructure of knowledge	Internal organization and distortion	Restructure of knowledge
Humanism	O	Proactive	Built-in process	None	None

Contemporary Theories of Learning

Five diverse contemporary theories of learning are presented in table 6.2. These theories, which include the essential characteristics of a wide spectrum of learning theories, are **traditionalism, behaviorism, neobehaviorism, cognitivism,** and **humanism.** The underlying assumption of the information given in this table is that learning events involve three elements: situation, internal processes, and observable performance. In the notation under learner-situation emphasis, S means **stimulus,** stimuli, situation or environment; O means organism or learner; and R means **response,** behavior or performance. As these elements can be on a general or a specific level, the symbols can stand for different levels of complexity.

A large letter for S, O, or R indicates that the element is given major consideration. A small letter for s, o, or r indicates that the element is given minor consideration in the theory. If the letter is absent, it means that the element is not a part of the theory. Direction under learner-situation emphasis refers to assumptions made about the relative contribution of the learner and the situation as influences on the learning outcomes. The subscripts p, r, and f stand for punishment, reinforcement, and feedback respectively.

Traditional Theory Let us consider the basic orientation of each theory and then we shall compare their implications for education. The traditional theory represents a col-

Motivation to Learn	Nature of Readiness	Nature of Goals	Nature of Outcomes
Fear of consequences	Planned learner unreadiness	Assumed that learner is to learn as many facts as possible	Reproduction of as many facts as possible
Obtainment of reinforcers	Readiness is a learned behavior	Clearly specified behavioral objectives	Performance of behaviors in a natural setting
Confirmation of expectancies	Readiness is a learned behavior	Identification of learning objectives	Performance of learning in a realistic setting
Need to know and understand	Modify situation to learner	Learning process objectives	Production of solutions to new problems
Self-actualization	Let learner decide own readiness	Student-determined objectives	Student-determined experience

lection of principles and assumptions of learning that have been passed down through the years. This theory serves as a straw man with which to compare other theories. However, it may also be a popular theory today. Weber found this theory to be most popular among teachers as late as 1965. The results of Weber's study are presented in table 6.3.

Table 6.3   How Do Students Learn?

Rank	Learning Condition	*Percentage of Responses
1	Drill and repetition	47
2	Imitation of others	38
3	Do not know, had not thought about it	33
4	Hard work	26
5	Following directions of teachers	21
6	Trial and error	17
7	Maturation	12
8	Miscellaneous	7

From "Do Teachers Understand Learning Theory?" by C. A. Weber, *Phi Delta Kappan,* 1965, *46,* p. 434. Reprinted by permission.

* Respondents could give multiple responses to the question, How, in your opinion, do children learn?

> "Viewed from the traditional orientation, the learner is endowed with natural tendencies to relate actively to the environment. Unfortunately, with the advancement of civilization, these natural tendencies are often undesirable responses."

Viewed from the traditional orientation, the learner is endowed with natural tendencies to relate actively to the environment. Unfortunately, with the advancement of civilization, these natural tendencies are often undesirable responses. Hence, these behaviors must be curbed and replaced with knowledge behaviors that are desirable in today's society. Through rote memorization of vast amounts of information, the learner acquires self-control and **mental discipline.** Retention is improved through the use of the **memory faculty;** lack of retention occurs through not using the memory faculty. Nothing is forgotten, but something can't be remembered if it was never acquired. Transfer of knowledge occurs automatically.

When a learner's natural ways of relating to his experiences are undesirable, **motivation** must be imposed from an external source. Fear is the motivation to learn; that is, the pain principle is the basis of motivation. This might be considered an $O-R-s_p$ approach in that no use is made of prior situational conditions that might enable the learner to accomplish the desired goal, while major consideration is given to the importance of the learner's predisposition, his response, and the post-situational condition of punishment (s_p).

Due to the vastness of information needed for the learner to achieve mental discipline, our first definition of learning would be a satisfactory one for this traditional theory: *Learning is the acquisition of knowledge.*

Behaviorism and Neobehaviorism

The second and third theories, behaviorism and neobehaviorism, are both a part of what is known as the behavioristic family of learning theories. Associationistic, conditioning, behavioral, stimulus-response, or simply S-R, are labels that have been given to these theories. The underlying assumption of these theories is that one's behavior results from one's experiences or situational conditions.

Behaviorism refers to a theory that does not consider internal processes of the learner and that does not distinguish between learning and performance. In recent years, behaviorism has been used as a label for a collection of similar orientations—operant conditioning, instrumental conditioning, and behavior modification.

Neobehaviorism, on the other hand, refers to new behaviorism in the sense that learning is distinguished from performance and provisions are made for learner processes as **intervening variables** between learning condi-

> "When a behavior is reinforced, the probability of its reoccurrence is increased. When a behavior is not reinforced, the probability of its reoccurrence is decreased."

tions and outcomes. There is only one other major difference between these two orientations: **Reinforcement** is the *only* situational condition in behaviorism but it is merely one situational condition in neobehaviorism. The situational conditions prior to the response are always important in neobehaviorism, while these conditions are only important sometimes in behaviorism.

From a behavioral position, situational conditions are the only variables that are used to explain learning. The learner is assumed to be passive in the sense that the learner is the product of his experience. The basic notation for behaviorism is $R-S_r$. The particular situational variable that is instrumental in producing the behavior of the learner is the reinforcing stimulus (S_r) that occurs after a response.

Since some simple responses will not be made by a learner without minimal cues in the environment and some complex behavior will not be made by the learner without maximal cues in the environment, it is necessary to introduce a prior situational condition into the notation, that is, $s-R-S_r$, to account for some behavior. When a learner makes a response with no known prior situational condition, the behavior is referred to as an operant. If a prior situational condition is known, the resultant behavior is called a **respondent.** A special instance of behaviorism is when the behavior is so complex that several responses are required for a learner to perform the behavior. In this case, **shaping** is the concept used to refer to the learning conditions.

When a behavior is reinforced, the probability of its reoccurrence is increased. When a behavior is not reinforced, the probability of its reoccurrence is decreased. Absence of reinforcement will eventually extinguish a behavior. In addition, immediate reinforcement is more likely than delayed reinforcement to increase the probability of a behavior reoccurring. Acquisition and retention of behavior are based on reinforcement. To acquire new behavior, continuous reinforcement is required when the appropriate response is made for the most efficient and effective outcomes. If shaping is required to elicit the new behavior, then appropriate partial responses or **successive approximations** of the complete behavior must be continuously reinforced until the complete behavior is performed. When the complete behavior can be **emitted,** then it operates like any other behavior.

Behavior that has been acquired through intermittent reinforcement is more resistant to extinction than behavior acquired through continuous rein-

Figure 6.2 Effects of Enforced and Withdrawn Post-Situational Conditions. From "A Taxonomy of Instrumental Conditioning" by Paul J. Woods, *American Psychologist,* 1974, *29 (8),* p. 585. Copyright © 1974 American Psychological Association. Adapted and used with permission.

		Enforcement of condition	Withdrawal of condition
Condition	Positive or desirable	Positive reinforcement (reward)	Penalty
	Negative or aversive	Punishment	Negative reinforcement (relief)

forcement. There is no basis for transfer in the behaviorism theory since transfer, as usually defined, involves internal processes. However, transfer-like behaviors can be acquired through the same conditions as any other behavior.

Motivation is also interpreted as a situational condition, reinforcing stimulus. Of course, what is reinforcing to a learner depends upon the particular person. That is, not only do one's experiences determine a person's behavior but they also determine the particular reinforcers that will control one's behavior. While **punishment** (aversive stimuli) can suppress one's behavior, it does not extinguish it. The reinforcement (negative) that results from the termination of punishment directs the learner to the aversive stimuli rather than to the response that preceded the aversive stimuli. The effects of punishment on a person's future behavior is unpredictable. However, mild aversive stimuli can be used in an immediate situation to suppress an undesirable behavior until a desirable one can be performed and reinforced. The effects of these reciprocal conditions are presented in figure 6.2.

The best known contributor to this theory today is B. F. Skinner. Actually, Skinner does not call behaviorism a theory; rather, he refers to his position as a descriptive functional analysis of behavior. Skinner's primary reason for choosing not to call his system a theory is that he has tried to define terms and explain his results precisely. Theoretical explanations are inferences that may distort facts as they are generalities based on the relationships between two or more principles. Skinner is interested in being able to predict phenomena, not to explain them.

Other well-known proponents of this orientation are Donald Baer, Sidney Bijou, Leonard Krasner, John Krumboltz, Murray Sidman, J. M. Stephens, and Leonard Ullmann.

The definition given by Travers (1972) is an appropriate one for contemporary behaviorism: *Learning occurs when a response shows relatively permanent modification as a result of conditions in the environment.*

Neobehaviorism places primary emphasis upon associations between S and R rather than on the associations between R and S_r. The occurrence of S and R at approximately the same time in a situation is called contiguous

The Psychology of Learning

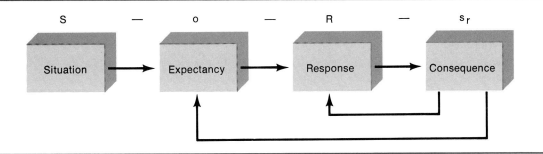

S — o — R — s_r

| Situation | Expectancy | Response | Consequence |

Figure 6.3 Relationships Among Elements of Neo-behavioral Notation

conditioning. In neobehaviorism, reinforcing stimuli serve the purpose of confirming the expectancies of the learner in relation to an anticipated goal. The relationship among the various elements of the theory is given in figure 6.3.

The only condition required for learning is the contiguity of S and R. Performance requires reinforcement, however, if a person's observable behavior is to be an accurate estimate of what has been learned. Unless optimal incentives are present in the situation (or optimal expectancies in the learner), one's performance will be a low estimate of what has been learned. The relationship between level of arousal and performance are represented in figure 6.4. Arousal level is equivalent to the degree of motivation. As arousal level increases, so does anxiety. When one's arousal level is high, a person may be described as anxious.

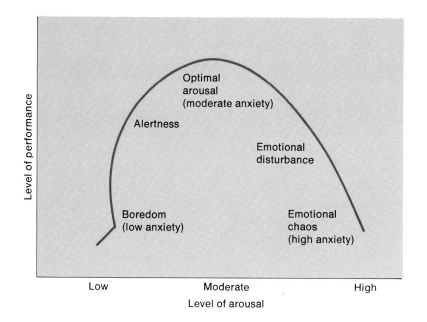

Figure 6.4 The Relationship Between Level of Arousal and Performance. From *A Textbook of Psychology*, 3rd ed., by Donald O. Hebb (Philadelphia: W. B. Saunders Company, 1972). Adapted with permission from display on p. 199.

The primary condition for the acquisition of new behavior and, subsequently, learning is reinforced practice of S-R associations. Reinforcement is required because effective performance increases learning. Overlearning of the associations are important in minimizing forgetting that occurs through interference with similar stimuli and responses in the environment. Transfer of a response occurs if the stimuli are similar in a new situation. Transfer is accomplished by the learner through the processes of generalization and discrimination of stimuli and responses.

The basis of motivation is the expectation that a goal will be obtained. Confirmed expectatives are also acquired, retained, and transferred as any other behavior. Through the learning of the probabilities of certain goal expectancies, a person reacts accordingly to experiences that are in his future.

Albert Bandura, Robert Gagné, Donald Hebb, Neal Miller, Robert Sears, and Arthur Staats are well-known proponents of neobehaviorism. The definition given by Hilgard and Bower (1966) is quite adequate for this theory: *Learning is the process by which an activity originates or is changed through reacting to an encountered situation, provided that the characteristics of the change in activity cannot be explained on the basis of native response tendencies, maturation, or temporary states of the organism.*

Cognitivism   The fourth theory, cognitivism, is sometimes referred to as cognitive-field, field, or gestalt theory. At one time, cognitive theory was concerned with the general nature of perception and thinking. Through the course of time, situational conditions as well as the relationship between thinking and observable performance have been incorporated into the theory.

The word *cognitive* means *to know*. The focus of cognitivism is on the individual's thinking processes; on the ways in which the individual comes to know something. Consequently, from the cognitive perspective, learning is examined in terms of the processes within the person. For example, a cognitivist would be extremely interested in studying the different ways in which people can arrive at the same conclusions. To the cognitivist, unlike the behaviorist, it is not the observable behavior that is of paramount importance—not the conclusion (outcome) itself, but rather the mental processes that lead to that conclusion. Cognitivists recognize, however, that the person's observable performance is a useful clue to the person's internal organization and use of knowledge.

The introduction of a feedback loop (s_f) indicates that cognitivism has become an interaction theory insofar as the relationship between the learner and the situation are concerned. From this viewpoint, thinking precedes learning. When a cognitivist is speaking of the learner as active, he is referring to the learner thinking rather than doing. The learner is active in the sense

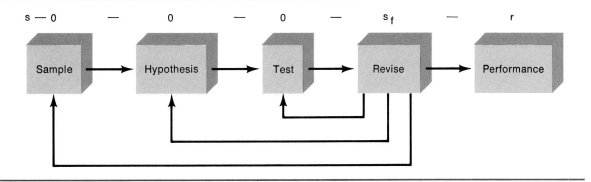

$$s - 0 \quad - \quad 0 \quad - \quad 0 \quad - \quad s_f \quad - \quad r$$

| Sample | Hypothesis | Test | Revise | Performance |

Figure 6.5 Relationships Among Elements of Basic Cognitive Notation

that he samples situations, constructs hypotheses, tests them out, and revises them as need be. A representation of the cognitive orientation is given in figure 6.5.

Acquisition is based on the assimilation of new knowledge into existing knowledge structures and changes in old knowledge structures through accommodation to new knowledge. In processing information, the learner develops decision-making strategies to deal with future learning experiences. Since the learner is continuously testing hypotheses, organization of knowledge is continuous. That is, life is a constant open-ended learning experience. Retention is based on a sound internal structure of knowledge. Forgetting occurs because of distortions in memory resulting from the continuous revision in the internal structure of knowledge. Because of the learner's sensitivity to new information through hypothesis testing, transfer is considered to be general in the sense that previously learned principles can be applied to new situations, and changes can be made by the learner in the principles previously learned to solve problems through sampling and hypothesis testing.

Motivation is based on the need to know and understand. **Equilibration** is the concept used to refer to the learner's sensitivity in differentiating between information that can be **assimilated** or **accommodated** and the capability to integrate the new information into the internal knowledge structure. This, of course, is accomplished through hypothesis testing.

David Ausubel, Jerome Bruner, and Ulric Neisser are well-known proponents of cognitivism. Many ideas have also been borrowed from the extensive work of Piaget on the development of logical thinking in children. Of the five orientations, the cognitive position has been influenced most by developmental theory and research. The definition given by Ausubel (1968) is appropriate for this theory: *Learning is the long-term acquisition of stable bodies of knowledge and of the capacity needed for acquiring such knowledge.*

> "The source of motivation is the need to self-actualize. To this end, it is assumed that a person has a built-in need to become all that one can."

The humanistic approach emphasizes self-actualization —a type of creative growth.

Humanism

Humanism is a theory representative of a number of points of view, including dynamic psychology, **phenomenology, existentialism,** and perceptualism. Perhaps the position, as presented here, should be called natural humanism, or romanticism, because humanism is a term that has been used in many ways through the years to refer to the ideals and circumstances of the human condition. However, the label "humanism" has been adopted by what is sometimes referred to as the *third force* in psychology; that is, a force interested in putting the will and free spirit of the person back into psychology. The two deterministic positions constituting forces one and two are behavioral and psychoanalytic theories that have been most dominant during much of the twentieth century.

In the humanistic theory, the learner is viewed as having a built-in mechanism to foster his own development through experiences. Mechanisms that are not available at birth will naturally unfold in the course of development. The position advocates allowing the learner to choose his own situational conditions rather than having them imposed upon him by others. This is based upon the premise that the learner is in the best position to understand his needs and how to meet them.

There is no attempt to explain the acquisition, retention, or transfer processes. The source of motivation is the need to self-actualize. To this end, it is assumed that a person has a built-in need to become all that one can. A

The Psychology of Learning

"From a traditional viewpoint, readiness is an undesirable characteristic of the learner. If a learner is eager to learn, then there is no disciplinary value in the lesson for him."

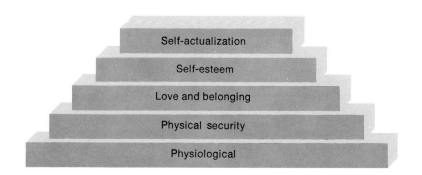

Figure 6.6 Hierarchy of Needs from a Humanistic Viewpoint. Adapted from "A Theory of Human Motivation" by Abraham Maslow, *Psychological Review*, 1943, *50*, pp. 370–96.

hierarchy of needs from a humanistic viewpoint is given in figure 6.6. Arthur Combs and Carl Rogers are well-known proponents of humanistic psychology. The definition given by Garry and Kingsley (1970) would serve the theory well: *Learning is the process by which an organism in satisfying its motivation adapts or adjusts its behavior in order to reach a goal.*

Historically, there have been many individuals who have contributed to one or more of the learning theories. As you may wish to read or may be required to read some of these authorities' works in addition to those previously cited, we shall align these historical figures with their orientations. Major contributors to the behavioristic family have been Edwin Guthrie, Clark Hull, Ivan Pavlov, Kenneth Spence, and E. L. Thorndike. Major contributors to cognitivism were Johann Herbart, Kurt Koffka, Wolfgang Kohler, and Max Wertheimer. Major contributors to humanistic psychology were Gordon Allport, Kurt Lewin, Abraham Maslow, Jean Jacques Rousseau, and Donald Snygg. William James and Edward Tolman made major contributions to both cognitive and behavioral theory, and John Dewey contributed to behaviorism, cognitivism, and humanism.

Implications of Theories for Teaching-Learning Processes

As indicated in table 6.2, the nature of readiness, goals, and outcomes are major factors to consider in conditions of learning. Readiness is defined as being emotionally, intellectually, and physically prepared to learn particular school curricular goals.

From a traditional viewpoint, readiness is an undesirable characteristic of a learner. If a learner is eager to learn, there is no disciplinary value in the

> "The behaviorist views readiness as any other behavior. A teacher starts at the point of readiness in relation to the goal and helps the student to attain the desired outcome."

lesson for him. In addition, the teacher who is not able to instill fear in the learner as punishment or threat of punishment is ineffective. Two common ways to create unreadiness for learning are to assign difficult or noninteresting tasks to the learners. These conditions can be planned in a manner consistent with the theory, as the actual factual goals are not as important as the development of mental discipline. Indirectly, the number of facts learned gives an indication of the amount of mental discipline that has taken place.

The behaviorist views readiness as any other behavior. A teacher starts at the point of readiness in relation to the goal and helps the student to attain the desired outcome. Reinforcers that are appropriate for the particular learner are used. The outcomes are performed in a setting identical to the one in which the behavior is expected to be performed at the present or in the future, as there is no transfer. Since many responses and reinforcement events will likely be needed to attain the desired outcomes, it is often necessary to use programmed materials and mechanical devices such as **computer-assisted instruction.** The programs used should be **linear** or in small progressive steps from simple to more complex behavior.

The neobehaviorist views readiness in the same way as the behaviorist does. In neobehaviorism, however, it is not as important for a teacher to specify the goals or the conditions under which the behavior is to be performed. Several goals can be accomplished efficiently at one time through demonstrations, observation, models, or a lecture. The learner does not actually have to perform every response, as learning occurs through vicarious experiences and activated internal processes. Hence, a goal for every meaningful response does not have to be specified. However, a teacher should be able to specify goals if need be. The conditions under which the behavior is to be performed do not have to be identical to those of the real world because of the transfer process. It might even be viewed as desirable that the conditions of learning are not identical to the real world since it would be rare that identical elements would occur in two situations. Simulations, programmed materials, and mechanical devices would be consistent with this point of view.

From a cognitive viewpoint, the task and method must be adapted to the readiness of the learner. In contrast to the two previous positions, behaviorism and neobehaviorism, readiness is not viewed as something that can be taught. If a teacher persists in trying to teach a particular goal by a particular method, it may be necessary to wait until the learner has sufficient readiness

through maturation to attain the goal. However, if the method is varied in accordance with capabilities of the learner, the outcome may be attained. Since the learner is actively sampling and hypothesizing from experiences, it is necessary to redefine goals as learning progresses toward the general goals.

The **discovery method** is a technique commonly used by cognitivists. The learners have the task of solving a problem through sampling of information and hypothesis testing, and the teacher has the task of creating a climate in which it is acceptable for students to make mistakes. The teacher also has to stimulate guessing in order to get the learners to restructure their knowledge and try various strategies in solving problems. Since thinking rather than experience is the foundation of learning, errors are considered as meaningful as correct solutions to problems. The nature of outcomes is never the same as the original goals. New problems are introduced to determine whether the learner can transfer knowledge and previously learned strategies to new problems. In a sense, performance always involves a new learning experience. If programmed materials or mechanical devices are used,

Theories of Learning and Motivation   227

> "Basic assumptions of the humanistic position are that the learner is the best judge of what his developmental and momentary needs are. Consequently, the learner not only has the responsibility to choose his own method but also his goals of learning."

the programs should be in large-step progressions with branching subroutines, and they should be interactive with the learner.

Basic assumptions of the humanistic position are that the learner is the best judge of what his developmental and momentary needs are. Consequently, the learner has the responsibility to choose not only his own method but also his goals of learning. In addition, the learner has the responsibility of deciding upon the nature of the outcomes and how they are to be measured and assessed.

The role of the teacher is to create a permissive climate for the students, to serve as a resource person when called upon by a learner, and to have such interpersonal skills as **acceptance, empathy, trust,** and **sincerity** in order to facilitate students' learning. Programs and mechanical devices are perceived as any other resource for the learner.

Having considered the orientations and implications of the systematic theories, it might be helpful to return to table 6.2 on pages 216 and 217 and to see if you can identify the theory that is most closely in agreement with the following statements:

(1) I have come to feel that the outcomes of teaching are either unimportant or harmful.

(2) We begin with the hypothesis that any subject can be taught in some intellectually honest form to any child at any stage of development.

(3) Give me a dozen healthy infants, well-formed, and my specified world to bring them up in and I'll guarantee to take any one at random and train him to become any type of specialist I might select—doctor, lawyer, artist, merchant-chief, and yes, even beggarman and thief, regardless of his talents, penchants, tendencies, abilities, vocations, and race of his ancestors.

The first statement was made by a humanist Carl Rogers (1961, p. 276); the second statement by a cognitivist Jerome Bruner (1960, p. 33); and the third statement was made by a behaviorist John Watson (1930, p. 82).

Answers to Teachers' Questions

At the beginning of the chapter, three questions were raised about problems that teachers often face. How would a theorist of a particular orientation attempt to answer these questions in a round table discussion?

Traditionalist: "Anything worthwhile is difficult to learn. I have found that using threats and punishments gets students to work—a little sweat and tears, as they say, will take care of that problem."

Behaviorist: "It is probably difficult because the goals of the lesson are not clearly specified and/or the content is not sequenced in a simple to complex manner."

Neobehaviorist: "It could be that the behaviorist is right. It could also be that the students do not have the necessary prerequisite behaviors for the goals of the lesson."

Cognitivist: "You are probably using the wrong method, given the readiness of the students. Perhaps, you are using the wrong mode of representation or the content is not structured properly."

Humanist: "The topic is likely not relevant to the students' needs. A student can learn anything he or she wants to with remarkable ease."

Why is a particular topic so difficult for students to learn?

Traditionalist: "I have not observed this. Drill has worked well for me in getting them to learn."

Behaviorist: "It is primarily due to the previous reinforcement history of the students. If you would like to have them learn better under the condition that is the 'other method,' I suggest you set up reinforcing contingencies for that method. Then it may work just as well."

Neobehaviorist: "I agree."

Cognitivist: "Naturally, some students have developmental readiness for one method, and other students have developmental readiness for another method."

Humanist: "I can see how different methods would meet the needs of different students. However, you will find that the students would have achieved better outcomes had they been allowed to choose their own methods."

Why do some students learn better under one method than another?

Traditionalist: "Students naturally want to avoid hard work, but it's essential to learning."

Behaviorist: "The students have a different reinforcement history than the teacher."

Neobehaviorist: "There is probably not adequate incentive in the situation."

Cognitivist: "I suspect there is not an opportunity for students to understand the goal, to sample and to test a hypothesis."

Humanist: "The key phrase here is that the teacher thinks the goals are important. Only when the student chooses the goals is he or she really interested in the learning experience."

Why aren't the students interested in learning the goals of a unit that the teacher considers important?

> "It has been generally recognized for some time that when all the facts are considered no one theory is adequate to deal with the diversity of goals, conditions of learning, and learning styles found in our schools."

We have tried to present a fair picture of each theory insofar as the processes and conditions of learning are concerned. Perhaps we have been somewhat harsh with traditionalism, but we used it as a straw man for comparative purposes. We know of no one who ascribes to traditionalism, at least in its entirety, as presented here.

There are limitations to any systematic theory. If you would like to test the limits of systematic theories, consider the following question: Holding society constant as you know it, what would an 18-year-old person be like if from preschool through high school he had learning experiences based on just a behavioral theory? neobehavioral? cognitive? humanistic?

What Is Instructional Theory?

It has been generally recognized for some time that when all the facts are considered no one theory of learning is adequate to deal with the diversity of goals, **learning styles,** and **teaching styles** found in our schools. In addition, it is not easy to educate teachers to translate how people learn into how people teach. Consequently, an area has emerged recently that is called **instructional theory** or **instructional psychology** (Glaser, 1976). The goal of instructional theory is to identify the most effective conditions of learning for particular kinds of educational goals for particular kinds of learners. It is a broad generic term that includes all important aspects of the classroom learning environment. While learning theory is at the foundation of instructional theory, the goal of learning theory per se is quite different. The goal of learning theory is to identify general laws of learning. In effect, the goal of instructional theory is to identify specific laws of learning. We will consider here the relationship between learning and instruction.

In general, educational psychologists have a combined eclectic-functionalist orientation in this area. Such terminology as stimulus-response (behavioral), or process-product (cognitive), or input-output (computer model) is used. It is important to recognize that the terminology used by an eclecticist or a functionalist does not necessarily mean that he ascribes to the particular theory with which the terms are associated.

Various models have been conceptualized as a basis from which to consider the useability of knowledge provided by theories of learning. Per-

> "Essentially, the question is, What instructional procedures are most likely to optimally develop student learning for particular objectives and for particular learners in relation to performance outcomes?"

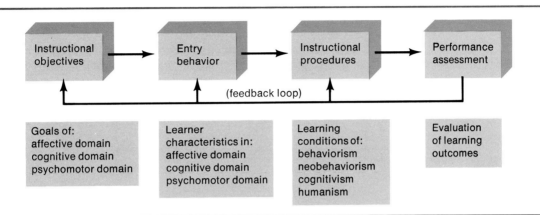

Figure 6.7 Basic Teaching Model. From Robert Glaser, "Psychology and Instructional Technology," *Training, Research, and Education*. (University of Pittsburgh Press, 1962). Adaptation of display on p. 6, used with permission.

haps the most popular model is one developed by Glaser (1962) that appears in figure 6.7. His model represents the basic components of classroom learning conditions.

Of the possible eclectic orientations involving the four systematic theories, the combinations of behaviorism-neobehaviorism, neobehaviorism-cognitivism, and cognitivism-humanism are the most common, as you might expect. Lee Cronbach, Francis DiVesta, N. L. Gage, Robert Glaser, and Ernest Hilgard are examples of educational psychologists who have developed at least the beginnings of knowledge related to classroom learning conditions. A word of caution is appropriate at this time. Models are designed for "thinking" about what might be. A model is not based on empirical evidence. Once the relationships among components of a model have been thoroughly investigated, the model has served its purpose. Relationships between variables that hold up in replicated studies become a part of a theory. Thus, this part of the chapter deals with where the "thinking" of educational psychology is rather than with its knowledge.

Essentially, the question is, What instructional procedures are most likely to develop student learning optimally for particular objectives and for particular learners in relation to performance outcomes? One way to approach this problem is to consider the nature of the components of the model, the empirical findings related to each component, the issues that separate the learning orientations, and then attempt a meaningful synthesis of the theories for the objectives, entry behaviors, and procedures.

Instructional Objectives

Instructional objectives are statements of educational goals. Objectives are often broken down into **affective, cognitive,** and **psychomotor** categories so that conceptualizations may more readily be made between and within categories. In addition, such conceptualizations are helpful in writing objectives that may be measured as performance outcomes. The hierarchical categories of the *Taxonomies of Educational Objectives* (Bloom et al., 1956; Harrow, 1972; & Krathwohl et al., 1965) are reported in table 6.4. These categories are presented here to illustrate the scope of what may be educational objectives in school curricula. The generality of the categories is such that they cut across all levels of development, skills, and subject-matter contents.

Table 6.4   Hierarchies of Educational Objectives

Affective	Cognitive	Psychomotor

	6.0 Evaluation
	   6.1 Internal criterion judgments
	   6.2 External criterion judgments
		6.0 Nondiscursive Communication
		   6.1 Expressive movement
		   6.2 Interpretive movement

5.0 Characterized by a Value
   5.1 Generalized set
   5.2 Characterization
	5.0 Synthesis
	   5.1 Unique communication
	   5.2 Plan or proposed operation
	   5.3 Set of abstract relations
		5.0 Skilled Movement
		   5.1 Simple adaptive skill
		   5.2 Compound adaptive skill
		   5.3 Complex adaptive skill

4.0 Organization
   4.1 Value conceptualized
   4.2 Organized value system
	4.0 Analysis
	   4.1 Analysis of elements
	   4.2 Analysis of relationships
		4.0 Physical Abilities
		   4.1 Endurance
		   4.2 Strength
		   4.3 Flexibility
		   4.4 Agility

3.0 Valuing
   3.1 Acceptance of a value
   3.2 Preference for a value
   3.3 Commitment
	3.0 Application	3.0 Perceptual Ability
		   3.1 Kinesthetic discrimination
		   3.2 Visual discrimination
		   3.3 Auditory discrimination
		   3.4 Tactile discrimination
		   3.5 Coordinated abilities

2.0 Responding
   2.1 Acquiescence in response
   2.2 Willingness to respond
   2.3 Satisfaction in response
	2.0 Comprehension
	   2.1 Translation
	   2.2 Interpretation
	   2.3 Extrapolation
		2.0 Basic Fundamental Movement
		   2.1 Locomotor movement
		   2.2 Nonlocomotor movement
		   2.3 Manipulative movement

1.0 Receiving
   1.1 Awareness
   1.2 Willingness to receive
   1.3 Controlled or selected attention
	1.0 Knowledge
	   1.1 Specifics
	   1.2 Ways and means of dealing with specifics
	   1.3 Universals and abstractions in a field
		1.0 Reflex Movement
		   1.1 Segmental reflexes
		   1.2 Intersegmental reflexes
		   1.3 Suprasegmental reflexes

Adapted from and reprinted by permission of the David McKay Company:
Taxonomy of Educational Objectives: Handbook II, pp. 176–185, by D. R. Krathwohl, B. S. Bloom, and B. B. Masia. Copyright © 1964 by Krathwohl, Bloom, and Masia.
Taxonomy of Educational Objectives: Handbook I, pp. 201–207, by D. R. Krathwohl, B. S. Bloom, and B. B. Masia. Copyright © 1956 by B. S. Bloom.
A Taxonomy of the Psychomotor Domain, pp. 96–98, by Anita J. Harrow. Copyright © 1972 by Anita J. Harrow.

Entry Behavior

Entry behavior or **readiness** is concerned with developmental and individual differences among learners in relation to instructional objectives or **instructional procedures.** The developmental theory of Piaget (Piaget and Inhelder, 1969), for example, has become of interest to psychologists in relation to the entry behavior of learners. The stages of cognitive development are presented in table 6.5. This information is presented to demonstrate possible developmental factors to consider in relation to readiness.

Insofar as individual readiness factors are concerned, there is little doubt that such variables as general cognitive ability and socioeconomic background experiences affect performance in school regardless of the objectives or instructional procedures.

Table 6.5 **Stages of Cognitive Development**

Stage of Development	Salient Features of Thinking	Approximate Age Range
Sensorimotor	Thinking occurs through coordination of sense and motor activities. Recognition that objects remain constant when seen from different angles and even when out of sight. Often referred to as preverbal and amoral stage.	Birth–2 years
Preoperational	Thinking about objects based on perceptual appearances. Classification of objects on the basis of only one feature such as height, rather than on the basis of the relationship between two or more features such as height and width. Behavior characterized by intuitive thought and egocentric speech. Often referred to as moral realist stage.	2 to 7 years
Concrete Operation	Thinking out problems previously performed. Understanding of concrete concepts such as classifying objects into a series and reversing operations. Behavior characterized by logical thought and socialized speech. Often referred to as moral relativist stage.	7 to 11 years
Formal Operation	Thinking about thinking. Understanding of abstract concepts such as reasoning about the future and contrary-to-fact propositions. Behavior characterized by logical thinking and both egocentric and socialized speech. Often referred to as moral idealist stage.	11 to 15 years

Developmental Psychology by John H. Flavell © 1963 Litton Educational Publishing, Inc. Reprinted by permission D. Van Nostrand Co.

"Insofar as individual readiness factors are concerned, there is little doubt that such variables as general cognitive ability and socioeconomic background experiences affect performance in school regardless of the objectives or instructional procedures."

Table 6.6 Individual Differences in Learning Styles

Motivation	Cognitive
Locus of Control	*Conceptual Integration*
Internal—great deal of responsibility for one's behavior	High—elaborate network of ideas
External—very little responsibility for one's behavior	Low—limited network of ideas
Conceptual Tempo	*Conceptual Style*
Reflective—slow, methodical pace	Categorical—tends to think in categories
Impulsive—fast, random pace	Descriptive—tends to think in details
	Relational—tends to think in themes
Structure of Instruction	
Learning via Independence—very little control in learning experience	
Learning via Conformance—great deal of control in learning experience	

Interest in entry behavior has focused on the identification of individual readiness factors that may result in different qualities of performances given the nature of the instructional procedures. It is well known that individual differences in the development of many cognitive and motivational factors at any age are as striking or more so than the predictability of sequences of developmental patterns for the same factors (Mischel, 1973). Consequently, some cognitive and motivational factors of developmental concepts have been hypothesized to function in interactive ways with instructional procedures (Glaser, 1972). There is little evidence that individual readiness factors do interact with particular methods. One reason that it cannot be concluded that they do so is that studies of so-called **trait-treatment interactions** (or aptitude-treatment interactions) are relatively recent and, consequently, there are few replicated results in this area. Examples of such individual factors are given in table 6.6. These factors were selected because there is some evidence to support the possibility that they do interact with instructional methods, and there is enough research activity in these areas that perhaps over the next decade we shall learn a great deal more about how they do interact with instructional procedures. An example of a trait-treatment interaction is illustrated in figure 6.8.

The Psychology of Learning

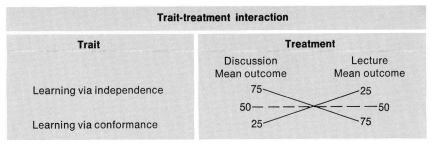

Trait	Mean outcome		Treatment	Mean outcome
Learning via independence	50		Discussion	50
Learning via conformance	50		Lecture	50

Trait-treatment interaction

Trait	Treatment	
	Discussion Mean outcome	Lecture Mean outcome
Learning via independence	75	25
	50 — — — — — — 50	
Learning via conformance	25	75

Figure 6.8 An Example of a Trait-Treatment Interaction

While neither the outcome difference in the trait or treatment condition results in a significant effect, the interaction between the trait and treatment condition does result in a significant effect. That is, only the interaction results in a difference.

Instructional Procedures

Instructional procedures are the methods used by teachers. A lecture, demonstration, discussion, reading, television, seat work, writing a theme, recitation, films and film strips, tapes, tutoring, and quizzes are all examples of vehicles for teaching methods. The ways in which the vehicles are used, that is, nature of objectives, reinforcement, feedback, criteria of acceptable performance, are the methods. A programmed text or computer-assisted instruction can have methods built into them, of course.

Performance Assessment

Performance assessment refers to an evaluation of learning outcomes. Meaningful evaluation of a student's performance can be made in relation to the objectives, entry behavior, and instructional procedures if the measurements are valid and reliable.

Through the years, empirical findings related to instructional objectives have focused on the question, Which method—specific or more general objectives—is best? This question has generally been asked about the cognitive domain. The results of many such studies indicate that it does not make any significant difference. Perhaps this finding has been replicated so many times because the component was studied in isolation rather than in integration with instructional procedures. That is, a statement of instructional objectives for a lesson or unit is also a vehicle, not a method.

Findings in the area of entry behavior indicate that general cognitive ability, previous achievement, or prerequisite knowledge of the objectives or

> "Findings in the area of entry behavior indicate that general cognitive ability, previous achievement, or prerequisite knowledge of the objectives or skills are significant factors in later performance. . . . While it would seem that a learner's interest in a learning task would also be a significant factor, it has not been found to be so."

skills are significant factors in later performance. Socioeconomic background experience is also a significant factor in performance. While it would seem that a learner's interest in a learning task would also be a significant factor, it has not been found to be so. This is likely because one's interest can be indirectly affected by a method. This is also the case with other motivational factors. They are process variables, which are affected by the method in connection with learning outcomes. The findings related to such factors is one of the reasons why trait-treatment interactions have become of concern to educational psychologists.

Instructional procedures have also been studied rather extensively in relation to the cognitive performance and attitudes toward the learning experience. Most of the studies have dealt with the question, Which method is best? but the methods studied were only vehicles. There have been many replications of the finding that there is no significant difference in the use of lecture versus discussion, film versus lecture, programmed materials versus lecture, and so forth. These findings indicate that a vehicle in isolation does not make any practical difference in student cognitive performance or attitudes toward learning (see Part Three).

Insofar as instructional methods are concerned, distributed practice has been found to be more effective than massed practice, certain schedules of reinforcement more effective than others, embedded questions more effective than pre-questions or post-questions in reading comprehension of text, reading more effective than listening in comprehension of text, and goal setting with corrective feedback more effective than merely corrective feedback. These are but some of the replicated findings that have been found in investigations of instructional methods (see chapter 8).

From table 6.4, behaviors represented in 1.0 to 3.0 in the affective domain, 1.0 to 4.0 in the cognitive domain, and 1.0 to 5.0 in the psychomotor domain can be measured reliably. Conceptually, the higher categories in the respective hierarchies represent ways in which we sometimes see people, particularly adults, behave, but it is difficult to conceive writing objectives for them or designing procedures to teach them. It is as though these behaviors must come from the learner and his or her experiences.

Issues separating the four theories involve each of the components of

"There is no significant difference in the use of lecture versus discussion, film versus lecture, programmed materials versus lecture, and so forth. These findings indicate that a vehicle in isolation does not make any practical difference in student cognitive performance or attitudes toward learning."

the basic teaching model. The issues are (1) maturation versus experience in readiness; (2) the nature of the goals of learning experiences; (3) the nature of the instructional procedures; and (4) the nature of the learning outcomes.

Both behaviorists and neobehaviorists recognize that a person inherits natural reflexes. Experience is viewed as the important factor in readiness. Readiness is seen as resulting from environmental conditions.

The cognitivist and the humanist believe that maturation is the more important factor in readiness. However, the two positions divide from this point. The cognitivist speaks of changing the environmental conditions to fit the learner. The humanist speaks of allowing the learner to use the environment to fit his needs.

We will consider goals of education from these stands on experience and maturation. The behaviorist and neobehaviorist would ask the teacher the following: What goals would you like to accomplish in this lesson? unit? course? curriculum? We will then define them more precisely; sequence them; determine where to start, given the readiness of the students in relation to the goals; design learning activities; and implement suitable learning conditions.

The cognitivist would ask the teacher: What goals would you like to accomplish in this lesson? unit? course? curriculum? We will then determine where to start, given the readiness of the student in relation to some methods; design learning activities; and implement suitable learning conditions.

The humanist would say to the teacher: What goals would the students like to accomplish this day? week? semester? We will then determine how to facilitate their initiating of some activities and taking some responsibility for completing the activities through suitable learning conditions.

Concerning instructional procedures, the behaviorist and neobehaviorist would say we are born equal; environmental conditions make us different. Let us do a better job of arranging environmental conditions to make us more equal than we have in the past.

A cognitivist would say we are not born equal. We can use different environmental conditions to make us more equal than if we used just one set of environmental conditions.

> A humanist would say. . . . let's allow people to make their own decision
> about what they need. This will allow our differences to
> contribute to the good of all humanity.

A humanist would say we are not born equal. We are not going to be equal, rather we are going to be more unequal with experience. Therefore, let's allow people to make their own decision about what they need. This will allow our differences to contribute to the good of all humanity.

The behaviorist, neobehaviorist, and cognitivist would assess the learning outcomes based on the original instructional objectives. The difference in original objectives would be that the behaviorist would have specified each behavior, the neobehaviorist would have specified sequences of behaviors, and the cognitivist would have indicated problems to be solved. The behaviorist would measure and evaluate each behavior after the unit of instruction; the neobehaviorist would measure and evaluate a sample of each sequence of behavior and a few transfer tasks; while the cognitivist would measure and evaluate student solutions to a few similar but new problems.

The humanist would allow the students to decide if and how they want to assess their experiences from the instructional unit.

If we would like to offer an opportunity for students to develop at least some behaviors from each of the major categories in the affective, cognitive, and psychomotor domains, we need some instructional procedures. Table 6.7 presents an orientation that appears to best align particular categories with the most effective learning outcomes.

Combination of theories appear to align logically with the stage of cognitive development (table 6.5). For the sensorimotor stage, humanistic and behavioral orientations seem appropriate. Behavioral and neobehavioral orientations appear to be appropriate for the preoperational stage. For the concrete operations stage, neobehavioral and cognitive orientations may be the most meaningful. Cognitive theory appears to be most helpful in relation to the formal operations stage. For individual differences in learning styles (table 6.6, p. 234), alternative instructional procedures can be speculated upon.

As defined in table 6.6, for elementary and secondary students with external, reflective, low integration and descriptive learning styles, the most effective instructional method would probably entail structural conditions such as those of behaviorism and neobehaviorism. For impulsive and relational students of the same ages, less structured conditions such as those of cognitivism and/or humanism may be more desirable. For internal, high-

> "In sum, the nature of the objectives as well as the stage of the development of the learner must be considered in the use of learning conditions that underlie a particular theory."

Table 6.7 Alignment of Educational Objectives and Instructional Procedures

Affective	Cognitive	Psychomotor
	Evaluation Humanistic	Nondiscursive communication Humanistic
Characterized by a value Humanistic	Synthesis Cognitivistic Humanistic	Skilled movement Neobehavioristic
Organization Cognitivistic	Analysis Cognitivistic	Physical abilities Behavioristic
Valuing Cognitivistic	Application Cognitivistic Neobehavioristic	Perceptual ability Cognitivistic
Responding Neobehavioristic	Comprehension Cognitivistic Neobehavioristic	Basic fundamental movement Behavioristic
Receiving Behavioristic	Knowledge Behavioristic	Reflex movement Behavioristic

elaborated, and categorical students, it would be necessary only to refer back to the basic developmental and objective alignment. There may be more options available to them.

There are two criteria of importance for making decisions related to interactions between learning styles and method. If the criterion is to achieve as effective learning outcomes as possible at a particular moment in time, then it would seem most appropriate to match a student with the most favorable method. This was done in the preceding paragraph. A second criterion is to help the student use a new way of learning effectively. If this were the goal, then a mismatch of method with the learning style would seem to be most appropriate—for example, using a cognitive approach with a low integrated or reflective student. It is important in making such decisions to consider that outcomes related to the method are sometimes as important as outcomes related to the goals.

In sum, the nature of the objectives as well as the stage of the development of the learner must be considered in the use of learning conditions that underlie a particular theory.

Summary

In this chapter we examined the major theories of learning: behaviorism, neobehaviorism, cognitivism, and humanism. Using each of these theories, we considered respective views of learning, as a process and an outcome, and the implications of the learning theory for subsequent instructional theory. Basic components of learning—acquisition, retention, and transfer—were examined in detail, and their relationships to each of the theories discussed were considered. Drawing from all this information, we examined, in some detail, instructional theory.

Suggested Additional Readings

Learning Theories for Teachers, Third Edition, by Morris L. Bigge (*New York: Harper & Row, 1976*)

Bigge analyzes the major theories of learning and their educational implications. Contemporary theories of learning—behavioral and cognitive —are compared to historical learning theories.

Psychology is not a field of study characterized by a body of theory that is internally consistent and accepted by all psychologists. Rather, it is an area of knowledge characterized by the presence of several schools of thought.

from *Learning Theories for Teachers*

The Affective Domain in Education by Thomas A. Ringness (*Boston: Little, Brown and Company, 1975*)

Ringness discusses the usefulness of contemporary learning theories within the context of the development of the teacher as well as the learner. The relative importance of the behavioral and the humanistic positions are considered throughout the book.

The point of this discussion is simply that behavioral and humanistic approaches have their place in teacher education programs. The choice of activities depends on one's personal objectives.

from *The Affective Domain in Education*

Learning Performance and Individual Differences, Essays and Readings, by Len Sperry (*Glenview, Ill.: Scott, Foresman and Company, 1972*)

Sperry attempts a definition of learning styles and instructional styles and problems of the match between them through an integration of selected articles.

Perhaps the reason there has been so little success in controlling and predicting learning performance is an inadequate understanding and model of learning performance.

from *Learning Performance and Individual Differences*

What Is Affective Learning?

Affective learning includes emotional learning, value learning, and character development, along with aesthetic appreciation. Through affective education, the raw materials of the emotions are translated into feelings, attitudes, and values.

The Taxonomy of Educational Objectives in the Affective Domain

The taxonomy lists levels of affective objectives in hierarchical order. The levels are receiving (attending behavior); responding; valuing; organization (of value systems); and characterization by a value or value complex. Since the taxonomy is hierarchical, it is necessary for the learner to master the objectives of a given level before demonstrating adequate functioning at the following level.

Emotional Growth in the Classroom

The recognition of the importance that a person's emotional state plays in all life functions leads us to the conclusion that the learner's emotional state is not incidental to his or her performance in school, but an integral part of it.

Emotional Conflicts and Affective Learning

Frustration may produce different types of conflicts. The four common models used to describe conflicts are *approach-approach; approach-avoidance; avoidance-avoidance; double approach-avoidance.* Unresolved conflict situations may result in the immobilization of the student.

The Healthy Person: Coping and Adaptation

Maslow's theory of needs is discussed. He found that as individuals learn to cope with their environments, they master the ways of satisfying what he calls the *hierarchy of needs,* which range from the basic physiological needs to the highest self-actualizing needs.

Continued

7 Conditions and Processes of Affective Learning

Self-Perception and Affective Learning

Although there is no clear-cut, unambiguous definition of the word *self,* we operationally define the term *phenomenal self* to account for the ways the individual perceives himself. The phenomenal self is basically a perceptual self. Insights on self-growth and personal development are summarized from the work of Boy and Pine (1971). This development includes four types of therapeutic experiences: the human therapeutic experience, the vocational therapeutic experience, the religious therapeutic experience, and the recreational therapeutic experience.

Character Development and Moral Learning

Different positions on character development and moral learning have been offered—ranging from Plato's philosophical doctrine to Freud's theory of the superego. It is generally agreed by all that character development is an integral part of the educative experience.

Russell's Theory of Character Development

Bertrand Russell cites four "virtues" that the learner should develop: *vitality, courage, sensitiveness,* and *intelligence.* Vitality is synonymous with good health and a strong body. Courage begins with the absence of irrational fears, but excludes bravado, or false courage. Sensitiveness includes both cognitive and emotional sensitivities. Intelligence relies heavily on curiosity and its stimulation. Intelligence is the virtue that links the qualities of character with the powers of intellect.

Piaget's Position on Moral Reasoning

Piaget conceptualizes the child's moral development as a progression from heteronomy (obedience to imposed rules) to autonomy (individual decision making). The child develops from a position of blind obedience— a "morality of constraint"—to a "morality of cooperation." Ultimately, the child develops what Piaget calls "distributive justice," the idea that rewards and punishments can be distributed in different ways, according to the act and the circumstances surrounding it.

Kohlberg's Theory of Moral Reasoning

Lawrence Kohlberg divides the development of moral reasoning into three stages: the preconventional level, the conventional level, and the postconventional level. The progress of the child's reasoning moves from avoidance of negative consequences to well-thought-out moral principles. At the highest level, the person acts according to autonomous moral principles that have validity apart from the authority of the groups or persons who hold them.

Evaluation of Kohlberg's and Piaget's Positions

Research studies have confirmed important aspects of both theories. In general, it has been noted that higher intellectual processes are prerequisite for higher levels of moral reasoning, but that moral behavior may be independent entirely of the reasoning behind it.

Moral Education: From Theory to Practice

A number of proposals have been put forth to facilitate moral development in the schools. Several specific programs are presented. The principle objective of moral education in the schools becomes the attainment of the next higher level of moral development.

Often, when we think of learning, we are thinking of what is technically called either **cognitive learning** or **psychomotor learning.** Some examples of cognitive and psychomotor learning are learning how to spell, learning the causes of the American Revolution, learning how to fly a kite, learning how to build a generator, learning how to divide numbers, and so on. Whenever we learn about facts, learn how to do processes, learn how to organize and analyze information, and so forth, we are experiencing cognitive learning (which will be discussed more fully in the following chapter). Whenever we learn to coordinate our body and to physically navigate reality, smoothly, efficiently, and with purpose, we are experiencing psychomotor learning. But there is another kind of learning as well; learning not about facts alone or how to process information, but rather a "learning to be human," a learning to feel, to experience, to value, to respond to others. This is called **affective learning.**

In this chapter, we shall look at some of the principles of affective learning and at some of the conditions and processes involved in affective education. But first, to understand better what affective education is all about, let us look at some of the objectives and purposes of affective learning.

What Is Affective Learning?

While it has been stated in many different ways—by educators, philosophers, social scientists, psychologists, politicians, and others—it is generally agreed that the total function of education includes not only the teaching of subject matter but the development of *character* as well. Some educational theorists such as Plato, Rousseau, and Bertrand Russell consider the development of character a prerequisite to the cultivation of intellect. For without character, they ask, to what uses can knowledge legitimately be put.

Plato points out in *The Republic* that when intelligence is cultivated in the absence of a sound moral foundation, the result is likely to be a person whose great capacities are used for evil purposes. "You must have noticed in dishonest men with a reputation for sagacity," he argues, "the shrewd glance of a narrow intelligence piercing the objects to which it is directed. There is nothing wrong with their power of vision, but it has been forced into the service of evil, so that the keener the sight, the more harm it works" (Plato, p. 518). What Plato meant, of course, is that knowledge can be a dangerous tool, and if we give a person knowledge without a moral foundation to accompany it, we risk the possibility that the person will use this knowledge to evil purposes. Likewise, Bertrand Russell, in *Education and the Good Life,* devotes the first section of the book to the "Education of Character" and the latter section to the "Education of Intellect," reasoning,

> "Through affective education, the raw materials of the emotions are translated into feelings, attitudes, and values."

as Plato did, that a sound character development should underlie any cognitive growth.

One aspect of character development, then, is moral development. An important task of affective education is to understand the nature of moral growth and how it can be positively influenced. We will consider this as one of the important topics in this chapter.

But **character,** an inclusive concept, means more than simply one's moral outlook. It includes the individual's self-perceptions, attitudes about self—self-concept, in general. Self-concept is not easy to define, but we know from many years of study that the individual's **self-concept** plays a vital role in all of the mental processes, including learning. The way a person treats others, the way he responds to the environment, the way he challenges the obstacles that confront him at every point in living, are all related, directly or indirectly, to the person's self-concept.

We can say, then, that another part of affective learning is learning about oneself—developing a self-concept, or self-image, that will enable one to survive and prosper in this world. We will also look at ways in which the self-concept is influenced, particularly in the school setting.

The word *affective* is often used synonymously with *emotional:* affective learning means emotional learning; affective education means emotional education. In fact, the dictionary (*Webster's New World Dictionary,* 2nd College Ed.) defines affective as "of, or arising from, affects or feelings; emotional."[1] While this is correct, it is not the whole truth—affective is more than simply emotional. We can say, in fact, that the affective domain— the part of the person's psychological existence—includes all of his perceptions, responses to others, feelings about self, feelings about others, characteristic behaviors, value orientations, and moral outlook. This means, in effect, that affective learning has an important cognitive dimension, and through affective education, the raw materials of the emotions are translated into feelings, attitudes, and values.

A Problem As we can see from the material above, affective learning includes a lot of different things, many of which are not easy to measure and define. One of the problems in defining educational programs is the tendency to leave out

1. With permission. From *Webster's New World Dictionary of the American Language,* Second College Edition. Copyright © 1976 by William Collins & World Publishing Co., Inc.

　　　　The Psychology of Learning

affective objectives as either frills, intangibles, or things irrelevant to the educational process. Recognizing this tendency, a major effort was undertaken in the mid-1950s by Benjamin S. Bloom, David R. Krathwohl, and Bertram B. Masia to classify the educational objectives of the affective domain. Speaking of the need for a classification system for affective objectives, the authors argued:

> When we looked for evaluation material in the affective domain we found it usually in relation to some national educational research project or a sponsored local research project (for which a report had to be written). Only rarely did we find an affective evaluation technique used because a group of local teachers wanted to know whether students were developing in a particular way. It was evident that evaluation work for affective objectives was marginal and was done only when a very pressing question was raised by the faculty or when someone wished to do "educational" research. (Krathwohl et al., 1964, p. 15)

Their work, which covered a period of several years, was devoted to a single task: to classify the educational objectives of the affective domain so that they could be properly evaluated and therefore worked toward. While their **taxonomy**—or classification system—is not entirely adequate, it is probably the single most comprehensive example of classifying affective objectives. For this reason, we shall begin with an examination of their scheme, and then proceed to a more detailed understanding of some of the processes of affective learning.

The Taxonomy of Educational Objectives in the Affective Domain

In explaining the purpose and structure of the **taxonomy,** Krathwohl (1964) says:

> We had at first hoped that somehow we could derive a structure by attaching certain meanings to the terms "attitude," "value," "appreciation" and "interest." But the multitude of meanings which these terms encompassed . . . showed that this was impossible. After trying a number of schemes and organizing principles, the one which appeared best to account for the affective phenomena and which best described the process of learning and growth in the affective field was the process of internalization.
>
> The term internalization is perhaps best defined by the descriptions of the categories of the affective domain. Generally speaking, however, it refers to the inner growth that occurs as the individual becomes aware of and then adopts the attitudes, principles, codes and sanctions that become a part of him in forming value judgments and in guiding the conduct. It has many elements in common with the term socialization. . . . (pp. 45–46)

The taxonomy is hierarchical; that is, each level is a prerequisite for the next level. Thus, it is necessary for the learner to master the objectives of a given level before demonstrating adequate functioning at the following level.

> "The taxonomy is hierarchical. . . . It is necessary for the learner to master the objectives of a given level before demonstrating adequate functioning at the following level."

Figure 7.1 The Affective Taxonomy

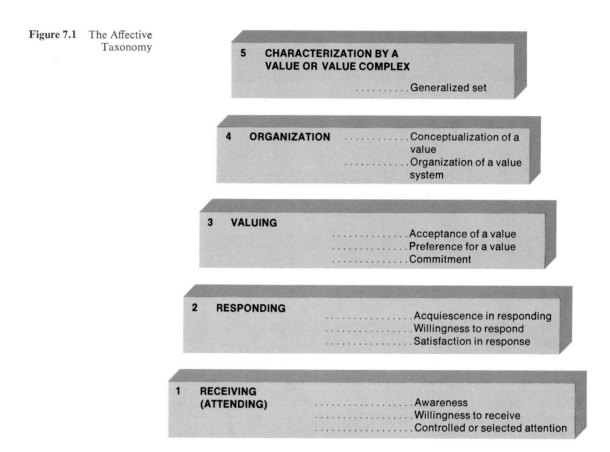

Figure 7.1 shows the basic construction of the taxonomy, and we will now consider each level in some detail.

Receiving: The First Level

The affective taxonomy contains five major classes: receiving (attending), responding, valuing, organization, and characterization by a value or value concept. **Receiving,** or attending behavior as it is sometimes called, involves sensitivity to the world around us. It is divided into three subcategories: awareness, willingness to receive, and controlled or selected attention. Receiving "is clearly the first and crucial step if the learner is to be properly oriented to learn what the teacher intends that he will" (Krathwohl et al., 1964, p. 176). *Awareness,* the simplest level of receiving, requires only that the learner "take into account a situation, phenomenon, object or state of

The Psychology of Learning

Without awareness, there can be no attending to the world around us.

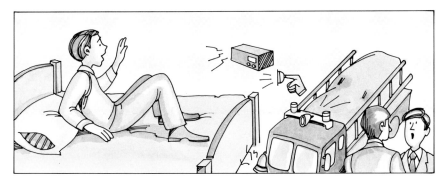

If we received everything around us, we would be confused and unable to act . . .

. . . so we discriminate in our environment those things that are most important at the moment.

affairs" (pp. 176–177). *Willingness to receive* describes "the behavior of being willing to tolerate a given stimulus, not to avoid it." A further level of orientation, however, is required when we attend to the world. We have to be able to differentiate stimuli into prominent and less prominent features —to focus our attention on the things around us that are important. *Controlled or selective attention* is the learner's ability to differentiate "a given stimulus into **figure** and **ground** at a conscious or perhaps semiconscious level—the differentiation of aspects of a stimulus which is perceived as clearly marked off from adjacent impressions" (pp. 177–178).

For example, a person may be forced to be aware of what is going on around him, but may show neither a willingness to receive this information nor the ability to discriminate the significant information from less significant, tangential material. This person would be functioning only on the first sub-category (awareness) of this class in the affective taxonomy. A person functioning on the level of the second category (willingness to receive) would not only be aware of what is happening around him but would also be open to this experience; would reach out to become more aware, when necessary. A person functioning on the third level (controlled or selected attention) can discriminate from those things happening around him what is important and what is not important. Thus, at each increasing level there is greater perceptual sophistication.

We see, then, that the first level of affective learning involves a multi-staged process in which the learner confronts his or her world, proceeding from a passive awareness to an openness to stimuli, to the ability to select from the many stimuli around and to differentiate among them.

A part of affective learning includes being open to experience.

Immediately after attending to the world around us, we respond to it. This level, like receiving, is divided into three stages: acquiescence in responding; willingness to respond; and satisfaction in response. A brief description of each stage should clarify the nature of this level.

Acquiescence means a passive agreement, and indeed this level involves a compliant learner; one who responds passively to the stimuli around. At this level, "the student makes the response, but he has not fully accepted the necessity for doing so" (Krathwohl et al., p. 179). Next, the learner develops a *willingness to respond:* ". . . the learner is sufficiently committed to exhibiting the behavior that he does so not just because of a fear of punishment, but 'on his own' or voluntarily" (p. 179). Finally, at the third level, the learner derives "a feeling of satisfaction, an emotional response, generally of pleasure, zest, or enjoyment" from the response. The difference between this stage and the other two that precede it can be typified in the difference between a person who reads a book because it is required for class and one who reads a book for pleasure. Not only is the qualitative experience different but the quantitative experience (of learning) also differs because of the increased motivation in the second instance.

At this level, we enter the more obvious area of affective education. Valuing is used in its common sense of the attribution of worth to a thing, a behavior, and so forth. It, too, is divided into three stages: acceptance of a value; preference for a value; and commitment.

Acceptance of a value is characterized by the learner holding a belief, but tentative beliefs that are held open to re-evaluation and external influences. When the student moves to the next stage, *preference for a value,* his or her behavior "implies not just the acceptance of a value to the point of being willing to be identified with it, but the individual is sufficiently committed to the value to pursue it, to seek it out, to want it" (Krathwohl et al., 1964, p. 181). Finally, as the belief achieves "a high degree of certainty," as the student "acts to further the thing valued in some way, to extend the possibility of his developing it, to deepen his involvement with it and with the things representing it," he reaches the third and final stages of valuing, *commitment.*

At higher levels of affective functioning, the learner has organized values into systems, or hierarchies, that help him make decisions in which there may be conflicts of values or lack of clarity about behavior. "Thus necessity arises for (*a*) the organization of the values into a system, (*b*) the determination of the interrelationships among them, and (*c*) the establishment of the dominant and pervasive ones. This level comprises two stages— conceptualization of a value and organization of a value system—to deal with these situations."

At the level of *conceptualization of a value,* the learner can consider personal values on an abstract level, which "permits the individual to see how the value relates to those that he already holds or to new ones that he is coming to hold" (Krathwohl et al., p. 183). The *organization of a value system* follows logically when the individual can "bring together a complex of values, possible disparate values, and to bring these into an ordered relationship with one another" (p. 183). When this is achieved, the learner is ready to function at the highest level—characterization by a value or value complex.

Characterization by a Value or Value Complex: The Fifth Level

At the previous level, the individual has integrated his or her values into an organized system; at this level, "the individual acts consistently in accordance with the values he has **internalized** at this level, and our concern is to indicate two things: (*a*) the generalization of this control to so much of the individual's behavior that he is described and characterized as a person by these pervasive controlling tendencies, and (*b*) the integration of these beliefs, ideas, and attitudes into a total philosophy or world view" (p. 184). The stages for this level are *generalized set* ("which gives an internal consistency to the system of attitudes and values") and *characterization* ("those objectives which concern one's view of the universe, one's philosophy of life, one's *Weltanschauung....*") (p. 185).

Practical Implications of the Taxonomy

We may be asking at this point, What is the value of having all these categories? Doesn't it just add confusion to have so many levels and stages that try to explain affective learning? The answer to these questions might be either yes or no!

On the one hand, the very nature of affective learning is not conducive to such categorization. Affective growth is expansive, often spontaneous, involving operations of mind and concomitant behaviors simultaneously. We cannot hope to touch so many of the mysteries of the human soul by setting up categories, no matter how careful our efforts for accuracy and inclusiveness are.

On the other hand if we recognize the importance of affective learning, then we will want ways of understanding the processes involved, and, more importantly, ways of measuring outcomes of affective education. The true value of this taxonomic system is in helping the teacher measure the outcomes—the objectives—of learning in the affective domain. In figure 7.2, we see some of the specific affective educational objectives for selected stages. The manual (Krathwohl et al., 1964) provides detailed suggestions for measuring these outcomes that are helpful in assisting the teacher determine the extent and breadth of affective growth in the classroom.

In the following sections, we will look at several areas that can be examined within the context of the affective taxonomy. First, we will consider the basis for emotional growth in the classroom and then examine some im-

Figure 7.2 Sample Objectives from *Taxonomy of Educational Objectives. Handbook II: Affective Domain.* By D. R. Krathwohl, B. S. Bloom, and B. B. Masia. Copyright © 1964 by Krathwohl, Bloom, and Masia. Reprinted by permission of David McKay Company, Inc.

1.1 Awareness	Develops awareness of aesthetic factors in dress, furnishings, architecture, city design, good art, and the like.
	Awareness of the importance of the prevention, early recognition, and treatment of marital discord and of behavior problems of children.
	An awareness that there is an interdependence of nations in the creation and preservation of a satisfactory postwar world.
	Recognition that there may be more than one acceptable point of view.
	Awareness of the feelings of others whose activities are of little interest to ourselves.
1.3 Controlled or selective attention	Listens to music with some discrimination as to its mood and meaning and with some recognition of the contributions of various musical elements and instruments to the total effect.
	Sensitive to the importance of keeping informed on current political and social matters.
	Alertness toward different types of voluntary reading.
	Appreciation of the contribution of the arts toward man's seeking of the good life.
	Listens for picturesque words in stories read aloud or told.
2.1 Acquiescence in responding	Willingness to force oneself to participate with others.
	Willingness to comply with health regulations.
	Visits museums when told to do so.
	Reads the assigned literature.
2.3 Satisfaction in response	Finds pleasure in reading for recreation.
	Enjoys reading books on a variety of themes.
	Responds emotionally to a work of art or musical composition.
	Uses various art media for recreation or emotional release.
	Develops a keen interest in his physical surroundings—in trees, flowers, birds, insects, stars, rocks, physical processes, and the like.
	Enjoyment of participation in varied types of human relationships and in group undertakings.
3.2 Preference for a value	Interest in enabling other persons to attain satisfaction of basic common needs.
	Initiates group action for the improvement of health regulations.
	Deliberately examines a variety of viewpoints on controversial issues, with a view to forming opinions about them.
	Writes letters to the press on issues he feels strongly about.
	Actively participates in arranging for the showing of contemporary artistic efforts.
	Preference for artistically appropriate choice, arrangement, and use of ordinary objects of the environment.
4.1 Conceptualization of a value	Attempts to identify the characteristics of an art object that he admires.
	Finding out and crystallizing the basic assumptions that underlie codes of ethics and are the basis of faith.
	Forms judgments as to the responsibility of society for conserving human and material resources.
5.2 Characterization	Develops for regulation of one's personal and civic life a code of behavior based on ethical principles consistent with democratic ideals.
	Develops a consistent philosophy of life.

Figure 7.2

> "The recognition of the importance that a person's emotional state plays in all life functioning . . . leads us invariably to the conclusion that the learner's emotional state is not incidental to his or her performance in school, but an integral part of it."

pediments to that growth. We will look at the psychoanalytic theory of defense mechanisms and the behavioral model for interpersonal and intrapersonal conflict. We will then turn our attention to the "healthy" learner to better understand those qualities that contribute to mental health and emotional growth. Finally, we will examine the processes and conditions of self-perception as an integral part of affective growth.

Emotional Growth in the Classroom

The recognition of the importance that a person's emotional state plays in all life functioning, including cognitive performance, social relationships, interpersonal perceptions, and so forth, leads us invariably to the conclusion that the learner's emotional state is not incidental to his or her performance in school, but is an integral part of it.

Consider, for instance, the depressed child. Every teacher is familiar with those students who hold in all their feelings and suffer in silence, who reveal in their bland expressions and passivity of spirit the abundant grief that infuses their inner being. Yet, teachers rarely make headway into these students' private worlds, since they are least likely to be the students who disrupt class, who exhibit aggressive behavior, who make their presence felt as a negative force in the classroom. Yet, can these students, so embittered in their own private misery, reach the very first level of affective learning: awareness?

Consider also how **anxiety,** another emotional state, influences in so many ways the learner's performance in school. Anxiety may accompany all learning, or may be specific to certain school-related situations such as participating in class, taking exams, working in group situations, or dealing directly with the teacher. Like all of our emotions, anxiety is one that the teacher is inevitably required to deal with since it impedes most directly the second level of affective learning: responding.

In both of these examples, we see how emotional states directly influence affective learning. To understand the qualitative and quantitative significance of emotion, it might be necessary for the teacher to examine the abundant research on this subject. Robison (1968) has summed up some of the general principles of this subject, which might hold particular relevance for the teacher:

1. Emotional development is not to be confused with observable behavior in a situation. Observable behavior is merely a form of expressing an emotion. A person suffering from frustration may react in many ways. He may run away, attack, or remain suspended, and he may do any of these in a socially acceptable manner. His level of emotional development, however, cannot be understood until the original source of frustration and the degree and type of reaction that takes place is understood.

2. Emotional reactions are not always negative. Certain levels of frustration can act as motivators toward very positive and profitable action on the part of some people.

3. Early experiences are very important to future emotional development. Some researchers feel that the emotional pattern of an individual is established within the first three to five years of his life and will not change basically after that time. Others feel that individuals are born with a built-in degree of emotional tolerance which they will carry with them through life.

4. Emotional development undergoes the greatest degree of fluctuation of any area of growth and development. The military services are not unaccustomed to the situations involving a young man who enlists in order to assert his independence and then spends his first night at camp crying in his pillow because he is homesick.

5. Emotional development is greatly dependent upon the degree and type of interaction between the individual and his *mother image* in early life and between the individual and his peers in later life.

6. Researchers are beginning to illustrate that emotional behavior can be predicted by analyzing patterns of behavior of an individual.

7. Emotional growth and development and intellectual growth and development are interacting forces which are highly dependent on each other.

8. Emotional behavior is the result of a reaction to a stimulus. The stimulus may be real or imaginary and it may be recognizable or beyond the realm of conscious awareness.

9. Emotional behavior causes concomitant physiological reactions. The degree of emotional maturity may therefore affect physical growth and development. (Robison, 1968, pp. 59–60, reprinted by permission)

These nine ideas briefly summarize many of the areas of research in this multi-branched discipline. As we examine some of the implications of this research for the teaching situation, we will get a better idea of how the emotional state of the learner is an important determiner in the educative

Moods and feelings are an important part of the affective domain.

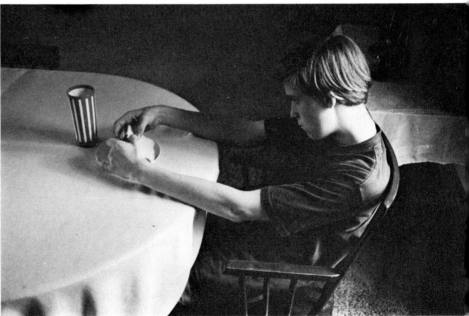

process, and how the teacher can play a role in that growth and therefore help the learner progress through the taxonomic hierarchy.

Implications for the Teacher

As we saw in chapter 1, many of the determinants of emotion are embedded in the preschool years and therefore not directly mediated by anything the teacher does. This is further confirmed in Robison's point 3 and point 4, as you have read. However, even if much of the emotional life is determined early on, as point 5 suggests, the emotions can undergo a great deal of change during any period of life. As point 8 suggests, emotions respond to various stimuli in the environment. The most important single stimulus in the school setting is the teacher, even though peer leaders do exert important peer pressure.

It would be impossible to adequately cover in so short a section the many complex issues that comprise emotional development, but let us look briefly at a few of the more pervasive issues, selecting those that are most likely to have specific classroom implications. The two areas we have selected are the defense mechanisms and emotional conflicts.

Defense Mechanisms

An important part of the person's efforts to preserve emotional stability is the use of defense mechanisms that, in many ways, distort or confuse the objective reality. While the use of defense mechanisms is considered quite normal and healthy, they can be misused, or overused, so that the goals of learning are impeded. When the learner is no longer able to deal objectively with his or her emotional state, a serious overuse of the defense mechanism may result. Let us consider some of the major defenses and their implications.

Repression

This is the most common defense mechanism, and in its most basic form, it simply means forgetting. Generally, we tend to forget painful, unpleasant, anxiety-producing situations. But we may also forget things that on their surface don't seem unpleasant but that arouse anxiety in us. When the teacher notes examples of **repression** in students, or in the entire class, it is best to treat these as manifestations of some emotional problem rather than to simply dismiss them as arbitrary examples of forgetting.

Illustration 1: Two students forgot to bring in their grab bag presents the day before the Christmas party. The teacher explored with these two students, in private, their feelings about having a grab bag. She found that although they had verbalized no disagreement in class, each, for her own reason, resented the idea of a grab bag. Once the teacher allowed expression of the negative feelings, she resolved the need for the repression, and the students were able to "remember" to bring the presents on the following day, *even though they still were able to feel the resentment.*

Many times, repression occurs because we are not in touch with our negative feelings. Getting in touch with these feelings allows us to act in an appropriate way and to feel our anger at the same time. Thus, as learners are encouraged to express their feelings, the likelihood of repression decreases.

Regression

Regression means *returning,* particularly returning to an earlier stage of emotional or intellectual development. When a person becomes overpowered by feelings that he can no longer handle, one way of dealing with the situation is to return to an earlier level of development in which one was able either to avoid such feelings or to feel comfortable with them.

Illustration 2: Andrew, a fourth-grader, suddenly begins wetting himself in class. As a result, the other children make fun of him, and he himself seems to make a joke out of it. The teacher, recognizing that such a return to earlier behavior means that the child is not able to deal adequately with a present situation, begins to examine the child's feelings by encouraging him to speak about these feelings. It seems that Andrew is not able to deal with some of his reading problems, and he feels he cannot progress with the other children in the class. His way of dealing with this is to become a "baby" again, to return to the days when he had his mother to "change his diapers," and therefore, symbolically, to give him protection he does not feel the teacher is giving him. Recognizing this, the teacher decides to show a little more concern and help to Andrew, thus minimizing his use of regression.

Regression takes many common forms in the classroom, including temper tantrums, excessive or unprovoked crying, babylike behavior, overdependency, and so forth. Recognizing each of these as manifestations of regression —a defense mechanism—the teacher can probe to determine what difficulties underlie the use of these defensive behaviors and then help the child overcome the underlying conflicts.

Projection

Projection, another common defense mechanism, is the process of attributing to another person or to an object in the outside world, feelings, thoughts, or beliefs that emanate from within. A student who feels that the teacher doesn't like him, for example, may be projecting his own internal feelings of hostility for the teacher since he cannot adequately recognize these feelings. Projection, which is often verbalized or exhibited in behaviors, allows the teacher to study the feelings that the student is unable to get in touch with.

Illustration 3: A new student, admitted to the class in mid-semester, complains that none of the other students like him and that they are talking about him behind his back. The teacher listens to these perceptions, but upon watching the other students, she does not see this as being the case. She begins to recognize that the new student bears this hostility toward the other students because they seem so much more comfortable in the class situation, and that he is projecting these feelings on to the other students even though they are really his own feelings. In addition to allowing this new student to express his feelings, she helps the other students express positive, accepting feelings to help the new student overcome his anxiety.

Projection occurs quite commonly in the classroom situation and may become a major cause for acting out behaviors. Individual counseling or psychotherapy may be indicated in severe cases in which the projected fantasies replace the child's reality orientation.

Displacement

This defense mechanism involves shifting the feelings we have about one person or thing to another person or thing, generally safer. A student, for example, may express some of the aggression he feels toward his older brother or sister onto other students in the class who are "safer" objects. The word *safer* is used to mean less threatening emotionally.

Illustration 4: Alonzo continually picks on little Daniel in the classroom, even though Daniel, to the teacher's knowledge, does nothing to provoke these continued attacks. After exploring his feelings with Alonzo, the teacher recognizes that Alonzo's mother recently had a new baby, and Alonzo lost much of the attention he had enjoyed in the family. At the same time, the mother kept telling Alonzo how much he should be "enjoying" his new baby brother, and how he should love him. In short, Alonzo displaced his feelings of aggression toward the new baby onto little, cherubic Daniel, who served as the helpless scapegoat.

In addition to repression, regression, projection, and **displacement,** other defense mechanisms that also play a role in the classroom are reaction formation, rationalization, denial, and identification. Each of these, when used inappropriately by the student, works toward stunting emotional growth. **Reaction formation** involves acting in a way that is in total contradiction to the way one really feels. For example, a sixth-grade boy goes around "beating up" the girls he really feels most attracted to. **Rationalization** involves either attributing false motives to one's behavior or explaining behavior with false explanations. Commonly referred to as sour grapes, rationalization is typified

> "In terms of character development, resolution of inappropriate defensive patterns is a paramount task in the development of the fully-functioning individual."

by the famous Aesop fable of the fox who tried repeatedly without success to get at a bunch of grapes. Failing time and again, the fox finally gave up his attempts, rationalizing that the grapes looked sour anyway. One student who couldn't master the multiplication table used rationalization to convince herself that learning these tables wasn't at all important. **Denial** is exhibited when the learner's conscious mind denies feelings from within or situations from outside that prove threatening. Although Jill had failed her three history exams, she couldn't believe that the teacher was going to fail her in the course. Thus, she denied an inevitability that she couldn't accept. **Identification,** as a defense mechanism, involves identifying with an important psychological figure. In its most persistent use, the individual confuses his identity with the identity of someone else. Students whose egos lack sufficient strength to deal with reality problems may identify with the more aggressive children in class rather than trying to cope with their own problems.

Emotional Growth and Defensive Behavior in the Classroom

The taxonomic levels most consistently affected by the employment of defense mechanisms are *receiving* and *responding,* and their respective substages. Defense mechanisms, and consequent defensive behavior, prevent the learner from fully becoming aware of and responsive to the environment around him or her. Since success at these levels is a basic prerequisite to success at the higher levels, the implications of failing to respond appropriately to defensive behavior patterns is quite serious. In terms of character development, resolution of inappropriate defensive patterns is a paramount task in the development of the fully functioning individual.

One prominent thinker, Lawrence S. Kubie, a psychiatrist profoundly concerned with educational problems and human development, has suggested the idea of "educating for maturity," which touches directly upon some of the problems we have been looking at in this section (Kubie, 1959). Kubie argues that the cognitive goals of education—critical and creative thinking—are not independent from emotional growth, but are an integral part of it. He goes on to suggest that the schools must become involved, along with social institutions, in helping people (particularly students) overcome their neurotic problems. He says that the great cultural institutions of human society have failed in their three basic missions; "namely, to enable human nature itself to change; to enable each generation to transmit to the next whatever wisdom it has gained about living; to free the enormous untapped creative potential which is latent in varying degrees in all men" (p. 561). He goes on to criticize these institutions, particularly the school, for failing to directly confront the human problems that children universally bring with them to the school setting, and, as a result, education inadvertently "increases the power of the neurotic processes in our culture" (p. 562). He goes on to state specifically what can be done, and we can examine some of his ideas in light of our discussion of defensive behavior in the classroom:

Every adult bears the imprint of the child. The unconscious projection of the years of childhood onto the screen of adult years anchors us to the past. Consequently, the educator who is interested in making education assist the individual to move toward maturity must study how such projections from the past influence education, and whether the educational process tends to perpetuate their influence.

First of all, we face the obvious fact that the schoolroom and school as a whole confront the child with substitute parents and siblings. This provides an opportunity to resolve the fateful and destructive conflicts of the nursery. Yet the opportunity is not utilized. Instead, the child in school merely relives and buries even deeper the hates and loves and fears and rivalries which had their origins in his home.

The schoolroom may partially balance or neutralize these conflict-laden feelings; but it fails utterly to render them less fixed and less rigid *by bringing them within the reach of conscious selection, direction, and control.* Self-control, as it is taught, is almost invariably concentrated on control of the secondary consequences of such conflicts, rather than on focusing on the elimination of their inner sources. (p. 563)

One such way of focusing on the inner sources of conflict-laden feelings, with the hope of resolving the conflicts, is to recognize the defense mechanism involved in the behavior. This can usually be accomplished simply by observation, but at times the teacher may have to probe beyond the superficialities of behavior to determine which defenses are being used.

Emotional Conflicts and Affective Learning

Defense mechanisms are one of several manifestations of emotional conflict. When the student experiences conflicts, these may directly impede cognitive learning, and they are always considered obstacles to affective growth. But, as we all know only too well, life is filled with conflict, and the ability to resolve conflicts is an important part of living. It may be of some help to the teacher to understand the different types of conflicts that people typically experience. We will use a paradigm for conflict that is generally used by behavioral psychologists, but which should have application to all types of conflicts. First, let us examine one of the major causes of emotional conflict: frustration.

We've all experienced feelings of **frustration** at one time or another, but there are certain situations that are more likely than others to create frustration. School is one such situation. In the school setting, no matter how good the teacher, no matter how interesting the subject matter, no matter how motivated the student, there are a variety of elements that are particularly conducive to producing frustration. First, we have the group setting in which the student has to function. In any group setting (as we shall see in chapter 15), there are abundant opportunities for individuals to find themselves pitted against the group, and this confrontation is often a source of overt or covert frustration in the classroom setting. Secondly, the competition for attention in the group situation is greater than it is in the one-to-one learning situation. As the student finds himself competing with other members of the group for attention, he or she may experience frustration. The tasks of learning and mastery—which are always subject to objective measurement in the classroom—further increase the likelihood of frustration.

Lundin (1974) describes three common causes of frustration, each of which has many specific instances in the classroom. *Frustration by delay* occurs because of the "withholding of the reinforcement that ordinarily occurs from an organism that has already been conditioned in a particular way" (p. 295). An example of this might occur when a student is accustomed to receiving immediate approval after giving a right answer. He has learned this from his first-grade teacher, but when he enters the second grade, the teacher no longer does this; and every time the student gives a correct answer, he feels frustration because he does not receive the response he was prepared to receive. *Frustration by thwarting* results "when a barrier is introduced and behavior is prevented" (pp. 295–98). Consider a student who is highly motivated to learn but is prevented from doing so by an undiagnosed learning disability that prevents the student from accurately perceiving the material that has to be learned. Or, consider a student who is pushed to be a superior athlete, but whose physical capacities are not adequate for this. This student will also feel a frustration by thwarting. Finally, Lundin describes *frustration from a conflict situation,* and we shall look at four types of conflict situations that can serve as models for most of the conflicts experienced in the school setting.

Conflict Situations

Conflict occurs whenever we are faced with a choice that involves the pairing of two or more conflicting motives or goals. The four common models of conflict situations are *approach-approach, approach-avoidance, avoidance-avoidance,* and *double approach-avoidance.* We'll consider examples of each.

The Psychology of Learning

An approach-approach conflict results from a situation in which the person has two possible goals, each equally attractive, and cannot decide between the two. A student can choose between honors English and honors Social Studies, and cannot decide between them. This is, of course, a relatively easy conflict to resolve, since either choice is a positive one. An avoidance-avoidance conflict is much more difficult, since it involves two possible alternatives, both of which are negatively perceived by the person. A student either has to work at an after-school study center or be held back, and neither of these choices is pleasant to the student.

In both of these types of conflict situations, the student may become immobilized and unable to act or may resolve the conflict through some decision. A typical way of resolving such conflict situations is to make one of the goals more positive than the other, thus disequilibrating the block that has resulted in a behavioral stalemate.

With an approach-avoidance conflict, there is only one goal, but it has both strong positive and negative characteristics. If there are two goals, each with strong positive and negative characteristics, it is called a double approach-avoidance conflict. These types of conflicts are particularly difficult to resolve because of the ambiguity of the situation, ambivalent feelings, and the tendency to duck the conflict situation rather than face up to it.

Much research focuses on how people attempt to resolve these conflicts in which a single pole has both negative and positive characteristics. Berelson and Steiner (1964), in reviewing the literature, conclude that "when goals are at once satisfying and threatening . . . people's behavior vacillates at a point near, but not too near, the goal: at a distance the tendency to approach predominates; near the goal the tendency to avoid is greater. The result is a stable of self-maintaining conflict that tends to keep the organism at the point where the two tendencies cross" (p. 272).

Let us look at a classroom situation that results from unresolved conflicts.

Illustration 5: In a sixth-grade class, the teacher becomes aware of a certain tension in the air although he is not able to pinpoint the problem. He just senses that lately some of the students have been troubled. After a few weeks of careful observation, noting especially subtle innuendos that have been expressed, he realizes that some of the students in the class are beginning to use drugs, and other students, who are not using them, are upset about this. Yet no one has brought this to his attention.

Because he knows his students well, he is able to analyze some of the conflicts that are present. He knows (again, from the innuendos) that three of the students want to tell him what's going on, but are afraid of peer disapproval. This is a typical approach-avoidance conflict. Some students, he suspects, might be on the verge of being pressured into using drugs; particularly those students who typically respond to group pressure. On the one hand their consciences may be telling them not to, while the group encourages them to do so. They are experiencing an avoidance-avoidance conflict.

Recognizing that in such conflicts the student may become immobilized and unable to act, the teacher decides to help the students resolve their conflicts. He knows that if the avoidance pole becomes negative, the approach will become more positive, and vice versa. Thus, he includes in his lessons information about the dangers of drugs and illustrative examples of how people are pressured into using drugs by their peers. He allows the students to experience, in fantasy situations, how the group can pressure people into doing what they really don't want to do. He also teaches them a responsibility to discourage their classmates from using drugs.

This teacher has used behavioral principles of conflict resolution to help his students overcome a conflict that was not only interfering with their schoolwork but had the potential for causing them great harm as well.

The Healthy Person: Coping and Adaptation

One of the weaknesses inherent in many psychological theories—Freud's psychoanalytic theory particularly—is that it concentrates on people who are in the midst of turmoil and conflict and fails to study in depth the healthy, well-adjusted individual. Abraham Maslow, a noted American psychologist, cognizant of this weakness, made a systematic study of healthy, successful individuals to learn about their psychology—a psychology of growth and self-actualization.

Maslow found that as individuals learn to cope with their environment and adapt to changing situations, they master ways of satisfying what he calls the *hierarchy of needs*. These needs are the physiological needs (food, shelter, sleep, etc.); the safety needs (freedom from illness, controlled and predictable environment); the need for love, for esteem; and finally, the need for self-actualization. Maslow (1954) explains this highest need:

Even if all these needs are satisfied, we may still often (if not always) expect that a new discontent and restlessness will soon develop, unless the individual is doing what he is fitted for. A musician must make music, an artist must paint, a poet must write, if he is to be ultimately happy. What a man *can* be, he *must* be. This need we may call self-actualization.

In Maslow's scheme of things, the healthy person develops in the affective realm by satisfying levels of needs, ultimately reaching the self-actualizing needs—the highest level. This growing process takes many years, of course, and one could hardly expect the preschool-age child to be self-actualizing. In fact, at this early age, the child is barely able to satisfy any of its needs and depends almost entirely on the parents. However, the learning during this period prepares the child to satisfy all of these needs later in life, and by the time the child reaches high school, we already see the markings of self-actualization in progress. One way of looking at affective growth, therefore, is to examine the success or failure of the individual in satisfying the basic needs.

> "One way of looking at affective growth is to examine the success or failure of the individual in satisfying the basic needs."

In terms of the taxonomic levels, this means that the individual can meet the following objectives:

1. The individual is self-sufficient; that is, can function without exhibiting over-dependence upon other people, but . . .
2. The individual also indicates a gregariousness; a recognition of others, an interest in interpersonal interactions, and a sincere and genuine warmth and empathy for others.
3. The individual is not passive to his or her environment, but is an active participant, attempting to change the environment rather than be changed by it.
4. The individual is able to experience feelings of love for others and able to accept being loved by others. While not feeling "hungry" for love, he or she is able to feel satisfied with love.
5. The individual acts according to moral principles, although he or she demonstrates a moral flexibility when dealing with others.
6. The individual integrates his beliefs into his actions, and shows, through his behavior, consistency.

Self-Perception and Affective Learning

So far, our examination of the affective learning processes has looked at emotional growth, paying particular attention to defense mechanisms and their uses, and to the behavioral model that attempts to explain conflict situations in terms of the individual's behavior options. These areas are related most directly to levels one and two of Krathwohl's taxonomy: receiving and responding. Our ability to perceive the world and to react to what we perceive is crucial to all other affective processes.

Unfortunately, none of these areas helps us understand how the transition is made in the affective domain between these lower levels and the three higher levels—**valuing, organization, and characterization**—which together are certainly the most significant and advanced levels of the affective human experience. To understand this relationship, we have to abandon the objective perspective we have been using and look deeply into the hidden recesses of the learner's mind; namely, at the learner's concept of self, which, as we shall see, is the integral cohering force that underlies all affective growth.

Although we use the word quite frequently in our conversations, with an implicit understanding of what it means, there is no generally accepted definition of **self.** In fact, it has been argued by several psychologists (and philosophers, too!) that the question, What is self? is essentially unanswerable. Gergen (1971), for example, in a book-length study of the concept of self, argues that the question, What is self? is "inappropriate because the way in which it is formulated does not lead to conclusions that are scientifically useful" (p. 38). He goes on to explain what he has done in his efforts:

> Rather, we have first hypothesized a process by which the individual defines and categorizes his own activities, both internal and external. The resultant *concepts* of self are multiple and often inconsistent. Concepts, particularly self-concepts, play a crucial role in orienting the individual to the world around him and in enabling him to increase his rewards and avoid punishments. (Gergen, 1971, p. 38)

This would be considered a process approach to understanding the concept of self—an approach that begins with the individual's processes of perception as the basis for understanding the individual's perception of self.

Yet, despite such objections, which are rife in the literature, the word *self* persists in its usage, rich with denotations and connotations that acquire meaning through its continued use. Drever's *Dictionary of Psychology,* for example, defines self:

> Usually in the sense of the *personality* or *ego,* regarded as an agent, conscious of his own continuing identity; often used widely of an animal or even material object regarded as an agent. . . .[1]

So, again we don't find much help in a technical definition. The unabridged dictionary confuses us even more when we find four separate entries under *self,* with over twenty-five different meanings.

If we wish to understand and study the self in the educative process, we first must have an understanding of what self means. This, as we see, is a most difficult task.

Fortunately, there is a solution at hand. If, instead of using the broad term *self,* we propose an alternative term that embraces self in its specific meanings and yet has application to the problems we are concerned with, we can avoid these pitfalls. The term that has been suggested, and which we shall use, is **phenomenal self.**

This term has been comprehensively defined, studied, and evaluated by Arthur W. Combs and Donald Snygg. Before examining its implications in affective learning, let us look at some selections from their lengthy definition and clarification of the term:

1. From James Drever, *A Dictionary of Psychology* (Revised edition, 1964) © the estate of James Drever, 1952. Reprinted by permission of Penguin Books Ltd.

> "The phenomenal self is not limited to the body proper, but extends to all those things in the world which we feel a part of."

By the phenomenal self we mean those aspects of the perceptual field to which we refer when we say "I" or "me." In common with the rest of the perceptual field it has the feeling of complete reality. Its physical boundaries are roughly the skin or clothing surface. Man can extend these boundaries; for example, when he uses a cane, or when he drives a familiar vehicle. It is a common observation that many a man reacts to a crumpled fender as though it were a violation of his own person.

   The perceived, or phenomenal, self includes far more than the physical aspects of the self. Perceptions of the self as strong, honest, good-humored, sophisticated, just, guilty, and a thousand other qualities may be a part of the phenomenal self in a particular individual. . . . The phenomenal self, it should be understood, is not a physical entity, that is, it does not exist someplace in our bodies. To the individual himself the phenomenal self is real. It *is* himself. To the outsider observing the individual, the phenomenal self is pure abstraction inferred from the observed behavior and representing only an approximation of the self experienced by the behavior. Such a concept is useful in helping us to understand and deal with problems of human behavior. It helps us to focus attention upon those aspects of the perceptual field of particular importance in understanding behavior, and at the same time makes it possible to exclude many aspects of minor importance. (Combs & Snygg, 1959, pp. 44–45)

Two important points emerge from this definition. One, that **phenomenal self** is not limited to the body proper, but extends to all those things in the world which we feel a part of. Two, observations of an individual can offer us only an approximation of self, since the phenomenal self is basically a perceptual self.

   With this in mind, we can turn our attention to the crucial issue of self and **perception,** and examine how the phenomenal self influences our perception of the world and how this perception of the world coheres and clarifies our valuative processes.

"The phenomenal self," Combs and Snygg (1959, p. 145) argue, "is the individual's basic frame of reference." What this means, in terms of the taxonomic categories we have been using, is that not only is the learner's awareness of and response to the world affected by the phenomenal self but this same self serves as a reference point for forming values, for organizing these values into systems, and for characterizing one's behavior in terms of the organized value systems. Thus, the **phenomenal self** is an integral part of levels three, four, and five of the taxonomy.

   The structure of the self is often revealed in the classroom. Its manifestations include the learner's ability to perform work, to socialize with others, to

The Phenomenal Self and Personal Growth

Therapeutic experiences take many different forms in the school setting. . . .

. . . learning to work with their hands, these students develop the foundations for later vocational therapeutic experiences.

The Psychology of Learning

interact on a personal level with the teacher, and other learner behaviors that are open to the teacher's scrutiny. Moreover, the teacher touches this self through his or her communications with the student, both individually and through the group. The relevance of self to all learning experiences has been discussed by Staines (1971), among others. In pointing out the relevance of self for educators, Staines argues that, "the educational significance of the Self is reaffirmed when it is realized that changes in the Self-picture are an inevitable part of both outcomes and conditions of learning in every class-room, whether or not the teacher is aware of them or aiming for them" (p. 407).

As the teacher is able to change the self-picture, or self-image, or self-concept—alternative terms—the teacher not only promotes affective learning and emotional growth but lays the foundation for cognitive and psycho-motor mastery as well. For the teacher to ignore self-development as tangential to the aims of education is to deny one of the most important components of the educational experience.

But self-expansion, or self-growth, is an easier term to bandy around than to actually do something about. Many of the teaching practices discussed in chapters 10 and 11 are designed to help the teacher reach this oft-hidden area of the affective domain. Of course, the basic prerequisite to making an impact on the students' senses of self is that the teacher be in touch with his or her own self—that the teacher's phenomenal field be intact, realistic, and functional. In a book devoted entirely to expanding the self, and directed toward the teacher's own self-growth, Angelo V. Boy and Gerald J. Pine suggest four areas of therapeutic experiences through which the teacher, and subsequently the student, can grow. The **human therapeutic experiences** include positive interpersonal experiences with others. **Vocational therapeutic experiences** are the riches derived through one's work; not as work is a job, but as work is a commitment for the individual. **Religious therapeutic experiences** are growth through religion, defined broadly "to be man's relationship to that which he regards as being holy" (p. 67), whether it is through formal religion or any other overriding beliefs that influence the person's actions. **Recreational therapeutic experiences** occur in a pleasant social context, and facilitate interpersonal communications and understanding. Boy and Pine's book, *Expanding the Self: Personal Growth for Teachers* (1971), is one of the most important documents on self-growth to appear since Combs and Snygg's work in the late '50s. Their conclusions on self-growth and personal development in the affective domain apply as well to the student as to the teacher. A major portion of their conclusions is contained in display 7.1, but the insights that lead to these conclusions can only be provided through the book itself.

1. *The self expands because of a balanced, integrated, and continuous involvement in therapeutic human work, religious, and recreational experiences.*

A balanced involvement in the four therapeutic experiences means that man must have contact with his visceral in order to ascertain the degree of therapeutic balance that exists in his life. He must translate this visceral sensitivity into conscious awareness so that he knows when the balance does or does not exist. When there is balance, the self feels itself expanding and reinforces this expansion. When there is imbalance, the self must be aware of what is causing the imbalance and move toward a particular therapeutic experience which has the potential for creating the desired behavior....

2. *The extent to which the self expands is proportionately related to the degree of qualitative involvement in each of the four therapeutic experiences available.*

... In order to expand, the self must immerse itself in each of the four therapeutic experiences in an effort to discover its heretofore unknown depths. The self becomes involved in a search for the hidden treasure of each therapeutic experience, but there must be a deep desire to seek; a desire to plumb the depths of each therapeutic experience in order to penetrate and absorb its personal relevancy.

3. *The self cannot fully expand by engaging in only one, two, or three of the four therapeutic experiences available.*

When the self limits itself to an involvement in either human, vocational, religious, or recreational experiences, or a combination of two or three of these experiences, it decreases the degree to which it can be expanded. The self becomes more whole, more fully expanded, when it absorbs the inherent value contained within each of the four therapeutic experiences and realizes how each contributes to the fullness of the self. ... Whenever the self senses a void in its existence, it is typically due to the absence of one or more of the therapeutic experiences in the life-style of existence ...

4. *Among the four therapeutic experiences, man devotes more psychic energy to the one which expands the self more fully than do the others.*

To divide the time available for the four therapeutic experiences into quartiles would hamper the expansion of the self.... Among the four therapeutic experiences, one usually has more visceral relevancy than the others and, hence, contributes more to the expansion of the self than the others. When one discovers which of the four therapeutic experiences impacts the self more qualitatively than the others, he intuitively expends more psychic energy when engaging in that therapeutic experience....

5. *Involvement in therapeutic human experiences is the catalyst which enables the self to discover the visceral relevancy of therapeutic vocational, religious, and recreational experiences.*

The self that is expanded more fully than others typically experiences more personal relevancy in therapeutic human relationships. These therapeutic human experiences become the base whereby the self feels comfortable enough to project itself toward therapeutic vocational, religious, and recreational experiences....

6. *The self which has been expanded by a qualitative engagement in the four therapeutic experiences will transcend itself and consciously and humanly extend itself toward man.*

... Man returns to man when he is free to do so; when he feels sufficiently fulfilled as a person, he completes a therapeutic cycle by returning to a caring attitude toward man. When he is fulfilled, he is no longer suspicious or distrustful of man....

7. *The expanded self attempts to replace the tolerance of man with an empathic sense of unconditional positive regard for man.*

The expanded self refuses to "put up" with his fellowman—to tolerate his existence.... The expanded self realizes that the true test of its expansion is its ability to have reverence for the differences among men.... The expanded self accepts differences; it sees beauty in differences and realizes that the self can be further expanded when it evolves toward an unconditional positive regard for the differences among men....

8. *The expanding self values the direction of its own expansion but has no inclination to move other men in the same direction; it respects pluralism because it is evidence of the existence of personal freedom.*

The expanded self realizes that there can be human convergence among men only if the individual is freely allowed to determine his own values. Man attempts to impose his values on another only when he feels that his own values are superior to the values held by the other person; but the expanded self doesn't feel the need for such a psychological crutch. . . . Instead, the expanded self creates an atmosphere of communication in which the person can reach toward his own crystallization of personally relevant values. . . .

9. *The expanding self has a reverence for the people of the past who have contributed to the civilization of man, is more relevant in its present state of being, and possesses a psychic temperature which insists that a viable legacy be passed on to future generations of man.*

The expanding self knows and values its own existence. The expanding person conceives himself to be a valuable part of mankind in the here-and-now, but he is also appreciative of the unknown men of the past who have contributed to the evolution of whatever degree of humanness exists in the world today. . . . Because he is an expanded person, he realizes that his life, his existence, is important only insofar as it is a contribution to the human evolution of man. He doesn't want to play games with his life—to exist only at a superficial and uninvolved level; he wants to live and sense the thunder and the rainbows of his existence. . . .

10. *Participation in the four therapeutic experiences is a self-expanding process for all age groups regardless of nationality, race culture, socioeconomic status, political affiliations, or religious inclinations.*

. . . In all countries and cultures, the self can experience personally relevant human experiences, can seek out the intrinsic values in the work being performed, can spiritually link itself to man, can enjoy itself through recreation. The only barriers which prevent the self from expanding are those self-conceived barriers which one can easily construct. . . .

11. *The expanding self senses an internationally emerging convergence of man in various areas of human thought; it possesses a deep sensitivity to the psychosocial, philosophical, technological, and biological evolution of man and the importance of his place in that evolution.*

The development of sophisticated communications media . . . have developed among formerly divergent peoples a sense of their commonness, a sense that they are essentially alike. . . . This international convergence of man is a new and refreshing experience. . . . For the first time in the history of man, he is truly beginning to sense a link between himself and the international community of man. . . . As this occurs more frequently, it will become psychologically more difficult for a person to want to kill others. . . .

12. *All educational institutions should make provisions whereby students have qualitative access to each of the four therapeutic experiences.*

One of the major functions of educational institutions is to produce positive, psychologically whole persons. School settings should make it possible for students to have qualitative human, vocational, religious, and recreational therapeutic experiences. A school cannot help the self to expand by merely providing cognitive experiences for its students. Within the context of organized education, teaching for knowledge is important, but facilitating the development and expansion of self is just as important and is a primary educational goal. The self is a consequence of experience, and in schools, we provide a host of experiences. . . . Any institution which hopes to expand the selves of its clientele must make provisions whereby they can become involved in each of the four therapeutic experiences. . . .

13. *It is impossible to expand the self into perfection; man will always be involved in the process of becoming more adequate, but he will never achieve full personal adequacy because his reach will always exceed his grasp.*

A qualitative involvement in each of the four therapeutic experiences will not result in the self becoming expanded in its fullest and most perfect sense. Such perfect expansion is impossible because the nature of man is evolutionary; he progresses, in self-expansion, from one stage to the next, but he never achieves his apex, since today's sense of self-fulfillment . . . will not, and should not, be satisfying tomorrow. . . .

Angelo V. Boy and Gerald J. Pine, "Expanding the Self: Some Tentative Conclusions," *Expanding the Self: Personal Growth for Teachers* (Dubuque, Iowa: Wm. C. Brown Company Publishers, 1971), pp. 98–106. Used with permission.

> "The respect the teacher shows to the student—through allowing diversity of opinion, through encouraging creative thinking and problem solving, by allowing individual expression—provides an enriching therapeutic experience that can serve as a basis of growth."

Classroom Implications

For the teacher to provide avenues for affective learning in the classroom, some careful, well-balanced planning would be helpful. Fortunately, each of the four areas of therapeutic experiences are natural consequences of the classroom setting, some more obvious than others. *Human therapeutic experiences* are ubiquitous, of course; in the classroom setting, the teacher's own interpersonal relationships with students can serve as a facilitative basis for human encounters. The respect the teacher shows to the student—through allowing diversity of opinion, through encouraging creative thinking and problem solving, by allowing individual expression—provides an enriching therapeutic experience that can serve as a basis of growth.

Since the students are not yet immersed in the adult world of work, the educational (cognitive) experience becomes the equivalent for the *vocational therapeutic experience.* How enriching and relevant is the subject matter for the student? What can the student bring to the subject matter, and how can the teacher integrate what the students bring, to give subject matter a personal, transcendent dimension? Are the students in the process of developing positive attitudes toward learning or is learning a burden to them —an irrelevant, cumbersome bane in their existence? The answers to these questions will help determine how therapeutic the vocational-educational experience is for the student.

Religious therapeutic experiences, in the nontraditional sense in which this term is used, refers to the development of beliefs and values through education. For the student to develop these, he must be encouraged to explore, articulate, challenge, and reflect amongst his peers. The teacher's openness to such explorations helps the student discover values within the school setting.

The informal **socialization** that is characteristic of some aspects of students' school behavior constitutes the *recreational therapeutic experiences.* While often the appearance of such socialization in the classroom is viewed as a disruption—which it may well be—students experience new social modes of communication within and outside the classroom. The school may provide ample opportunities (such as socials, clubs, dances, etc.) to facilitate socialization and broaden the students' base of **recreational therapeutic experiences.**

Let us pause for a moment to see where we stand as of now. We've taken in so much material in this chapter that we need a brief period to digest it.

We began the chapter by embracing a broad view of affective learning as something more than emotional learning; something that helps the person develop his or her sense of humanness. Because this was a vague statement, we've attempted to clarify it by examining the specific categorization of educational objectives proposed by Krathwohl, Bloom, and Masia in the Taxonomy of Educational Objectives for the Affective Domain. *The progression of levels in this* **taxonomy** *moved from simple* receiving *of the world around to* responding *to this world. Next, the progression of levels moves to valuing, organizing values into systems, and finally to characterization by value, in which the individual's behavior is fully integrated into the value systems that underlie it. This listing of taxonomic categories served as a map of the territory we would explore in this chapter.*

Our exploration necessarily involved looking into the emotional life of the learner. We considered the relationship between emotions and performance in school; between emotional growth and personal development and fulfillment in the educational setting. Then, we looked in detail at two crucial areas of emotional conflict: the defense mechanisms, which color perception of the world (Krathwohl's level one) and how we respond to what we perceive (level two), and conflict situations, which either immobilize us or make appropriate actions difficult.

Finally, we directed our attention to the primary agent *of affective learning, the self. We suggested the use of* phenomenal self, *in the sense proposed by Combs and Snygg, and examined the implications of self in other learning endeavors. Then, using Boy and Pine's work in self-growth, we listed thirteen basic principles of self-expansion that have relevance to the teacher.*

Where does this leave us? Unfortunately, still far afield. While we have explored some of the foundations for affective learning, we still have not touched upon one of the most important areas, moral learning. *Moral learning is involved in levels three, four, and five of the taxonomy, and is also one of the areas in which the greatest amount of research has been done. What we want to determine specifically is how the child develops a sense of moral values, how these values can be changed and molded by others, and how the child (or adult) reasons when he or she makes moral judgment. These will be the subject of the following section of this chapter.*

We shall examine four positions on moral development and moral reasoning: the psychoanalytic, the behavioral, Piaget's and Kohlberg's—the last two in some depth. To provide us with a perspective of these theories so that we can ultimately integrate them into what we have learned, we will begin with a general statement on the development of character in the educative process, which has generally been considered one of the most important components of affective learning and one of the chief goals of affective education.

Character Development and Moral Learning

As we mentioned near the begining of this chapter, in the *Republic,* Plato speaks of the development of character as both a prerequisite for and an integral part of the learner's intellectual (or cognitive) development. It is dangerous, he argues, to help a person acquire intellectual skills without first helping him develop a sense of values—of *right* and *wrong,* of *goodness, justice,* and *proportion.* For if the person has the powerful tools of intellect at his disposal, they can be put to good use or they can be abused; the person's character, above all else, assures that the strengths of the mind will also prove to be its virtues.

Two thousand years after Plato, Bertrand Russell, in his book *Education and the Good Life,* raises much the same point. He includes in this important work a detailed discussion on the development of character. Significantly, this discussion precedes the section on intellectual development; for Russell, like Plato, believes that a strong, moral character is the best foundation for intellectual growth. We shall look at Russell's position shortly.

Independent of the philosophical tradition (at least insofar as the methodology and lines of reasoning are concerned), psychologists have attempted to understand how character develops and what forces shape the acquisition of character, the inculcation of values—and moral outlook, in general. Freud's psychoanalytic theory of moral development is the first distinctively psychological theory, although in many respects it supports philosophical positions that have been espoused (Belkin, 1974).

To Freud, the young child is basically amoral, a creature of impulse, motivated by selfish drives, which Freud called the *id.* The id strives for immediate gratification of instincts and is oblivious to the needs of others and to the constraints of the society. This leads inevitably to conflict, and Freud's theory attempts to explain how such conflicts are avoided.

The process of **maturation,** according to psychoanalytic theory, requires that the child learn that many of its needs cannot be gratified immediately; some not at all. As the child matures, it moves through a series of stages (see chapter 2), during which two other aspects of personality develop that assist in the socialization process. The first of these, the *ego,* is the realistic aspect of the person. The other aspect is the *superego,* or conscience, which is strict, moralistic, and often unrealistic. The child develops its sense of conscience through internalizing the parents' values, which form a coherent unit in the concept of superego. In the healthy person, the ego is the strongest part of the personality, since it must orient the individual to reality.

The **superego,** according to psychoanalytic theory, is responsible for telling the person "right" or "wrong," "should" or "shouldn't." Whenever the person acts contrary to the injunctions of the superego, he or she feels guilt, a powerful psychological force that becomes the basis for many psychoneurotic conflicts. To the Freudians, then, these values—or "moral introjects"—which are integrated into the structure called superego by the time the child is six or seven years old, become the basis for most moral decisions.

A contrary position, the behavioral (or learning theory) position, rejects the Freudian concept of superego and argues instead that all moral behavior is learned through various conditioning processes. Alexander (1969) presents in summary the behavioral position on moral development:

Moral behavior can be defined as a response system developed as the result of perception of the pleasure and satisfaction occurring in other persons. It is likely that in early childhood, perhaps by the age of three years or earlier, the child comes to understand that some behavior brings parental approval and praise and other behavior brings disapproval or perhaps even disgust and anger. . . . The child during his first five years, however, can differentiate only minimally among types of behavior that might be termed 'moral'. . . . teaching about morality is in a context similar to that of teaching about other behavior, and the moral significance of behavior is only realized at a later age.

The fact that the child does not understand the significance of moral behavior does not mean that the so-called 'moral learnings' do not occur in early childhood; it simply means that the child does not differentiate moral behavior from any other taught behavior. However, a child does begin the internalization of emotional responses of others in association with actions labeled 'good' and 'bad'." (p. 95)

In many ways, the positions of the Freudians and behaviorists are quite compatible, although the language differences between the two "-isms" often obscure the similarities. For example, Bandura's position (Bandura & McDonald, 1963; Bandura, 1969), that the major mechanisms in moral behavior are imitation and social reinforcement, fits in quite well with the Freudian point of view and avoids the pitfalls of Freud's metaphysical language. Bandura has conducted a number of empirical studies to support his position that children learn moral behavior through the behavioral process called modeling.

The debates between the Freudians and behaviorists are still heated and no clear resolution is on the horizon. But actually the two theories share a common weakness: neither discloses the processes by which we reason out moral choices; each describes the behaviors and the psychodynamics underlying the behaviors, but neither probes fully into the cognitive and affective processes that shape our moral reasoning. A little later in this chapter, we will be looking at two theories that provide some details in this area: Piaget's and Kohlberg's theories.

Let us return now to our original problem: how character is shaped, and which forces influence its development. In some ways, *character* is preferable to *moral outlook* since it includes more than the moral behavior and the moral reasoning of the person. But theories of character development are far scarcer than theories of moral development, so the latter has attracted far more attention. Probably the most detailed position on the development of character—and a position with direct implications for the classroom teacher —is the one articulated by Bertrand Russell. Let us direct our attention to Russell's position.

Russell's Theory of Character Development

Russell's position, as we have mentioned, is a derivative of Plato's original formulation on **character development,** but it is designed to be more practical in today's world. Russell himself ran an experimental school during the 1920s and attempted to put into practice many of the ideas that later appeared in his educational writings. "To what developmental ends should moral education be directed?" Russell asks (1926, 1927, 1930, 1932), and he attempts to answer the question with some specificity.

He argues that the child must develop four "virtues" in order for his education to prove helpful to him and to society. These virtues are the connecting links between the needs of the individual and the needs and demands of the world in which he lives. They are **vitality, courage, sensitiveness,** and **intelligence.** An understanding of the sense in which Russell uses these words will help the teacher see how his ideas can be readily translated into classroom applications.

Vitality is synonymous with good health and a strong body. It is attained by keeping the child fit through a good diet and a well-balanced schedule of exercise. It gives one a feeling of pleasure in being alive and consequently encourages the person to take an interest in the outside world, "and thus promotes objectivity, which is an essential of sanity." It also acts as a safeguard against envy by giving a person pride in himself and by making his whole existence more pleasurable. Plato's idea of "a sound mind and a sound body" is embodied in this virtue.

Certainly, the degree of vitality is predominantly controlled in the home rather than in the school. What the child eats, what activity is allowed, what nutrients are ingested are mostly a matter of the parents' concern and education. But we have long recognized that we cannot educate a starving, physi-

> "The child who comes to school hungry each day is less likely to develop a healthy character than the child who comes to school well-fed."

cally deficient child, and the schools (particularly in poor urban and rural areas) have traditionally made efforts to compensate for deficiencies of the home by providing free lunches and breakfasts and by setting aside a period or two each day for healthy physical exercise. What the teacher might want to consider is that an assessment of the child's vitality (observed or inferred from information) can be useful in understanding learning or personality deficiencies. The child who comes to school hungry each day is less likely to develop a healthy character than the child who comes to school well-fed, according to this position.

Courage, the second virtue, begins with an absence of irrational fears. It is always achieved by instruction, not by suggestion, coercion, or undue persuasion. The child is shown the groundlessness of his irrational fears and taught to approach and manipulate the object that he fears. Both example and experience, Russell argues, are a part of instruction—the example of the parents dealing with the feared object and then permitting the child to have his own experience with it.

A fifth-grade teacher, recognizing the importance of developing courage in her students, asked the students which ones were brave and bold. Several raised their hands; and some looked down, ashamed. The teacher then explained that she knew every person in that class had courage, and she would show them why. First, she asked them to explain what they meant by courage, and many gave examples of reckless bravado instead of courage. She then explained that courage is not venturing into dangerous situations for the excitement or danger, but rather that courage is being able to handle difficult situations for which we are unprepared or which startle us. "What would you do if you were walking to school and you saw your friend get hit by a car?" she asked; and then, "What do you do if you see a house on fire?" Through the discussion following these questions, the teacher was able to help the students understand the meaning of courage—as the ability to deal rationally with dangerous situations. Then the teacher asked the students to verbalize some of the things that frightened them, and as they did so, she attempted to reassure them in a rational, logical manner and to teach them how to handle some of these difficult, often terrifying situations. One boy told of how frightened he became when his father, coming home drunk, beat his mother with a belt. Although the teacher could not intervene directly in this situation, she showed the boy how he could deal with his feelings about what was happening, and how he could deal with his parents' feelings about what

> "The teacher can be an active participant in the process of emotional sensitiveness by bringing into the classroom real and hypothetical situations that the children are encouraged to discuss."

was happening, and how he could appeal to his father in more rational moments. Before this intervention, the boy had never discussed this with his father—he did not have the courage to bring it up with him. Now he would be better equipped to deal with the problem.

This fifth-grade teacher recognized that courage was an important part of character development, and that classroom time was well spent in helping the students understand what courage means (and, importantly, how it differs from temerity and bravura) and in showing them how they could become more courageous.

Avoidance of fear is only a part of the cultivation of courage. The child must also realize what is really dangerous and must experience fear appropriately. Russell uses the example of his son's ignorance of the dangers of a steep cliff. Russell illustratively taught the child what would happen if he fell down the cliff, and instilled in him an appropriate sense of danger. The classroom teacher can be especially helpful in teaching students courage by making them more rational beings. Just as the parents may have induced in the child unhealthy, neurotic beliefs through irrational, fear-inducing training, the teacher can counteract these irrational forces by using reason, logic, and example in the classroom.

Sensitiveness, Russell's third virtue, assumes two forms: emotional sensitiveness and cognitive sensitiveness. Emotional sensitiveness consists of the ability to react appropriately to a situation; to properly sort out and handle oncoming stimuli. Sympathy is a form of emotional sensitiveness and should be properly cultivated while the child is young. It should be cultivated, however, to occur in the right situations. The teacher can be an active participant in the process of developing emotional sensitiveness by bringing into the classroom real and hypothetical situations which the children are encouraged to discuss. The teacher also teaches by example when he presents to the students the consequences of his own emotional maturity.

Cognitive sensitiveness is almost synonymous with intelligence, but contains more subjective elements, therefore placing it in the category of a character (affective) trait rather than a purely intellectual trait. For example, the intelligence to listen to the other side of an issue with which we are passionately concerned is a part of cognitive sensitivity. One exercise that teachers can use is to have students debate two sides of a controversial question, giving each student the opportunity to use his or her intellectual and rhetorical skills in defending each position. The opposite of cognitive sensitiveness is closed-mindedness.

Intelligence is the fourth virtue and the one that most closely links the virtues of character with the strengths of intellect. It is the connecting virtue that gives continuity to the scheme. Intelligence, Russell says, relies heavily on curiosity, and the stimulation of curiosity increases the possibilities of intelligence. While all children have some sense of curiosity, goal-directed, purposive curiosity—the backbone of intelligent thinking—must be cultivated early in life. When the child's primitive motor actions during the first year of life seek out and explore his world, the parents should encourage this budding **curiosity** so it flowers and multiplies. Teachers can foster attitudes of curiosity in the students by promoting an active interest in the subject matter and by allowing students to question freely and engage in lively debate.

While Russell's theory of character development has many strong points, it is not based on either clinical or empirical evidence. In the following material, we shall look at some psychological theories that fall into broader categories of developmental positions. These positions, unlike the ones we have looked at so far, present a detailed description of how we go about making moral decisions—what processes of reasoning are involved.

Piaget's Position on Moral Reasoning

In 1932, Piaget published *The Moral Judgment of the Child,* a landmark study that elaborated a theory of moral development using much of the same methodology that characterizes Piaget's other research, namely, close observations and interviews with children. Piaget's moral theory in many ways parallels his position on intellectual growth, and he takes great pains to point out the interrelationship between cognitive reasoning and moral reasoning. Just as in Piaget's cognitive theory, the child progresses from simple, automatic behaviors to more complex, organized behaviors, so, too, in his moral theory does the child progress from naive beliefs and simple motor behaviors to more sophisticated, hypothetical, abstract reasoning. As in his cognitive theory, Piaget's moral theory consists of stages of development, with each stage proving a prerequisite to successive stages. He uses three basic motifs to construct his theory—**rules, realism,** and **justice**—and he relates each of these motifs to patterns of behavior and reasoning. Let us look at each basic motif individually.

The earliest signs of moral development occur as the child goes from unruled **Rules** behavior to what Piaget calls a "morality of constraint." In early forms of play, the child acts without any awareness of rules. Around the beginning of the latency period, the child begins to recognize the differences between right and wrong, as defined by the rules of the game. When the child first learns rules, he sees them as fixed, unchanging principles, which are sacrosanct and laid down by higher authorities. His moral behavior is dominated by constraints, by rules that he has learned to obey. Even when he disobeys rules, he does not question the validity of the rules, which appear to him to be beyond challenge.

Around the age of ten or eleven, the child begins to see that rules can be fixed by agreement, that they can be changed, that they can be questioned. He may still abide by the rules, but he is more willing to negotiate new rules. Piaget calls this the "morality of cooperation," because the child's moral behavior now involves a volitional element that was absent in the earlier stage.

From "Moral Realism" to "Moral Relativism"

When the child first realizes the concepts of wrong and punishment, he thinks in absolute terms rather than in relative, situational terms. The child regards the objective consequences of an act rather than the subjective circumstances surrounding it. For example, in one series of experiments, Piaget told a group of children two short stories and invited their comments. In one story, a little boy *accidentally* broke fifteen of his mother's cups as he was on his way to dinner. In a second story, another little boy broke one cup as he was trying to sneak jam from the cupboard while his mother was out of the house. When the children were asked which of these little boys was more naughty, they answered that the first one was *because he broke more cups*. Piaget calls this type of reasoning "moral realism," and it is characteristic of children to about seven years of age. These children weigh an act strictly according to the consequences and ignore the intentions and extenuating circumstances. Later on, they develop a sense of moral relativism that enables them to consider extenuating circumstances in their moral judgments.

From Immanent Justice to Distributive Justice

The idea of justice develops slowly during the early years, but it ultimately becomes the highest principle of morality. Early in life, the child has an idea of *immanent justice:* the belief that justice is inherent in the order of things, that evil deeds inherently produce evil consequences for the perpetrator. Pulaski (1971, p. 86) refers to this principle as the idea "that knives cut children who have been forbidden to use them." We hear this general principle referred to in such common sayings as "If you play with fire, you are going to get burned."

> "When the child first realizes the concepts of 'wrong' and punishment, he thinks in absolute terms rather than in relative, situational terms."

As the child matures, his sense of justice becomes more sophisticated. He recognizes *distributive justice:* that rewards and punishments can be distributed in different ways. The development of the sense of distributive justice undergoes various transformations. At first (before eight years old), the child considers just and right whatever punishments or rewards the authority figures wish to dispense. During the latency period (about 8 to 11), the child believes that all "bad" acts should receive the same punishment, regardless of the circumstances. A boy who lies out of a noble motivation should receive the same punishment as one who lies out of malice and deceitfulness. After latency, the child begins to recognize the principles of equity, of fairness, and develops a "kind of relativistic egalitarianism in which the strict equality will sometimes be winked at in favor of higher justice" (Flavell, 1963, p. 294).

When we fully understand the specific categories through which Piaget explored moral development, a picture emerges of the developmental progress that characterizes the learner's transition from a fixed-rule oriented perspective to a relativistic, rational morality that transcends the narrow limitations of rules. The first type of morality, which Piaget calls a "morality of constraint," is based on fear and punishment; on the belief that we do not do wrong because we are told not to. In describing this stage, which comprises "rules of the game," "moral realism," and "immanent justice," Jantz and Fulda (1975) point out:

Piaget's Position on Moral Development: From Heteronomy to Autonomy

> During this period children view teachers as authority figures who are to be obeyed to the point where "tattling" may occur. During this stage, teachers need to consider the "constraints" they place upon children. Children need some guidance during this period, and it would be unfair to them if teachers did not set down some guidelines for children to follow. However, if the teacher totally restrains her pupils by making and dictating all of the moral decisions, her class may be slower in moving towards the next stage, a morality of cooperation. (p. 25)

Piaget calls the morality of this period *heteronomous morality*. The word *heteronomous* means "subject to another's laws or rule" (*Webster's New World Dictionary,* 2nd College Ed.),[2] and this again refers to the **constraint** that dominates the child's moral thinking. As the child grows, intellectually, socially, and emotionally, he moves toward what Piaget calls *autonomous*

2. With permission. From *Webster's New World Dictionary of the American Language,* Second College Edition. Copyright © 1976 by William Collins & World Publishing Co., Inc.

morality—a personal, individual morality, based more on cooperation than on constraint. The **autonomous morality** is not independent of the heteronomous morality, but a consequence of it; that is, the child must first learn the rules and pressures of real living in order to learn ways to break free of them when it becomes necessary. Table 7.1 (Summary Characteristics of Levels of Moral Thinking) shows how the concepts of control, justice, responsibility, motivation, and rights are characterized under the **heteronomous**

Table 7.1   Summary Characteristics of Levels of Moral Thinking

Concept	Morality of Restraint	Morality of Participation

Control	Duty is obeying authorities
	  Good defined by obedience to rules
	  Rules or laws not analyzed
		Mutual agreement
		  Lessening of adult constraint
		  Rules can be modified

Justice	Letter of the law
	  Anxiety over forbidden behavior
	  Concern for violation of game rules
	  Punitive justice
	  Any transgression is serious
		Restitutive justice
		  Concern for inequalities
		  Concern for social injustices
		  Spirit of law considered

Responsibility	Objective view
	  Intentions not considered
	  Egocentric position
	  Judgments in relation to conformity to law
		Subjective view
		  Motives considered
		  Rights of others to their opinions respected
		  Judgments by situation

Motivation	External motivation
	  Punishment by another
	  Rewards by another
		Internal motivation
		  Disapproval by others
		  Censure by legitimate authorities followed by guilt feelings
		  Community respect and disrespect
		  Self-condemnation

Rights	Selfish rights
	  No real concept of right
	  Rights are factual ownership
		Rights of others
		  No one has right to do evil
		  A right is an earned claim on the actions of others
		  Concept of unearned, universal rights
		  Respect of individual life and personality of others

Table 1, Summary Characteristics of Levels of Moral Thinking, from R. K. Jantz and T. A. Fulda, "The Role of Moral Education in the Public Elementary School," *Social Education,* January, 1975, p. 28. Reprinted with permission of the National Council for the Social Studies and R. K. Jantz and T. A. Fulda.

The Psychology of Learning

> " 'With advances in social cooperation . . . the child arrives at new moral relationships based on *mutual respect* which lead to a certain autonomy.' "

morality—"morality of restraint"—and under the autonomous reality—"morality of participation."

Piaget and Inhelder (1969) offer a clear picture of autonomous morality and, at the same time, show its derivation from its heteronomous roots:

> With advances in social cooperation . . . the child arrives at new moral relationships based on *mutual respect* which lead to a certain autonomy. . . . First, in games with rules, children before the age of seven who receive the rules ready-made from their elders (by a mechanism derived from unilateral respect) regard them as "sacred, untouchable, and of transcendent origin". . . . Older children, on the contrary, regard rules as the result of agreement among contemporaries, and accept the idea that rules can be changed by means of a democratically arrived at consensus. . . .
>
> Second, an essential product of mutual respect and reciprocity is the sense of justice. . . . As early as seven or eight and increasingly thereafter, justice prevails over obedience itself and becomes a central norm. (p. 127)

Piaget does not present a single, ordered scheme of developmental stages, but rather views a "major underlying developmental progression from a 'heteronomous' to an 'autonomous' attitude or orientation" (Graham, 1972, p. 202).

At a later point, we will examine the implications of Piaget's positions in the educational setting, but let us first turn our attention to a contemporary theory of moral development that rivals Piaget's in importance, and in some ways supports some of Piaget's major assumptions. This is a theory of moral reasoning and moral development proposed by Lawrence Kohlberg.

Kohlberg's Theory of Moral Reasoning

Kohlberg, like Piaget, developed his theory by actually interviewing children and adolescents and studying their responses to certain hypothetical situations. In his studies, he was particularly interested in the ways that subjects arrived at moral decisions—their reasoning—rather than the specific decisions arrived at. The results of his studies indicate that moral thinking progresses through three developmental levels, each of which comprises two related stages. There are, in other words, six specific stages in all.

> "At Kohlberg's conventional level, the person not only conforms to the expectations and rules of conduct of the family, group, or nation, but is concerned with maintaining them because of identification with and out of loyalty to the persons or groups involved."

The Preconventional Level—I

At this level, the child begins to think in a "moral" way, interprets good and bad in terms of their physical consequences (rewards and punishments), or in terms of the physical power of authority figures. In stage 1, the child reasons according to the principle of avoiding punishment and unquestioning obedience to authority figures, such as the parents. Fear, specifically in the form of physical punishment ("You'll have to stay in after school. . . .") plays an important part in the determination of behavior. In stage 2 of the preconventional level, the child is governed by the principle of self-satisfaction and at times recognizes and responds to the satisfaction of the needs of others whom he cares for. Reciprocity, at this stage, is a matter of "You do one thing for me and then I'll do something for you," not of loyalty, gratitude or justice.

The Conventional Level—II

At this level, the person not only conforms to the expectations and rules of conduct of the family, group, or nation but is concerned with maintaining them because of identification with and out of loyalty to the persons in the groups involved. At stage 3 (the first stage of the conventional level), the child demonstrates what Kohlberg calls the "good boy-good girl" orientation. The child internalizes the values of significant others and believes that "good behavior is that which pleases or helps others and is approved of by them. . . . One seeks approval by being 'nice' " (Kohlberg, 1968, p. 26). The individual is primarily motivated to gain the approval of others. Consequently, the child will conform to stereotyped images of what is natural behavior and for the first time will judge other's actions by their intentions. For example, the science teacher asks for a volunteer to stay after class and help her in the lab. Jeffrey knows that this would mean giving up playing basketball with his friends, but he reasons this way: "If I give up the game and offer to stay, the teacher will like me, and this is important."

During stage 4 (the second part of the conventional level), the individual is oriented toward fixed rules and the concept of duty—of obedience to recognized authority. There is a strong tendency, during this stage, toward maintaining the social order, and it is therefore sometimes referred to as the law-and-order stage. Characteristic of moral reasoning during this stage is the relationship to the authority figure. Consider, for example, a student who has the opportunity to steal a final exam, but reasons, "The teacher trusts me, it's

> "At the postconventional level, the person acts according to autonomous moral principles, which have validity apart from the authority of the groups or persons who hold them and also apart from the individual's identification with those persons or groups."

against the rules to see the exam in advance, and therefore I won't give into this temptation."

The Postconventional Level—III

Also called the autonomous or principled level, this is the highest level of moral development. At this level, the person acts according to **autonomous moral principles,** which have validity apart from the authority of the groups or persons who hold them and also apart from the individual's identification with those persons or groups. In other words, obedience to authority and social recognition are secondary to the higher values and principles that are recognized as paramount by the individual. In stage 5 (the first half of the postconventional level), the individual demonstrates a social-contract orientation, generally with legalistic and utilitarian overtones. Right action is defined in terms of general rights and in terms of standards that have been critically examined and agreed upon by the whole society. There is a clear awareness that values, opinions, and laws are relative and can be changed. There is emphasis on the legal point of view, but also on the possibility of changing the law through elections rather than freezing it in terms of stage 4's law-and-order type of thinking. The type of moral reasoning during this stage corresponds roughly to Piaget's concept of a **morality of cooperation,** as opposed to a **morality of constraint.**

Clearly this stage calls for a great deal of abstract reasoning, of which the preadolescent child is still not capable.

During stage 6 (the second half of the **postconventional level**), the person is oriented toward the decisions of conscience in accordance with ethical principles, which are rational, organized, and intended to be applied universally. Rules at this stage are "universal principles of justice, of the reciprocity and equality of human rights, and of respect for the dignity of human beings as individual persons" (Kohlberg, 1968, p. 26).

We see, then, from these stages how the child's naive moral outlook may progress gradually during the years of preadolescent and adolescent growth into a sophisticated, ethical moral system, although many individuals never reach these higher levels. In a number of ways, Kohlberg's stages parallel the levels of affective competency postulated by Krathwohl et al. in the *Taxonomy.* Figure 7.3 shows some specific examples of the moral reasoning model, using Kohlberg's own case material.

Moral problem presented to subjects
In Europe, a woman was near death from cancer. One drug might save her, a form of radium that a druggist in the same town had recently discovered. The druggist was charging $2,000, ten times what the drug cost him to make. The sick woman's husband, Heinz, went to everyone he knew to borrow the money, but he could only get together about half of what it cost. He told the druggist that his wife was dying and asked him to sell it cheaper or let him pay later. But the druggist said, "No." The husband got desperate and broke into the man's store to steal the drug for his wife. Should the husband have done that? Why? (Kohlberg, 1969, p. 379)

PRECONVENTIONAL LEVEL

Stage 1:
"If you steal the drug, you will be sent to jail, so you shouldn't do it."

"If you don't steal it, then you'll get in trouble for letting your wife die."

Principle: Avoidance of negative consequences.

Stage 2:
"If you get caught, you'll probably get a light sentence, and your wife will be alive when you get out."

"Your wife may not be around to appreciate it, anyway, and it's not your fault if she has cancer."

Principle: Act to your own advantage, using the principle of quid pro quo.

CONVENTIONAL LEVEL

Stage 3:
"No one will condemn you for stealing the drug, but they will hold you responsible for her death if you don't."

"By stealing it, you'll bring dishonor on your dying wife, and everyone will think you a thief."

Principle: Act according to how you think others will approve or disapprove of your actions.

Stage 4:
"Your duty is to your wife, and therefore you must steal the drug for her."

"Your duty is to obey the law, and you should not steal the drug."

Principle: Adherence to law and order.

PRINCIPLED LEVEL

Stage 5:
"The fact that you *feel* you have a right to violate the law does not actually give you the right to do so."

"The druggist is abusing his license to hold a public trust, and therefore has violated his implicit obligations to the society in which he works."

Principle: The rule is a social contract which can be changed by agreement.

Stage 6:
"I live by the principle that to save a human life takes priority over all matters of property, and therefore feel no compunctions about taking the drug."

"I live by the principle that property is sacred and cannot be expropriated, and will therefore let my wife die."

Principle: An organized set of values which comprises the conscience acts as the basis for decision making.

Figure 7.3 Kohlberg's Stages of Moral Development

> "The higher moral processes demand higher processes of intellect as well. Thus, moral development depends to a large extent upon intellectual growth and the ability to reason abstractly."

Evaluation of Kohlberg's and Piaget's Positions

While Kohlberg's and Piaget's positions are saying quite different things, they are not in opposition to each other. Both are the direct result of observations with subjects, and both deal with hypothetical moral dilemmas that the subjects are given to resolve, although Piaget also concentrated on observing the spontaneous behavior of children. Both systems are developmental in that they require that the child pass through one stage before he or she can move on to a higher one. Both systems, moreover, move from very concrete "naive" reasoning to hypothetical reasoning about abstracts and principled behavior. The higher moral processes, in each system, demand higher processes of intellect as well. Thus, moral development, according to both of these schemes (as opposed to the behavioral model), depends to a large extent upon intellectual growth and the ability to reason abstractly.

A number of research studies have attempted to evaluate each of these positions. In one early study, Bloom (1959) offers several general criticisms that have become the basis for later studies. Bloom argues that Piaget did not sufficiently take into account the part that cultural and class factors may play in determining the child's judgment; nor does he adequately explain why the child's major reference group shifts from adults to peers. Nor, Bloom argues, is the influence of intelligence made clear, since the IQ's of the subjects are not reported. Also neglected is the role that conflicting or changing standards within the society have on the child's moral development. "The lack of attention to conflict," Bloom (1959, p. 10) says, "in the child's world of moral development . . . is perhaps derived from Piaget's tendency to emphasize the intellectual and logical aspects of thinking."

Dolores Durkin (1959, 1960), in two studies of the child's concept of justice, using 119 children in grades two, five, eight, and eleven as the subject and using Piaget's method of storytelling, found support for Piaget's concept of equity, but not for the principle of **reciprocity.** In a more recent study, Buchanan (1973) interviewed forty-eight boys between six and ten years old and had them make "two quantitative moral judgments about characters in stories where levels of damage and intent differed systematically." As you learned earlier in this chapter, in Piaget's framework, younger children place more emphasis on damage while older, more mature children consider intent as well. His findings are summarized on page 288.

In accordance with Piaget's predictions, damage was the most important factor in moral decisions for younger children while intent information was more important to older children. However, unlike Piaget's clinical procedures, the experiment's methodology allowed substantiation of the ability of children to simultaneously weigh damage and intent information when making a moral judgment. (Buchanan, 1973, p. 186)

Kohlberg's theory has also been empirically investigated, by Kohlberg himself, among others. In light of the cross-cultural criticisms, Kohlberg and his colleagues have explored the development of moral thought in other cultures, such as in Great Britain, Canada, Mexico, Turkey, and other countries, and have found that the sequence of moral development is the same in these other cultures, although the *rate* at which individuals progress through the sequence may vary under other social, cultural, and religious conditions (Kohlberg & Kramer, 1969). This finding adds further support to Kohlberg's position and is compatible with the culturally relativistic positions that argue that values are the result of cultural conditioning. It merely asserts that the level of reasoning by which ethical decisions are made is a result of growth. Kohlberg and his colleagues have also studied subjects of different religious backgrounds and again found no important differences in the development of moral reasoning.

Other studies have tested the presumed sequentiality of the moral stages. Turiel (1966) attempted to induce stage change in seventh graders by discussing the moral dilemmas with them and giving them additional pro and con arguments. The research demonstrated that the subjects were somewhat more susceptible to arguments aimed one stage above their own than to those two stages above or one stage below. This, again, provides strong support for Kohlberg's position.

Reviewing these and other studies, Wrightsman and Brigham (1973) state that there is solid indication that children do move from stage 1 to stage 2 to stage 3, . . . but that the proposed sequence through the remaining stages has much less support. In other words, the theory provides a good description of the child's moral progression, but not so strong a description of the adolescent's development.

Moral Education: From Theory to Practice

During the late 1960s and early 1970s, an increasing social awareness and revitalized political consciousness precipitated an intense interest in the school's role in developing moral values in students. Parents, educators, clergymen, public figures, newspeople—and students themselves—began to ask, "Are the schools doing a sufficient job in instilling in young people a sense of right and wrong, an ability to make appropriate moral judgments, and, above all, encouraging them to develop a personal ethos that is compatible with the higher ideals of a democratic, humanistic society?"

These challenging questions did not arise in vacuo, but rather as a reaction to a complex chain of public events that shook the very foundations of our sense of stability, order, and progress. Let us review some of these major social events and consider the implications of these for the learner, teacher, and educator.

1. The assassination of President John F. Kennedy in 1963 shocked the American public deeply. For the first time in the lifetime of most Americans, the mortal vulnerability of the nation's leader was incontrovertibly brought to our attention. The massive psychological repercussions of this event are felt not only in the many books and articles that question the validity of the *Warren Commission Report* but in novels like Wright Morris's *One Day,* in films such as *The Parallax View* and *Executive Action,* and in the many magazine and newspaper articles that help us relive, year after year, the moments of this tragedy. Perhaps the great skepticism that beclouds the *Warren Commission Report* reflects the growing distrust in government—a distrust that was to take many forms during the decade that followed.

2. The presidency of Lyndon Baines Johnson proved to be a period of further divisiveness among the American people, and between the generations in particular. Deeply divided over the Vietnam war, the nation split into factions: left against right, young against old, hawks against doves, academics and intellectuals against hardhats and the silent majority, and so forth. Young people in particular began to distrust the government more openly and more strongly than during any other point in recent history. Questions were raised, and these questions were not answered despite their furied rhetoric, but invariably led to complex moral issues that demanded equally complex answers. The youth culture began to form as a cohesive social unit, defined by the media, by adults, and at times by the youth themselves.

3. Riots on college campuses added fuel to the already turbulent attitudes toward young people. Martin Luther King, Jr. and Robert F. Kennedy were slain—easy victims of the mad passions that ran wild—and people were more and more convinced of the uncertainty of our future as a country. Popular rock music reflected the angst and anger of this time:

> "You say you want a revolution
> Well, you know
> we all want to change the world. . . ."
> Paul McCartney and John Lennon, "Revolution"[3]

3. "Revolution" (John Lennon and Paul McCartney) © 1968 Northern Songs, Ltd. All rights for the United States, Canada, Mexico and the Philippines controlled by Maclen Music, Inc. Used by permission. All rights reserved.

> "The American public has become increasingly sensitive to the moral climate of our time, increasingly preoccupied with morality, with values, with ethics. And where do we look in such times of crisis: to the clergy, to our political leaders, to our culture heroes, and, of course, to the schools."

Media coverage was overgenerous in bringing to the attention of the American public the new "radicalism" of young people.

4. Increasing and flagrant use of drugs—marijuana, hallucinogens, tranquilizers, and so on—gave birth to the drug culture, offending a large segment of older, more conservative adults. This group, which reacted to the changing social patterns of young people, was dubbed "Middle America" by the press and media.

5. Radical groups, such as SDS, the Weathermen, and the Black Liberation Army, engaged in increasingly violent behavior and intentionally offensive rhetoric. Because most of the members were young, older people generally blamed such attitudes on youth as a group.

6. NIXON ELECTED PRESIDENT: Promising to unite this factionalized America, Nixon set about instituting policies to bring together all Americans, but, instead, came . . .

7. WATERGATE—the year of scandal, of lies, of denials, finally of resignation. Once again, the American public was shamed into asking, "Where are we? Where do we stand? Don't we have any values left?"

There are, of course, hundreds of other significant events that could be added to a list such as this one. But the net effect remains the same: The American public has become increasingly sensitive to the moral climate of our time; increasingly preoccupied with morality, with values, with ethics. And where do we look in such times of crisis: to the clergy, to our political leaders, to our culture heroes, and, of course, to the schools.

Love Is Not *All* You Need In a recent book on moral education, William Kay (1975) emphasizes the need "to advance the cultural evolution of mankind" toward "compassionate reasoning." His emphasis in moral education is that "children must be taught to love one another," since this is a strong basis for positive moral action. Kay's book, written more from a philosophical-sociological point of view than from a psychological point of view, stresses a position that reflects in many ways the moral constructs that evolve from the changing morality of the 1960s and 70s: as the Beatles put it, "All you need is love."

But when we look deeply, we find that love is not all you need; it's just a part of the total picture. As Piaget's and Kohlberg's theories of moral reasoning clearly show, knowledge is also an important part of the ability to make sound, sensible, progressive moral judgments. You will note how both Piaget's and Kohlberg's positions parallel the taxonomic levels in many ways. At the beginning levels of moral reasoning, the child is capable only of receiving the world around him, of picking up and repeating moral constraints. Piaget calls this a "morality of constraint," and Kohlberg refers to it as a "preconventional" moral reasoning. The responding level would be embodied in Piaget's "moral realism" and in Kohlberg's "law-and-order" stages. Both of these stages involve the ability of learners to respond appropriately to the world in moral ways, but to do so without fully evaluating the consequences of their responses. Finally, at Piaget's level of **"cooperative morality"** or Kohlberg's stage 5, the learner is functioning at taxonomic levels three or four: valuing, which is implied in both levels, or organization of a value system, which certainly is a part of Kohlberg's stage 5. Full autonomy as a moral agent (Piaget) or reasoning (Kohlberg's stage 6) would require skills from taxonomic level five—characterization by a value or value complex.

A number of recent books have attempted to apply these insights in practice. Many of these works refer to the turmoil discussed previously and try to come to grips with the many problems inherent in rapid social change. In 1971, the National Council for the Social Studies (NCSS) published its forty-first yearbook, called *Values Education: Rationale, Strategies, and Procedures* (Metcalf, 1971). The theme of this yearbook is summed up in this passage from the opening chapter:

Current fashion in educational theorizing encourages us to conceptualize educational objectives as being either cognitive behaviors or affective behaviors, or a set of behaviors both cognitive and affective. Testing student achievement is then viewed as a process of observing to see if students exhibit the appropriate behaviors in appropriate circumstances.

It is instructive to consider the objectives of helping students make rational judgments about the value object in question from this point of view. Is our objective to produce a cognitive outcome in the student or an affective outcome? Are we perhaps attempting to produce outcomes of each type? . . . We come back to the point emphasized earlier: the outcome sought is that students will have acted according to certain standards in making their decisions. It is difficult to see how this outcome could be described in terms of the cognitive-affective behaviors dichotomy. Assessment of student achievement with respect to this objective must be based primarily on performance during value analysis, not on behaviors exhibited after it. (p. 26)

One of the important implications of this argument is that moral education transcends the cognitive-affective dichotomy; that it involves skills that are parts of both domains. Specific objectives for moral reasoning (or value clarification or value analysis) can be stated and then assessed within the classroom situation.

> "Moral education transcends the cognitive-affective dichotomy . . . it involves skills that are parts of both domains."

In answer to the question, What exactly are the legitimate objectives of value analysis in the classroom? authors in the NCSS report argue five major points:

1. It is possible to describe our use of value language and the rules governing our reasoning about matters of value without thereby making any value judgments.
2. Value judgments are neither judgments of fact nor mere expressions of attitude.
3. Standards of rational value judgment can be specified but they apply to the process of value decision making and not to the product of such a decision. These standards include:
   a. The purported facts supporting the judgment must be true or well confirmed.
   b. The facts must be genuinely relevant. . . .
   c. Other things being equal, the greater the range of relevant facts taken into account in making the judgment, the more adequate the judgment is likely to be.
   d. The value principle implied by the judgment must be acceptable to the person making the judgment.
4. Since standards of rational value judgment can be specified, the following objectives of value analysis in the classroom are defensible.
   a. Helping students make the most rational, defensible value judgments they can make.
   b. Helping students acquire the capabilities necessary to make rational value decisions and the disposition to do so.
5. There are no logical grounds for deciding that value criteria ought never to be taught nor for deciding that resolution of conflict about value matters is an illegitimate objective of value analysis. (p. 27)

Moral Education in the Classroom

We see from these five points some major objectives of moral education in the schools. While they serve as valid guidelines, they are open enough to accommodate a wide range of subject matter. Of course, the position that moral education is an important part of the educative process did not originate in the NCSS report; in fact, as we pointed out in the introduction to this chapter, it can be traced back to Plato. Many recent writers, including Kohlberg (1966), who cites "moral maturity as an aim of education," argue much the same point. Probably the most important contribution in recent years is embodied in those efforts that attempt to specify to some extent how to achieve these aims—what they really mean.

Arguing that students are "philosophers" intent on organizing their lives into universal patterns of meaning (Kohlberg & Turiel, 1973; Kohlberg, 1968), Kohlberg, probably more than any other contemporary thinker, fuses the intellectual and moral realms into a unified conception of growth and development within the school setting. He attempts to fuse affective (moral) and cognitive growth: ". . . the problem of insuring correspondence between developing moral judgments and the child's action is not primarily a problem of eliciting moral self-criticism from the child. One aspect of the problem is the development of the ego abilities involved in the non-moral or cognitive tasks upon which the classroom centers. . . . The encouragement of these attentional ego capacities is not a task of moral education as such but of general programming of classroom learning activities" (p. 25). We see in this passage how integral a part of education affective learning is; and, more importantly, we see how the general emotional health of the learner is an integral part of the affective learning experience, including the learning of values—moral development.

Jantz and Fulda (1975) have explored the role of moral education in the elementary school. "If the role of moral education is to be stressed in public education," they argue (p. 28), "then knowledge on the part of educa-

Classroom posters communicate to students the values that are characteristic of the school and society.

tors as to the moral growth of children is essential." They advocate that the elementary school teacher be familiar with Piaget's and Kohlberg's positions, and that the teacher work toward helping the learners reach consistently higher levels of moral development. "Recognition of the levels of moral thinking should result in clearer statements of objectives for the elementary grades. This recognition can aid the teacher in helping her pupils move from one stage level to the next. *The principal objective of moral education in the schools then becomes the attainment of the next higher level of moral development. To accomplish this, students must be provided with opportunities to make moral decisions that are within realistic expectations of their level of moral thinking"* (p. 28, our italics).

Other educators have argued much the same point. Graham (1975) argues that moral education is integral to the child's total development and defines it as a joint responsibility of the home and school. In the following selection from his article, Graham capsulizes his point of view:

Whatever the effect of moral judgment on one's own or private life, it seems certain that the development of moral judgment as an aim of education will have effect on things public, on the role and conduct of citizens. To be sure, moral judgment alone does not determine one's actions. Intensity of attention to issues or strength of will and other factors influence what one does. But principled judgment tends to produce principled behavior. There is then reason to have greater hope for the world, since the processes of education that most effectively prepare a person to deal with the intricacies of a technological living are those which tend to develop logical reasoning. And it is in logical reasoning that the underpinnings of moral judgment are developed. If we adopt programs of education that stimulate moral development as well, there is reason to believe that we can become a society that not only has the technological ability to create problems as complex as those involving the uses of nuclear power and of genetic engineering but one that possesses the principled judgment needed to deal with them. (pp. 307–308)

The teaching of ethics, or applied moral reasoning, is a major part of this effort. Many teachers are no longer satisfied teaching issues alone, but demand that issues—historical, scientific, and social—be presented within the context of an ethical framework. Benson and Forcinelli (1975) provide a well-reasoned argument for teaching ethics in the high school, and offer a sampling of some of the efforts already under way. Other researchers and educators (Craig, 1974; Edwards, 1974; Stanton, 1974; McBride, 1973; Duffey, 1975) have directed their attention to Kohlberg's position (and indirectly to Piaget's as well) in attempts to evaluate its applicability to the school setting, and have reached similar conclusions to those cited above.

One of the best specific applications of Kohlberg's theory to the classroom situation is provided by Galbraith and Jones (1975), who offer practical teaching strategies to help students understand and resolve moral dilemmas. Figure 7.4 outlines their suggested teaching process for use in this area. "Teachers must help students to *confront* a moral problem involved in a dilemma, to *state* a position on the dilemma, to *test* the reasoning behind

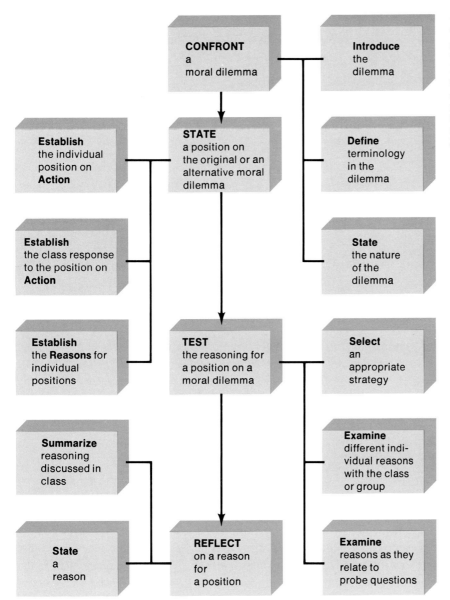

Figure 7.4 Diagram of the Teaching Process for Teaching a Moral Dilemma. From "Teaching Strategies for Moral Dilemma" by R. E. Galbraith and T. M. Jones, *Social Education*, 1975, p. 21. Reprinted with permission of the National Council for the Social Studies and R. E. Galbraith and T. M. Jones.

their position, and to *reflect* on their reasoning and that of others during a discussion" (p. 19). The specific strategies involved in each of these processes is illustrated in this figure, and the stories that are used to illustrate types of dilemmas are similar to the ones used by Kohlberg in his research (discussed earlier in this chapter).

Raths, Harmin, and Simon (1966) have presented a thorough analysis of values in the classroom, also from a developmental point of view. While they too see a direct integration between cognition and valuing, they are care-

The objective processes of valuation and moral reasoning are easily beclouded by human passions, such as anger.

ful to distinguish between the thinking process and the valuing process; the former being directed toward understanding, the latter toward decision making. Within the classroom setting, the two are combined both in the curriculum and in teacher presentation. Specifically, the goals and processes of value education, according to Raths, Harmin and Simon (1966) are to—

help children: (1) make free choices whenever possible, (2) search for alternatives in choice-making situations, (3) weigh the consequences of each available alternative, (4) consider what they prize and cherish, (5) affirm the things they value, (6) do something about their choices, and (7) consider and strengthen patterns in their lives. . . . As the teacher helps students use these processes, he helps them find values.

The implications of the above positions are that the teacher is inevitably engaged in value teaching, whether this is intentional or not. Since values are the basis of character development, and since character development is the basis of growth within the school setting, it is imperative that the teacher confront directly the challenges of value education that stand before him. "The educationist," Bantock (1965) points out, "is unavoidably a moralist, by the very logic of his position." To conscientiously and purposefully help students develop their independent, yet organized, systems of values is one of the higher and most productive functions of the teacher.

A variety of innovative and effective methods by which the teacher may do this have been presented in the literature. Simon (1973) has suggested methods of "values clarification strategy," based on his work with Howe and Kirschenbaum (Simon, Howe & Kirschenbaum, 1972). These strategies can be used in the classroom to encourage students to deal with

The Psychology of Learning

moral dilemmas by helping them get in touch with their feelings, and by having them observe their own moral behavior in various arranged situations.

In a more recent effort, Hawley (1975) has expounded a system of value exploration through role playing. The eleven problem-solving objectives of this system span the width and breadth of affective education, particularly in the realm of valuing, value organization, and characterization by value. These objectives are:

1. To help students to identify the real problem.
2. To help students see that behavior is purposive.
3. To help each student to explore and clarify his own frame of values.
4. To help students test their values through simulated action.
5. To help students realize that their decisions have consequences.
6. To help students enlarge their problem-solving capability through the habit of seeking alternatives.
7. To help students identify the underlying influences in decision making.
8. To confront and evaluate the ways in which we tend to solve interpersonal problems.
9. To demonstrate the effectiveness of group problem solving.
10. To help students distinguish between the over demand and the underlying desire in interpersonal conflict situations.
11. To demonstrate the necessity of open communication in problem solving. (pp. 128–32)

These objectives are achieved through specific role-playing exercises that allow the student to explore a range of possibilities of behaviors and different approaches to decision making.

We see in these objectives that the developmental theories of moral reasoning have many practical implications and that many serious efforts have helped translate these findings into applicable classroom procedures.

Summary

In this chapter we have examined the processes of learning in the affective domain, using the *Taxonomy of Educational Objectives in the Affective Domain*. The five taxonomic levels are receiving, responding, valuing, organization of values, and characterization by value or value complex.

Since affective learning can also be construed as emotional learning, we also studied the processes of conflict resolution, defense mechanisms, and healthy growth that are likely to manifest themselves in the classroom setting. We next examined the idea of self-development as an integral part of affective learning, using Comb and Snygg's concept of the "phenomenal self" as our reference point.

Finally, we turned our attention to moral development and theories of moral reasoning. The ideas of Russell, Piaget, and Kohlberg were examined in detail, and strategies for moral education in the schools were explored.

Suggested Additional Readings

Becoming: Basic Considerations for a Psychology of Personality by Gordon
W. Allport (*New Haven: Yale University Press, 1955*)

While this is ostensibly a book on personality theory, there is probably no
better introduction to the area of affective education. Allport's concepts reflect
not only the essence of humanistic thought, but outline the basic dimensions
of affective growth and development as well.

*The goal of psychology is to reduce discord among our philosophies of man,
and to establish a scale of probable truth, so that we may feel increasingly certain
that one interpretation is truer than another.*

from *Becoming*

Values and Teaching: Working with Values in the Classroom by L. Raths,
M. Harmin and S. Simon (*Columbus, Ohio: Charles E. Merrill Publishing
Company, 1966*)

This noted book is the foundation for a course in the teaching of moral
reasoning and value clarification approaches. It is rich in practical applications
of moral decision theory, with a special relevance for the teaching setting.

*The goals of value education are to help children: (1) make free choices whenever
possible, (2) search for alternatives in choice-making situations, (3) weigh the
consequences of each available alternative. . . . As the teacher helps students use
these processes, he helps them find values.*

from *Values and Teaching*

Moral Education in the Schools: A Developmental View by Lawrence Kohlberg
School Review, 1966, 74, 1–30.

This is a fine application of Kohlberg's research to the school setting. It
outlines the argument of making "moral maturity" a primary goal in the
school curriculum, and offers some suggestions and guidelines for doing so.

*One aspect of the problem is the development of the ego abilities involved in the
non-moral or cognitive tasks upon which the classroom centers. . . . The encouragement of these attentional ego capacities is not the task of moral education
as such, but of general programming of classroom learning activities. . . .*

from "*Moral Education in the Schools: A Developmental View*"

Facts and Feelings in the Classroom, ed. by Louis J. Rubin (*New York: Walker & Company, 1973*)

This book presents different essays on the role of emotions in successful learning. It goes into some detail in examining the relationship between feelings and intellectual gains in the school. It is strong in its emphasis on educating the total person.

☙♥❧

There is reason to believe . . . that anxiety, fear, and the threat of failure—in dosages too large to be borne comfortably—may preclude successful learning for many of our students. Even high-achieving students often excel at the cost of permanent insecurity and anxiety.

from *Facts and Feelings in the Classroom*

Education and Values by G. H. Bantock (*Atlantic Highlands, N.J.: Humanities Press, 1965*)

Although the orientation of this book is the educational system of Great Britain, the essays, which deal with all aspects of moral education and value clarification, are equally germane to our concerns in American education.

☙♥❧

. . . the educator is inevitably involved in the world of values; and here, it seems to me, literature provides some measure of protection against many of those over-simplifications of outlook and procedure which mar so much of current educational discourse. . . .

from *Education and Values*

The Concept of Self by Kenneth J. Gergen (*New York: Holt, Rinehart and Winston, 1971*)

A thorough introduction to theories of self and self-development. Research from different positions is included.

☙♥❧

The individual's presentation of self may be determined by his motives in a relationship. If a person wishes to be treated with deference, his demeanor may be marked by superiority; if he wishes to be trusted, he may insure that his behavior is always consistent.

from *The Concept of Self*

Processes of Cognitive Learning

Cognitive learning is the kind of learning we generally associate with formal schooling. It involves both the acquisition of information and the development of the processes necessary to transform information into a usable form. Cognitive learning includes the processes of acquisition, retention, and transfer.

Goals of Education

The perspectives of William James, John Dewey, and Alfred Whitehead, among others, are presented. Thorndike's complete list of school goals is examined. Parallel analyses by other noted educators and psychologists are also compared.

Goals of Cognitive Learning

The learning of organized bodies of knowledge, intellectual skills, processes of thinking, and attitudes about knowledge are the goals of cognitive learning. The specific learning goals include language skills; categorizing skills; memory skills; critical thinking skills; creative thinking skills; problem-solving skills; flexibility in the application of information-processing strategies; quantitative and relational concepts; general knowledge; facility in the use of resources for learning and problem solving.

Contents and Processes of Cognitive Learning

Content can be classified by subject-matter areas, by the nature of the symbols used, or by the difficulty of the content. Process can be classified by the type of learning or by the type of thinking.

Conditions of Learning on Which Educational Psychologists Tend to Agree

Learner conditions include cognitive ability, previous cognitive achievement, and motivation. Situational conditions that are agreed to be relevant include the goal, the organization of knowledge, the activity of the learner, practice, reinforcement, and type of learning process.

Continued

8 Conditions and Processes of Cognitive Learning

Learning Processes

Acquisition is a change in performance due to experiences from which learning can be inferred. *Retention* is a relatively permanent change in performance due to practice. *Transfer* is the influence of previous learning on performance in a new situation.

Are Systematically Oriented Learning Theorists Concerned With the Same Processes and Outcomes of Learning?

Learning theorists' concerns with processes and outcomes represent a continuum from extreme situation-oriented positions to extreme learner-oriented positions. Skinner holds the position that the learner can be shaped to acquire, retain, and use knowledge through discrimination of stimulus cues. Gagné argues that learning proceeds most effectively from the simple to the complex for the purposes of problem solving and proposes a model to account for this. Ausubel has devised a system to increase the learner's retentive abilities. Bruner stresses the importance of the structure of knowledge in relation to the curriculum and to the content of instruction. Rogers focuses on the fully functioning person, advocating a strong learner-oriented approach.

Something to Think About

Two classical studies have been done concerning outcomes of acquisition, retention, and transfer of knowledge. From these studies, several aspects of processes and conditions of learning are explained.

Goals and Conditions

A resolution of the National Association of State Boards of Education is presented to include many of the goals and conditions of learning discussed in this chapter.

When we think of the term *learning,* especially the type of learning we associate with formal education, we are actually thinking of cognitive learning. Cognitive learning may be defined as the acquisition of information and the development of processes necessary to transform the information into some usable form. Information that has been learned is referred to as knowledge. The ways in which the individual gains new knowledge are called the *processes* of cognitive learning, the factors that influence these processes are called the *conditions* of learning.

Processes of Cognitive Learning

The processes of cognitive learning include acquisition, retention, and transfer, which were discussed in chapter 6. In evaluating learning, we consider *what* knowledge has been acquired (acquisition), *how long* one can retain the acquired knowledge (retention), and *how well* one can apply the knowledge to new learning situations (transfer). These factors may be external and observable through changes in the learner's behaviors (outcome), or they may be internal and not readily observable (process). In the latter case, testing may be used to make the changes observable.

Cognitive learning—and knowledge, in general—may assume different forms. Gilbert Ryle, the language philosopher, distinguishes between "knowing-that" and "knowing-how"; between knowing about something and knowing how to do something. An example of the former might be, "I know all the parts of an automobile and why the car runs." An example of the latter is: "I know how to drive a car." Cognitive learning generally includes both types of knowing, the abstract and the practical. As we examine the conditions and processes of cognitive learning, then, we should keep in mind that the *content* of this type of learning includes ideas and skills. In the preceding chapter, on affective learning, we focused more directly on subjective ideas as the contents of learning. In the following chapter, on psychomotor learning, we will focus more explicitly on learning motor skills.

The **conditions** of learning refer to the learner and the situation in which learning occurs. Since the learner and situational conditions are interrelated (e.g., **meaningful learning** involves the readiness of the learner as well as the nature of the task), the concept of the **teaching-learning process** is often used in discussing the conditions of learning. While there are a few conditions that are important in all cognitive learning, most learning conditions are dependent upon the goals of the particular experience. Conditions of learning are not of much value until we know what is supposed to be done with the knowl-

Conditions of Cognitive Learning

edge—acquire it, retain it, or transfer it. Before we concern ourselves with the conditions for different learning processes, we need to discuss the goals of cognitive learning within the contexts of education.

Goals of Education

Educational goals are general statements of *what* the student is expected to learn in school. Schools have served many functions for the societies that have established and maintained them through the centuries. Educational goals have been reviewed continuously by participants in the educational process as well as by society in general (e.g., American Council on Education, 1944; Commission for the White House Conference on Education, 1955; Educational Policies Commission, 1938, 1961; National Educational Association Commission, 1918; Office of Child Development (Anderson & Messick), 1974; Phi Delta Kappa (Shane), 1973; Russell Sage Foundation (French et al.), 1957, (Kearney), 1953).

Although the goals of education are by no means limited to cognitive learning (as we saw clearly in the preceding chapter), we repeatedly find references to cognitive learning in the literature of educational goals. Since learning in school comprises learning from all three domains, it is often convenient to use cognitive learning structures as focal points through which we can scrutinize the total impact that the school has had upon the learner. As we examine some prominent thinkers' positions on educational goals, let us keep this redoubtable bias in mind. We will then be in a better position to appreciate their creative approaches toward understanding the problems of establishing educational goals.

Three well-known thinkers provided some perspectives on the context of cognitive learning in education. These perspectives, although formulated in a past era, are still timely today. William James gave the following account in 1892:

We are too apt to measure the gains of our pupils by their proficiency in directly reproducing in a recitation or an examination such matters as they may have learned, and inarticulate power in them is something of which we always underestimate the value. . . . Although the ready memory is a great blessing to its possessor, the vaguer memory of a subject, of having once had to do with it, of its neighborhood, and of where we may go to recover it again, constitutes in most men and women the chief fruit of their education. . . . Be patient, then, and sympathetic with the type of mind that cuts a poor figure in examinations. It may, in the long examination which life sets us, come out in the end in better shape than the glib and ready reproducer, its passions being deeper, its purposes more worthy, its combining power less commonplace, and its total mental output consequently more important. (pp. 100–101)

In 1902, John Dewey stated:

If, once more, the "old education" tended to ignore the dynamic quality, the developing force inherent in the child's present experience, and therefore assume that direction and control were just matters of arbitrarily putting the child in a given path and compelling him to walk there, the "new education" is in danger of taking the idea of development in altogether too formal and empty a way. The child is expected to "develop" this or that fact or truth out of his own mind. . . . Nothing can be developed from nothing. . . . Development does not mean just getting something out of the mind. It is a development of experience and into experience that is really wanted. . . . (pp. 17–18)

Alfred Whitehead voiced the following view in 1929:

Culture is activity of thought, and receptiveness to beauty and humane feeling. Scraps of information have nothing to do with it. A merely well-formed man is the most useless bore on God's earth. What we should aim at producing is men who possess both culture and expert knowledge in some special direction. Their expert knowledge will give them the ground to start from, and their culture will lead them as deep as philosophy and as high as art. We have to remember that the valuable intellectual development is self-development, and that it mostly takes place between the ages of sixteen and thirty. As to training, the most important part is given by mothers before the age of twelve. A saying due to Archbishop Temple illustrates my meaning. Surprise was expressed at the success in after-life of a man, who as a boy at Rugby had been somewhat undistinguished. He answered, "It is not what they are at eighteen, it is what they become afterwards that matters."
In training a child to activity of thought, above all things we must beware of what I will call "inert ideas"—that is to say, ideas that are merely received into the mind without being utilized or tested or thrown into fresh combinations. (p. 1)

There have been many conceptualizations of educational goals. For our purposes, we will use two types of goals: **ultimate** and **immediate objectives.** Ultimate objectives are those that guide school experiences over the long duration of formal education. Immediate objectives (i.e., proximate goals) are those that guide school experiences for a relative short duration (e.g., a year-long course).

E. F. Lindquist (1951) has succinctly summarized the relationship between ultimate and immediate goals of education. Lindquist stated:

Many of the basic objectives of school instruction cannot possibly be fully realized until long after the instruction has been concluded. For guidance in specific courses of instruction, however, it is common practice to set up less remote objectives—objectives which are capable of immediate attainment. Ideally, these immediate objectives should in every instance have been clearly and logically derived from accepted ultimate objectives, in full consideration of all relevant characteristics of the pupils who are to receive the instruction. . . . Finally, the content and methods of instruction should, ideally, be logically selected, devised, and used with specific reference to these immediate and ultimate objectives. . . . (p. 121)

There are several perspectives that can and must be considered in answering the question, What are the goals of education? One perspective is derived from our personal observations. A second perspective comes from the observations of others. A third perspective is based on wisdom of the past, knowledge of the present, and prophecy of the future by prominent educators.

In order to establish some parameters on the goals of education, let us consider perhaps the most complete list of goals ever compiled. The following summary of the aims of education is taken from E. L. Thorndike's (1906) interpretation of the views of educational theorists of that time:

> ... These aims of education in general—goodwill to men, useful and happy lives, and noble enjoyment—are the ultimate aims of school education in particular. Its proximate aims are to give boys and girls health in body and mind, information about the world of nature and men, worthy interests in knowledge and action, a multitude of habits of thought, feeling and behavior, and ideas of efficiency, honor, duty, love and service. The special proximate aims of the first six years of school life are commonly taken to be to give physical training and protection against disease; knowledge of the simple facts of nature and human life; the ability to gain knowledge and pleasure through reading and to express ideas and feelings through spoken and written language, music and other arts; interests in the concrete life of the world; habits of intelligent curiosity, purposive thinking, modesty, obedience, honesty, helpfulness, affection, courage and justice; and the ideals proper to childhood.

> The special proximate aims of school life from twelve to eighteen are commonly taken to be physical health and skill; knowledge of the simpler general laws of nature and human life and of the opinions of the wisest and best; more effective use of the expressive arts; interests in the arts and sciences, and in human life both as directly experienced and as portrayed in literature; powers of self-control, accuracy, steadiness and logical thought, technical and executive abilities, cooperation and leadership; habits of self-restraint, honor, courage, justice, sympathy and reverence; and the ideals proper to youth.

> With respect to the amount of emphasis upon different features of these general ideals, the best judgment of the present rates practical ability somewhat higher and culture of the semi-selfish sort somewhat lower than has been the case in the past. ...

> The best judgment of the present gives much more weight than has been the case previously to health, to bodily skill and to the technical and industrial arts. ...

> Very recently thinkers about education have dwelt more and more upon the importance of aiming not only to prepare children for adult life and work but also to adapt them to the life of childhood itself. Aim more to make children succeed with the problems and duties of childhood and less to fit them for the problems and duties of twenty years after ... such are the recommendations of present-day theories of education. ...

> ... The energy of any teacher, and of scholars as well, is limited. All that can be expected is that none of the aims of school education shall be willfully violated and that energy should be distributed among them all in some reasonable way. (pp. 3–5)

Thorndike's interpretation of the views of educational theorists of his time has probably not been surpassed. Recent statements tend to be more restricted, based on current changes in society. During the past three-quarters of the century, most of Thorndike's objectives have at one time or another been included in a statement of educational goals. We will present recent statements of educational goals by current theorists as illustrations of these points.

Shane (1973) proposed the following resolution related to the question of educational goals:

That as professionals in education we honor in our schools the human need of children and youth to learn, to find acceptance, to empathize, to feel satisfaction, to discover dignity and take pride in one's self-concept, and to develop skill and thus wisdom in coping with personal and group problems. . . . (p. 329)

Kagan (1973) presented his ideas related to the role of the school in society:

I want to see schools begin to serve the needs of society. Ancient Sparta needed warriors, Athens needed a sense of the hero, the ancient Hebrews needed knowledge of the Testament, nineteenth-century Americans needed managers and technicians—and the schools responded beautifully in each case by providing the kind of people the society needed. What do we need now? I believe that we need to restore faith, honesty, humanity. And I am suggesting in deep seriousness that we must, in the school, begin to reward these traits as the Spartans rewarded physical fitness. I want children rank-ordered on the basis of humanism as we rank-order on the basis of reading and mathematics. . . . (p. 43)

Bruner (1971) also reflected on the goals of education. Bruner stated:

. . . They were innocent days. But beware such judgments rendered in retrospect. At worst, the early period suffered in excess of rationalism.
. . . The prevailing notion was that if you understood the structure of knowledge, that understanding would then permit you to go ahead on your own; you did not need to encounter everything in nature in order to know nature, but by understanding some deep principles you could extrapolate to the particulars as needed. Knowing was a canny strategy whereby you could know a great deal about a lot of things while keeping very little in mind. . . .
. . . What would one do now? . . . in my view, through my perspective, the issues would have to do with how one gives back initiative and a sense of potency, how one activates to tempt one to want to learn again. When that is accomplished, then curriculum becomes an issue again—curriculum not as a subject but as an approach to learning and using knowledge. (p. 20)

These three statements—by an educator, a developmentalist, and a learning theorist—reflect a return to the ideas expressed by Thorndike more than seventy years ago. It is not so much that we seek a return to the traditional, but that we desire a plan for education based upon sound, scientific insights rather than popular pressures. Of course, whether the goals of education "are being distributed in some reasonable way" at the present time can only be verified by the future.

Despite the scientific and educational soundness of any statement of goals, public concern over immediate matters always generates an influence over policy, if not philosophy. It is for this reason that we seek out the educated insights of specialists in the field to gain a clearer picture of what is really happening in the classroom. For instance, if we wish to compare what has been happening with respect to cognitive learning, let us consider two observations, twelve years apart. In 1958, Jerome Bruner wrote:

... I have been struck during the past year or so, sitting in classrooms as an observer, by the passivity of the process we call education. The emphasis is upon gaining and storing information, gaining it and storing it in the form in which it is presented. ... One of the great inventions of man—elementary number theory —is presented as a cookbook. I have yet to see a teacher present one way of doing division and then put it squarely to the class to suggest six other ways of doing it— for there are at least six other ways of doing it than any one that might be taught in a school. So too with algebra. Algebra is not a set of rules for manipulating numbers and letters except in a trivial sense. It is a way of thinking, a way of coping with the drama of the unknown. ... How does one ask questions about the unknown? Well, algebra is one technique, the technique for arranging the known in such a way that one is enabled to discern the value of an unknown quantity. It is an enriching strategy, algebra, but only if it is grasped as an extended instance of common sense. ...

So knowledge-getting becomes passive. Thinking is the reward for learning, and we may be systematically depriving our students of this reward as far as school learning is concerned. (p. 186–187)

By 1970, Silberman had the following observations about what goes on in the classroom:

... There is a great deal of chatter, to be sure, about teaching students the structure of each discipline, about teaching them how to learn, about teaching basic concepts, about "postholing," i.e., teaching fewer things but in greater depth. But if one looks at what actually goes on in the classroom—the kinds of texts students read and the kind of homework they are assigned, as well as the nature of classroom discussion and the kinds of test teachers give—he will discover that the great bulk of students' time is still devoted to detail, most of it trivial, much of it factually incorrect, and almost all of it unrelated to any concept, structure, cognitive strategy, or indeed anything other than the lesson plan. ... (p. 172)

Note the similarities in these two expert's observations. Each criticizes the school's emphasis on the trivial, the implied lack of creative, divergent thinking, the failure of teachers (or of curriculum planners) to see some type of design, or purposeful order in what is taught.

The point is this: For education to be truly meaningful, educators will have to come to grips with the problem of strengthening students' cognitive processes instead of simply trying to fill their minds with facts. As the goals of education come to coincide more closely with the goals of cognitive learning, the educational experience will become more valuable in preparing students for a life of thoughtful living.

Goals of Cognitive Learning

In 1961, the Educational Policies Commission issued the following statement concerning the primary purpose of the school in society:

The purpose which runs through and strengthens all other educational purposes —the common thread of education—is the development of the ability to think. This is the central purpose to which the school must be oriented if it is to accomplish its traditional tasks or those newly accentuated by recent changes in the world. To say that it is central is not to say that it is the sole purpose or in all circumstances the most important purpose, but that it must be a pervasive concern in the work of the school. (pp. 11–12)

But what is the meaning of thinking as referred to in the commission's statement? What is its role in school learning? Let us see how five theorists of different viewpoints answer these questions. From these statements, we will then define the goals of cognitive learning.

Robert Hutchins (1965), one of the editors of *Great Books of the Western World,* has stated:

The world is new and is getting newer every minute. Anything may happen, and what is most likely to happen may be what we least expect.

Almost every "fact" I was taught from the first grade through law school is no longer a fact. Almost every tendency that was proclaimed has failed to materialize. The "facts" and tendencies of today are those that nobody foresaw fifty years ago. . . . (p. 1)

The special function of our educational institutions is to supply the intellectual tools, the intellectual discipline, and the intellectual framework necessary to understand the new problems we shall face. . . . One might almost say that now the most practical education is a theoretical one; the man with the theoretical framework will comprehend the new situation, whereas the man without it has no recourse but to muddle through. (p. 4)

Robert Ebel (1972), a specialist in educational measurement and research, made the following comments:

. . . What schools were primarily built to do, and what they are most capable of doing well, is to help the student develop cognitive competence. . . .

What is cognitive competence? Two distinctly different answers have been given. One is that it requires acquisition of knowledge. The other is that it requires development of intellectual skills. . . .

Knowledge, as the term is used here, is not synonymous with information. Knowledge is built out of information by thinking. It is an integrated structure of relationships among concepts and propositions. A teacher can give his students information. He cannot give them knowledge. A student must earn the right to say "I know" by his own thoughtful efforts to understand. . . .

. . . Those who advocate the development of intellectual skills as the principal cognitive aim of education often express the belief (or hope) that these skills will be broadly transferable from one area of subject matter to another. But if the subjects are quite different, the transfer is likely to be quite limited. . . . (p. 5)

B. F. Skinner (1973) has observed:

No one learns very much from the real world without help. Much can be learned without formal instruction in a social world, but not without a good deal of teaching. Formal education has made a tremendous difference in the extent of the skills and knowledge which can be acquired by a person.

A much more important principle is that the real world only teaches what is relevant to the present; it makes no explicit preparation for the future.

... It has always been the task of formal education to set up behaviors which would prove useful or enjoyable *later* in the student's life. (p. 43)

Jerome Bruner (1960) made these comments:

The first object of any act of learning, over and beyond the pleasure it may give, is that it should serve us in the future.... There are two ways in which learning serves the future. One is through its specific applicability to tasks that are highly similar to those we originally learned to perform. Psychologists refer to this phenomenon as specific transfer of training; perhaps it should be called the extension of habits or associations. Its utility appears to be limited in the main to what we usually speak of as skills. A second way in which earlier learning renders later performance more efficient is through what is conveniently called nonspecific transfer or, more accurately, the transfer of principles and attitudes. In essence, it consists of learning initially not a skill but a general idea, which can then be used as a basis for recognizing subsequent problems as special cases of the idea originally mastered. This type of transfer is at the heart of the educational process —the continual broadening and deepening of knowledge in terms of basic and general ideas....

Mastery of the fundamental ideas of a field involves not only the grasping of general principles, but also the development of an attitude toward learning and inquiry, toward guessing and hunches, toward the possibility of solving problems on one's own.... (pp. 17–20)

Finally, Carl Rogers (1969) had the following thoughts:

... The only man who is educated is the man who has learned how to learn; the man who has learned how to adapt and change; the man who has realized that no knowledge is secure, that only the process of seeking knowledge gives a basis for security. Changingness, a reliance on *process* rather than upon static knowledge, is the only thing that makes any sense as a goal for education in the modern world. (p. 104)

In summary, these five viewpoints indicate that the learning of organized bodies of knowledge, intellectual skills, processes of thinking, and attitudes about knowledge are goals of cognitive learning. Anderson and Messick (1974) have identified in some detail ten goals of cognitive learning based on a synthesis of diverse points of view such as the ones we have just discussed. A summary of these goals is presented in table 8.1.

Now that the goals have been identified, what are some possible ways in which to improve upon what teachers and learners have been doing in the classroom to enable learners to acquire knowledge more efficiently, to retain knowledge more effectively, and to transfer knowledge more accurately and more frequently? The position we will take here is that the most direct way is to improve upon the conditions of learning used in schools. This position

Table 8.1 Synthesis of Cognitive Learning Goals Valued by Society in the 1970s

Cognitive Learning Goal	Description
Language Skills	Labels, retells, describes, makes requests, and gives instructions—first in words, then sentences, then within a body of texts—first by listening, then speaking, then reading, then writing, and applies this knowledge in his or her own spoken and written communications.
Categorizing Skills	Recognizes and can verbalize whether objects or events are similar or different; categorizes objects or events on the basis of attributes, generic classes, or relationships, and verbalizes the principles underlying categories.
Memory Skills	Retrieves information on the basis of relevant cues over time. These skills include appropriate strategies of attending, organizing, and rehearsing the content.
Critical Thinking Skills	Identifies problems, analyzes the elements of situations, and evaluates concepts, processes, and products. Essential to these analyses and evaluations is the child's ability to appraise his own capabilities and resources in the context of situational demands.
Creative Thinking Skills	Generates multiple responses (language and motor, conceptions and hypotheses) to situations. In generating these responses, the child moves flexibly across content and form. Some of the responses are original or aesthetically satisfying. Some responses are initiated by the child and some are initiated by others.
Problem-solving Skills	Applies memory, critical thinking, and creative thinking skills in order to identify, analyze, and solve problems and evaluate his own responses and products in the process. In decision-making situations, problem-solving skills include weighing alternative solutions and their consequences.
Flexibility in the Application of Information-processing Strategies	Recognizes that there are different approaches to exploring the environment to obtain and process information from it; further recognizes these approaches are effective in different situations. That is, he does not limit his exploration to isolated components of the situation but rather considers the situation as a whole and the relationships among components.
Quantitative and Relational Concepts	Understands and has skills related to number, number properties, seriation, ordinality, conservation, relation, comparison, causality, measurement, estimation, enumeration, counting, arithmetic and other formal operations.
General Knowledge	Has a reasonable amount of knowledge in areas such as health and safety, social norms and customs, physical facilities, consumer behavior, games, art, music, and literature. Such general knowledge facilitates the acquisition of more advanced knowledge, interpersonal communications, and aesthetic satisfaction.
Facility in the Use of Resources for Learning and Problem Solving	Knows where and from whom he can obtain information and knows how to use these external resources effectively.

Adapted from "Social Competency in Young Children," *Developmental Psychology*, 1974, *10(2)*, 282–293, by permission of the authors, Scarvia Anderson and Samuel Messick, and the American Psychological Association.

is supported by basic research, applied research, and the experience of educators and psychologists throughout the past century.

In 1892, William James stated:

... and the only really useful practical lesson that emerges from this analytical psychology in the conduct of large schools is the lesson already reached in a purely empirical way, that the teacher ought always to impress the class through as many sensible channels as he can. Talk and write and draw on blackboard, permit the pupils to talk, and make them write and draw, exhibit pictures, plans, and curves, have your diagrams colored differently in the different parts, etc.; and out of the whole variety of impressions the individual child will find the most lasting ones for himself. In all primary school work, this principle of multiple impressions is well recognized, so I need say no more about it here.

This principle of multiplying channels and varying associations and appeals is important, not only for teaching pupils to remember, but for teaching them to understand. It runs, in fact, through the whole teaching act. (p. 99)

In 1938, John Dewey concluded:

The word "interaction" [which has just been used] expresses the principle for interpreting an experience in its educational function and force. It assigns equal rights to both factors in experience—objective and internal conditions. Any normal experience is an interplay of these two sets of conditions. Taken together, or in their interaction, they form what we call a *situation*. The trouble with traditional education was not that it emphasized the external conditions that enter into the control of the experiences but that it paid so little attention to the internal factors which also decide what kind of experience is had. It violated the principle of interaction from one side. But this violation is no reason why the new education should violate the principle from the other side—except upon the basis of the extreme either-or educational philosophy. . . . (p. 42)

J. M. Stephens observed in 1967:

One of the psychological phenomena to be explained is the remarkable constancy of educational results in the face of widely differing deliberate approaches. Every so often we adopt new approaches or new methodologies and place our reliance on new panaceas. At the very least we seem to chorus new slogans. Yet the academic growth within the classroom continues at about the same rate, stubbornly refusing to cooperate with the bright new dicta emanating from the conference room. . . .

. . . True enough, our frantic manipulation of the administrative externals of schooling has produced no such improvement. . . . These efforts have tried to produce improvement while ignoring the humble, basic processes by which schooling proceeds. When we honestly turn to a realistic study of these ancient, earthy, and pervasive forces themselves, who knows what improvement may result? By directing the attention of thousands of teachers to these basic processes and to the principles so far adduced to explain them, we might facilitate a more profound and more relevant understanding of the machinery responsible for schooling and the schools. . . .

An adult with a strong interest in, say, algebra, and with a liberal supply of the communicative tendencies will automatically induce children to respond to some of the notions of algebra. He will also reinforce or accept proper responses, will correct erroneous responses, will point the way to the right answers, and will sharpen the pupil's insight into the relations between procedures and outcomes. In these events we find a composite list of the mechanisms of learning. . . . (pp. 9, 14)

Finally, B. F. Skinner concluded in 1973:

The natural, logical outcome of the struggle for personal freedom in education is that the teacher should improve his control of the student rather than abandon it. . . . The teacher who understands his assignment and is familiar with the behavioral processes needed to fulfill it can have students who not only feel free and happy while they are being taught, but who will continue to feel free and happy when their formal education comes to an end. They will do so because they will be successful in their work (having acquired useful productive repertoires), because they will get on well with their fellows (having learned to understand themselves and others), because they will enjoy what they do (having acquired necessary knowledge and skills), and because they will, from time to time, make an occasional creative contribution toward an even more effective and enjoyable way of life. Possibly the most important consequence is that the teacher will then feel free and happy, too. (p. 44)

To implement this position, it will be necessary for us to analyze more specifically cognitive learning goals, learner conditions, and situational conditions.

Contents and Processes of Cognitive Learning

Cognitive goals of education consist of **content** and **process.** Content can be subdivided into many levels. The content can be very specific (numbers), less specific (arithmetic), more general (mathematics), or very general (knowledge). Process can also be very specific (addition), less specific (arithmetical operations), more general (mathematical problem solving), or very general (general problem solving).

The contents and processes of learning are subject to various schemes of categorization. Content, for instance, can be classified by subject matter areas (e.g., social studies, language, math), by the nature of the symbols used in the content (verbal, numerical, spatial), or by the difficulty of the content (e.g., simple, complex, concrete, abstract). In the school setting, content is generally categorized according to subject-matter areas since this conveniently meshes with teachers' areas of concentration. On standardized tests, such as the Scholastic Aptitude Test, content is categorized according to its symbolic components (verbal and quantitative). Within the classroom, or in the development of curricula, content is frequently categorized according to level of difficulty in order to provide students with a stage-by-stage progression of mastery.

The processes of learning are also classified in different ways. Processes may be classified in terms of the type of thinking (e.g., memory, generalization, discrimination, convergent thinking, divergent thinking) or by the type of learning (acquisition, retention, transfer). The way in which the categorization is determined depends upon the learner and the situation.

Table 8.2 Taxonomy of Cognitive Domain

Category	Definition	Examples of Goals
Knowledge	Remembering specific and universal information from previously encountered communications	
Specifics	Recalling specific information with concrete referents	Define technical terms by giving their attributes, properties, or relations
Ways and means of dealing with specifics	Recalling or recognizing ways of organizing, studying, judging and criticizing	Knowledge of the standard representational devices and symbols in maps and charts
Universals and abstractions in a field	Recalling or recognizing major schemes and patterns by which phenomena and ideas are organized	Knowledge of the basic elements (balance, unity, rhythm) which can be used to judge a work of art
Comprehension	Understanding of communication previously encountered	The ability to translate a problem given in technical or abstract terminology into concrete or less abstract terminology
Application	Using abstractions in particular and concrete situations	The ability to apply principles, postulates, theorems, or other abstractions to new situations
Analysis	Breaking down a whole communication into its constituent parts	The ability to check the consistency of hypotheses with given information and assumptions
Synthesis	Combining parts to form a whole communication not clearly there before	The ability to formulate appropriate hypotheses based upon an analysis of factors involved, and to modify such hypotheses in the light of new factors and considerations
Evaluation	Judging the value of content and/or method for a given purpose	The ability to identify and appraise judgments and values that are involved in the choice of a course of action

Adapted from *Taxonomy of Educational Objectives: Handbook I: Cognitive Domain* by B. S. Bloom et al., pp. 62–200. Copyright © 1956 by Bloom. Reprinted by permission of David McKay Co., Inc.

Such fragmentation inevitably leads to confusion. Many theorists have attempted to identify specific types of learning and their component parts (Gagné, 1965; Spence, 1959; Tolman, 1949). Several schemes have also been proposed to classify cognitive learning into cross-disciplinary subject-matter areas not commonly found in the traditional school curriculum (e.g., Bloom et al., 1956; Gagné, 1970; Guilford, 1959). The model most commonly cited in educational practice as a basis for classifying cognitive learning is found in *The Taxonomy of Educational Objectives: Cognitive Domain* (Bloom et al., 1956).

Table 8.2 summarizes the major categories of this taxonomy. A taxonomy is a hierarchical arrangement of elements, the purpose of which is to show the relationship between categories. The criteria used in this taxonomy are simple-to-complex and concrete-to-abstract, with respect to content and process. Thus, if we examine the categories in the order listed, we find that they involve progressively more complex types of learning and progressively greater levels of abstract thinking.

The purpose of the taxonomy is not simply to list, but rather to enable the educator to identify precisely different kinds of objectives and to measure the success of learning outcomes. Each major category is subdivided into component parts, and the authors suggest specific types of questions that identify mastery over the skills categorized in that part. Let us consider briefly the characteristics of the taxonomy.

The taxonomy is divided into six categories: knowledge, comprehension, application, analysis, synthesis, and evaluation. Within the knowledge category, a number of different abilities are hierarchically ordered. Ability, as it is used here, refers to the learner's being able to make a correct or desirable response or to solve a problem correctly. The ability to recall a fact taught in class (knowledge) is far less sophisticated than the ability to understand what that fact means (comprehension), which in turn is less sophisticated than the ability to judge the relative truth, falsity, or value of that fact (evaluation). Thus, the taxonomy represents a grouping of abilities in order of increasing sophistication. More importantly, it is implied that mastery of any given level of ability is contingent upon mastery of the preceding levels. One cannot judge if one cannot understand. Likewise, one cannot understand if one does not know the "facts" of the matter. With this in mind, let us consider each of the major categories.

Knowledge is the content base upon which intellectual abilities and skills are used and from which they are developed. Knowledge as defined within the context of the taxonomy refers to the exact reproduction of information.

If knowledge is defined in this way, then comprehension is an important ability necessary in order to improve upon one's learning. Comprehension involves one's ability to put knowledge into his or her own words and to give examples. It involves not only acquisition but also retention; the learner is required to relate previous experiences to newly encountered knowledge.

It is important to note that the ability to rephrase and give examples must come from the learner. A learner's recall or recognition of someone else's phrase or idea (e.g., book, teacher, peer) is knowledge. This type of knowledge is the starting point. However, unless one can reproduce ideas and give examples from his own experience or recognize newly encountered ideas and examples, it is not likely that he or she comprehends the knowledge. Which goals described by Anderson and Messick (table 8.1) are most closely related to knowledge and comprehension?

Application involves the transfer of universals and abstractions to new situations. The way a learner goes about solving a new problem by applying in a new way knowledge already learned determines the level of application. For instance, if a student has learned to multiply but has never multiplied the number 76 by the number 584, doing so would be an example of low-level application since a known principle is involved—only the numbers are different. But, if a student can apply the principles of multiplication to solving another kind of problem (say in algebra), this could be indicative of a high

level of application. What goal described by Anderson and Messick is most similar to application?

Analysis is sometimes referred to as **critical thinking** or **convergent thinking.** One analyzes existing knowledge for the purpose of finding flaws (critical thinking) or for the purpose of finding logical explanations to situations (convergent thinking).

Synthesis is sometimes referred to as **creative thinking** or **divergent thinking.** The learner recombines elements of existing knowledge in a novel way to solve a problem or to extend knowledge in some way. Creative thinking refers to one's being able to recombine elements to form a unique outcome. Divergent thinking explains one's ability to suggest a variety of possible reasons for a situation. Divergent thinking, then, is a part of creative thinking.

In the knowledge category, the learner's previously encountered information is held back except for recall and, in part, for recognition. In the comprehension category, all or at least relevant aspects of previously encountered information is available to the learner. In the application category, it is necessary that the learner have relevant information available if needed. Knowledge of the situation, however, is not available to the learner in application.

In analysis, synthesis, and evaluation, it is critical that the entire communication be available to the learner. The problem in analysis is to detect logical errors based on some criteria; the problem in synthesis is to correct the errors for a more satisfactory solution to a problem from the outcome of analysis. Evaluation is a judgment of the value of the knowledge and outcomes resulting from the various processes based on some criteria. It may involve analysis and/or analysis and synthesis.

Unlike application, these higher order **problem-solving skills** do not involve supplying the learner with previously identified principles related to the situation. Both the relevant principles and aspects of the situation must be identified by the learner. In the process of synthesis, a new principle has to be created in relation to one's previous knowledge or borrowed from another context to satisfactorily solve the problem. Did Anderson and Messick identify and describe goals similar to analysis, synthesis, and evaluation?

If one is taught to solve a problem in a particular situation and does so accordingly, knowledge was used to resolve the situation. The person may possess some very useful knowledge; however, the person has not used the processes of analysis, synthesis, or evaluation in the problem solving.

Examples of questions that can potentially solicit processes and outcomes of the various categories of the taxonomy are given in table 8.3.

Table 8.3   Examples of Questions for Solicitation of Different Aspects of Cognitive Learning for Learners of Different Cognitive Developmental Levels

Category	Examples of Questions
Knowledge	Who wrote the book, *Walden II?* Was it Bruner, Ebel, Hutchins, Rogers, or Skinner?
	What clues, in order, did the Three Bears use to find out that someone had been in their house?
Comprehension	Give an example from your own experience of what reinforcement is.
	In your own words, what is a heroine?
Application	How would you use positive reinforcement to increase the amount of time a child spends doing . . . in this situation. . . ?
	What is a circumstance common to Goldilocks and Snow White?
Analysis	What would need to be changed in the reinforcement procedures in the following behavioral modification program . . . in order to attain these effects . . . (1) . . . (2) . . .
	What are some differences and similarities in the circumstances of Goldilocks and Snow White?
Synthesis	If Carl Rogers had written *Walden II,* how would the story have differed?
	If Goldilocks had not left the Three Bears' house, what do you think might have happened to her?
Evaluation	How effective do you believe the following Behavioral Modification program . . . would be for this purpose . . . ?
	Do you think Goldilocks was the heroine or villain in the story of the Three Bears?

Questions are not only an important means of facilitating different kinds of learning and thinking but they also represent a convenient way to demonstrate different kinds of learning. Do you detect any differences in what is required of the learner as you progress from one category to the next?

While the objectives of the taxonomy are apparently clear enough to construct tests of educational outcomes, they are considered by many educators to be too general to use as instructional objectives for the purposes of prescribing conditions of learning (e.g., Mager, 1962, Gronlund, 1970).

For instructional purposes, the two major problems with the goals stated in the taxonomy of cognitive learning objectives are the ambiguity of the infinitives used (process), and the globalness of their direct objects (content). To define a word is a less ambiguous process than to understand what a word means. Content that includes all of the technical terms in a field is very global as compared to content that contains only ten technical terms. Translating goals for each category of the taxonomy into curriculum, course, unit, lesson and moment in a lesson requires greater and greater specificity. Some representative infinitives (process) and their direct objects (content) suggested by Michael, Metfessel, and Kersner (1969) for the different categories of the taxonomy are given in table 8.4.

Table 8.4 Processes and Content of Cognitive Learning Objectives

Category	Examples of Infinitives	Examples of Direct Objects	Goals of Anderson and Messick
Knowledge			
Specifics	To acquire, to recall, to define, to identify	Terms, sources, names, dates, events, places	Memory
Ways and means of dealing with specifics	To acquire, to recall, to recognize, to identify	Trends, classifications, criteria, methods	Categorization, resources
Universals and abstractions	To acquire, to recall, to recognize, to identify	Generalizations, theories, organizations, implications	General knowledge
Comprehension	To comprehend, to rephrase, to interpret, to explain	Meaning, conclusion, consequence, relevance	Language and quantitative
Application	To apply, to use, to generalize, to transfer	Principles, methods, conclusions	Application
Analysis	To analyze, to detect, to discriminate, to distinguish	Facts, assumptions, points of view, hypotheses	Critical thinking
Synthesis	To synthesize, to originate, to modify, to combine	Solution, plan, hypothesis, theory	Creative thinking
Evaluation	To evaluate, to standardize, to judge, to validate	Accuracy, consistency, efficiency, utility	Problem-solving

From "Instrumentation of Bloom's and Krathwohl's Taxonomies for the Writing of Instructional Objectives" by William Michael, Newton S. Metfessel, and Donald A. Kersner, *Psychology in the Schools*, 1969, *6(3)*, pp. 227–231. Used with permission.

The goals discussed earlier by Anderson and Messick (1974), arranged in a hierarchical order in accordance with the taxonomy, are also presented in table 8.4. You might want to return to the description of these goals by Anderson and Messick and consider them in light of a hierarchy.

In summary, an understanding of the nature of cognitive learning content and process is important in order to translate ultimate educational objectives into immediate educational objectives for the purpose of prescribing learning conditions.

While acquisition, retention, and transfer are separate processes, they are not usually considered in isolation from one another in relation to learning. All three processes are a part of gaining and using knowledge and skills, and a meaningful plan must be conceptualized so that conditions of learning are arranged in a way that there will be minimal interference from one phase of learning to another. With this continuity of learning process in mind, let us turn our attention to the conditions of learning.

Conditions of Learning on Which Educational Psychologists Tend to Agree

A number of the more applied-oriented educational psychologists have attempted to synthesize the practical applications of learning theory and research (Bigge, 1964, 1971, 1976; Bugelski, 1964, 1972; Burton, 1958; Dale, 1972; Hilgard & Bower, 1966, 1975; Travers, 1967, 1972; Watson, 1960). We will consider learner and situational conditions of the teacher-learning process in which there is considerable agreement among theorists.

Learner Conditions

Principles related to the nature of the learner are of potential value to the teacher. These principles are involved with cognitive ability, previous cognitive achievement, and motivation of the learner. While we might assume that the cognitive characteristics of a learner are important to learning cognitive goals of education, we must be aware that learning theorists give motivation a major role in terms of its effects on present learning outcomes and its effects on one's motivation in future learning situations.

It is important to consider the principles related to learner conditions (page 320) in arranging situational conditions of learning. Situational conditions of learning may be used to change the readiness of the learner and make provisions for them. In general, the younger the learner the more likely the readiness characteristics can be changed. The older the learner the more likely that provisions for the readiness are of greater importance.

The following are useful principles related to learner conditions:

1. Readiness of the learner for new cognitive learning is a product of the interaction among many affective, cognitive, and psychomotor characteristics. Readiness characteristics that have been studied most extensively are cognitive abilities, cognitive achievement, and motivation.

2. Learners vary not only in general cognitive achievement but also in general cognitive ability. The latter represents their potential level of cognitive achievement.

3. The importance of specific cognitive abilities in learning a complex skill or body of knowledge may depend upon the level of cognitive learning. Such cognitive abilities have been referred to as cognitive strategies or cognitive styles; this depends upon whether the focus is on the task or the learner. Aptitude has also been used to refer to more specific abilities. Strategy or style is conceived of as a process variable while aptitude is conceived of as a product variable.

4. A learner progresses in any area of cognitive learning only as far as necessary in order to achieve his or her goals. With optimal motivation, cognitive achievement can improve. Rate of learning is related to the arousal level of the learner. Learning may be inefficient because the arousal level of the learner is either too high or too low. Arousal level may be controlled through the amount of stimulation experienced by the learner. The level of arousal for optimal learning may differ, depending upon the level of complexity of the skill or body of knowledge.

5. A learner internalizes the evaluation of his performance by significant others in his environment. The self-esteem of a learner is affected by previous experiences and affects one's performance in future experiences. If a learner experiences much criticism, failure, and discouragement, the effects are detrimental to his or her well-being.

Group Atmosphere Learning situations in schools usually involve groups of students, and it is important to consider the social setting in which learning occurs. See chapter 15 for an in-depth discussion on group processes. Cognitive learning is largely an individual matter, but listed on p. 321 are important factors that are related to the individual's learning in a group rather than learning in isolation. These group atmosphere conditions represent important modifications to learner conditions. It is within the social setting that situational conditions of learning occur.

The following are useful principles related to group atmosphere:

1. Learners grouped in a situation based on one readiness trait will vary considerably on other readiness traits.
2. Interactions among group members provide sources of reinforcement—with both positive and negative effects—related to the goals of cognitive learning and the procedures used by the teacher and the learners in an attempt to accomplish them.
3. A learner tends to be more productive when he or she is in a group situation rather than working in isolation.
4. Students learn much from one another—both positive and negative. Students who have been together for an extended amount of time learn new knowledge and skills more readily from one another than they do from students who are strangers to them.
5. Strict control of a group by a teacher through punishment is associated with more conformity, anxiety, shyness, and acquiescence in learners. Excessive punitive control may result in apathy, defiance, or escape from the situation. Less strict control of a group by a teacher through positive reinforcement is associated with more security, initiative, and attempts to learn the goals of schooling.

Goal

Situational Conditions

Principles of potential value to the teacher for the purpose of prescribing situational conditions of learning involve goals, organization of knowledge, activity of the learner, practice, reinforcement, and the type of learning process. It is the interrelationships among these factors that make up principles of situational conditions.

The goals of learning should be defined clearly so that the learner knows what it is that he or she is trying to learn; the process and content of teacher-assigned objectives should be clearly specified. The conditions under which the student will be expected to demonstrate his or her proficiency and the consequences of performance should be specified at a meaningful time during the learning experience.

The learner benefits from experience in setting realistic goals for himself or herself. Goals should be neither so low as to elicit little effort nor so high as to result in failure. Realistic goal setting leads to more satisfactory improvement than unrealistic goal setting. Goal setting can be related to the standards for acceptable performance, time needed to complete a task, or the procedures the learner will use in achieving the goals.

Organization of Knowledge

A body of content should be organized from simple and concrete to complex and abstract, or vice versa, depending upon the particular learning processes and the nature of the content. The developmental level of the learner may be important in determining how the content should be structured or sequenced. In general, the older the learner is, the more likely it is that the complex and abstract to simple and concrete will be the better structure.

Activity of the Learner

The learner gains from being an active rather than a passive listener or viewer. Considerable activity involves the learner's *learning by doing* rather than passively receiving information such as listening to a lecture or an audio tape, or viewing a film or television. When less active participation is a part of the instructional program, the activities should be designed to elicit some mental activity on the part of the learner. The latter, of course, is an efficient means of presenting information. Coupled with active learner participation following such presentations, learning by doing can be effective for retention or transfer purposes.

The learner should also be provided opportunities to sample information in situations, set up hypotheses and test them. The learner should be encouraged to *learn by thinking* as well as by doing.

Learners who are provided with opportunities for exploration are encouraged to "learn by thinking," as well as by doing.

The Psychology of Learning

Practice

There is no substitute for frequency of repetition for attaining goals of cognitive learning. Practice is important to insure retention. Intentional recall following original learning decreases the amount forgotten. Learning from printed material is improved by practicing recall. Time spent on recalling what has been read is often more effective than time spent on rereading for retention purposes. This may also be the case in connection with tapes, films, and television.

Practice without progress indicates inadequate learning. Practice should be arranged so that knowledge of results and corrective information can be supplied to the learner based on his or her responses.

Practice is most profitable when the learner has adequate readiness. Meaningful learning requires less practice than learning for which the learner has inadequate readiness. Practice of knowledge should occur in varied contexts so that learning will become appropriate to a wider (or more restricted) range of stimuli.

Reinforcement

A reinforcer is any stimulus that strengthens the probability of a behavior reoccurring. Reinforcers may be compiled into different categories, e.g., positive and negative; internal (self-imposed) and external (other-imposed); affective and cognitive (knowledge of results, information feedback), tangible and intangible. It is generally known that positive reinforcement is more effective than punishment.

Performances that are reinforced are more likely to reoccur than those that are not reinforced. However, to be most effective, reinforcement must almost immediately follow a desired performance. Delayed reinforcement may be effective if the learner remains oriented to the task.

New learning is most efficiently learned through a continuous reinforcement schedule (i.e., 100%). Well-established performances are best maintained through the use of a schedule of reinforcement that is less than 100 percent, i.e., intermittent. Such intermittent schedules are most effective if the reinforcers occur randomly rather than systematically. Using money, grades, stars, etc. as reinforcers often distract from the goals of cognitive learning. However, such incentives can be used to orient a student to learning tasks.

Punishment may have variable and uncertain effects upon learning. It may make the desirable performance more likely or less likely to occur and may set up avoidance tendencies for the situation. When punishment is used,

it should be mild and directed primarily at the performance that is incompatible with the response to be learned. Punishment is most effective if the appropriate response is reinforced when it occurs. In most situations, there are inhibitions that must be learned in order for learning to proceed.

Extinction is an effective way to eliminate unwanted behavior if it is possible to arrange for the manifestation of the behavior without reinforcement, and to reinforce the desirable behavior when it does occur. Extinction involves withholding a reinforcer for a behavior that has been previously reinforced. Extinction is sometimes used in a different manner in educational practices by ignoring undesirable behavior. This is an effective technique if the behavior is not one which has been strengthened from a previous reinforcement schedule. If such a schedule is in use, then behavior must be considered as an extinction problem as defined earlier.

The more closely the reinforcement is to a natural outcome of the learning process, the better the effect. Learning is stimulated, and undesirable side effects, such as attention being given to the external reinforcement, are minimized. In addition, the external reward may assume more value than the object of the lesson. A learning experience initiated by the goals of the learner is likely to be motivated by its own incompleteness.

The successful completion of a task or discovery of the solution to a problem may be reinforcing for the behaviors leading up to the event.

Learning Processes

Acquisition   Acquisition is a change in performance due to experiences from which learning can be inferred. New learning can be positive or negative in relation to the desirable or correct performance. Learning occurs in two stages. Early learning (novel learning) is slow and involves the acquisition of basic discriminations. Later learning (meaningful learning) builds upon the foundation of early learning and involves the acquisition of generalizations.

Retention   Retention is a relatively permanent change in performance due to practice. While it is not critical that many new acquisitions are retained for a lifetime, it is important that they are retained long enough that further learning based upon them can occur. The retention curve initially declines rapidly and then declines gradually. The initial decline represents the first hour after the acquisition of new learning. The amount forgotten depends upon the manner in which retention is measured (e.g., recall or recognition) and the meaningfulness of the learning.

Meaningful content is more easily learned and retained than novel content because it represents content that has already been partially learned. Learning with understanding is more permanent and more transferable than rote memorization or learning by formula. Learning with understanding is highly dependent upon readiness for the task, practice in varied contexts, and the conditions under which practice occurs.

Concepts represent classifications of experiences. The learning of concepts involves identification of the defining attributes of the class of phenomena included in the concept, and opportunities to classify exemplars and nonexemplars of the concept under conditions that provide the learner with information of the acceptability of his classifications. A good way to enable a learner to improve his or her understanding of a concept is to present the concept in a variety of specific situations contrasting experiences with and without the concept, then to encourage precise formulations of the concept and its application in situations different from those in which the concept was learned.

Time devoted to the learning of principles provides better possibilities for the transfer of what has been learned in new situations than the same amount of time devoted to the learning of specific facts.

Transfer

Transfer is the influence of previous learning on performance in a new situation. Transfer may be positive, negative, or zero. Positive transfer occurs in situations in which previous learning facilitates subsequent performances. Negative transfer occurs in situations in which previous learning interferes with subsequent performance. Zero transfer occurs in situations in which previous learning does not affect subsequent performance. What is learned will most likely be available for further use if it is learned in a situation similar to the one in which it is to be used. The closer together the time of learning and the time it is needed for use, the more likely the learning will be available.

Transfer is more likely to occur with well-practiced skills and knowledge when the situation in which the learning is to be transfered is similar to the one in which the original learning occurred. Transfer depends upon sudden insight of the learner. Practice will not affect the learner's performance. That is, transfer depends upon the learner's previous knowledge and skills. Transfer is enhanced if the learner can discover some relationships among concepts and principles on his own.

Sudden insight into the solution of a problem is not likely to occur in situations in which the learner has not had previous experience with related problems and with transferring what has been learned to new problems.

Transfer is not likely to occur automatically. The learner will most likely need assistance in establishing an appropriate set, consideration of principles that might be applied to a particular setting, and conditions to which they might apply.

Table 8.5   Comparison of the Interpretations of Behavioral and Cognitive Theories of Learning Processes, Conditions, and Outcomes

Concept	Behavioral	Cognitive
Readiness of Learner	Task readiness	Developmental readiness
Goal	Assigned goal	Practice in goal-setting
Content	Content sequenced logically	Content structured psychologically
Activity of Learner	Active—learning by responding (doing)	Active—hypothesis testing and sampling (thinking)
Motivation	Reinforcement—primarily effect	Cognitive feedback—primarily information
Acquisition	Task readiness results in meaningful learning	Developmental readiness in relation to task results in understanding
Retention	Practice under conditions for retention	Structure knowledge for retention
Specific Transfer	Practice in varied contexts will allow proper generalizations to new situations	Focus on problems and cognitive strategies will result in transfer
General Transfer	If novel (creative) behavior is reinforced, it is most likely to reoccur	Focus on development of creative thinking and other learning to learn skills

Table 8.6   Comparison of Interpretations of Behavioral and Cognitive Theories in Relation to Categories of Cognitive Learning

Bloom et al.	Gagné	Guilford
	Behavioral	Cognitive
Knowledge	Verbal information	Information
Specifics	Verbal associations	Memory of symbolic units
Ways and means of dealing with knowledge	Multiple discriminations	Memory of semantic classes and relations
Universals and abstractions	Concepts and principles	Memory of semantic systems
Comprehension	Knowledge	Convergent production of symbolic classes relations, and systems
Application	Problem solving	Convergent production of symbolic relations
Analysis		Convergent production of semantic systems
Synthesis		Divergent production of symbolic transformations
Evaluation		Evaluation of semantic implications

As you may recall from chapter 6, there are two learning theories that focus on the situational conditions of learning—behavioral and cognitive. The conditions we have considered represent processes and synthesis of conditions of learning based on these theories. A summary of the different emphases in the behavioral and cognitive theories as related to the conditions of learning and learning processes are given in table 8.5. Table 8.6 contains examples of classifications that a behaviorist and cognitivist might use in relation to categories of the taxonomy (Gagné, 1965; Guilford, 1959). This summary may enable you to consider the consistency of the situational conditions of learning we have presented.

Are Systematically Oriented Learning Theorists Concerned With the Same Processes and Outcomes of Learning?

Several systematically oriented learning theorists have attempted through the years to demonstrate the implications of their work for educational practices. Five theorists who have had a major impact on conditions of cognitive learning in practice during the past quarter-century include Ausubel, 1963, 1968; Bruner, 1960, 1966; Gagné, 1965, 1970; Rogers, 1951, 1969; and Skinner, 1954, 1968. Their theories of the direction of learning processes are presented in table 8.7.

The information contained in this display—moving from left to right—represents a continuum from extreme situation-oriented to extreme learner-oriented positions based on these theorists' contribution to conditions of learning outcomes. A represents the beginning point of the learning process, and the highest letter (for example, C) represents the end point, or learning outcome. When there are no letters for a theorist in a particular category, this category is not a part of their system.

Table 8.7   Comparison of Five Theorists on Goals and Processes of Cognitive Learning

	Skinner	Gagné	Ausubel	Bruner	Rogers
Category					
Knowledge	A	A	B		
Comprehension		B	A		
Application		C		C	
Analysis				B	
Synthesis				A	B
Evaluation					A

> "If transfer behavior is systematically shaped, it still would not be known whether
> a person could transfer the behavior to still another new situation."

The important points of overlap are between Gagné and Ausubel on the role of comprehension; between Gagné and Bruner on use of application; and between Bruner and Rogers on the role of synthesis in learning. In each case, there is a difference in goals. Ausubel is concerned with comprehension as an aid in retention while Gagné is concerned with comprehension as an aid in application. Gagné's work includes application as an outcome in itself, while Bruner's interest lies in application as a means to develop general transfer skills. Bruner demonstrates the role of synthesis (divergent thinking) as a means to facilitate transfer, while Rogers examines synthesis (creative thinking) as an outcome. There is little overlap when the theories are considered from a goal perspective. Let's look at some of the similarities and differences in their theories and contributions to teachers on a practical basis.

Skinner B. F. Skinner was an experimental learning theorist before dedicating his efforts to educational practices. His extensive research on principles of operant conditioning and schedules of reinforcement were based on lower organisms.

Skinner makes no distinction between learning and performance. The learning process and outcome are identical. The learner can be shaped to acquire, retain, and use knowledge through discrimination of **stimulus** cues. Knowledge results from **responses** made to information under **reinforcement contingencies.** While comprehension, application, analysis, synthesis, and evaluation can be shaped through reinforcement, they lose their meaning in the context of the way they are typically defined. All of these intellectual abilities and skills involve some aspect of transfer on the part of the learner.

If transfer behavior is systematically shaped, it still would not be known whether a person could transfer the behavior to a new situation. This is a critical point concerning the assumptions made by Skinner about the learner and the situation. An important principle from this position would be to reinforce these behaviors (as any other behavior) whenever the learner makes them, if it is desirable that they reoccur. As Skinner has limited confidence in a learner's ability to transfer knowledge, it is critical that the school gives careful attention to the goals that will be needed by the learner in the future.

The most direct contribution to the teaching of cognitive learning has been Skinner's work on applying **operant conditioning** to instructional materials. Programmed materials or instruction based on Skinner's system are called **linear** programs. Linear programs involve relatively small step-by-step frames for content organized from simple to complex behavior (e.g., letters to words, words to sentences, concepts to principles, principles to problems, etc.) depending on the content. An example of a linear program is presented in figure 8.1 (Holland & Skinner, 1961).

In a linear program, the number of the stimulus (frame) and the response correspond (e.g., 18–2; 18–8). The stimulus requires an **overt** (or **covert) response,** and the correct response is given on the following page. Making the response is one manner of learning by doing. The correct response is both a reinforcer and corrective feedback. The reinforcement is immediate and continuous in this type of program as the knowledge is being newly acquired.

The small step-by-step approach is used to prevent the learner from making a mistake. However, if a mistake occurs, the correct response is immediately available so that the learner will not practice errors. Given the human facility to reinforce one's self, errors can be difficult to extinguish. Notice that Skinner is particularly concerned that the reinforcer be a natural consequence of the situation. One adjusts his or her performance on the basis of the consequences of the corrective feedback. In addition, the rewards are small.

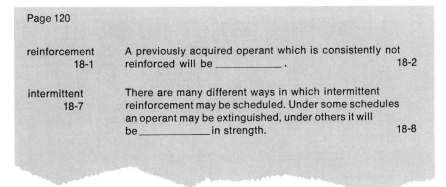

Figure 8.1 Example of Linear Program. From *The Analysis of Behavior* by J. Holland and B. F. Skinner. (New York: McGraw-Hill, 1961). Adapted from pp. 120–21 with permission.

Figure 8.2 Example of Branching Program. From Robert F. Mager, *Preparing Objectives for Programmed Instruction,* 2nd ed. (Belmont, Calif.: Fearon Publishers, 1975). Adapted from pp. 7–13 with permission.

page 7

A general survey of the organizing and administration of elementary and secondary school libraries, with emphasis on methods of developing the library as an integral part of the school; includes functions, organization, services, equipment, and materials.

What does the above statement represent? Does the statement look more like an objective of a course, or does it look more like a description of a course?

An objective of a course. Turn to page 11.

A description of a course. Turn to page 13.

page 11

You said the statement was an objective of a course. Apparently I didn't make myself clear earlier, so let me try again...

page 13

You said the statement was a description of a course, and right you are! One final word about...

Skinner makes two important justifications for his idea of linear programming. First, new learning requires continuous reinforcement to be efficient and effective. Second, the learner can progress at his or her individual rate. These are two of the more difficult problems confronting education—effective reinforcement contingencies and **individualized instruction.**

A **branching program,** based on principles of a cognitive theory, is illustrated in figure 8.2 (Mager, 1975); you may want to compare the linear program to it. Note the allowance for errors, the generous use of additional information as cognitive feedback, and large steps in comparison to small steps used in a linear frame. Both programs are presently used in programmed materials. The principles of branching programs are the basis of computer-assisted instruction.

Skinner's work has been applied to disciplinary and motivational problems in schools. Operant conditioning is the foundation for behavior modification procedures and behavioral management of classroom programs. Principles of reinforcement are potentially useful in any situation. These procedures will be considered in Part III.

> "Ausubel has been primarily concerned with . . . . knowledge and comprehension, not application. However, he would assume that mastering knowledge would more likely lead to transfer than not mastering knowledge."

Robert Gagné was a military psychologist before turning his attention to schools. One of his interests was the task analysis of intellectual and psycho-motor skills. His primary concern has been to develop effective principles of transfer. Gagné's hierarchy of learning was presented in part in table 8.6. Unlike the taxonomy, this hierarchy is collapsible from the top to the bottom except in the case of signal learning. Signal learning (classical conditioning) is an aspect of all types of learning.

For Gagné, learning proceeds most effectively from the specific to the general (i.e., **inductive**) for the purposes of problem solving (application). Design of instruction should begin by defining the terminal behavior (problem solving), and then breaking it down from the general to the specific. Learning and teaching then proceed inductively from the bottom to the top of the hierarchy. At this point, Gagné would call upon the principles of behavioral and cognitive psychology. However, he has also synthesized some aspects of these theories into his work and more recently has begun to develop his own theory (1974). Through the years, his perspective has become more and more that of a cognitive learning theorist.

Gagné's model is potentially helpful in building curriculum, writing objectives, designing materials and activities, and constructing pre- and post-tests. The use of his system of **task analysis** may be effective whenever the content can be interpreted effectively on the basis of his model.

David Ausubel was a physician before embarking upon studies in psychology and becoming an educational psychologist. Ausubel has been primarily concerned with how to enable a learner to retain knowledge efficiently from relatively large bodies of content. He refers to his theory in terms of **meaningful verbal learning.** His concern is with knowledge and comprehension, not application. However, he would assume that mastering knowledge would more likely lead to transfer than not having mastered knowledge.

Starting from the observation that people tend to remember more general ideas and forget more detailed specifics, Ausubel devised a procedure to facilitate retention of specifics. The procedure consists of an advance organizer supplied to the learner before the body of knowledge is presented. An example of an advance organizer is given in display 8.1.

Gagné

Ausubel

Since the psychology of classroom learning is concerned with the acquisition and retention of large bodies of meanings, it is important that we make very explicit at the outset what we mean by meaning and meaningful learning. In this chapter, we shall explore the nature of meaning, examine some alternative theories of meaning, and consider the relationship of meaning to meaningfulness and meaningful verbal learning. In so doing, we shall also be concerned with issues as the general significance of meaningful learning in acquiring knowledge, how words, concepts, and propositions acquire meaning, the distinction between logical and psychological meaning, and the difference between cognition and perception. Lastly, we shall attempt to illustrate and concretize this abstract discussion of meaning and meaningful learning by showing briefly how important such conceptions are for understanding how we learn the syntax of our native language, how we learn to read, and how we learn second languages.

From David P. Ausubel, *Educational Psychology: A Cognitive View* (New York: Holt, Rinehart & Winston, 1968), p. 37. With permission of the publisher.

Since the most general ideas are retained, then these ideas provide a foundation on which the learner structures the detail. Better retention results as compared to simply practicing isolated specifics. In time, the detail is forgotten, but the general ideas that remain will be more accurate generalizations than before the experience. An advance organizer consists of the most critical abstractions on which the content of a body of knowledge (e.g., chapter in a book) can be secured. The advance organizer is composed of first abstract concepts, then less abstract concepts and, finally, concrete concepts. Topics and subtopics are then designed in a similar manner. This is a **deductive** model. A comparison of Gagné's inductive model and Ausubel's deductive model for comprehension are given in figure 8.3.

Ausubel's procedures can be helpful to a teacher in designing materials and presentations whenever the content can be interpreted effectively on the basis of his theory.

Figure 8.3 Comparison of Knowledge Acquisition

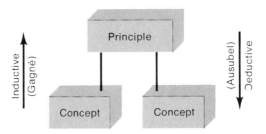

Bruner   Jerome Bruner studied the psychology of **perception** and cognition many years before becoming concerned with education. Bruner has stressed the importance of the structure of knowledge in relation to the curriculum as well as to the content of instruction. Structure of knowledge as defined by Bruner refers to the modes of representation of content—that is, **enactive** (physical manipulation), **iconic** (perceptual features), and **symbolic** (formal language of logic). He contends that the learning of concepts and principles is based not only on the developmental age of the child but on the mode in which the content is represented. While the phases *enactive, iconic,* and *symbolic* are similar to Piaget's stages of cognitive development, their use refers to the transition that knowledge undergoes for any learner. That is, we first acquire learning enactively, then iconically, and finally symbolically. Bruner proposed that the curriculum be designed on the basis of these modes of representation in relation to the developmental age and to the nature of the content. Bruner's inductive approach to concept learning is referred to as the discovery method.

Bruner is also concerned with methods to enable learners to synthesize knowledge in order to develop general transfer skills. He contends that knowledge is merely a vehicle from which such skills can be developed. Bruner has proposed a deductive model as represented in figure 8.4. It is compared in this display to Gagné's inductive model. Bruner has advocated conditions of learning such as encouraging guessing, allowing for errors, and a generally relaxed atmosphere for the purpose of developing general transfer skills. Bruner's ideas are most useful in attempting to encourage a learner to focus on the process of transfer itself, particularly when it is known that the learner has the prerequisite knowledge.

Jerome Bruner's work in learning has extended our understanding of how classroom conditions can maximize learning effectiveness.

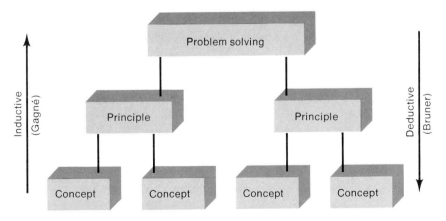

Figure 8.4 Comparison of Knowledge Utilization

Rogers   Carl Rogers was a counseling psychologist for many years before he attempted to apply some of his ideas to education. His approach originates from the ultimate goal of the individual in society—that is, a **fully functioning person** within the ideals of a democracy. Evaluation of one's self and one's environment in terms of what is and is not meaningful is critical in becoming a fully functioning person. Due to our uniqueness as individuals, such an undertaking results in a meaningful synthesis of our experiences.

Lack of meaning in life is a continuous problem for many adults who seek counseling. As an experienced therapist, Rogers has tried to isolate characteristics of the counselor that tend to be of help to the client in his or her attempts to derive meaning from life. Under the assumption that children are like adults, he has advocated that teachers arrange the conditions therapeutically so that children can become fully functioning people.

When the meaning of the goals and conditions of learning come into inevitable conflict, Rogers's ideas about the facilitating characteristics of the teacher would appear to be sound and may be helpful in assisting children to set up goals for themselves.

Given their respective differences, one might conclude that these positions are irreconcilable. On the contrary, however, the practitioner can draw freely from each of these positions, depending upon the needs of the learner, what the teacher is trying to accomplish, and the nature of the subject matter to be taught. Taken together, these theorists have put together important pieces of a puzzle depicting the processes and conditions of learning. Skinner, in his studies of animal behavior, Gagné, in his studies of adult learning, Bruner, in his studies of children, Rogers, in his work with clients, Ausubel, in his studies of the gifted—each in his own way has contributed to our understanding of the total person in the processes of learning.

Carl Rogers, the founder of client-centered therapy, has contributed a wealth of insight for educators.

Something to Think About

Two classical studies have been done on the outcomes of acquisition, retention, and transfer of knowledge. The first study was conducted by Tyler (1934) and the second by Gagné and Brown (1961) at a period in which there was heated debate concerning the relationship of knowledge and its transfer. Tyler's study involved college students' prerequisite knowledge in a biological science course and the ease with which they acquired and retained knowledge and skills for different categories of learning. Results of the Tyler study are reported in table 8.8.

The second investigation was undertaken by Gagné and Brown (1961), who focused on the acquisition and transfer of principles of mathematical

Table 8.8   Acquisition, Retention, and Transfer of Different Kinds of Cognitive Learning

Category of Learning	Pretest *Prerequisite Knowledge*	Course Tests *Acquisition at Time Course Taken*	Percent of Gain From Pretest	Posttest *Retention 1 yr. later*	Percent of Original Acquisition Retained
Knowledge of Specifics (identifying technical terms)	20%	83%	63%	67%	75%
Knowledge of Universals and Abstractions (recalling facts)	21%	63%	42%	54%	79%
Application (applying principles to new situations)	35%	65%	30%	65%	100%
Evaluation (interpreting new experiments)	30%	57%	27%	64%	126%

Adapted from "Some Findings from Studies in the Field of College Biology" by Ralph Tyler, *Science Education*, 1934, *18*, p. 141. Used with permission.

Table 8.9   Comparison of Three Approaches in Terms of Amount of Time Needed to Acquire and Transfer Concepts and Principles

Condition	Time in Minutes *Acquisition*	Number of Hints Required *Transfer*	Time in Minutes *Transfer*
Rule-Example	28.8	6.5	27.4
Discovery	18.5	2.2	19.8
Guided Discovery	33.2	1.5	16.7

Adapted from "Some Factors in the Programming of Conceptual Learning" by Robert M. Gagné and Larry J. Brown, *Journal of Experimental Psychology*, 1961, *62*, p. 317. Copyright © by the American Psychological Association. Used with permission.

problems by high school students (table 8.9). The conditions of learning were similar to those advocated by Ausubel (rule-example), Bruner (discovery) and Gagné (guided discovery). The problems would be classified as application in accordance with the taxonomy.

Several aspects of processes and conditions of learning are illustrated from these data. Tyler's data concludes that the prerequisite knowledge of complex and abstract concepts in the context of applied settings are higher than facts. Performance in problem-solving is also higher than for factual knowledge. Are these data in agreement with Ausubel's notions about retention? At the time of regular course examinations, what category of learning was most readily learned? Which was least readily learned? What learning was best retained?

Gagné and Brown's study demonstrates that the discovery of principles facilitates transfer (compare rule example with guided discovery). The ability to verbalize the principle during acquisition also facilitates transfer (compare discovery and guided discovery). Which approach would be most efficient for acquisition? Which approach would be most efficient for transfer?

In view of this limited information, what is your theory about the relationships among acquisition, retention, and transfer? In attempting to answer this question, you will find yourself in a situation similar to learning theorists in their efforts to consider the processes and conditions of cognitive learning.

Goals and Conditions

In recent years, goals of education have been concerned with learning conditions as well as goals. The following is a resolution adopted by the National Association of State Boards of Education (1976).[1] See if you can identify items that are referring to goals and conditions of learning from this resolution:

1. To assure a free society, children at all levels of learning should have instruction in the rights and responsibilities of citizenship and in the ethical, moral and legal bases for that citizenship.
2. The basic skills of reading, writing and mathematics must receive priority. The effective use of basic skills requires the development of communication and logical thinking skills in students, with the result that they be able to express themselves lucidly, evaluate information factually and make critical judgements affecting their lives.
3. Comprehensive health and safety education for all students should stress causes, prevention and cures of major national problems including chemical dependency, malnutrition and venereal disease.
4. To maintain the integrity of the family unit, high school curricula should emphasize the privileges and responsibility of marriage and parenthood.
5. Appropriate programs to identify and to meet the needs of all handicapped children should be available to all such children.

1. Adaptation of material from resolution adopted by the National Association of School Boards of Education, 1976. Used with permission.

6. Programs should insure that gifted and talented children are afforded the opportunity to progress according to their abilities thereby permitting them to achieve full potential.

7. Early childhood education should be family-based with appropriate public support whenever possible. It should start as early in life as proven desirable by research and experience, especially for children with special needs.

8. Career education, as an integral part of the educational program, should develop respect for work, workers and employers, motivation to learn by emphasizing the satisfaction in useful and stimulating careers, and awareness of alternative careers.

9. Vocational and technical education are necessary parts of comprehensive education programs, should train persons to competence in salable skills, and should provide opportunities for retraining as circumstances and interests change.

10. Bilingual education is necessary in schools where there are significant numbers of limited English-speaking students who should become fluent in both languages.

11. Foreign language instruction should lead to conversational fluency.

12. Consumer education is necessary for all students in order to prepare them to be intelligent in the use of goods and services and in personal management.

13. To prepare people to function in a world-wide technological society, schools must insure that students are conversant with *a*. History, culture, language and art of the various civilizations *b*. Economic principles under which societies are based *c*. Scientific principles describing the operation of the physical world *d*. Law education, the rights and responsibilities of citizenship, and the legal process as it applies to their daily lives.

14. Education for national conversion to the metric system should be provided.

15. The education process should be free of bias on the basis of race, sex, national origin, or religion.

16. Because students learn at different rates and learn best within varied environments and because children should have an opportunity to be in a suitable learning situation, learning options should be made available within the public school system.

17. Environmental education should be provided which emphasizes the need to preserve the natural quality of life balanced by recognition of mankind's need for natural resources, energy, goods and services [pp. 2].

Summary

In this chapter, we considered historical and contemporary perspectives of the cognitive learning goals of the school. As we have seen, processes and conditions of learning are necessarily related to the goals and outcomes of education. Distinctions were made among acquisition, retention, and transfer of learning. Contributions of several systematic theorists—Skinner, Gagné, Ausubel, Bruner, and Rogers—were discussed. In addition, we have examined conditions and processes of cognitive learning from a synthetic viewpoint. Finally, we discussed the goals of cognitive learning for the latter part of the twentieth century from the viewpoint of the school and society.

Suggested Additional Readings

Taxonomy of Educational Objectives: Handbook I: Cognitive Domain by Benjamin Bloom et al. (*New York: David McKay Co., 1956*)

A comprehensive discussion of educational objectives in the cognitive domain is presented. Numerous examples of each type of learning are given for goals and outcomes.

We were reluctantly forced to agree with Hilgard that each theory of learning accounts for some phenomena very well but is less adequate in accounting for others. . . . We are of the opinion that our method of ordering educational outcomes will make it possible to define the range of phenomena for which such a theory must account.

from *Taxonomy of Educational Objectives*

Fundamentals of Human Learning and Cognition by Henry C. Ellis (*Dubuque, Ia.: Wm. C. Brown Company Publishers, 1972*)

The basic foundations of cognitive psychology are explained in this book.

Despite instances in which transfer is minimal, the assumption of transfer underlies much of what is taught in the American classroom. . . . Therefore, the issue is not if transfer occurs, but rather the conditions under which transfer occurs.

from *Fundamentals of Human Learning and Cognition*

Fundamentals of Learning and Motivation, Second Edition, by Frank A. Logan (*Dubuque, Ia.: Wm. C. Brown Company Publishers, 1976*)

The basic foundations of behavioral psychology are explained in this book.

Psychology should be studied as a living subject matter; indeed, it is the most personal and intimate subject matter in the world. Nothing is quite so close to us as our own behavior, and nothing is quite so important to us as the behavior of others.

from *Fundamentals of Learning and Motivation*

Learning: A Survey of Psychological Interpretations, Revised Edition, by Winfred F. Hill (*Scranton, Pa.: Chandler, 1971*)

Hill examines the major learning theories. The primary emphasis is upon the cognitive and the behavioral positions.

For most of us, the various learning theories have two chief values. One is in providing us with a vocabulary and a conceptual framework. . . . The other is in suggesting where to look for solutions to practical problems.

from *Learning: A Survey of Psychological Interpretations*

What Is Psychomotor Learning?

Psychomotor learning is defined as the acquisition, retention, and transfer of voluntary movement. Sensorimotor and perceptual motor skills are terms often used synonomously with psychomotor skills.

Processes and Outcomes of Psychomotor Learning

Essentially, the process is the internal movement (motor movement) and the outcome is observable movement. A taxonomy of the psychomotor domain includes the following categories: reflex movements; basic fundamental movements; perceptual abilities; physical abilities; skilled movements; nondiscursive communication. Each of these categories comprises several subcategories. Perceptual ability may be further differentiated into kinesthetic, visual, auditory, and tactile discriminations.

Conditions of Psychomotor Learning

The conditions of psychomotor learning are similar to those of cognitive learning. Distinctions between factors such as the degree of continuity of movement and coordination are taken into account.

Relationships Among the Affective, Cognitive, and Psychomotor Domains

While the goals of the different domains can be somewhat differentiated, we cannot assume that a learner will shut off all systems and direct activities toward the goal of a single system.

Movement Education

Movement education involves the application of psychomotor skills to learning in other areas. Three math lessons are presented that demonstrate how movement can be used to teach mathematical concepts.

9 Conditions and Processes of Psychomotor Learning

We sometimes spin off into an *affective* or a *cognitive* world. Eventually, though, we will return to the physical world; a headache, heartache, indigestion, or another physical need will require our attention. In addition, we always return for action; we move our tongues, legs, arms, hands, fingers, and even our torso to act on our feelings and thoughts. Without such movements, feelings and thoughts would often serve little purpose.

While societal attitudes are slowly changing, we have valued the development of the **psychomotor** system of a person far less in the recent past than the other two systems—the affective and the cognitive. To some people, it is disgusting even to discuss the psychomotor aspect of our existence. To others, it is a disgrace to our species for someone to demonstrate a well-developed psychomotor skill. Still other people can separate their psychomotor system from themselves. People try to play guitars and drive automobiles with their affective and cognitive systems rather than with their psychomotor system. Who among teachers has the courage to say, "I help kids learn psychomotor skills," without emphasizing the importance of cognitive and affective learnings in the task?

How did psychomotor learning come to occupy such a low position in the **hierarchy** of human experiences in our society—and school? Perhaps, it is our heritage. We don't want to be reminded of a time in which we were primitive as a people—a time in which proficiency in psychomotor skills was essential to daily survival. Perhaps it is because of trends in the job market of the work world over the past century. Perhaps it is status. Social status in a community may depend upon one's having a nonphysical job. Perhaps it is because the psychomotor potential of an individual is more determined by heredity than cognitive and affective potentials are. For example, an athlete was "just born that way." The long hours spent refining the skill might be called "exploitation" or "indulgence" rather than an earned "gift." Perhaps it's because one's psychomotor skills are so observable to others. Individual differences in a psychomotor skill are so blatantly clear to observers that a refined instrument is not often needed to measure them. In addition, movements are not as readily hidden as feelings and thoughts are. We can deny their importance; not make very many movements when others are watching; and refuse to try a movement when someone is interested in teaching us one. These are all possible reasons why psychomotor learning has come to occupy such a low position. You have probably thought of others.

If society rejects a part of the human condition, it also rejects a potentially important part of each of us. While we will not attempt to discuss psychomotor learning in great detail, we have chosen to include some aspects of this domain for three reasons. First, we considered it important to study the total person in his or her environment. Second, some areas of the school curriculum include an important psychomotor component, i.e., fine arts, business, physical and vocational education, and reading and writing. Finally, some educational activities developed in recent years for students with special educational needs (as well as for students in general) make use of psychomotor skills.

What Is Psychomotor Learning?

Psychomotor learning may be defined as the acquisition, retention and transfer of voluntary movement. A distinction is often made between **movement** and **motor.** Movement refers to an external observable motion, while motor refers to the internal unobservable response (Kephart, 1960). Movement can be involuntary. Hence, the word *psychomotor* is commonly used rather than *motor* alone to indicate that the domain of interest is movement under voluntary control of the person. The concern of psychomotor learning in general, then, is the movement or "muscular activity that is directed toward a specific objective" (Stallings, 1973, p. 7).

Other important distinctions have been made in this area. Psychomotor ability is considered to be a more general concept than psychomotor **skill** (Fleischman, 1962). An **ability** is an attribute that contributes to proficiency in several motor skills. For example, manipulative and limb coordinations are abilities that contribute to proficiency in sports, typing, drawing, or playing a guitar.

There are many similarities in the nature of the methods used to study psychomotor learning and those used in cognitive learning. For many years, in fact, psychomotor tasks were used as vehicles to study cognitive issues rather than for their own possible importance (Irion, 1966). A study of psychomotor learning is also a study of psychomotor **development.** This occurrence is not unique to the psychomotor domain. Extensive studies of development have usually charted the direction for practical studies of learning phenomena. Of course, research in learning and development contribute simultaneously to our understanding of an area.

Sensorimotor and **perceptual motor** skills are also terms often used synonymously with psychomotor skills. For our purposes, we will use the term *psychomotor* as a general concept to include all of the above skills, abilities, and proficiencies. Harrow (1972) has given the relative importance of psychomotor learning in life experiences in the following statement:

Movement is the key to life and exists in all areas of life. When man performs purposeful movement he is coordinating the cognitive, the psychomotor, and the affective domains. Internally, movement is continuously occurring and externally man's movement is modified by past learnings, environmental surroundings and the situation at hand. Therefore, man must be prepared to understand muscular, physiological, social, psychological, and neurological movement in order to recognize and efficiently utilize the components of a movement totality. (pp. 6–7)

Processes and Outcomes of Psychomotor Learning

The **processes** and **outcomes** of psychomotor learning are relatively simple compared to affective and cognitive learning. Essentially, the process is the internal movement (motor) and the outcome is the observable movement. Thus, psychomotor learning labels both the internal movement and the observable movement. It is important to remember that both a process and an outcome are involved. Only in one aspect of psychomotor learning is there a complexity of cognitive learning, i.e., perceptual abilities. Perceptual abilities can then be considered cognitive abilities.

There have been a number of **taxonomical** schemes developed in this domain also (e.g., Harrow, 1972; Kibler, Barker & Miles 1970; Ragsdale, 1950). Again, we have chosen the most frequently used one in education, the *Taxonomy of the Psychomotor Domain* developed by Harrow (1972). Since both the major categories and subcategories of the psychomotor domain are presented in chapter 6, only the major categories are presented here, in table 9.1.

The taxonomy represents a hierarchy of mutually exclusive categories. Like the taxonomies for the affective and cognitive domains, there are some overlaps across categories. The relationships among categories are based on maturation-learning and simple-complex behavior continua.

Reflex movements, the lowest category, are the precursors of basic fundamental movements, the second lowest category. Reflex movements are functional at birth and develop primarily through maturational processes. Display 9.1 illustrates the reflexes of the newborn baby (Dennis, 1934).

Basic fundamental movements are the foundation for specific skilled movements. Like reflex movements, basic fundamental movements are thought to develop primarily from maturational processes. It should be pointed out that unless an infant, toddler, or child is deprived of sufficient physical and social stimulation and/or has a sensorimotor handicap, the movements in these two categories are very predictable in relation to age. That is, the age of the person is related to the onset of the movement while learning experiences are not.

Perceptual abilities represent a diverse set of factors. The area of perceptual abilities is not very well organized, to say the least. Consequently, it is difficult to place these abilities into a taxonomy. Anderson and Messick (1974) have suggested that two aspects of perceptual abilities as well as two aspects of basic movements are important goals of education. These are presented in table 9.2.

Because of the diversity of the subcategories within the category of perceptual abilities and their relative importance in general school learning

Table 9.1   Major Categories of the Psychomotor Domain

Category	Definition	Examples
Reflex Movements	Movement in response to a stimulus without conscious control on the part of the person	Flexing of limbs, straightening of limbs, alternating arm swings and foot pats, postural adjustments, grasping of objects
Basic Fundamental Movements	Patterns of movement that form the foundation for specialized complex skilled movement	Crawling, walking, running, jumping, hopping, sliding, rolling, climbing, pushing, pulling, stooping, twisting, grasping, releasing, and handling objects
Perceptual Abilities	Modalities used to carry information received from stimuli to central nervous system for interpretation	Body balance, catching a ball, bouncing a ball, separating a figure from its ground, eye-limb coordinations, discriminating textures by touch, repeating sounds, orientation in space
Physical Abilities	Functional characteristics of organic vigor that form the foundation for complex skilled movements	Muscular and cardiovascular endurance, muscular strength, flexibility in range of motion in joints, agility in movement
Skilled Movements	Outcome of the acquisition of proficiency in performing a complex skilled movement	Sports, dance, typing, piano playing, fine arts, industrial skills
Nondiscursive Communications	Outcome of the acquisition of effectiveness in performing communicative, aesthetic, and creative movement	Posture, gestures, facial expressions, dance movements and choreographies

we will discuss the subcategories in this category in a little more detail. The subcategories of perceptual abilities are presented in table 9.3.

There are four major kinds of perceptual abilities involving the psychomotor system: **kinesthetic, visual, auditory,** and **tactile** discriminations. In addition, a person coordinates these abilities in order to make movements involved in fine and gross motor skills.

Perhaps there is no aspect of a person's experiences that affects one's **self-concept** more than the degree to which one uses perceptual abilities effectively. The possible exception to this is one's physical appearance as it is interpreted in terms of "attractiveness" by one's self and others. Both physical appearance and movements resulting from perceptual abilities are very obvious. Perhaps this is one of the basic reasons why psychomotor movement is often not emphasized in our society. We can play it down and even ridicule it so that we can accept ourselves as "just human" and move on with other daily survival activities.

Eyelid Responses

Opens and closes eyelids; this appears spontaneously and in response to a variety of external stimuli.

Pupillary Response

Pupils contract and expand in response to light. The pupils tend to be consensual (when one is stimulated, the other eye also responds).

Ocular Response

There are pursuit movement and saccadic movements which are quick, jerky movements used later in reading.

There is coordination of the eyes, with convergence being rare. Eyes in sleep are up and sideways like the adult.

Tear Secretion

Tear secretion is unusual in the newborn but has been observed during crying and with nasal irritation.

Facial and Mouth Response

Opens and closes mouth; lips move in response to touch; sucking occurs either spontaneously or in response to tactual or taste stimuli; smiles; yawns; frowns; wrinkles forehead; grimaces.

Throat Responses

Crying is usually accompanied by activity of arms and legs. Swallowing occurs in all newborn infants, vomiting may occur, hiccoughing may occur, sneezing may occur, and holding the breath has been reported.

Head and Neck Responses

Moves head upward and downward and turns face to side in response to some stimuli. As early as two days of age, the baby can balance his head in response to changes in bodily positions.

Head and Arm Responses

Closes hand in response to tactual stimulation of fingers and palm. Arm flexion can be elicited with pricking the hand or a tap on the hand. Rubs his face, and moves his arms. The startle response is evident—throws arm outward if startled.

Trunk Reactions

Arches back—can be produced by pinching the nose.

Twisting—head rotates one direction, shoulders and pelvis in the opposite direction.

Abdominal reflex—draws in stomach in response to needle stimulus.

Sexual Responses

Cremasteric reflex—raising of testes to stimulation of inner thighs.
Penis erection.

Foot and Leg Responses

Achilles tendon reflex is present in most newborn babies.

Flexion of leg—this action is accompanied by plantor flexion of the foot.

Kicking consists of a pedaling action and a simultaneous flexion and extension of both legs.

Stepping movements occur when the child is held upright with its feet touching a surface.

Toe phenomena consists of spreading the toes when the sole of the foot is stroked.

Coordinate Responses of Many Body Parts

Resting and sleeping position—the legs are flexed, fists closed, upper arm straight out from the shoulders with forearms flexed at right angles so they are lying parallel with the head.

Opisthotonis position—this is a strong dorsal flexion from head to heels, often occurs in crying.

Backbone reflex—this is a concave bending of a side that is stimulated with a stroke or a tickle.

Lifting head and rear quarters simultaneously.

Fencing position—this occurs when the baby's head is rotated to one side, the arm toward which the head is rotated will extend and the opposite arm will flex.

Springing position—this occurs when the infant is held upright and inclined forward. The arms extend forward and the legs brought up.

Startle response—this response consists of throwing the arms apart, spreading the fingers, extending the legs and throwing the head back. It sometimes occurs with no apparent stimulation but is usually a response to stimuli which could frighten it, such as noise, falling, or other sudden occurrences.

Mass activity—general unrest and crying.

Creeping—this may occur when newborn is placed in a prone position. The legs and arms are drawn under the body and the head lifted. The legs push and the arms become more active.

Nursing posture—if an infant is hungry and given a nipple, it begins to nurse and at the same time it flexes its arms so they are pulled across the body with the fists toward the chin. The legs and toes are raised. The position relaxes as the child's hunger subsides.

Abridged by William L. Hottinger in *A Textbook of Motor Development* by Charles B. Corbin (Dubuque, Iowa: Wm. C. Brown Company Publishers, 1972), p. 12. From Wayne Dennis, "A Description and Classification of the Responses of the Newborn Infant," *Psychological Bulletin*, 1934, *31*, pp. 5–22. Copyright 1934 by the American Psychological Association. Used by permission.

Table 9.2 *Psychomotor Learning Goals for the 1970s*

Psychomotor Learning Process Variable	Description
Gross Motor Skills	The child walks, runs, jumps, and reaches without excessive clumsiness and within the limits of his physical development.
Fine Motor Dexterity	The child manipulates small objects and uses tools within his limits of physical development.
Perceptual Skills	The child perceives a form separately from its background, discriminates between similar forms, analyzes forms into parts, and synthesizes parts into an organized form with the visual, auditory, tactile, and kinesthetic sense modalities.
Perceptual Motor Skills	The child coordinates visual, auditory, and motor behavior within the limits of his physical development.

Adapted from "Social Competency in Young Children" by Scarvia Anderson and Samuel Messick, *Developmental Psychology*, 1974, *10* (2), pp. 289–292. Copyright © 1974 by the American Psychological Association. Used with permission.

The Psychology of Learning

Table 9.3 Subcategories of the Psychomotor Learning Domain

Perceptual Ability	Definition of Ability	Labels for Different Abilities Within the Category
Kinesthetic Discrimination	One's concept of the body, body surfaces, and limbs; judgments of body in space; and one's sensorimotor orientation used in making such spatial relation judgments.	Body awareness—bilaterality, laterality, sidedness, balance; body image, body relationship to surrounding objects in space.
Visual Discrimination	One's ability to attend to, differentiate, reproduce, coordinate, and interpret aspects of spatial relations involving sight.	Visual acuity, visual tracking, visual memory, figure-ground differentiation, perceptual consistency.
Auditory Discrimination	One's ability to attend to and differentiate sounds, and make distinctions among the origin of sounds.	Auditory acuity, auditory tracking, auditory memory.
Tactile Discrimination	Ability to attend to and differentiate among textures through tactile means.	Tactile discrimination.
Coordinated Abilities	Ability to coordinate two or more perceptual abilities.	Eye-hand coordination, eye-foot coordination.

Perceptual abilities and physical abilities result from the interaction between maturation and learning. Both perceptual and physical abilities set limits on one's learning of skilled movements and nondiscursive communications.

The last two categories of the psychomotor domain—skilled movements and nondiscursive communications—are usually a part of a specialized program in secondary school. However, Harrow points out the importance of including activities for both of these categories over the full developmental span of schooling. The degree of proficiency in skilled movements and the degree of effectiveness in nondiscursive communications result primarily from learning and practice.

In so far as educational goals are concerned, the first and second categories represent movements that are not usually learned in school. In individual cases, however, basic fundamental movements of a student may need remediation, e.g., sensorimotor handicapped children. The remaining categories may be a part of the elementary and secondary program either in the form of curricular or extracurricular activities.

Stallings (1973) has given an interesting verbal picture of the course of psychomotor development. It is reproduced in table 9.4.

Table 9.4   The Development of Psychomotor Skills

Adulthood	Adolescence	Late Childhood	Early Childhood	Infancy	Prenatal
Peak proficiency dependent on nature of the skill.	Three factors combine to affect performance:	Increasing proficiency in basic abilities and basic skills.	Basic locomotor skills being perfected: walking, jumping, throwing, kicking, galloping and skipping.	Developing postural stability with crawls and squats.	Slow, asymmetrical, diffuse, uncoordinated movements by nine to ten weeks.
Proficiency can remain relatively high with experience.	Growth spurt may lead to temporary decrements.	Great variability in performance and sex differences overlap.	Critical period for acquiring motor skills; need ample opportunity, space, equipment.	Begins to achieve upright locomotion.	Total pattern response but reflex action increasing by ten to twelve weeks.
Less inclined to take up new activities.	Hormonal changes lead to changes in body shape.	Increasing interest in games and sports activities.		Prehension and preferential handedness developing.	Every joint has mobility and reflexes more complex by thirteen weeks.
Aging slows perceptual and muscular capacity.	Cultural expectations influence type and intensity of activity.	Extent of participation a function primarily of family interest.		Development of otogenetic activities requires practice.	Motor development is cephalo-caudal and proximal-distal in direction.

From Loretta M. Stallings, *Motor Skills: Development and Learning* (Dubuque, Iowa: Wm. C. Brown Company Publishers, 1973), p. 147. Used with permission of the publisher.

Conditions of Psychomotor Learning

Not surprisingly, the conditions for psychomotor learning are very similar to those for cognitive learning. In particular, the work of Gagné (1970) on task hierarchies and the work of Skinner (1968) on **reinforcement** can be of help. In general, **behavioral** and **neobehavioral** theory is called upon quite extensively in this area.

Distinctions between such factors as the degree of continuity of movement (e.g., bicycling involves continuous movements and typing discrete movements) must be taken into consideration in analyzing tasks and arranging for the amount of practice needed for a student to attain a given degree of proficiency (Fitts, 1962). Behavioral objectives have been found to be useful in this domain (Harrow, 1972).

The role of the teacher in psychomotor learning is the concern of Stallings (1973) who has summarized work in this area on the effective uses of verbal, manual, and visual teaching functions. These principles are presented in table 9.5. As you can see from this information, principles of *cognitive* and *humanistic* theories can also be helpful in facilitating the student's learning in the psychomotor domain.

Table 9.5   Teaching in Psychomotor Domain

Verbal	Manual	Visual
Keep explanation to a minimum in the early stages of learning.	Give the "feel" of the spatial pattern or point of force.	Give the learner a clear objective and plan of action.
Direct attention to the essential aspects of the skill.	Use only when the learner has a positive attitude toward it.	Demonstrate correctly; learners will differ in what they see.
Avoid excessive analysis of movements of body parts.	Employ only after exploring other methods.	Demonstrate at normal speed to retain essential timing.
Increase verbalization only as skill understanding increases.	Limit to early trials so that individual kinesthesis can occur.	Present more than once, especially for beginners.

From Loretta M. Stallings, *Motor Skills: Development and Learning* (Dubuque, Iowa: Wm. C. Brown Company Publishers, 1973), p. 125. Adapted from Aileene Lockhart, "Communicating with the Learner," *Quest,* Monograph Series 6, pp. 57–67, 1966. Used with permission.

Psychomotor learning is integral to mastering almost any complex task.

> "It has become apparent that we must consider the total learner in his or her effort to attain the goals of education."

Relationships Among the Affective, Cognitive, and Psychomotor Domains

We have considered goals, processes, conditions, and outcomes of affective, cognitive, and psychomotor learning. How are they related? There is not an easy answer to this question. From time to time, however, there is an insight. For example, Harrow (1972) pointed out the importance of the psychomotor domain in one's attaining a goal, whether it be affective, cognitive, or psychomotor. Kohlberg (1968) has taken the position that a student can attain affective goals most effectively through cognitive learning. Likewise, Rogers (1969) has stressed the importance of affective learning in one's attaining cognitive goals.

Perhaps the most important conclusion to be drawn is that we can define a goal that is primarily affective, cognitive, or psychomotor, but we cannot assume that the learner (or the teacher) will (or can or even would want to) shut off all systems but the one most direct to the goal. It has become apparent that we must consider the total learner in his or her effort to attain the goals of education.

Movement Education

Movement education and its counterpart, movement therapy, have gained wide acceptance in recent years as innovative, practical methods for allowing the learner to "get in touch" with his body, for encouraging creative expression through physical movement, and for helping the person refine and develop the motor skills. Movement education, of which movement therapy is a part, is also a valuable tool for developing self-insight, self-awareness. "Self-realization," Henry (1976) points out, "is physical as well as mental. The body is a medium of expression and emotion. . . . Ideas and attitudes are demonstrated by the individual through movement alone, and through this activity an individual may gain insight into the interaction of body movement and mental attitudes through spontaneous reaction to given stimuli." The overriding purpose of movement education is to enable the student to develop a "physical vocabulary" of expression, which supplements the verbal vocabulary and helps develop a psychological externality through musculature. This leads to integration, the condition in which the learner's body expresses, along with words and ideas, the feelings and thoughts of the mind.

Moreover, movement education can be a valuable pedagogical tool for teaching in the subject-matter areas. Project MOPPET, a federally funded Title III program in Woodbridge, New Jersey, has developed a number of lessons, on all grade levels, for teaching subject matter through movement. The rationale behind these lessons is that since psychomotor learning involves the voluntary coordination of the body, this effort can be used to help the child learn subject-matter areas. While many of us recognize the application of psychomotor skills to the humanities, it takes some persuasion to recognize their applicability to the "hard sciences" or to mathematics. For this reason, we have selected a MOPPET lesson in which movement and psychomotor skills are used to teach mathematical concepts.

Figure 9.1 illustrates three math lessons that use movement as their medium. In the first lesson, "Design I/Qualities," (pp. A, B, C), the learner approaches the difficult subject of dimensionality, which is essential to proficiency in geometry. The mathematic concepts of *dimension* and *symmetry* are learned not as abstracts, but by students moving their bodies through space to produce symmetrical and asymmetrical designs. The input part of the lesson represents what the teacher does: She shows slides, asks the class to move their legs, and so forth. The interaction part is a dialogue between the class and the teacher: Questions are asked and answered, and so forth. The experience part is what the learner experiences. In this lesson, the learner plays an instrument, moves around, and gets in touch with the idea of what it means to move through dimensions of space.

The second lesson, "Design II/Mirrors," reinforces this understanding. It is sequentially structured so that the skills developed during the first lesson are used. Again, one of the objectives is that the student is able to "identify planes and dimensional aspects of objects": a goal that will, later in the term, be related to purely mathematical concepts. The third lesson, "Design III/Structures," again strengthens this understanding through movement. Also, the idea of quality is understood through the physical reality of qualitative experience. Further information about these lessons may be obtained by writing to Dr. Alfred D. Kohler, Director of Project MOPPET, Indiana Ave. School, Iselin, New Jersey 08830.

Figure 9.1 Junior High Math Lessons Using Movement as Their Medium. Three lessons, Design I, II, and III, from "Math Movement," *Teacher's Manual of Lessons for Seventh Grade*. Published by Project MOPPET, Dr. Alfred D. Kohler, director, Iselin, New Jersey. Copyright © 1975 Board of Education, Woodbridge Township, New Jersey. Developed with ESEA Title III/IV-C grant through New Jersey State Department of Education. Used with permission. *(See pages 354-358.)*

First lesson

Grade—seventh		**"Design I/qualities"**
Objectives	**Equipment**	**Materials**
At the end of this lesson the student will be able to: Physically demonstrate two and three dimensional design. Physically demonstrate difference between percussive and sustained movement and sound. Demonstrate symmetrical and asymmetrical design. Have a basic comprehension of isolation. Move isolated parts of their body. Demonstrate concept of levels.	Carousel projector Screen	MOPPET kit Slides of individual plants, animals, sculpture, people, objects taken from different angles containing symmetrical and asymmetrical design. Claves, triangle. Slides of non-objective—free form—3-dimensional designs.

Lesson scheme		**Math/movement**
Input	**Interaction**	**Experience**
Show the slides—ask class to notice how shapes change, depending on where in space they are observed.	Discuss horizontal, vertical and diagonal as planes.	Play claves; have class put just their heads on different planes each time the claves is struck. Emphasize that only the head moves; *not* the back.
Ask that they notice also how much more interest there is according to the variety of planes and dimensions contained in the object observed.	Discuss symmetrical and asymmetrical design.	Play claves, ask class to put their arms into a different asymmetrical design each time the claves is struck. Stress that only the arms are used, not the back nor the head.
Show slides that clearly illustrate symmetric or asymmetric design.	Let class call out which slides illustrate which. Ask which design makes for more variety, interest, planes and dimensions.	Similarly, have them change their backs. Ask them to change their whole shape *including their legs,* and remind them that they too must make asymmetrical designs.
Play some tones on the triangle.	Ask whether they would move the same way to this sound as they would to the sound of the claves.	Playing the triangle, have them move their heads in one direction for as long as a tone sounds and to change the direction each time the triangle is struck;

Figure 9.1

First lesson — continued

Lesson scheme		Math/movement
Input	**Interaction**	**Experience**
		a) their arms, one at a time, right then left, each time the triangle is struck reminding that the form must be asymmetrical;
		b) their backs;
		c) whole body.
Show slides of objects in varying levels from the ground.	Discuss relationship between object being seen and their own bodies with relationship to level, planes and dimension.	
Introduce instrument: Claves (percussive), triangle (sustained)—Have class move as long as the tone sounds—quasi slow motion—alternate claves and triangle.	Students move as long as they hear sound; freeze at ending.	Ask class to rise in four percussive strikes and fall on four sustained tones taking only one movement per tone. Vice-versa.
Show some three dimensional free form painted slides.	Ask class to relate them to sounds of instruments and kind of movement.	Let someone play and let rest of class move.

(Developed by Carol Henry)

Second lesson

Grade—seventh		Design II/mirrors
Objectives		**Materials**
At the end of this lesson the student will be able to:		Claves, triangle, tambourine.
Distinguish between the qualities of percussive, sustained and vibratory sound and movement.		
Concentrate on other people's movements and imitate.		
Comprehend the difference between same/obedient and contrary/opposite/disobedient.		
Distinguish between symmetrical and asymmetrical body positions.		

Second lesson — continued

Lesson scheme		Math/movement
Input	**Interaction**	**Experience**
Play claves.	Ask the class to move just their heads each time you strike the claves.	Class moves just their heads each time you strike the claves. Name the direction in which they should look so that the directions are clear.
Play single sustaining tones on the triangle.	Discuss whether or not they would move the same way.	Play and ask that they move their heads in the way this sound makes them move.
Play the triangle again . . .	Find one child doing it properly and ask that he/she demonstrate for the class.	Have the class move again to the triangle, moving as long as they hear the sound—quasi slow motion.
Play the tambourine.	Ask if this sound is in any way like the other two.	Have the class move just their hands to the sound.
Review: Play, demonstrate and illustrate— the claves is percussive— (move freeze); triangle is sustained— (quasi slow motion movement); tambourine is vibratory— (quivering, trembling)		Ask for 3 volunteers—singly, let them play and tell the class what part of their body they should move to the sound—let several sets of children have a chance to play.
	Ask the class what does obedient mean? (Same) Contrary? (opposite)	a) Play the claves—ask that they move their backs contrary/opposite to the sound. b) triangle—head same. c) triangle—arms opposite—a second opposite (claves/percussive; tambourine/vibratory).
		Let 3 new people play and assign same or contrary and parts of the body.
Let class sit. Do hand, back and arm movements in mostly sustained movement and then in variety of percussive movements.	Ask class to do the same movements in sustained or vibratory quality.	Let class pair up. One person does percussive movement and the other will do sustained movement. Advise that the leader, the percussive movement person, must give the other person a chance to reach the position before moving to the next position. Give each partner a chance to lead. Watch each half of the class separately.
		(Developed by Carol Henry)

The Psychology of Learning

Third lesson

Objectives	Equipment	Materials
At the end of this lesson the student will be able to:

Relate his body to an inanimate object with regard to design.

Reinforce comprehension of qualities.

Identify planes and dimensional aspects of objects. | Carousel slide projector
Screen
Students' own chairs | MOPPET kit
Slides of individual sculptures and plants, trees or shrubs taken from different angles containing symmetrical and asymmetrical design examples.

Slides of other classes working on the chairs taken from various angles.

Also:

Claves, triangle, tambourine. |

Lesson scheme

Math/movement

Input	Interaction	Experience
Show slides of sculptures and trees.	Point out how the planes and dimensional aspects of the objects change according to how they are viewed.	Ask students to arrange their chairs, as they would themselves, in a place of their own, away from the walls and separated from everyone else.

If this doesn't work and the class is still too "bunched up", ask that they walk around the room to the beat you play, listening to the beat, avoiding the chairs, using the whole room, and not touching each other and stopping when you stop.

a) Change beats several times.

When class is finally spread out, direct that they sit in a chair near them. |
| Show slides of other classes working on chairs. | Ask them to pick out most interesting designs. | Playing the claves, direct that while you play 8's (1 2 3 4 5 6 7 8), they are to change their shape *on* or *in* the chair on 1 and freeze for the other counts. They *must* keep *contact* with the chair, and be aware of changing their *total* shape in relation to asymmetrical designs with their entire bodies. |

Third lesson — continued

Lesson scheme		Math/movement
Input	**Interaction**	**Experience**
		Allow them several minutes to work on this.
		Now play the triangle and still counting 8's direct that they must move in only one direction for making their shape through the entire eight counts—so that all movement is seen in slow motion.
		Allow several minutes for this. Then divide the class in half. Ask for one student to play the claves and one group is to move percussively. Simultaneously, play the triangle, and the other group is to move sustained. Both groups move for several minutes. Then, let groups change qualities.
		After several minutes, divide class into two groups, let one group work while the other watches—performing both qualities.
	Ask for comments from the group that watched.	
		Exchange groups and do the same thing.
	Request comments.	
		Have class come to the center with chairs: Again, walk to the beat and mix up around the room.
		Arbitrarily divide class down the center, let one group work while the other watches—performing both qualities.
	Ask watching group/class to comment on whether they could tell the difference between those sustained and those percussive.	
		Exchange again.
	Same as above.	
		Let students play both instruments while you clarify and remind students of the problem while they work.
		(Developed by Carol Henry)

The Psychology of Learning

Summary

In this chapter, we have focused our attention on the psychomotor domain. Psychomotor learning was defined as the acquisition, retention, and transfer of voluntary movement. A taxonomy of psychomotor learning comprising the following categories was presented: reflex movements, basic fundamental movements, perceptual abilities, physical abilities, skilled movements, and nondiscursive communication. The relationships among cognitive, affective, and psychomotor learning were considered.

Movement education was presented as an alternative teaching modality. Three math lessons using the principles of movement education were outlined.

Suggested Additional Readings

A Taxonomy of the Psychomotor Domain by Anita J. Harrow (*New York: David McKay Co., 1972*)

A thorough discussion of educational objectives in the psychomotor domain is presented by Harrow.

❧

This growing interest in psychomotor behavior will inevitably lead to a concern for explicit educational theory and meaningful efficient learning strategies to promote optimum development of each learner in the area of movement behavior.

from *A Taxonomy of the Psychomotor Domain*

Motor Skills: Development and Learning by Loretta M. Stallings (*Dubuque, Ia.: Wm. C. Brown Company Publishers, 1973*)

Processes and conditions of psychomotor learning are presented within a developmental framework in this book.

❧

As teachers, we are notoriously delinquent in trying new techniques. We must realize that even the most promising technique is seldom successful until we practice it.

from *Motor Skills: Development and Learning*

Part 3

A teacher who can arouse a
feeling for one single good
action, for one single good
poem, accomplishes more
than he who fills our memory
with rows on rows of natural
objects, classified with name
and form.

Goethe, *Elective Affinities,*
Book II, chapter 7

Teaching: Art and Science

In the first two parts of this book we have considered how people develop and learn. You may be thinking, "This is all very interesting, but when do I find out about how to teach?" Teaching is the subject of the third part of the book. It is included as the final section because we believe that principles of teaching have their greatest potential value within the context of understanding development and learning.

Is teaching an art or a science? Is a good teacher born that way? Does one become a good teacher through practice? Does one become an effective teacher by imitating a good model? Does a knowledge of teaching theory contribute to one's becoming an effective teacher? These are questions that educators of teachers have used for many years in helping teachers-to-be focus on the question, How does one become a good teacher?

Theories of teaching have been studied throughout the greater part of the twentieth century without reference to theories of learning and development. Such studies have focused on teaching methods and personality characteristics of teachers. Around 1960, a major change in direction occurred in the area of teaching theory. The new direction was an attempt to synthesize teaching and learning theories. In the eyes of many educational psychologists, such an approach seemed necessary in light of the little practical knowledge that had been gleaned from the study of these theories separately (Bruner, 1966; Gage, 1964; Spence, 1959).

By 1970, a comprehensive review of teaching theory in the *Encyclopedia of Educational Research* (Gage, 1969) had a very strong learning theory orientation. Likewise, a large section of Hilgard and Bower's book *Theories of Learning* (Fourth Edition, 1975) was on the topic of theories of instruction. The wedding of teaching theory and learning theory has resulted in what is commonly called instructional theory.

Before we look at studies of teaching theory, let's define some of the terms used in the preceding questions. A universal principle of teaching would be one that works to accomplish some purpose across a wide range of classroom settings. (A theory of teaching comprises assumptions of the universal principles.) For example, "Students obtain higher performances in academic achievement when a teacher uses a democratic approach in classroom decision making than when a teacher uses an autocratic approach" would be a theory (if it were supported empirically).

Effective and *good* are used synonymously in connection with outcomes. They refer to a desired outcome for an educational objective such as academic achievement or psychological adjustment. It is important to observe that the validity of a theory of teaching is based on a single utilitarian principle: Does it work? For a theory of teaching to be tested, it should be compared to at least one other theory. It might be helpful for you to refer back to chapter 6 and consider the similarities and differences of the characteristics of teaching and learning theories.

The results of many studies of teaching theories have been reviewed. Teaching theories have been categorized into four areas: *instructional methods* (e.g., lecture versus discussion); *teacher characteristics* (e.g., good verbal facility versus poor verbal facility); *classroom climate* (e.g., student-centered versus teacher-centered atmosphere); and *administrative arrangements* (e.g., size of class). The criteria for effectiveness have been such outcomes as academic achievement, group morale, and attitudes toward the learning experience. Extensive reviews of many studies have rarely found one teaching theory to be superior to another (Anderson, 1959; Coleman, 1966; Duschatal & Merrill, 1973; Gage, 1967; Getzels & Jackson, 1963; Stephens, 1967; Templeton, 1972; Wallen & Travers, 1963). What do these results suggest to you about the role of teaching theory in educational practices? Let us consider some of the possibilities.

One position is that the conclusion reached by reviewers is an accurate account of the situation. Educational researchers have usually tested alternative theories that are logical and sound. For example, the lecture and discussion methods have stood the test of time. It does not seem surprising that one of these methods would be no better than the other. This is essentially the position reached by Stephens (1967). The implication of this view would be that as long as alternative theories are among those previously tested, a teacher should feel free to select the theory that best fits one's personality and the situation.

A second position is that there are many valid theories of teaching substantiated by studies. These theories, however, tend to be narrow rather than broad. It may be argued that reviewers are insensitive to the characteristics of the educational setting in their quest for universal principles (Light & Smith, 1971). A closer scrutiny of the studies might illustrate that a teaching method interacts with a characteristic of the teacher. For example, a teacher who is extroverted might be more effective with a discussion method than a teacher who is introverted, while a teacher who is introverted might be more effective with a lecture method than a teacher who is extroverted. Thus, the only modification needed for a teaching theory would be to consider the personal dimension along with the general theory.

A third position is that an interaction between instructional variables and learner variables may be a more helpful model to uncover theories of teaching than a classical teaching theory model (Bracht, 1970; Cronbach, 1957, 1975). For example, a student who is autonomous of others may achieve more in a student-centered atmosphere than a student who is dependent on others, while a student who is dependent on others may learn more in a teacher-centered atmosphere than a student who is autonomous. A proponent of this position would discard previous research related to teaching theory.

A fourth position is that studies of teaching theory have been weak methodologically. A possible solution would be to refine procedures so that universal principles might be uncovered (Flanders, 1960; Gage & Unruh, 1967; Travers, 1972). For example, variables related to student-centered and teacher-centered atmospheres might be defined in detail. A study investigating the validity of a theory would avoid an overlap of variables.

The fifth position is that the result of reviews may or may not be an accurate account of the situation. At any rate, it is difficult to see how a teaching theory would be of much value to the teacher (Travers, 1972). Essentially, the argument is that teaching theories cannot be adequately explained; hence, it would be nearly impossible for a teacher to use such theories effectively in the classroom setting. A proponent of this point of view would replace teaching theory with miniature theories related to learning tasks, developmental readiness, or learning theories (Ausubel, 1968; Bloom et al., 1971; Bruner, 1966; Gage, 1969; Gagné, 1970; Skinner, 1968). For example, a discovery method may be more effective than the receptive method of learning in an eight-year-old child's learning mathematical concepts. On the other hand, the receptive method may be more effective than the discovery method in a fifteen-year-old youth's learning mathematical concepts. If this is the case, these principles would be explained on the basis of the developmental theory.

Each of these positions has a ring of truth. Given the lack of previous success in finding universal principles of teaching, it would seem appropriate to remain open to the possibility that each of the orientations may be helpful in understanding better the consequences of teaching. Certainly the five views in combination allow one to consider the classroom environment in its full complexity. A teacher who has a spirit of inquiry and alternative ways to analyze the classroom setting may have the best teaching theory of all.

The Teacher's Personality

The personality of the teacher is examined from three perspectives: the psychodynamic, the humanistic, and the behavioral. The psychodynamic position emphasizes the *integrated personality*. The humanistic thinkers stress *growth* and *self-actualization*. The behaviorists pay little attention to the teacher's personality, but lay emphasis instead on the way the teacher intentionally influences the learning environment.

The Teacher's Problems

Some of the personal problems that may affect the teacher's performance are considered. Meaninglessness, the feeling of lack of purpose in life, is contrasted with meaningful existence. Alienation, as a pervasive state of mind, is examined in its component parts: powerlessness, meaninglessness, normlessness, isolation, and self-estrangement. The teacher's confrontations with his own freedom has direct ramifications in the classroom. A comparison is made, in five classroom situations, between the teacher who experiences a condition of freedom or feels a loss of freedom.

The Rewards of Teaching

Teaching is viewed as a healthy, productive, satisfying activity. One reward is that by teaching we learn again —we confront anew the challenges of the subject matter. The teacher also enjoys a personal, satisfying relationship with the student; a relationship characterized by a quality we call "communion." There also are many deeply personal satisfactions in teaching.

Characteristics of the Effective Teacher

Generally, the more effective teacher is simply the more effective person in helpful, healthy living. Specific qualities that contribute to teaching effectiveness include understanding others, relating to others, and self-knowledge, each of which is divided into subcategories here.

John Powers: The Growth of a Teacher

A case study of John Powers, a black teacher from the South who comes North, is presented. By watching John's growth as a teacher, we see embodied the principles and characteristics we have been discussing throughout the chapter.

10 The Teacher as a Person

> ### "The 'personal side' of the teacher should be the starting point for exploring the teacher's role in the teaching process."

It is generally agreed that the two key **variables** in the educative process are the teacher and the learner. While other factors do indeed come into play, they are intervening variables, subordinate to the tremendous impact that teacher and learner have upon each other. To deny or limit the presence of the teacher-as-person (as opposed to the functional role of the teacher) is to ignore key influences in what transpires in the classroom. Indeed, the better we understand the teacher in depth, the clearer we see the person behind the facade, the more sensible and explicable becomes the educational process.

"The teacher," Maxine Greene (1973) points out, "is frequently addressed as if he had no life of his own, no body, and no inwardness." She goes on to describe the problems attendant to such an oversight:

> Lecturers seem to presuppose a 'man within a man' when they describe a good teacher as infinitely controlled and accommodating, technically efficient, impervious to moods. They are likely to define him by the role he is *expected* to play in a classroom, with all his loose ends gathered up and all his doubts resolved. The numerous realities in which he exists as a living person are overlooked. His personal biography is overlooked; so are the many ways in which he expresses his private self in language, the horizons he perceives, the perspectives through which he looks on the world. (pp. 269–270)

This "personal side" of the teacher should be the starting point for exploring the teacher's role in the teaching process. Just as we began this book with a considerable examination of the learner's development, we will begin this section with a detailed analysis of the teacher as a person. Since the teacher is also a learner, the developmental processes discussed in Part One are relevant for the teacher as well as for the learner. In this chapter, we will devote our attention to ways in which the teacher's "biography," fully realized in the classroom setting, becomes an integral force. We will pay particular attention to those qualities that contribute to effective teaching.

In this sense, we are going to look at what Maxine Greene calls "the numerous realities in which [the teacher] exists as a living person." To accommodate, as comprehensively as possible, the many topics that are subsumed under this rubric—realities—we have selected five categories that include most of the relevant material: the personality of the teacher, the teacher's problems, the rewards of teaching, characteristics of effective teachers, and a case study, "John Powers: The Growth of a Teacher," which will illustrate some of the points we have made along the way. Let us begin, then, with a general examination of the teacher's personality and how it can be effectively used in the classroom.

The Teacher's Personality

It is generally agreed that at least a minimal level of personality development —of **maturation**—is an important prerequisite to effective teaching. While partisans of different positions might state differently exactly what is required of the teacher on a personal level, most educational psychologists can easily identify those qualities that are beneficial or detrimental to the goals of teaching. Since we have been using three personality positions throughout the text —the psychoanalytic, the humanistic, and the behavioral—we will again use these three perspectives to examine the personality of the teacher and its relationship to the teacher's behavior in the classroom.

Psychoanalysts use the term *integrated personality* to describe a fully functioning, healthy, mature adult personality. From the Freudian perspective, this means that the parts of the personality—the instincts (id), the reality orientation (ego), and the sense of values and conscience (superego)— work harmoniously together. This is demonstrated by the person's ability to engage in socially productive activities that give him a sense of satisfaction and fulfillment. The word used by the Freudians to describe this process whereby instinctual energy is transformed into socially productive, satisfying behaviors is **sublimation.** When an individual is able to sublimate his "psychic energies," according to Freud, he avoids the "intra-psychic conflicts" that form the bases of neuroses. The neurotic, in fact, is a person who is unable to channel the energy into socially appropriate form because this energy is blocked by conflicts that are unconscious.

From the Psychoanalytic Perspective

Other psychoanalytic positions, most notably those of Alfred Adler, Karen Horney, and Erik Erikson, portray the healthy personality along similar lines. Each, in its own terminology, argues that the healthy person is able to function in accord with the rules of society. This does not mean that the healthy person is a conformist, nor that he has "given up" his individuality and uniqueness. Rather, it simply implies that the goals of living for the person are not in contradiction to the goals of social progress and societal health, but that the two are compatible and can work together.

Since teaching is a socially productive activity that leads to an ultimate good, according to this position, the teacher should derive job satisfaction by subliminating his or her instinctual drives. Moreover, neurotic conflicts that prevent the release of this energy are likely to result in ineffective teaching or teaching problems in the classroom. In the following sections, we will note how many different writers cite the teacher's personal problems as a major source of disturbance in the classroom.

Growth is the keynote of humanistic psychology. While humanists express their ideas in different forms, they all agree that, as Cardinal Newman said,

From the Humanistic Perspective

> "If the teacher provides a climate of health in the classroom, a climate that can never exceed his own healthiness, the learner will change, will grow, will ripen—in feeling and intellect."

"Growth is the only evidence of life." From the humanistic perspective, the healthy teacher is one who is in the processes of growth and who facilitates growth in his students.

Carl Rogers, an advocate of this position, speaks about the group leader as a "facilitator," which refers to his role as an agent of change. "A facilitator," Rogers (1970) says, "can develop, in a group which meets intensively, a psychological climate of safety in which freedom of expression and reduction of defensiveness gradually occur" (p. 6). The humanists conceive of the role of the teacher through this central theme. Later in this chapter, we will examine Abraham Maslow's concept of the **Taoistic teacher,** which is a derivative of this idea.

Growth implies change, and the term *change* can refer to both emotional and intellectual growth. *Stasis,* the impairment of growth, is the most visible sign of an unhealthy personality. Health itself blooms into change when nurtured in the appropriate atmosphere. Thus, if the teacher provides a climate of health in the classroom, a climate that can never exceed his own healthiness, the learner will change, will grow, will ripen—in feeling and in intellect.

But before the teacher can do this, he must be in touch with the limitations of his own personality. Reichart (1969), who has written extensively on the subject of change and the teacher, points out some of the questions "which each teacher needs to ask himself. His answers should reflect the painful process of deep introspection wherein he sees himself as he really is, wherein he is guided by honesty and integrity and directed by the obligation to produce quality out of his energies" (p. 109). Some of these questions are:

Is my attitude healthy and responsive toward change?
Is my skill capable of translating change into classroom practice?
Is my knowledge sufficient to meet the changing content in the world of ideas?
Is my technique sufficiently flexible to the changing technology in the world of instruction?

These are not pro forma questions, but are actually designed to help the teacher assess how well he is capable of encouraging change at a given time.

A second concept that is central to the humanistic position is **self-actualization,** a specific type of growth leading to personal fullness. While this is discussed in some detail in chapter 7, we need only point out here that education as a process should lead to self-actualization. This implies that the teacher should be in the self-actualizing process if he is to be an effective

Teaching: Art and Science

facilitator, or teacher. The healthy personality, according to the humanistic position, is in the process of **self-actualizing growth,** which indicates a positive, socially productive, personally fulfilling dimension.

The personality of the teacher is not as significant a factor to the behaviorist as it is to the other positions. Since the teacher's primary job, according to behaviorism, is to provide an environment in which contingencies (reinforcements) are appropriately intertwined, it is the teacher's behavior, rather than personality, that is of primary importance.

Consider, for instance, Skinner's (1968) description of the teacher:

... It is he who is directly in contact with students and who arranges the contingencies of reinforcement under which they learn, and if he fails, the whole establishment fails. ...

... Teaching is defined by the change induced in the student. Men learn from each other without being taught. A man may once have learned to use a digging stick by watching someone else use one, but the digger was not therefore a teacher. *It was only when the increased effectiveness of the learner became important to the digger that he became a teacher and changed his behavior in order to facilitate learning*—moving more slowly or exaggerating his movements so that they could be more easily imitated, repeating some part of an action until it could be successfully copied, reinforcing good digging with signs of approval. ... (pp. 249–251, italics ours)

We note in this brief description the central theme that runs through the behavioral position, namely, that the teacher creates a learning environment, in which the contingencies of reinforcement work toward maximizing the learner's abilities.

According to the behavioral psychologists, the teacher positively reinforces appropriate responses.

> "The teacher brings into the classroom all of his personal problems and conflicts, and these difficulties, despite all of his efforts to conceal or bury them, will exert a powerful force on him and his students during his teaching activity."

While the behaviorists do not directly refute the importance of teacher personality characteristics, they pay little attention to the subject. In Skinner's book, *The Technology of Teaching,* for instance, personality is not even included in the index. To the behaviorists, it is what the teacher intentionally sets out to do in the classroom, the teacher's observable and measurable behaviors, that are important—not the underlying qualities that others refer to as personality.

The Teacher's Problems

It would be nice if when the teacher entered the classroom setting all of his personal problems and adjustment difficulties were to miraculously disappear, or at least, be put aside so that they do not interfere with his teaching. It would be nice, but unfortunately this is not the case. On the contrary, the teacher brings into the classroom all of his personal problems and conflicts, and these difficulties, despite all of his efforts to conceal or bury them, will exert a powerful force on him and his students during his teaching activities. The mature and well-adjusted teacher can control these factors so that they do not exert a disruptive force upon his work, but to do so he must first be intimately aware of the types of problems he has, the effect of these problems on his behavior, the types of interference these problems are likely to cause in the teaching setting.

The teacher has, in effect, the same types of problems as all other people. There are family problems, financial problems, relationship problems, sexual problems, health and medical problems, problems in self-esteem and confidence, social problems, and all the other problems the human being is heir to. While circumstances beyond his control may dictate the extent to which these problems interfere in his daily living and teaching practice, it is the teacher's responsibility to govern his own life and shape his own destiny in an intelligent, effective, and productive manner. He must, if he is to serve himself and his students well, have his own house in order; for his performance in the classroom will in many ways reflect the condition of his life, particularly in regard to stability, purpose, consistency, and direction. His teaching and his presentation of self in front of the classroom is in many ways a reflection of himself as a person.

> "Whether one chooses religion, politics, philosophy, or some other system, the search for meaning is a search for coherence and purpose in the order of things."

As we attempt to understand the teacher as a person, in all of his or her dynamic complexity, we have to look at various categories of the teacher's perception, feelings, and interests. Three basic problems that inhibit the full realization of a person's potential are particularly relevant to this end. They are the problems of meaninglessness, alienation, and loss of freedom. Let us explore each of these briefly, and consider their collective and individual effects upon the teacher as a person and upon the teacher's performance in the school setting.

Meaningfulness is an integral part of psychological health, and its absence, meaning*less*ness, has profound implications, not only for the individual's functioning, but for his survival as well. Victor Frankl, a Viennese psychiatrist who was imprisoned in Dachau and Auschwitz during the Nazi era, found that the degree of meaningfulness in a prisoner's life very much influenced the probability of the prisoner's surviving the catastrophic experience. In his famous book, *Man's Search for Meaning,* Frankl (1962) discusses the importance of each man developing a sense of meaning in his life and how this sense of meaning keeps him alive, gives him a purpose of living, and generally tends to minimize the neurotic component of his existence. It is only as the individual comes to understand and strive toward ultimate and ideal purposes and goals—meanings—that his life becomes full and rich, that his existence as a person becomes important and special to him. "The psychological health of the individual," suggests Katz (1960), "seems to hinge on this search for meaning."

Individuals have a wide variety of ways of finding meaning in life. They may hold religious values, political values, humanitarian values, hedonistic or solipsistic values, or any other values that hold together their beliefs, color their perceptions, and influence their actions. Whether one chooses religion, politics, philosophy, or some other system, the search for meaning is a search for coherence and purpose in the order of things. Meaning holds together the universe; it makes sense of the contradictions we inevitably experience. Seeman (1959) indicates that meaninglessness "is characterized by a low expectancy that satisfactory predictions about future outcomes of behavior can be made" (p. 786). It is, in other words, a pessimistic, deterministic view of the future, a relinquishing of one's right to choose freely one's destiny. In its most concrete form, meaninglessness is experienced as a sense of

Meaninglessness

The Teacher as a Person   373

futility, of hopelessness, of what the Germans call *weltschmerz* (a pessimism over the state of the world).

Meaningfulness, on the other hand, offers a sense of order and coherence to the universe. It not only gives us purpose but makes our individual life a thing of importance, a significant event in the history of mankind. Without meaning, the world is reduced to an inconsequential play of events—much like that characterized by the playwrights who developed the *theatre of the absurd.*

The problem of meaning*less*ness, then, is a serious problem for the teacher. **Meaninglessness** cuts the teacher off from the world, restricts the dimensions of his emotional and intellectual interchanges with others, prevents him from experiencing life to the full. The teacher who has meaning in his own life, on the other hand—if he is truly conscientious and dedicated to his work—will find within the contexts of his life's meanings, the meaning of his work as a teacher, and this will help him function more effectively. To the teacher whose life holds meaning, teaching holds meaning as well.

Alienation   In recent years, the term *alienation* has been bandied about quite freely, in the popular press, in the academic world, and in professional journals. It is often suggested that alienation is a "sign of the times," a result of some complex of social, political, and economic problems. In fact, however, alienation is a condition of the individual and his relationships with others—not a condition of the society, although the structure and operation of society may exert some influence in the degree of alienation.

Rollo May (1967), the great existentialist, discusses alienation in terms of modern man's loss of significance in the world. There are a number of factors that contribute to this loss of significance—ranging from rapid technological change to the danger of nuclear war—but whatever the cause, "when the individual loses his significance, there occurs a sense of apathy, which is an expression of his state of diminished consciousness." This apathy may be appropriately called alienation.

R. D. Laing, the existential psychiatrist, views the individual's feelings of separateness from himself as the normal condition of modern man. He uses the word *alienation* to express this condition, and it becomes integral to his understanding of the person. "The condition of alienation," he says, "of being asleep, of being unconscious, of being out of one's mind, is the condition of the normal man" (Laing, 1967, p. 28). What forms does alienation assume? Many forms, according to Laing, including a sense of isolation and loneliness, a separation from others, and a loss of a coherent sense of self:

Our alienation goes to the roots. The realization of this is the essential springboard for any serious reflection on any aspect of present interhuman life. . . . No one can begin to think, feel, or act now except from the starting point of his or her own alienation. (Laing, 1967, Introduction)

Laing, in a sense, offers a positive use of alienation in helping us better grasp the intense nature of human interactions. There are many possibilities for the teacher who is able to experience his or her sense of alienation to use it constructively in the classroom.

Example: Vivian R. teaches a junior high school social studies class. Through her own introspective honesty and open self-appraisal, she has come to grips with her own feelings of alienation, of purposelessness in life. "I feel," she says, "like one small cog in the great educational machine that processes people from birth to death. The students pass through my class on their way from and way to other classes, and it hardly makes any difference to them at all." She has decided that to give her own work some meaning, and at the same time to lessen the students' feelings of alienation, she will teach social studies as a way of understanding oneself in the contemporary world. "I don't have them learn about feudalism for the sake of historical knowledge," she says. "Instead I try to help them see how their lives, how their parents' lives—how their children's lives—are very much a result of a series of historical processes that occurred hundreds of years before they were born. This not only makes the subject interesting for them—I hope— but also lets them understand how and why they are where they are today."

Vivian is not an alienated person, but rather a person who has come to grips with her *feelings* of alienation; feelings that we all experience in one form or another at some time in life. The truly alienated person would not be able to act as effectively as a teacher as someone who has resolved these feelings.

Erich Fromm (1955), one of the more prominent thinkers in this area, presents a concise but accurate picture of the truly alienated individual:

By alienation is meant a mode of experience in which the person experiences himself as an alien. He has become, one might say, estranged from himself. He does not experience himself as the center of his world, as the creator of his own acts—but his acts and their consequences have become his masters, whom he obeys, or whom he may even worship. The alienated person is out of touch with any other person. He, like the others, is experienced as things are experienced; with the senses and with common sense, but at the same time without being related to oneself and to the world outside productively. (p. 111)

Fromm attributes this condition of alienation to a variety of social, economic, political, and psychological causes. But regardless of the cause, he feels strongly that many individuals in our society are alienated above a healthy level.

Seeman (1959) attempts to clarify further the specific qualities of alienation by breaking the concept down into its five component parts: **powerlessness, meaninglessness, normlessness, isolation,** and **self-estrangement.** By focusing his critical eye on each of these components, he attempts to

Table 10.1   The Teacher's Feelings of Alienation

Component	Teacher Statement	Possibilities of Growth
Powerlessness	"I can't do anything to change the system. . . . I can only stand by and watch. . . . I can only become a part of it, even though I despise it. . . ."	The teacher can make *small* changes in the system through the various channels of input available. If many teachers made small changes, their sum would produce some major changes.
Meaninglessness	"The work I am doing is worthless. The kids don't change. They don't even take me seriously. I punch in at 8:30 and punch out at 3:00. That's my job. . . ."	Even if the work really is worthless, isn't there something the teacher can do to make it more worthwhile? Maybe when this feeling occurs it is time for the teacher to take stock of himself and of his teaching.
Normlessness	"I really don't know what good teaching is, and although I'm ashamed to say it, I don't know *how* to educate these kids. What are we educating them *for?*"	This feeling reflects a basic lack of value structure in the teacher's life. The teacher should examine his own sense of values and determine what education means for *him*.
Isolation	"I feel so alone in my work. I don't get support from anyone, my supervisors don't know what I'm doing. . . . They just tell me 'Don't rock the boat.' "	Teacher-discussion groups, where teachers are able to share these similar feelings, can provide valuable support. An honest nonthreatening talk with the supervisor may also be helpful.
Self-Estrangement	"I am not really myself in front of the classroom. I am playing a role—the role of teacher—and this is how I feel—like a role-player. Sometimes I see my own teachers in myself, and this is frightening."	The teacher should find those parts of himself that he can share with the class. The teacher who hides his 'true self' behind his professional role is not in touch with some feelings that are threatening to be exposed in the classroom; feelings that may be helpful, not harmful.

draw a picture of the alienated individual from a sociological point of view. Like Fromm and Laing, Seeman recognizes the preponderance of alienation in our culture today.

The five components Seeman cites are particularly relevant in our attempts to understand the classroom teacher's sense of alienation. While the teacher may bring feelings of alienation into the classroom, it is not uncommon to find the teaching situation producing additional feelings of alienation. Table 10.1 shows teacher responses that are typical of these five categories.

Loss of Freedom   Certainly, no single force has exerted a more profound influence upon the course of human events than the persistently turbulent force of men passionately engaged in their struggles to be free. In their strivings for freedom, particularly in their efforts to break off the social and legal shackles imposed upon them by despots, conquerors, monarchs, and otherwise repressive societies, men have sacrificed wealth, love, family, security, and almost everything else that in peaceful times would have been too dear to sacrifice. This is understandable, for the allure of freedom is a powerful force in people's lives. Ironically, attaining the social condition of freedom is often not enough;

> "The teacher must be free to perceive and reconstruct the world in a usable manner and to act and behave in a rational well-thought-out way. The first is a prerequisite to the second."

it is a promise more than a reality. For the person needs more than the opportunity to be free, he or she has to learn how to be free as well.

Although each of us has a sense of what freedom is and what it means to us personally, formulating an objective, encompassing definition of freedom is difficult. Wilson (1966), using the philosophy of Maurice Merleau-Ponty, deals with this problem by delineating two types of freedom. There is the subconscious freedom, which he defines as "the continual activity of 'constituting' the perceived and experienced world, of which we only become aware when it breaks down. . . ." Then there is the conscious freedom "that enters into my act of deciding to protest about the H-bomb or any other issue" (p. 150). This is a rather complex definition, but one which is helpful in placing the teacher's feelings of freedom into perspective. The teacher must be free to perceive and reconstruct the world in a usable manner and to act and behave in a rational, well-thought-out way. The first is a prerequisite of the second.

Because being free requires that the individual be able to exercise his freedom, and because the individual always functions within the context of a social order, the society's willingness to allow freedom becomes the fundamental precondition for the individual to live freely. This is the basic premise of all discussions of freedom. Often, a society may allow more freedom than the individual can ever hope to take advantage of. In this respect the problem of freedom is a psychological problem, not a social problem. Erich Fromm (1955) points out that although—

man had won his freedom from clerical and secular authorities, he stood alone with his reason and his conscience as his only judges, but he was afraid of the newly won freedom; he had achieved "freedom-from" . . . without yet having achieved "freedom-to" . . . to be himself, to be productive, to be fully awake. Thus he tried to escape from freedom. (pp. 308–309)

This situation—where an individual is unable to exercise the fullness of his freedom—is typical of many teachers who feel a loss of freedom instead of their inability to fully exercise the freedom that they do have. A teacher may complain of the limitations placed upon him by an imposed curriculum without exercising his options to make that curriculum more exciting to the students. A teacher may feel that the "educational system" is restricting, without exploring how he can transcend some of its limitations. There are ways

> "Freedom is a condition involving the individual in relation to the society. The one can never be distinctly separated from the other. The society offers the option; the individual exploits the possibility."

in which the teacher can find greater degrees of freedom even in a potentially restricting situation.

But there are also barriers to discovering freedom in one's life. A person may lack the training skills necessary for him to exercise his intellect freely; he may lack appropriate information needed to make sound vocational and social choices, to take advantage of many of the resources available; he may lack the self-understanding requisite for making a constructive choice of a lifetime mate, thus permanently encumbering himself in an intolerable, frustrating, ungratifying situation. Moreover, throughout his training, the student and prospective teacher may be subtly coerced into giving up part of his essential freedom. He is taught, time and again, the values of cooperation, conformity, and acquiescence—often at the expense of independence, originality, and innovation. At times, when choices that fall outside the mainstream occur to him, he is encouraged to abandon these choices with a false certainty, never giving them the seriousness and credence that are due them. This is not to suggest that rebellion itself is a desirable end, but only to emphasize what the great philosopher Socrates said: "The unexamined life is not worth living."

We see from this discussion that freedom is a condition involving the individual in relation to the society. The one can never be distinctly separated from the other. The society offers the option; the individual exploits the possibility.

In considering the problem of *loss of freedom* as a barrier to effective teaching and to living effectively as a person, we mean this inner type of freedom that is not directly manifest in most social actions. Jacques Maritain, in his beautiful little book *Education at the Crossroads* (1943), discusses the individual's internal freedom:

> The chief aspirations of a person are aspirations to freedom—I do not mean that freedom which is free will and which is a gift of nature in each of us. I mean that freedom which is spontaneity, expansion, or autonomy, and which we have to gain through constant effort and struggle . . . the freedom of which we are speaking is not a mere unfolding of potentialities without any object to be grasped, or a mere movement for the sake of movement, without aim or objective to be attained. . . . A movement without aim is just running around in circles and getting nowhere. (pp. 10-11)

Rather, the freedom to which Maritain is referring is the freedom to grow in the way and in the direction that one wants to grow. It is a spiritual as well as practical freedom: a freedom-to more than a freedom-from. It is a freedom to explore, test, and finally discover and passionately embrace new truths and beliefs. "This conquest of being, this progressive attainment of new truths, or the progressive realization of the . . . significance of truths already attained, opens and enlarges our mind and life, and really situates them in freedom and autonomy" (p. 12).

When we lose our freedom, we lose the possibility of this growth and exploration. We become isolated from the future, a victim of circumstances rather than a master of opportunities. Especially for modern man, who "has lost all the metaphysical certainties of mediaeval brother" (Jung, *Modern Man in Search of a Soul*), this freedom is important to assure the continuity of his own experiences and the continuity of generations. It is a cultural as well as an individual, psychological necessity.

Since teaching is in part a mutual engagement in a freeing activity (education) between teacher and student, it is crucial that the teacher be ever sensitive to his own limitations of freedom, that he show not only a readiness and willingness but an incentive and drive to explore the possibilities of his freedom, that he be aware of the alienation and anxiety that result from a loss of freedom.

In the classroom this can take many forms. Table 10.2 shows how some typical classroom situations are dealt with from the conditions of freedom and the loss of freedom.

The Teacher's Problems: Conclusions and Implications

In conjunction with each other, the problems of alienation, meaninglessness, and loss of freedom are three variables that directly threaten the integrity and continuity of the teacher's "wholeness," of his ability to draw out the best of himself and share it with others. While none of these is directly a condition of the time in which we live, each is present in our age and each must be confronted within the context of the conditions of our age that govern our values, technologies, and approaches to teaching. The teacher whose commitment to his work infuses all his activities will recognize at every juncture of human interaction the play of these variables on his feelings and on the feelings of others. He will understand his human limitations and strive to overcome them, to transcend them, to deal with them in order to function more effectively as a person and as a teacher.

In the classroom, such a teacher will give freely of himself and allow the student to express himself freely. Subject matter will be viewed as a means rather than an end, and the relevance of most subject matter will become compellingly clear when viewed within the contexts we have described. As the teacher comes to recognize that his problems are the problems of all people, his efforts to resolve his problems will translate into constructive efforts to help his students resolve their problems, within the setting of the classroom, within the microcosmic universe of the school.

Table 10.2   Freedom and Loss of Freedom in the Classroom

Classroom Situation	The Condition of Freedom	Loss of Freedom
Presenting Subject Matter	The material is not presented as incontrovertible fact, but as something that can be challenged and questioned.	The student is told to "learn" what is presented to him in the same way a child is told to swallow his food.
Attitudes Toward Students	Students are viewed as fully functioning, free people able to act and make decisions. They are above all else people, with their peculiarities, idiosyncracies, and personal needs, interests and preferences.	Students are viewed within the contexts of their role-as-student. They are expected to conform to the teacher's expectations of what students should be.
Discipline	Behavioral problems are interpreted in light of what they mean to the student. How voluntary is the behavior, and what degree of control does the student have over it? What is the student trying to communicate through disruptive behavior, and are there other channels of communication that the student does not know of?	Rules are set by the teacher, and the establishment of these rules makes them "right." When infractions occur they must be dealt with, but the rules themselves do not have to be changed.
Attitude Toward Profession	The teacher recognizes that his feelings about teaching are reflected in classroom behavior. He openly and questioningly attempts to explore his own feelings and attitudes about what he is doing with his life's work.	The teacher tries to isolate his personal feelings and perceptions from what goes on in the classroom. He acts in accordance with a prescribed role and diminishes the importance of his personal presence.
Personal Experiences	The teacher recognizes that sharing many of his personal experiences, through which he has grown, can help the students grow. He is willing to give of himself.	The teacher sees his job as helping the students *learn:* growth is out of his purview. While he is willing to share his knowledge, he is unwilling to give of his own feelings.

The Rewards of Teaching

We have spoken at length about the problems that influence the teacher's behavior in the classroom, but this is only half the picture. In fact, the teaching situation itself offers rich rewards to the teacher who is capable of appreciating them, and these rewards can have a positive, therapeutic effect on the teacher. Thus, teaching, as a human activity, can be as productive and healthy as the best of interpersonal relationships. In these paragraphs, we will look at some of the rewards of teaching.

"Teaching Is Learning"   Joseph Joubert, the great French moralist and essayist, said, "To teach is to learn twice!" This is certainly true for all teachers, and especially relevant for the best of teachers. Whenever we teach anything, even subject matter we have been teaching for years, we confront once again the challenge of learning the material. If we open our eyes to the wonders of learning, if we

> "Whenever we teach anything . . . we confront once again the challenge of learning the material. Joseph Joubert, the great French essayist, said, 'To teach is to learn twice'!"

are able to see anew the material we are teaching, not only will we continue to learn but we will communicate to our students the freshness and excitement of the subject matter. The teacher who immerses himself in his subject, whose commitment to teaching is entwined with his interest in the material to be taught indeed does relearn as he teaches. With the effective teacher, the following statement is true: "No teacher teaches the same thing twice!"

The teacher enters a very special, very personal relationship with the student. This relationship transcends the subject matter itself, and, in one perspective, provides the continuity between generations by recapitulating the parent-child relationship. The teacher acts, according to the law, **in loco parentis** (in the place of the parents). In the Hippocratic Oath, to which all physicians subscribe, are the words, "I swear . . . to hold my teacher in this art equal to my own parents." This is not some offshoot of Freudian theory (although it certainly can be, and has been, so interpreted), but is a reflection of the fundamental reality that teaching is the process by which the past is brought into the present, by which the learner grows and acquires necessary skills, by which values and cultural patterns are transmitted from generation to generation. The teacher is the individual responsible for this. Belkin (1974) calls this unusual aspect of the relationship "communion in teaching":

"Communion In Teaching"

> The sense of communion in the teacher-student relationship is not only a convergence of spirit and mind between the teacher and the student, but an emotional reunion between the early mother, embodied in the person of the teacher, and the growing child, reenacted by the student. The power of the relationship is explained by this reunion. . . . The job of teaching and the goal of instruction is also clarified by this conception. Just as the job of a concerned parent is to make his children good parents by instilling in them the requisite character traits and necessary knowledge, so is the job of a teacher to make his students good teachers, to themselves and to others. . . .
>
> *This communion between the teacher and the student, between the mother and child, between generation and generation, maintains the continuity of education as a progressively civilizing endeavor.* (Belkin, 1974, pp. 181–182)

In addition to the general satisfactions of teaching, there are many personal satisfactions. There is the satisfaction of knowing that you have helped a student emotionally, socially, intellectually. There is the satisfaction of knowing that by your actions you are fulfilling the promise of your own finest teachers. There is the pleasure in realizing (if your ego is strong!) that your

Personal Satisfactions

better students will, in time, know more than you. There is a feeling of usefulness that is captured in very few other personal or business relationships.

Moreover, as a teacher, you know how important a person you really are. You know that what you say and what you do goes beyond the walls of your classroom. You know that, like the physician, lives are in your hands. As Henry Adams said, in his biography, "The teacher affects eternity; he can never tell where his influence stops." This is the greatest reward of teaching.

Characteristics of the Effective Teacher

Much has been written about what makes one teacher more effective than another, what qualities of a given teacher are beneficial to the tasks at hand and what qualities are detrimental, and what the teacher can do to increase his or her effectiveness. In recent years, an emphasis on skill and attitude-related training programs has led to a spate of research on how teachers can be made more effective. In this section we are going to consider some of research findings and examine their implications. Our goal is to understand what makes a teacher effective and how we can become more effective as teachers.

Research Perspectives A number of studies have attempted to determine what qualities are related most positively to effective teaching. Aspy (1969, 1972), Truax and Tatum (1966), Morse, Bloom and Dunn (1962), among others, have investigated this question from different perspectives. George M. Gazda has applied most of the known research in this area to developing a training plan to make teachers more effective. His book, *Human Relations Development: A Manual for Educators* (1973), attempts to provide exercises that will allow the teacher to develop effective characteristics. Naturally, this task involves a substantial understanding of the research findings and applications of these findings in the training paradigm. Gazda explains the purpose of his program:

The human relations training program . . . is designed to help develop one's vast capacities for improved functioning. . . . We will concentrate on the development of a fundamental group of personal and interpersonal skills—that is, skills that facilitate living effectively with oneself and others. . . .

Through one's own efforts, the facilitative skills that are developed may be carried into one's relations with one's students and their parents, fellow classmates, fellow teachers, principals and other school personnel, "the man on the street," friends, and loved ones. In short, these abilities may be employed in relating to all human beings. As a person becomes more proficient in the art of helping, he may find that he moves from a condition of "techniquing it" to one of living it—helping may become a way of life! (p. 17)

To this end, the manual provides exercises that test and strengthen the students' perceptions and responses in order to make them more *facilitative*. **Facilitative** is the key word; a word that underlies all discussions of teaching effectiveness. It is an encompassing term that includes all the individual's behaviors that prove helpful to others. This help may take many different forms: increasing the ability to learn, lessening anxiety, increasing self-assurance and self-esteem, strengthening positive behaviors, and so on. Gazda's approach, which is indicative of most contemporary approaches, is based on the principle that an effective person, a person who lives his life to the fullest and experiences all the riches of existence, will prove to be the most effective teacher.

A facilitative attitude includes many components that are referred to by many different terms. For simplicity, we have selected three basic categories that include all of the traits generally associated with the effective "helper," be he teacher, counselor, or friend. We shall consider in some detail the respective traits subsumed in these categories. The categories are *understanding others, relating to others,* and *self-knowledge*. Within these fall all the characteristics of the effective teacher.

Understanding Others

To teach the learner, one must first understand the learner. This is easier said than done, for our perceptions of others are blocked and distorted under many different circumstances. But just as awareness is the first level of affective growth (see chapter 7), so too the ability to understand others is the first level of teaching development. This ability transcends any individual characteristic and includes many diverse but related qualities of interpersonal and personal development. The core qualities generally associated with the ability to understand others are open-mindedness, sensitivity, empathy, and objectivity. Let us consider each quality individually.

Open-mindedness

Our awareness of the world around us—our perceptions of and feelings toward others in that world—is always relative to the frame of reference through which we perceive the world and its inhabitants. We see, hear, touch, speak, and experience in respect to reference points, parameters, against which we measure our sensory and emotional stimulation. The more fixed and inflexible our frames of reference, the less able we are to experience things that fall outside of and are incompatible with the boundaries of the reference frame. Likewise, the greater our ability to alter frames of reference to suit the needs and criteria of situations, the more likely it is that we will be able to understand and adapt to changes that are not entirely compatible with our usual reference points. The first quality of open-mindedness, therefore, is *flexibility*.

Open-mindedness in the teaching setting is demonstrated by the teacher's freedom from fixed preconceptions and perceptual biases that limit his ability to perceive what "is there" by an attitude of open receptivity to that which the student is trying to communicate, either directly or indirectly. The open-minded teacher is able to accommodate the students' values, insights, and perceptions that are different from his own. Moreover, he is able to experience and interact with students throughout a wide breadth and range of feelings, since his flexible frame of reference does not find itself restricted by set expectations. Open-mindedness, in its sense of accommodation and receptivity combined, produces the second important quality of the effective teacher: *perceptiveness*.

The quality of open-mindedness also implies the ability to listen, to respond, to interact with the student—free from the constraints of imposing value criteria. The open-minded teacher is functionally nonjudgmental. This does not mean that the teacher holds no judgments or communicates no values to the student. Rather, that the teacher accepts the students' values while encouraging the student to question these values when the teacher feels they are in need of clarification or critical rethinking. But the effective teacher is equally willing to question his own values. Students will often express feelings about the subject matter that are at odds with the teacher's feelings. While the judgmental teacher will try to "correct" the students feelings, the nonjudgmental teacher will accept these feelings, examine them, and then question his own feelings.

Sensitivity

Webster's *Third New International Dictionary* defines sensitivity as "the capacity of an organism to respond to stimulation . . . the capacity of a person to respond emotionally to changes in his interpersonal or social relationship."[1]

1. By permission. From *Webster's Third New International Dictionary*. Copyright © 1976 by G. & C. Merriam Co., Publishers of the Merriam-Webster Dictionaries.

> " 'The chronological distance and psychological chasm that separates children from adults can be bridged only by genuine empathy—the capacity to respond accurately to a child's needs, without being infected by them.' "

This capacity to respond, this "sensitivity-to" something, is a prime factor in contributing to teacher effectiveness. While open-mindedness makes possible a comprehensive and accurate view of the student, sensitivity—a cognitive as well as emotional response to the student as a total person—makes possible a deeper and more spontaneous response to his needs, feelings, conflicts, doubts, and so on. **Open-mindedness** makes possible what sensitivity actually accomplishes.

Empathy

The question arises, How does sensitivity differ from perceptiveness? (both of which terms we categorized under open-mindedness). The distinction between the two terms is small but significant. Whereas perceptiveness is the ability to see and understand the student (both as subject and object), sensitivity implies a deeper response on the part of the teacher—an emotional response, an ability to feel and see the world as the student is seeing it, an ability to experience along with the student his struggles in learning, his excitement in mastery, his "ups" and his "downs." This particular manifestation of sensitivity is usually referred to as *empathy* or *empathic understanding*.

"To see the world through children's eyes," Ginott (1972) points out, "a teacher needs infinite emotional flexibility. The chronological distance and psychological chasm that separates children from adults can be bridged only by genuine empathy—the capacity to respond accurately to a child's needs, without being infected by them" (p. 64). Ginott's concept of empathy is derived from Carl Rogers, the original spokesman on the subject. Referring to **empathy** as an integral part of the counseling setting, Rogers (1957) describes the process in a way that is relevant to teaching as well as counseling:

> To sense the client's private world as if it were your own, but without ever losing the "as if" quality—this is empathy, and this seems essential to therapy. To sense the client's anger, fear, or confusion as if it were your own, yet without your own anger, fear, or confusion getting bound up in it, is the condition we are endeavoring to describe. . . . (p. 77)

This definition, originally applied to the counseling setting, is equally applicable (with appropriate modifications) to the classroom setting. Since the teacher is dealing with the student as a total person, it is the teacher's sense of empathic understanding that allows him to experience fully the feelings and perceptions of the student as they relate to the teaching-learning process.

Two conditions are important in Rogers's definition. First, the teacher must be able to experience the student's feelings as the student is experiencing them, in the same way, with the same degree of affect and personal meaning. He must, therefore, put himself emotionally and intellectually in the student's place, he must *be the student momentarily,* and think and feel as the student does. Thus, if the student is experiencing boredom during a classroom lesson, the empathic teacher will not only recognize this, but will understand the sources of the boredom, its qualities as the student experiences it, and its ramifications. While the defensive teacher may deny the presence of boredom, the empathic teacher will use students' feelings of boredom to better understand the students' needs and to find ways of communicating more effectively with them.

Second, and of equal importance, the teacher must maintain his or her own identity and remain sensitively aware of the differences between himself and the student. This is what Rogers refers to as the "as if" condition, and it is an important qualifier of empathic understanding. **Empathy** is a *temporary* bridge, joining the purposes, perceptions, and feelings of teacher and student, establishing a working unity between them as they face each other in the classroom; but empathy is not a permanent merging of the two into a single feeling or perception. In short, empathy, in addition to being an important personal quality of the teacher, is also a teaching method, inasmuch as it allows the teacher better understanding of the students and their needs.

Objectivity

To remain objective, in the teaching sense as well as in the counseling sense, means to be able to stand back and observe what is happening from a neutral, or nonimposing, frame of reference. In one respect, objectivity seems to imply the very antithesis of empathy: when one is objective, one is not involved to an extraordinary degree with another. However, in terms of our discussion of empathy, we can see objectivity as the extension of the "as if" quality to the intellectual realm of experience. In terms of practical classroom application, objectivity is especially important in communicating the subject matter, in answering students' questions, in establishing contingency systems, and in evaluation. To the degree that the teacher can perform these activities on a level that is appropriate and effective, he is acting objectively.

One aspect of objectivity is **cognitive flexibility.** This term refers to "an ability to think and act simultaneously and appropriately in a given situation,

> "The teacher who places too much of his life energy in teaching will lose the capacity for cognitive flexibility . . . and attempt to derive all types of intellectual and emotional benefits, which are unrealistic to expect, from teaching."

and to dimensions of open-mindedness, adaptability, and a resistance to premature closure" (Whitely et al., 1967). As the teacher is better able to control his emotional involvement in what is happening, as he avoids the temptations to discriminate and perceive selectively, he increases his potential for seeing objectively and in true perspective what is happening in the teaching setting. On the other hand, as the teacher becomes encumbered by his own personal problems and by his own maladjustments, his cognitive flexibility diminishes.

Typically, the teacher who places too much of his life energy in teaching will lose the capacity for cognitive flexibility. Such a teacher *over*values the teaching situation, and attempts to derive all types of intellectual and emotional benefits, which are unrealistic to expect, from teaching. Teaching, as a part of the *total* life activities of the teacher, must be kept in its realistic perspective. "In effect," Peck and Mitchell (1969) point out, "the teaching situation is one which provides many opportunities for the development of personal autonomy, the realization of self, self-acceptance, and a respect for others. Thus, the mental health impact of the teaching situation has a good many positive influences—or it *can* have, if one permits it." However, if the teacher has nothing in life besides teaching, then difficulties are likely to occur. Peck and Mitchell (1969) elaborate this point:

The classroom teacher whose satisfactions in life are totally dependent on his work . . . will usually fall short of achieving a sense of balance and contentment in life. No matter how rich the satisfactions from one's work, one can rapidly reach a point of satiety with any occupation if it is the *sole* focus of one's life. It is most important, therefore, that the teacher develop out-of-school interests that are a vital and satisfying part of his life. The form that these activities should take is very much dependent on the personality involved, but in most cases, these activities should probably be quite dissimilar to typical work tasks. . . . (pp. 274–275)

The obvious connection between this insight and our definition of cognitive flexibility is this: If the teacher has too much value invested in teaching, it becomes too difficult to maintain an open mind, which is the basis of cognitive flexibility.

Relating to Others

Generally, it is the qualities of relating to others that are given priority in discussions of teaching. We have considered the qualities of understanding first, because we believe that to relate one must first understand. Thus, we can consider the qualities discussed in the preceding paragraphs as prerequisites to the qualities discussed in this section. Again, we can use the basic principle that *the teacher can only relate to students as well or as poorly as he is able to relate to others in life.* Teaching, as we have been suggesting, is an integral part of living, and the teacher's life and life-style can never be fully severed from his capacities and performance as a teacher. The four qualities we will direct special attention to under this heading of relating to others are genuineness, nondominance, positive regard, and communication skills.

Genuineness

An extremely difficult concept to define operationally—**genuineness**—overlaps in meaning and in implications with such terms as honesty, sincerity, veracity, and candor. Rogers (1957) himself, speaking of genuineness in the counseling situation, says:

> It means that within the relationship he is freely and deeply himself, with his actual experience accurately represented by his awareness of himself. It is the opposite of presenting a facade either knowingly or unknowingly. . . . It is not necessary (nor is it possible) that the therapist be a pargon who exhibits this degree of integration, of wholeness, in every aspect of his life. It is sufficient that he is accurately himself in this hour of the relationship, that in this basic sense he is what he actually is, in this moment of time. (p. 75)

In its most basic sense, then, genuineness is acting without a facade, functioning openly without hiding behind the veneer of one's role or one's professional status. All too often a teacher may be tempted to use his position for protection, to conceal his human frailties behind an authoritarian veneer. When this happens, he cuts himself off from the students, dissolves the common bond of the relationship between them in an acidic solution of insincerity and pretension. The *genuine* teacher is willing to give of himself during the time that he and the students interact in their mutual aims.

To appreciate fully the idea of genuineness, we must be sensitive to the many roles we are expected to play during the course of our daily lives. A role is a social mask—a persona—which we wear in the presence of others in order to define and reinforce a situation by establishing clear limits as to the participation of each character. When the teacher wears a mask, he is saying in effect to the students, "I am the teacher and you are the students. Don't you forget it!" The student, acquiescing to the situation, agrees to recognize the role of the teacher and to respond to that role, not to the teacher as a person. In this way, the cues of the one determines the feedback of the other; ambiguity and uncertainty are avoided at the expense of genuineness.

Erving Goffman (1959) describes this process as one of "team co-operation," in which both members of the team (teacher and student) "cooperate to maintain a given definition of the situation" (p. 238). Such a situation, although common on one level, is directly in conflict with the idea of genuineness we are attempting to put forth. For when a genuine quality of the relationship emerges, the dependence on this type of artifice should diminish. *The genuine teacher, in other words, minimizes his dependence upon role and increases his giving of self to the students.* He is open, honest, and at all times "himself."

It is important, however, that genuineness not be confused with self-indulgence. The teacher should not offer those feelings that he simply desires to offer, but rather those that his experience and training tell him will be beneficial to the class. Often the inexperienced teacher tends to be *over* genuine, thinking that this is helpful to the students. The teacher may try to rap with students when they are not ready to; he may try to identify with the students, speaking their patois and proclaiming himself a supporter of their values when this actually confuses the students, who do not expect such behavior from the teacher. Genuineness, like any affective personal quality, represents a proportioned and well-reasoned mean, in this case between the temptation to be overbearing and forcing oneself upon the student and the need to give something of oneself in a honest, open way.

Nondominance

It is an ever-present temptation for the teacher, in his position of authority and in his enthusiasm to help the learner, to become inadvertently dominant and to attempt to direct the learner more than is necessary. Dominance may take a number of forms, some subtle and others more blatant: imposition of values, tendency to speak too much, insistence on conformity in the classroom, manipulation of the students. Despite the good intentions that may motivate the dominant teacher, there is more to be said for the nondominant approach.

A teacher's enthusiasm over student-initiated activities reflects the teacher's quality of nondominance.

Bremer and Bremer (1972) point out how teacher dominance may work against the goals of education:

> ... Many teachers, especially the most able, know that it is not hard to interest children, but they are fearful of stimulating that interest too greatly because there is always a point at which teachers lose control of the situation. The interests of the children come to outweigh the authority of the teacher. However much teachers operating conventionally may recognize the educational values of child-centered activities and the desirability of utilizing children's interests for effective learning, they have not generally been able to find a way of putting their beliefs into practice.... (p. 35)

In this respect, dominance stifles the natural expression and creativity of the learner. The nondominant teacher, who suppresses the urge to dominate, allows this tendency to blossom into fruitful classroom endeavors.

These qualities are the ones most generally associated with effective teaching; for, after all, teaching is no more than communication. Effective communication can be broken down into many component parts. *Order* is an integral part of any communication. Words themselves only become meaningful within the context in which they are used. The teacher's ability to communicate requires that he order his communications (whether this be subject matter, disciplinary communications, or personal comments) in such a way that he can best be understood by the students. Beechhold (1971) outlines the various tasks of the classroom teacher, and in doing so provides us with a model of how the teacher orders (or arranges) his communications in the classroom. In speaking of the things that the teacher must do, Beechhold lists the following as primary:

1. He conceives and plans. But his planning must be far more flexible than the usual "unit" and "lesson plan" system. . . . Detailed advanced planning supposes a curriculum, and unless the curriculum is itself concerned with the process of learning, it is largely fraudulent, for the curriculum developer assumes that he can predict the needs and intellectual behavior of each student and each class without having met either student or class.
2. He introduces. . . . There are occasions when an entire class is ripe for the challenge the teacher wishes to offer. By the same token, the teacher must be ready to deal with the critical moments of each student. Never should the teacher feel obligated or be obligated to require all students to do the same thing at the same time.
3. He questions. There is no use in the teacher's pretending to be universally knowledgeable. . . . What the teacher should have is wisdom born of experience, appreciation of the process of learning, respect for the student, and a reasonably well stocked and agile mind. . . .
4. He expedites. In a sense, the teacher is like an executive or project chief. He keeps the operations of the classroom moving (toward, we would hope, some worthy goal, a goal that can perhaps be anticipated by the class at large and re-examined from time to time along the way). . . .
5. He encourages. . . . Like the conductor of an orchestra, he tries by a variety of means to draw all that he can from each student. . . .
6. He learns. Teaching and learning are not two things, they are the same thing. And the teacher must approach his task with the full appreciation that he will learn as much from his students as they will learn from him. . . . (pp. 38–40)

Table 10.3 shows how these six categories of teacher activity are integral to the way that the effective teacher orders and arranges what transpires in the classroom. Effective communication involves effective timing, appropriate interventions, and structuring that is flexible but not arbitrary.

Because teaching is essentially a verbal process in which words are used to transmit feelings, perceptions, and ideas on various levels of abstraction, the effective teacher must have a proficiency in language that enables him to understand and communicate with the student under a wide variety

Table 10.3   Teacher Activities and Effective Communication

Activity	Utilizing Effective Communication Skills
He Conceives and Plans	The teacher structures the material in a way he thinks can be useful, but recognizes at every moment that the material can be restructured—may have to be restructured to meet the needs of the students. Planning is always tentative—open to evaluation and amenable to change.
He Introduces	The teacher recognizes that his desire to introduce new material may not coincide with the students' readiness to learn. Before introducing any new material, the teacher openly assesses the class's readiness.
He Questions	The teacher uses questions not only to see what the students have learned but to evaluate his own teaching as well. Questions are used, as they were used by Socrates: as an effective pedagogical tool that enables the student to reason out his answers—instead of repeating by rote.
He Expedites	The teacher tries to maintain a productive balance in class. As he controls the flow and substance of information in the classroom, he observes the reaction of the learner: Is more or less information needed? Is the information clear? Can some confusion be avoided, some ambiguity cleared up? These are the questions the expediter tries to answer.
He Encourages	The teacher studies the kinds of reinforcement that should be used, and then dispenses reinforcement at appropriate times. Encouragement is not only given because the student did something to please the teacher but whenever it is needed to increase the learner's performance.
He Learns	Part of effective communication is willingness to learn; for when we communicate, we always communicate *with* someone. Our openness to the other person's responding is directly related to our effectiveness as communicators.

of circumstances, about many different topics. By proficiency in language, we mean not only a good vocabulary, acceptable speech patterns, and the like, although these are each important, but we also mean that the teacher should be able to direct his communications to the levels for which they are intended—*that he be able to communicate in the language that the student is best able to understand.* For communication, in its real sense, is a cooperative effort by two people to "speak the same language," and this can only be accomplished if the teacher has a fluency in many different tongues.

One criterion of good communication is the ability to anticipate the effect that words will have upon another, to know in advance, before saying

> "One criterion of good communication is the ability to anticipate the effect that words will have upon another, to know in advance, before saying them, the inferences, denotations, connotations of the words used and the messages transmitted."

them, the inferences, denotations, connotations of the words used and the messages transmitted. The science that studies words and their meanings is *semantics,* and an individual who specializes in this study is known as a *semanticist.* To some degree, every teacher is a semanticist in that he is profoundly concerned with the shades and levels of meaning each word has in the student's thinking. As a semanticist, a teacher never assumes that a word has the same meaning to the student that it has to him; he never assumes that the subject matter he is teaching is perceived and processed by the student as it would be by the teacher. This is especially true where feelings are communicated. A student might, for instance, say to the teacher, "I know you *hate* me," when the teacher knows the student does not feel this way. The teacher, aware of his own feelings, might be tempted to disagree at once. However, the student may be using the word *hate* in a specialized sense, different from the sense of the word that is familiar to the teacher, and it is necessary for the teacher to first explore with the student the meaning of the word *hate* to him. Such analyses of language, particularly as they deal with the personal meaning of words, are crucial to effective teaching.

A second criterion of good communication is called **consonance.** Every communication is conducted on two levels. The first level, on which the conversational voices speaks its words, we call the **level of content.** This is the audible level of communication—the level that the student hears. The other level, the silent one that has no need for words, we shall call the **level of intent.** This is the level of meanings and implications, of connotations and inferences, the level that the student really feels.

The two levels work differently. While the ear hears the content of an utterance, the heart feels the intent. The level of content speaks logically to the mind, while the level of intent speaks silently to the heart. The level of content is verbal. Information is transmitted on this level in the form of comments, questions, criticism, commands, and so on. The verbal dimension of teaching is conducted on the content level, where subject matter is presented and reasonable discourse ensues. The purpose of the level of content is to inform.

The level of intent is silent. Important feelings are communicated on this level, craftily concealed behind the unassuming content, which serves as a distraction or a shield. The purpose of the level of intent is to express feeling that cannot be openly verbalized. The level of intent is deeper, more profound than the level of content. Both levels communicate, but they do so in different ways.

The two levels of communication function simultaneously in the teaching setting. Every content-laden utterance conceals an intent, which charges the neutral content with an emotional meaning. When they speak the same message, they are said to be in harmony—they are consonant. When they speak different, or opposing messages, they are said to be in discord—they are dissonant. The effective teacher strives in his communications for consonance.

For example, if a teacher is having trouble with a class—and does not recognize the anger the class is producing in him—he may give overly long homework assignments. He tells the class, "This is to help you learn the material better," but they get the feeling that they are being punished—which they really are. Many times the teacher (like the parent) will tell the student that something is good for him, when what the teacher is really doing is expressing his own anger.

Or, the teacher may express anger through criticisms of the student's work. No matter how much objective validity a criticism has, it is the context in which it is presented, the tone in which it is given, that determines how the student will react to it.

Self-Knowledge (and Emotional Health)

The personal qualities of the teacher, especially as the teacher is able to objectively perceive himself as others perceive him, are of paramount importance in contributing to teaching effectiveness. The teacher's feelings of security, trust, and personal self-esteem are revealed through all of his teaching efforts, regardless of how independent they seem from personal feelings. Even the reserved teacher who lectures to the class reveals a part of himself through his manner as well as through his words.

For this reason, among others, the teacher's mental health is central to his teaching effectiveness. Mental health is an imprecise term, but it is generally used to include the following characteristics: ability to recognize one's feelings; congruence in perceptions and behavior; recognition of the reality that is agreed to by others; realization of growth potential. At the source of many mental health difficulties are anger and anxiety that, when inappropriately expressed, may contribute to ineffective interpersonal functioning and a loss of perspective. In speaking of the teacher's anxiety, Jersild (1965) points out:

. . . The anxieties of teachers are as diverse as the anxieties of people in general. Some special conditions exist in the teaching profession, however, that may in distinct ways express or give rise to anxiety.

Anxiety springs from a condition of inner conflict. It is especially likely to prevail if a discrepancy exists between a teacher's avowed motives and the motives that actually impel him. When such a discrepancy occurs, the teacher is, in a sense, acting in a devious fashion—playing false with others, with himself, or both.

A teacher is likely to feel anxious if he uses the teaching situation to satisfy needs in his own life while trying to convince himself that everything he does is for the welfare of his pupils. One teacher reported that, as a beginner, she encouraged her pupils to be dependent upon her, to view her as a precious person. She got a great deal of satisfaction because many of them cried when they said goodbye to her on the last day of school.

Then this young woman examined her motivation. She decided that she had been fostering dependence to gratify her need for power or to be assured of her adequacy.... (pp. 23–24)

This is one of many examples of how a teacher's unresolved personal conflicts can block effective teaching, can make the teacher feel anxious, can prove counterproductive in the goals of education. It is generally agreed that self-knowledge is an important first step in achieving better levels of mental health. Psychologists note how self-knowledge begins with a feeling of security that blossoms into trust. Together, the secure and trusting person is said to have a high sense of self-esteem. Let us consider each of these qualities.

Security

The prerequisites to **security** are self-confidence and self-respect. These are the foundations of any healthy personality, and the types of feelings that these create within the individual are inevitably communicated to all with whom he comes in contact. The secure teacher is able to relate to a class through the individual students because he does not have the need to manipulate the class to his own ends. The personal quality of security, translated into classroom practice, becomes a willingness and ability to be oneself and share oneself with students, to feel comfortable in the teaching role, to know with certainty but approach with flexibility one's goals and purposes in teaching.

Insecure teachers tend to act more defensively with their classes than secure teachers do. They fear the students' anger and rejection and consequently either act to suppress these feelings in the class or they try to please their students more than they try to teach them. An insecure teacher, hungry for approval and praise, will embrace as his main value that the students like him, and this may at times be in contradiction to what is required of him. On the other hand, if the teacher knows who he is and is comfortable with the knowledge, he is then more likely to allow the students to be themselves. The secure teacher has no need to shape the students' opinions of him, for he is

"To be able to trust and to be trustworthy are different sides of the same coin. . . .
Most educators and psychologists agree that a sense of basic trust is an
essential ingredient of effective teaching."

willing to accept any and all feelings that the students show; he is confident enough to know his "good worth," and to believe that his students will recognize it in time, as he conducts himself in accordance with his principles.

William Glasser, the founder of *reality therapy,* suggests that there are two basic psychological needs: "the need to love and to be loved [and] the need for achievement and self-worth, the feeling that you are worthwhile as a person both to yourself and to others" (Glasser, 1971, p. 366). When these individual psychological needs are satisfactorily met, the individual—be he teacher or student—feels a sense of security; a sense that is communicated to others. But as we pointed out above, it is not advantageous if the teacher tries to have all these needs met by the students. On the contrary, they should be met outside the school in order that the teacher come to the classroom with a feeling of security. In this way, the teacher requires less from his students than he is willing to give to them.

Trust

Trust is a basic quality that develops during the early stages of life. To be able to trust another, in its simplest form, is to be able to give to another, to receive from another, and to depend upon another. To be able to trust and to be trustworthy are different sides of the same coin: People who experience difficulties trusting others are usually themselves untrustworthy.

Most educators and psychologists agree that a sense of basic trust is an essential ingredient of effective teaching. In speaking of the kind of teacher who uses a "student-centered approach," Rogers (1971) suggests that "one of the requisites for the teacher who would facilitate this type of learning is a profound trust in the human organism." He goes on to clarify the relationship between trust and teaching:

If we distrust the human being, then we *must* cram him with information of our own choosing, lest he go his own mistaken way. But if we trust the capacity of the human individual for developing his own potentiality, then we can permit him the opportunity to choose his own way in his learning. Hence it is evident that the kind of learning I am discussing would be possible only for a teacher who holds a somewhat confident view of man. (p. 54)

This "confident view of man" is a translation of an underlying feeling of basic trust. So integral is this feeling to the teacher's classroom performance that almost everything the teacher does, from structuring subject matter to answering students' questions, reveals his trusting or untrusting nature.

Expanding this concept of trust, and security as well, Abraham Maslow speaks about the "Taoistic teacher," which is derived from the combined insights of the Chinese philosophy of Lao-tse and Western humanism. It is a teaching approach that implies "not only accepting the style of another person, but accepting the style of nature, the style of things as they are. . . ." The foundation of this approach is a deep feeling of trust:

If you trust them sufficiently—that includes birds, trees, monkeys, human beings —then you discover there is considerable wisdom of the body, self-reparation and self-healing. It requires that kind of Taoistic trust to keep from interfering. With that kind of trust, inevitably you move toward each person as an individual. Taoism means respect for yourself as well, paying attention to your own impulses. If you can't do something, forgive the defect and build on your strength. . . . (p. 152)

What type of teacher is the **Taoistic teacher?** He is a teacher who recognizes, above all, "that the function of education, the goal of education—the human goal, the humanistic goal, the goal so far as human beings are concerned—is ultimately the self-actualization of the person, the becoming fully human, the development of the fullest height that the human species can stand up to. . . ." (p. 153). Consequently, he is a teacher who avoids "a mastering, manipulating, controlling outlook toward nature," a teacher who recognizes the art of helping as an integral element of teaching, as a basic goal of education. The Taoistic teacher combines perspectives from many different ideologies into a single commitment to helping the learner grow and develop in every way possible—emotionally, socially, morally, and intellectually.

Trust, which is so basic to teaching effectiveness, is, unfortunately, a difficult quality to learn later in life. It is either there or not there. Training models, such as those developed by Gazda (1973), can be helpful in allowing the teacher to "get in touch" with his feelings of trust, and to work on problematic areas that need attention.

John Powers: The Growth of a Teacher

In this case study we will see how a teacher, over a period of several years, was transformed from a relatively insecure, defensive person (who reflected this in his teaching) to a comfortable, secure, progressive, and therapeutic teacher. The story is basically true, although some of the details have been changed.

John was a participant on Operation Reclaim, a federal program whose purpose was to reclaim and retrain black teachers from the rural South, many of whom had been displaced after the schools were integrated, to be teachers in Northern urban schools, where in the mid-60s there was a shortage of teachers. The idea of the program was to bring these teachers to Northern cities where the demand for experienced black teachers exceeded the supply, and to slowly acclimate them to the city milieu and the city school system. They were to enroll in relevant graduate courses in education and sociology, which would "broaden their educational horizons and acquaint them with the everyday problems faced by a city teacher." After being thus broadened and acquainted, they would spend several months observing and practice teaching in the city schools. Finally, they would enjoy a brief period of guidance and counseling, provided by the university to which they were attached, after which they would become full-fledged teachers in the city school system, with all the rights and privileges thereof.

Unfortunately, things didn't work out quite the way they were supposed to. Funds were cut, bureaucrats shifted to new posts, key sponsors of the program were not reelected, and crucial files and dossiers got lost in the shuffle. So, when John Powers met with his training supervisor on his second day in New York City, he was immediately assigned to Cotton Mather Junior High School in distant Queens county to teach social studies.

"But what about the training?" he asked.

"We'll get that all straightened out in a few weeks," answered the training supervisor. "We have to wait for your file to arrive."

This author met John Powers six months later when he was mistakenly enrolled in an undergraduate educational psychology course that I was teaching instead of in the appropriate graduate section, a few doors down the hall and a few digits away on the computer. "Well, since I'm here, I'll stay," he said, in his recently acquired tone of weariness and resignation. John Powers no longer challenged fate and error; he had learned well about urban living and urban universities.

By this time, he had already taught for six months at the junior high school, to which he was still assigned. Much of his lively participation in my class consisted of his telling and retelling, in a deep rich voice—a gift from his father who was a preacher in Savannah—the incredible stories of what he had gone through at that school. He couldn't understand what had happened, and he desperately sought an explanation. He was disgusted with his life here, and he spoke often about returning home, maybe finding a different type of job, making a new start for himself. What he was really saying was "I have failed as a teacher. Why?"

We'll let John tell his own story of what happened to him at Cotton Mather Junior High School.

John Powers Tells His Story

"It's this old school in Glendale, you see—one of those special service schools for disciplinary problems, et cetera, et cetera. It seems that if a kid has two strikes against him, they send him to Mather, where we watch over him until strike three, when he can legally be thrown out for good. So, you see, we have a good deal of disciplinary problems here to start with—more than a regular school.

"Well, the schools here work a little different from the schools back home. For one thing, back home we all know each other—everybody knows everybody else's family, et cetera. You see the kids after school—some of them even visit at your house—it's not all so impersonal as it is up here. Also, I never taught in front of a white class before, and at first, the thought of it made me kind of scared. I mean in the South you just don't do that kind of thing—it's just not done. But up here, I thought it would be different—that it wouldn't matter much. And when I got to the school and saw other colored teachers—quite a few, now that I think about it—I figured that since I wasn't the only one there, everything would be fine and dandy. I was in for a surprise, as you know.

"Things didn't go well from the very beginning. You can't really imagine what it was like—I mean those kids and my being colored and all—it just didn't mix. It was kind of like a bad dream—the way they acted and treated me—you wouldn't believe it—no respect, no . . . no nothing. The first day there, I swear, I didn't think I'd ever come back. 'One day,' I figured—'that's enough for me, thank you.' It was quite a day, I tell you.

"In the first class, I walked into the room and said 'good day'—just elementary politeness—and they started to laugh and carry on like you've never seen. They're an ugly looking bunch—long hair, very untidy, pock marks on their faces—I mean they look like gangsters. Well, I tried to quiet them down, to interest them—I had prepared a fine lesson—but they became worse. Why, some of them just walked out in the middle of class—no words, no excuses—they just walked out on me.

"The second class was just as bad. They raved and carried on, et cetera, until a teacher from across the hall came in and took a couple of them out. Someone put chewing gum, or some kind of glue, on my seat, and I ruined a pair of trousers. 'What kind of joke is that?' I asked them. But they weren't even ashamed—they were proud of it, can you imagine?

"In the third class—really the fourth class, the third class was pretty good by comparison—after I introduced myself, 'I'm Mr. Powers,' I said, they start murmuring among themselves. 'He's a nigger, he's a nigger,'—very quietly so I can't really make out who's saying it. When I try to quiet them down—and believe me I tried every trick in the book—they became worse. It was almost as if they were challenging me, like they were asking me to do something about it.

"So this is what my first day at Mather was like. A typical day, eh?

Well, I didn't completely give up—I figured in a day or two I could have everything straightened out.

"But the next day I walk in and NIGGER is written on the board. NIGGER, in big pastel letters—here in New York City—Nigger—do you believe it? Well, I immediately erased it with my hand—someone had stolen the eraser—and I say in a really angry voice, 'Who wrote this?' No one says a thing, so I repeat the question, twice as loud and twice as angry. 'Who wrote this?' From the back, some voice calls out, 'Eberman wrote it—Paul Eberman.' I say, 'All right, who is Eberman—where is he?' and I look around the room real threatening. Now, they see fire in my eyes and they get scared. 'He's cutting,' someone yells out, 'he never comes to class.'

"Well, I figure I can't let this type of thing go on, so I sit down—they're all talking and fighting—and I write a note to Mrs. Perrin—she's supposed to help me out in the school—and I tell her what this Eberman character did and that I don't want him in my class, et cetera, et cetera. I send some kid out with the note, and he never comes back.

"Then, I tried to do some teaching—which is what I'm being paid for, I guess. 'I'm a teacher,' I tell them, 'a t-e-a-c-h-e-r, not a warden, and I'm here to teach you.' But it's no use—they keep carrying on and talking like I wasn't even there. 'Tell us about the Civil War, Mr. Powder,' they keep saying, 'C'mon, teach us about the Civil War, Mr. Powder.' Mr. Powder! they can't even remember my name. Well, I know damned well why they want to talk about the Civil War, and I just won't do it. One of the boys calls me Rap Brown, and when I tell him he'd better cut it out, he says, 'You gonna make me, man?' What can I do, I ask you. This just goes on all period, three periods a day, and I'm good and sick of it. They hate me, I tell you.

"Anyway, at lunch I go to the teacher's cafeteria, and I walk in and everyone is sort of looking at me funny. Not vicious or anything—maybe even a little sympathetic. 'They must know what kind of classes I have to cope with,' I figure. I know many of them from the day before, so I smile back friendly. But I still have this funny feeling—the intent as you'd say—that I'm on display or something.

"Then, this tall, gray-haired gentleman—very distinguished looking—comes up to me and says, 'You must be our new Mr. Powers.' I nod. 'I'm the principal of Cotton Mather' he says, 'and I'd like to welcome you to our school.' I put my hand out to shake, and he says, 'Paul Eberman is my name.' Well, everybody just looks at us and starts laughing—they'd all heard, I guess—and I get flustered and don't know what to say. He tries to make me feel better—'These kids—they're clever sometimes, don't worry, the same thing happened to me many years before'—but the more he says, the more flustered I get. The sons-of-bitches had done it; they made a nigger out of me, after all.

"Anyway, to make a long story short, I couldn't teach them a damned thing all term. Not a damned thing. And believe me, I tried. I sent away for maps from a company that specializes in maps for classroom use. I paid for them out of my own money. One got ripped, and the others, no one would even pay attention to. What good does it do? I ask you. They just don't want to learn.

"Now don't get me wrong, I'm not saying these techniques you've been teaching us for lowering resistance are not good or useful, et cetera. But, believe me, they're just not going to work on classes like I had. As a matter of fact, I tried to be informal and friendly with them—lots of the things you've been saying—but nothing worked. They don't want to learn. Not from me, anyhow. That's the sad part about it. *They just don't want to learn!*"

_____

That last sentence—THEY JUST DON'T WANT TO LEARN—sums up the enormous frustration that John Powers and many other teachers feel. "They just don't want to learn!" "What am I doing here anyway, trying to teach them?" "Isn't it all a waste of time?" Anne and John Bremer, in their sensitive little book, *Open Education: A Beginning* (1972) cite the question that teachers inevitably ask in the face of frustration: *"What more can I do?"* This is the counterpart to John Power's expression of frustration—*"They just don't want to learn."*

The Bremers make an important point about this question—a point that will help us understand John Powers better:

"What more can I do?" This is the question teachers ask. There is no shortage of answers. There must be more discipline, more books, more money, more materials, more schools. Lessons must be better prepared. Teachers must be better prepared. There are vast quantities of information available to help them. . . . But teachers still ask. Their question is not answered. They are told what can be done, but that is very different from what they can do.

In this they are like the children who cannot read. All sorts of help is given, but the children still say, "I can't." And really this is not too much different from the young child who cannot walk. He has to take the first step. There is no other way. When he can walk he can be helped to walk better, further, faster, but the walking is his skill alone. So too a child must read the first word, and when he can read he can be helped to read even better. So too a teacher must learn to teach, and the action of teaching has to be the teacher's alone. . . . To answer the question, "What more can I do?" the "I" has to "do" something. That something has to be a part already of the "I." What is done will be done because intuitively it is felt to be appropriate, to be the next step, the next learning action. (Bremer & Bremer, 1972, pp. 1–2)

What this passage suggests is that the teacher must *act*—must "do something" —in a way that is compatible with the personality of the teacher—"the I"— as a first step to successful teaching. The frustration John Powers experienced in this retraining, the frustration that most teachers experience when they are enmeshed in a bureaucracy over which they have little or no control, becomes a dominant motif when they enter the classroom. The frustration carries over, the expectation of frustration infuses the teaching setting, and the teacher is doomed to failure and frustration even before he begins. If we look at this situation from John Powers's point of view it becomes abundantly clear how he ended up in such a quagmire. First, he was uprooted from his native soil and transposed without preparation to a totally different environment. Promised training and a period of acclimation, instead he found himself placed in front of a hostile class whom he could not understand and who could not understand him. The point is this: *It was not lack of technical pedagogical training that proved to be John Powers's weakness, but a lack of perspective and psychological soundness that inhibited him from functioning at his full capacity.*

If we look further at what happened to John Powers we will understand how the personal growth of the teacher can affect his or her teaching.

John Powers Comes Into His Own

John was still actively teaching at the time he was enrolled in my class, although he was in the process of looking for another kind of job—one with "less hassles" as he put it. I used the fact that he was in the classroom on a day-to-day basis to encourage him to bring into class his experiential material and at the same time to take what he learned in class and apply it in his own classroom, which would be used as an "educational laboratory." He was willing to do this, although reluctantly. After several months of speaking with John, five major insights made an impression on me and were simultaneously recognized by John:

1. John had a need to be liked by his students. When they rejected him or in some other way refused to show appreciation, he felt that he had failed, that he was no good as a teacher—*that he was no good as a person.* It was actually more important to him that his students like and respect him than that he was liked and respected by his colleagues (although this was of secondary importance).
2. Being brought up in the South during an era of racial discrimination, John was very sensitive about being black. Although he did not view his blackness as an integral part of his total identity, he was easily hurt when someone made racial remarks that were unflattering. His expectations of being

accepted in the North were unrealistic and he was unprepared to deal with the prejudice he found.

3. When John found himself in a frustrating situation, he lost his ability to plan rationally and to take appropriate actions. Instead, he panicked and reacted spontaneously, often inappropriately, in a highly defensive manner.

4. In his interactions with students, John often appealed to their putative "fear of authorities" to try to gain order and control. He did not recognize that his presence and power as a person—as John Powers, the individual—could be used as a powerful force in the classroom. He tended, particularly in times of stress, to rely on his authority and to identify himself with his position. "I AM THE TEACHER . . . I AM IN CHARGE HERE," he wanted to shout, and he implied this by his actions.

5. John did not recognize the interrelationships between the students' attitudes as they were verbalized in class and their readiness, motivation, and interest in learning. He felt, as many teachers do, that a class is not ready to learn until they are orderly and attentive; until they display an attitude of seriousness and purposefulness. In fact, at the very moments when they are in rebellion they can be mobilized into learning—even if the learning is not exactly what the teacher had in mind.

Acknowledging these insights to be true, John Powers indicated, "So what?" Is there anything that could be done to change him—or to change the situation? I explained that it would be far easier to change him than to change the situation, and that if he were to change, then he would be able to change the situation itself. He agreed to this and we went to work.

The first stage involved the use of role playing in class. John would stand up in front of the class and act as the teacher, while the students in the course would give him all the problems and aggravation he was likely to find in a real classroom. Some difficulties he handled brilliantly, others he foiled. When he foiled one, we explored with him what went wrong. Often manifestations of the five insights just listed became clear, and we were able to understand how John's problems contributed to the problems he had in the classroom. *He* began to see how his personality—his feelings, his values, his perceptions—were brought into the classroom setting and what influences they had.

Once he recognized this, he was able to change; but slowly, and with some difficulty. He realized that he would have to take a good, hard look at himself—an honest self-portrait—to evaluate his strengths and weaknesses, and to consider the influences of these in the classroom. Using value clarification strategies (discussed in chapter 7), we examined John Powers's value structure. Particular attention was paid to those insights (1) to (5) enumerated previously, and we examined how they contributed to disruptive processes in the classroom. A detailed analysis of these teaching techniques—as they were extensions of his personality—showed ways in which his classroom manner could be improved. All of the efforts paid off.

John began to experience personal growth. He knew when it was happening—"it was a change within," he said. This growth enabled him to respond better in the classroom, to be healthier as a person, to function in all of his capacities more fully, more realistically, more effectively.

This is not to suggest that John no longer had any problems as a teacher. He experienced the pains and frustrations that all teachers experience. But now he was able to deal with these situations better, to recognize the needs of the learner at a given time, to find in himself those feelings that are appropriate to a situation and to act on them. In short, John Powers's development as a teacher and his growth as a person are one in the same. The possibility of one and the reality of the other are not distinct; they are joined in the presence of John Powers as a person.

Summary

In this chapter, we considered the personal dimensions of the teacher as an integral variable of the teaching-learning process. The teacher's personality was examined from three perspectives: the psychodynamic, the humanistic, and the behavioral. We went on to look at how some of the teacher's personal problems might affect his performance.

The rewards of teaching—which include satisfying relationships with the students, a sense of personal fulfillment, and intellectual and emotional growth—were discussed. We then turned our attention to the characteristics that are associated with effective teachers. In general, we concluded, the more effective teacher is the more effective person in everyday living. Categories in which we include the specific qualities are understanding others, relating to others, and self-knowledge.

The case of John Powers was presented to demonstrate ways in which a teacher may grow through his experiences.

Teaching: Art and Science

Suggested Additional Readings

The Skilled Helper: A Model for Systematic Helping and Interpersonal Relating by Gerard Egan (*Belmont, Calif.: Brooks/Cole Publishing Co., 1975*)

The crux of this book is in its focus on all of the personal qualities that are necessary for helping another individual, regardless of the setting. It is ideal not only for the prospective teacher but for the prospective counselor, therapist, school psychologist, and effective person as well.

This book has been written primarily for those who will be learning about helping by practicing the skills that constitute the helping process. Since helping is an art, it is learned by doing. . . .

from *The Skilled Helper*

Teacher as Stranger by Maxine Greene (*Belmont, Calif.: Wadsworth Publishing Co., 1972*)

A landmark work that deserves to be read by every teacher. Applying many of the ideas of existentialism and phenomenology, the author examines the responsibilities and decisions of the teacher in a style of writing that is literary and stimulating.

This book is specifically addressed to the teacher or teacher-to-be who is in the process of choosing as his "fundamental project" the activity of teaching in a classroom. The vantage point of the reader is conceived to be that of a person who is involved and responsible, someone who looks out on the educational landscape from inside a specifiable "form of life."

from *Teacher as Stranger*

How Children Fail by John Holt (*New York: Delta, Paperback, 1972*)

This classic offers as much insight into the person of the teacher—as a critical variable in learner success or failure—as it does into the problems faced by the learner. Still the best of Holt's writings.

It doesn't take children long to figure out their teachers. Some of these kids already know that what pays off with us is plenty of talk, lots of ideas, even if they are wild. What can we do for the kids who may like to think but don't like to talk?

from *How Children Fail*

The Presentation of Self in Everyday Life by Erving Goffman (*Garden City, N.Y.: Doubleday Anchor, 1959*)

An unusual sociological examination of the different ways in which we present ourselves to others. A theory of role and role-region is presented that is especially valuable in helping the teacher understand the relationship between himself and his role-as-teacher.

Within the walls of a social establishment, we find a team of performers who cooperate to present to an audience a given definition of the situation.

from *The Presentation of Self in Everyday Life*

Philosophical Fragments by Sören Kierkegaard (trans. by David Swenson & Howard V. Hong) (*Princeton, N.J.: Princeton University Press, 1962*)

The great Danish philosopher and theologian examines the effects of the teacher on the disciple in this important book. Using such great teachers as Socrates and Christ, Kierkegaard attempts to understand what it is about the teacher that makes such an indelible impact on the learner.

As between man and man, no higher relationship is possible; the disciple gives occasion for the teacher to understand himself, and the teacher gives occasion for the disciple to understand himself.

from *Philosophical Fragments*

Theories and Processes of Teaching

A Definition of Teaching

A number of possibilities for defining teaching are considered. We use an operational definition suggested by Smith: "Teaching is a system of actions intended to induce learning." From this definition a pedagogical model, accounting for teacher variables and learner variables, is derived.

The Teaching Process: A Theoretical Overview

The implications of applied psychological models—behavior modification, humanistic psychology, psychoanalysis, and cognitive-developmental psychology—are considered in terms of teacher and student behaviors and performance in the classroom. Other specific teaching models are presented and evaluated: a "three-step process" model; a "helping" model, designed to facilitate the education of human potential; and an analysis of Joyce and Weil's sixteen models of teaching.

Emotional Education in the Classroom

Psychotherapy and education are compared and contrasted as two processes that have as their goals the betterment of the person. The applications of psychotherapeutic principles to the educational setting are then considered. The psychoanalytic approach focuses on resistances to learning, transference, and the importance of the unconscious. The humanistic approaches to teaching include the client-centered psychology of Carl Rogers, the existential position, and Maslow's psychology of self-actualization. These approaches have in common their emphasis on growth and learner potential.

Unfortunately, we have all had experiences with bad teachers. Who of us has not sat through a class, doodling and counting the minutes as the teacher's dull drone lulls us into a bored trance, helping us forget altogether about the subject matter? Who of us has not had the experience of learning from the textbook totally independent of—and sometimes in spite of—the teacher's efforts? We all know how the unsuccessful teacher can be irrelevant to or even harmful to the learning process.

We can learn a lot from poor teachers. They glaringly demonstrate many of the important principles that are less evident in good and effective teachers. Just as we take for granted the efficiency of our auto mechanic, year after year, until we are stuck in a remote town with an incompetent mechanic who is unable to fix the car—and then recognize what a fine mechanic we have had all along—we are sometimes unable to recognize good teaching until a poor teacher comes along. Even then, there is a tendency to denigrate all teachers with the exception of Mr. X or Ms. Y, who were the only good teachers we have ever had.

More realistically, most teachers are effective some of the time and ineffective other times. Rarely is there such a thing as a "good" teacher or "poor" teacher per se. Mr. X may be my favorite, but to my friend, Jan, X was a pompous fool who completely repressed his interest in the subject matter. There are several key interactions that the teacher is a part of that determine his or her effectiveness or ineffectiveness:

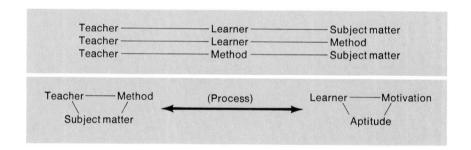

All of these are critical variables in the teaching process—variables that interact with each other and with external variables—and make discussions of teaching very difficult.

In the previous chapter, we looked at the teacher from a personal point of view—as a unique individual with special needs, interests, abilities, commitments, and so on. In this chapter, we will focus a more objective and critical eye on the work of the teacher, examining some of the variables of the teaching process. While research in this area is often technical and theoretical—as it should be, considering the complexity of the problems—we will attempt to translate the research into practical insights that can be helpful to the teacher in his or her work.

We will begin with the most basic question, What is teaching? and present a model that accounts for a host of variables that play a part in the classroom situation. Next, we will look at the teaching process, not as a unidirectional transaction (*from* teacher *to* student), but rather as an interactive process in which feedback and, often, subjective interpretation play an important role. In examining the total teaching process, we will apply the positions we have discussed throughout this book—**psychoanalysis, humanism, behaviorism,** and **cognitivism**—to the elements and goals of teaching. In this way, we will have in our grasp a coherent, if not unified, idea of what the teaching process is all about.

Following this general introduction, which outlines the major approaches to teaching, we will focus in more detail on the psychological perspectives of the teaching process. We will note how the goals of affective development and the processes of affective learning, elaborated in chapter 7, become realities in the classroom setting. If we recognize that the emotions are the foundation of personality and the substructure of all personal growth, and that critical learning variables such as **motivation, readiness, interest** and **attention** are intricately entwined with one's emotional profile, then we can readily attempt to translate therapeutic insights into pedagogical principles. We will also attempt to understand the conditions and processes of emotional education in the classroom and to consider how the learner's frame of reference can be made most adaptable to the classroom's demands and realities.

We can best understand the thrust of this chapter, and of the next two chapters on classroom management and instructional principles, if we think of teaching as a comprehensive activity that touches all areas of human behavior.

> Toward a fully developing person.
> Education is for better, more productive living.
> Appreciating each learner's individual capacity.
> Clarifying and facilitating individual goals.
> Helping the learner overcome obstacles to achievement.
> Instruction of specific subject matter.
> No man is an island—we each learn to live with others.
> Growth through learning.

Each of the points embodied in the *T-E-A-C-H-I-N-G* acronym will be covered in these chapters. It is with the idea of teaching as a comprehensive activ-

> "Does teaching occur every time one person tells another person something
> that the other person did not know before?"

ity, which touches the total person, that we begin our discussion of theories and processes of teaching.

A Definition of Teaching

Does teaching occur every time one person tells another person something that the other person did not know before? Can teaching be differentiated from instruction? Are there certain characteristic behaviors of a person that, taken together, can be defined as teaching? These questions have been debated for centuries—by philosophers mainly—and there still are no clear-cut answers. But modern approaches to answering these questions have yielded some clear criteria that will help us in defining teaching.

Smith (1961), a language philosopher, argues that the definitions of teaching that are used lead to "controversial discussions in pedagogical circles," and that therefore some attempts should be made at precision in defining the term. He points out these three widely used definitions of teaching:

Teaching: arrangement and manipulation of a situation in which there are gaps or obstructions which an individual will seek to overcome and from which he will learn in the course of doing so.
Teaching: intimate contact between a more mature personality and a less mature one which is designed to further the education of the latter.
Teaching: impartation of knowledge to an individual by another in a school. (p. 87)

He cites a variety of weaknesses inherent in each of these definitions, and argues his own view that avoids the pitfalls of specific definitions altogether. "Teaching," he says, "is a system of actions intended to induce learning" (p. 88). With this definition, he can then go on to propose **models** to examine the system of actions that best induce learning, and therefore study teaching without ever having defined it.

In order to undertake this difficult task, Smith proposes a pedagogical model that is derived from the writings of Edward C. Tolman. This model considers the variables in the teaching process, both from the teacher's and the learner's **performance** criteria (see table 11.1). The behaviors accounted for are grouped into three types: linguistic (verbal), performative (achieve-

Table 11.1   A Pedagogical Model

I **Independent Variables**	III **Intervening Variables**	II **Dependent Variables**
Teacher	*Pupils*	*Pupils*

1. Linguistic
   Behavior
	These variables consist of postu-
	lated explanatory entities and
	processes such as memories,
	beliefs, needs, and associative
	mechanisms.
		1. Linguistic
		   Behavior

2. Performative
   Behavior
		2. Performative
		   Behavior

3. Expressive
   Behavior
		3. Expressive
		   Behavior

Reprinted with permission of *Teachers College Record* and B. O. Smith.

ment and performance variables), and expressive (affective, often nonverbal, behavioral variables). The learner, according to this model, comes to the classroom setting with "memories, beliefs, needs," and so forth, which are treated as **intervening variables.** The dependent variables comprise the kinds of behavior exhibited by the pupil: linguistic, performative, and expressive.

We see that this model encompasses a wide variety of behaviors that can be analyzed and assessed, but only three types of variables—independent, intervening, and dependent—thus making the analysis far simpler than it would otherwise be.

While it would be possible to find faults in this model and to propose counter models, for our purposes it takes into account not only the major variables of the teaching process but their relationships among each other, and therefore, from a practical point of view, it is immensely helpful. We shall, therefore, in the subsequent sections, use this model when we refer to the teaching process and direct our efforts to analyzing the variables of the process, beginning with general approaches to teaching, paying special attention to their theoretical underpinnings.

The Teaching Process: A Theoretical Overview

Educational psychologists, curriculum planners, teachers, teacher-trainers, and others in the educational field have been at odds concerning the teaching process since time immemorial. Over two thousand years ago, Socrates battled the Sophists over what the best approach to teaching is, and what the difference between teaching and demagoguery really is. In Plato's dialogue, *Meno,*

Socrates uses a geometry lesson to demonstrate that what Meno learns is already in his mind, and that it is the teacher's task to bring out this knowledge —to help the learner "recollect" what is already in the mind. Some of the questions raised then are still persistently troublesome today. For example, consider the following questions:

1. Is the teacher limited in teaching only as much as he knows?
2. Who is more influential in the teaching process—the teacher or the student?
3. What is the difference between knowledge and opinion?
4. Can values be taught? If so, how are they taught?
5. How can the teacher avoid propagandizing students, or is all teaching a subtle form of propaganda?

These questions, sometimes in different forms, are still asked today. While there are no unequivocal answers, a number of teaching models have been proposed that come to grips with some of the issues underlying these questions. In this section, we will examine these models, comparing their conceptions of the teaching process.

Applied Psychological Models

There are a number of clearly defined areas of human behavior for which an adequate teaching model must account. A model should shed light on what motivates a student to learn, on teaching methodology, on objectives and curriculum, on classroom management and discipline, on the relative values of different types of learning and presentation. Frostig and Maslow (1973) have translated the implications of four psychological theories—behavior modification, humanistic psychology, psychoanalysis, and cognitive-developmental psychology—for education. Table 11.2 shows how these psychological models can be applied to the teaching setting.

Three important points emerge from their analysis. First, it is clear that there are similarities and differences when we compare these models and that these similarities and differences are related to their underlying view of the person. Second, whatever theory we accept, there are clear-cut educational guidelines implicit, and, as teachers, we should be eager to discern these guidelines and see if they are in accord with our own thinking. Finally, we note that it is possible to select from the different positions—to form an eclectic perspective—and make different applications to different areas of behavior and development. For instance, a teacher could use behavior modification for classroom management, humanistic psychology to formulate curricular objectives, and psychoanalysis to understand the individualization of the learner. Other combinations are possible; in fact, each teacher has to select his or her own unified approach to teaching.

A Three-Step Process Model

Becker, Engelmann and Thomas (1971) conceptualize teaching as a three-step process in which the teacher presents a stimulus; the learner responds to

Table 11.2 Comparison of Implications of Behavior Modification, Humanistic Psychology, Psychoanalysis, and Cognitive-Developmental Psychology for Education

	Behavior Modification	Humanistic Psychology	Psychoanalysis	Cognitive-Developmental Psychology
Individualization	Individualization of task assignment taking the child's level of functioning into account. Individualization of rewards and of discipline.	Individualization of total approach according to needs and individuality of child, on an intuitive basis as a consequence of shared experience.	Individualization in relation to differences of needs and maturational level, task assignments, personal relationships, and total approach.	Adaptation of tasks to child's developmental stage and previous experiences.
Motivation	The child's interests and needs are not accepted as a "given"; they are to be changed and manipulated, whenever this seems of advantage. A reward system motivates the child. Motivation is extrinsic. Rewards may be material, social, or fulfill other needs. In contrast to psychoanalysis and humanism, satisfaction of needs is the consequence and not the precondition of learning.	Satisfaction of needs is necessary for optimum learning ability. The child's need for experience, his wish to be helpful and to communicate with others—in short, social motives and need for experience—are emphasized. Motivation is mainly intrinsic.	Satisfaction of needs regarded as the prime source of motivation ("the pleasure principle"). Needs for love, security, and mastery and emotional and social needs must be satisfied before energy and interests are available for learning. Motivation is both extrinsic and intrinsic.	Interests are the expression of a "drive" toward equilibrium. Knowing is a motive in itself. Motivation is intrinsic. The need for equilibrium is as compelling as physiological needs.
Degree of Systematization	Very specific methods of classroom management and teaching are prescribed. Systematization is emphasized. Programmed material is suggested.	A balanced curriculum and balance between freedom and discipline is advocated. Recognition of developmental progression is only one of the factors to be taken into account in adjusting to the child's needs. The teacher must be attuned to the child's intellectual, emotional, and social needs.	Systematization is not especially stressed; the classroom environment must be stable but flexible. Teaching takes developmental level of child into account. Curriculum usually shows progressive steps, except in the type of school like Summerhill.	Progress in teaching is systematic, but classroom environment free enough for exploration and discovery. Theory of cognitive development results in definite teaching approaches suitable for the child's developmental level.
Methodology	Extensive and detailed methods and sequences to develop skills and specific knowledge are advocated. Use of computer and other machine technology to assist teacher.	Emphasis on integrated project approach, with particular stress on social studies.	No special developments or innovations, except in the type of school like Summerhill where total freedom prevails.	Materials and curricula to develop basic cognitive skills, such as classification, seriation, conservation, imagery, and problem-solving have been developed, as well as specific curricula in science, math, and social studies.
Curricular Objectives	Focus on academic knowledge and skills and on socially defined personal and social behavior characteristics.	Focus on social development, communication skills, and sensitivity to beauty and other humanistic values. The child's sensitivity to group needs as well as to individual needs is to be enhanced. Social influences are more emphasized than biological ones. The goal is optimum interrelationship with the environment, not adjustment.	Focus on emotional development, communication skills, and social institutions. Social interaction is used as a tool to further emotional growth. Academic knowledge and skills are tools to achieve the main objectives of later mature adjustment.	Focus on total development: sensory-motor, language, and cognitive. Social interaction serves as a tool to develop decentration, intelligence, and logical thought.

Table 11.2 Continued

	Behavior Modification	Humanistic Psychology	Psychoanalysis	Cognitive-Developmental Psychology
Form of Classroom Management	Teacher-centered. The teacher prescribes curriculum and classroom procedures. Social relationships are not emphasized as goals but utilized as means.	Child-centered. The teacher assists child but does not direct him in his learning. The classroom structure permits freedom of choice for the child and fosters creativity and exploration. The importance of human relationships is recognized. The classroom situation permits and should foster social learning.	Opinions among this group vary. In certain schools it is partly child-centered, with the roles of teacher and child specified in relation to each other. The teacher's role includes her influence on character formation and adjustment of the child. In others, a Summerhill-like atmosphere prevails, and the school is totally child-centered. The value of peer relationships is emphasized.	Child-centered. The teacher assists the child and guides him in his learning, explorations, and discovery. The classroom structure permits and fosters self-direction.
Making Teaching Meaningful	Emphasis is usually not on integration of topics but rather on a linear progression in teaching content and skills. Behaviorists are not concerned with "meaning" except as meaning is derived from understanding previous steps. Mastery is emphasized in behavioristic terms of specific mastery of subject matter or adjustment to classroom demands. Mastery or attainment of extraneous rewards makes learning meaningful.	As in psychoanalytically influenced teaching, meaning derives from integration of topics and relating the content to child's personal needs. Additional emphasis is put on human needs in general, on creativity and involvement, and on developing the child's feeling of "being in the world" and awareness of the world around him.	Meaningfulness of material taught is achieved through integration of topics, and by relating topics to satisfaction of the child's past experiences, present needs, and future goals. In certain schools, the child chooses the topic he wants to study and even whether or not he wants to learn.	Integration of knowledge is emphasized. Integration is not merely achieved by associations between thoughts or between contents of curricula or by addition of new knowledge. The hierarchical order of concepts and skills must be grasped to make meaningful what has been learned. Concepts are related to other coordinated, supraordinated, and subordinated concepts.
Active Participation	Behaviorists are little concerned with activity, except if the activity is the behavior to be elicited. The child may be a rather passive recipient of knowledge, and should follow directions. The behavior is shaped, not guided.	Experience requires action. The child needs to relate himself actively to the environment and to share with others in common activities. Also, the child's need for play and activity has to be satisfied.	Activity is deemed necessary, first, because it is the mode in which younger children can best express thoughts and feelings. Activity, including play, also helps the child to understand and to adjust to the environment. Finally, the physiologic need for movement has to be satisfied.	Activity is regarded as the basis of all mental development. The child learns by exploring and experimenting. In new learning, he proceeds from activity (enactive learning) to perceptual learning (iconic) and then to symbolic learning. To make symbolic learning possible, he must learn to read, write, make graphs, use mathematical language, etc.
Use of Early Symbolic Abilities (not including language)	The topic of symbolic play and imagery has not been discussed by behaviorists, as these are activities which are not at all or only partly overt. Repetition, modified repetition, and imitating a model are methods used extensively in teaching.	Experience involves imagery. Empathy requires imagery and is developed by imagining playing another person's role. Imagery is basic to all understanding and must be developed; one method is symbolic (dramatic) play.	Imagery and role-taking are forms of learning. Imaginative and symbolic play assist the child in adjusting to reality and in his emotional growth. Imitation helps the child to learn behavior patterns.	Imitation, symbolic play, and imagery are basic to symbolic behavior. Imitation and symbolic play are therefore utilized in instruction. Development of images (kinetic and anticipatory) must occur prior to logical thought and can be developed through planning and self-direction.

Table 11.2 Continued

	Behavior Modification	Humanistic Psychology	Psychoanalysis	Cognitive-Developmental Psychology
Language Instruction	The approach to language teaching is structured. Syntax, vocabulary, and articulation are taught specifically. Imitation is used in the teaching of language, as well as modified imitation and the learning of rules. Correct use of language is the goal of language instruction, and includes oral and written language.	Language is developed through use of creative language, poems, story-writing, and dramatic play. Expressions of feelings and ideas are furthered. Language includes body language, gestures, and creative expression.	Language is enhanced through social contacts and small group learning. Little formal teaching of language. Reading and writing are introduced late. The child is taught to substitute language for "acting out" in achieving need satisfaction.	Language and thought cannot be separated in instruction. Language is the most important form of symbolic expression. Language needs to be used to describe and explain action. Written language is taught very early, together with beginning reading.
Rote versus Insight Learning	Rote learning and associational learning in small steps are emphasized. Skills are greatly emphasized.	Emphasis is on insight learning and understanding, in contrast to mere acquisition of knowledge.	Emphasis is on insight learning and understanding. The importance of understanding current behavior in light of the child's previous experiences is also stressed.	Emphasis is on insight learning and understanding.
Goals	A person able to fill a job well or to continue with his education because he has mastered skills and knowledge taught on a lower level. Competence is the goal of education.	A loving, creative human being with a strong social conscience, aware of the needs of others, feeling fulfilled, and helping others to feel fulfilled. Self-fulfillment and understanding are the goals of education.	A person free of neuroticism and not suppressed by cultural demands who is socially aware and responsive, cherishes human values, is self-assured, and feels enriched by his culture, to which he adjusts and attempts to contribute. Adjustment and interaction with society are both goals of education.	A person who has optimally developed his cognitive functions and who is innovative and flexible in his thought processes. Most important, he is a person who can decenter, especially by taking into account the points of view of others as well as all possible outcomes in making decisions and carrying out actions. Intelligence used equally well in decisions pertaining both to oneself and to others is the goal of education.

From M. Frostig and P. Maslow, *Learning Problems in the Classroom.* (New York: Grune & Stratton, Inc., 1973), pp. 97–103. Reprinted by permission of Grune & Stratton, Inc., and the authors.

this stimulus; and then the teacher follows with a consequent stimulus "to strengthen and maintain right responding." Figure 11.1 demonstrates some examples of this model.

While this is a useful model, certain weaknesses are inherent in it. It conceptualizes teaching as a one-way process, when experience tells us that the teacher is always influenced by the learner. It does not explain how the teacher's first stimulus is related to the learner's readiness at a given point. However, the authors do break down the process into small components that can be extremely useful in the presentation of subject matter as well as

Figure 11.1 Teaching as a Three-Step Process. From *Teaching: A Course in Applied Psychology* by Wesley C. Becker, Siegfried Engelmann, and Don R. Thomas. © 1971, Science Research Associates, Inc. Reprinted by permission of the publisher.

S ⟶ R ⟶ S

Teacher presents preceding stimulus (signal)	Child responds	Teacher presents following stimulus (consequences)
1. "When did Columbus discover America?"	"In 1492."	"Good."
2. "How much is 2 plus 2?"	"Four."	"That's right."
3. "How many times will 3 go into 12?"	"Three."	"No. That's wrong."
4a. Teacher shows the letter *m* and asks: "What sound is this?"	No response.	No consequence.
4b. Teacher then says, "This is mmmm; say 'Mmmm'."	"Mmmm."	"Good! You're getting it."
5. Child is sitting at his desk. Teacher instructs him to take out his reading workbook and complete the exercise beginning on page 41.	Child works at the task for twenty minutes, completes task, and raises hand for teacher to check his answers (or turns exercise in for checking).	Teacher checks answers right and wrong; writes *B* on the top.
6. A display of ten objects, all different shapes. Teacher says: "Touch all the red objects."	Child touches the four red objects.	"Fine. You're smart."

Teaching: Art and Science

in helping the child reach the level of readiness where learning can be maximized.

Their definition of teaching crystallizes their view of the teaching process:

> When a child does things at one point in time that he could not do earlier, we are likely to say he has *learned* something new, especially if the changes follow behavioral interactions with the environment. When the behavior of someone else (a playmate, a parent, or a teacher) is responsible for his new learning, the process is called *teaching*. Teaching is changing what children do or say (*responses*) under particular environmental circumstances. . . . Environmental events that influence responding are called *stimuli*. A teacher accomplishes a teaching objective by effectively arranging the occurrence of stimulus events for the child—that is, by controlling when and how she talks, praises, shows things, and prompts responses. (p. 1)

Some models conceive of teaching as a process that helps the individual realize his full potential. Such models, usually of the humanistic variety, do not isolate intellectual, emotional, and physical growth. For it is the sum of these three that adds up to the fulfilling of the person's potential.

The Helping Model: "The Education of Human Potential"

Mann (1972), in his fine little book, *Learning to Be: The Education of Human Potential,* offers an educational approach "which draws from both traditional and progressive approaches and reaches beyond either toward an educational experience in which the goal is to teach the student how to *understand, direct,* and *develop* himself" (p. 9). The core of this approach involves describing "categories in terms of which the organism can be described and analyzed," and explicating the functions associated with each category. Fifteen human functions are discussed, and educational (teaching) methods for "cultivating" these functions are described, along with "applications of these methods to traditional subject matter." The goal of the book is to help the teacher identify and effectively influence all of the human organism's functions. Table 11.3 shows these fifteen functions and offers a brief description of each.

The central theme of Mann's argument—that teaching directs itself to all of the learner's functioning—is common to many of the helping models. Most of these models are derived from the philosophy and psychology of humanism, with strains of sociocultural influences pervasive throughout. They conceptualize teaching as a process that touches all the mysteries and depths of the human organism with a single goal in mind—*helping* the person develop his potential most fully. Robert R. Carkhuff, who has written extensively on the subject of helping, from both the counseling, teaching, and human interaction perspectives, speaks of the development of human resources: that is, "to help someone to do things differently from how he did them before, since

Table 11.3   Fifteen Human Functions "Cultivated" by the Teacher: "The Education of Human Potential"

Function	Description
Sensing the Human Organism	The sensory awareness of self—"the grounding of our experience."
Perceiving the Environment	Taking in more perceptions, improving the motivation to perceive, and stretching one's awareness.
Moving in Space	"To be aware of the sense of moving and the impact of the movement on others."
Emotional Expression	"Emotions . . . are the water of life. . . . Because emotions are among the most powerful motivators we have, utilizing their power in teaching vitalizes the enterprise."
Visualization and Imagination	"Visualization is the ability to picture clearly a given object. . . . Imagination is a broader concept. A person with a vivid imagination can create an inner world of events."
Empathy	"Our ability to put ourselves into the position of another."
Paranormal Abilities	"The unexplained and the misunderstood [which] represent something real in human nature even though science has not succeeded in clarifying the issues that are involved."
Creative Expression	Artistic expression, originality of thought, and creative problem solving.
Intelligence	"There are five major operations: cognition . . . memory, convergent thinking . . . divergent thinking. . . . and evaluation."
Ethical Values	"Ethics consists of a set of empirically derived guides or principles that the individual develops in the process of maturing."
Attending and the Will	"The principal means of attaining control over one's organism is through selective attention and willing. . . . Willing and attending are closely related to the act of choice."
Meditation	"Meditation requires the conscious control of attention." Although there are many different types, "all methods demand that the person must be on guard to avoid losing the particular focus he has undertaken to hold."
Role Behavior	Meeting social expectations in terms of our behaviors. "Such training is necessary for the survival of institutions within which these roles are enacted. It also produces some measure of predictability in social behavior without which we would live in uncertainty and anxiety."
Conditioning	People generally act "in such a way as to maximize pleasure and avoid pain."
Environmental Reorganization	"This reorganization concerns three distinct levels: (1) the relation between the student and the material he is studying, (2) the physical surroundings in which the learning takes place, (3) the social structure within which education is applied. *The ability to institute planned change on all three levels is a peculiarly human function.*"

From *Learning to Be: The Education of Human Potential* by John H. Mann. Copyright © 1972 by John H. Mann. Used by permission of the publisher, The Free Press, a division of Macmillan Publishing Co., Inc.

> "While the helping model does attempt to reach all areas of human functioning, it includes a diversity of techniques and approaches that transcend any single point of view."

the way he did them before didn't work out well for him" (p. 177). Note that this general definition extends to all areas of human functioning in the same way that Mann's does. A simplified paradigm of Carkhuff's model is presented in display 11.1, which divides functioning into three basic areas (that, by the way, include all of Mann's human functions): *physical, emotional-interpersonal, and intellectual.* The key word that underlies this model is *optimum;* for it is the purpose of the "helping model" to enable the learner to achieve optimum functioning on all levels, in all areas of living.

Students are often confused between the *helping* model and the humanistic model, since both emphasize the whole person in interaction with his environment. While there are some striking similarities between the two, the helping model is in some ways a broader conception than the humanistic model. For while the helping model does attempt to reach all areas of human functioning, it includes a diversity of techniques and approaches that transcend any single point of view. Thus, we can say that the helping model is an integrated approach that uses myriad methods to touch all areas of human functioning. Applications of all the psychological positions we have considered are integrated into the helping perspective.

Display 11.1   *Goals of the "Helping Model"*

Physical

Optimum physical readiness attained by proper rest including periodic relaxation periods and diet including vitamin intake or therapy, etc.

Optimum physical functioning attained by exercising body in making it functional for attaining intended goals, with particular emphasis upon those exercises such as running which influence most positively overall cardio-vascular functioning.

Emotional-Interpersonal

Optimum interpersonal relationships attained by training in interpersonal skills, with special emphasis upon responsive and initiative dimensions.

Optimum constructive personality change attained by experience of helper(s) offering high levels of responsive and initiative dimensions.

Intellectual

Optimum development of intellectual powers attained by systematic reading in area(s) of specialized interest.

Optimum development of effective, working cosmology attained by recording insights in a systematic manner in an intellectual journal.

From *The Development of Human Resources: Education, Psychology, and Social Change* by Robert R. Carkhuff. Copyright © 1971 by Holt, Rinehart and Winston, Inc. Reprinted by permission of Holt, Rinehart and Winston.

In a major work that analyzes different teaching approaches, Bruce Joyce and Marsha Weil (1972) point out "that there are many kinds of 'good' teaching, and that the concept 'good' when applied to teaching is better stated 'good for what?' and 'good for whom?' " (p. 3). Rather than selecting any single model as adequate and sufficient in itself, they present sixteen major models and examine each in some detail. In this way, we find the relative strengths and weaknesses of each model, and, more importantly, we can draw freely from different models.

The models are grouped in four major categories: (1) the social interaction models, (2) the information-processing models, (3) the personal models, (4) the behavior modification models. The designation of each model refers to its sources, the theoretical roots from which it is drawn. "The social interaction sources," the authors point out, "emphasize the relationships of the person to his society or his direct relationships with other people" (p. 8). A group problem-solving model might serve as an example of this approach. The information-processing models share "an orientation toward the information-processing capability of the student and systems which can be taught him so as to improve his information-processing capability" (p. 9). The widely used model of inductive teaching is representative of this group. The models based on personal sources share "an orientation toward the individual person as the source of educational ideas. Their frames of references spotlight personal development and they emphasize the processes by which the individual constructs and organizes his reality" (p. 10). The client-centered Rogerian approach would be indicative of this family of models. Finally, the behavior modification models are based on the empirical principles of conditioning, and Skinner's operant conditioning models serve as a primary example. Table 11.4 presents an overview of the models, indicating their family source, the major theorist who has written about each, and their goals. Joyce and Weil's analysis is especially helpful in understanding the diversity of teaching strategies.

So Many Models: What to Do?

There is bound to be some confusion at this point after reading about so many different approaches to teaching. How can I, as a teacher, you may be asking, prove most effective in the classroom? This question is most easily answered if we keep in mind that these models are derived from the work of effective teachers—teachers do not necessarily become effective because they have learned these models.

When we speak of teaching approaches, the first question we must answer is: Is a teaching approach or teaching technique an explanation of what the teacher is doing, or is it, as has been suggested, designed to assist the teacher prior to making decisions? Techniques should serve as guidelines—tentative parameters of approach—in helping the teacher maintain the delicate balance of the teacher-student relationship. This question will

Table 11.4   The Methods of Teaching Classified by Family and Mission

Model	Major Theorist	Family or Orientation	Missions or Goals for Which Applicable
1. Inductive teaching model	Hilda Taba	Information processing	Primarily for development of inductive mental processes and academic reasoning or theory-building, but these capacities are useful for personal and social goals as well.
2. Inquiry training model	Richard Suchman	Information processing	
3. Science Inquiry model	Joseph J. Schwab (also much of the Curriculum Reform Movement; see Jerome Bruner *The Process of Education* for the rationale)	Information processing	Designed to teach the research system of the discipline but also expected to have effects in other domains (i.e., sociological methods may be taught in order to increase social understanding and social problem-solving).
4. Jurisprudential teaching model	Donald Oliver and James P. Shaver	Social interaction	Designed primarily to teach the jurisprudential frame of reference as a way of processing information but also as a way of thinking about and resolving social issues.
5. Concept attainment model	Jerome Bruner	Information processing	Designed primarily to develop inductive reasoning.
6. Developmental model	Jean Piaget, Irving Sigel, Edmund Sullivan	Information processing	Designed to increase general intellectual development, especially logical reasoning, but can be applied to social and moral development as well. (See Kohlberg.)
7. Advance organizer model	David Ausubel	Information processing	Designed to increase the efficiency of information-processing capacities to meaningfully absorb and relate bodies of knowledge.
8. Group investigation model	Herbert Thelen John Dewey	Social interaction	Development of skills for participation in democratic social process through combined emphasis on interpersonal and social (group) skills and academic inquiry. Aspects of personal development are important outgrowths of this model.

Table 11.4 Continued

Model	Major Theorist	Family or Orientation	Missions or Goals for Which Applicable
9. Social inquiry model	Byron Massialas Benjamin Cox	Social interaction	Social problem-solving primarily through academic inquiry and logical reasoning.
10. Laboratory method model	National Training Laboratory (NTL) Bethel, Maine	Social interaction	Development of interpersonal and group skills and through this, personal awareness and flexibility.
11. Nondirective teaching model	Carl Rogers	Person	Emphasis on building capacity for self-instruction and through this, personal development in terms of self-understanding, self-discovery, and self-concept.
12. Classroom meeting model	William Glasser	Person	Development of self-understanding and self-responsibility. This would have latent benefits to other kinds of functioning, i.e., social.
13. Awareness training model	William Schutz Fritz Perls	Person	Increasing personal capacity for self-exploration and self-awareness. Much emphasis on development of interpersonal awareness and understanding.
14. Synectics model	William Gordon	Person	Personal development of creativity and creative problem-solving.
15. Conceptual systems model	David E. Hunt	Person	Designed to increase personal complexity and flexibility. Matches environments to students.
16. Operant conditioning model	B. F. Skinner	Behavior modification	General applicability. A domain-free approach though probably most applicable to information-processing function.

Bruce Joyce and Marsha Weil, *Models of Teaching*, © 1972, pp. 11–13. Reprinted by permission of Prentice-Hall, Inc., Englewood Cliffs, New Jersey.

Teaching: Art and Science

> "Areas of individual growth are not separated from each other, but related theoretically and functionally within the organic context of the total person."

be dealt with in greater detail in the following chapter in which we examine the elements of instruction.

At this point, we shall turn our attention to an issue that invariably precedes questions of instruction or technique, namely, how can the teacher foster emotional growth and development in the classroom. What can the teacher do to increase the possibilities of affective learning? In answering this, we shall examine in greater detail the outline of psychological models applied to teaching presented in table 11.2.

Emotional Education in the Classroom

We mentioned at the beginning of this chapter—as we have implied throughout the book—that intellectual, social, and emotional development go hand-in-hand. Areas of individual growth are not separated from each other, but related theoretically and functionally within the organic context of the total person. For this reason, in Part One and Part Two of this book we examined the needs, interests, tendencies, and problems of young people, paying particular attention to how these needs can be met, how these interests can be constructively stimulated and used as motivating forces, how these tendencies can be modified or channeled into constructive outlets, and how these problems can be resolved within the context of the school situation. Now we shall turn our attention to various systems of counseling, psychotherapy, personal enhancement and human resources development, behavioral modification procedures, and other perspectives that make a direct contribution to teaching efficacy. We shall look at insights from these systems, not as counselors or therapists dealing with the problematic or disturbed individual, but as teachers dealing with the natural processes of growth and development through the educational process. As such, we shall not attempt to fully reconstruct the rationale behind the various therapeutic approaches, but merely to examine those insights that have been derived from positions that are directly applicable to the teaching situation.

Both psychotherapy and education have as their goals the betterment of the person, but each goes about its tasks in different ways. Psychotherapy has as its central focus the inner consciousness (feelings) of the person; the dynamic processes and their influence on behavior and actions. Education is also

Psychotherapy and Education: Two Approaches to Human Growth

> "The recognition of the importance of the unconscious mind
> is essential for understanding the
> psychoanalytic contribution."

concerned with this inner-subjectivity, but it has a concomitant interest in intellectual growth, which is not a part of the psychotherapy paradigm. There are other differences as well: the gross dissimilarities between the expectations, rules, and observable behavior in the psychotherapy setting and the school setting, the discrepant goals of psychotherapy and formal education, the dependency upon diagnostic evaluation in psychotherapy as opposed to the reliance upon learning-achievement evaluation in the school setting.

Despite these differences, there are many important parallels between psychotherapy and education. Both strive toward helping the individual adjust to and function in his social setting; both attempt to correct deficiencies in early upbringing; both work toward helping the individual maximize his potential, live harmoniously with others, increase the accuracy of perceptions, and to relate to the world in a way that is both congruent, integrated, and productive. Furthermore, in practice, psychotherapy is a type of "reeducation," as Freud called it, which ideally should work concomitantly with the goals of teaching.

With this in mind, let us examine the contributions of five therapeutic approaches to teaching: psychoanalysis, behavior therapy, client-centered therapy, and existentialism.

Contributions of the Psychoanalytic Approach

Several important concepts in psychoanalytic therapy are directly relevant to the teaching situation. Most clearly relevant to the teaching situation are the concepts of the unconscious, transference, resistance, countertransference, and defense mechanisms.

The recognition of the importance of the unconscious mind is essential for understanding the psychoanalytic contribution. Belkin (1974) points out, for example, that—

> . . . the starting point for developing a psychodynamic teaching model, based upon the insights and categories of psychoanalysis, must be the unconscious mind. While most of the educators throughout history certainly demonstrated an intuitive recognition of an unconscious—or at least of forces beyond the individual's conscious awareness—no person was capable of developing comprehensively a *theory* of the unconscious and its application to teaching. (p. 14)

Freud was the first to do so. He argued that the basis of all our actions is energy that emanates from the unconscious mind and is channeled into our

> "The psychoanalytic recognition of unconscious conflict has profound implications for the practicing teacher. It impels him to deal with the hidden, elusive forces that play in the classroom interaction."

conscious minds, and ultimately into activities that we call *behavior*. In cases where our unconscious motives are in conflict with our conscious motives, it is likely that either our unconscious motives will win out or that some compromise between the two—what we call a symptom—will appear. Let us consider, for instance, the following cases where the principle of unconscious conflict is illustrated:

Case 1: A third-grade boy develops a sudden case of school phobia. Although he had been performing above average in school, he is suddenly too fearful to attend. Consultation with the mother reveals that prior to the development of the phobia, the boy overheard a conversation between his parents in which they discussed the possibility of divorce.

Case 2: A seventh-grade girl, of average IQ and performance in school, has extreme difficulty learning her social studies material. Her previous school history reveals no difficulties in this area, and the teacher cannot explain the failure. Consultation with the school counselor reveals an unconscious conflict between the girl and her teacher that is affecting her performance academically in that one subject area.

Case 3: A college-bound high school student suddenly changes his plans and decides not to attend college. After a lengthy discussion with his physical education teacher, with whom he has great rapport, it is revealed that the boy has an underlying fear of failure in a competitive situation.

Each of these cases would be interpreted differently by a behaviorist, who would deny the importance of unconscious conflict and concentrate on the symptom itself. To the psychoanalytically oriented educator, however, unconscious conflicts are best dealt with by the traditional methods of psychoanalytic psychotherapy: talking, on the part of the patient, and interpretation, on the part of the analyst. Thus, in Case 1, the school psychologist met with the boy and encouraged him to verbalize his fears of abandonment and how they precipitated the phobic response. In Case 2, the school counselor, at an emotionally appropriate moment, interpreted to the girl her feelings about the teacher that were interfering with learning. In Case 3, the physical education teacher helped the student explore causes in the past that contributed to the fear of failure in competitive situations. As it turned out, the student had two older siblings who were over-achievers and received lavish praise from the parents, who tended to neglect their youngest child.

The psychoanalytic recognition of unconscious conflict has profound implications for the practicing teacher. It impels him to deal with the hidden, elusive forces that play in the classroom interaction and to recognize that it is not only the conscious, subject-matter oriented interactions that are valid parts of the educational process. Particularly important manifestations of the unconscious are found in resistance and transference. Let us look at each of these.

In psychoanalytic therapy, resistance is anything that impedes the course of treatment. In the classroom situation, we can define resistance as anything that impedes the progress of education. This would include inappropriate behavior, psychological "learning blocks," as well as chronic absenteeism, tardiness, and other disturbances of the learning process. The contribution of psychoanalysis in this area is in the methods it provides for dealing with resistances psychodynamically. For while the behavioral approach would treat resistances as undesirable behavior and attempt to quell them as symptoms, the psychoanalytic approach views them as inevitable attendants to all learning efforts, and treats them as unconscious conflicts (or blocks) that have to be resolved before meaningful learning can begin. Let us examine two ways of dealing with resistances: the classical psychoanalytic approach and the modern psychoanalytic approach.

In the approach developed by Freud, resistances are interpreted by the analyst to the patient. This brings the patient into contact with his unconscious, and through awareness, the patient is presumably able to control the resistances. Unfortunately, the interpretation of resistances has little relevance to the classroom situation, where most resistance will not respond to psychological interpretation. For this reason the modern psychoanalytic approach is especially useful.

Modern psychoanalysis, as defined by its originator, Hyman Spotnitz (1961, 1969, 1976), differs from the traditional, classical psychoanalytic approach in that instead of using interpretations to resolve resistances (which would be inappropriate to the classroom setting), it responds to the unconscious unmet "maturational needs" of the individual that are revealed through his or her resistances. These are unmet needs from childhood that, when fulfilled later in life, will help the person grow. Applying the insights from this approach to the classroom setting, Kirman (1976) argues that "modern psychoanalysis is extremely useful in helping students on the road to emotional maturity." He proposes that teachers recognize and deal with transference and resistance when they make their appearance in the classroom. Kirman points out that resistances may be cognitive, emotional, or social resistances, each of which impedes learning and disrupts the normal flow of teaching. One modern psychoanalytic technique for dealing with these resistances is known as *mirroring the resistance*.

In the following situation the teacher attempts to resolve the resistance to forming a cooperative peer relationship by mirroring the student's unconscious.

John, a 7th grade student, is like a shark: he pounces on other students in the class when he senses they are weak. He has a leer on his face like a hyena moving in for the kill. When a student gives an incorrect answer, John calls him a "retard"; if someone trips and falls, John laughs in glee; if a member of the class has a cold and sneezes, John gloats that he is very healthy. He also tries to goad the teacher to laugh with him—to have contempt for those inferior creatures, too. The teacher intervenes to interrupt John's destructive interpersonal patterns:

Teacher: You're very lucky to be so healthy—I am often sick and feel terrible and weak—sometimes I think I shouldn't even come to school.

John: Why shouldn't you come to school, "teach"?

Teacher: Because they'll all laugh at me when they see how weak I am—and besides when I feel sick I also feel stupid—they might find out how stupid and weak I am and fire me.

John: (Laughing wildly) Teacher is a retard!—Teacher is a retard! But why tell all the kids if you're so stupid, "teach"? Once they find out—boy, are you gonna get it.

Teacher: Well, I thought you should know about it; perhaps you can help me. What do you suggest I do?

The teacher here, by mirroring John's repressed feelings, enables the student to deal with his own dreaded feelings in terms of the teacher's ego. At the same time the hostility is deflected from the more vulnerable students to the teacher. And if the "important" teacher himself is weak, then weakness cannot be quite so despicable. . . . (Kirman, 1976, pp. 397)

From the modern psychoanalytic perspective, the teacher uses free discussion to help resolve student resistances.

> "The teacher is often the object of feelings that are transferred from figures that made a profound impression on the child early in life."

In addition to resolving resistance, adequately dealing with transference feelings is critical in psychoanalytic teaching. "It is important to recognize," Kirman (1976) points out, "that once the transference is recognized, the teacher has the most powerful tool ever discovered to influence the lives of the students." This tool can be used advantageously or harmfully, depending in part upon the teacher's conscious intentions and in part upon the teacher's sensitivities to what the student is communicating and what type of intervention will be helpful to the student at a given moment. Basic techniques for responding to transference have been discussed fully by Nelson et al. (1968), and direct application to the classroom setting has been illustrated by Belkin (1974) from a philosophical point of view, and by Kirman (1977), who has translated the complete modern psychoanalytic approach into a classroom application.

"Everyone who wishes to explain, to teach anyone anything," argues Ferenczi (1966), "becomes a substitute for the father- and teacher-imago (mind images), and takes upon himself all the disbelief these personalities formerly roused in the child" (p. 215). The teacher, in other words, is often the object of feelings that are transferred from figures that made a profound impression on the child early in life. If the teacher fails to sense the discrepancies between the way he or she behaves and acts toward the learner and the way the learner perceives and responds to the teacher, this can become a basis for much misunderstanding. Thus, analysis of the transference is crucial to operating a classroom on a level that is meaningful to the unconscious mind as well as to the conscious mind.

Other writers have discussed in detail the application of basic psychoanalytic principles to teaching and learning (Cantor, 1972; Freud, A., 1947; Hellman, 1958; Hill, 1965), but this is still a flowering ideology, beset by controversy. The chief points, agreed to by most of these writers, can be summed up as follows:

1. The analysis of resistance and transference is essential to successful communication (teaching) in the classroom.
2. The recognition of the power of the unconscious mind is of paramount importance.
3. In the classroom, emotional growth occurs simultaneously with cognitive and social development.

Approaches that emphasize the self-actualizing, free-will, independent nature of the human being are called humanistic approaches. In addition to humanism per se, these also include the client-centered approach, developed by Carl Rogers, and the existential approach, which is credited to many developers. These approaches have five basic postulates in common, even though they may differ in specific areas. The five postulates underlying these systems follow.

1. When we consider the individual we have to look at the whole person; that is, the person in continual interaction with the environment.
2. The person is always in the process of growth and change. Living is growing; life is never static.
3. People are essentially free. Inability to understand the potentials of our free will result in the inability to exercise it.
4. People tend toward self-actualization, the realization of their full potentiality. The direction in which growth occurs, ideally, is toward the satisfaction of all life's needs.
5. People are essentially good.

These principles, while they are general to the humanistic approach, vary from specific philosophy to philosophy. In this section, we shall try to present an overview of "humanistic education," concentrating on those aspects that are particularly relevant with respect to theories and processes of teaching. First, we will look at the basic tenets of the client-centered and existential approaches; then, we will note their specific teaching applications.

In the early 1940s, Carl Rogers, an American psychologist, introduced what he then called *nondirective therapy,* but which has subsequently become more widely known as Rogerian, or *client-centered therapy.* Objecting to the strict, dogmatic tenets of Freudian psychoanalysis, and arguing that the therapist should not be above the client, but equal to him, Rogers founded a therapeutic ideology built on the idea that the movement and progress—the course—of therapy is determined by the client, not by the therapist. Even replacing the term *patient* with *client* showed Rogers's more humanistic view of the person seeking help.

The Client-Centered/
Learner-Centered Approach

From these beginnings, client-centered therapy became more than just a new therapeutic approach. It blossomed into a living ideology—a philosophy of life—that includes views on marriage and the family, society, religion, and, particularly, on education and teaching. Rogers, through his prolific publications (Rogers, 1942, 1951, 1962, 1967, 1970, 1975) has translated the

> "Underlying client-centered teaching is a consistent philosophy that reaffirms faith in the essential goodness of man and assurance in the person's natural tendency toward growth and improvement."

essential tenets of the client-centered philosophy into a number of practical applications. Underlying all of these practical applications is a consistent philosophy that reaffirms faith in the essential goodness of man and assurance in the person's natural tendency toward growth and improvement.

The specific changes Rogers (1959) expects therapy to produce in the individual are consistent with his expectations of the positive changes a *facilitative* educational experience should produce. These changes, according to Rogers, are:

The person comes to see himself differently.
He accepts himself and his feelings more fully.
He becomes more self-confident and self-directing.
He becomes more the person he would like to be.
He becomes more flexible, less rigid, in his perceptions.
He adopts more realistic goals for himself.
He behaves in a more mature fashion.
He changes his maladjustive behaviors.
He becomes more acceptant of others.
He becomes more open to the evidence, both to what is going on outside of himself, and to what is going on inside of himself.
He changes in his basic personality characteristics in constructive ways. (p. 232)

We note the general thrust of all these changes: toward a more concrete, valid, openness to experience and to others. Education, Rogers argues, produces these changes in the same ways that therapy does; through the crucial interaction between teacher and learner (counselor and client), in which each experiences the inner core of the other, and grows from the experience.

The Client-Centered/Learner-Centered Teacher

The qualities that Rogers argues are essential to therapeutic progress are also essential to progress in the classroom. These basic qualities (which were discussed more fully in chapter 10) are empathy, genuineness, warmth, and positive regard. The teacher who has these qualities will transmit the subject matter along with the emotional experience necessary for growth and learning. Specifically, Rogers speaks of "learning to be free," an important element in his educational philosophy. "The goal," he says, "is to assist students to be-

> "At first, the student may experience 'a period of frustration, disappointment, disbelief,' not sure of how to cope with the experience of *learning to be free.*"

come individuals who are able to take self-initiated action and to be responsible for those actions." He goes on to state that such students are ones—

who are capable of intelligent choice and self-direction;

who are critical learners, able to evaluate the contributions made by others;

who have acquired knowledge relevant to the solution of problems;

who, even more importantly, are able to adapt flexibly and intelligently to new problem situations;

who have internalized an adaptive mode of approach to problems, utilizing all pertinent experience freely and creatively;

who are able to cooperate effectively with others in these various activities;

who work, not for approval of others, but in terms of their own socialized purposes. (Rogers, 1971, pp. 52–53)

This description closely parallels the goals of client-centered therapy, stated previously, and Rogers continually emphasizes in his writings the concordance between the two.

The Student

Rogers goes into some detail outlining the processes of development that the student experiences in the client-centered/learner-centered school setting. At first, the student may experience "a period of frustration, disappointment, disbelief," not sure of how to cope with the experience of learning to be free. After coming to grips with these feelings, students go through a period of individual initiative and work, when they realize "that they can express, in class, the way they really feel; that issues can be discussed in class which are real to them, not simply the issues set forth in a text." They develop a sense of what Rogers calls "personal closeness" among themselves and with the teacher. Finally, they begin to experience individual change "in the direction of greater freedom and spontaneity."

The client-centered/learner-centered approach, as we can see, is an integrative method that combines cognitive and affective development in order for the learner to be able to meet goals that are both intellectually important and therapeutically beneficial. Now, we will turn our attention to the less specific, but equally important, existential approach.

> "The convenient catch phrase that expresses the basic idea that underlies all the diverse philosophies found under the rubric of existentialism is *existence precedes essence.*"

Contributions of the Existential Approach

The existential approach derives from the European philosophy of existentialism that made its appearance in the writings of Sören Kierkegaard, a nineteenth-century Danish philosopher and theologian who argued passionately that the person becomes what he or she is through actions—not through birth, station, or rhetoric. Martin Heidegger, a German philosopher, and Jean Paul Sartre, a French philosopher, contributed substantially to developing the philosophy of existentialism, which today is a multifaceted philosophy that embraces religious and nonreligious points of view, communistic and capitalistic proponents, and other contradictory partisans. This attests to the large degree of interpretation that existentialism allows.

During the 1940s, psychoanalysts began to recognize the implications of existentialism for therapy, and the existential therapy movement began. Ludwig Binswanger, a Swiss psychiatrist, and Victor Frankl, an Austrian-born psychiatrist who was imprisoned in a German concentration camp, made important contributions in developing a rich, practical existential psychotherapy. Frankl's therapy, called **logotherapy,** emphasizes the person's "will to meaning," which is a powerful motivating force throughout his life. Rejecting both Freud's argument that the person strives primarily for pleasure and Adler's argument that the person is motivated primarily by a will to power, Frankl sees the will to meaning as the underlying basis of existential striving:

> In the last analysis, it turns out that both the will to pleasure and the will to power are derivatives of the original will to meaning. Pleasure . . . is an effect of meaning fulfillment; power is a means to an end. A certain amount of power, such as economic or financial power, is generally a prerequisite for meaning fulfillment. Thus we could say that while the will to pleasure mistakes the effect for the end, the will to power mistakes the means to an end for the end itself. (Frankl, 1967, p. 6)

During the past twenty years, the insights that Frankl and others have had about counseling and psychotherapy have been applied to the teaching situation. We will examine here what these insights mean for the teacher.

The Existential Point of View

The convenient catch phrase that expresses the basic idea that underlies all of the diverse philosophies and methodologies found under the rubric of existentialism is *existence precedes essence.* In its most simple form, this

means that what a person does with his life—the way he lives it—determines what he is. We are not born to be anything in particular, argues the existentialist, but we become what we are through our actions and our commitment to those actions. We make choices between alternatives, exercising our free will and judgment, and then accept complete responsibility for the choices we have made. In this way, we govern our own lives, shape our destinies, and develop our essential, individual natures.

Martin Heidegger (1962) speaks of **authenticity:** a mode of being in which the person, seriously engaged in projects that are meaningful to him, exhibits concern for the project, commitment to its goals, and responsibility for its results. This term—*authenticity*—pretty well sums up the belief of all existentialists regarding the importance of meaningful activities, of commitments, of responsibility in the person's life. We cannot simply live our life as if it were a part in a play, prearranged and inevitable; but rather, we must actively participate in making our life something special—that which we desire. Paul Tillich, the existential theologian, calls this *the courage to be.*

The popular conception of existentialism as a morbid philosophy derives from the existentialist's view of death and the importance attached to it. Heidegger speaks of "the fear of non-being . . ." the fear of death, which causes anxiety for all people. Our knowledge and recognition of death can either corrupt our authenticity, by forcing our submission, or make us more authentic by our continual striving to create in the shadow of this impending doom.

Two other basic existential concepts are *choice* and *commitment,* which function as a single action. Man as a free agent is constantly choosing between possibilities of action. He alone is responsible for his choices and for the consequences of those choices. Since whatever choices he makes helps determine his existence, and hence, *who* he is, choosing is an essential part of being. The validity of his choices is not determined by how successful the choices were in executing the ends (as they would be, for example, in philosophical pragmatism), but in how willing the individual is to accept the consequences of the choices as his own doing—as a part of himself. "For the existentialist," Greene (1973) points out, "the self is devoid of character or coloration before action is undertaken. When the individual begins devising projects and purposes, he begins creating an identity. No outside factor or force, no science or set of rules or moral law, can make decisions for him" (p. 256).

The Educational Perspective

Existentialism has enjoyed much attention and application in the school setting. Teachers and educators, recognizing its emphasis on the individual person and his or her responsibility to choose and develop in his or her own unique way, have integrated many of its fundamental principles into educational practice. Since the main emphasis of existentialism is on *freedom,* the existential teacher strives to have his or her students come to grips with their essential condition of freedom. As Morris (1966), who has written a book on existentialism and education, explains it:

The policy of freedom has certain consequences we had better be prepared for. It means no hierarchy of authority in the school, no dominion of teacher over pupil, no external standards of achievement or success visited upon the young. It means that the students shall have not only a freedom *from* such standards but a coordinate freedom *to* establish their own standards in terms of which they choose to learn. . . . Finally, *the teacher comes to realize that successful teaching in the Existential mode ends, as it began, in paradox: such teaching succeeds by doing itself out of a job.* It succeeds by becoming unnecessary, by producing an individual who no longer needs to be taught, who breaks loose and swings free of the teacher and becomes self-moving. (p. 153)

We can say, then, that the existential approach to teaching is not so much a specific methodology as it is a general attitude toward goals and processes in education, toward the learner's place and the learner's movement in the teaching-learning process. Existentialism, as it is applied to teaching, becomes a rationale for acting and behaving in a certain way—but the way is never specified.

Probably the greatest contribution to existentialism and education has been made by Maxine Greene, an existentialist who has devoted over twenty years to writing and lecturing about the existential teacher. Professor Greene, who teaches existentialism at Columbia University, sees the teacher as "stranger," an important existential concept that she explains this way:

To take a stranger's vantage point on everyday reality is to look inquiringly and wonderingly on the world in which one lives. It is like returning home from a long stay in some other place. The homecomer notices details and patterns in his environment he never saw before. . . .

We do not ask that the teacher perceive his existence as absurd; nor do we demand that he estrange himself from his community. *We simply suggest that he struggle against unthinking submergence in the social reality that prevails.* If he wishes to present himself as a person actively engaged in critical thinking and authentic choosing, he cannot accept any "ready-made standardized scheme" at face value. He cannot even take for granted the value of intelligence, rationality, or education. . . . (pp. 267–269)

What Maxine Greene is suggesting—and what is essentially the underlying perspective of the existential teacher—is that the teacher approach the educational setting afresh, without preconceived biases that influence the course of teaching, but with a flexibility and willingness to see, experience, and understand the learner as he or she is. The teacher's presence as a person is the most important influence in education. "If he is able to think what he is doing while he is vitally present as a person, he may arouse others to act on their own freedom" (Greene, p. 298). Since this attitude involves a great personal struggle on the part of every teacher, the existential position is especially relevant in understanding the teacher as a person, and this was considered in some detail in chapter 10.

Teaching for Self-Actualization

Other humanistic psychologists, who are neither distinctly existential nor distinctly client-centered, have also made significant contributions to teaching style and instructional methodology. Abraham Maslow, one of the seminal thinkers in this field, points out how humanistic philosophy, which "conceives of the human being as having an essence, a real self to be discovered and actualized . . . [which] must be sought for and uncovered," has translated this into educational practice:

Abraham Maslow's humanistic psychology has had a profound effect on teaching.

Generated by this new humanistic philosophy is also a new conception of learning, of teaching, and of education. Stated simply, such a concept holds that the function of education, the goal of education—the human goal—is ultimately the self-actualization of the person, the becoming fully human, the development of the fullest height that the human species can stand up to or that the particular individual can come to. In a less technical way, it is helping the person to become the best that he is able to become. (Maslow, 1973, p. 153)

Maslow recognizes that such a goal is easier said than done. "Teachers and other kinds of professionals," he points out, "suffer from having been indoctrinated into a mastering, manipulating, controlling outlook toward nature, toward people, especially toward children."

All humanistic writers emphasize much the same point, although they express it in different words and highlight different areas. Bugental (1967) has edited a comprehensive and thorough anthology of humanistic psychological thought, and the recurrent themes throughout the book are the quality of the human experience; the growth of the individual; the power of the human encounter to expand awareness of self and others; the interrelationships between cognitive and emotional learning. The cohering motif that holds together these themes is that the person is always in the process of self-actualizing, a key process in the humanistic philosophy. Maslow describes this process in some detail:

Teaching: Art and Science

Self-actualization is a lifelong process that begins in childhood where we learn the basics of self-expression.

. . . self-actualization means experiencing fully, vividly, selflessly, with full concentration and total absorption. It means experiencing without the self-consciousness of the adolescent. At this moment of experiencing, the person is wholly and fully human. This is a self-actualization moment. . . . (Maslow, 1967, p. 281)

He goes on to describe the process in more detail. "Self-actualization is not only an end state but also the process of actualizing one's potentialities at any time, in any amount. It is, for example, a matter of becoming smarter by studying if one is an intelligent person. . . . Self-actualization can consist of finger exercises at a piano keyboard. *Self-actualization means working to do well the thing that one wants to do.* To become a second-rate physician is not a good path to self-actualization. One wants to be first-rate or as good as he can be" (Maslow, 1967, p. 283).

What does this mean in terms of humanistic teaching? It has many implications. First, that we, as teachers, help students discover those things that they can do well and that they enjoy doing. As we help them in this direction, without impinging our own values on them, we are helping them in the self-actualizing process. Second, that we try to provide an environment for learning that affords the students opportunities to experience what Maslow calls "peak experiences," which are essential not only to self-actualization but to growth itself. The joy of learning is not some myth left over from the Renaissance, but a true possibility that exists every moment for every child in every classroom, but is continually threatened by blind adherence to tradition, by fears and doubts on the teacher's part, by false expectations on the part of the students, and by other factors, all of which bring to bear an almost overwhelming pressure to conform. Finally, that we recognize the unitary nature of human growth; its inseparable elements of mental, emotional, and intellectual energy all channelled within the organism. Rubin (1973) articulates this position succinctly:

In its highest form, learning is holistic and organic. Encouraging emotionality at the expense of logic, or rationality at the expense of feeling, results either in the subjugation of man to the tyranny of his passions or in raw intellectualism. *In both instances we achieve but half a person.* (p. 20)

He goes on to differentiate between an *explicit* curriculum and an *implicit* curriculum; between that which we intend to teach and have so organized into subject matter, and that which the environment of the school itself communicates. "If true learning in the explicit curriculum is experiential," he points out, "then the corollary for our implicit curriculum can be said to be; *what is experienced is learned.*" Beyond what is taught, then, the school itself must provide an environment that is nurturing and through which the learner can grow and self-actualize.

Summary

In this chapter, we have examined a variety of approaches to teaching, while keeping in mind the principles embodied in our *T-E-A-C-H-I-N-G* acronym that directs itself to the total person. We arrived, early in the chapter, at a functional definition of teaching that includes the host of variables that contribute to the process. This definition was general enough to account for the different specific models presented, but specific enough to enable us to see the variables omnipresent in all teaching interactions. We then examined how theory becomes practice by considering the implications of different theoretical positions for the teaching process. We noted that there are consistencies and inconsistencies (contradictions) between positions, and we suggested that an eclectic point of view, derived from several of the positions, could be logically arrived at.

Finally, in our discussion of psychological perspectives, we looked at the issue of emotional education in the classroom. We suggested that emotional readiness is an important prerequisite to cognitive readiness, and that retarded maturation lessens the probability of effective learning. Looking at the psychoanalytic, existential, client-centered, and humanistic positions, we noted how each contributes, in its own way, to our better understanding of the theories and processes of teaching.

In the following chapter, we will focus on some principles of effective classroom management, applying the insights from behavioral learning theory to the classroom setting.

Suggested Additional Readings

Modern Psychoanalysis in the Schools by William J. Kirman (*Dubuque, Iowa: Kendall/Hunt Publishing Co., 1977*)

> This is the first book to thoroughly apply the principles of modern psychoanalytic thought to the school setting. The first part outlines the basic concepts of modern psychoanalysis (maturational needs, transference, resistance, countertransference), and the second part applies these principles to such educational problems as evaluation, presenting subject matter, dealing with parents, helping students overcome blocks, and so forth.

Frequently evaluation is experienced by the student as reinforcing existing attitudes. The student's "value" as seen in the teacher's low grade may be taken as confirmation of an already established negative self-concept. This negative evaluation can then become a self-fulfilling prophecy.

from *Modern Psychoanalysis in the Schools*

Existentialism in Education by Van Cleve Morris (*New York: Harper & Row Publishers, 1966*)

A fine little introduction to existential education. The author covers the philosophical foundation and educational application of existential thought. The book avoids much of the technical jargon and abstraction that turns off the beginning student and focuses instead on the personal, relevant dimensions of existentialism.

The policy of freedom has certain consequences we had better be prepared for. It means no hierarchy of authority in the school, no dominion of teacher over pupil, no external standards of achievement or success visited upon the young.

from *Existentialism in Education*

Person to Person: The Problem of Being Human by Carl R. Rogers and Barry Stevens (*New York: Pocket Books, 1971*)

An overview of the client-centered approach, drawing heavily from the writings of Carl Rogers. There are some particularly excellent sections that apply to teaching and learning and some personal reflections that concretize much of the client-centered philosophy.

It is clear from the experience of Aichorn, Neill, or the many individuals who have tried a student-centered approach to teaching, that one of the requisites for the teacher who would facilitate this type of learning is a profound trust in the human organism.

from *Person to Person: The Problem of Being Human*

Modern Humanistic Psychotherapy by Arthur Burton (*San Francisco: Jossey-Bass, 1967*)

While this book concentrates primarily on humanistic and existential approaches to psychotherapy, there are enough important insights between the covers to justify its use by teachers and prospective teachers. Particularly valuable are the chapters on acting-out behavior and artistic productions in psychotherapy.

If you observe children at play, and observe mothers observing their children at play, you come to see that the play of the child creates anxiety in the mother. She attempts to limit not only the child's playmates, but the kind of play experience he has.

from *Modern Humanistic Psychotherapy*

Teacher and Child: A Book for Parents and Teachers by Haim G. Ginott (*New York: Avon Books, 1973*)

There are some excellent insights in this book that transcend any single theoretical orientation. Ginott is able to communicate his sense of the right thing to do at the right time. While the book is simply written, the ideas are quite penetrating at times, and the examples are usually very interesting.

Praise consists of two parts: What we say to the child and what he in turn says to himself. Our words should state what we like and appreciate about his efforts, help, work, and accomplishments. The child then draws conclusions about himself.

from *Teacher and Child*

Contributions of Behavioral Learning Theory to Teaching Theory

Basic learning principles are applied to the classroom setting. Operant conditioning, extinction, positive reinforcement, negative reinforcement are each defined and examples of their uses given. Punishment is discussed in both its positive and negative manifestations. It is pointed out that while punishment itself is not a fully effective tool, if used constructively and combined with other methods, it can be an extremely helpful method in the classroom. Nine principles of constructive punishment are deduced from the research and discussion. The uses of modeling, or learning by example, are examined.

Designing and Implementing a Behavior Modification Program

Specific procedures for choosing the type of program and then implementing it are considered. It is pointed out that the teacher should attempt to strengthen positive behaviors while weakening negative behaviors. A method of keeping track of behaviors, by the use of coded index cards, is detailed, and suggestions for selecting reinforcers are explored. A case illustration of two third-grade boys whose behaviors were treated by the behavior modification paradigm is presented.

Effective Classroom Management

The position is put forth that we try to educate the total person, and that management decisions should be governed by this rationale. Several principles of effective classroom management are then derived. Classroom discipline is examined as a positive teacher influence. Particular cautions, involving the imprudent use of discipline, are also presented.

12 Approaches to Classroom Management

The application of behavioral learning theory to the teaching process deserves special attention since this one theory has been shown to be compatible with the goals of both affective and cognitive learning. Moreover, the application of this learning theory is directly relevant to a problem that concerns all teachers: how to manage the class effectively. This will be the primary concern of this chapter.

In addition to examining the basic nomenclature of the behavioral theory of teaching, we will explore in some detail the mechanics of a behavior modification program. A step-by-step analysis of how to implement a program will be directed toward the practical application of behavioral principles. Attendant issues, such as the pros and cons of punishment in the classroom, will also be considered, and some synthetic principles of "constructive" punishment will be presented.

Finally, we will integrate the insights from these different areas in the section, "Effective Classroom Management," in which we will try to come to grips with ways of dealing with learners in the most effective way. Beginning with the principle that it is the teacher's job to educate the total person, we will look at related issues, such as classroom discipline and teacher intervention. Again, our purpose in these sections is to better understand ways of bringing the learner to the level where efficient learning (and thus, effective teaching) becomes a reality.

Let us begin, then, by examining the contributions of behavioral learning theory to teaching theory.

Contributions of Behavioral Learning Theory to Teaching Theory

The methods comprising the behavioral learning approach are derived from the two theories of conditioning discussed in chapter 2. Briefly, behavioral learning theory distinguishes between two types of conditioning: respondent (classical) conditioning and operant (instrumental) conditioning. Respondent conditioning is explained by the following paradigm: A stimulus, which elicits an automatic response not requiring prior learning (called the *unconditioned stimulus*), is paired with a neutral stimulus that does not elicit any particular (or predictable) response. This neutral stimulus is called the *conditioned stimulus*. After being thus paired, the conditioned stimulus soon begins to elicit the same response as the unconditioned stimulus did:

Illustration: A student at Mather Junior High School has been assigned to Room 101 six times in the past two years to take final examinations. He suffers from test phobia, so he experiences anxiety whenever he goes to take an exam

> " 'When a learned response is repeated without reinforcement, the strength of the tendency to perform that response undergoes a progressive decrease.' "

there. By pairing the unconditioned stimulus (taking the exam) with the conditioned stimulus (Room 101), in a short time he begins to experience anxiety whenever he approaches that room—*even if he is not on his way to take an exam.*

Operant conditioning is defined by the following paradigm: Desirable behavior is rewarded and undesirable behavior is either ignored or punished. This type of conditioning refers to behavior that operates on the environment. For the most part, this is *voluntary* behavior. The desired responses to specified stimuli are strengthened by reinforcing these responses with positive reinforcers, such as food, praise, money, tokens, privileges, or other types of gratification:

Illustration: A student is given an extra dessert at lunchtime whenever he behaves on the lunch line (positive reinforcement), but given no dessert when he misbehaves (extinction). Or he may be deprived of his gym period, which he enjoys, whenever he severely misbehaves (punishment). After several days of such conditioning, he misbehaves less frequently, and his tendency to behave positively is strengthened.

Many different methods of behavior therapy that are applicable to the classroom situation derive from these two basic paradigms. We shall look closely at four such methods in this section: extinction, positive reinforcement, negative reinforcement, and modeling. We shall also consider, in some detail, the specific steps involved in setting up a behavior modification program. Finally, we will examine aspects of punishment, considering the advantages and disadvantages of punitive practices. Several books that can help the teacher utilize behavior modification principles discussed here are listed at the end of this chapter.

Extinction

"When a learned response is repeated without reinforcement, the strength of the tendency to perform that response undergoes a progressive decrease" (Dollard & Miller, 1950). This is the most concise and accurate definition of **extinction.** Let us say that a teacher has been giving a star to each student who hands in a homework assignment. When her supply of stars runs out, she inadvertently forgets to buy a new box. After a period of time, according to the theory of extinction, if the reward of the star was the primary motivation for the positive behavior, then the students will lose this positive behavior because the reinforcement they had been receiving is no longer forthcoming. Of course, there are a number of factors that influence the rate of extinction, including "the irregularity with which the behavior was reinforced in the past, the amount of effort required to perform it, the level of deprivation

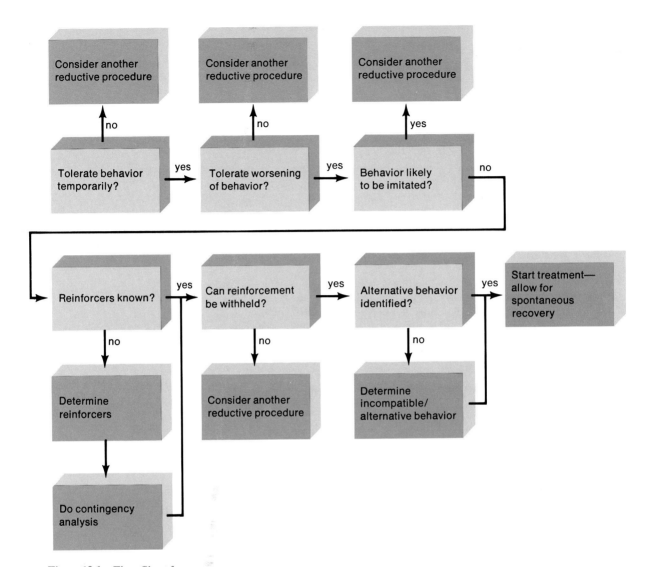

Figure 12.1 Flow Chart for Extinction. From "Extinction: Guidelines for Its Selection and Use" by R. B. Benoit and G. R. Mayer, *Personality and Guidance Journal*, 1974, *52*, p. 291.

present during extinction, the ease with which changes in conditions of reinforcement can be discerned, and the availability of alternative modes of response" (Bandura, 1969, p. 335).

Benoit and Mayer (1976) have discussed in detail the uses of extinction as a classroom behavior modification technique. They point out the questions that the teacher must ask before employing this technique: Are the reinforcers of the behavior that is to be extinguished known? Can these reinforcers be withheld? Have alternative behaviors been identified? Figure 12.1 provides a flow chart that can be useful for the teacher who is considering implementing an extinction program. By following the arrows on the flow chart, the teacher can see the appropriate questions that must be asked and the alternatives that must be considered. Particularly important is the idea that with the extinction technique the negative behavior is likely to get worse before it gets better. Consider, for example, the situation in which a teacher gives a child attention every time he behaves negatively. When the teacher decides to use extinction, it is necessary to withhold the attention. But, at first, this will only encourage the child to misbehave more in the hopes of ultimately getting the attention (reinforcement) that is being withheld. This is why it is so important to decide what reinforcement actually can be withheld and to decide what alternative behaviors are going to be positively reinforced, and how. In general, extinction is more effective if it is combined with a positive reinforcement program.

Positive reinforcement is perhaps the most widely used behavioral technique in the school setting. This technique simply involves providing a reward for positive behavior. The reward (positive reinforcement) can be anything ranging from a high grade to candy to a smile to a verbal compliment. The principle underlying positive reinforcement is that the tendency to repeat a response to a given stimulus will be strengthened as the response is positively rewarded.

Positive Reinforcement

The teacher who wishes to use positive reinforcement is confronted at the outset by a number of questions. Which behavior should be rewarded? What type of reward should be used and how frequently should it be dispensed? Should the positive reinforcement be combined with another technique, such as extinction or negative reinforcement? What is probably most important for a teacher to remember is that positive reinforcement is used all the time, even if the teacher is not aware that he or she is using it. So long as the teacher treats some student behavior differently than other behavior, it seems likely to the student that the teacher is rewarding some behavior and not rewarding other behavior.

Illustration: A teacher walks Johnny back to his seat whenever he jumps out and runs around the room. To Johnny, this extra attention is a reward, and thus the teacher is inadvertently rewarding the very behaviors she wishes to stop.

One of the most debated questions among teachers, educational psychologists, and concerned parents is, To what extent is punishment an effective tool in classroom discipline? Arguments on this subject often become heated, while the objective evidence, which is plentiful, becomes lost in the smoke of the battle. All too often, one's personal opinion on the subject is more a result of one's individual beliefs than a result of the careful, unbiased consideration of all relevant issues. In this section, we shall explore the issue in some detail, and if we do not come to firm conclusions, we will at least have gained a familiarity with the many complex issues involved.

Punishment

> " 'Punishment should be examined not only as an alternative but in light of existing evidence be considered the method of choice in certain instances.' "

Punishment, as a behavioral technique, has been down-rated from the time of Thorndike to the present. "Reward positive behavior more than you punish negative behavior," educators have been crying out. While there may be much strength in this injunction, evidence does indicate the efficacy of punishment as well. Macmillan, Forness and Trumbull (1973), in a thorough review of the literature on the subject, conclude that in certain instances punishment may be required in addition to or instead of positive reinforcement and extinction. According to some educators, whenever a person is systematically punished for certain behavior, the principle of negative reinforcement is in operation. Although, technically, negative reinforcement differs from punishment, the two terms are often used interchangeably to describe teacher behaviors designed to decrease the recurrence of inappropriate student responses.

Research Findings Macmillan, Forness and Trumbull (1973) have examined the role of punishment in the classroom by critically presenting the wealth of literature on the subject and extrapolating some very cogent conclusions. They point out that theoreticians who are writers of education texts and journal articles tend to downgrade punishment and emphasize the techniques of extinction and positive reinforcement instead. However, it is "evident that teachers and parents alike continue to use punishment whether theoreticians like it or not" (p. 88).

They go on to suggest "that punishment should be examined not only as an alternative but in light of existing evidence be considered the method of choice in certain instances" (pp. 88–89). To this end, they propose a rigorous scrutiny of the variables affecting punishment in order to objectively, unemotionally examine the efficacy or inefficacy of punishment as a method of classroom management.

The important variables cited are the timing of punishment, consistency of punishment, intensity of punishment, adaptation to punishment, alternatives to the goal, relationship between the punishing agent and the recipient, and cognitive variables. We shall now look at each of these variables, bringing in other evidence where applicable.

Sommers (1972) discusses the idea of "positive punishment." This type of punishment is designed to produce more positive behavior without reinforcing the child's feelings of shame and guilt about the misbehavior that prompted the punishment. She offers an example of what she told her class after they had wasted half a period throwing a red ball across the room:

> "Punishment by itself is not an effective tool for either correcting aberrant behavior, facilitating emotional and intellectual growth, or maintaining classroom control."

"Since I figure you wasted about 15 minutes with the 'red ball incident,' " I told them the next day, "I think you each owe it back as your punishment. Remember, I want this to be something which you retain in your mind with a positive value. Each is to spend 15 minutes between now and the end of the year doing something helpful around school. Clean cupboards, work on the floors—use your imagination, as other teachers and the staff show you how you may help. . . ." (p. 55)

The negative values of punishment are discussed also at some length by Marsico (1965), who argues against the traditional forms of punishment—through fear—and suggests instead that the hostile, disruptive child be treated in the same way as the withdrawn child; namely, as someone in need of help rather than someone who needs to be punished.

In a famous study, Hollenberg and Sperry (1951) found that when verbal punishment was administered after aggressive behavior, there was an immediate, but temporary, decrease in the behavior. Azrin (1960) also reports the resurgence of the undesired behavior when the punishment is discontinued. Adams (1973), in reviewing these and other studies, concludes that punishment in itself is not an effective method for controlling or changing inappropriate classroom behavior, since it does not produce long-lasting effects. Kounin and Gump (1961) compared the attitudes of 174 first-grade children, half of whom were in classes run by punitive teachers and half of whom were in classes conducted by nonpunitive teachers. Their survey revealed that "as compared with children who have nonpunitive teachers, children who have punitive teachers manifest more aggression in their misconducts, are more unsettled and conflicted about misconduct in school, are less concerned with learning and school-unique values, show some, but not consistent, indication of a reduction in rationality pertaining to school misconduct" (p. 49).

The implicit conclusion of these and many other studies and theories is that punishment by itself is not an effective tool either for correcting aberrant behavior, for inducing calmness in the classroom, or for facilitating emotional and intellectual growth. Now, using the variables cited by Macmillan, Forness and Trumbull (1973), let us examine some possibly constructive applications of punishment, extracting principles that can be helpful to the teacher.

Timing of Punishment

To be effective, punishment should be administered immediately after the inappropriate behavior. The longer the delay between the behavior and the

"If the child is continually subjected to punishment, he loses the ability to distinguish between which behaviors are acceptable and which are not acceptable."

punishment, the less effective it will be. Through the "law of association . . . ideas, experiences, events or objects which frequently occur together in space or time come to be associated, or linked in the minds of observors" (George, 1973, p. 146). Because of this principle, the punishment should be administered in temporal proximity to the offense so that it becomes associated with the offense.

Consistency of Punishment

If a student is punished sometimes for a certain behavior but not punished at other times, then the punishment is less effective than it is if it is consistently administered. Parke (1970), in reviewing the literature, finds that consistent punishment is requisite to positive behavioral change. Macmillan et al. (1973), after a review that includes the Parke paper, conclude that "if a teacher or parent is inconsistent in reacting to a behavior, that behavior will be more difficult to weaken either via extinction or punishment" (p. 90).

Intensity of Punishment

Types of punishment range from a disapproving look to corporal punishment to severe electric shocks (in the laboratory setting only!) A number of studies have shown that very aversive stimuli produce more permanent changes than mildly aversive stimuli, and that intense punishment is effective—at least in the experimental setting (Rachman & Teasdale, 1969).

Generally, the most intense type of punishment used in the school setting is corporal punishment, although this is legally prohibited in many states. An all-too-willing public has recently applauded the recrudescence of corporal punishment as an answer to the overwhelming discipline problems in the schools (*Nation's Schools,* 1972). However, most educational organizations suggest that the weaknesses of this approach far outweigh any potential benefit and that it should be eschewed completely (Langer, 1973; *American School Board Journal,* 1973; National Education Association, 1972). The deficit of concrete, empirical research in this area, however, severely limits any cogent conclusions, and presently, only opinion prevails in this heated debate. The ethical repugnance many feel toward this form of punishment has restricted wide-scale experimentation regarding its efficacy.

Adaptation to Punishment

If the child is continually subjected to punishment, he loses the ability to distinguish between aversive and nonaversive situations, between which behaviors are acceptable and which are not acceptable. Azrin and Holz (1966), in discussing the relative merits of continual versus intermittent punishment, point out:

Continuous punishment produces more suppression than does intermittent punishment for as long as the punishment contingency is maintained. However, after the punishment contingency has been discontinued, continuous punishment allows more rapid recovery of the responses, possible because the absence of punishment can be more rapidly discriminated.

This conflicts somewhat with Azrin's earlier statements (Azrin, 1959), in which he argues that extended periods of punishment diminish its effectiveness. Macmillan et al. (1973) suggest that the teacher who uses punishment with great frequency vary the types of punishment to facilitate the discriminative abilities of the students.

Alternatives to the Goal

One question the teacher must always ask when administering punishment is, What alternative behaviors are available to the student? A number of experiments have demonstrated that if an organism is punished for behavior that has no alternatives, serious psychoneurotic side effects can be produced. "By providing alternatives," Macmillan et al. (1973) point out, "a teacher also facilitates the child's discrimination between what is acceptable and what is unacceptable" (p. 92). The teacher may combine positive reinforcement with punishment to strengthen the positive alternatives to the undesirable behavior that he or she is trying to eliminate.

Relationship Between Punishing Agent and Recipient

This variable can be simply stated: Who can hurt us more—a person whom we deeply care about or one for whom we have only negative feelings? Clearly, the person about whom we care can hurt us more deeply.

This has several implications for the teacher. If the teacher has a positive, highly motivating relationship with a student, the teacher is then more capable of dispensing punishment. By the same token, such a teacher must carefully weigh whether the administration of punishment will jeopardize the positive values of this relationship.

One way of dealing with this dilemma for the teacher who wishes to punish a child with whom he has rapport is to combine some positive affection with that punishment—to make the student realize that, although he is being punished, the teacher still feels positively about him. The following dialogue between Stephen and his teacher illustrates how this is done:

Teacher: . . . So, Steve, since you did cut, I want you to spend some extra time in school to make up the work. I realize you don't like this, but I feel that this will help you with your work and also teach you that you have to come to class.

Stephen: So what you're saying, really, is that I'm getting punished. Isn't that it?

Teacher: Yes, I think that would be a fair assessment. But I'm trying to punish you in a way that will also help you.

Stephen: If you really cared about me, then I think you would let me go. It's clear you don't care!

Teacher: But, you're wrong—I do care. Just as you care about me, but you cut the class anyway. You have to realize that sometimes punishment can be helpful, and I honestly believe it will be in this case.

> "When punishment is used, it should be used advantageously, to the benefit of the student; not simply as a retributive measure by the teacher."

In this way, the teacher was able to maintain a positive relationship with the student at the same time he administered "constructive punishment"—or, as Sommers (1972) calls it, "positive punishment."

Conclusions and Implications

We have examined in this section several views of punishment and a review of the research regarding its efficacy and legitimate application. Some conclusions are now in order.

First, we realize that when punishment is used, it should be used advantageously, to the benefit of the student; not simply as a retributive measure by the teacher. The research on punishment is plentiful, and Azrin and Holz (1966) have written a comprehensive review of it. Their conclusions are well worth stating in some detail, since they summarize many of the insights we have presented in this section:

We have seen that punishment can be quite effective in eliminating behavior. Let us imagine that we are given an assignment to eliminate behavior by punishment. Let us summarize briefly some of the circumstances which have been found to maximize its effectiveness: (1) The punishing stimulus should be arranged in such a manner that no unauthorized escape is possible. (2) The punishing stimulus should be as intense as possible. (3) The frequency of punishment should be as high as possible; ideally the punishing stimulus should be given for every response. (4) The punishing stimulus should be delivered immediately after the response. (5) The punishing stimulus should not be increased gradually but introduced at maximum intensity. (6) Extended periods of punishment should be avoided. . . . (7) Great care should be taken to see that the delivery of the punishing stimulus is not differentially associated with the delivery of reinforcing properties. (8) The delivery of the punishing stimulus should be made a signal or discriminative stimulus that a period of extinction is in progress. (9) The degree of motivation to emit the punished response should be reduced. (10) The frequency of positive reinforcement for the punished response should similarly be reduced. (11) An alternative response should be available which will not be punished but which will produce the same or greater reinforcement as the punished response . . . (12) If no alternative response is available, the subject should have access to a different situation in which he obtains the same reinforcement without being punished. . . . A reduction of positive reinforcement may be used as punishment when the use of physical punishment is not possible for practical, legal, or moral reasons.

Rachman and Teasdale (1969) discuss each of these points in considerable detail. While some are applicable primarily to the laboratory of behavior modification setting, others are directly relevant to the question of classroom punishment. We have extracted those principles that are applicable to the classroom setting, and display 12.1 offers the teacher a number of specific

1. Punishment should be used as a last resort. Although it has been shown to be an effective tool, it is not the most effective tool—and should be used sparingly!
2. Punishment, when administered, should immediately follow the undesirable behavior. It should also be consistently applied, to avoid arbitrariness.
3. As a constructive technique, punishment should be coupled with positive reinforcement to strengthen the student's desirable behavior.
4. Students should not be punished until it is determined that alternative behaviors are available to them. When necessary, the teacher may point out to the student some of these alternative behaviors.
5. Teachers should take great care that punishment administered by them does not destroy the positive qualities of their relationship with the student.
6. Constructive, positive punishment should be used instead of retributive punishment. Ideally, the student should be able to learn from his punishment.
7. The teacher should be careful to reward at no time the behavior that is usually punished. This leads to confusion in the student's mind. The principle of consistency must be enforced.
8. Since research regarding the efficacy of corporal punishment is scant, it should be avoided. Other strong, aversive punishing stimuli should be found. In general, the stronger the punishment, the more efficient it is.
9. The teacher must take care to avoid the tendency to repeat punishments that were administered to him in the past.

principles to be used in determining the frequency, strength, and indications for punishment in the classroom.

One last point should be mentioned. "Many teachers," Cangemi and Kahn (1973) point out, "use discipline methods that were used on them when they were in school." They feel that "the way their classroom forefathers treated them, although often harsh, was beneficial because they succeeded, they got their diplomas, their degrees, and their jobs" (p. 118). This compulsion to repeat the discipline of one's past, whether it is a teacher who is compelled to repeat it in the classroom or a parent compelled to repeat it in the home, should be avoided. It does little good, lacks all the credibility of scientific validity, and prevents the teacher from tackling the real question of what methods of punishment are most effective and which can be used most beneficially to facilitate growth in the classroom. The teacher should analyze his own feelings toward the ways he was punished to resolve any unconscious tendencies to repeat these patterns of punishment in the classroom.

Modeling

The behavioral learning principle of modeling occurs when an individual models himself or herself after another's behavior, even if not consciously aware of doing so. It is not even necessary to repeat the observed behavior in order to learn it through modeling: "When a person observes a model's behavior, but otherwise performs no overt responses, he can acquire the

> "In its most obvious form, modeling is learning by example. If the example is a positive one, then positive behavior will be the likely outcome; if the example is a negative one, then undesirable behavior will be the outcome."

modeled responses while they are occurring only in cognitive, representational forms" (Bandura, 1969).

In its most obvious form, modeling is learning by example. If the example is a positive one, then positive behavior will be the likely outcome; if, on the other hand, the example is a negative one, then undesirable behavior will be the outcome. Thus, the child who models himself or herself after the best behaved child in the class (perhaps because of the teacher's attitude toward this "good" child) will try to behave well, while the child who uses the class troublemaker as a model (perhaps because the teacher gives this student more attention) will tend toward disruptive behavior.

Krumboltz and Krumboltz (1972) point out that in all of our living, "the process of learning by modeling is inevitable. If teachers and parents could deliberately avoid being models themselves and refrain from providing examples of desirable behavior for youngsters, the youngsters would simply turn elsewhere for their models." They offer many examples of how we learn from modeling, one of which is:

Robbie enrolled in tenth-grade biology with the same perfunctory spirit with which he enrolled in any course. It was merely to fulfill a requirement.

The biology teacher, Mr. Barnett, was a favorite among many of the students in Robbie's class, especially the boys. He would occasionally plan short field trips during laboratory periods. At the request of some of the students he also devoted some of his Saturday mornings to taking longer field trips with students who volunteered. . . . Mr. Barnett asked many questions and encouraged his students to ask questions also. He was never satisfied with mere opinions. He insisted that the students answer questions from their own direct observations or the observations of scientists who wrote biological or reference books.

Robbie became an avid information seeker. He spent much of his free time on hikes looking for insects for his new collection. He kept a notebook on his "research work" and shared his findings enthusiastically with his classmates and family. (Krumboltz & Krumboltz, 1972, p. 62)

We see in this example the teacher as a positive model in the learner's intellectual and attitudinal development.

Designing and Implementing a Behavior Modification Program

There is at the present time a wealth of literature on the design and implementation of a behavior modification program in the school setting (Krumb-

> "One rule the teacher might keep in mind while designing a program is, Always strengthen positive behavior while weakening negative behavior."

oltz & Thoresen, 1969; Fargo, Behrens & Nolen, 1970; Bradfield, 1971), and we could do little justice to the complexity of this topic in the limited space available in this textbook. Instead, let us outline the general criteria of when to use a behavior mod program, and cite appropriate sources so that the teacher can refer directly to the most appropriate literature.

The first question that the teacher must ask is whether or not a behavior mod program is in order. Generally speaking, the indications for such a program are present in all classrooms. Often such programs are used to calm disruptive students or to increase motivation for learning. Besides these instances, however, we can say that wherever there are behavioral problems—whether it involves intellectual, emotional, or disciplinary problems—a behavior mod program should be considered.

After ascertaining that a behavior mod program is indicated, the teacher must then ask the critical question of what type of program should be considered. As noted above, there is a wide variety of behavior mod techniques available to the teacher. O'Keefe and Smaby (1973) discuss seven behavioral techniques particularly applicable to solving classroom disciplinary problems: positive reinforcement, extinction, contingency management, negative practice, pairing, time and systematic exclusion, and behavioral contract. Some of these techniques were discussed previously, and the others will be dealt with later in this section.

Generally, a combination of techniques is preferable to the use of a single technique. Extinction, for example, is best when combined with positive reinforcement. In the section on punishment, the basic rules of negative reinforcement were presented, and these included the combination of punishment with other behavioral techniques. In general, the teacher should remember this basic rule in determining the type of program to use: *Always strengthen positive behavior while weakening negative behavior*. Also, always look at the student's behavior as a whole—as a total response of the organism to its environment. In considering the type of program to be used, do not isolate some behaviors and disregard others. For example, if the child is misbehaving in the classroom, is this a bid for attention or is it a sign of the child's inability to control his actions, possibly even his musculature? Are other alternative behaviors available to the child? Display 12.2 lists some of the guiding principles that should help the teacher in determining what type of behavior modification design to use.

Once the type of program to be used is selected, the teacher must begin

1. What are the target behaviors to be changed? Are they readily identifiable?
2. Is the program to be directed at individual students or at the entire class? Would different target behaviors be appropriate for different students?
3. What type of contingencies have been planned and what input did the students have in selecting reinforcers?
4. Are the students aware of the appropriate behaviors that will lead to positive reinforcement?
5. How was the choice of conditioning techniques made? Was reference to the literature used to support the hypotheses?
6. Within what limits is the teacher required to work (i.e., is the teacher allowed to withhold a student's lunch, can she give the students money, what kinds of aversive stimuli can be used)?

implementing the program. The first step in implementation is the establishment of baseline data. This simply means recording and evaluating the behaviors at the beginning of the program. The simplest way to do this is with the use of color-coded index cards. Remember, what we want to find out is the total variety of student behavior, not just the negative behavior. We also want to know the degree of behavior—how frequently it occurs.

The indexing of behaviors is easily recorded in the following way. First, the teacher prepares five to ten index cards for each student, indicating the student's name on the top of each. Different-colored cards should be available so that each student can have his own color. Since there may be twenty-five to thirty-five students in a class, this is not always possible, so, instead, the teacher might use five different colors (white, salmon, green, blue, and buff are readily available), and cut the right corner off one batch and the left corner off another. In this way, the five colors and two diagonal cuts offer fifteen different, readily recognizable possibilities. In addition, the teacher can stripe with a bold, colored felt marker the tops of the cards, so that the color, cut, and stripe together offer well over thirty possibilities needed in the average classroom. Starting with a plain white card and using this system, here are some of the possibilities:

white rectangle, as is
left corner cut
right corner cut
as is, red-striped top
left corner cut, red-striped top
right corner cut, red striped top

Multiply by five colors and we have thirty different possibilities. Why is it so important to have easily identifiable cards, different for each student? Because the teacher will place these cards on the desk, and whenever a student exhibits a striking positive or negative behavior, the teacher will record it on a card, drawing out the student's card from the "deck." The easier it is to locate a

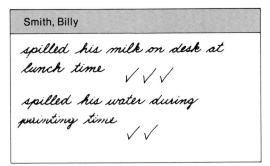

Smith, Billy

spilled his milk on desk at lunch time ✓ ✓ ✓

spilled his water during painting time ✓ ✓

The teacher records on each index card one type of behavior and then checks off the frequency of occurrence. On this card, two closely linked behaviors are recorded, with the idea of possibly combining them into one later on when the baseline list is prepared.

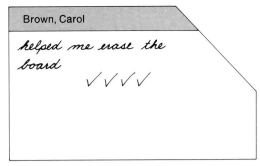

Brown, Carol

helped me erase the board ✓ ✓ ✓ ✓

Cutting the right or left upper edge off a card enables the teacher to more quickly find a student's card. The top of the cards may also be striped with a colored felt marker.

Figure 12.2

student's card, the less disruptive this recording process will prove to be. In a matter of days, the teacher will become familiar with each student's individual card, and will naturally reach for it upon noticing a student's particular behavior.

Figure 12.2 shows how these cards look when the teacher records behavior on them. The check marks indicate that the behavior was repeated again, and in this way the teacher keeps track of frequency as well as type of behavior.

When the teacher feels that he has enough information to design the program (and this usually takes two to three weeks), he tallies the information on master cards, one for each student. No color coding is necessary in this case, since the cards will be used for out-of-sight references. Figure 12.3 shows what one of these cards might look like. The negative behavior is recorded

Figure 12.3

Covington, Walter		TOTAL	
no homework	−4	answered ques.	+3
hit Mary	−2	washed bd.	+8
ran out of room	−9	did work at	
stole from supply		desk	+12
cab.	−7	told me when	
cried	−2	others were	
blew whistle	−12	fighting	+4
lost lunch money	−10		
fell asleep	−7		

After the teacher tallies each of the students' individual cards, a composite card such as the one above summarizes the positive and negative behaviors, along with the frequencies. This card will be used in determining the behavior that will be strengthened or weakened.

Approaches to Classroom Management 459

in one column on the card, and the positive behavior is recorded in a second column.

At this point, the first step of implementing a behavior modification program is completed. The teacher has in front of him a thorough inventory of behaviors, both those that should be strengthened and those that should be weakened. He may now begin to intervene, using the behavior modification techniques he has selected. One general principle should be elaborated here: While you continue to reinforce frequently occurring positive behaviors, special attention should be given to reinforcing those positive behaviors that occur with less frequency. The high frequency positive responses ("did work at desk"—Walter Covington) are probably already being positively reinforced and do not require any particular interventions.

Let us now look at some of the specific problems the teacher faces as he begins to use the behavior mod techniques.

Selection of Reinforcers The first question the teacher must ask if operant conditioning techniques are being used is, What are the most appropriate reinforcers? Laymen often think that tokens, toys, and candy are the most typical reinforcers, but this is simply not so. Reinforcers range from subtle gestures, to verbal compliments, to material rewards. The matter of most concern at this point is how the teacher selects the reinforcers: what criteria and guidelines govern the process of selection.

Viel and Galloway (1973), in tackling this problem, suggest that the students themselves determine the reinforcers. The teacher can use the method of "paired comparisons," in which "incentives are grouped in pairs and students are asked to select the one item from the pair that he likes best and would prefer to have," in order to determine the most effective reinforcers. The teacher can then easily prepare a list of the most and least effective reinforcers, which may also be used in future programs with the same group as was surveyed.

Addison and Homme (1966) have designed a "reinforcement menu," which presents to the student, in line drawings, a smorgasbord of possible rewards. This menu is shown to the student prior to his mastering a specific learning exercise, and if he satisfactorily completes the exercise, he is brought to a reinforcement area where he is immediately provided with his selection. One advantage of this technique is that it directly allows the student to select the reinforcement that is most motivating to him at the moment.

Premack's law may also be applied in the selection of reinforcement. "When a person's probability of choosing between any two responses is known," Premack (1965, p. 34) has stated, "one can increase the frequency of the less probable response. This is accomplished by making the availability of the more probable response contingent upon the prior occurrence of the less probable response." More simply, Premack's law says that one activity may be used to motivate a student to engage in another activity.

Example: In a junior high school, a separate room is designated as an audio room, in which several stereo sets, earphones, and a large record collection are provided. Students are shown the room and allowed to experiment briefly with the equipment. They are then given a behavioral task (i.e., to maintain order during lunchroom period), and promised an hour in the audio room if they complete the assignment. Immediately after they successfully complete the assignment, they are given the promised reward.

In a study using Premack's generalization on a second-grade class of culturally deprived children, Wasik (1970) found that the principle was effective in increasing the frequency of desirable behavior. Homme (1969) and his colleagues have applied the principle extensively to classroom management, and their manual would certainly have to be consulted by any teacher planning to apply this principle to classroom use.

The selection of reinforcers is critical to the ultimate success of the behavior modification program. While reinforcers are typically thought of in

terms of tokens or tangible rewards, many studies have demonstrated that praise, attention, and social esteem (peer approval) may be used equally as well for reinforcement. The teacher will have to assess the resources, and use his or her familiarity with the individual students, to determine the most effective reinforcements.

Implementing the Program The first part of the implementation, after the baseline data is established and the reinforcers selected (if operant methods are to be used), is establishing with all the subjects either a verbal or written contract that carefully sets forth the rules, contingencies, and consequences of various types of behaviors. Since every behavior mod program is a learning program, the teacher should take the same care and show the same specificity in creating the contract as he or she would ordinarily take in preparing material for and then teaching a lesson. The contract should avoid vagueness and arbitrariness; it should state specific behavior that will be rewarded and punished and pinpoint the exact rewards and punishing agents that will be consequent to each type of behavior. If behaviors that are not covered by the contract occur later, they may be written into the contract, but until they are, they must be considered outside the province of the program. The legal principle of ex post facto—that legislation cannot be enacted to punish crimes that have already occurred—applies equally as well to a behavior modification program. In many ways, the tightness of the contract will determine the strength of the program and its reinforcers.

A second and equally important consideration must be taken into account while the teacher is drawing up the contract. Who, besides the teacher, will be involved in the dispensing of reinforcement? If possible—and we are quick to recognize the difficulties involved—the parents and other school personnel should be drawn into the program as contingency agents, to work along with the teacher. If the program can be extended into the home, its effectiveness increases more dramatically. Moreover, Lindsley (1970) found that of five hundred behavior modification cases that were managed by nonprofessionals—mostly parents—85 percent succeeded on the first try, and all succeeded by the third try. Parents can be effective managers of behavior mod programs because they are with the child for so many hours and have the resources to observe all facets of behavior and dispense rewards and punishments.

The program is then implemented by carrying out the terms of the contract. At first, the students may attempt to have certain conditions of the contract waived, to find loopholes (if they are clever and sophisticated enough), or to get away with as much as they can. This should not disturb the teacher, for it is expected, natural behavior. The teacher may find that things don't work quite as well or quite as quickly as he or she expected, and may become discouraged, but again, this is natural. Nowadays, behavior modification is enshrouded in some type of mystique, so that hopes for immediate, permanent change raises expectations to levels that are sometimes higher than realistic.

During the implementation phase, the teacher will want to assess carefully which aspects of the program are working and which are not. By continuing to keep the coded index cards discussed earlier, the teacher will be able to ascertain the extent to which various parts of the program are effective. After several weeks, the teacher may wish to negotiate a new contract with the students in light of the assessment. A specific quantitative measure will be available as the teacher studies the new tallies of appropriate and inappropriate behaviors, and at some point the teacher may feel that new positive behaviors need to be strengthened and new negative behaviors need to be weakened.

Evaluating the Program

Briskin and Anderson (1973) report a case in which the inappropriate behaviors of two third-grade boys were treated through the use of behavior modification techniques. A careful look at this case will illustrate some of the points we have been discussing as well as demonstrate an innovative technique in which sixth-grade boys were used as the contingency managers.

Case Illustrations

Two troublesome third-grade boys, who were acting particularly disruptive, were the subjects of the program. During the stage of baseline observation, two major categories of disruptive behavior were noted:

1. verbal disturbances, including shouting, interrupting, making gutteral noises, whistling, and talking loudly without permission; and
2. physical altercations, including hitting, pushing, tripping, and throwing objects at classmates.

Two sixth-grade boys were selected as "learning assistants" who would manage the program. They were taught two behavioral techniques: time-out and positive reinforcement. In time-out, immediately after the occurrence of negative behavior, the subject is separated from the environment for a period of a few minutes. When one boy misbehaved, one of the learning assistants would take him out of the classroom for four minutes. "The only verbal interaction during the time-out was a short statement by the learning assistant telling the boy why he was asked to leave the room" (p. 264). If the boys required no or only one time-out during the period, they were positively rewarded by the learning assistant.

During the second phase of the intervention, the teacher took over the role as the chief contingency manager. "She was encouraged by the counselor to be specific in describing their appropriate behaviors to them" (p. 264). The principal also came into the program by speaking with the boy if he failed to leave the room when time-out was indicated. The counselor assisted the entire implementation. In this way, various concerned professionals and two nonprofessionals (the sixth-graders) worked as a team to help the third-grade boys develop appropriate behaviors.

The analysis of the results of the program consisted of comparing the number of inappropriate behaviors before the intervention procedures and afterwards. The data included in the analysis follows:

	Before intervention*	During*	After*
Boy 1	104	1.2	16
Boy 2	64	.7	8

* Average number of inappropriate behaviors per hour

We see that even though there was some resurgence of inappropriate behaviors after the implementation phase, on the whole, the program was quite successful.

This particular experiment illustrates several important points. First, the establishment of accurate, specific baseline data enabled the teacher to identify the behaviors that needed change and, later, to evaluate the effectiveness of the program. We see again how important the establishment of the baseline data is. Second, older students were used to assist in the program. This has the advantage of leaving the teacher free to work with the rest of the class, especially where time-out procedures are used. Third, a combination of procedures was used, rather than a single technique. And, finally, we see how successful the program was in correcting the inappropriate behaviors.

Effective Classroom Management

In chapter 10, "The Teacher as a Person," we pointed out how the personality of the teacher—his or her attitudes, interests, values, problems, conflicts, and fundamental beliefs—are integral to what happens in the classroom. Then, in chapter 11, "Theories and Processes of Teaching," we examined objective and subjective approaches to teaching methodologies. We considered ways in which the variables of the teaching-learning interaction can be organized into comprehensive models of teaching that explicate the process. In this chapter we have looked at the way in which behavioral techniques are employed to control and modify classroom behavior. Now, let us tie together the strands of our discussions to consider basic rules and applied principles for effective classroom management.

When the teacher approaches the teaching task, what is his or her attitude? Does the teacher view the task as the transmission of subject matter? Does the teacher concentrate on affective or cognitive growth at the expense of the other? How does the teacher view the role of the learner and what expectations of the learner are present at the outset? The answers to these questions determine, to a large extent, not only the teacher's style, method, and attitude but effectiveness as well.

The most effective approach to teaching is characterized by the teacher's recognition of the learner as a total person. This term, which is used unsparingly in professional literature, is not always clearly defined. We will use the definition provided by Carkhuff and Berenson (1967), which is compatible with most definitions offered: "The whole person does not merely live in the external world. *The life of the whole person is made up of actions fully integrating his emotional, intellectual, and physical resources in such a way that these actions lead to greater and greater self-definition*" (p. 197). The key point in this definition is that the whole person integrates his psychological, intellectual, and physical attributes in a productive way. Whenever the teacher directly or indirectly isolates one realm of the learner's experience from the other realms, the teacher inadvertently denies the existence of the whole, integrated, fully functioning person.

What this means in practice is that if the teacher emphasizes subject matter to the exclusion of personal growth, or uses behavioral techniques to the exclusion of psychodynamic principles, he or she is failing to deal with the total person.

On the other hand, when the teacher does recognize the total person— does consider the student's needs, interests, and abilities that manifest themselves at the moment—new opportunities for all kinds of growth open up. "The school," Montessori (1967) says, "must give the child's spirit space and opportunity for expansion. . . . This is the starting point of education." She goes on to describe this process in language that reveals her recognition of the total person:

If the teacher cannot recognize the difference between pure impulse, and the spontaneous energies which spring to life in a tranquilized spirit, then her action will bear no fruit. The true foundation of the teacher's efficiency consists in being able to distinguish between two kinds of activities, each of which has the appearance of spontaneity, because the child in both acts of his own free will, but which are in fact directly opposed. Only when the teacher has learned to discriminate can she become an observer and a guide. . . . This power to know good from bad is the light which disperses the shadows hiding the path to that discipline which leads to perfection. Is it possible to specify the symptoms, or syndromes, with sufficient clarity and precision to permit even a theoretical description of the stages through which the infant soul has to pass in its ascent towards discipline? Yes, it is possible. . . . (pp. 264–265)

What Montessori is suggesting is that when the teacher *really* understands the learner, he or she is able to distinguish between similar behaviors, some of which are constructive and lead to productive activities and some of which are detrimental to learning.

We can state, then, our first principles of effective classroom management:

1. The teacher recognizes that he or she is educating the total person. This means that the learner's intellectual, psychological, and physical development are recognized as integral to each other.
2. The teacher learns to distinguish between behaviors that are productive or detrimental to personal growth and development. This means understanding why the learner is behaving in a certain way, and appreciating what such behavior means.

We now turn our attention to ways in which the teacher manages those behaviors that have been determined to be detrimental—to the processes of classroom discipline.

Classroom Discipline

The term *discipline* evokes punitive connotations; we might, for example, picture the child with his hand outstretched waiting for the lash of a hickory rod, or sitting at his desk copying "I will be good" one hundred times as punishment. In reality, however, discipline is not synonomous with punishment, but if used properly, discipline is likely to be a constructive tool in the classroom. In a recent panel discussion on discipline, four educators and psychologists—John Holt, Haim Ginott, Lee Salk, and Donald Barr—considered what discipline means and if (and how) it can be used constructively in the classroom. "To me," Dr. Salk said, "discipline is an extension of an adult's concern for a child's welfare. Discipline is the limits set for a child so that he knows what's acceptable and what's not acceptable" (Holt et al., 1972). This view of discipline reveals one of its more positive sides. It shows the child that the teacher is concerned. Emphasizing that discipline is not punishment, Dr. Ginott defines discipline as "finding effective alternatives to punishment," pointing out that when the child is punished he becomes enraged, and "to enrage a child is to arouse hate in him. It makes him uneducable, unreachable, and unteachable. . . ." Donald Barr emphasizes a different aspect of the disciplinary process, one which is not traditionally included under the rubric of discipline: *conscience*. "One would hope that children developed a moral conscience," he argues, indicating that this development involves learning the values from parents and teachers. This learning is facilitated if the teacher makes *explicit* his or her values; if the teacher, in other words, is firm, but in a value-oriented and consistent manner. Holt's comment perhaps sums up all these positions: "It's not what we tell people," he says, "but how we treat them." In other words, if the child is treated in a manner that reflects order, discipline, and logical responses to situations, he will be much more likely to behave in such a way.

In the literature on discipline, which is extensive, certain key points are repeated over and over again. First, the recognition of discipline as a positive classroom approach is pointed out. Bossone (1964), for instance, sees discipline as "the training in self-control and in orderly social conduct brought about by desirable, effective classroom management" (p. 218). Discipline, when used properly, does not restrain the learner's natural curiosity and spontaneity, but actually encourages its natural, effective expression. This is what Montessori was talking about when she indicated that the teacher needs to develop the perspicacity to differentiate between spontaneous constructive expression and behavioral problems. The same theme recurs throughout many other educators' works. Pickering (1972) puts forth a cogent argument along the same lines:

> . . . a sound approach to childhood education will include both structure and freedom of choice, and will foster the development of freedom and discipline—that, in a system of conceptualizing the world which includes the ideas of society and interpersonal relations, discipline and freedom are coincidental, both in development and practice. (p. 115)

We see here again the emphasis on the compatibility between freedom and discipline. Pickering (1972) goes on to examine the conclusions of his position:

> . . . good programs for young children will be structured sufficiently to enable the young child to learn and to value social behaviors; such programs will be sufficiently "free" to enable children to pursue their own interest and, thus, to learn individual responsibility. *Well-rounded educational programs for young children will foster attitudes and behaviors which will promote the attainment of the ultimate freedom which is attainable in society—the ability to discipline oneself.* (p. 116)

Thus, one other positive advantage of discipline is that it leads to self-discipline, which leads to greater freedom. At this point, we can introduce two other principles:

3. As the teacher uses discipline constructively, the learner learns from the discipline behaviors that are socially productive and compatible with his or her own feelings and beliefs.
4. Discipline should be integral to the educational program itself. It is not intended exclusively for problem situations.

Of course, discipline does become an especially important issue when the teacher attempts to quell classroom disturbances. Here again, we can differentiate between discipline and punishment and examine how discipline can be used to bring the individual or class to order without causing damage

Constructive discipline can be an integral part of effective classroom management.

in the process. Carnot (1973) identifies three types of approaches generally used by teachers to establish discipline: (1) the authoritarian approach, (2) the permissive approach, and (3) the democratic approach. The democratic approach, he argues, is the best method, since it allows the child to develop internal controls upon himself and also shows the child that the teacher respects him as a person. "Democratic discipline," he argues, "usually provides guidance without domination and freedom without laxity. . . ." Again, we see the use of discipline as a learning tool.

Recognition of the constructive values of discipline impels us to find ways of making discipline more effective (in this positive sense). Purkey (1971) points out that the teacher's beliefs about pupils plays an important part in determining the pupils' conduct, and therefore conduct problems can be alleviated as the teacher gets in touch with his or her beliefs. Ediger (1973) suggests a number of steps to lessen the disciplinary problems in a classroom: examining lessons (to insure that the expectations of the teacher are in accord with the students' abilities), providing stimulating classroom lessons, keeping abreast of the students' progress, positively reinforcing the students' achievements. Most teachers do these things instinctively, but the teacher may have to honestly reevaluate each of these areas when confronted with an inordinate amount of disciplinary problems. It is not unusual for the teacher to find that he or she has seriously, although inadvertently, neglected one of these areas and that this has been the root of the problems.

Certain cautions are also involved in the dispensing of discipline. Before acting as disciplinarian, the teacher will want to be sure that he understands the causes of the problems. It is never sufficient to suppress disruptive behavior before it is understood. Quay et al. (1966) point out that "the environment, through discriminative stimuli and through response-reinforcement contingencies, is seen as the major influence determining the precise behavior repertoire of an individual child" (p. 510). The teacher might pay special attention to what, if anything, in the classroom environment is causing the disciplinary problems. Kaplan (1973) makes the important point that since behavior problems in the classroom generally involve student interaction, to decrease classroom behavior problems it is necessary to recognize and understand this interaction rather than just being concerned with restoring order as quickly as possible. He proposes a model (see figure 12.4) "that relates pupils' social adaptations in the classroom to various combinations of actions and feelings . . . The action dimension of a pupil's responses to his surroundings can be active or passive. . . ." By using this model, the teacher can better understand the feeling and the mode of adaptation used by the child and

Feelings	Actions	
	Active	Passive
Positive	(1) Initiator (seeks out success-oriented activities)	(2) Compliant follower (does exactly what is expected of him)
Ambivalent	(3) Competitor (fluctuates between success and failure)	(4) Fence sitter (does not finish work—makes simple errors)
Negative	(5) Disrupter (consistently refuses work—defiant)	(6) Withdrawer (consistently avoids work—evasive)

Figure 12.4   A Model for Relating Interactional Behaviors to the Dimensions of Action and Feeling. From "Classroom Discipline Is More than Technique," *Elementary School Journal,* 1973, *73,* p. 244. Used with permission.

get to the "root" of the problem rather than concentrating only on its superficial sign.

Two more principles can now be introduced:

5. When discipline is used to quell disruptions, the teacher should make every effort to recognize the causes and details of the problem before attempting to suppress the symptom.
6. The teacher should study how pupils interact to produce disruptive behavior in order to better understand the dynamics of the classroom and the source of problems.

Once the teacher has established that an intervention is necessary, the question becomes, What kind of intervention should be made?

Teacher Interventions   Several types of behavioral interventions have been discussed in this chapter. The use of an appropriate intervention depends upon the situation, the learner, and the teacher's repertoire. After all, we recognize that there are some teachers who know only one or two interventions, and are therefore limited in what will be used. The well-rounded teacher who recognizes the importance of educating the whole person tries to develop a repertoire of interventions that will be appropriate to the largest number of learners in the greatest number of situations.

Any given intervention, although effective in some situations, may not be effective in other situations. Palardy (1970), for example, cites weaknesses of behavioral interventions and stresses the need to instill self-discipline in students. Koppel (1972) points out several ways in which teachers mishandle discipline problems, including punishing the entire class when only a few of the students were misbehaving. We all know, from our own experiences, how damaging the wrong intervention can be. Using the right technique at the right time is something that only the teacher's intuition and sensitivity can insure.

Conclusions and Implications

In this chapter, we examined ways in which the application of behavioral learning theory contributes to effective classroom management. Using the principles of operant conditioning, extinction, positive reinforcement, negative reinforcement, and punishment, we paid special attention to the role of the teacher as an organizer of contingencies, a dispenser of rewards and punishments.

In considering the implementation of a behavior modification program, we have tried to maintain our perspective of the total person. While it is easy enough to focus on behaviors and exclude the more complex totality of the individual, we believe that it is necessary to view every behavior within the interpersonal context of the individual. Several principles of effective classroom management, based on this point of view, were elaborated.

Combining the insights of this chapter with those of the two preceding chapters, we can draw several conclusions, which we list in the form of statements. These are not prescriptive statements, designed to tell the teacher what to do, but rather ideas that every teacher—who takes his task seriously—has to think about, make decisions about, and cannot afford to ignore. The statements are as follows:

1. Teaching and learning are related concepts, but not in a one-to-one ratio. Because something has been learned does not mean something has been taught; because something has been taught does not mean something has been learned. Teaching involves much more than simply showing someone how to do something. It is this "much more" that every teacher has to decide about.
2. There are recognized and unrecognized variables in the teaching process. Two key variables—usually recognized—are teacher and learner. But beyond these, each brings to the classroom setting other variables—personality variables, attitudinal variables, intellectual variables, physical variables, aptitudinal variables, ideological variables, and so forth—and these too must be recognized. In addition, there are variables present in the setting itself (the administration, prescribed curriculum, the physical plant) over which the teacher and learner may have little, if any, control. The more variables that are recognized, the more effective the teacher becomes.
3. Teaching can be conceptualized broadly or narrowly. On the one hand, we can think of teaching only in terms of subject matter: What is it that is to be taught? On the other hand, teaching can be viewed as an almost transcendental encounter between two people. Teaching models help us to articulate our view of the teaching process, and the range of these models is as vast and diverse as the range of teaching styles found in the classrooms of our schools.
4. Any considerations of the teaching process must take into account such categories as motivation, readiness, method of instruction, goals, perception of the learner, role of the teacher, and other factors. The way a teacher arrives at conclusions about each of these is generally a reflection of his or her view of the person. Each of us brings into the teaching setting a philosophy; and this philosophy is invariably reflected in our teaching.
5. There are a number of practical questions that all teachers have to consider at one time or another. How stern or flexible should I be in the classroom? Is a laissez-faire approach practical with the children in my class?

Do I approve or disapprove the material I am required to teach? What support do I have from my colleagues and from the administration? There are hundreds of other questions, too, but the point is this: *Each teacher strives toward what he or she considers effective classroom management, and this goal is linked to many other questions that should be articulated.* Empirical research can support many different points of view—pro and con corporal punishment, for example—and the teacher should honestly ask why he is selecting what he is selecting from the bulk of research; what biases influence his choices.

6. The taxonomy of the affective domain, which was discussed in chapter 7, is indicative of the stages of growth that are integral to all kinds of learning. The effective teacher will want to ask, "How well am I responding to the emotional needs of my students? What am I doing to facilitate growth in all areas of human functioning?"

Summary

In this chapter, we applied basic principles from the psychology of learning to the classroom setting. Specific procedures for choosing the type of behavior modification program were discussed, and the practical aspects of implementation were considered. Some principles of effective classroom management, based on the recognition of educating the total person, were presented. These principles included the pros and cons of discipline as a teaching (or classroom) technique.

Suggested Additional Readings

Changing Children's Behavior by John D. Krumboltz and Helen B. Krumboltz (*Englewood Cliffs, N.J.: Prentice-Hall, 1972*)

This practical guide offers the teacher and counselor step-by-step directions for using behavior modification techniques to change specific behaviors. Many excellent case illustrations are used throughout.

In real life rewards are not always presented immediately after improved behavior. In some cases rewards are delayed weeks, months, or years after the behavior occurs.

from *Changing Children's Behavior*

Behavior Modification of Learning Disabilities, ed. by Robert H. Bradfield
(*San Rafael, Calif.: Academic Therapy Publications, 1971*)

This book is more technical than the one above. It is rich in research, but maintains a practical dimension. The contributions each offer are specific guidelines for modifying learning disabilities with the use of behavioral techniques.

Involving a parent or teacher in the evaluation process enables the referring agent to collaborate with the diagnostician on the determination of target behaviors specified for subsequent treatment.

from *Behavior Modification of Learning Disabilities*

Specializing Education Behaviorally by R. Douglas Greer and Laura G. Dorow
(*Dubuque, Iowa: Kendall/Hunt Publishing Co., 1976*)

This book represents a detailed application of behavioral principles to special education. The reader is shown how to set up a behavior-modification program, and numerous exercises are included for review. An index of behaviors that are corrected is appended.

Behaviors increase because there are reinforcers in the environment which cause them to increase; behaviors decrease because there are punishers in the environment which decrease them. The reason the behaviors change is a function of environmental factors.

from *Specializing Education Behaviorally*

Instruction

An attempt is made to differentiate instruction from teaching: Instruction is viewed as a part of the total teaching process. Several instructional approaches are considered. Competency-based instruction, which relies on individualized programming, is discussed, and the basic axioms of CBI (competency-based instruction) are outlined. Peter's model of individual instruction, which uses the concepts of *elicitor*, *behavioral response*, and *reinforcer*, and Glaser's division of instruction between *component* and *content* repertoires are considered individually.

The Contributions of Cybernetics to Instructional Theory

Cybernetics is a discipline that attempts to explain how a system regulates itself through the processing of information. This can include the system "teacher-learner," and thereby has special applicability to the school setting. The concepts of "closed" and "open" feedback loops as information-processing models are discussed. Examples are given of teachers using each type of model. Some applications of cybernetic principles to instructional procedures include computer-assisted instruction (CAI) and using evaluative tools to assess how much information the learner is processing at a given time.

Methods of Teaching

A teaching method differs from an instructional method in that it is more comprehensive. The teaching method is always colored by the teacher's biases, values, and personality in general. The purpose of a teaching method is to maximize the student's readiness to learn; to make available the subject matter in a way that can be appreciated; to provide rewards for learning; and to resolve intellectual or emotional problems that are thwarting teaching or blocking learning.

Continued

13 Elements of Instruction: A Survey and Synthesis

Presenting Subject Matter

Several methods for presenting subject matter are examined: the lecture method, discussion method, project method, and recitation. The simulated environments technique involves setting up classroom models of real social situations. Teaching games and programmed instruction, two other methods used for the presentation of subject matter, are also considered. The analysis of "structure in teaching" by O. Roger Anderson is discussed, and his pedagogical model evaluated.

The Lesson

A lesson model involving three main sections—input, interaction, and experience—is presented. INPUT includes all print, media, verbal, and environmental contents of the lesson. INTERACTION represents the teacher-learner dialogue and may be structured toward convergent or divergent experiences. The EXPERIENCE is the student's reaction to the *input* via the *interaction*. Specific components of these three sections of the lesson are examined with respect to the basic ordering and structuring of the classroom lesson. The design of a traditional lesson plan is outlined.

Elements of Instruction: A Synthesis

Instruction is an integral part of the teaching process, and there are a number of things the teacher can do to facilitate its effect. Fourteen principles of learning, which embody the goals of instruction, are considered.

476

There is an apocryphal story about a professor of educational psychology who studied for years the unusual methods of teaching used in Zen Buddhism. No matter how many books he read, however, he was unable to grasp fully how this strange system of teaching worked, for, after all, it was a far cry from what we, as Westerners, think of when we use the term teaching.

During his sabbatical year, he travelled to Japan, where high in the mountains, inaccessible to most travelers, lived a famous teacher of Zen. It took the professor many weeks to make arrangements for a guide to lead him to the teacher, and many more weeks to make the arduous journey through the rugged mountain terrain. Finally, weary almost to the point of exhaustion, he reached the famous Zen teacher's house.

The teacher welcomed him in, and the professor explained his purpose. "I have come to you," he said "to learn the Way of Zen."

The teacher laughed. "I will be glad to teach you the Way of Zen. But first, a cup of tea."

He handed the professor a cup and poured from an empty kettle. Of course nothing came out, and the professor looked up quite startled.

"Tell me when you have enough tea," the Zen teacher said, quite seriously.

"But nothing is coming out!" the professor protested.

"Then you shall never have enough," the Zen master answered, quite cheerfully.

"Of course not," the professor responded, with a hint of agitation.

"Well, then," the master retorted, fully satisfied, "you do understand the Way of Zen."

If this little story, called a **koan** in Zen terminology, makes little or no sense to you, don't feel bad; it's not supposed to. Zen is, after all, a system that is not directly expressed through words; words are far too limiting for its purposes. "Zen Buddhism presents a surface so bizarre and irrational," Barrett (1956) points out, ". . . that some Westerners who approach it for the first time fail to make sense of it. . . ." But although we cannot make sense of it, although the koan is a "bizarre and irrational" idea of a teaching method, it will shed some light on the distinctions between teaching and instruction, between types of instruction, and between the different elements of instruction that merge together in the teaching process.

D. T. Suzuki, the single individual most responsible for introducing the teachings of Zen Buddhism to the English-speaking world, explains the derivation and contemporary meaning of the koan:

Ko-an literally means "a public document" or "authoritative statute". . . . It now denotes some anecdote of an ancient master, or a dialogue between master and monks, or a statement or question put forward by a teacher, all of which are used as the means for opening one's mind to the truth of Zen. . . . The *koan* is neither a riddle nor a witty remark. It has a most definite objective, *the arousing of doubt and pushing it to its furthest limits.* (Suzuki, 1949, p. 236)

The koan about the professor and the Zen master should, if nothing else, encourage us to think about what will soon emerge as the subject matter of this chapter. What is instruction? What principles are behind theories of instruction, and what are the processes of instruction? Is there some way to integrate the many different approaches to instruction, to formulate a comprehensive model? These are but a few of the questions we will attempt to answer in this chapter.

We will begin with an examination of the concept of **instruction** and differentiate *instruction* from **teaching,** while discussing several specific instructional theories. We will then turn our attention to the contribution of **cybernetics** to instructional theory and examine some of the implications of this research. Later, we will expand our view to include instructional and teaching methods and their applications in the classroom. Finally, we will examine the lesson itself as a natural synthesis between teaching and instruction, between learning and growing, between **convergent** and **divergent** thought, between conformity and spontaneity; in short, we will examine the lesson as the ideal means through which learning can take place.

Instruction

There is no clear-cut distinction between the terms *instruction* and *teaching,* although it is generally agreed that instruction is one type of teaching. The etymology of the word *instruction* may shed some light on its meaning. It is a derivative of the Latin verb *instruere,* which means to erect, pile up things, arrange, or build. If we look at the dictionary definitions of *instruct* and *instruction,* something quite interesting is revealed:

in·struct (in-strukt′), *v.t.* [< L. *instructus,* pp. of *instruere,* to pile upon, put in order, erect; *in-,* in, upon + *struere,* to pile up, arrange, build], 1. to communicate knowledge to; teach; educate. 2. to give the facts of the matter to; inform: as, a judge *instructs* the jury. 3. to give directions or orders to: as, the officer *instructed* the sentry to shoot.—*SYN.* see command, teach.

in·struc·tion (in-struk′shən), *n.* [ME. *instruccioun;* OFr. *instruccion;* L. *instructio*], 1. an instructing; education. 2. knowledge, information, etc. given or taught; any teaching; lesson. 3. *pl.* directions; orders.[1]

We see that although there are three different meanings for the verb and for the noun, the tendencies of these meanings is toward the idea of direction,

1. With permission. From *Websters New World Dictionary of the American Language,* Second College Edition. Copyright © 1976 by William Collins, World Publishing Co., Inc.

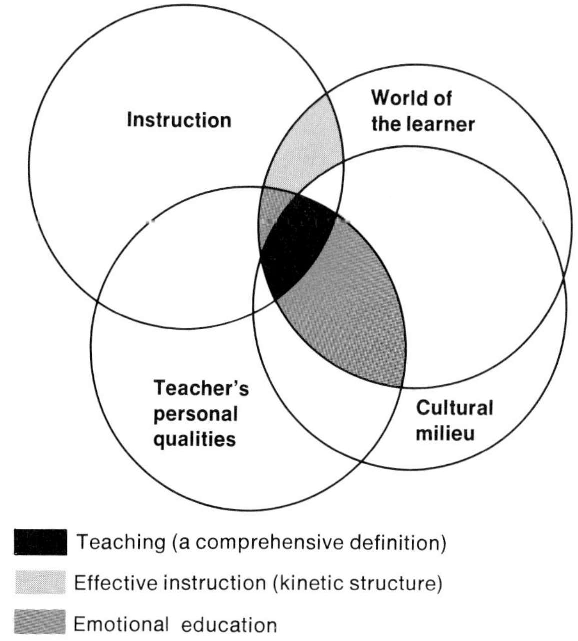

Figure 13.1 Instruction as an Element in Teaching

Teaching (a comprehensive definition)

Effective instruction (kinetic structure)

Emotional education

command, orders. When we instruct someone we show them what to do, we "give" them some kind of information, we "direct" them. Teaching is a broader category, as we pointed out in chapter 11, of which instruction is an important element.

Thus, the difference between teaching and instruction is this: *teaching includes instruction and other activities that are psychological, social, and personal.* Figure 13.1 shows the relationship between these factors.

This idea of a broader inclusive term—teaching—and a more restricted term—instruction—enables us to gain a better perspective of the total teaching situation. While we directed our energies in chapter 11 to conceptualizing and analyzing teaching as a theory and as a process, in this chapter we will look more specifically at instruction, and its relevant elements. To avoid mechanistic reasoning, we shall attempt to integrate into our discussion some of the major points of view from the preceding chapters.

While the general idea behind all instructional approaches involves the transmittal of information, of subject matter, from teacher to student, the means by which this is accomplished varies a great deal. One popular instructional approach that has gained increasing recognition in recent years is called **competency-based instruction.** "Competency-based instruction," Nagel and Richman (1972) point out, "is a rather high-sounding collection of words that means in essence a flexible, individualized program that frees both stu-

Instructional Approaches

Figure 13.2 The Axioms of Competency-Based Instruction. From *Competency-Based Instruction: A Strategy to Eliminate Failure* by T. S. Nagel and P. T. Richman (Columbus, Ohio: Charles E. Merrill Publishing Co., 1972). Reprinted by permission.

1. In traditional programs
time is held constant while achievement varies,
while in a competency-based program
achievement is held constant while time varies.

2. Traditional programs place greatest weight
on entrance requirements,
while competency-based programs place greatest stress
on exit requirements.

3. If you want somebody to learn something,
for heaven's sake tell him what it is!

4. Competency-based instruction equals
criterion-referenced instruction plus
personalization of instruction

dents and teachers to work at their own rates without the fear of failure" (p. 1). They list axioms that differentiate CBI from traditional instructional models (figure 13.2, above). The major advantage of CBI is that it allows students to master material at a rate that is appropriate for them, and eliminates unnecessary and counterproductive competitiveness that infuses so many educational efforts.

A closely related model is Peter's model of *individual instruction*. This model, which is similar to Becker, Englemann and Thomas's three-step-process model of teaching (see p. 418) utilizes three elements: **elicitor** (E), **behavior** (B), and **reinforcer** (R). Figure 13.3 shows the basic components of the model. The theory of instruction behind this model is essentially the behavioral theory, although specific applications of behavioral psychology produce special instructional adaptations. While one might argue that this is a teaching model as well as an instructional model, according to the criteria of figure 13.1, it would probably be more accurate to include it under instructional models (since it does not account for the personal and socio-cultural elements implicit in teaching).

Analyses of instruction generally take one of two basic forms: an analysis of behaviors involved in the instructional process and/or an analysis of the content, or subject matter, of the instructional process. Robert Glaser (1969) who has written in detail on the subject of instruction, differentiates between what he calls *component* and *content* repertoires: "The importance of the analysis of subject matter competence is emphasized by the distinction between *component* and *content* repertoires. **Content** repertoire refers to a

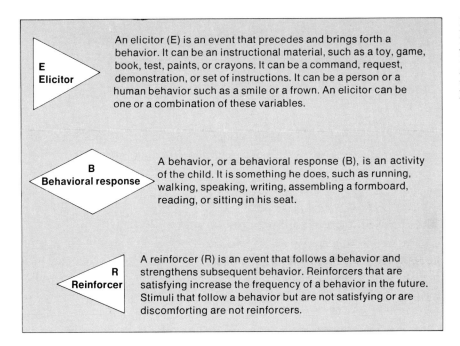

Figure 13.3 Peter's Model of Individual Instruction. Laurence J. Peter, *Competencies for Teaching: Individual Instruction* (Belmont, Calif.: Wadsworth Publishing Company, Inc., 1975), pp. 15–16.

An elicitor (E) is an event that precedes and brings forth a behavior. It can be an instructional material, such as a toy, game, book, test, paints, or crayons. It can be a command, request, demonstration, or set of instructions. It can be a person or a human behavior such as a smile or a frown. An elicitor can be one or a combination of these variables.

E
Elicitor

A behavior, or a behavioral response (B), is an activity of the child. It is something he does, such as running, walking, speaking, writing, assembling a formboard, reading, or sitting in his seat.

B
Behavioral response

A reinforcer (R) is an event that follows a behavior and strengthens subsequent behavior. Reinforcers that are satisfying increase the frequency of a behavior in the future. Stimuli that follow a behavior but are not satisfying or are discomforting are not reinforcers.

R
Reinforcer

subject matter analysis; component repertoire refers to a behavioral analysis" (p. 181). He directs attention to **component** repertoire and examines its implications:

From the point of view of instruction, the practical requirement for component repertoire analysis is to identify the kind of behavior involved so that the learner can be provided with instructional procedures and environmental conditions which best facilitate the learning of that kind of behavior. The underlying assumption is that the learning of various kinds of component repertoires requires different kinds of teaching procedures, and a research task is to identify the learning processes and appropriate instructional procedures associated with different component repertoires. (p. 182)

The implications of this, he points out, are that greater focus is directed toward the *processes* of learning, and that instructional procedures are guided by "process," or "instructional objectives." "Emphasis is placed on such behaviors as generating hypotheses, selecting fruitful hypotheses, testing hypotheses and deciding upon experiments, and on the more generalized traits of a scientist, such as perseverance and curiosity." In other words, it is not the curriculum of learning itself that becomes of paramount importance, but rather the curriculum of behaviors that comprise (in toto) the processes of learning through which the learner masters the subject matter. This recognition of the learner's world in relation to the content (subject matter) repertoires is indicated on figure 13.1 by the dotted area (effective instruction).

Having now considered a few of the general instructional approaches, or models, let us examine the basic principles of cybernetics, which we shall then apply to these approaches, expanding our understanding and exploiting their rich possibilities.

The Contribution of Cybernetics to Instructional Theory

Cybernetics is a discipline developed by Norbert Weiner, an American mathematician, during the late 1940s. It is a science of communication that analyzes control and regulating principles, generally between machines and persons, but defined more broadly, between one person and another or between one system and another. In this section, we shall explain briefly the science of cybernetics, and then apply these principles to educational problems. No attempt will be made to explicate comprehensively the many subtleties of cybernetics; but rather, to extrapolate and interpret in nontechnical language those principles that are particularly relevant to the classroom teacher.

The Science of Cybernetics   **Cybernetics** attempts to explain how a system regulates itself through the processing of information. By *system,* we can mean a computer, an automobile, a teacher, a student, an entire society, an educational institution, or almost anything else. By *regulates,* we mean that this system changes in some respect—either in behavior, in tendency, in organization, or in its ability to process new information or process old information in a new way. Most important to the study of cybernetics is the interaction between more than one system as information is transmitted between them.

It is important to mention that cybernetics, although it is often associated with computers, robots, and complex mechanical equipment, takes into its purview any system—human or mechanical—that can be analyzed as a functioning system. It is a synthetic discipline, drawing from many different areas of science in "an attempt to bring together and reexamine lines of research that had formerly been pursued in isolation. We might call it a 'crossroads of the sciences'. . . . Its only function is to devise new and fundamental techniques of research and analysis, which each specialist can then apply in more specific forms to his own field" (Guilbaud, 1959, pp. 4–5). What holds cybernetics together as a discipline is its focus on the processing and feedback of information within and between systems.

> "In a closed-loop system 'the desired behavior of the system is compared with the actual behavior and the difference is used to constrain the actual behavior of the system to approach the desired behavior.' "

There are a number of basic ideas that underlie all cybernetic thinking. First, and foremost, is the concept of the **feedback loop.** When two systems interact, with the first conveying information to the second, the second effecting a change, which in turn requires the first to communicate new information to the second—this is the concept of the feedback loop. The most common example of this is the interaction between a household thermostat and the heating system. A continuous feedback loop exists between them.

A feedback loop may be closed or open. An open-loop control system might be illustrated as follows (Porter, 1969, p. 6):

A

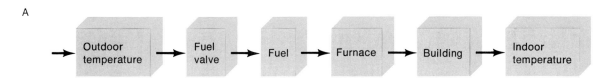

In this system a central heating system is controlled by measuring the outside temperature and varying the amount of heat according to this temperature. It is an open loop because the heat in the house does not feed back to the central sensor as would occur in a closed-loop system, illustrated as follows:

B

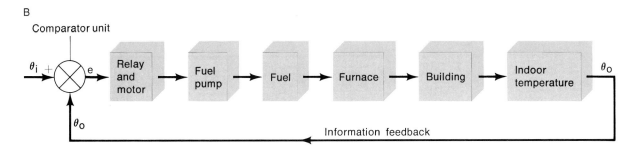

In this illustration—typical of a home thermostat—as the house temperature changes, the heat output is regulated accordingly.

The difference between close-loop and open-loop systems may be stated simply as follows: In a closed-loop system "the desired behavior of the system is compared with the actual behavior and the difference is used to constrain the actual behavior of the system to approach the desired behavior" (Porter, 1969, p. 8).

This seems complex, but it can be illustrated quite simply, using the classroom as a situation and the student and teacher as the two systems:

Example: Teacher A prepares a plan of individualized student assignments, based upon the student's reading scores on a test administered at the beginning of the school year. No matter how well or how poorly the students do on the assignment, the basic plan remains the same because it is based on the information from the test at the beginning of the year. The plan is changed as the students' scores change on subsequent tests, but not directly in response to their performance on the assignments themselves. This is an example of an open-loop system.

Teacher B, on the other hand, does not prepare the plan of assignments in advance, but rather looks at the student's performance on the last assignment to determine the next assignment. Thus, actual performance (how the student did) and desired performance (what the teacher expected he could do) are compared before the next assignment is made. This is an example of a closed-loop feed-back system.

A second concept, which is basic to cybernetic thinking, is the idea of measurement of information. How can we adequately measure the amount of information communicated between one system and another in such a way that our measurement is most basic and simple to use and apply? In order to answer this question, it is first necessary to define ways in which information can be measured. The smallest unit of information is called a "bit," and all other information is made up of bits. While this type of system is particularly useful in computer technology, it can be helpful, too, to the classroom teacher by enabling the teacher to carefully measure what is taught and what is learned in small units of information. Some of the techniques of measurement, discussed in chapter 16, can be used to evaluate the flow of information in the classroom setting between the teacher and the learner, using some of the basic principles of information measurement derived from cybernetic theory.

Finally, cybernetics has contributed the concept of *model,* which is a mathematical, or other, representation of a system or interaction of systems. When we attempt to represent the teacher-student interaction in some type of symbolic format we are drawing directly from the theory of cybernetics. For example, the basic teaching model described in chapter 6 is based on the principles of cybernetics.

Cybernetics and Instructional Methods

We have now looked at some of the basic principles of cybernetics, albeit rather hastily and without engaging in some of the technical mathematical and engineering principles that this discipline comprises. Now we shall examine some specific principles of cybernetics applied to problems and strategies of instruction.

First, and foremost, since instruction is in part—perhaps to the greatest part—a process that involves the transmission of information to effect changes in behavior—the "systems" concept of cybernetics is particularly

> "Since instruction is in part a process that involves the transmission of information to effect changes in behavior, the 'systems' concept of cybernetics is particularly relevant in thinking about teaching problems."

The use of technology for instructional purposes is indicative of cybernetic principles.

relevant and helpful in thinking about teaching problems. Our definition of **system,** as you recall, was rather global, allowing for such diverse systems as a thermostat, a nuclear sensor, or a teacher or student. The student can always be considered a separate, integrated, functioning system, as can the teacher, or teaching machine—whatever the case may be.

The student-as-system, of course, comprises a number of subsystems. Broadly, we may speak of the motor coordination system, the cognitive system, the system of processing affect, and so forth. All of these systems interplay in the relationship between the teacher and student, and the teacher may at times direct his efforts toward one system or another or toward all systems together—toward the total person.

Central to the implementation of cybernetic principles is the conscientious and carefully planned use of a closed feedback loop. What this means, in practical terms, is that the information from the student is used by the

teacher in the planning and presentation of subsequent lessons. When we look at teaching methods in the following section, we will see how some methods fail to use this principle (the lecture method, for example) and how other methods make full use of it (the discussion method). We will also consider the techniques employed with programmed learning approaches, particularly teaching machines, which are clear examples of the application of cybernetic principles to teaching.

In every classroom, there are numerous occasions in which the insights from cybernetics are helpful to the teacher in understanding problems—particularly learning blocks. Since learning involves the processing of information, usually in sequential stages, teachers can break down the processes of learning into relative steps—into bits of information—and attempt to determine at what level the information is no longer being adequately processed. In this sense, cybernetic principles are used as diagnostic aides.

Finally, we should mention the use of cybernetics in curriculum development. Harnack (1968), who has written about the teacher as a decision maker and curriculum planner, speaks about the teacher's role in making choices about what to teach and how to teach it. These choices are multiple contingencies, related to each other, and application of basic cybernetic principles of decision making can certainly prove helpful. To this end, some knowledge of decision theory (in cybernetics) can be beneficial.

Probably the most notable application of cybernetic principles to education is the use of **computer-assisted instruction.**

Computer-assisted instruction (CAI) is not designed to replace the teacher, nor is it intended as an end product in itself; rather, as the key word, *assisted,* tells us, it is primarily of adjunctive value. Stolurow (1969), who has written extensively on this subject, sees CAI as a possible means for the problem of getting a grasp on the plethora of media available to the teacher today. CAI is primarily a tool designed for efficiency. It enables individual instruction to take place without compromising the resourcefulness of the teacher, student, or programmer. "If we look at the problem of information dissemination as a teaching problem," Stolurow (1969) argues, ". . . then the mass media in general are deficient. It is obvious that all of these media—books, film, radio, audio systems, and television—suffer from the same problem. *None of them communicates on an individualized basis"* (pp. 270–271). CAI is designed to resolve this difficulty.

CAI is a direct application of cybernetic principles:

In a CAI system, the computer integrates sensory and motor devices into a response-dependent, or cybernetic, instructional system which, at a minimum level, provides a multi-media environment for learning and all the capabilities of extant programmed instruction. (p. 277)

Thus, CAI represents a true merging of personal teaching and cybernetic principles of instruction.

Now, we shall turn our attention to methods of teaching, keeping in mind these principles of instructions we have considered in this chapter.

Methods of Teaching

There are certain difficulties inherent in attempts to discuss teaching method as if it were some abstract principle distinct from the teacher and learner themselves. In most cases, teaching is a very personal relationship between teacher and student, an echo of the harmony between them, and any attempt to present the method apart from its application could only turn out an unprofitable exercise in abstraction. Although a teaching method is built on a formal foundation, an underlying theoretical basis (such as a learning theory),

> "The classroom method, as it is applied by the teacher, is colored by the idiosyncratic tints and shades of his own personality."

the actual method, as it is practiced by each teacher, adapts to his or her unique individuality. In unapplied form, as it appears on the printed page of a textbook, the method is as indistinctive and universal as a typical artst's palette; the teacher, like the artist, blends and applies the elements from the palette in his own unique style, transforming an infinity of possibilities into a concrete, personal expression, distinctively his own. The classroom method, in other words, as it is applied by the teacher, is colored by the idiosyncratic tints and shades of his own personality, which ultimately give it its form.

A teaching method differs from an instructional method in that it is more comprehensive: It takes into account all of the problems that attend classroom efforts. These problems are not limited to what we ordinarily call "learning problems": that is, obstacles which block or impede the learning process itself. Actually, a method includes within its purview not only the students' pre-learning and post-learning problems, but the teacher's pre-teaching and post-teaching problems as well (as we saw earlier in Smith's paradigm). Because a teaching method is concerned with classroom situations that are universal—readiness, motivation, presentation, reinforcement, communication and feedback, and so forth—it must be relevant to all disciplines as well as to all levels of education. It should be as appropriate for the teaching of science as it is for the teaching of art; as applicable in a first-grade classroom as it is in a graduate seminar.

The purpose of a teaching method, if we wish to cite a single purpose, is to maximize the student's readiness to learn, to make available the subject matter in a way that it can be appreciated, to provide rewards for learning (either built-in intrinsic reward or teacher-dispensed extrinsic rewards), and to resolve intellectual or emotional problems that are thwarting teaching or blocking learning; in short, to make the educative process as pleasurable, productive, and conflict-free as possible. This can be accomplished by recognizing and controlling, within the boundaries of the classroom, the myriad forces (variables) that influence all learning efforts.

Psychotherapeutic methods differ from most teaching methods in their emphasis on the **psychodynamic,** affective dimensions of learning. They are designed more for motivation than inculcation; they are concerned more with the desire for learning than with the mechanics of learning; they are directed more to what the student *feels* than to what he *thinks*. While the ultimate goal of these methods is effective teaching and personal growth, their emphasis is on the psychology of the learner, and not subject matter per se. More tra-

> "Traditionally, the teacher has been thought of as a guide, whose job it is to lead his pupils through the winding and elusive paths of knowledge to intellectual mastery."

ditional methods, on the other hand, focus primarily on subject matter and measure performance by how much has been learned. We shall consider both types of methods in this chapter, paying particular attention to how they can be combined in order to educate the total person.

Each method has certain implication about how we view the teacher. The discrepancies between these approaches reflect an underlying discrepancy about how the teacher is perceived, what is the appropriate role of the teacher in the educative process, what *should* the teacher be doing (which leads to the question of *how*).

Traditionally, the teacher has been thought of as a guide, whose job it is to lead his pupils through the winding and elusive paths of knowledge to intellectual mastery. He is a leader (*pedagogue*), and adviser (*mentor*), and a builder (*instructor*), as the roots of these words show. The tradition of teaching methodologies, built on this assumption, is held together by a common pursuit, to find the most expeditious way to navigate this path.

Most traditional teaching methodologies, therefore, are concerned with such matters as how to make a class behave so that they will be ready to learn; how to make the subject matter interesting and stimulating so that they will want to learn; how to organize and present subject matter so that they will be able to learn; how to test and measure knowledge to find out what they have learned. And, indeed, if the teacher is a guide, this may well be his itinerary.

But is he a guide? Is he a man of wisdom, leading his pupils along the paths of knowledge? Is he a direction post, advising his students where to turn at every juncture? While there is a tendency to say yes to all of these questions—let us consider them for a moment.

Let us consider, for example, a situation where the teacher is clearly not a guide, but rather, a man who teaches in silence. There are many such cases. John Singer, the deaf-mute in Carson McCullers's novel, *The Heart Is a Lonely Hunter,* taught his friends to look into their own hearts without ever uttering a single word. Rabbi Saunders, in Chaim Potok's *The Chosen,* following a Hasidic tradition, teaches his own son in silence. Zen tracts are replete with stories of great teaching masters who never spoke, and yet taught magnificently. How can we reconcile this with the image of the teacher as a guide? How can we call a silent man a teacher?

Or, consider another problem: the teacher who speaks, but is not heard. The teacher whose words echo noiselessly through the corridors of empty schools. The teacher whose roar resonates as a whisper. If he is a guide, he is a guide without followers. What good is a teaching method to this man if it does not include ideas for engaging a following?

Then, again, there is the teacher whose pupils hear but do not listen, or, listen but do not heed. The teacher whose students waylay him along the path to knowledge and rob him of his patience, time, and effort. He is the guide of a mutinous crew. Of what benefit can a teaching method be to this man, when the negativity of his presence defies his purpose?

It is not enough then to say simply that the teacher is a guide. He is sometimes not a guide, and he is sometimes more than a guide. He is not a guide when he teaches in silence. Nor is he a guide when he has no followers. He is not a guide until he makes his students want to hear him. He is more than a guide—he is the imposer of order—in front of a chaotic class. He is more than a guide—he is the quarry—when his class makes him feel he is less than a person should be. To say that the teacher is a guide is simply not enough.

But if he is not a guide, what is he? He is, in fact, many things—different to each student. Because each student approaches the learning situation with different needs, expectations, and abilities—because each student comes to the teacher with all of his feelings about himself and about teachers intact and at the fore—the teacher is not the same person to every student. To some, the teacher is a nonevent, barely credible in his presence. To some, he is a heroic figure, a mythical creation of their own imagining. To some, he is a fountain of inspiration, whose waters nourish the wish to learn. To some, the teacher is an occasion, an opportunity; to be loved, to be rejected, to be accepted, to be rebelled against, to be pleased or displeased, to be sanctified or crucified. To some, he is everything; to some, he is nothing. Some love him and some hate him; many don't even care. At times, even the teacher himself is not quite sure of what (or who) he is.

With all of these contradictions and discrepancies in mind, let us attempt to look at teaching methods, with the hope of resolving some of the problems we have brought up. We will begin with methods that are directed primarily at the transmission of subject matter—cognitive methods. We will then look at cognitive lessons, and move on to lessons that relate to the affective domain. Then we will try to consolidate and synthesize all of these insights in the final section, "Elements of Instruction: A Synthesis."

Presenting Subject Matter

Over the years, much has been written about different ways of organizing and presenting subject matter to students. Kuethe (1968) cites the four major traditional teaching methods as lecture method, discussion method, project method, and recitation. "A lecture is a formal discourse intended for instruction. . . . By using the lecture method, the teacher is able to present exactly the material he chooses in the way he prefers" (p. 128). One weakness of the **lecture method** is that it does not invite student participation and feedback and, therefore, may be misdirected either in content, level, or tone. The **discussion method,** on the other hand, involves interaction between either teacher and student, or between student and student. "Perhaps the most important aspect of group discussion as a teaching method," Kuethe (p. 130) suggests, "is that it involves the active participation of the students in the teaching-learning process. Students enjoy an opportunity to express their opinions, and when they know that they can contribute, they direct their attention toward the classroom activity more than when learning is a passive experience. With only passive participation, the students' attention can easily drift away from the learning situation." Lecture and discussion are often combined during a typical class session.

The **project method** "is a general name for the form of the teaching-learning process that consists of students working on some task with relatively little direct interaction with the teacher" (Kuethe, p. 132). A science teacher may, for example, allow the students to develop their own science projects from which they will learn the basic principles of science. One important advantage of the project method is that it encourages *learning by doing,* which research has demonstrated is particularly effective in making learning meaningful and helping the learner retain information. Finally, Kuethe cites recitation (or drill), a method which, when used by itself, "can easily become meaningless, and without meaning there is reduced retention and, of course, little interest" (p. 133).

Kuethe goes on to discuss some specialized teaching techniques, too. The **simulated environments** techniques, which represent in the classroom setting models of real social situations, "are successful to the degree that they teach the content and skills that are needed for success in the world outside the classroom" (p. 134). An example of this technique is presented in this illustration offered to us by a sixth-grade teacher:

Illustration: "Before I came to teaching, I had been in the world of business for several years, and therefore knew quite a bit about how the business world *really* worked. When the curriculum called for teaching the class about business, I decided the best way to learn was by doing, so we set up our own business. The fourth graders were making potholders—they had dozens of them—and we asked the teacher if we could buy up all of them. We bought them for a few cents each, and the fourth-grade class became our manufacturer.

"We then divided our class into a typical organizational pattern. Several students wanted to go out and sell them right away, and these became our sales staff. Other students assumed managerial and executive tasks, without even realizing that this is what they were doing. We found that the students could sell

Elements of Instruction: A Survey and Synthesis 491

a few potholders to friends and family, but to really "build the business" we would need some innovation. The class and I discussed it, and we decided to package the potholders in a small cardboard box which was designed by Mr. Prenner's art class, who was paid, out of our sales money, for their efforts. At one point, when the supply was dwindling, the fourth-grade class was no longer making potholders, and we learned how risky it is to have your whole business depend on one manufacturer. Other problems cropped up along the way and we dealt with them. What was most interesting was to observe situations occurring that I hadn't planned, but which really paralleled what happens in business. Ethical questions arose and had to be dealt with. Record keeping led to math lessons. Our advertising, in a local paper, helped us in grammar lessons. In retrospect, I realize that the students learned much more than only business: they were able to learn their subject matter in other areas, as it could be applied to the business world.

We see in this illustration two of the main advantages of the *simulated environments* approach. First, it helps the student master real-life skills that may sometimes be omitted from the school curriculum. Second, it often integrates subject matter from diverse areas in a practical way.

Two other methods mentioned by Kuethe are **teaching games** and **programmed instruction.** Teaching games provide extrinsic reward (in winning or doing well), involve student participation in a positive, nonthreatening way, and help the student master skills. Programmed instruction, which involves little direct participation of the teacher, can be a useful aid to teaching:

The main advantages claimed for programmed instruction are the immediate feedback provided to the learner and the fact that each learner determines his own rate of progress. The bright student can proceed rapidly and be given more difficult material, whereas the slower individual can find the pace that is most comfortable for him. (p. 138)

Programmed instruction, particularly as it is presented through the medium of the *teaching machine,* has been the subject of controversy for a number of years now. B. F. Skinner, who has been a vociferous proponent of the idea, argues that teaching machines are an effective educational tool. "If our current knowledge of the acquisition and maintenance of verbal behavior is to be applied to education," Skinner (1968) argues, "some sort of teaching machine is needed." He describes the criteria for such a machine, including the ability to process individual responses to questions and to assure that the student's progress is in a logical, step-by-step progression. He then summarizes the advantages of such a machine, and these arguments have been especially taken to task in recent years.

The machine itself, of course, does not teach. It simply brings the student into contact with the person who composed the material it presents. It is a labor-saving device because it can bring one programmer into contact with an indefinite number of students. This may suggest mass production, but the effect upon each student is surprisingly like that of a private tutor. The comparison holds in several respects. (i) There is a constant interchange between program and student. Unlike lectures, textbooks, and the usual audio-visual aids, the machine induces sustained activity . . . (ii) Like a good tutor, the machine insists that a given point be thoroughly understood . . . before the student moves on. Lectures, textbooks, and their mechanized equivalents . . . proceed without making sure that the student understands and easily leave him behind. (iii) Like a good tutor the machine presents just that material for which the student is ready. . . . (iv) Like a skillful tutor the machine helps the student come up with the right answer. . . . (v) Lastly, of course, the machine, like the private tutor, reinforces the student for every correct response using this immediate feedback not only to shape his behavior most efficiently but to maintain it in strength in a manner which the layman would describe as "holding the student's interest." (Skinner, 1968, pp. 7–8)

The concept of the teaching machine as well as its practical application have been criticized in the professional literature, and the fact that in the almost twenty years since teaching machines have been marketed they have not made a great inroad in education is perhaps the strongest criticism. Wohlwill (1968), in a rejoinder to Skinner's position, argues that teaching machines are not capable of teaching the complex skills that are characteristic

Table 13.1   Comparison of Seven Teaching Methods

	Directs Attention	Promotes Motivation	Maintains Interest	Provides Immediate Feedback	Allows Student to Progress at His Own Rate	Avoids Excessive Frustration and Failure	Promotes Transfer	Develops Positive Attitudes
Discussion	Usually	Usually	Usually	Yes	Usually	Usually	Can, with a little effort	Usually
Games	Does, but indirectly	Usually	Usually	Yes	Usually	Often does not	Seldom	Usually
Lecture	Can, with a little effort	Can, but often fails to	Can, but often fails to	No	Rarely	Usually	Rarely does without special care	Can, if interesting
Programmed Instruction	Almost always	Does, at least in beginning	Depends on material	Yes	Yes	Usually	Usually does not	Uncertain
Projects	Usually	Usually	Usually	Yes, when projects or parts of it are completed	Usually	Often does not	Often does not	Does, if project is successful
Recitation or Drill	Always	Rarely	Rarely	Yes, when oral No, when written	Usually, but not for better students	Rarely	Rarely, if ever	Rarely, if ever
Simulations	Often does not	Usually	Usually	Usually, depending on specific simulation	Usually	If well designed	Always, if simulation is adequate	In majority of cases

From *The Teaching-Learning Process* by James L. Kuethe. Copyright © 1968 by Scott, Foresman and Company. Reprinted by permission of the publisher.

of human teaching. Also, teaching machines cannot adequately deal with the psychological dimensions of human learning and growth.

In summary, we can say, then, that the method of programmed instruction, particularly as it is embodied in the teaching machine, while it may be effective for certain basic, structured, learning tasks, is not particularly effective in teaching complex learning that involves the interaction of several skills simultaneously (such as learning citizenship, for instance).

Structure in Teaching   In 1969, *Structure in Teaching,* by O. Roger Anderson, appeared in print, synthesizing the research of many early pioneers in this area. Two years later, Anderson published a quantitative analysis of structure in teaching, elaborating many of the insights of the earlier work. In this section, we will review Anderson's position and make reference to parallel and antipodal positions as well.

Anderson (1969) begins by arguing against a single theory of structure,

Teaching: Art and Science

Table 13.2   Classes of Structure in Teaching

Stimulus Structure	Cognitive Structure
The Patterns of Stimuli Emitted by the Teaching Source	*The Patterns of Responses Acquired by Pupils*
Kinetic stimulus structure (the order in which materials are presented by the teaching source)	Kinetic cognitive structure (the order in which the pupil describes what has been learned)
Static stimulus structure (the logical relationships among substantive areas presented by the teaching source)	Static cognitive structure (the logical relationships a pupil makes among the substantive areas learned)

Reprinted by permission of the publisher from O. R. Anderson, *Structure in Teaching: Theory and Analysis* (New York: Teachers College Press, 1969, © 1969 by Teachers College, Columbia University), p. 9.

pointing out that theories of structure lack the ability to be tested empirically and do not account for the complexities of the teaching interaction. He suggests that teaching can be analyzed through what he calls a **kinetic structure:**

Kinetic structure in simple terms is the specification and serial ordering of subject-matter content in verbal units in accordance with organizational principle. An *organizational principle* is a rule stating the necessary qualities a teaching sequence must have to achieve a high degree of kinetic structure. . . . The organizational dimension can be viewed as a kind of lesson outline; and it can serve as a criterion for assessing the amount of kinetic structure in a communicated sequence. (p. 7)

Table 13.2 shows the classes of structure in teaching, divided into classes of emitted stimuli (by the teacher) and cognitive responses (by the learner). The essence of Anderson's conceptualization is found in two basic ideas. First, kinetic structure is represented in terms of teacher and learner:

Stimulus kinetic structure is the ordering of teacher-emitted stimuli in accordance with specified organizational principle.
Cognitive kinetic structure is the serial order in which the learner presents responses in accordance with such a principle. (p. 9)

Second, Anderson speaks of three types of organizational dimensions: (1) spatial, (2) chronological, (3) derived. These dimensions—or organizational principles—refer to the serial order in which content is presented (stimulus kinetic structure) or in which information is learned (cognitive kinetic structure). The spatial organizational principle "requires that stimulus or response units representing objects occur in a serial order identical to that of the spatial array of the represented objects" (p. 23). For instance, if we were teaching human physiology, we would teach as a unit the mouth-esophagus-stomach-small intestine-large intestine-colon-rectum, since these are spatially related; that is, one is next to the other.

The chronological organizational principle "requires that stimulus or response units representing events occur in a serial order identical to the

> "At the core of any considerations about teaching method lies the question of what we teach and how it is organized. The organization of material to be learned, along with its presentation, is called the lesson."

temporal sequence of the represented events." In the example just cited the order of elements is also chronological since food must pass through one before it reaches the next. Thus, the organizational principle behind the structure of this lesson involves both spatial and chronological organization.

"A derived organizational principle requires that stimulus or response units be arranged in a series such that contiguous statements will contain symbolic elements in common" (p. 23). For instance, in teaching the idea of *justice* we may cite a variety of historical events that took place in different places at different times. Instead of arranging these events geographically or chronologically, we arrange them and present them to the student in terms of the concept of justice, which is the subject matter.

The particular value of Anderson's theory is that it allows empirical investigation. In a later book (Anderson, 1971), detailed analyses of teaching interactions are conducted using these (and some more complex) categories of structure. Although Anderson does not refer directly to cybernetic principles, it is evident that his theory of structure in teaching is an informational theory that accounts for the way information is transmitted and the way that the cumulative transmittals produce a teaching (or lesson) structure. It is also, when studied in depth, a challenging interpretation of the relationship between language and teaching and an insightful explanation of the way people learn.

The Lesson

At the core of any considerations about teaching method lies the question of what we teach and how it is organized. The organization of material to be learned, along with its presentation, is called the lesson. While the dictionary refers to the lesson as "a piece of instruction," a better definition would be that the lesson is a complete step in the learning process. Whether this step is significant or insignificant, whether it leads to progress or stasis, whether it is compatible or incompatible with future and past steps depends upon the teacher's organization of the lesson, the effect of the lesson upon the learner, and the lesson's place in the total curriculum. In this section, we will examine some basic principles behind the planning and implementation of the lesson, paying particular attention to two general types of lessons: divergent and convergent.

Lessons contain three main sections, each of which must be thoroughly dealt with in order for the proper outcomes to occur.

I	II	III
INPUT	INTERACTION	EXPERIENCE
(Content)	(Dialogue)	(Doing)

In figure 13.4 under INPUT we include all print, media, verbal, and environmental contents of the lesson. This would include the books and printed materials the teacher uses, any audiovisual equipment (such as slides, charts, an overhead projector, etc.), the teacher's own verbal communications, and the setting of the classroom itself (environment). In a creative lesson, the INPUT is customarily very well thought out in a manner that corresponds to the objectives of the lesson. Frequently, the A–V presentations are elaborate because they are intended to be the primary motivational force, and their impact must extend throughout the lesson. Enthusiasm, curiosity, and willingness to discuss the INPUT are the customary student responses teachers may look for in order to evaluate the appropriateness and effectiveness of the presentation.

In figure 13.5 under INTERACTION we describe the **convergent** nature of the conventional cognitive teaching process, which is teacher-oriented with specific goals in view.

The extent that a lesson follows this convergent-cognitive format depends on the goals of the teacher and the teacher's style. Lessons that attempt to focus on affective areas, such as creativity and emotional growth, will minimize the convergent element, which is more applicable to cognitive learning tasks. In any case this convergent element is virtually never completely absent.

In figure 13.6 under EXPERIENCE, we describe the outcomes that are aimed for in the *cognitive* mode. Figure 13.6 gives a reasonable picture of the conventional teaching process. This process is familiar to all teachers and is geared primarily to cognitive learning. It allows for little differences on the part of the learner. A number of theoretical rationales for this type of lesson structuring are found in the literature. These rationales are examinations of different types of teaching styles.

A recent book by Muska Mosston (1972), *Teaching: From Command to Discovery,* describes a continuum of teaching styles ranging from the *command style* (completely teacher controlled) on the one extreme, to the *individual program* (completely student controlled) on the other. Mosston (1972, p. 35) says this of the command style:

---

* Written by Alfred D. Kohler and taken from "Moppet: An Elementary (K–6) Humanities Program Devoted to the Development of a Lesson Process Promoting Creativity in Children." Doctoral diss., Teachers College, Columbia University, 1975, pp. 43–50. Reprinted by permission of the author.

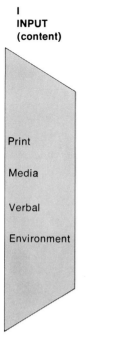

I
INPUT
(content)

Print

Media

Verbal

Environment

Figure 13.4 Input-Convergent

When all decisions are made by the teacher there can be no development of democratic procedures, and certainly no experience by the student of a freeing process that would maximize the individual's freedom and uniqueness.

Obviously, the completely student-controlled style virtually implies that the students are so advanced that the presence of the teacher is hardly necessary. Consequently, this style has little relevance for a program designed primarily to be introduced into traditional classroom situations since it would not fit into the convergent lesson model in figures 13.4, 13.5, and 13.6. However, what Mosston identifies as the problem-solving approach has many possibilities. It is completely teacher controlled only in the planning or pre-impact stage, and even in that stage there is room for student input. But more important, in the impact and post-impact stages there is ample room for students to express their own wishes.

As the students become more adept at taking responsibility for their own progress, the teaching style becomes more and more indirect—more and more student-centered. It is in this neighborhood of trust and increasing self-responsibility that students seem to learn best. This idea is consonant with the research of Flanders (1967), who points out that "in general, the more the teacher accepts and encourages pupils in contrast to directing or criticizing them the more pupils seem to learn and the better they like it" (p. 4).

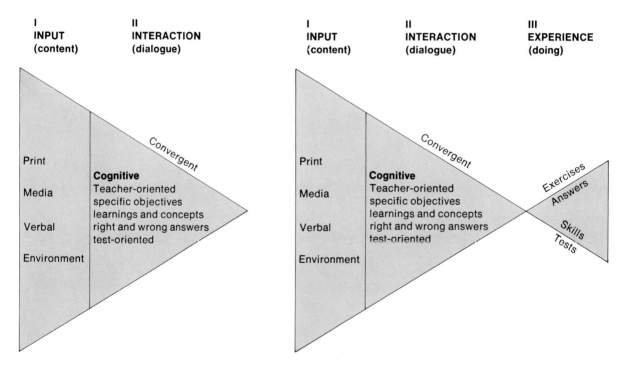

Figure 13.5 Interaction-Convergent

Figure 13.6 Experience-Convergent

Teaching: Art and Science

> "As students become more adept at taking responsibility for their own progress, the teaching style becomes more and more student-centered. It is in this neighborhood of trust and increasing self-responsibility that students seem to learn best."

This type of distinction—between authoritarian, highly structured and convergent teaching as opposed to student-centered, flexible, divergent teaching—has been recognized for many years, but appears in the literature under a variety of different names. Torrance (1963) has discussed this issue in terms of the differences between teaching by authority (which would correspond to Mosston's command style) and learning by thinking creatively. He describes learning by authority:

.... when we are told what we should learn, when we accept an idea as true on the word of some authority, perhaps a teacher, a textbook, a newspaper, an encyclopedia, or the like. Authority frequently represents the majority opinion, the consensus of the peer group. (p. 47)

Conversely, "a child learns creatively by questioning, inquiring, searching, manipulating, experimenting, even by aimless play; in short by always trying to get at the truth" (p. 47).

The conflict between these two modes of teaching encompasses both the ancient and modern conflicts over authority and freedom described by John Dewey (1963) in *Freedom and Culture*. Regarding the slow evolution of the ingredients of a democratic consciousness, Dewey says, "The idea that mind and consciousness are intrinsically individual did not even occur to any one for much the greater part of human history" (p. 21). Thus the very idea of the individual consciousness, which is the main avenue of creative thinking, is dichotomous with external authority. Therefore it should not be unexpected that, despite political and philosophical doctrine that virtually sanctifies the individual, the actual daily practice is so deeply rooted in authoritarianism that even well-meaning people typically practice authoritarian behavior while maintaining the belief that they are democratic in tendency. This is particularly true of teachers, who are prone to justify their authoritarian practices by the apparently obvious fact that one cannot teach a class that one cannot control. They will tell you that as the children grow older, they will mature and, consequently, teacher domination can relax, without recognizing that relaxation of domination will help the learner grow and mature. Bellak et al. (1966) have shown, for example, that in high school classrooms there is very little evidence to support the idea that teachers relax their dominance in the higher grades. This is the reason behind Mosston's (1972) statement, "Our argument is not with the teacher's philosophy, but with the teacher's blindness." The works of Bellack, Flanders, Mosston, and others in analyzing the interaction of the classroom is based on the premise that teachers need to become conscious of what they are doing and of the alternatives for change before they will be able to modify their teaching styles to accommodate alternative approaches.

One suggested alternative for change is in a **divergent** lesson that relies on a learner-oriented, democratic style of teaching. This is especially important in affective teaching, the goals and processes of which are discussed in detail in chapter 7. The convergent teaching model, illustrated in figures 13.4, 13.5, and 13.6 fails to produce positive results in this domain.

Recently, significant strides have been made in conceptualizing the affective mode and in designing lessons accordingly (Kohler, 1975, 1976). In figure 13.7 the divergent (dotted) lines branch out under INTERACTION, which represents the broad nature of the process involved in increasing a student-oriented situation in which the usual instructional mode of "pouring in" is reversed and replaced with a "drawing out" of the person through the teaching process.

The drawing-out process encourages the learners to conceptualize their own personal responses and ideas. Note that the test orientation and the resulting tests and exercises have disappeared from the cognitive model. This

Figure 13.7 Interaction-Divergent

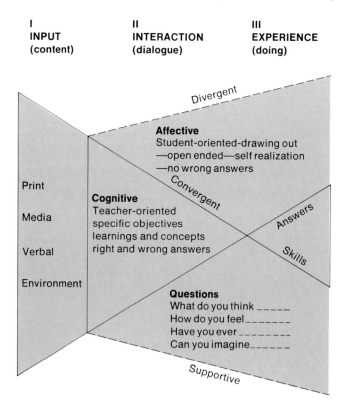

I
INPUT
(content)

II
INTERACTION
(dialogue)

III
EXPERIENCE
(doing)

Divergent

Affective
Student-oriented-drawing out
—open ended—self realization
—no wrong answers

Convergent

Print

Cognitive
Teacher-oriented
specific objectives
learnings and concepts
right and wrong answers

Answers

Media

Verbal

Skills

Environment

Questions
What do you think _____
How do you feel _____
Have you ever _____
Can you imagine_____

Supportive

is done to remove impediments to the free flow of student expression. In short, the test-oriented approach is now absent in both cognitive and affective realms.

In the course of the INTERACTION dialogue, the questioning of the teacher should focus on drawing out as many unique responses from as many students as possible. In order to do this successfully, the teacher must exercise tolerance for poor quality responses. This does not mean that poor responses should be highly praised, but that the teacher should refrain from comments that will inhibit further exploration. *The objective at this point is not to evaluate responses, but rather to help children formulate their personal responses into ideas that can be used in the EXPERIENCE part of the lesson.*

In figure 13.8, the EXPERIENCE is extended to enable students to engage in arts experience. During this process the teaching approach must consistently be noncritical and accepting of *all* student statements. This is necessary in order to promote growth in all of the students regardless of their initial level of competence. The resulting student statements should represent them and not the preconceptions of the teacher.

The question of suspending the customary system of rewards and criticisms may bother some teachers. This problem will be discussed in greater detail later in this chapter.

Figure 13.8 Experience-Individual Statements

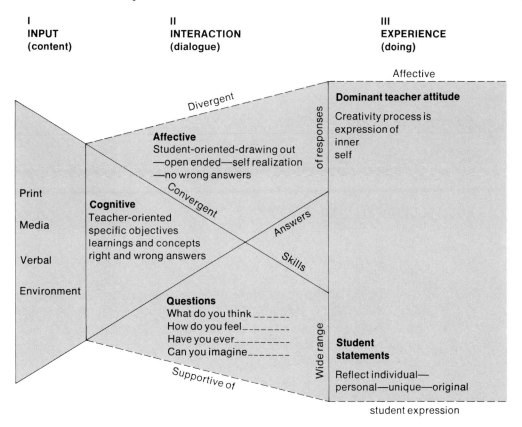

> "When all the children are brought dynamically into the positive spirit of creative activities, the teacher need not worry about quality."

Figure 13.9 Experience-Wide Range of Responses

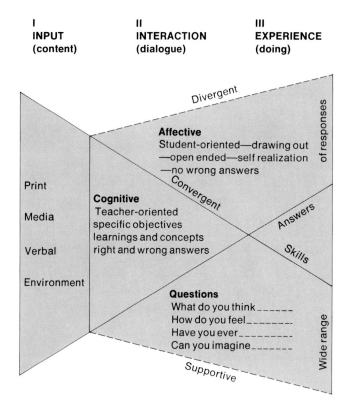

I
INPUT
(content)

II
INTERACTION
(dialogue)

III
EXPERIENCE
(doing)

Divergent

Print

Media

Verbal

Environment

Affective
Student-oriented—drawing out
—open ended—self realization
—no wrong answers

Convergent

Cognitive
Teacher-oriented
specific objectives
learnings and concepts
right and wrong answers

Answers

Skills

Questions
What do you think _____
How do you feel _____
Have you ever _____
Can you imagine _____

of responses

Wide range

Supportive

In figure 13.9 under EXPERIENCE we note that the range of reactions now includes the cognitive, but the range has been greatly widened to include the individual responses of all the children.

When all the children are brought dynamically into the positive spirit of creative activities, the teacher need not worry about quality. The best the children have to offer is usually on a high level and frequently astonishingly so.

In evaluating the success of a divergent lesson, teachers should look first at the work of the group as a whole. If the work displays great variety, it is likely that the children have consciously departed from the customary pattern of seeking to produce the *correct* response expected by the teacher. In short, children should seek the individual, and they must have confidence that the teacher will accept it.

In addition to diversity of expression within the group, the teacher should look for eloquence and evidence of deep personal involvement in the individual statements. Those responses that are of poor quality should not be held up for unfavorable comparison, but should be taken for what they are—the best the student can or will produce at that point. Therefore, such statements should be viewed as an exercise along the road to becoming. The following are examples of positive comments the teacher might use: "You are using your voice much better now in drama." "Your movement is showing more variety." "I like the closing line of your poem." "Where is this picture going?" Usually there is something in a child's statement that can be used as a basis for encouragement.

The cognitive element has not ended in figure 13.10, but rather the concepts and skills, which were kept simple in deference to the limited arts background of the classroom teachers, are brought into interaction with the personal ideas of the children, which results in imaginative applications. The steadily widening cognitive lines point out that the affective contents are merging with the cognitive, resulting in an increasing self-realization by the child. The cognitive lines never reach the extreme outside lines because there always remains an element of the unknown in the creative process.

Figure 13.10 Experience-Imaginative Applications

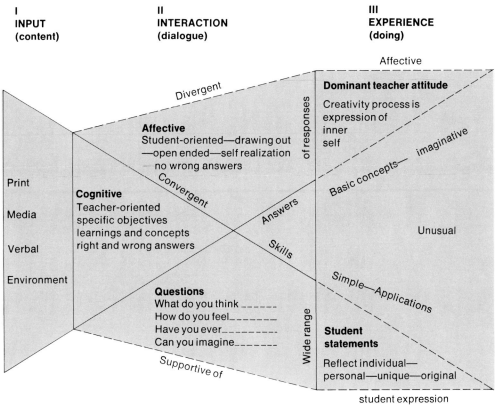

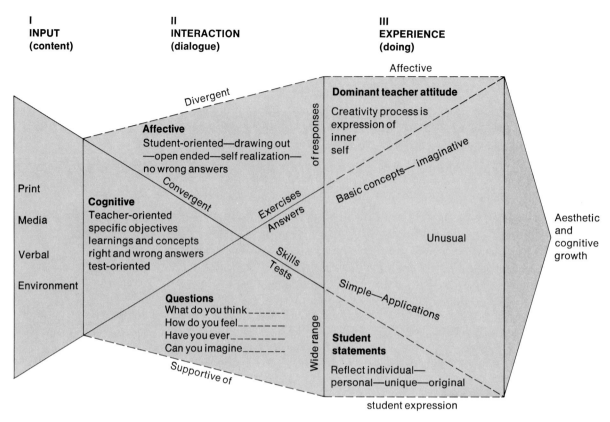

I
INPUT
(content)

II
INTERACTION
(dialogue)

III
EXPERIENCE
(doing)

Affective

Divergent

Affective
Student-oriented—drawing out
—open ended—self realization—
no wrong answers

Convergent

Print

Media

Verbal

Environment

Cognitive
Teacher-oriented
specific objectives
learnings and concepts
right and wrong answers
test-oriented

of responses

Exercises
Answers

Skills
Tests

Dominant teacher attitude
Creativity process is
expression of
inner
self

Basic concepts—imaginative

Unusual

Aesthetic
and
cognitive
growth

Questions
What do you think _____
How do you feel _____
Have you ever _____
Can you imagine _____

Wide range

Simple—Applications

**Student
statements**

Reflect individual—
personal—unique—original

Supportive of

student expression

Figure 13.11 Complete Lesson Process

In figure 13.11 the final bracket denotes that when this process is brought successfully to a conclusion, the result is both aesthetic and cognitive growth.

Now that we have examined some general considerations about teaching method and structuring the lesson, let us consider the practical uses of the traditional lesson plan.

The Lesson Plan   A **lesson plan** can be a useful tool, but if it is used inflexibly it can also prove detrimental. At best, a lesson plan is a *tentative* plan that takes into account the learner's entry level, the subject matter that is to be taught, and the instructional processes to be utilized.

The traditional framework of a lesson plan consists of:

AIMS	MOTIVATION
Knowledge	MATERIALS
Skills	PROCEDURE and PRESENTATION
Attitudes	EVALUATION

This is a rather formal structure and may include some inherent redundancy, but the teacher himself can introduce flexibility into the lesson by his own presentation of the material.

In writing a lesson plan, what is more important than the elements under each heading is the relationship of these elements. The materials must be appropriate to the procedure; the evaluation must relate directly back to the aims, and so forth. Often, the beginning teacher will have a tendency to concentrate on one element of the plan at a time, failing to integrate all of its parts into a unified whole.

Elements of Instruction: A Synthesis

The reader, like the educational psychologist mentioned at the beginning of this chapter, has travelled a difficult, rugged terrain in search of some answers. Hopefully the reader, unlike the educational psychologist seeking the Way of Zen, will feel more pleased by the answers (even if he is less enlightened). We began this chapter with a Zen koan because it served to make a point: that there are no easy answers when we deal with subjects as difficult as teaching. We shall conclude this chapter with some attempt to synthesize the material we have covered into a coherent idea.

Instruction as a Process

In examining the different approaches to instruction, what we were really considering was the question, What are the most effective ways of getting students to learn? We looked at different models, each of which conceptualized the instructional process in terms of its elements, but none of these models went so far as to integrate the elements into a viable, procedural prescription for effective instruction. We shall make this effort by looking at instruction in terms of the environment through which learning occurs. Using the term *environment* in the same sense as it was used by those we have discussed, let us consider what kind of environment best facilitates learning.

Leonard (1968) speaks of a strongly interactive environment as a prerequisite for meaningful learning. "The human organism is incredibly flexible," he argues. "If there are limits on the human ability to respond to learning environments, we are so far away from the limits as to make them presently inconsequential. Throughout human history to date, it has been the environments, not the human beings, that have run up against limitations" (p. 39).

There are a number of things the classroom teacher can do to promote an effective learning environment. He must first recognize the interplay of needs that are manifest in the learning situation. Regardless of which instructional model we are guided by, the presence of the students' needs is invariably and persistently felt. Students' needs include not only the need for recognition and approval but intellectual needs, social needs, familial needs that are

unsatisfied at home, and creative aesthetic needs. Not all students enter that situation with a positive attitude, with a willingness to learn, with an optimism about their capabilites. On the contrary, many students, turned off for years by the educational experience, come into the classroom with a sense of disillusionment, with a morbid pessimism, with an expectation of frustration and failure.

As figure 13.1 indicated, instruction is a critical element of the teaching process, but it is not the only element. The world of the learner must be taken into account; the sociocultural framework in which learning takes place has an enormous relevance; the teacher's personal characteristics are brought forth in the teaching interaction. It is the blending of all these elements together that becomes the crux of the educational experience.

All that this really means is that instruction is always a positive, therapeutic process, as is teaching. Pine and Horne (1969) have expounded a list of fourteen principles of learning that "incorporates and integrates the basic therapeutic experiences," and these principles are well worth looking at since they are compatible with much of what we have suggested in this chapter.

1. Learning is the process of changing behavior in positive directions.
2. Learning is an experience that occurs inside the learner and is activated by the learner.
3. Learning is the discovery of the personal meaning and relevance of ideas.
4. Learning is a cooperative and collaborative process.
5. Learning (behavioral change) is a consequence of experience.
6. Learning is an evolutionary process.
7. Learning is sometimes a painful process.
8. One of the richest resources for learning is the learner himself.
9. The process of learning is emotional as well as intellectual.
10. Learning fuses work and play.
11. Learning is a "religious" experience.
12. The learner is a free and responsible agent.
13. The processes of problem solving and learning are highly unique and individual.
14. Teaching is learning.

These fourteen principles are inclusive and comprehensive. They represent a working axiom for the teacher who endeavors to use therapeutic instructional approaches in the classroom. Whether the teacher uses competency-based instruction, computer-assisted instruction, kinetic structure, behavioral methods, or psychodynamic techniques, or any other system, it is the climate of learning—the classroom environment—that is the ultimate variable among variables in the educational process.

Summary

In this chapter, we examined *instruction* as an activity differentiated from teaching per se. Types of instruction and elements of the instructional process were presented and discussed. Special attention was directed to the contribution of the cybernetic approach to teaching theory. We examined the principles of closed and open feedback loops, which help explain the interactive learning process.

The lesson was examined according to its component parts, and structures for convergent and divergent lessons were elaborated. Finally, fourteen general principles of instruction, which represent a synthesis of the ideas covered, were enumerated.

Suggested Additional Readings

A Teacher Is Many Things by Earl V. Pullias and James D. Young (*Blooming-ton, Ind.: Indiana University Press, 1968*)

Although this book is more about "teaching" than "instruction," it offers many valuable insights for the teacher who is engaged in instruction. The book describes, in great detail and with fine perceptions, the many different things a teacher *does* and *is* (to the students).

By its very nature, the teaching experience is artificial in the best sense of artificiality. The teacher-to-be spends money, time, and energy in preparing for the role of "teacher." He masters subject matter, improves his personal skills, and develops his own ability to transfer that subject matter.

from *A Teacher Is Many Things*

Individualized Teaching in the Elementary Schools by Dona Kofod Stahl and Patricia Murphy Anzalone (*New York: Prentice-Hall, 1970*)

This is a clearly written, direct introduction to the important subject of individualized instruction. Topics covered include the rationale for individual-ized instruction; basic strategies and techniques; the preparation of instruc-tional materials and designing a program.

Some of the most vital learnings that take place in our schools never appear in the objectives in the teacher's plan book. They are the things a child is learning to think about himself.

from *Individualized Teaching in the Elementary Schools*

Programmed Instruction: Bold New Venture ed. by Allen D. Calvin (*Bloom-ington, Ind.: Indiana University Press, 1969*)

This is a more advanced, detailed look at programmed instruction. After some general introductory material, programmed learning is discussed in terms of specific subject matter areas: spelling, reading, social science, foreign languages, mathematics, in nongraded schools, and in other settings. The book is replete with much practical information.

The case for programmed texts is not a case for everything on the market in programmed form: it is the case for the possibility of significant benefits when this technique is applied properly. And proper application refers not only to the writing-testing-rewriting process, but to the proper classroom use of the result which we shall discuss.

from *Programmed Instruction: Bold New Venture*

MOPPET: Theory and Practice
MOPPET: Teachers' Manual of Lessons for Elementary Grades (K-6)
MOPPET: Teachers' Manual of Lessons for 7th or 8th Grade
(Published by Project MOPPET, Indiana Avenue School #18. Iselin, N.J. 08830)

MOPPET stands for Media-Oriented Program Promoting Exploration in Teaching. It was a federally funded program in a suburban New Jersey community, which from 1970–1976 developed new teaching and curriculum strategies designed to encourage creative, divergent thinking within the context of normal subject matter areas. The program was closely evaluated at every step of development, and considerable evidence now exists that not only were students affected by this new approach, but that participating teachers were able to develop new, radically different, more effective teaching styles. Despite a small staff and limited budget, over the six years several significant publications evolved, including a general theoretical outline and hundreds of specific lessons that can be applied in any classroom.

MOPPET is interdisciplinary in concept in that various areas of the curriculum are consciously drawn upon for subject matter for lessons. In this context the arts are not viewed solely as ends in themselves but are utilized as avenues to perceive and communicate in different ways. Thus, the individual student can find means for individual expression—even amidst subject matter that would not ordinarily interest him or her as generalized facts or information.

from MOPPET Lesson Manual/ 7th Grade

Extremes of Intelligence

Although *intelligence* is an elusive concept to define, psychologists have relied primarily on IQ tests to assess the individual's intelligence, which is then expressed as an IQ score. While the majority of learners score within the normal range of IQ, there are many students at both ends of the spectrum: the gifted and the retarded. The slow learner requires remediation, supplementary training, and a curriculum geared to his or her capabilities. The gifted learner, which we define as a person not only of high intelligence but with any valuable gift or talent, can benefit from enrichment, acceleration, and advanced placement. The underachiever, who may be average, gifted, or slow, is a person performing far below his potential. Special considerations for dealing effectively in the classroom with the slow learner, the gifted learner, and the underachiever are considered.

The Learning Disabled Student

Learning disabilities may be detected early in the child's schooling. Teacher observation is the first step in diagnosis; further psychological testing can pinpoint the nature and quality of the specific disability. The two most common learning disabilities are dyslexia and minimal brain dysfunction (MBD), both of which are broad terms that cover several different areas of learning problems. The confusion over terminology in this area is sorted out, and the teacher is encouraged to view the total learner as a functioning organism rather than as a victim of a learning disability.

The Hyperactive Child

The distinction between the terms *hyperactive* and *hyperkinetic*—and their frequent interchangeability —is pointed out. Specific methods for helping the hyperactive child include drug treatment in conjunction with therapy, arranging lessons in brief units to accommodate short attention spans, and using behavior modification to decrease the child's impulsivity.

Continued

14 Teaching the Exceptional Learner

The Exceptional Learner in the Classroom

Parallel approaches to understanding the exceptional
learner are pointed out. The communication gap,
precipitated by the overwhelming nomenclature in
this area, is translated into the ways a layman, a reading
teacher, and a learning disabilities teacher would
perceive the same situation.

**Features of Emotional Disturbance Manifested
in the Classroom**

The basic emotional disturbances are detailed. A high
degree of anxiety is common to all categories of
emotional disorders in childhood. Impulse control
poses problems for many children and their teachers.
Specific methods for dealing with emotional disturbances,
through the use of *selective programming* and *modification
of curriculum content,* are discussed.

**The Classroom for the Learning Disabled
and Emotionally Disturbed**

The characteristics of the classroom environment are
reexamined in light of the special needs of the learning
disabled and emotionally disturbed student. Components
of the room that are given special attention are
location, size, shape, sound control, arrangement,
furniture, and use of wall space. Practical suggestions
for maximum organization of the classroom facilities
are highlighted.

The discussion of theories and processes of teaching that we considered in the preceding chapters is relevant to helping all types of students in a variety of teaching situations. It is generally recognized, however, that teaching strategies are designed with the so-called **normal** or **typical** learner in mind. It is also acknowledged that many of the students in a school will deviate from this normal profile in at least one area, and possibly in several different areas. Thus, while an understanding of the theories and processes of teaching, of the elements of a lesson, and of the methods used to communicate within the context of the **teacher-learner interaction** are of importance, they do not directly account for the many idiosyncratic possibilities that become manifest in the classroom. In chapter 10, "The Teacher as a Person," we directed our attention to the individuality of the teacher as a critical variable in the classroom. In this chapter, we will focus equal attention on the learner—particularly on the exceptional learner—to come to grips with the fundamental problem of teaching: How can the teacher make an effective impact upon a given learner?

Each learner presents to the teacher specific needs and individual problems that require attention if the teacher's educational efforts are to bear fruit. Learners enter the classroom with different abilities that are not always evident to observation alone. **Evaluation** procedures can help the teacher better understand where a learner stands at a given point with respect to the tasks that lie ahead. Certain learner characteristics may prove frustrating to the teacher or may take the form of disruptive behaviors in the classroom. In short, the teacher's understanding of the specific learner-as-a-person—as a unique individual with his own capabilities, interests, and problems—is a prerequisite to all successful teaching efforts.

The purpose of this chapter is to better understand ways in which the teacher can evaluate and assess the needs of a learner, can appreciate the implications of special needs, and can communicate effectively with the **exceptional learner.** While the concept of the typical learner is certainly valid, in reality, most students demonstrate exceptional performance—either in the positive or negative direction—in different academic, social, and psychological areas. When any learner shows such exceptionalities, it poses special challenges to the teacher, who, as a rule, tends to direct attention to the hypothetical norm. For instance, if a teacher is teaching a class of **"slow" children,** the teacher may be slow to recognize that one of these children has excellent mechanical abilities, which can be exploited and developed fully. In a class of **intellectually gifted children** (IGC), the teacher may not immediately recognize some of the children's retarded **socialization** or may ignore important **psychomotor** deficiencies. In heterogeneously grouped classes, the problems are multiplied when the teacher is expected to deal simultaneously with each student functioning at different levels.

One group of exceptional learners, with whom we will not deal specifically in this chapter, is the physically handicapped. This group includes the cerebral palsy and birth defect victim, the sightless and deaf student, the chronically ill, and the student with mild to severe motor problems. These learners may function in the mainstream or may require special classes. In general, the problems they encounter in the school, and the specialized approaches used to deal with these problems, are beyond the scope of this chapter, which will direct itself to more general kinds of exceptionalities.

In recent years, studies of exceptionalities have come to grips with two basic questions: How can we identify the exceptional learner before it is too late to help him? and, What classroom procedures can facilitate growth for the exceptional learner? These are very complex questions that transcend the purposes of an introductory educational psychology text. We will consider in this chapter the major exceptionalities, focusing on their classroom symptoms and viable teaching procedures. The detailed clinical analyses—particularly the sophisticated tests for diagnosing some exceptionalities—will be left to the more specialized books on this subject.

We will begin with an examination of the extremes of intelligence, paying attention to the slow and gifted learners. We will then focus on the group of exceptionalities known as learning disabilities, and then consider the special case of the hyperactive child. Finally, we will delve into some classroom procedures for educating the exceptional learner.

Extremes of Intelligence

The traditional, and most criticized, method of assessing a learner's intelligence is through the use of an **IQ test.** This test, developed originally in the early part of this century by Alfred Binet, a French psychologist charged with identifying slow learners, attempts to give a score that indicates how intelligent a person is compared with others of the same age group. In 1905, with the help of a colleague, Theodore Simon, Binet published the first test that stressed the aptitudes associated with success in education. The test was widely adopted and translated into many languages. In the United States, Lewis Terman of Stanford University revised it for use in this country's public schools, and it appeared in 1916 as the Stanford-Binet Test of Intelligence, the name it is still known by.

Binet recognized that **intelligence** was not a single ability, but a number of related abilities that worked together. His test comprises a number of sub-tests that measure each of the abilities that he associated with intelligence. He also recognized that as the child grew older each of these abilities would increase, but not always at the same rate as their chronological age increases (since this is invariable). To account for the difference, the child's score on the test was converted into a **mental age;** that is, the age for which his intelligence (or, performance on the test) would be normal. An eight-year-old child with a mental age (MA) of six is therefore about two years below the norm for his age, and equal to the average six-year-old.

To express the relationship between the chronological age and mental age, Stern developed the **intelligence quotient,** or **IQ.** IQ expresses intelligence as a ratio of mental age (MA) to chronological age (CA), multiplied by 100 to avoid the inconveniences of using decimals. Thus, if a person's mental age is eighty months and **chronological age** is sixty months, the IQ is—

$$\frac{80}{60} \times 100 = 133 \text{ (IQ)}$$

The IQ expresses the person's relative position mentally in the population. If we graph the distribution of IQ in the population, we find a normal curve, with a mean (or average) IQ of 100, and a **standard deviation** (SD) of 16. This means that if we know a person's IQ we can place that person in relation to the entire population.

Over the years, a number of criticisms have been levelled at the Stanford-Binet test. A test designed to meet some of these criticisms is the Wechsler Adult Intelligence Scale (WAIS), which was developed by David Wechsler of the Bellevue (New York City) Psychiatric Hospital. Another test, the Wechsler Intelligence Scale for Children (WISC), has also been widely distributed. Group intelligence tests, widely used in the school setting, enable an entire class to be tested and are therefore economically feasible, whereas the WISC, WAIS, and Stanford-Binet are individual intelligence tests.

Regardless of which test is used, the IQ score is considered a reasonably reliable and valid index of intelligence. Although an IQ of 120 means something slightly different on different tests, it indicates on all tests that the person's IQ is well above average. So, too, an IQ of 80 indicates that a student is well below average regardless of which test was used. A person whose IQ is 100 is considered average—right in the middle of the range of scores.

The question that has challenged educators in recent years is how valid an index of intelligence are IQ scores? This general question breaks down into a number of subquestions, each of which seriously challenges the ubiquitous acceptance of the IQ test. Some of the questions more commonly raised are:

1. Are there kinds of intelligence that are not tapped by IQ tests? Doesn't the scope of material on a typical test limit our definition of intelligence?
2. Are the IQ tests culturally biased? Do they appeal primarily to subjects from a white middle-class background? Can they ever be constructed to account for various ethnic idiosyncracies?
3. Can test anxiety and test phobia obscure a subject's true intelligence by precipitating inadequate performance on the test?
4. Do the IQ tests really measure innate ability or do they actually measure what has been learned? If they measure what has been learned, then they do not legitimately test innate human potential.

It is not within our scope to answer these difficult questions, but we should keep in mind that the value of the IQ score is under increasing challenge. Nevertheless, this score is used as the basis for identifying those students who are considered brighter than average and duller than average. These learners, at the extremes of intelligence, often require specialized treatment in the classroom, including curricular revisions. To avoid the pitfalls of over-reliance on IQ scores alone, we will use a model that includes additional factors in assessment and that divides exceptional learners into six categories. Figure 14.1 shows these categories: the **gifted,** the **retarded,** the **underachiever,** the **learning disabled,** the **hyperactive child,** and the **emotionally disturbed.** In some cases, as we see, IQ scores play a prominent part, and in other categories it plays a lesser role. What is most important is that we integrate factors other than the IQ score into our assessment. In this way, the individual is not limited in categorization by his or her performance on one test alone.

In the following sections we will examine in more detail the mildly retarded, the gifted, and the underachiever, using this integrative perspective to better help us understand their needs and the specialized techniques available for helping them in the classroom context.

The Slow Learner

The group of slow learners includes the approximately two-and-a-half percent of the population whose IQ falls below seventy and who are classified as mentally retarded. While it is typical to show a range of IQ scores, each of which bears a different label such as severely retarded, mildly retarded, educable,

Category	Relative importance of IQ	Other relevant factors
The gifted	Usually above 2.0 Stand. Dev.	Any single talent that distinguishes the person from his peers.
The retarded	Usually below 1.5 Stand. Dev. Mild retardation is a higher score	We recognize that the score may not be an accurate reflection of the person's intelligence because of test performance factors.
The underachiever	Irrelevant in itself. Important only in comparison with the person's performance	The discrepancy between the IQ as aptitude and the measured achievement.
The learning disabled student	Usually about average or above average	An inability to perform in one specific area (such as visual tasks) or a problem that generalizes to many areas.
Hyperactivity	Irrelevant, except for extremely low scores	The observed behavior in the classroom. Short attention span, et cetera
Emotionally disturbed	Totally irrelevant	The psychological profile of the learner.

Length of line indicates respective *importance* of IQ score.

Figure 14.1 The role of IQ Scores in Assessing Exceptionalities.

and so forth, we will abandon this in favor of a more synthetic approach since we are attempting to decrease our reliance on the IQ scores alone. Among the group of retarded are some who can perform on fifth-grade level, some who can perform on fourth-grade level, some on third-grade level, and some who will never learn the rudiments of personal hygiene and care necessary for independent survival. While the IQ score may be a useful *initial* index, a more in-depth examination of the learner's capabilities is necessary to determine to what extent he is educable and in which direction his education could probably be most adequate.

Since the severely retarded learner is not included in the traditional school population, we will focus our attention in this section on the **educable mentally retarded (EMR)** learner who typically does find a place in the public schools. In some cases the EMR learner is put in special classes, while in other cases he is integrated into the regular classes. Which is the best approach has been a matter of contention for many years.

Baldwin (1958), in an early study, investigated the social position of the mentally retarded child in the regular grades. Three questions were explored:

1. To what extent were the educable mentally retarded children in the regular grades of the public school accepted socially?
2. What was the social position of the children of different levels of mental

retardation, of chronological age, of public-school grade level, and of socioeconomic status?

3. What desirable or undesirable characteristics seemed to be related to the degree of social acceptance of the mentally retarded child?

Her conclusions showed "that the mentally retarded children . . . were less accepted socially by their classmates than were the non-mentally retarded children" (p. 112). In a later study, Johnson (1962) cited some possible advantages for placing the EMR in the regular classes and points out that the attitude of the teacher may be partially responsible for the low acceptance of the EMR student in instances where this occurs. "The teacher should approach the education of the mentally handicapped children with a positive rather than a negative attitude. *This is what they can learn to do*" (p. 69). The key point is that the attitude of the teacher toward the EMR learner is critical to successful teaching. Johnson (1962) expands this point:

With an understanding of the performance level of the child at all times, daily goals are set that require each one to strive and by striving to reach the goal. The goal, then, is raised slightly from day to day as the child grows and improves his performance. Only in this way will the mentally handicapped child leave school having learned the most efficient use of the tools and greatest understanding of the content and concepts that will promote his most effective personal, social, and economic adjustment for the rest of his life. (p. 69)

What can we conclude? Should the EMR be placed in the "regular" classes or should they be segregated? Can the appropriate attitude on the part of the teacher assure acceptance of the EMR by his peers, as Johnson suggests, or is the EMR learner ostracized as Baldwin and others have suggested?

In an impressive set of recent studies, Jay Gottlieb and his associates (Gottlieb, Gampel & Budoff, 1975; Gottlieb, 1975) made several significant findings. One of the studies concerned the effects of labeling. An actor was instructed to show some "acting-out" behavior to a group of third-grade students. At one time the class was told that the actor was EMR, and at another time no label was given. There was a significant difference in the class's attitude toward identical behaviors by the same actor when he was labeled and when he was not labeled. In general, the students responded more negatively when they believed the actor was EMR. The implications of this study are clear: The labeling of children as EMR isolates them from the "regular" group and increases negative reaction to the child.

In the second study, Gottlieb, Gampel and Budoff (1975) investigated whether there were positive changes in the behavior and social acceptance of EMR who were integrated into regular classes. It was concluded that there was no degree of social acceptance of the EMR by the regular pupils, but there was a decrease in the incidence of antisocial behavior by the EMR pupils. These results, as unfortunate as they are on a human level, indicate that it is perhaps best for the EMR to be placed in special classes. However, when they are placed in the regular classes, the teacher should be especially sensitive to the social needs of these slow learners and should make every effort to attempt to increase their acceptance by the rest of the class.

It is generally agreed that EMR students show more positive social behavior when they are integrated into regular classes. In addition to the study cited above, Gampel et al. (1974) showed an increase in positive behavior after mainstreaming EMR into integrated classes. The contradiction is this: While the behavior of EMR students improves in an integrated class, the classmates do not readily accept them:

In the context of the data available on these children, the disturbing finding is the consistent data from three school systems that regular-class non-EMR peers do not choose integrated EMR children as friends. . . . Given the generally positive nature of the integrated experience for the EMR children, research must focus on the reasons for this continued lack of acceptance by their normal peers and on the means by which it may be ameliorated. (Gottlieb, Gampel & Budoff, p. 151)

The Gifted Learner

Unlike most of the other groups of exceptional learners, the **gifted** are not in need of remediation and corrective services, but rather in need of enrichment, stimulation, and appropriate exploitation of their gifts. Ironically, this group, which constitutes a major national resource, has been sorely neglected in the school setting. Too often it is assumed that the gifted can get by on their own, and the special services provided to the less able are not extended to the gifted. Cost-conscious administrators are wont to limit enrichment programs when they should be expanded. In this section we will look at the special needs and interests of the gifted learner, with a view toward better understanding what can be done in the school setting to bring the fruits of their gifts to full ripeness.

Who Are the Gifted?

Most individuals are gifted in one area or another. Some have talents in music, some in sports and physical activities, some in social functioning, some in intelligence, some in other areas. But the gifted, as a group, are individuals of general talent and ability, although most gifted people have particularly strong

> "The gifted, as a group, are individuals of general talent and ability, although most gifted people have particularly strong talents in one area or another."

talents in one area or another. The single area that is most integral to defining the gifted is intelligence, often as measured by IQ tests. However, there are gifted individuals who are not in the top 5 percent of the IQ range, but who display some extraordinary talent that separates them from their peers. These are called *prodigies*.

For the most part, intelligence is the single criterion for determining the gifted child. This view of giftedness is "stated in terms of rank or IQ on an intelligence test, most frequently the Binet scale. The gifted child was one whose cognitive development was advanced beyond children of comparable

　　　Teaching: Art and Science

age" (Hildreth, 1966). The specific cutoff point may vary, as it does in different studies, but the relative positions of a child with respect to his or her group remains essentially the same:

Children with intelligence quotients (IQ's) of 120 or over make up about 10% of the population and are considered to have superior intelligence. Only 2.27% of children have IQ's of 130 or over, and only 0.5% have IQ's of 140 or over. Children with IQ's of 140 or better are commonly referred to by psychologists as "gifted." (Bakwin & Bakwin, 1967, p. 287)

This is a rather extreme cutoff point and excludes many children who surely possess great gifts. Since IQ tests are known to be somewhat inaccurate at the very high range, this arbitrary cutoff is especially unfortunate. In recent years, educators and psychologists have suggested less restrictive (and more realistic) standards of giftedness.

The Fifty-seventh Yearbook of the National Society for the Study of Education of the Gifted (1958) provides a well-rounded, practical definition that we shall use throughout this section:

The talented or gifted child is one who shows consistently able performance in any worthwhile line of endeavor. Thus, we shall include not only the intellectually gifted but also those who show promise in music, in graphic arts, creative writing, dramatics, mechanical skills and social leadership. Although most of the attention of educators has been directed towards the intellectually gifted . . . we think of such special attention to the intellectually gifted as a weakness or shortcoming in the kind of program for gifted children we would like to see in existence.

This expanded definition not only allows us to include more learners in the group but offers us a broader perspective of giftedness.

It is helpful in approaching the subject of giftedness, as many recent writers have pointed out, if we look beyond the measurement of IQ as the defining criterion. Getzels and Jackson (1958), in a perceptive paper that attempts to come to grips with a workable definition, argue against this single criterion approach to giftedness:

. . . . First, there is the limitation of the single metric itself, which not only restricts our perspective of the more general phenomenon, but places on the one concept a greater theoretical and predictive burden than it was intended to carry. . . . Second, within the universe of intellectual functions themselves, we have behaved as if the intelligence test represented an adequate sampling of *all* these functions. For example, despite the growing body of literature concerning intellectual processes which seem closely allied to the general concept of "creativity," we tend to treat the latter concept as applicable only to performance in one or more of the arts. . . . Third, there has been a failure to attend sufficiently to the difference between the *definition* of giftedness as given by the I.Q. and the variations in the *value* placed upon giftedness so defined. It is often taken for granted, for example, that the gifted child is equally valued by teachers and by parents, in the classroom and at home . . . It can be demonstrated that none of these assumptions . . . can be held without question. (pp. 75–76)

Getzels and Jackson conclude that the concept of giftedness be expanded to "include other potentially productive groups." While they do not elaborate a system for so doing, we can assume that they mean individuals with special talents in areas outside those normally measured by IQ tests.

Special Needs and Problems of the Gifted Learner

The one researcher most closely associated with studies of the needs and problems of the gifted learner is Lewis M. Terman who conducted a longitudinal study of gifted children that extended over thirty years. Using about fifteen hundred gifted children in the public school system of California, Terman followed their development between the 1920s and 1950s until the time of his death. IQ scores on the Stanford-Binet were used as the determining factor of giftedness, although teacher reports were also considered. The results of this massive research effort have been used continually to draw a psychological and social portrait of the "typical" gifted child.

Terman and Oden (1951), in summarizing the results from this study, draw a composite picture of the gifted child. He or she is a better than average physical specimen and is generally somewhat accelerated emotionally. This contradicts the stereotypical image of the gifted child as a reclusive, withdrawn, awkward, myopic outcast—who becomes the butt of other's jokes. During the years of follow-up, it was found that the physical and mental health of the gifted subjects were about average. Their adult intelligence also remained above average, but not quite as far above (on the whole) as it had been during childhood. Educationally, the gifted population was much further advanced than the general population to which it was compared. The gifted group also achieved a much higher rate of employment and occupational level and a higher income than the norm. Terman and Oden offer many specific examples to illustrate the lives of these subjects. It should also be mentioned that a small part of this group developed into unequivocal failures in life: alcoholics, institutionalized psychotics, and so forth. But this group was in a very small minority, and it can be attributed to the largeness of the sampling rather than to the giftedness itself.

Other research has generally supported Terman's findings (Groth, 1973; Hollingworth, 1942; Miller, 1959; Strang, 1951; Thom & Newell, 1959), although certain specific anomalies have been noted. Hollingworth (1942), for instance, has investigated the social adjustment of children with an IQ above 180. She views the major adjustment problems of gifted children as arising from the "combination of immaturity and superiority." These problems disappear as the child grows older because maturity catches up with intelligence. Gifted children, she goes on to point out, present adjustment problems, for the most part to themselves, not to society, so society tends to pay little attention to them.

She discusses in detail the problems of the gifted child, using three categories. First, there are "the problems of work." School may prove too easy for the gifted child, and lacking sufficient challenges, the child may become lax and apathetic. "The problems of play," too, she argues, are of importance. The gifted child has more "play knowledge" than the average child. He prefers games requiring more intellectual skill and less sensorimotor play. He likes organized games leading toward a "remote and definite climax as the goal." Other children do not like that kind of play and so they may reject the gifted child because he or she doesn't fit in. Moreover, children of similar **mental age** are chronologically older than the gifted child, bigger and more developed, and may not want to play with him. Thus, the gifted child may be forced to play by himself.

Gifted girls, according to Hollingworth, are "less interested in traditional girls' play. . . . The special problem of gifted girls is that they have strong preferences for activities that are hard to follow on account of their sex, which is inescapable." Gifted children, both boys and girls, often have trouble conforming to the expectations of adults around them. They find it hard to suppress their own initiative, to defer to authority when it contradicts their own insights. Gifted children become concerned with "problems of origin and destiny" at an age when they cannot handle these problems emotionally. "It is especially to be noted," Hollingworth concludes, "that many of these problems are functions of immaturity. To have the intelligence of an adult and the emotions of a child combined in a childish body is to encounter certain difficulties" (p. 282).

Hollingworth's study, although it is over thirty years old, is just as accurate a description today as it was when it was written. However, we should keep in mind that she is dealing with the problems of the gifted, and that the positive aspects of giftedness far outweigh the problems.

The Gifted Learner in the Classroom

The teacher of the gifted is faced with special challenges that the average learner does not present. But these challenges, when met, can yield handsome rewards and personal fulfillment. While most educators agree that the gifted have special needs, it is not always clear how these needs should be met. Should the gifted be placed in special classes or should they be integrated into the mainstream? What kind of stimulation is best to cultivate their abilities? How can their socialization skills be developed to the fullest? These and other questions are still the lively subject of debate in professional circles.

> "The gifted learner needs special stimulation within the classroom. The 'typical' curriculum and methodologies that prove effective for other students are prone to failure with the gifted."

Ingenuity in providing appropriate stimulation is especially important in working with the gifted learner.

What is agreed upon is that the gifted learner needs special stimulation within the classroom. The "typical" curriculum and methodologies that prove effective for other students are prone to failure with the gifted. The teacher must honestly assess his or her own abilities to meet the demands of the gifted learner. If the teacher is not up to the task, consultation with specialists may be of assistance. The teacher's failure to openly assess this issue may lead to counterproductive negative feelings directed at the gifted learner.

Example: Mrs. Robinson complained to the school counselor about Teddy, who she said was acting obnoxiously in class. When the school counselor consulted Teddy's records, he found that Teddy had an IQ of 165 and a reading level five years above his grade. How strange, the counselor thought to himself, that Mrs. Robinson never mentioned how intelligent Teddy was. He brought this up the next time he met with the teacher, and she confessed, "Oh, sure, he's bright, but he's also cocky and fresh."

Upon exploring this, the counselor found that Mrs. Robinson secretly resented Teddy's brightness. The boy asked questions she couldn't answer, pointed out, in one instance, a mistake the teacher had made, and finished the work far ahead of the other students. These behaviors brought out feelings of inadequacy in Mrs. Robinson—feelings she did not recognize—and these resulted in her negative feelings.

Often, the teacher will feel threatened by the gifted child, and this is natural. If the teacher is able to openly acknowledge these feelings, they need not be counterproductive; it is only when the teacher fails to recognize them that they become problematic.

In addition to dealing with personal feelings, the teacher can help the development of the gifted child in a number of ways. Careful planning is essential to assure that the learner is given material that meets his intellectual needs. Many gifted children are especially strong in one area and weak in another, and the teacher can help the learner build strength in deficit areas. In **heterogeneous** classes, the special socialization problems of the gifted should be taken into account, and the teacher can be very helpful in assisting the gifted child in resolving these problems. Moreover, if the teacher uses one of the expanded definitions of giftedness discussed above, it is likely that gifted students who would not otherwise be so identified can emerge in the classroom, and their special talents can be developed. Many a budding musical prodigy or mathematical wizard was neglected during the critical years of learning because of the failure of teachers to identify the student as a gifted learner.

Once the gifted learner has been identified, and recognized by the school administration, there are a number of effective ways of helping this learner maximize his or her enormous potential. Acceleration, in which the student is placed a year ahead, is one popular approach. There are both advantages and disadvantages to acceleration. The advantages are that it provides the learner with enrichment, paces his activities with his abilities, provides him with challenges, and enables him to complete his schooling in less time. The disadvantages of acceleration are that the child may be prematurely separated from his peers, or that he may not be maturationally capable of adequate socialization. On balance, however, acceleration is an effective approach to encouraging the gifted learner to develop to his full capacity.

Compatible with the ideas of acceleration are early admissions (to college) and advanced placement. Early admissions is the broader category in which the student is admitted to college before the completion of the senior year in high school. Advanced placement may be limited to certain subject-matter areas in which the student excels. However, advanced placement circumvents some of the pitfalls of both acceleration and early admissions since it more accurately assesses those areas in which the learner's competency is the greatest.

Enrichment, the approach in which the curriculum is strengthened, has been shown to be of some value. Enrichment programs may be oriented toward the entire class of gifted learners, or may include individualized approaches in which each learner's special abilities and aptitudes are tapped. While there are certainly many compelling reasons to advocate enrichment programs, there is some evidence that acceleration is the more productive approach.

Whichever approach is used, there are several clear-cut benefits for the learner. Boredom, an inevitable consequence of being a gifted person in an ungifted world, can be avoided if the learner is provided with sufficient opportunities to develop himself. More importantly, giftedness is our greatest natural resource and its cultivation works always to the benefit of the society. Finally, by appropriately meeting the needs of the gifted group, we are recognizing our obligation to this group; an obligation that, translated into practice, means the best of teaching for the best and most capable learners—those who will benefit most.

The Underachiever

One special class of gifted students deserves additional attention. The underachiever is a learner whose performance falls far below his capabilities. It is not unusual to find a student with an IQ above 140, whose performance in the school is average or even below average. Many studies have attempted to understand the contributing factors that result in underachievement. Most of these studies compare underachievers with bright children who perform well. Comparisons have been made on such factors as parental concern, socioeconomic background, siblings, personality traits, and so forth. But there is still no definite explanation of this phenomenon.

One of the more interesting characteristics of underachievement is that it is primarily a male problem. Shaw (1961) found in a review of the studies that have investigated underachievement that "approximately half of all males who are above average in ability may be considered underachievers." The corresponding figure for females is only 25 percent. In two case studies, Kimball (1952) investigated adolescent male underachievers. She found in many instances that these boys had poor father-son relationships. They revealed in various interviews and projective exams that their relationships with their fathers were neither close nor warm. Also, their fathers were seen as extremely authoritarian or domineering or else they were extremely hard workers, which subsequently resulted in emotional distance between parent and child. Kimball also noted that many of the boys showed feelings of inferiority and dependent needs.

Other factors have also been identified in contributing to underachievement: The education of the mother is negatively correlated with underachievement; parent absence is positively correlated, as is socioeconomic level. However, it is generally agreed that the most accurate understanding of underachievement can be attained only through interviewing the underachieving learner and by determining what needs are not being met, what problems are blocking the ability to fully exploit the learner's capabilities, what the teacher can do to mitigate the situation.

Underachievement is not limited to the gifted student. The normal student and the EMR may also underachieve; in fact, it has been suggested

Teaching: Art and Science

> "Underachievement is not limited to the gifted student. . . . in fact, it has been suggested that the EMR are the largest group of underachievers in the school system."

that the EMR are the largest group of underachievers in the school system. It is all too easy to dismiss the EMR as not capable of tasks that he may be readily capable of. But the criterion for identifying underachievement remains the same: the failure to perform commensurate with one's abilities.

Early identification of underachievement is critical for remediation. Jackson, Cleveland and Merenda (1975) conducted a longitudinal study on the effects of early identification and treatment (through counseling) of academic underachievers. The identification was made in the fourth grade, in which one group received psychological treatment while the other group did not. The group that received the treatment performed significantly better over a four-year period than did the control group that did not receive treatment. As with most learning and behavioral disorders, the earlier it is treated, the more likely will be the success of the treatment.

The Learning Disabled Student

The broadest definition of a learning disability would be any condition or set of conditions that prevents a person from functioning at grade level in one or several areas. This would include such conditions as perceptual disorders, motor disorders, brain damage (mild), or what are generally called learning blocks that affect only one area of endeavor. Several conditions may interact to produce a learning disability: A perceptual disability may be compounded by motor problems, with the result that the student cannot learn to write, even though he is intellectually capable of doing so. The diagnosis and remediation of learning disabilities is primarily the job of the classroom teacher, who has the most opportunity to observe and evaluate the student. In most instances, a learning specialist is called in for specific diagnosis, prognosis, and treatment approaches. In this section, we shall examine some of the broader issues in this area, avoiding the technicalities that would be more appropriate to an advanced course in the treatment of **learning disabled students.**

Usually the manifestation of a learning disability will be apparent to the teacher during the first two years of the child's schooling. A number of factors may lead the teacher to the conclusion that a child has a learning disability: inability to follow simple instructions or to repeat processes; func-

Identifying the Disabled Learner

tioning that is far below grade level; confusion in orientation; performance anomalies (such as turning to the left when told to turn to the right). The first process by which a learning disability is identified is *teacher observation*.

It is generally agreed that systematic observation is the basic screening technique for identifying the learning disabled student. Studies have demonstrated that this procedure does have value. Forness and Esveldt (1975) report the results of a study that indicate that teachers are able to identify disabled learners through observation. DeGenaro (1975) has described informal methods for assessing children suspected of having a learning disability. In attempting to answer the teacher's question, What can I do before the psychometrist arrives? DeGenaro argues in favor of "informal assessment." He presents informal methods by which the teacher can assess fourteen basic areas that include all of the learning disabilities:

1. Visual discrimination and memory
2. Auditory discrimination and memory
3. Letter identification
4. Writing the alphabet sequence
5. Phonetic knowledge
6. Tactual ability
7. Reversals and rotations
8. Verbal skills (oral)
9. Copying at near and far points
10. Reading levels
11. Self-concept
12. Eye-hand coordination and written language
13. Following directions
14. Gross motor skills

These fourteen areas, he argues, are sufficient to provide enough information to enable the teacher to make a general assessment that can then be confirmed by a psychometrist. More importantly, these informal procedures will allow the teacher to develop programs until more specific diagnoses can be made.

Although observation is an important tool, a caution must be stated. The teacher may show bias in observation; bias that can lead to incorrect, damaging diagnosis and treatment. McAvoy (1970) has explored the issue of systematic observation, defining it as a "formalized system of classifying, recording, and quantifying any form of teacher or pupil behavior which occurs in the classroom. Measurable variables in the classroom can be defined in one of three categories: presage, process, and product" (p. 10). Presage variables are "those characteristics which a teacher or pupil brings to the classroom." Process variables "include those behaviors, moves or strategies which are employed by a teacher or pupil in a classroom situation." Product variables "are measures of instructional outcomes." Using these categories, McAvoy suggests several possibilities for using systematic observation to increase teaching effectiveness. Applications of these procedures are especially helpful in identifying and treating the disabled learner.

The disabled learner may find outlets of creative expression outside the traditional curriculum.

The teacher's familiarity with different types of learning disorders will be an important factor in his or her ability to identify a specific disorder. We will consider some of the major learning disabilities in the following section, but it should be kept in mind that these constitute only a small percentage of the total disabilities.

The two disabilities most often encountered in the classroom are **dyslexia** and **minimal brain dysfunction (MBD).** Both of these are broad diagnostic terms that include a host of symptoms, some of which overlap. The most typical symptom of either or both of these is reading problems.

Types of Learning Disabilities

Dyslexia

Broadly defined, dyslexia is any retardation of normal learning ability with regard to reading; that is, where the ability to read is far below the intelligence of the learner. "Most reading difficulties" Bakwin and Bakwin (1972) point out, "may be included under the heading of developmental dyslexia. The characteristic feature is an inborn difficulty in comprehending written language" (p. 410). Often dyslexia is thought to be the disorder in which the learner sees reversed letters or groups of letters (*was* for *saw*), but this is only one type of dyslexia, and the term should be used more broadly.

> "The diagnosis of dyslexia is much easier than the treatment. . . . It is generally emphasized in the literature that the type of treatment will vary from child to child, depending upon a number of factors."

The diagnosis of dyslexia is much easier than the treatment. A variety of proposals have been put forth, some of which claim high rates of success, some of which are still in the experimental stages. McCoy (1975) has suggested the use of Braille "as an alternative language for the severely learning disabled student." She used this system to teach her daughter, a fifteen-year old dyslexic who could neither read nor write, and it worked. But it has not been tested, and at the present time its efficacy for mass educational efforts remains in question.

It is generally emphasized in the literature that the type of treatment will vary from child to child, depending upon a number of factors, such as the child's general intelligence; the nature of the dyslexia; the child's particular strengths; the motivation and home environment that the child brings to school. In addition, the type of treatment will depend to a large extent on whether the learner suffers from visual or auditory dyslexia. Johnson (1969), in discussing treatment approaches, considers both types of dyslexia. Speaking of visual dyslexics, she says:

> . . . characteristically they have a tendency to reverse, rotate, or invert letters or transpose letters within words. Some attend to details within words or to the general configuration but not to both. . . . Because they cannot perceive and remember whole words, we use an elemental or phonic approach in remediation. Letter sounds are introduced (a few consonants and short vowels) and the student blends them into meaningful words. . . . The objective is to help the student unlock the code, to convert the visual to the auditory as simply as possible. . . . *The basic approach to reading for the visual dyslexic circumvents his basic weakness and capitalizes on his strengths.* . . . (pp. 81–82)

This brief excerpt sums up the basic approach to treating the *visual* dyslexic, although there are hundreds of specific treatment models available, and it is usually a specialist in this area who will be most successful in remediative efforts. Research has demonstrated that the major problem for the visual dyslexic is in processing information that is sensed through the eyes. Stanley and Hall (1973), in a recent study, confirmed results of several earlier studies that show "significant differences exist between dyslexics and normals at early stages of visual information processing" (p. 843).

The *auditory* dyslexic, whose difficulties are in processing information obtained through audition, presents somewhat different problems, and there-

> "Despite the medical and organic implications of the term, minimal brain dysfunction (MBD) is not *necessarily* a physical disorder, and its chief diagnostic criteria are clinical . . . rather than neurological."

fore requires a different treatment strategy. Johnson (1969), speaking of this group, points out:

> . . . the auditory dyslexic usually cannot learn phonics and therefore is taught to read whole words. Characteristically these children have disturbances in auditory perception, rhyming, blending, analysis, and memory. . . . Many have difficulty with oral reading. Because of these learning patterns, the children are taught with an intrasensory visual approach during the initial stages of remediation. *They are taught a sight vocabulary which consists largely of nouns and verbs, that is, words which can be associated with an object, experience, or picture. In this way no oral response is required.* . . . (p. 82)

Again, treating the auditory dyslexic requires specialization, and an expert in this area will usually prove to be most effective.

The job of the regular classroom teacher is primarily to identify visual and auditory dyslexics, and this should be done early—by the first grade, if possible. The earlier the identification is made, the better the chance for improvement. It is those dyslexics who are not properly diagnosed, and who move on from grade to grade unable to master reading, that suffer the most.

Minimal Brain Dysfunction (MBD)

Minimal Brain Dysfunction (MBD) is a general term that characterizes a variety of behavioral and learning disorders that are commonly evident in the classroom. Despite the medical and organic implications of the term, MBD is not *necessarily* a physical disorder, and its chief diagnostic criteria are clinical (through observations in the classroom) rather than neurological. Many writers, such as Abrams (1975), define MBD in terms of inadequate ego functioning or in terms of specific learning disabilities, avoiding any physiological implications. His comments on the interchangeability of terms is revealing:

> Many of you have probably noted . . . that I have used MBD and reading disability almost synonymously. Essentially again, *whatever term is utilized depends primarily upon the orientation and interest of the individual assessing the problems.* [our itals.] When an individual is concerned particularly with a comprehensive diagnosis following a medical model, with the assessment of

biological concomitants and antecedents of the condition, and with the role of medical management, MBD is the label of choice. When the individual is concerned primarily with assessment of reading disabilities and techniques of remedial education, specific learning disability (SLD) often becomes the label. The difference and emphasis is reflected in the literature: authors who write from the medical orientation prefer the term "minimal brain dysfunction" or its equivalent, whereas those who write from an educational point of view tend to use the term "specific reading disabilities" or its equivalent. . . . (p. 220)

The important point for the teacher to remember is this: There are many fancy-sounding technical terms used interchangeably to describe what is essentially the same condition. Display 14.1 shows almost fifty technical terms

---

Display 14.1   *"What's in a Name"*

Teachers are apt to become confused and overwhelmed by all the technical jargon used to describe the exceptional learner. But, in reality, the situation is not as complicated as all the technical jargon implies. Ellingson (1975, p. 40) cites all the terms that are used interchangeably to describe what is actually a single disorder—a learning disability:

As with most learning disorders or disabilities, terminology is always a major problem. Every discipline, in fact every professional, seems to have a favorite term to describe the minimal brain damage or dysfunction syndrome. Some of the names applied and used interchangeably to describe this disorder are:

Aggressive Behavior Disorder
Aphasoid Syndrome
Association Deficit Pathology
Attention Disorder
Auditory Handicap
Brain Dysfunction
Cerebral Dysfunction
Cerebral Dyssynchronization
Character Impulse Disorder
Choreform Syndrome
Clumsy Child Syndrome
Conceptually Handicapped
Diffuse Brain Damage
Disorders of Attention
Disorders of Concept-formation
Disorders of Impulse Control
Disorders of Motor Coordination
Disorders of Perception
Distractibility
Dyscalculia
Dysgraphic
Dyssynchronous
Hyperexcitability Syndrome

Hyperkinetic Behavior Disorder
Hyperkinetic Behavior Syndrome
Hyperkinetic Impulse Syndrome
Hyperkinetic Syndrome
Hypokinetic Syndrome
Interjacent Child
Mild Neurosensory Defects
Minimal Brain Damage
Minimal Brain Dysfunction
Minimal Brain Injury
Minimal Cerebral Damage
Minimal Cerebral Injury
Minimal Chronic Brain Syndrome
Minor Brain Damage
Neurophrenia
Organic Behavior Disorder
Organic Brain Dysfunction
Organic Driveness
Organic Language Disorder
Organic Language Dysfunction
Perceptual Cripple
Perseverative
Psychoneurological Learning Disorders
Scatter Child
Visual-motor Perceptual Lag

Obviously so many names for the same general disability leads to confusion—especially when, in the majority of cases which fall under one of these descriptions, *the child does not necessarily display any visible handicap.*

---

that one author (Ellingson, 1975) has found can be used interchangeably to describe the same learning disabilities syndrome.

With this nomenclatural redundancy clearly in mind, we can proceed to describe some of the clinical signs of MBD. Weil (1973) differentiates between *congenital* and *acquired* MBD. The congenital type is indicated by a developmental lag, by "a slowness and initial deficiency in the maturation of certain centers and tracts, with the consequent clinical lag in the development of the corresponding functions" (p. 553). Areas affected may include speech, visual-motor coordination, psychomotor functioning, early reading failures, and so forth. Acquired MBD is usually the result of a childhood disease (especially encephalitis) or trauma (accident). It is diagnosed by sudden changes in the child's characteristic behavior and performance before and after the onset of the disease or trauma. Essentially, however, the symptoms of the two types are the same.

In describing the most typical symptomatology, Weil (1973) points out that "their motility may be damaged by focal lesions or diffusely affected in obvious awkwardness, jerkiness, or clumsiness, or pathology may be revealed only on very special scrutiny and testing" (p. 555). The teacher can be an effective diagnostician in both categories: in the former, through classroom observation; in the latter, through referral to the school psychologist for testing.

As we see from the symptomatology, the signs of MBD do not differ significantly from types of dyslexia or hyperactivity, and differential diagnoses between these three are often regarded as nitpicking. What is most important, rather than attempting to pinpoint a diagnosis, is to attempt to understand how the exceptional learner can be helped within the classroom setting. This requires not only an understanding of the behaviors (as we have explored in this section) but a sensitivity to the nuances of the classroom environment that can help or hinder the exceptional learner's growth and development. We shall consider this in the concluding section of this chapter.

The Hyperactive Child

Although this syndrome was first described in great detail in a humorous poem by a German physician, Heinrich Hoffman, in the mid-nineteenth century, it was not until the past decade that the term *hyperactive child* has entered the professional nomenclature. Nowadays, it is not uncommon to find teachers, school psychologists, parents—and even students—referring to manifest behavioral disorders as hyperactivity. Unfortunately, with the popularization of the term has come a loss of clarity and precision in its meaning, and it is

> "A hyperactive child, as the term implies, is an *overly* active child, in the physical sense of the word. Often, the term *hyperactive* is used synonymously with *hyperkinetic,* and this can be misleading."

probably abused more than any other diagnostic term today. We are prone to label any disruptive child—any student who gives the teacher a great deal of trouble—as hyperactive, and this is often incorrect and certainly unfair to the child. In this section, we will attempt to clarify what hyperactivity is, how it appears in the classroom, and how it can be dealt with by the teacher.

Who Is the Hyperactive Child?

A hyperactive child, as the term implies, is an *overly* active child, in the physical sense of the world. Often, the term **hyperkinetic** is used synonymously with **hyperactive,** and this can be misleading, especially since hyperkinetic is so technical sounding. In commenting on the interchangeability of these terms, Zukow (1975) argues:

Unfortunately, the medical literature and lay press use the terms *hyperactivity* and *hyperkinetic* interchangeably. In my opinion, they are not the same. The problems which arise in using the terms . . . . interchangeably is more than semantic. For instance, frustrated adults reacting to a child who does not meet their standards can easily exaggerate the significance of the child's occasional inattention or restlessness and label the youngster hyperkinetic. (p. 39)

He goes on to clarify the differentiation between hyperactivity and hyperkinesis. The hyperactive child is overly ebullient and may be disruptive; the hyperkinetic child shows "purposeless physical activity and a significantly impaired span of focused attention. The inability to control physical motion and attention may generate other consequences, such as disturbed moods and behavior within the home, at play with peers, and in the schoolroom." This leads to the conclusion that the teacher must make a qualitative assessment of the student's behavior. What does this excited activity mean? Does it have purpose or is it purposeless? Is the child overly active *and* unable to focus attention and concentrate, or is the activity also manifest in the child's ability to attend to the world around him? Are there concomitant learning problems or is the child's disposition toward gregariousness and spontaneity? These kinds of questions lead to the qualitative assessment.

Cantwell (1975) has provided a comprehensive guideline for the diagnostic evaluation of the hyperactive child. His diagnostic strategy is particularly useful in differentiating between overt hyperactivity and deeper rooted hyperkinesis because it is intensive and thorough. He proposes six aspects to the evaluation: interview with the parents; interview with the child; behavior rating scales; physical examination; neurological examination; and laboratory studies. The first two aspects can be easily managed by the classroom teacher. A school psychologist and psychiatrist would have to be called in for the remaining four stages. It is important to keep in mind, however, that to be able legitimately to diagnose a student as hyperkinetic (or *clinically hyperactive*) it is imperative that a physical (neurological, especially) examination be administered. This not only determines possible organic causes for the disorder—which may be metabolic, minimal brain dysfunction, or other—but assures the teacher that his or her perceptions of hyperactive behavior are not being misused for an invalid judgment.

Whenever the teacher acts as a diagnostician, there is the implicit danger of subjectivity and bias in the diagnosis, and this is especially true in cases of hyperactivity. There is a tendency on many teachers' parts to label all children who misbehave or are otherwise obstreperous in the classroom as hyperactive, when, in fact, it may be no more than the teacher's inability to understand the behavior that is the cause of the problem. Several objective rating scales are available whereby the teacher can assess the presence and degree of hyperactivity. McConnel, Cromwell, and Bialer (1964) have developed a child-rating scale that measures the activity level of the child through the rater's (teacher's) responses to questions. Conners (1969, 1970, 1973) has developed several rating scales that can be used by teachers and parents to assess hyperactivity. These scales offer a qualitative and quantitative dimension to the measurement and are particularly useful.

Having now examined some of the criteria by which hyperactivity is diagnosed, let us consider ways of dealing with the problems of the hyperactive child in the classroom.

The most controversial topic in this area is the efficacy and ethics of drug treatment for hyperactivity. During the past decade, a number of drugs have been used to manage the hyperactive child's behavior, both in the classroom and in the home. Ritalin (*methylphenidate hydrochloride*), a stimulant drug, has been shown effective in "calming" the hyperactive child. Although it is still a source of controversy among physicians as well as educators, as of 1976 the Food and Drug Administration has classified Ritalin effective in the treatment of minimal brain dysfunction in children, which is defined broadly enough to include hyperactive children: ". . . as adjunctive therapy to other measures" (psychological, educational, social). It is clear from this restriction that Ritalin is not a *cure* for hyperactivity, but merely a stopgap measure that must be accompanied by positive therapeutic experiences.

Deaner (*deanol acetamidobenzoate*) is another drug often prescribed in the treatment and management of hyperkinesis. The Food and Drug Administration has classified Deaner as "possibly effective" for the following:

Managing the Hyperactive Child

1. Learning problems—learning in deficit of that usually associated with apparent level of intelligence, including IQ and reading difficulties. Shortened attention span.

2. Behavior problems—hyperkinetic behavior problem syndrome characterized by distractibility, motor disinhibition, dissociation and perseveration.
3. Or, as more frequently encountered, hyperkinetic behavior and learning disorders incorporating varying combinations of both of the above. Underachievers, reading and speech difficulties. Impaired motor coordination. Hyperactive, impulsive/compulsive behavior, often described as asocial, antisocial, delinquent, stimulus governed.

Final classification of the less than effective indications requires further investigation. (*Physicians Desk Reference* 1976)

While the disorders listed make Deaner appear almost a panacea, it must again be emphasized that this drug has not yet been proven effective in the treatment of any of these disorders.

Cylert (*Pemoline*) has also gained some prominence in the treatment of hyperactivity. It is generally considered effective and safe in the treatment of hyperkinesis. Page et al. conducted comprehensive research on the efficacy of Cylert and found that it "is a highly useful clinical alternative to the amphetamines and methylphenidate as an adjunct in the management of hyperkinetic children." Again, we must stress that these drugs are valuable as adjuncts to therapeutic experiences.

The amphetamines, which are powerful stimulants, were the first drugs used in the treatment of hyperkineses, but they are prescribed less widely today as the three drugs listed above—much safer to use—have come into prominence. Grinspoon and Singer (1973), in reviewing the extensive research on amphetamine use in the treatment of hyperkinetic children, conclude that there is insufficient evidence to justify the frequency with which these drugs are prescribed; and currently efforts are underway to ban the use of amphetamines altogether. Questions about the propriety of using drugs to control children's behavior deserves attention from all teachers, even though it is not they who prescribe the drug.

To Drug or Not to Drug?

John Holt, an outspoken opponent of prescribing drugs to quell hyperactivity, calls this practice "quackery." In strong language, he vents his feelings on this issue:

We take lively, curious, energetic children, eager to make contact with the world and to learn about it, stick them in barren classrooms with teachers who on the whole neither like nor respect nor understand nor trust them. . . . Then, when the children resist this brutalizing and stupefying treatment and retreat from it in anger, bewilderment, and terror, we say that they are sick with 'complex and little-understood' disorders, and proceed to dose them with powerful drugs that are indeed complex and of whose long-run effects we know little or nothing, so that they may be more ready to do the asinine things the schools ask them to do. (Holt, 1970)

> "Despite the criticisms, there is much evidence that drugs *can* help the hyperactive child maintain himself long enough to benefit from good educational practice."

Other writers have echoed the same feelings, chiding the schools—as well as the medical profession—for dispensing drugs promiscuously, when there is not sufficient evidence that they are either required or beneficial. Grinspoon and Singer (1973), for example, argue that "using drugs to 'modify' classroom behavior constitutes a covert subversion of what *should* be our educational ideals. If an important aim of our educational institutions were really to help young people deal with and learn to regulate their 'self-destructive' or even 'anti-social' tendencies, it would make little sense to give them drugs as soon as they exhibited restless or unruly behavior" (p. 544).

Despite these criticisms, there is much evidence that drugs *can* help the hyperactive child maintain himself long enough to benefit from good educational practice. Teachers, who have to deal on a day-to-day basis with these children, are especially resentful at times of "ivory tower" theorists who condemn the use of drugs.

Both advocates and critics of drug administration agree on one important point: Drugs do not cure the disorder. Those who argue against the use of these drugs suggest that the teacher rely solely on sound educational and therapeutic techniques; those who favor drug administration emphasize its adjunctive function and seek simultaneous treatment modalities. Let us now consider some classroom strategies for dealing with the hyperactive child.

Classroom Strategies for the Teacher of the Hyperactive Child

In recent years, as the recognition of hyperkinesis as a common syndrome has increased, there has been a sudden outburst of innovative approaches that the teacher can use in dealing with the hyperactive child. Forness (1975) cites three areas in which educational approaches can be particularly helpful: attentional deficits, impulse control, and motivation. We will consider each of these separately since they constitute the major categories of problematic behavior.

"The attention problems of the hyperactive child," Forness (1975) points out, "render it less likely that information acquisition will be complete and that effective learning will take place" (pp. 163–164). While there is no universally accepted method for increasing the attention of the hyperactive child (drugs are clearly most effective in this!), several innovative designs have been suggested. In a thorough review of the literature, Alabiso (1974) found "that attention appears to be a multi-behavioral process that is incompatible with hyperactive behavior." The most important finding from this survey is that operant conditioning procedures (which are discussed in detail in chapter 12) are valid methods for increasing the hyperactive child's attention span. He cites a wealth of evidence that these techniques can be used successfully to increase the child's attention span. Maier and Hogg (1974), in another study, investigated the use of operant conditioning in increasing the hyperactive child's sustained visual fixation. They found, as have other studies, ". . . that the behavior of the hyperactive child is amenable to modification through the appropriate management of discriminative stimuli and reinforcement contingencies" (p. 297). Several implications of this and other studies can be translated into a few basic principles that will help the teacher deal with the brief attention span of the hyperactive child:

1. Organize the classroom so that there is a minimum of distracting stimuli. Bright colors and lights as well as noise can "set off" the hyperactive child.
2. Structure lessons in short, complete units, requiring no more than fifteen minutes of sustained attention. A rest period, in which the child can run around and discharge his energy, should punctuate lessons.
3. Calmness on the part of the teacher helps induce calmness in the children. This, in turn, increases the attention span.
4. Coordinate visual and aural stimuli so that the child is not overwhelmed. For example, writing a word on the blackboard as the teacher is saying the word is helpful.
5. Develop conditioning programs that are directed toward increasing, bit by bit, the child's attention span.

In addition to research on increasing attention span, much research has been done on decreasing the child's impulsiveness. Again, **operant conditioning** proves the method preferred (where drugs are not being used). Mitchell and Crowell (1973) report on a **behavior modification** program with three nine-year-old boys who were classified as hyperactive. They were informed that they would be observed during their art class and rewarded for good behavior by use of a point system. The boys' behavior improved significantly, and this in turn positively affected their classmates' behavior. Six conclusions were made from this study:

1. A behavior modification program can bring about change if the behavior to be changed is pinpointed, recorded, and modified by reinforcement.
2. A periodic review of class rules seems to be an effective way to remind children of the expected class procedures.
3. Teacher consistency is extremely important.
4. Modifying the behaviors of selected students in a class seems to affect the behavior of other students within the same class.

Physical play may serve to discharge the hyperactive child's need for physical expression.

5. A counselor can be effective in serving as a consultant to teachers in setting up such a program.
6. Instructors report that teaching is more enjoyable and the work of students is improved when students receive positive reinforcement. (p. 41)

In another paper, Kauffman and Hallahan (1973) describe how "an unruly, hyperactive boy was managed in a free-play setting, using reinforcement techniques: A highly structural directive teaching program (DISTAR) contributed to his tractability while developing his academic skills" (1225). These and many other papers that have appeared in the professional journals are reassuring to the teacher of the hyperactive child. They show that, despite the many difficulties of working with such children, there can be effective means for educating them, even if they are not on medication. Still, the combination of medication and adjunctive educational and therapeutic programs proves the treatment of choice for this condition.

Conclusions

At the present time, hyperactivity is diagnosed by certain characteristic behaviors including short attention span, unruly active behaviors over which the child appears to have little control, attendant learning disorders, lack of motivation, and inability to follow instructions (including psychomotor anomalies at times). Rating scales are available for the teacher to determine the presence and extent of this condition, and it is suggested that a medical examination be conducted for a complete diagnosis.

A number of medications have proven effective in the management of hyperactivity; Ritalin, Deaner, Cylert, and amphetamines have demonstrated

> "There are a number of things the teacher can do to help the hyperactive child. . . . Lessons should be broken down into short, complete units. The classroom atmosphere should not be distracting, and the child should not be asked to concentrate on several things at once."

efficacy. But no drug is curative; rather, each is recommended for use with adjunctive treatments (educational or psychological) that can be implemented in the classroom. Debate persists over the efficacy and ethicality of using drugs to quell disruptive students' behaviors, and each teacher (or parent) has to make his or her own decision on this matter.

There are a number of things the teacher can do to help the hyperactive child adjust in the classroom. Recognizing the child's brief attention span, it is imperative that the lessons be broken down into short, complete units. The classroom atmosphere should not be distracting, and the child should not be asked to concentrate on several things at once. Behavior modification programs have been used to increase attention span and to facilitate learning. It is helpful if other members of the educational team—such as parents, the school psychologist and counselor, the physician—be used in conjunction with the teacher to provide a comprehensive program of treatment. The teacher should allow for physical activity during the day so that the child has the opportunity to discharge some of his excessive energy.

The Exceptional Learner in the Classroom

After reading the preceding section, you are probably tempted to ask, "What can I do to help with the exceptional learner?" This is the question we will attempt to answer in this section.

Identification is, as we have stated, the first step. The teacher must be able to assess the needs of each learner and to understand special learner problems that require intervention before successful learning behaviors can occur. From that point, specialized teaching approaches can be helpful. The most challenging problems facing the teacher are often obscured in unnecessary technical language, which may act as a barrier to effective teaching. We have already discussed this point, but it still requires emphasis. Niensted (1975), in talking with teachers of students with learning disabilities, concluded that many disagreements between learning disability teachers and reading teachers are the result of communication gaps between them. He, like many others in the field, argues for a joint vocabulary. Table 14.1 shows the parallel ways of viewing a phenomenon based on one's theoretical approach. Perhaps some integrative perspective will better enable *all* teachers to work better with the

Table 14.1   Parallel Approaches to Understanding the Exceptional Learner

Language of the layman	Language of the reading specialist	Language of the LD teacher
When you show the child a letter, can he give you its sound?	When shown a phonogram, can the child respond with the correct phoneme?	Does the child associate a visual clue for a phoneme with its auditory motor expression?
When you pronounce a sound, can the child point to the letter for that sound?	After a list of words with the same initial phoneme are pronounced to him, does the child select the appropriate grapheme?	When presented with an auditory clue is the child able to select the associated visual symbol? Or, does he have visual recall for auditory input?
If you pronounce a word, can he write its first letter?	After hearing a word pronounced, can the child write its initial phonogram?	Can he integrate his visual recall with the necessary motor expression?

Parallel versions of Grace Fernald's (1943) tracing technique

LD teacher	Reading teacher
Because lack of closure claims a child's attention, don't pronounce the word being studied before you begin to write it.	Because a child has little reason to pay attention if he already knows what you're going to write, don't pronounce the word being studied before you begin to write it.
Then begin giving auditory input as you give visual input.	Write the word as you say it.
Next provide kinesthetic and tactile stimuli associated with auditory and visual input so that the child can associate his channel of strength with his channel of deficit.	Have the child trace the word as you pronounce it. He is hearing it as he sees it, as he traces it.
Next give practice in strengthening visual memory.	Ask him to take a picture of the word in his mind's eye.
Give opportunity for visual-motor expression of his visual short-term memory.	Cover the word and ask him to write it from memory.
Let him provide his own immediate feedback.	Uncover the word and have him check letter by letter to see if he wrote it correctly.
At this time, the goal is not putting the visual pattern into his long-term memory, but of forming visual-motor-auditory associations.	At this time, he is learning sound-letter correspondence rather than memorizing the spelling of words.

Serena Niensted, "Talking with LD Teachers," *Reading Teacher,* Vol. 28 (1975): p. 664. Reprinted by permission.

learning disabled student. To this end, we propose that specific classroom applications be given priority over theoretical considerations (even though in many cases the latter is a prerequisite to the former).

Both the structure of the classroom and the methods employed require some modification in working with both the learning disabled and exceptional learner. Special motivational techniques may be needed to increase the child's

> **"Common to all categories of emotional disorders of childhood is the high degree of anxiety suffered by the child."**

ability to concentrate on a task. The teacher may have to restructure the order of presentation to circumvent some of the problematic areas in which the learner shows signs of deficit. After-school tutoring can also be helpful if the class time does not prove sufficient to get across the subject matter. In a later section of this chapter, we will look at more specific classroom modifications.

In addition to the types of exceptionalities we have been discussing, the category of *emotionally disturbed learner* is of major importance. Unfortunately, the term is often used too loosely, and many of the learning disabled students are unfairly placed in this category. However, if used cautiously, the term *emotionally disturbed* can be meaningful—even helpful in identifying specific learning, social, or behavioral problems that share a psychological origin. In the next section, we will consider the main features of emotional disturbance manifested in the classroom, and in the concluding section we will examine specific classroom practices designed to help the exceptional and emotionally disturbed learner.

Features of Emotional Disturbance Manifested in the Classroom*

Anxiety Common to all categories of emotional disorders of childhood is the high degree of anxiety suffered by the child. The sources and manifestations of this anxiety may differ with each disorder. The psychotic child's anxiety frequently centers around his confusion of identity, perceptual distortions, inability to separate real and unreal, and fear of survival in the face of the wide assortment of dangers he perceives around him. The neurotic child's anxiety centers around his inner psychic conflicts with fear of disaster if he either meets his needs or gives up his constricting symptoms. The anxiety of the child with the behavior disorder centers about his inadequacy in coping with external forces which he perceives as liable to starve, destroy or control him. Brain-damaged children are anxious about their poor performance and the exposure of their failure to the world.

* Reprinted with permission of the publisher from *Educational Therapy*, Vol. 1, "Clinical Principles of Curriculum Selection" by R. S. Cohen & R. LaVietes, edited by Jerome Hellmuth, Special Child Publications, 4535 Union Bay Place, N.E., Seattle, Wash., 98105 © 1966.

The skill of the teacher in working with these children depends on his ability to recognize the numerous manifestations of the child's anxiety and particularly on his ability to reduce anxiety in the child and in the group situation. This reduction of the child's anxiety level is the first step in increasing his educational capacity and academic achievement. Careful daily programming as well as selection or modification of the content of curriculum can serve as important educational tools to accomplish this reduction.

Common to many emotionally disturbed children is their difficulty in control of instinctual drives and primitive impulses. The urge to gratify needs is very insistent in emotionally disturbed children who do not have the tools to understand or regulate these emotions. The inability to delay gratification or tolerate frustration of immediate desires, to hold back his urges in favor of long-range goals, contributes to the child's difficulties in the learning situation. In addition, his expectation that he will be deprived of gratification as well as his confused time sense create difficulties in control for the child and difficulties in management for the teacher.

Difficulty in Impulse Control

Since aggressive and sexual drives can either promote or interfere with learning, these need to be understood and regulated so that they can be used to promote learning. Modification of programming and content of curriculum can serve to channel and counterbalance the force of these drives and keep them under appropriate control.

While manifestations of anxiety and acting-out behavior present the greatest difficulties in these special classrooms, many other features of emotional disturbance impinge on the learning process and lead to school disabilities. In the next section we will attempt to suggest some ways of dealing with these manifestations of disorder through selective *programming* and *modification of curriculum content*.

1. Timing: Disturbed children have vague and distorted perceptions of time. They often become anxious under pressure of time limits. The teacher's strategic timing of the introduction and termination of activities, his use of time allotments and schedules, and his flexibility in adapting these to changing group needs, influence the effectiveness of the learning situation and the child's ability to function in the group.

Principles of Program Modification

2. Pacing: Because of the child's brief attention span, intolerance of frustration and extreme emotional reaction patterns, suitable sequences of activities are necessary for effective teaching of emotionally handicapped children. Alternation of sedentary and motor activities, challenging and easily mastered projects, anxiety raising and anxiety lowering activities, gratification and frustration, solitary and group, manual and cognitive, must be constantly incorporated into all daily programming in order to enhance

the child's learning capacity. For example, the provision of food after a challenging activity, the change of pace after a lunch period, with a quiet structured activity like handwriting, help to reduce tension and anxiety in these classrooms.

3. Transitions: Changing from one activity to another causes a rise in tension with groups of emotionally disturbed children. This is often due to the child's inability to detach himself from what he is doing, his fear of the unfamiliar and the disorganizing effect of loss of focus. Impulse release may follow and these times become difficult ones in the school day. The handling of transitions in a relaxed and thoughtful manner is part of the teacher's armamentarium of skills. For example, talking about the project to follow helps to prepare the child for the next experience. Provision of simple, non-challenging and repetitive activities during the necessary waiting periods—coloring and dot books—helps to make such transitions smoother. Sustained emotional contact with children during these transitions prevents disorganization due to loss of object.

4. Routine: While routine is, by definition, part of every child's school day, it is of particular importance to the disturbed child. The use of repetition and routine has unquestionable value in ordering and stabilizing the world of the child, establishing a connection with the outside world, encouraging identification with peers, providing opportunity for mastery and limiting the danger of the unknown. However, this must sometimes be measured against the possibility of boredom, passivity, lack of stimulus to creativity and reinforcement of compulsive patterns.

5. Control of sensory input: Emotionally disturbed children tend to be distractible by virtue of their blurred focus and greater tendency towards impulse release. In addition, they are often acutely sensitive to intense auditory and excessive visual stimulation. These factors necessitate control of sensory experiences which might increase these difficulties. For example, an open classroom door tends to distract children as they respond to the variety of irrelevant stimuli and are unable to concentrate. A cluttered table or work page tends to divert the child from the task at hand. At the same time consideration must be given to providing experiences which promote interest, curiosity and healthy excitement in the balancing of the school day.

6. Sensory distortions and preferences: Emotionally disturbed children tend to show strong preferences for specific sensory modalities and to distort many sensory experiences. To deal with this, the teacher needs to select curriculum materials based on an assessment of the need to emphasize or de-emphasize a sensory modality for the particular child. Gradual and strategic introduction of exposure to other modalities would help children whose fixed preferences for one modality impede learning.

> "The therapeutic climate of a classroom is strongly influenced by quantity, distribution, control, and variation of material."

7. Spatial arrangement: The need of the emotionally disturbed child for proximity to the teacher, particularly when delay of gratification is required, or conversely, the need for distance on the part of the child who fears physical contact, the availability of private corners of the room for children who need the privacy of being away from the group at times, the provision of ample work space to avoid mutual irritation and tension are all factors that enter into making suitable physical and spatial arrangements in classrooms of emotionally disturbed children.

8. Use of materials: The therapeutic climate of a classroom is strongly influenced by quantity, distribution, control and variation of material. An economy of scarcity tends to increase the child's sense of deprivation and leads to consequent tension and acting-out. On the other hand, an atmosphere of abundance tends to reduce anxiety about deprivation and leads to a more relaxed classroom atmosphere. An abundance of well sharpened pencils at the beginning of a work period can prevent many a classroom explosion caused by the child's irritations at defects or scarcity of tools. Problems of waiting, sharing, and the symbolic significance of giving and receiving are raised by the method of distribution of materials. Aggressive acting-out and destruction caused by a rise in the child's tension and anxiety about possible deprivation can be avoided by availability of plentiful supplies accompanied by techniques of distribution which minimize competition and rivalry. In addition, avoidance of overstimulating materials like glass jars of paints or hammers which can be used as lethal weapons can prevent unwanted behavior.

9. Intervention to control behavior: The ability to set appropriate limits and establish classroom controls is the first step in establishing a secure learning environment for emotionally disturbed children. Effective and appropriate intervention of a teacher into interactions between disturbed children or into destructive use of materials provides much ego support and relief of tension. If intervention is too early when a problem is self-limiting or too late when it is unresolvable, it can lead to group chaos and compound the child's already heavy load of burdensome difficulties, making classroom management impossible.

Awareness of potential danger spots in terms of materials and immediate removal is effective in preventing explosions. For example, the instant removal of milk containers when children are finished prevents many a temptation to throw or spill remaining contents.

The means by which the teacher conveys approval or disapproval and sets moral standards for classroom behavior must be evaluated in terms of the child's readiness and ability to perceive and respond to the teacher's message. Because of the emotionally disturbed child's frequent anti-adult feelings and distorted concepts of pain-pleasure, conventional punishment-reward systems for enforcing discipline are often inapplicable. On the other hand, many classical nursery school techniques of control seem to be effective with emotionally disturbed children.

Principles of Content Selection and Curriculum Modification

1. Affectivity: Emotionally disturbed children often experience intense emotional upheavals and an urgent need for emotional response from others. Teacher's maintenance of emotional contact with the child tends to reduce his anxiety centering around loss of object.

In addition, these children are often deficient in their comprehension of emotions, the motivations of behavior and its interpersonal effects. A therapeutic curriculum for emotionally disturbed children would therefore include the development and use of materials with meaningful emotional content which could be used to explain human action as a result of feeling, clarify emotional distortions, define and classify emotions in terms of appropriateness or inappropriateness and teach the meaning of facial expressions and gestures.

2. Cognition: Emotionally disturbed children have deviant patterns for intake of information due to anxiety, selective inattention, ego-boundary confusions, and asocial attitudes. While some of these patterns may have served former defensive needs, they impede current learning capacity. Understanding of these obstructions to intake can help the teacher to select curriculum content which circumvents the barrier of these deviant patterns.

Distorted thinking, frightening fantasies and bizarre preoccupations about death and destruction pervade the emotionally disturbed child. Curriculum materials can be geared to decreasing the fear produced by such fantasies, avoiding proliferation of further fantasies and fortifying the child's sense of reality.

3. Fantasy and reality balance: Many emotionally disturbed children have difficulty in perceiving and evaluating reality. The child who cannot distinguish between fantasy and reality finds learning all the more difficult due to this confusion. Constant clarification of reality through pictures and materials that are clear representations of meaningful parts of the world can help children with this difficulty.

With children who do not suffer from the inability to distinguish fantasy from reality, fantasy may often be used to promote learning. Some emotionally disturbed children suffer from a paucity of fantasy material and are unable to use fantasy as an aid to resolution of conflicts. Such children need to be exposed to varieties of fantasy material.

A balance of reality and fantasy through selection of appropriate content in accordance with each child's need in this area can be used to promote desirable learning goals, especially in language arts and social studies.

4. Body Image: Confusion about the self and bodily limits, exaggerated fears of external threats to bodily integrity are a common source of learning difficulty. Curriculum must be modified and new materials developed geared to minimizing fears of bodily disintegration, confusion of body parts in relation to each other and the outside world, and to correcting distorted concepts. Large realistic pictures of children can be used to teach body parts. This can be accompanied by the child's tactile experience of touching his own face, nose, etc. and to help differentiate sensations of touching another's body. "Put your finger on your head," and verses of this popular childhood song is a useful technique. On the other hand, pictures with distortion of size, shape and proportions of the human body should be avoided. A popular toy like Mr. Potato-Head in which body parts are interchangeable and distorted, as well as popular card games like Mixies in which faces and body parts of different persons are separated and then put together in amusing designs should also be avoided in classrooms of emotionally disturbed children.

5. Orientation and identity: Distorted concepts of person, confusion of sexes, disorientation in time and place are special areas of aberrant functioning in these children. The teacher's awareness of these difficulties and the learning impediments created by them helps in selection of educational activities to correct this disorientation. Personal Identity books, mirror or beauty parlor play, body drawings and outlines are helpful to children with these identity disturbances. A daily calendar, date on board, clock in classroom and a daily orientation period help to orient the child in time and place. Names of children on cubbies and desks help to solidify the child's sense of self and his place in the classroom world. Discussions of important events in the group life of the classroom help to reduce uncertainty and clarify reality for these children. Discussions of absent children as well as the practice of telephoning them at home tend to solidify the child's sense of group belonging as well as to reduce his fear of death through disappearance from the scene.

6. Concrete-abstract balance: To move from the sensory experience to the abstract or symbolic is the natural learning sequence in areas of read-

> "The classroom is a way of communicating to your children. It is a way of telling them what you think of them, what the purpose of this place is, what needs of theirs are going to be met here."

ing, language arts and number work. Emotionally disturbed children often tend to be either overly concrete or at times overly abstract. They may be inflexible and unable to shift from one level to another. The teacher needs to be aware of each child's style of thinking and its limitations and how to help move him to other styles. Selection and use of materials can help the child improve his ability to move from one level to another appropriately.

7. Autonomy and personal care: Emotionally disturbed children invariably have difficulties in caring for themselves, and in ordering and organizing their environment to enhance their own functioning. A basic curriculum sequence proceeding from self-care to more complicated social functioning with emphasis on development of personal and social know-how and based on cause-and-effect principles in social interaction would help the child to deal with this deficiency in functioning.

The Classroom for the Learning Disabled and Emotionally Disturbed*

The classroom is a way of communicating to your children. It is a way of telling them what you think of them, what the purpose of this place is, what needs of theirs are going to be met here. The room is a reflection of the teacher and of the relationship between teacher and child, and of the way the class is going. The classroom is both an expression of the philosophy of a program and an important tool in carrying out this philosophy.

When one walks into a room in which the walls are bare, no materials are in sight and screens surround each child's place of work, it is immediately apparent what the guiding philosophy of this program is. It is one of limiting the amount of stimuli which these children have to deal with. This room says

* Taken from mimeographed material prepared by the Bureau for the Education of Socially Maladjusted and Emotionally Disturbed Children, Board of Education of the City of New York, 1976. Gloria J. Lee, Assistant Director; Administrator, Special Education Services for Emotionally Handicapped Children; Aurelia Allen, Acting Supervisor, Junior Guidance; Wendy Lehrman, Acting Supervisor, Classes for Emotionally Handicapped; Edith Wolf, Acting Supervisor, Junior Guidance; Judy Schmidt, Curriculum Consultant, Junior Guidance; Sadie Stein, Acting Supervisor, Junior Guidance; Rachel Zurer, Psychiatric Social Worker, Junior Guidance. Used with permission.

to the children, "I am going to help you by presenting you with only as much stimulation as you can handle." If one enters a room where the walls are covered with children's work, recent and carefully displayed, where stories about the . . . children and pictures of them abound, then another philosophy, or at the least, a different emphasis is apparent. Here the room says, "I value and understand each one of you, your efforts and your achievements. I will try to help you value yourself more."

In thinking of classrooms for disturbed children, one must re-examine every aspect of the physical environment in the light of the special needs of these children. Some of the aspects of the room which have to be examined include size and shape, sound control, lighting, color, kind and arrangement of furniture, kind of storage facilities, use of wall space, location of equipment and supplies. The relation of the room to strategic school centers, such as the gymnasium, toilet, lunchroom, also deserves consideration. Planning will take into account the common needs of all children and the special needs of disturbed children. The philosophy of the program, the limits and possibilities in terms of the physical environment, the materials or finances available and the ingenuity of the teacher will all combine to mold the room and the program.

What are the needs and characteristics of disturbed children which have implications for room planning? Following is a list of some of these needs and their implications:

Characteristics of Disturbed Children Which Have Implications for Room Planning

1. *The need to withdraw from the group.* All children, but disturbed children in particular, can't always function in a group. There are times during the school day when the presence of other children or the presence of a whole class of children and the need to interact with them becomes too stimulating or upsetting. There has to be a place for an upset child to withdraw to. This suggests perhaps a room with one or two partitioned-off cubicles; or a room with nooks and crannies into which desks and chairs can be moved; or an L-shaped room so that mutually destructive children don't have to be constantly within sight of one another; or two adjoining rooms with a wide-open doorway between them; or it could suggest sectioning off a corner of a room with room dividers for this purpose. This withdrawal space should be a temporary haven; with growth, the need for it should diminish.

"Planning classrooms to give privacy or semiprivacy or the illusion of privacy for small groups provides relief from constant membership in large groups. . . ." "Curriculum and the Elementary School Plant," p. 54

A child may be able to tolerate the presence of three other children painting at easels set off from the main group of the class while the close proximity of and grouping with eight or ten other children may prove to be too stimulating or frightening. A phonograph with earphones can be kept there. A primary typewriter or a viewmaster with a few, carefully selected slides might also serve the purpose of calming and absorbing a distraught child.

2. *Hyperactivity.* Since these children are characterized by more diffused mobility it is valuable to seek acceptable movement and activities that are directed and limited, and constructively channeled as an area of sublimation. Music, dance and other forms of rhythmic activities in which the explosive centrifugal directions are limited can be combined towards acceptable outlets. (Genuine physical activities usually appropriate to the gymnasium should not be encouraged in the classroom. They disorganize the children and make definition of the function of the classroom difficult.) The need for gross movement activities suggests the need for a large open space within the classroom. This space can best be provided at special times during the day by rearrangement of movable furniture or equipment. Large open spaces when not in use can excite and incite the children to uncontrolled and inappropriate movement.

Space allowances should include movement opportunities for the children while they are seated. Arms and legs need room to stretch and twist and shake. Seating arrangements should take into consideration the individual movement needs of the children.

3. *Disorientation in Space* implies the need for consistency in physical arrangement of the room. It implies the need for a place of anchor for each child from which he can orient himself; a desk and seat attached may be better suited to meet the needs of hyperactive children with spatial disorientation. In some cases fixed furniture may even be called for, although fixed furniture in and of itself is insufficient to meet the needs of a class; the built-in rigidity of fixed furniture interferes with the possibility of meeting temporary needs and stages of growth. In classes with fixed furniture, all of the extra desks should be removed to make room for other kinds of equipment.

4. *Poor Motor Coordination.*

"In general, the stumbling, tumbling, bumping, spilling, dropping that goes on reminds one of a group of much younger children—sometimes kindergartners, sometimes those in nursery school." Montgomery Board of Education, p. 21

To take into account a child's poor motor control would mean to provide wide aisles and pathways for access to all areas which the children use; it would mean eliminating small objects from places where they can easily be knocked down; it would mean storing materials in such a way that they're easy to get at and easy to return; it would mean readying the class to accept and deal with spilled liquids, broken objects and other accidents.

5. *Lack of Initiative (or Destructive Initiative), Inability to Make Choices and Dependence; Feelings of Helplessness.* The placement and storage of materials has direct relevance to the problem of developing initiative. When materials are kept in closed shelves and are chosen and distributed by the teacher or a monitor exclusively, the children are deprived of the experience necessary to the development of initiative. On the other hand open shelves with attractive materials in sight may prove too great a distraction and temptation to children when the teacher is trying to get them involved in a group activity or in a formal academic learning situation.

Some materials may probably be left on open shelves in any classroom without proving themselves too disruptive. These include library and reference books, magazines, drawing paper and writing paper. Children can be encouraged to help themselves to these materials when they complete an activity before the rest of the class. Some materials such as jars of paint and fingerpaint and ceramic clay may have to be kept in closed closets which the children don't have access to. There is however a whole range of materials which the children should be encouraged to select from and use during parts of the class day. These might include table blocks and accessories, games, certain art supplies such as charcoal pencils, pastels and collage materials, and certain science supplies such as magnets, magnifying glasses, scales. One method which has proven itself valuable for storing these materials is the use of open shelves which are covered with curtains when these materials are not to be used; when these materials are to be used the curtain is picked up and left on the top of the shelf. With improvement over a period of time during the school year the children should become able to tolerate more materials in open or curtain-covered shelves.

6. *Abnormal Response to Stimuli—High Level of Distractability and Poor Impulse Control.* Several of the methods of using room components already discussed would aid in the development of impulse control and distractability. These include withdrawal space, room for movement at one's desk and the use of appropriate storage facilities. Storage facilities should not be located enticingly close to children's desks; materials should be out of reach if they need to be out of sight. Care should be taken to prevent mutually stimulating or destructive children from being seated near or in direct sight of each other. Centers of interest such as a block area, a wood-working area and a housekeeping center should be cut off from sight when not in use, by use of room dividers and screens or by dint of the room shape or arrangement. (Kindergarten classes or medical offices may have old screens or room dividers.) Evidence seems to support the hypothesis that poor reactions to stimuli are at least as much a result of the nature of stimuli present as they are of the intensity

of stimuli present. Also the need for stimuli reduction varies from child to child within the class and within any one child at different times. Thus a blanket attempt to produce as bland and non-stimulating a room as possible is inappropriate. In some cases it may lead to further withdrawal from the real environment and compound a sense of isolation. Furthermore this one need should not be stressed at the expense of other equally important needs.

7. *Poor Ability to Relate to Other Children. Anti-social Behavior or Withdrawal, Accompanied by Fear and Suspicion.* As already pointed up, care must be taken in the selection of children who are to sit near one another. One of the crucial factors in aiding the development of relationships of mutual support within a class is selection of children who will be given opportunities to work together. The children's own preferences are sometimes valuable guides but sometimes these preferences are based upon and reflect the child's illness. The teacher's best guide is her understanding of each child's dynamics and her observations of interaction in the classroom.

To foster the development of relationships between children requires a room and a program which allows for small group activities. This means either desks which can be grouped or tables to accommodate groups of two through six children.

Components of the Room Some of the needs of disturbed children which have implications for room planning have been discussed. We will now reverse our approach and focus on the components of the room, trying to develop pictures of rooms suitable for disturbed children.

1. *Location.* Children are put in a special class for the disturbed because they were unable to meet the expectations and demands of the regular class and school. Therefore every effort should be made to limit the interaction of the special class with the rest of the school until such time and only in such activities where they have the ability and tolerance to act in an acceptable way. (The school's definition of acceptable behavior may also be in need of modification.) In choosing a classroom therefore one would look for one which is not in the midst of comings and goings of large numbers of children, such as one would find near a play area or an auditorium.

If the class must use toilet facilities outside the classroom, the toilet facilities should be close to the room. There should also be an effort made to limit the number of other classes using these facilities. This is particularly necessary in view of the fact that many disturbed children manifest symptomatic problem behavior around toileting. If there are no drinking facilities within the room, it may be advisable to keep a pitcher of water in the room.

One would also want to look for a room which is reasonably close to a stairway and not above the second floor, since disturbed children find transitions an extremely trying time. A room located on the second floor would also provide some measure of control or reduction of stimulation from the outside environment. A room located on a high floor may lend to fears of hurting or being hurt and may result in panic during a fire drill.

2. *Size.* Teachers of classes for disturbed children often report that open spaces seem to invite movement and physical aggressiveness. Very large, undelineated open areas such as gymnasia seem to invite loss of control. Confined areas may have a repressive effect on some children and may lead to restlessness and friction and explosiveness within other groups. In determining how big a classroom or an area within the room should be, one must ask: What is the activity or activities to be carried on here and what are the needs of this group of children? During activities such as singing, listening to a story or looking at photographs, when the group is relaxed and interested, one might want to use a limited area to aid in developing group cohesiveness. On the other hand, during activities with high potential for friction one would want to use an area large enough to allow for movement and separation.

A major influence in the design of school buildings has been the increase in floor area of classrooms in response to the requirements of the changing elementary education program in recent years. Engelhardt, p. 56

Any blanket application of formulae such as a figure of 30 to 35 square feet per pupil, has been found to result in too small a room for the class group. In many cases, where communities have reduced the size of all classes to 20 or 25 pupils, the educational program includes an unusually wide variety of activities. Such schools tend to individualize the program so that more activities with fewer children involved in each are the general rule. The need for space, in such a situation, does not decrease in proportion to the reduction in class size. Ibid., p. 56

The figure 30 to 40 square feet of floor space per child, which had been generally accepted as a guide for classroom size, is now being questioned in light of the greater need for space of modern programs of learning through experience. In classes for disturbed children where registers generally range from five to fifteen children, 30 to 40 square feet per child is inadequate; the number of activities and materials cannot decrease in proportion to the decrease in class size. Forty-five to 55 square feet per child is probably a more appropriate figure for such classrooms. This figure will vary also according to the number of class activities which are carried out in other areas such as gymnasia, shops and outdoor areas.

3. *Shape.* Various shapes other than rectangular or square have already been discussed. These include an L-shaped room, a room with nooks and crannies, a room with partitioned-off cubicles and two adjoining rooms.

These rooms would better allow for reduction of disturbing stimuli, including separation of mutually destructive children, and would allow for more variety in learning experiences.

4. *Sound Control.* In thinking of sound control one must consider the arrangement of work centers and the seating arrangement. How many work centers which produce a high level of sound, such as a wood-working and block center, can a room house? What kind of work centers should be located near one another? Which children should be allowed to work together in a group or to sit near each other? The answers to these questions should be based on a knowledge that some disturbed children are hyperactive and loud; that some disturbed children may require a greater opportunity for being noisy as part of a coming-out of withdrawal stage; that some disturbed children show an exaggerated, painful reaction to auditory stimuli; that a high intensity or volume of sound will cause withdrawal in some children, loss of control in others. The program must be balanced to meet these needs and tolerances within a particular class. Sometimes the whole tone of a classroom can be quieted by a reduction in the volume of the teacher's voice, or the intensity of the teacher's voice. Screens and room dividers placed between separated groups can cut down on the amount of interfering sounds which children get.

Sometimes a "loud" classroom is partly the result of a room with hard, sound-reflecting surfaces which cause "thousands of almost imperceptible echoes and overtones" and "a fog of distracting or covering noises." (McQuade, p. 37) This situation can be remedied by the use of porous, sound-absorbent plaster tiles on the ceiling and/or the abundant use of bulletin boards (corkboards).

Moreover, sometimes noise can be necessary and beneficial.

5. *Arrangement.* Room arrangement cannot be meaningfully discussed apart from the content of the program. Following is a diagram drawn to scale of a possible classroom for ten children ages 7 and 8 (figure 14.2). Some of the principles of room arrangement which guided the drawing of this arrangement are:

5.1 The main area in which all the children's desks are located should be set apart from the special work centers and these special centers should be cut off from the children's view when not in use.

5.2 Children with high movement needs or children who become negatively involved with their neighbors should be seated in aisle seats.

5.3 Although the children's desks are kept apart there is the opportunity of moving together the desks of children who can work well together.

5.4 Toilet facilities and a sink are located in an inconspicuous part of the room, away from the main work area.

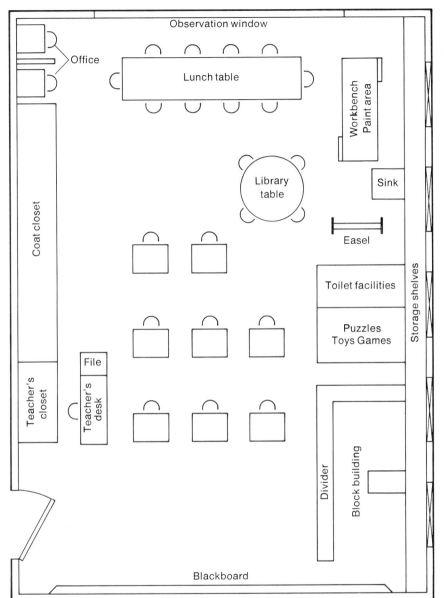

Figure 14.2 An ideal classroom arrangement for working with emotionally disturbed children.

Observation window

Office

Lunch table

Workbench
Paint area

Sink

Library
table

Easel

Coat closet

Toilet facilities

Storage shelves

Puzzles
Toys Games

File

Teacher's
closet

Teacher's
desk

Divider

Block building

Blackboard

5.5 If a child must be located close to the door, he should be a dependable, stable child.

5.6 A withdrawal area is provided for.

5.7 Work centers are clearly delineated.

5.8 Care is taken not to concentrate a large number of children in one area of the room, when the class is divided into groups.

5.9 Painting area is located near washing facilities.

5.10 Special work areas are self-contained so as to cut down on the amount of traffic and wandering, i.e., all the accessories for block play are stored within the block area; all painting supplies are located in the painting area.

6. *Furniture.* The value of different kinds of movable furniture or of a combination of movable and fixed furniture has already been discussed. It will be quickly noted that just as the individual emotional needs of disturbed children must be met, so must the individual physical differences be recognized. Desks and chairs should be ordered in three different sizes instead of one standard size for a particular age level. Desks which open up so that a child can inspect their contents have a decided advantage in satisfying disturbed children, over desks which have a fixed opening on the side. In the latter type of desk the children have to kneel on the floor to see what's inside.

Some compulsive children are quite disturbed by not being able to arrange and control their desk contents. Most other children just stuff things into their desks and have difficulty finding anything in this kind of desk. Since a child's desk is his home base in the room, it should be a piece of furniture which the child admires or wants to take care of. Old, disfigured desks should be sanded and shellacked, by the children if necessary and/or feasible.

In addition to individual desks, at least one large round table and a couple of small rectangular tables are needed for group work and displays. Round tables seem to be particularly inviting of group cohesiveness. Two semi-circular tables which fit together have the advantages of the round table plus additional flexibility. If no round table is available a large circular piece of wood can be bought cheaply and this can be placed atop two desks to give the advantages of a large circular table.

7. *Use of Wall Space.* Walls are for bulletin boards, blackboards and display

shelves. Blackboards are excellent devices not only to help the teacher teach but also to help the children learn. Many children will look forward to the opportunity to work at the board, whether in teacher-directed academic work or in drawing or group games.

> The chalkboard should be a workspace for a group of children. Children, especially in the elementary school, are ever ready and anxious to get out of cramped seats (all seats are cramped when one is a child) and to work at a chalkboard . . . Larger muscle movements are developed. Children learn much from each other through interaction. From a central position the teacher can observe the work of many students. . . . *Planning American School Buildings,* p. 58

Bulletin boards can serve many purposes in a classroom. Perhaps their most important function in classes for disturbed children is as a tool with which the teacher communicates her recognition and respect of the children, their efforts and their achievements. Current events are not only major occurrences in our city, country or world but also events in the lives of the children in the class. Displays of photographs of the children in school and at home might serve as the nucleus of a display centered around the individual children. The care with which their work is displayed, the trouble which the teacher is ready to take to preserve and exhibit their work proves to the children that their work is valuable to the teacher. This forms the basis for the children's own attitude towards their work (Kraker, p. 42). Every effort is made to comply with each child's wishes concerning the choice of his pictures to be displayed. "The teacher accepts any work which constitutes a child's genuine effort. . ." (ibid. p. 42).

Summary

In this chapter we examined some of the special situations that affect the exceptional learner and explored ways of helping the learner grow in the classroom setting. We directed attention to six major groups: the gifted and slow learners, the learning disabled student, the hyperactive and MBD student, and the emotionally disturbed learner.

Several important points emerged from our discussion. First, we noted a redundancy and lack of precision in the terminology used to identify special groups. Second, we pointed out that the teacher should first assess and then attempt to meet the special needs of *every* learner—that all people are really exceptional. Third, we suggested that the teacher can provide a specific classroom environment, in both homogeneous and heterogeneous classes, that will maximally deal with the needs, interests, and abilities of these students.

Suggested Additional Readings

MBD: The Family Book about Minimal Brain Dysfunction by Richard A. Gardner (*New York: Jason Aronson, 1973*)

This is an excellent nontechnical introduction to a very controversial topic. Although it is intended for MBD children and for their parents, it should be on every teacher's shelf, readily available to those who need its guidance. Part One is for parents and Part Two is for boys and girls classified as MBD.

Children are much more capable of accepting painful realities than is generally appreciated and are far less fragile in this regard than most parents realize. More difficult for them to handle . . . are the anxieties associated with ignorance and parental furtiveness. . . .

from *MBD: The Family Book about Minimal Brain Dysfunction*

Children with Learning Problems, ed. by Selma G. Sapir and Ann C. Nitzburg (*New York: Brunner/Mazel, 1973*)

This comprehensive anthology covers the gamut of learning problems, including such major topics as MBD, perceptual and motor disorders, behavioral problems, dyslexia, reading problems, and organic disorders. The contributions focus not only on identification but on treatment procedures as well.

Schools have changed from a traditional skill-oriented, teacher-centered program to one in which there is little consistent philosophy or attitude. . . . While there have been attempts at curriculum reform, in many cases we seem simply to have gone full cycle back to previous approaches.

from *Children with Learning Problems*

Art for Exceptional Children by Donald M. Uhlin (*Dubuque, Iowa: Wm. C. Brown Company Publishers, 1972*)

This most creative and unusual resource book provides the teacher with theoretical and practical concepts designed to help the exceptional child increase his expression and understanding through art. The uses of art "therapy" for all types of exceptional conditions is considered.

An exceptional child was once observed in the activity of drawing a man taking his dog for a walk, but in his drawing the dog appeared to be at least twice the size of the man. After short inquiry the child stated, "Well, dogs are *nicer than people!"*

from *Art for Exceptional Children*

The Hyperactive Child: Diagnosis, Management, Current Research, edited by
Dennis P. Cantwell *(New York: John Wiley & Sons, 1975)*

This is a solid introduction to hyperactivity, presenting a thorough overview
of issues, problems, and concepts. Although the book is somewhat technical
at points, the development of ideas is clear and the style is interesting.

*Symptoms of hyperactivity are usually present from an early age. Parents report
that the child has always seemed to have an unusual amount of energy, with less
need for sleep than his sibs, and that he wore out shoes, clothes, bicycles, etc.,
faster than other children.*

from *The Hyperactive Child*

Origins of the Group

Groups evolved as a social institution to enable individuals to solve common problems relating to survival. The first, and primary, group is the family. Individuals are joined in the group through shared goals, group identification, and identification with the group leader. Different types of leadership are discussed, with the conclusion that an individual's leadership status in groups is a joint function of his personality and the particular group setting.

Psychological Perspectives of the Group

From the psychodynamic perspective, an important educational function of the group is learning what can and cannot be said in group. This helps the group member develop impulse control and learn appropriate socialization. To the behaviorally oriented group leader, the group provides *models* for individual members to learn new behaviors and reinforcers to strengthen or weaken group members' behaviors. Since humanism is primarily concerned with the individual's self-actualization, growth, and personal fulfillment, the purpose of a humanistic group is to achieve these ends.

Teaching Process and the Group

The models of teaching and instruction discussed in earlier chapters are reexamined within the framework of the group context. A STRUCTURE-PROCESS-ATTITUDE model is used to illustrate some advantages of the group format. Cooperativeness is an essential part of effective group functioning. White's applied research findings on groups are presented.

Other Group Applications

The teaching group, guidance group, and group counseling are considered. The teaching group is defined as the group of professionals and paraprofessionals cooperatively working together for the betterment of the student. The concept of "faculty team" is examined in contrast to traditional school organizational models. Group guidance includes informational services and objective discussions of role area problems. Group counseling, which is more intensive, is a particularly helpful method for working with disruptive adolescents.

15 Group Processes in the Classroom

Throughout this book we have been discussing the "learner" and the "teacher," each stated in the singular. In practical situations, however, it is usually many teachers and many learners involved jointly in educational endeavors. Students rarely work on a tutorial basis with a single teacher; nor do teachers work with a group of students without participant feedback from other teachers. For these reasons, we are setting this chapter aside for special consideration of the phenomenon of group psychology.

Although the chapter is entitled "Group Processes in the Classroom," we will attempt a broader examination in the chapter of group psychology as it is applied in the school setting. While the classroom is certainly our primary concern, we cannot overlook the myriad instances of group interaction that contribute to the ultimate success or failure of all educational endeavors. A detailed examination of the sociopsychology of group process is beyond the scope of this book, but too narrow a focus could prove to be misinformative. Thus, we will examine briefly the origins of the human group from a **phylogenetic,** or sociopsychological perspective. Why did people band together in groups? What structure has been associated with the group over the years? How have these structures been modified, and what is the relevance of group structure for group performance today? We will then examine the attendant issue of the role of the group leader and attempt to apply some of these insights to the school setting.

After this introductory material, which should orient us to the group as a functioning unit, we will examine the three psychological perspectives we have been using throughout this book—psychoanalysis, humanism, and behaviorism—as they apply to group processes. We will then be in a better position to apply all this information to the school situation.

Groups as they exist in the school setting will be studied in two ways. First, we will present the topic "Teaching Process and the Group," which will focus directly on classroom activity. Then we will look at "Other Group Applications," which will open up the way to more expansive uses of the group for educational purposes. We will conclude this section with a detailed examination of the use of group counseling to help disruptive adolescents: an approach that can be used by teacher or counselor, or by a teacher-counselor team.

Origins of the Group

As long as individuals have needed and relied upon others for survival, companionship, or other areas of social interest, the formation of groups has been inevitable. Groups have existed in different forms over the years. The hunting groups of primitive tribes closely parallel the "herd" instinct in animal societies. The rise of political systems, by which people govern themselves, is rooted in the phenomenon of "grouping." The rise of religious factionalism reflects the inherent strength of man's tendency to group. Culture itself, which is transmitted from generation to generation through the socialization process, reflects the cumulative ideas and values of chronologically successive groups.

The first, and primary, group, from which other groups are derived, is the family. Each of us is born into a family structure, although different societies (and different socioeconomic situations within a single society) have different types of family life styles. We can say, therefore, that the family unit is the prototype of all group behavior.

We saw in Part One of this book how the influence of the family extends to the person's later socialization patterns. This fundamental principle is just as applicable in terms of group organization. Groups reflect, in many different ways, the upbringing of the group participants. Of course, groups have their own psychological idiosyncracies, as do individuals; but on the whole, there exist general principles by which we can understand human behavior, and these principles apply to groups as well as to individual situations.

Because the group was formed originally for survival—or social benefit—cooperation is integral to effective group functioning. If members of a group fight among themselves, and if factionalism outweighs cooperative participation, then the group is doomed to failure and destruction through *implosion*. On the other hand, if each member of a group is oblivious to other members, if each member functions primarily as an individual rather than as a group member, then the group will not hold together and will be doomed to failure and destruction through *explosion*. To avoid these problems, two important phenomena arose to accompany the formation of groups: group identification and shared goals. Group identification is the process wherein the individual identifies *a part of himself* with the larger group. If I say, "I am an American," or "I am a Democrat," or "I am a capitalist," these are all identifications with groups. So, too, the fraternity or sorority member who sees himself or herself as a member of the group shows signs of this group identification. This does not imply that the person gives up his own identity; but rather, that a part of his identity becomes merged with the identity of the group.

A group has goals of its own that may be in harmony or discord with the members' goals. At times, every member of the group feels the same way about the goals, but often there are conflicts. The essence of the democratic

> "Because the group was formed originally for survival—or social benefit—cooperation is integral to effective group functioning."

Figure 15.1 Group Synergy

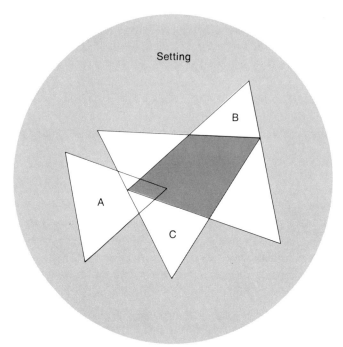

The interaction of more than two people is the immediate field of the group experience. The setting of the group is background environment.

system is based on the idea that if people come together openly and honestly, they can find common meeting points where they share similar or identical goals. While each person has many different goals in life, most of us share several goals with others. We belong to many different groups, and we identify with each to the extent that we share common goals. I may belong to the American Psychological Association, to the Society for the Prevention of Cruelty to Animals, to a church group, to a football team, to a fraternity, and so forth. I share certain of my goals and identify certain parts of myself with each of these groups.

Since rarely is any individual fully committed to any one group, and since even within the group identification is only partial, it is essential that there be some cohering force to hold together the members of the group and to help them achieve the goals that they share. That person is the group leader.

Just as the child learns that within the family there is a leader (or leaders!), each member of a group comes to recognize the existence of and to acknowledge the place of the group leader or leaders. The football captain (or coach), the political system's president, the church's clerical figurehead are all examples of the group leader.

Different types of groups require different types of leaders, and the role of the leader may vary greatly from group to group. One question that has interested psychologists and sociologists is, Are some people born leaders and others born followers? The personal quality called **leadership** has been studied under a variety of circumstances to determine if it is a quality bestowed upon an individual by a group, a quality an individual imposes upon a group, or somewhere in between. Mann (1959) points out some of the complexities of this issue:

> Viewed historically, the study of leadership has stimulated more than its share of controversy. The trait approach to leadership, the view that leadership is an attribute of the individual, has received the harshest treatment throughout the years. To have spoken of an individual as possessing a measurable quantity of leadership was perhaps an unfortunate choice of words. The clear implication of such a statement is that since leadership is specific to the individual, it will remain constant for the individual regardless of the situation in which he finds himself. . . . On the one hand, the trait approach has been modified to imply that an individual's achieved leadership status is a function of his personality. On the other hand, sufficient evidence has been accumulated to give impetus to the situation approach to leadership, which maintains that leadership is an emergent phenomenon, created through the interaction of individuals (leaders and followers), and that selection and stability of any leadership pattern is a function of the task, composition, and culture of the group. *From all this work has emerged some such summary formulation as that an individual's leadership status in groups is a joint function of his personality and the particular group setting.* (pp. 246–247)

These conclusions, written almost twenty years ago, are still valid today. Subsequent research has shown that there is an interactive quality that produces group leadership, although there has also been special emphasis on the personality characteristics that make for effective, charismatic, democratic, autocratic, or ineffective leadership qualities.

Schmuck and Schmuck (1975), writing more recently on the subject, argue that "the human striving to wield influence in relation to important others . . . enters into classroom life whenever the quality of leadership is demonstrated by the teacher or by students." They too agree with Mann's conclusion that "research has not led to consistent results about the traits or behaviors of great leaders. The ability to lead successfully appears to involve more than just a single set of personality characteristics" (Schmuck & Schmuck, p. 64).

With this in mind, we can fully appreciate how the leader came into being in the historical development of groups. The members of the group had certain goals that they shared, and one of the members of the group showed

the members that he or she was best able to help the group reach these goals. As the "appointed" leader carried out the delegated responsibilities, the group shared with him a part of its identification, thus strengthening the leadership role. "To die for King and country," the English used to say, indicating their willingness to give their lives not only for the group (*country*), but for the leader too (*King*). Later in this chapter, we will consider the implications of leadership in the classroom setting.

Psychological Perspectives of the Group

Each of the psychological positions we have considered has directed itself to the group phenomenon, in one way or another. In this section, we will look briefly at the role of the group, as it is perceived by the psychoanalytic practitioner, the behaviorist, and the humanist.

The Psychoanalytic Perspective   The psychoanalytic group leader emphasizes the parallels between group and individual counseling, but also recognizes the differences. As Kirman (1976) points out:

You proceed with groups much as you do with individuals, from the Modern Psychoanalytic point of view. In individual counseling, you want the client to say whatever comes to mind. But everything can't be said in a group. *An important educational function of the group is learning what can and cannot be said in group.*

"The psychoanalytic group leader believes that within the group context each member repeats his early situation within the family structure."

This important function carries over into the classroom (which is, of course, a group), where students have to learn to constructively control their statements.

You sometimes have to learn not to speak when you are not going to get attention because something more urgent is being attended to by the group leader. The student may recognize his impulse to speak at the wrong time, and then he may be able to learn to control this impulse. It is especially important to learn how to get your own needs met while not damaging anyone else. (Kirman, 1976)

Generally, the psychoanalytic group leader believes that within the group context each member repeats his early situation within the family structure. Needs which were not met in childhood cry out for satisfaction in the group; but the individual attempts to satisfy these needs in the same way that failed during the early years. One of the important roles of the group leader, therefore, is to teach the individual *how* to satisfy his legitimate needs in an appropriate, effective way.

Teachers using the psychoanalytic approach are sensitive to the phenomenon of group transference. This simply means that the group-as-a-whole perceives the teacher as a parental figure. The teacher, recognizing this, attempts to respond to group communications by acting in the way that a "good" parent would act. This phenomenon, it should be pointed out, works in conjunction with all of the individual transference relationships that also form between student and teacher in the classroom.

The Behavioral Perspective

The group serves two important purposes to the behaviorally oriented group leader. First, it provides rich behavioral resources after which individual group members can model themselves. The group leader may attempt to point out to members types of behaviors that he feels will be beneficial to them. The member is able to learn these new behaviors by observing others within the group.

The second purpose of the group is that members of the group can be used for positive or negative **reinforcement.** Peer pressure can be brought to bear on any member to encourage or to discourage certain specified behaviors. While reinforcers can be emitted by the group leader, it is far more effective on a deeper level if the group-as-a-whole withholds or dispenses reinforcement.

The teacher, who wishes to use the behavioral viewpoint, might combine these two applications. On the one hand, the teacher will make the most of students whose behaviors are constructive and attempt to use these as the

> "The humanistic group leader is accepting of the person's level of functioning and works toward helping the person reach higher levels."

facilitative models. In addition, the teacher will create an environment in which peer pressure works toward producing positive rather than negative behaviors. Contingency systems work as well in the group setting as they do in individual behavior modification programs.

The Humanistic Perspective

Since **humanism** is primarily concerned with the individual's self-actualization, growth, and personal fulfillment, it is the purpose of a humanistic group to achieve these ends. Moreover, group processes have played a more significant role in humanistic psychology than in any of the other psychological perspectives for two reasons: (1) humanism emphasizes the individual's interactions with others as a part of personal development; and (2) humanism's emphasis is entrenched in democratic problem-solving techniques.

Carl Rogers, a leading proponent of the humanistic point of view and a prominent group leader who is at the forefront of the encounter group movement, describes his way of facilitating the group experience, and in so doing reveals the humanistic group leader's perspective:

I tend to open a group in an extremely unstructured way, perhaps with no more than a single comment: "I suspect we will know each other a great deal better at the end of these group sessions than we do now. . . ." I listen as carefully and as sensitively as I am able. . . . I wish very much to make the climate psychologically safe for the individual—I have found that it 'pays off' to live with the group exactly where it is. Thus I have worked with a group of very inhibited top-notch scientists, mostly in the physical sciences, where feelings were rarely expressed openly, and personal encounter at a deep level was simply not seen. Yet this group became much more free and innovative, and showed many positive results of our meetings. . . . I am willing for a participant to commit himself to the group. . . . I am willing to accept silence and muteness in the individual, providing I am quite certain it is not unexpressed pain or resistance. . . . I tend to accept statements at their face value. . . . I try to make clear that whatever happens will happen from the choices of the group . . . When talk is generalized or intellectualizing, I tend to select the self-referent meanings to respond to out of this total context. (Rogers, 1971, pp. 275–278)

We see from this passage that the humanistic group leader is accepting of the person's level and works toward helping the person reach higher levels. It is this personal willingness of the leader and the leader's personal qualities that make for an effective humanistic group experience.

Table 15.1 shows the relationship between these three group approaches. In the following section, we will look more directly at the teaching process in a group context, synthesizing the elements we have presented in this section.

Table 15.1   Three Psychological Models of Group Processes

Category	Psychoanalysis	Behaviorism	Humanism
Actions of Group Participants	Repeat the infantile behaviors of the family setting.	Responses to stimuli from within the group setting.	Inhibited or uninhibited tendencies toward growth and change.
Methods of Facilitating Change	Pointing out (*interpreting*) the unconscious meanings of behaviors as they are revealed in the group.	Positive and negative reinforcement; modeling.	The leader's own personal capacity to "give" to the group members.
Role of the Leader	To encourage the transferring of feelings; to resolve resistances; to teach the individual to satisfy needs from childhood in a socially appropriate manner.	To reinforce positive behaviors and to provide models whereby the member can learn appropriate behavior patterns.	To accept; to clarify; to teach; to participate. In all, to help the group attain a high level of expressive freedom.
School Applications	Resolving resistances in the classroom. Lessening neurotic interference to mastering learning tasks. Meeting maturational needs that arise in a social context.	Direct behavior change. Increasing the rate of learning. Resolving school phobias, test anxiety, underachievement, etc. Drug prevention programs.	In all areas: the full inclusive growth of the total person.

Teaching Process and the Group

In examining the teaching process within the group context, we need not modify the earlier discussion of the teaching process (in chapter 11), but simply restate it in a new framework. Gorman (1969) has proposed an interactive model of teaching that uses the group situation as its primary reference point. The theory is based on the idea that "true interaction produces a cohesive classroom group where teacher and students share responsibility for the defining, carrying out, and evaluating of the learning experience" (p. 31). He cites a major advantage of the group model:

Creation of a group by a collection of individuals releases the creative potential of the total membership. The business of teaching and learning does not become easier (it is one of the most difficult human enterprises), but the abrasive little problems of motivation and discipline largely disappear. The students unite with the teacher to get the job done, which is much more satisfying than the situation where the teacher tries to do the whole thing by himself. (Gorman, 1969, p. 31)

Thus, cooperativeness is a clear advantage of the group format. Gorman then examines in great detail the class-group interaction in terms of what he calls the STRUCTURE-PROCESS-ATTITUDE model (SPA). Applying this model to the classroom setting, Gorman points out, its structure may include thirty students seated in chairs facing the teacher in front of the room, or it may include a smaller number of students seated in a circle around a central nexus of interacting communications. Figure 15.2 illustrates these two possibilities. "Changing the STRUCTURE changes PROCESS (though it may take many students some time to get used to the change) and eventually changes ATTITUDES. In this changed STRUCTURE, the students have more responsibility. They talk to each other as well as to the teacher, all communication does not have to flow through the teacher, and there is more student participation expected in terms of planning, executing, and evaluating" (p. 34).

Gorman's analysis probes deeply, and his book, *Teachers and Learners: The Interactive Process of Education* is well worth reading. But the main point emerges from the selections we have quoted: namely, that the group structure increases the cooperative participation of student and teacher alike in the learning process. Another way of stating this is: By using the group, the teacher avoids many of the disruptive, nonproductive situations that might arise in a one-way structured classroom.

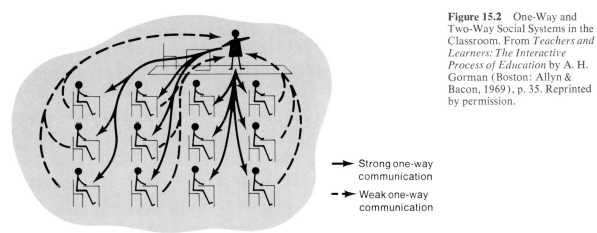

Figure 15.2 One-Way and Two-Way Social Systems in the Classroom. From *Teachers and Learners: The Interactive Process of Education* by A. H. Gorman (Boston: Allyn & Bacon, 1969), p. 35. Reprinted by permission.

→ Strong one-way communication

⇢ Weak one-way communication

One-way social system: the classroom.

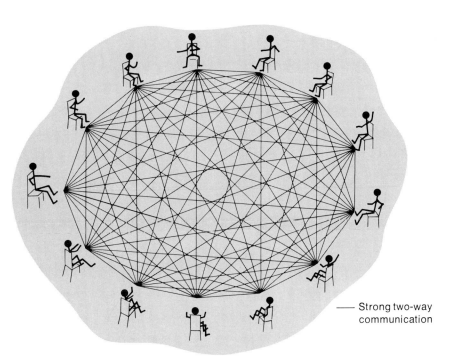

—— Strong two-way communication

Two-way social system: the classroom.

> " 'Students' attempts for classroom leadership are a function of their personal motive for power, their expectation for success, and the external incentives they perceive.' "

Figure 15.3 Communication in the Group

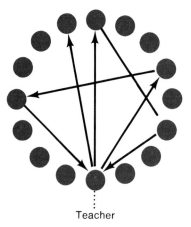

Teacher

Note how many communications are directed back to the teacher. The teacher "deflects" these communications back to other group members.

Despite this advantage of the group procedure, there is a tendency on the part of many educators to ask what relevance the group model has for the teaching of "hard" subject areas, such as math and science. "Sure, we can understand why a group would be good for a speech class or even a history class," they argue, "but how can the group model contribute to the teaching of science or math?" This frequently asked question does deserve an answer.

Lifton (1966), who has written extensively on all aspects of group behavior, responds to this question by citing the implications of using group techniques in the subject-matter classroom:

When the leader can accept the feelings of hostility that arise from youthful rebellion to societal limits, the group is free to use its energies toward discovering ways in which the course involved can be made personally meaningful to them. At this point it is most helpful for the group to be given responsibility for getting answers to the question of the value of the material.

One example comes to mind. A chemistry teacher who was accustomed to having students groan on the first day as he outlined the concepts to be learned decided to reverse his approach and ask the group about the ways in which chemistry was affecting their lives. After giving a few socially approved schoolbook answers, the children went off on a more personal basis. "I'd like to know what makes lipstick kissproof." "I want to know if detergents really make washing easier." . . . . At this point the instructor indicated on the blackboard what he expected them to know at the end of the semester. . . . He then asked the group to see if they could see any relationship between the questions they wanted answered and the skills they needed to learn. *Together* they mapped out projects that would answer their questions, while involving school skills needed in getting answers. (p. 181)

Schmuck and Schmuck (1975) have examined the implications for teachers of their role as classroom leader:

—All human beings want to feel some influence in relation to important others.

—Leadership is interpersonal influence; it is *not* the characteristic of an individual.

—Because of their legitimate status, teachers hold the most potential power in the classroom for executing leadership.

—Functional leadership involves interpersonal influence in relation to group tasks and social-emotional concerns.

—Students' attempts for classroom leadership are a function of their personal motives for power, their expectation for success, and the external incentives they perceive.

—Students frequently attempt leadership in classrooms with positive social climates.

—Influence attempts in the classroom can facilitate or hinder academic learning. Goal-directed influence of either teacher or students, by definition, facilitates learning.

—A teacher's leadership will have a significant impact on the climate of the classroom.

—The influence structure of a classroom group can be changed. Teachers should take the initiative in working toward a dispersed influence structure.

—Students will feel influential and learn to be self-controlling and responsible for their own behavior when they are helped to share classroom leadership with the teacher (pp. 81–82).

Again, we see the cooperativeness—the working *together*—as a central motif of the group organization. But in this instance we see a specific example of how the group can be used in the teaching of the "hard area" subject matters, such as chemistry.

It is sometimes assumed that for effective instruction to take place, a formal class organization—such as that with the teacher at the center of activity—must be utilized. Gibb (1966), among others, has argued quite effectively that the informal group structure can be equally beneficial to in-structional goals. "Many of the organizational functions of the instructional group," he points out, "are carried on at levels that are highly informal. The control system, for instance, is embedded in a system of norms which are dif-ficult for instructional group members to violate. . . . [While] certain formal controls may be lacking in the organization of the instructional group . . .

many informal regulatory mechanisms may create a relatively stable organizational pattern" (p. 131). It is not, we can conclude, the quantitative formality or informality in itself that affects the instructional process, but rather the qualitative dimensions that are revealed in the group processes that transpire in the classroom.

While studies have generally concentrated on one area of group behavior or another, William F. White (1969) has attempted to apply the research of psychosocial behavior to the class group setting. Display 15.1 shows seventeen applied principles derived from his research. These principles, as we can see, are directly supported by the positions in Part One and Part Two of this book; in other words, the group behavior recapitulates the individual behavior in the social setting.

One specific application of group technique within the school setting is role playing. Role playing may be structured or unstructured. "Some groups employ available scripts depicting scenes representing areas of common concern to the group. Others have the individuals in the group describe situations they desire to work out. The leader selects the other roles needed to develop the setting and he instructs group members in the kind of person they are to play" (Lifton, 1966, p. 149). Teper-Singer (1975) has suggested an innovative use of role playing, which is presented in display 15.2.

Probably the single most important factor in the group process is the role of the leader, which was discussed earlier in this chapter.

Other Group Applications

In addition to our discussions of group processes in the classroom, we would be remiss if we did not consider other aspects of group behavior in the school setting. Although the number of additional possibilities is almost inexhaustible, we will confine ourselves to the two most prominent examples: the teaching group and the guidance group.

The Teaching Group   The teaching group, as we will define it, is the team of professionals and paraprofessionals cooperatively working together for the betterment of the student. This team may include teachers, administrators, counselors, school psychologists and social workers, mental health personnel, the school nurse,

Applications

1. The definition of group cohesiveness has not changed much since 1950. Lott and Lott reaffirmed earlier positions about cohesiveness, calling it a group property that is inferred from the number and strength of mutual positive attitudes among members of a group.

2. Personal contact seems to be the most determining variable in bringing about and increasing positive affect toward individual members.

3. Physical contact or "living near one another" appears to be an overwhelming determiner of attractiveness among dyads and small groups of children. With adults, more exceptions are reported in the principle of proximity.

4. Cooperativeness seems to be the key word for increasing the "liking" of one another, acceptance of group membership, or for developing friendliness among middle-class children of elementary school age.

5. Children who participate successfully and cooperate on a task demonstrate more signs of friendship and acceptance than those who work separately.

6. The definition of the democratic classroom is not always synonymous with a cohesive group. At least an attempt should be made to operationally define the elusive construct "democracy." Open discussion in small groups, however, is known to be a meaningful stimulus for more risk taking by the group's members.

7. Members of the same high-status group or members of mixed-status groups occupying a high position tend to like one another.

8. Individuals who are compatible in race or religious background tend to be attracted to one another and associate frequently.

9. The need for affiliation determines how effectively group members develop their attraction for one another. From a needs-theory interpretation, affiliation explains the behavior of cohesiveness in groups better than any other need.

10. Students with positive, healthy self-concepts are more liked than children with negative self-concepts.

11. The attractiveness of an individual in group interaction is increased by warmth, equalitarianism, good judgment, sensitivity, and helpfulness.

12. There seems to be little doubt that we choose friends who are compatible with us in interests, goals, and personality behavior. There are exceptions, however.

13. When groups are successful, members of the group can be expected to be more favorable to one another than when groups fail. Members of failing groups who consider their failure justifiable may cohere very closely and project their negative attitudes outside the group, e.g., on the teacher.

14. Leadership is not merely a trait or attribute of personality. At least two types of leaders can be inferred from studies of leadership in small groups: a task specialist and a socio-emotional specialist. These possibilities do not preclude the possibility of the great-man theory. A few leaders seem to have both specialist qualities.

15. The majority of studies conclude that problem solving among small groups is superior to the performance of individuals.

16. The risky-shift phenomenon is that group decisions are riskier than the average of decisions made by individual members. Group discussion seems to bring about the tendency to be riskier in group settings.

17. Personality has some influence on the risky-shift phenomenon.

Role playing as a classroom technique has provided a marvelous environment for the exploration of health concepts. In the February 1971 issue of *School Health Review* a step by step procedure of the traditional role playing situation was presented in an article entitled, "Role Playing as a Tool in Mental Health Education." Briefly the steps included:

1. *Sensitizing the group*—present a situation where the class discovers that each person perceives a given situation differently based on past experience, assumptions, and expectations
2. *The Warmup*—describe the role playing situation with limited information
3. *The Enactment*—spontaneous dramatization
4. *The Replay*—the same people switching roles
5. *Student Observation*—discussion by the students about their reactions
6. *The Evaluation*—draw conclusions

At this time I would like to present three alternative approaches to role playing. Although any area in mental health can be explored through these procedures, the following are examples for use in drug education.

Example I

Structure

The class is divided into groups of four. Each group sits in a small circle within a large circle that the groups form.

x: role players

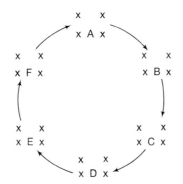

Situation

Student arrives home to a family that has discovered a "stash" of drugs hidden away in his/her room.

Roles

Each group will enact the following roles spontaneously without preparation other than deciding on a role. Mother and/or father, brother and/or sister, student.

Procedure

In sequence each group performs their presentation of what they think will happen. (Group A then B then C, etc.) Generally each group has a different approach. The teacher may stop the group and go on to the next group at any point.

Discussion

After all groups have enacted their presentation, the teacher will have several options for proceeding with the discussion depending upon the material presented. Some possibilities include:

1. The class may form new groups based on the behavior displayed by the parents. Students who think their parents would behave as the role was played, would group together with the role players. For example: parent who cries "How could you do this to me"; parent who kicks child out; parent who questions with concern; parent who lectures and does not allow a response, etc.
   Discussion questions may include: How do you feel when your parents approach you in this manner when they disapprove of your behavior? For what reasons do you believe your parents respond in this way? How would you approach your child if you were the parent?
2. The class may discuss their reaction to each group's performance.
3. The teacher may present questions for the small groups to discuss based on the diverse material that the teacher has been jotting down during the different presentations. For example:
   Describe the ways in which the person caught responded.

For what reason do you believe people would respond in this way?

What information about drugs do you believe was false, which was factual?

What are the penalties for breaking drug laws?

What was your reaction when alcohol was mentioned as alright for the adults but "pot" was put down?

Example II

Structure

Single group performance with stop-action directorship by the class. The performing group presents their interpretation of the situation in front of the class (the directors) who are sitting in a semi-circle around the classroom.

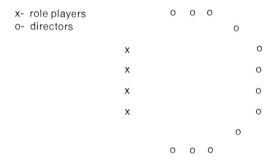

x- role players
o- directors

Situation

One student is trying to convince three friends to smoke a joint.

Roles

Person who does the convincing, person who refuses, person who is undecided, person who accepts.

Procedure

The group begins their enactment. At any point any member of the class, as well as the teacher, may stop the action by calling out "Stop Action" and

1. ask a question of a performer about how that performer feels at the moment.
2. assume the role of any of the players with a different approach.
3. ask the present players to switch roles.

Discussion

Questions for discussion may involve aspects dealing with group pressure and the decision-making process.

    a. In what ways were the situations realistic or unrealistic?

    b. How do you feel when someone tries to convince you to do something that you really don't wish to do?

    c. What feelings do you have when you want to convince someone to do something and they refuse?

Example III

Structure

One individual sitting on the edge of the circle who will enact two opposing aspects of himself while the remaining members of the class listen.

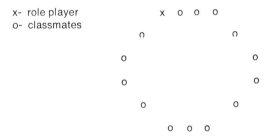

x- role player
o- classmates

Situation

The forces (feelings and attitudes) within the person that motivate him to use drugs versus those that influence him to refrain from using drugs.

Roles

The role is the dichotomy that exists within us that determines our decisions.

Procedure

The student holds up two hands (puppets may be used if appropriate for the age group). One hand is first used for emphasis "On the one hand why shouldn't I use drugs, everyone is doing it?" The other hand is then used "But on the other hand just because others do it doesn't mean I have to follow their example." The alternation of hands is repeated with each feeling and thought for or against the use of drugs.

Discussion

Questions for discussion may include:

1. In what ways are your feelings similar to and/or different from those presented?
2. What is your response in other situations where a conflict exists between your feelings, thoughts, and attitudes?

When teachers present role-playing situations it is most important for them to have a facility for questioning so discussions are meaningful. The teacher's responsibility in role playing is essentially to help students identify and define what they are experiencing, as well as to help them investigate their feelings and reactions. A non-judgmental setting is therefore a must.

Suggestions for Questioning

1. Avoid questions that merely yield a yes or no response or that call for judgments such as good or bad, should or shouldn't.
2. Explore several ramifications of questions:
   Clarify a point: If I understand you, you said. . . .
   Seek additional information: Would you tell us more about this?
   Evaluate: What do you think this might mean? How does the rest of the class feel about this?
   Conclude: What happened? Why is this a problem? How could the outcome be altered?
3. Provide an atmosphere where questions arise from and between students as well as from you.

From Lynn Teper-Singer, "The Many Faces of Role Playing," *Health Education*, Nov.–Dec., 1975, pp. 34–35. Reprinted by permission.

and so on. What makes this collection of individuals a group is the common goal that they share: namely, to help the students reach their full potential.

Moeller and Mahan (1971) discuss the concept of the "faculty team." This term is "chosen deliberately to denote a group of teaching colleagues committed to searching out ways collectively to improve educational quality." They point out the effectiveness of the team approach versus the conventional approach (in which the school personnel are organized on a vertical structure), and argue that productivity gains (in terms of educational objectives) are quite impressive. Table 15.2 compares the conventional organization with the faculty team organization in terms of participant functions. We can see that this approach is characteristic of the "two-way" communication model in figure 15.2.

The teaching group need not be as extensive as the model provided by Moeller and Mahan suggests. Glanz and Hayes (1967) suggest that "the more creative concept of faculty team teaching has presented a cross-disciplinary and cross-experiential group of teachers. The teachers form a group and use group techniques in their teaching." This is a flexible, practical definition that allows for experimentation and revision. Moreover, the emphasis in this model is that one group helps another; the teachers, working as a group, help the students working as a group.

Group guidance includes informational services and objective discussion of various role difficulties. "The primary goal of group guidance," Parks (1973) suggests, "is to prevent and ameliorate the development of problems rather than just remediation of existing problems, which differentiates group guidance from group counseling and group therapy." The content of group guidance, Parks goes on to point out, is primarily information: information about educational programs, about jobs, and about outside-school activities.

Group Guidance and Counseling

The guidance group may be conducted in the home room, in the regular class, or in a special setting. Many factors affect this decision: the abilities of the classroom teacher, the adjunctive staff, the needs of curricular demands, the specific information required, and so forth. Regardless of the setting, the process of the guidance group works toward solving similar types of problems and reaching similar groups.

Table 15.2   The Faculty Team

	Principal	Teacher
Conventional School Organization	Supervises teachers as individuals Transmits central office decisions to teachers Makes most other decisions himself Evaluates and supervises teachers individually according to their adherence to school rules Is solely responsible for the operation of the school Has little direct effect on actual classroom activities Largely unaware of many school problems because of inadequate or inaccurate communications from teachers and community	Concerned with his own class, not with other children in the school Responsibility for children ceases when they move to another teacher Largely isolated from one another Responsible to principal for adherence to school rules Has limited access to data; ranks children by giving them grades instead of measuring progress Tends to develop dependent rather than mature attitudes

	Faculty Team

Faculty Team Organization	Accepts collective responsibility for school program
	Analyzes present school program, develops new programs to achieve school-wide goals
	Emphasizes maximum growth for each child during his entire period of school attendance
	Monitors progress toward faculty team objectives, which are viewed as evolving rather than static
	Oriented to improvement by reason and education rather than by punishment
	Supervises its own membership; calls for other help when needed
	Helps team members become socially mature individuals, capable of effective interaction, initiative, and leadership
	Is most effective when continuous change is needed
	Insures pupil-teacher partnership in learning
	Seeks agreement between parents, students, and teacher about each child's learning objectives
	Makes decisions collaboratively
	    Principal and teachers share decision-making functions to the extent each agrees is desirable
	    Includes system-wide goals as well as local school goals
	    Quantity and quality of decision-making increase as mutual trust, confidence, team spirit, and sense of accountability grows
	    Uses a wide variety of measurements, including the knowledge of results to direct further planning
	    Each member accepts responsibility to the team (and to the principal) for contributions to group goals
	    Each member is expected to make improvements in his own professional competence and to help other members improve their skills
	    Each member has the trust and confidence of other members
	    All members actively participate in problem-solving
	    Accurate communication is encouraged and facilitated

Teaching: Art and Science

Student	School Board and Administration	Parents/ Community
Largely passive recipient of standard curriculum and teacher-planned instruction	Centrally plan and organize program	Elect school boards who run schools
Sees little stake in the school program except to attain needed credit or grades	Allocate resources by line-item budget	Largely passive except during elections
	Responsible for adherence of school system to state law	
	Evaluate principals and teachers according to state and local rules	
	Emphasize sending rather than receiving communications	

Participates as a full partner, according to his maturity level, with parents and teachers in the development of school and individual student objectives	Centrally plan and organize system-wide programs	Elect school board members who run schools
Accepts responsibility for helping other students learn	Allocate resources by comparing cost and benefits	Elect parent council linked to faculty team, which works with team to develop overall school goals and serves as an efficient two-way communication channel between community and school
Receives continuous feedback about his progress toward specified, measurable objectives that he has previously agreed on	Integrate all faculty team resources into a system-wide plan	Receive feed-back about student progress or barriers to progress
	Delegate responsibility and authority for local plans to faculty team	
	Control by results, not rules	
	Set performance criteria jointly with faculty team	
	Encourage open, accurate communication throughout organization	
	Inform students, parents, teachers, and community of results of learning	

From *The Faculty Team* by Gerald H. Moeller and David J. Mahan. © 1971, Science Research Associates, Inc. Reprinted by permission of the publisher.

Rothney (1972) offers seven justifications for group guidance:

1. Imparting of information not available from other sources.
2. Providing opportunity to recognize and discuss common problems which are met in making educational, vocational, and personal choices.
3. Giving students an opportunity to practice the acceptance of responsibility for their own learning in group situations.
4. Learning to use the democratic process in reaching common goals.
5. Developing interpersonal relationships which will help in group situations in the future.
6. Providing students and counselors with information which may be useful in the counseling situation.
7. Establishing relationships between students and counselors which create a demand for, and facilitate, counseling services. (p. 93)

We see from Rothney's seven rationales (objectives) how expansive an element group guidance can prove to be in the school setting.

Combining the teaching group and guidance group approaches, an integrated perspective begins to emerge: teachers, working among themselves, to help students—all within the context of a group setting.

Group Counseling with Disruptive Adolescents*

Group counseling with adolescents has been modeled on the group techniques used with adults. With some modification, these techniques have been successful with many adolescents. There are, however, adolescents who have not responded well to these traditional modes of group counseling. Among such are adolescents who are generally described as "disruptive."

In school, disruptive adolescents are unable to comply with the minimal rules. The term antiachiever aptly describes their school behavior. They are often truant, unprepared in their work and, consequently, poor students. They seriously interfere with the education of all; their own no less than others.

Outside of school, disruptive adolescents may be at the fringes of trouble with the law, if not already involved in delinquent acts. They commonly engage in such antisocial acts as vandalism, petty thievery and disturbing the peace of the community. Often, the only difference between disruptive and delinquent adolescents is that the latter have been caught or the former have received more protection from their families and communities.

* This section was written by Lester J. Schwartz, Queens College, City University of New York. Taken from G. S. Belkin, ed. *Counseling: Readings in Theory and Practice* (Dubuque, Iowa: Kendall/Hunt Publishing Company, 1976). Reprinted by permission.

Because the basic problem of disruptive youngsters is their inability to function constructively in social settings, group counseling is a logical therapeutic approach. Group counseling is particularly appropriate for modifying the behavior of disruptive adolescents because it provides a miniature but highly compacted social setting. A group creates the climate in which social behavior can be examined and understood and it affords an opportunity to practice change.

The dilemma for the group counselor, however, is that the very behavior that disruptive adolescents need to change can destroy the group in its early stages, or worse yet, cause the group members to act destructively towards each other. There is nothing more harmful to a group than all its members acting out their antisocial feelings promiscuously and without restraint. Such groups are doomed to failure.

Generally, it is wise for a group to be well balanced without one personality type dominating. Ideal conditions, however, seldom exist and counselors must often work with people who have very similar personality dynamics. Beyond the problem of homogeneity of group composition, other writers (Redl & Wineman, 1951) have pointed out the need for using different approaches with children who act out. Indeed disruptive adolescents cannot be expected to respond positively to traditional group counseling because such counseling is based on assumptions which apply to youngsters who have a reasonable degree of internalized social controls. To account for the differences between the disruptive and the more socialized adolescents, the group counseling process must be modified in relation to these assumptions.

The Basic Assumption of Group Counseling

The first such assumption is that individuals possess enough latent capacity to trust and to be concerned about other group members to permit group cohesion. This cohesion cannot be achieved without mutual concern on the part of group members and is essential to successful group process. It provides the atmosphere of support and security in which problems can be aired, shared, and worked through. In disruptive adolescents, however, the capacity for trust and appropriate social guilt has been severely damaged (Persons, 1970). Whatever the etiology—prolonged experience with harsh authority, an absence of any real affectional relationships, or impossible conditional standards for acceptance—the disruptive adolescents often feel that they can't trust others. Nor do disruptive adolescents feel that it pays to be concerned about others, because they are sure they will be disappointed or betrayed.

A second assumption made about group participants is that each individual has the potential to take responsibility for self change. Although he may come to the group with strong defenses it is expected that eventually he can understand that he can modify events and experiences in his life if he takes responsibility for his behavior. Kahn (1971) pointed out that acting out adolescents can not conceptualize this kind of responsibility. Disruptive adolescents perceive their life style as fixed and necessary; they feel powerless to deal with the social environment. They feel that restraints, selfishness and the control exerted by others leave them with no alternative but to deal with people by fighting, stealing, and deception. They do not say, "something is wrong or missing inside of me and I must try to do something about it;" rather they say, "the rotten world forces me into the situation I'm in and I'm going to beat them at the game." The only kind of responsibility disruptive adolescents may take for themselves is to try to be disruptive in the cleverest or in the most overpowering way.

The third assumption is that group members can learn and understand the objectives and methodology of group process in rather short order. This means that the group members can soon come to appreciate that the group process can be helpful, that personal goals can be set, that other group members have similar feelings and problems, and that affective interaction within the group is conducive to growth. These aspects of the group process, however, are beyond the ken of most acting out youngsters (Truax, Wargo, & Volksdorf, 1970). Instead of being goal oriented, they are impulsive. Instead of being interdependent, they act only in immediate self-interest. Instead of being emphathetic, they feel insulated. Instead of being in touch with their feelings, they avoid and deny.

In summary, the difficulties that disruptive youth have in being successful group participants are:

1. They have great difficulty in trusting and feeling concern for others.
2. They are unwilling to take responsibility for their own behavior and its modification.
3. They are unfamiliar with the skills and process of interpersonal and intrapersonal problem solving.

A group leader anticipates these problems in any group and he deals with them continuously, along with all the other problems that the group generates. The normal group process accommodates the problems and they are worked through in due course. The same can happen in a group of disruptive adolescents led by a skilled leader but in this kind of group, the degree of distrust, irresponsibility, and past defective social learning is so great that progress proceeds at a snail's pace, if at all.

An effective means for dealing with these problems is through a combined didactic-affective approach during the initial phase of a group's life. The problems, in fact, become the content of the initial phase. The following five points constitute the basic concepts employed by a group leader in using this approach during the initial phase of group counseling with disruptive youth:

1. *Expectations must be dealt with.* Disruptive youth approach the group with distortions, confusion, or ignorance about the group process. Many of them feel that the learner's objective is to reform them or to try to make them conform. The participants' expectations must not be unrealistic. To correct the misperceptions, the group leader teaches the group that each member must decide for himself what he wants to get out of the group and that each member has absolute control over the kind and degree of his own participation. The possible kinds of individual goals and participations are explained and discussed. The leader, also at this time, imposes a limitation on the behavior of every member. The group is told that no one may behave in any way that may seriously injure the group or any member of the group. This announced limitation helps the members feel less vulnerable to attack. It also helps contain dangerous acting out behavior. A discussion may then follow of goals and behaviors that are consistent with group enhancement and those that are group destructive.

2. *Didactic instruction facilitates affective learning.* Although interpersonal psychology is the major determinant of social behavior, cognitive and verbal learning play an important role. In counseling, insights are usually intellectually understood before they are integrated affectively. Similarly, didactic instruction does not in itself change behavior, but in group counseling with disruptive youth, it makes the process and goals of therapy explicit and provides the referents which mark the course to be taken by the group.

3. *Dealing with mistrust takes precedence.* Mistrust is an inhibiting force to group cohesiveness and whenever it emerges, it takes precedence. In the preparatory phase distrust is spelled out as a basic problem both in its etiology and how it influences behavior. The leader should impress the group with the importance and meaning of distrust in the group members' lives. This does not mean that the distrust can be dispelled or worked through at this point. In fact, in the preparatory phase, little would be gained by attempting to establish trust artificially. It is proper, however, for the leader to point out the elements of distrust that he observes within

> "The leader helps the group to examine how trust and concern are related and how the presence of one leads to and then relies on the presence of the other."

the group. He should also point out, without attempting to convince or assure, that he, as well as the group members, will have to earn each other's trust.

The issue for concern for others is the other side of trust. The leader helps the group to examine how trust and concern are related and how the presence of one leads to and then relies on the presence of the other. Again, the group members should not be urged to feel concern for others but they should begin to see why it is important and how it can develop.

4. *Self-responsibility is a primary goal.* The most difficult aspect of group work with disruptive youth is the learning of self-responsibility. The use of the existential concepts of choice, guilt, and anxiety is a helpful approach in this respect (de Beauvoir, 1946). The group members can be taught that guilt and anxiety are a normal and, in fact, necessary condition in interpersonal situations where choices must be made. This concept can be conveyed to the group through illustration. For example: Suppose one had to choose between visiting a sick friend in the hospital or keeping a date to go to a movie with a girl friend. Whatever decision is made, and no matter how understanding the girl friend and the sick friend are, one of them would have to be disappointed. The appreciation of this disappointment is guilt; but this kind of guilt is not pathological and it is something one must learn to accept. In the example cited the guilt is quite mild and not troublesome but when the choices are more difficult, the guilt becomes more intense. Without the guilt we are sociopaths, an incipient problem of disruptive adolescents. Consequently, a group leader attempts to help the group members not be afraid of the guilt and anxiety that accompany human decisions. This is accomplished during the initial phase of the group's life by using choice points as they come up: When should the sessions be scheduled? What should the ground rules be? Where should people sit? etc. The objective is for the members to learn that there is always a choice to be made, that the choice involves others, and most importantly, that an individual can control the choice he makes. Like the other points that are made during the preparatory phase, the process of what is happening is made explicit didactically.

5. *Problem-solving skills are learned.* Disruptive adolescents' problem-solving skills, generally, are inappropriate and self-defeating. To make good choices in conflict situations, they must relearn the method of problem

solving. A number of techniques can be used towards this end. Two such techniques are problem joining and stop action. Problem joining is demonstrating that a group member can assist other members with problems because he has or had problems with similar elements. As individuals talk, the leader delineates, compares, distinguishes and summarizes with an emphasis on the similarities among the group members' experiences. Stop action is role playing a problem to the point of critical action. The group then discusses possible solutions and the rationales for each proposed alternative. The proposed solutions are then role played with an ensuing discussion of how each solution felt. Whatever techniques are used, the important point is to help the members understand the skills and their use.

It is a mistake to assume that disruptive youth have the necessary social attitudes and skills to function effectively but can't or won't use them merely for psychological reasons. These skills and attitudes must be learned. The use of the process described above, during the early stages of group counseling, can shortcut the otherwise long, arduous, and often frustrating task of social relearning that disruptive youth must go through if they are to change. These social handicaps must be recognized and the gaps filled if the group and its members are to grow. Such a preparatory phase—which focuses on handicaps and which employs a combined didactic and process approach—can be an effective way of shortening the relearning process.

Summary

In this chapter, we examined the origins of the group as a social unit, the psychological approaches to understanding groups, and the implications of group processes in the school setting. Several major points emerged from our discussion:

1. The group can, if handled properly, be an effective educational unit in the school.
2. Group processes help explain teacher cooperation as well as teacher-student cooperation. Through team teaching, the faculty team, and group organizational patterns, the group is a viable unit for the instructional team.
3. The leader is an important part of every group. The leader increases the strength of the group and helps the group members attain their "shared goals."
4. Group counseling, in and out of the classroom, is an important school-related service.

Suggested Additional Readings

A Social Psychology of Group Processes for Decision-Making by Barry E. Collins and Harold Guetzkow (*New York: John Wiley & Sons, 1964*)

Despite the formidable title of this book, it is actually quite a readable, interesting little volume that examines the way decisions are made through the use of the social group. It is full of research and valuable insights and can help the teacher understand some of the underlying dynamics of class, school, and social groups.

An individual participant is profoundly influenced by the other individuals in the group. . . . The experience of interacting with (or merely being in the presence of) other human beings strongly affects the behavior of each individual.

from *A Social Psychology of Group Processes for Decision-Making*

Perspectives in Group Psychotherapy: A Theoretical Background by P. B. de Mare (*New York: Jason Aronson, 1973*)

Although this book is directed primarily to the group therapist, it contains so many valuable insights that every teacher could benefit from it. The dynamics of the group are examined psychologically, philosophically, sociologically, and in terms of communication and small group processes.

As far as process is concerned, in certain quarters the currency of exchange has been radically altered in favor of non-verbal communication, e.g. action, acting, playing, games, physical contact, relaxation, massage and oriental philosophy, Yoga, and mysticism.

from *Perspectives in Group Psychotherapy*

Beyond Words: The Story of Sensitivity Training and the Encounter Movement by Kurt W. Back (*New York: Russell Sage Foundation, 1972*)

This popular book examines the growing group movement, in terms of its social and psychological implications. Some excellent descriptions are provided of different types of groups and the theories behind groups. This is a fine non-technical introduction to the contemporary group movement, including T-groups, encounter groups, and their derivatives.

One of the striking facts about the period in which sensitivity training has spread is the increased affluence of a great part of the population. Simply stated, this means that a majority can avoid worrying about their subsistence.

from *Beyond Words*

Group Processes in the Classroom by Richard A. Schmuck and Patricia A. Schmuck (*Dubuque, Iowa: Wm. C. Brown Company Publishers, 1975*)

Directed primarily to the school setting, this is probably the best introduction to group processes in the school. All of the major topics are covered: leadership, dynamics, communication processes, norms and social behaviors.

The human striving to wield influence in relation to important others is basic. It enters into classroom life whenever the quality of leadership is demonstrated by the teacher or by students.

from *Group Processes in the Classroom*

Encounter: Group Processes for Interpersonal Growth by Gerard Egan (*Belmont, Calif.: Brooks/Cole, 1970*)

A strong plus for this book is the detail with which it examines group processes. A great deal of research is integrated into the discussion of such topics as the group contract, group goals, leadership, self-disclosure, and supportive behavior.

Most people hesitate to disclose themselves to a group. They balance on the edge of self-disclosure as they would on the edge of a diving board. But just as the shock and pain of entering the water are short-lived and certainly out-weighed by the pleasure of swimming, so the shock and pain associated with self-disclosure are mainly initial and short-lived and inevitably outweighed by the benefits of mutual sharing.

from *Encounter*

The Role of Evaluation in Learning and Teaching

Evaluation is the teacher's means of assessing changes in the learner that are a result of teacher interventions as opposed to changes that are a result of maturation.

Relationship Between Measurement and Evaluation

Evaluation is considered as the means of making a decision based on an interpretation of measurements. Evaluation requires decisions following measurement and is only as good as the measurement that underlies it.

Differences Between Educational and Psychological Testing

The purpose of psychological testing is to identify individual differences that may be helpful in predicting and explaining the person's learning and development. The purpose of educational testing is to identify the learner's capabilities that are a result of experiences in school.

Assumptions Underlying Testing

The type of distribution we find for a given test is viewed within the contexts of the educational decisions that have to be made. Usually, but not always, we use the normal curve as our model.

What Is a Standardized Test?

Standardized tests, unlike teacher-made tests, have been administered to a large sample of students from many different classroom settings. The value of a standardized test is that a student can be compared to other students outside of the immediate group and the group itself may be compared to a larger reference group.

Continued

16 Evaluation of Learning and Teaching

The Functions of Evaluation

Four functions of evaluation are described. *Selection* refers to the acceptance of a person into a general program. *Placement* refers to the acceptance of a person into a specific program. *Monitoring* refers to the acceptability of the learning conditions under which the student is trying to learn. *Terminal assessment* refers to a value placed on the student's capability at the end of a program.

Statistical Concepts in Measurement

Central tendency refers to the average score on a test. This may be expressed as the *median,* or middle score; the *mode,* or most recurrent score; or *mean,* the arithmetic average. Variability refers to the dispersion of individual scores, and the measure of variability most often used is the *standard deviation.* Correlation is the relationship between two variables, and it is expressed as a coefficient, which indicates the strength and direction of the relationship.

Criteria Used to Evaluate Measurement

Validity is the degree to which a test measures what it was designed to measure. Reliability is the degree to which a test measures something consistently. Objectivity is the degree to which responses to items on a test are scored consistently. Efficiency is defined in terms of the time it takes, for both test taker and teacher, to obtain a measurement.

Construction, Interpretation, and Uses of Classroom Tests

A case study is used to demonstrate how the teacher can effectively design and administer a classroom test. A detailed discussion of test item analysis is included in the case study.

We use moment-to-moment feedback from our learning experiences to evaluate our progress. Such feedback may come from an informal test that we personally improvise or from a more formal one improvised by someone else —a teacher, for instance. From the information we receive, we make decisions about what to do next—to continue, to adjust, or to end a course of action. Indeed, an ultimate objective of education is to enable each of us to devise tests and to use feedback from them to make effective decisions on our own.

When we hear the words *test* and *evaluation,* we immediately think of decisions that are made by teachers and other school personnel on the basis of our performance but that may have nothing to do with enabling us to improve upon our learning. We realize that tests should provide information for decision making that affects our future development as well as our present learning.

The Role of Evaluation in Learning and Teaching

Both **learning** and **maturation** are processes that result in changes in the capabilities of a person. While no clear distinction can be made between changes that result from the process of learning and those that result from the process of maturation, we can make some useful distinctions between educational outcomes due to learning and those due to an interaction between learning and maturation. Changes that result from both maturation and learning are referred to as development.

Learning is commonly thought of as a process of relatively short duration involving a small change in a capability of a person resulting from **situational conditions.** Development, on the other hand, is commonly thought of as a process of longer duration, involving a larger change in a capability of a person that cannot be clearly traced to situational conditions of learning.

For example, when a student's capability is tested at the beginning and at the end of a year in school, it would be difficult to attribute the change entirely to learning. On the other hand, change that occurs over a month in school may be largely due to learning. The younger the student, the more likely that development will be the significant factor in the change. For adults, we are likely to attribute change in capability to learning, even when it occurs over a relatively long period of time, such as a year.

The implication of this distinction is that the teacher can influence the student's learning over a relatively short period of time. Beyond these limits, the changes that occur are likely due to development. When the learning of the student is evaluated, so is the **teaching.** Since learning is a critical part of development, effective learning and teaching over a period of time affects the development of students (Farnham-Diggory, 1972).

Tests are used as a basis for making many decisions in school. Tests are also used as a basis for making many decisions in other societal institutions such as business and industry. In addition, tests are an essential aspect of educational research. Consequently, it is not surprising that much has been written on the topic of testing (e.g., Anastasi, 1976; Bloom, Hastings, & Madaus, 1971; Cronbach, 1970; Ebel, 1972; Gronlund, 1976; Mehrens & Lehmann, 1973; Thorndike & Hagen, 1977).

The ways in which tests have been used are issues of long standing. This is due in part to the fact that tests have been misused. It is also due to the fact that tests are such an important facet of decision making in schools. It is less threatening for us to criticize tests than to criticize one's self as a test taker, test constructor, or test user. It is important to sort out the subjective from the objective aspect in our evaluation of tests.

While a thorough discussion of testing is out of the mainstream of educational psychology, it is important that we consider the foundations of measurement and evaluation in relation to functions of teaching. We will define important concepts of testing and discuss their interrelationships. Then, we will discuss the construction, interpretation, and uses of tests.

Relationship Between Measurement and Evaluation

The term *testing* is often used to refer to both measurement and evaluation. It is important, however, to make a distinction between the two concepts. **Measurement** is a means of selecting, gathering, and analyzing information. Measurement may involve paper and pencil or a mechanical or observation instrument. Clocks, self-ratings, essay examinations, ratings by others, questionnaires, rulers, multiple-choice examinations, balances, and checklists are all examples of measurement. Measurement is used to refer to the test, the results, and the analysis of the results. Statistical procedures are commonly used to analyze the results of measurement.

Evaluation is a means of making a decision based on an interpretation of the measurement. That is, evaluation refers to the values attached to the measurement and subsequent decisions made on the basis of the value judgment. For example, if you obtain a score of 86 on a 100-point rating scale completed by the teacher, this is a measurement involving a test and a score. Furthermore, if you are informed that the average score on this scale is 97 and the range is from 85 to 100, this is still a measurement involving analysis of the results. Now if you conclude that this was a superior performance, and if the teacher concludes that this was a lousy performance, the student and the

Teaching: Art and Science

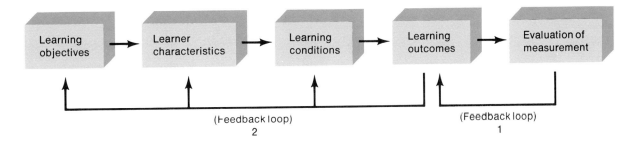

teacher have each made an evaluation. The question is, What is the criterion upon which each of the evaluations was made? After the criterion has been established, then the score can be evaluated.

Figure 16.1   Feedback Loops of Basic Teaching Model

Evaluation, of course, is only as good as the measurement that underlies it. Consequently, measurement is also subject to evaluation. The relationship between measurement and evaluation is illustrated in figure 16.1, based on the basic teaching model discussed earlier in the book. The first consideration is an evaluation of the measurement. If the measurement is judged to be sound, then the remaining components of the model and their interrelationships can be evaluated.

Differences Between Educational and Psychological Testing

Both educational and psychological tests are used in schools. In addition, many principles of the psychology of development, learning, and teaching (which are based on the results of tests) are used to discuss factors involved in one's school achievement. There is often confusion, therefore, about the differences in the nature of educational and psychological tests. The model in figure 16.2 may be helpful in clarifying these differences.

The purpose of psychological testing is to identify individual differences in the characteristics of people that may be helpful in predicting and explaining their learning and development. The purpose of educational testing is to identify as effectively as possible one's capabilities resulting from experiences in school.

Educational testing is concerned with the capability of the student to perform on measurements of educational outcomes. Skills and knowledge are examples of educational outcomes. Psychological testing is concerned with measuring the characteristics of students that may affect the outcomes of educational experiences. Attitudes, interests, and intelligence are examples of psychological characteristics that may affect educational outcomes. Psychological testing, then, is concerned with measuring and evaluating learner characteristics as predictor and interactive variables, while educa-

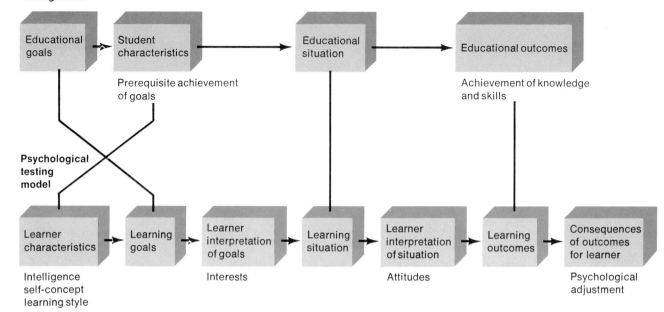

Educational
goals

Student
characteristics

Prerequisite achievement
of goals

Educational
situation

Educational outcomes

Achievement of knowledge
and skills

**Psychological
testing
model**

Learner
characteristics

Learning
goals

Learner
interpretation
of goals

Learning
situation

Learner
interpretation
of situation

Learning
outcomes

Consequences
of outcomes
for learner

Intelligence
self-concept
learning style

Interests

Attitudes

Psychological
adjustment

Figure 16.2 Comparison of
Educational and Psychological
Testing Models

tional testing is concerned with measuring and evaluating learner capabilities
as criterion or outcome variables.

Improved self-concepts, favorable attitudes toward learning, increased
intelligence, and psychological adjustment are often considered to be important educational outcomes in themselves. In addition, one's capabilities
today will become one's prerequisite achievement or learner characteristic
tomorrow. A conceptualization of the model in figure 16.3 can help you to
avoid the inherent confusion resulting from the different ways educational
testing and psychological testing can be used in educational practices.

Figure 16.3 Integration of
Psychological and Educational
Testing Models

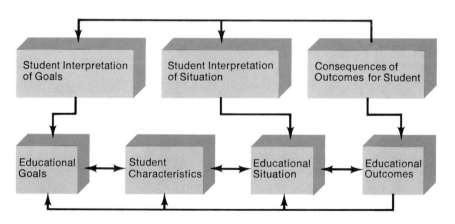

Student Interpretation
of Goals

Student Interpretation
of Situation

Consequences of
Outcomes for Student

Educational
Goals

Student
Characteristics

Educational
Situation

Educational
Outcomes

Teaching: Art and Science

Assumptions Underlying Testing

The underlying mathematical model of psychological testing is the familiar normal probability curve. A representation of this **normal curve model** is presented in figure 16.4.

The basic assumption of this model is that most psychological characteristics are distributed with a predictable frequency among the general pop-

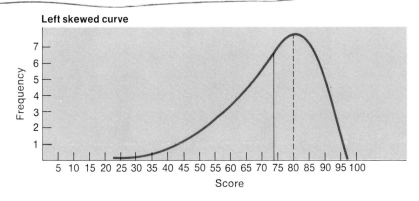

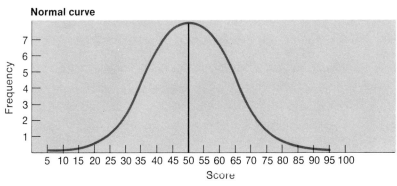

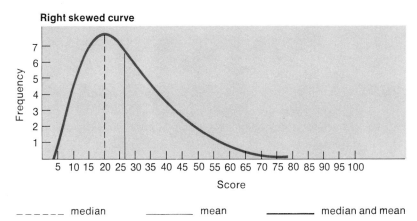

Figure 16.4 Models of Curves Underlying Measurement

_____ median   _____ mean   _____ median and mean

ulation. This means, in effect, that most people fall within the middle, or "normal," range.

There are extremes of most all personality characteristics, however, and there are individuals who differ enough in a particular characteristic to be considered unique. For any one characteristic, then, some of us would be considered unique. For instance, one might have low or high self-esteem.

The notion of the uniqueness of the individual comes from the observation of many different psychological characteristics—e.g., motivation, intelligence, dependency, aptitudes, friendliness, learning styles, self-concept, creativity, aggression, and so on. If we study a number of such characteristics in relation to other people, nearly all of us will be at the extreme ends of one or more characteristics.

Both **interindividual differences** (differences between people in a characteristic) and **intraindividual differences** (pattern of differences in characteristics for an individual) are of concern in psychological testing. Interindividual differences are of interest for the purposes of adapting learning conditions to the individual and enabling the individual to adapt to the learning conditions. Intraindividual differences are of interest for the purpose of identifying the strengths and weaknesses of an individual's characteristics in relation to future learning experiences.

The normal curve model also underlies much educational testing. Curiously enough, we are more apt to accept the notion of individual differences in learner characteristics than we are to accept the notion of individual differences in learner capabilities resulting from educational experiences. However, if we are interested in finding out about the successes and problems of all the students in a learning situation, we would use the normal curve model. Since this is usually our concern, the normal curve model underlies much educational testing.

There are instances in which a variation of the normal curve is a more satisfactory model in educational testing. For example, if we were interested in finding out who the students were that were having problems acquiring a skill, we might administer an easy test for the students as a group. Such a test would yield results in performances as illustrated in the **left skewed curve** in figure 16.4. The students in the left end of the curve are unique in that they are having problems learning the skill as compared to those students who are under the curve.

If we were interested in finding out who the students were that had already learned the skill, we might administer a difficult test for the students as a group. The results would be performances as illustrated in the **right skewed curve** in figure 16.4. The students in the right end of the curve are unique in that they have already learned the skill.

Test results for psychological and educational tests, then, depend upon the characteristics of the test as well as the characteristics or capabilities of the particular students taking the tests. The assumptions underlying the test are related to its purposes in decision making.

What Is a Standardized Test?

Mental Measurement Yearbooks (Buros, 1938, 1941, 1949, 1953, 1959, 1965, 1972) have included comprehensive reviews of educational and psychological tests through the years. Some of these tests have been **standardized.** Some are considered **experimental.** What does standardized mean? What does experimental mean? Is a **classroom test** standardized or experimental? We will answer these questions in this section.

As we indicated earlier, a test can be constructed by anyone. Students often make up tests in the course of their studies. Teachers sometimes construct tests. Texts sometimes include test items in an accompanying user's manual. Test specialists construct instruments that measure educational goals. Researchers make up tests to measure a particular phenomenon under investigation. All of these tests serve many different purposes. It has been said that a good test provides some of the best learning opportunities in school (Stroud, 1956).

It has been found through the years that the development of a "good" test requires a great deal of time and energy, and it became necessary to establish guidelines to define the quality of a test (e.g., American Psychological Association, 1974).

In educational testing, the most important distinction occurs between a classroom test and a standardized test. In psychological testing, the most important distinction is between an experimental and a "tried-and-true" test.

A classroom test refers to one constructed by a teacher and is designed to measure the immediate objectives of the educational program. The potential value of a classroom test is that the teacher can specifically adapt the test to the learning opportunities the students have had as well as to the capabilities of the students.

A standardized educational test refers to a test constructed for the purpose of supplying information about how students of similar characteristics (e.g., age, grade, or level) perform on an educational outcome at a particular point in time (e.g., beginning of year, midyear, or end of year). A test is standardized by being administered to a large sample of students from

> "Standardized tests can provide information about how effective the school curriculum has been in enabling the students to develop knowledge and skills and how well students have developed knowledge and skills that are not a part of the present curriculum."

many different classroom situations under similar conditions (i.e., standard administration conditions). The potential value of a standardized test is that a student or group of students can be compared to students in general on an educational outcome rather than just to those in the particular classroom situation. For example, a student may be about average compared to students in his or her class, yet may be well above average (or well below average) compared to students in the general population on the outcome. A classroom test, of course, could be standardized, but this is a rare event. If standardized, a classroom test may lose its value for the very purposes for which it can be useful, i.e., adaptation to the learner and the situation.

While it is not possible to make clear distinctions between classroom and standardized tests other than the establishment of norms across a representative sample of students, there are other potential values that we have come to expect from standardized educational tests.

Standardized educational tests often include subtests of different kinds of knowledge and skills. Since these subtests are administered to the same students in the course of standardization, scores from subtests can be converted to a standard (or common) scale. Hence, a profile of capabilities for an individual student or for a group of students can be meaningfully interpreted.

Standardized educational tests are usually based on a broader view of school curricular outcomes than those of a particular classroom or school. Standardized tests, therefore, can provide information about how effective the school curriculum has been in enabling the students to develop knowledge and skills and how well students have developed knowledge and skills that are not a part of, or at least are are not emphasized in, the present curriculum. While decisions related to how this information may be used is often the responsibility of a school administrator rather than a teacher, it is important for a teacher to consider the potential value of standardized test results in connection with the learning and development of students. It is also important because teachers often serve on curriculum committees.

Finally, reputable standardized tests are accompanied by a comprehensive manual that explains the characteristics and uses of the test. For further information, Buros (1972) gives independent reviews of and information about tests.

A psychological test that is called experimental is one in which the characteristics of the tests are unknown. It may turn out to be a "true classic" or it may turn out to be a "bomb." If it is found to be effective for its purpose, it may be placed into general use. A psychological test that is found to be useful for prediction or classification purposes may also be standardized. Standardization of psychological tests is usually necessary before they are used for non-research purposes. If they were not standardized, it would be difficult to understand the characteristics of the students in a particular school setting compared to the subjects who have been studied previously. If the psychological test is to be used to measure educational outcomes, then it is imperative that it be standardized. As with educational tests, reputable standardized psychological tests will have a user's manual. Psychological tests are reviewed by independent sources such as Buros (1972).

The most frequently used standardized tests in schools are educational achievement and general intelligence tests. Intelligence tests are sometimes called tests of mental maturity, cognitive ability, or similar terms that include the words *intellectual, mental,* or *cognitive.* **Aptitude** is a subset of intelligence. It may be a specific aspect of intelligence, such as mechanical aptitude, verbal aptitude, or quantitative aptitude. The term *ability* is often used interchangeably with both intelligence and aptitude. Intelligence is usually considered to be a general psychological characteristic and is used as an interindividual difference factor in decision making. Aptitude is commonly considered to be a specific psychological characteristic and is used as an intraindividual difference factor in decision making.

Because some items on standardized intelligence and achievement tests are similar (e.g., vocabulary and mathematical problem solving), there is often confusion about the differences in the nature of these tests. In general, intelligence tests are designed to measure one's cognitive functioning as it is related to life experiences rather than to school curriculum. That is, we speak of intelligence as being an indication of one's potential to learn. The content of an intelligence test is usually not specific to school curriculum, but the processes of the test are, since an intelligence test is usually developed to measure one's potential to learn in school.

Achievement tests, on the other hand, are designed to measure one's cognitive functioning in relation to school experiences. That is, we speak of achievement as being an indication of one's actualized learning and development. The content and the processes measured by achievement tests are based on immediate and ultimate objectives of school curricula.

The Functions of Evaluation

There are four functions of evaluation: **selection, placement, monitoring,** and **terminal assessment.**

Selection refers to the acceptance of a person into a general program. For example, being admitted to the regular reading program in the first grade, winning a part in a class play, making an athletic team, or being admitted into a college are examples of selection.

Placement refers to the acceptance of a student into a specific program. For example, after one is admitted to a general program such as the regular reading program, a cast, team, or college, one is given an assignment such as learning the alphabet or combinations of letters, a leading or supporting role in the play, a regular or reserve on the team, or advanced or fundamental composition in college. Selection and placement overlap, depending upon the definitions of general and specific program. The term **diagnostic evaluation** is sometimes used to refer to the decision-making aspects of selection and placement.

Monitoring refers to the acceptability of the learning conditions under which the student is trying to learn in a specific program. If conditions are judged to be unsatisfactory as indicated by one's progress, then the conditions will be modified. If they are judged to be satisfactory, then the conditions will remain the same. The term **formative evaluation** is sometimes used to refer to the decision-making aspects of monitoring.

Terminal Assessment refers to a value placed on the student's capability at the end of an educational program. Terminal means that a certain phase of educational experiences will not be returned to again. Graduation from high school is terminal, for instance. Moving from elementary school to junior high school is terminal in relation to the elementary school. A letter grade, particularly one at the end of a year in school, represents a terminal assessment. The term **summative evaluation** is sometimes used to refer to the decision-making aspects of terminal assessment.

Both educational and psychological tests can be a part of each evaluation function. In addition, a teacher may be involved in each aspect of evaluation. Table 16.1 presents one model of the role of evaluation in schooling.

As we have noted earlier, the soundness of an evaluation depends upon the quality of the information upon which it is based. Before we consider the functions of evaluation, it is important to consider the characteristics of the underlying measurement.

Statistical Concepts in Measurement

There are three statistical concepts that are critical in interpreting the results of a test: **central tendency, variability,** and **correlation.** These concepts, in turn, serve as a foundation for measurement concepts used to evaluate a test.

Table 16.1   Similarities and Differences Between Diagnostic, Formative, and Summative Evaluation

	Diagnostic	Formative	Summative
Function	Placement: Determining the presence or absence of prerequisite skills Determining the student's prior level of mastery Classifying the student according to various characteristics known or thought to be related to alternative modes of instruction Determination of underlying causes of repeated learning difficulties	Feedback to student and teacher on student progress through a unit Location of errors in terms of the structure of a unit so that remedial alternative instruction techniques can be prescribed	Certification or grading of students at the end of a unit, semester, or course
Time	For placement at the outset of a unit, semester, or year's work During instruction when student evidences repeated inability to profit fully from ordinary instruction	During instruction	At the end of a unit, semester, or year's work
Emphasis in Evaluation	Cognitive, affective, and psychomotor behaviors Physical, psychological, and environmental factors	Cognitive behaviors	Generally cognitive behaviors; depending on subject matter, sometimes psychomotor, occasionally affective behaviors
Type of Instrumentation	Formative and summative instruments for pretests Standardized achievement tests Standardized diagnostic tests Teacher-made instruments Observation and checklists	Specially designed formative instruments	Final or summative examinations

Table 5.1 from "Similarities and Differences Between Diagnostic, Formative and Summative Evaluation," Bloom, Hastings, and Madaus, *Handbook of Formative and Summative Evaluation of Student Learning* (New York: McGraw-Hill Book Company, 1971). Used by permission of the publisher and the authors.

Central Tendency

Central tendency refers to the average score obtained by students on a test. There are three different measures of central tendency that can be of importance in measurement: **mode, median,** and **mean.** A *mode* is the most frequent score from the results of a test. For example, if the scores on a test for five students were 19, 12, 11, 11, and 6, the mode would be 11. To find the mode, all one has to do is look for the most frequent score. Sometimes, there is more than one mode in a distribution of scores. If there are two modes (e.g., 19, 19, 12, 11, 11, 7), the result is called bimodal. If there are more than two modes, the result may be referred to as multimodal. While the mode is a crude measure of central tendency, it can be found quickly.

The *median* is the middle-most score for the results of a test. The following formula can be used to find the median position:

$$\frac{\text{Median}}{\text{Position}} = \frac{\text{number of scores} + 1}{2}$$

The median for the distribution 19, 12, 11, 11, and 6 is 11 (i.e., $\frac{5+1}{2} = 3$). The third score from the top or the bottom is 11. For the scores 19, 19, 12, 11, 11, and 7, the result is $\frac{6+1}{2} = 3.5$. Hence, the median is halfway between 11 and 12, or 11.5. The median then is the midpoint. It is the point in a distribution in which one-half of the scores are higher and one-half are lower.

The *mean* is the arithmetical average of a set of test scores. The formula for the mean is one you probably learned in school:

$$\text{Mean} = \frac{\text{sum of all the scores}}{\text{total number of scores}}$$

For the distribution of scores 19, 12, 11, 11, and 6, the mean is $\frac{59}{5} = 11.8$. When it is appropriate to use, the mean is the most accurate value for the average.

A mean does not represent the typical performance of the following scores (i.e., 20, 10, 9, 8; Mean $= 11.75$) as appropriately as the median (i.e., 9.5) does. Whenever a distribution of scores is **skewed** considerably in one direction, the median is a more accurate indication of central tendency than the mean. If we add a score of 0 at the end of the above distribution (i.e., 20, 10, 9, 8 and 0), then the mean (i.e., 9.5) is as representative of the typical performance as the median.

If a distribution of scores follow a normal curve, then the mean (arithmetical average), the median (middle-most score), and mode (most frequent score) will all be the same. If the scores are not normally distributed, it is necessary to compare the different averages in order to make decisions about the typical performance.

Variability *Variability* refers to how dispersed individual performances are for a distribution of scores. Like the mode for central tendency, the **range** is a crude indication of variability. The *range* is the difference in the value of the highest and the lowest score. Since a number has a numerical value from one-half above

> "A *correlation* is the relationship between two variables for a group of subjects. A *correlation coefficient* expresses the direction and degree of the relationship."

the number to one-half below, the range for the distribution 19, 12, 11, 11, and 6 would be 19.5–5.5, or 14. The range is often used to obtain a quick measure of variability.

A **standard deviation** is a measure of variability that is commonly used in measurement. Like the mean for central tendency, the standard deviation is a precise indication of variability based on the actual value of the scores. That is, a standard deviation measure takes into consideration the values of each score in a distribution in relationship to the mean. If the standard deviation is squared, we have, in effect, a precise measure of the range of a set of scores, i.e., **variance.**

One can estimate the standard deviation for a set of scores in a relatively simple way and yet lose little precision. The formula for estimating standard deviation is as follows:

$$\text{Estim. of Standard Deviation} = \frac{\text{sum of highest one-sixth scores minus the sum of the lowest one-sixth scores}}{\text{one-half the number of scores}}$$

For the distribution of 19, 12, 11, 11, and 6, we would appear to have a problem since there are but five scores. We will take 1/6 of the scores at either end; that is we will take 5/6 of 19, or 15.83, and 5/6 of 6, or 5. The result of 10.83 divided by 2.5 is 4.33. Thus, the standard deviation of the distribution is 4.33. If we square 4.33, we have 18.75 as the variance. It is important to use the exact value of 1/6 of the scores from either end if the obtained value is to be a reasonable estimate of the value obtained from the actual standard deviation formula. The standard deviation, then, enables us to determine individual variability within the group rather than just total group dispersion.

Correlation

A *correlation* is the relationship between two variables for a group of subjects. A **correlation coefficient** expresses the direction and degree of the relationship. Correlation coefficients can range from -1.00 through zero to $+1.00$. That is, the direction can be **negative** or **positive**. The degree of relationship can be from .00 to ± 1.00. A value of -1.00 represents a perfect inverse relationship between two variables. A subject would have exactly the opposite position in relation to other subjects on the two variables. A value of $+1.00$ represents a perfect direct positive relationship between two variables. A subject then has exactly the same position in relation to other subjects on the two

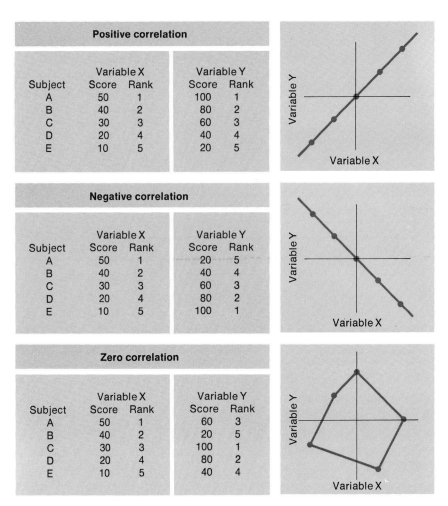

Figure 16.5 Numerical and Graphical Representations of Correlations

variables. A .00 value represents a correlation in which the scores for the two variables are distributed exactly at random in relationship to each other. These possible relationships are represented numerically and graphically in figure 16.5.

Two variables are rarely related in just one of these three ways, of course. Therefore, we have to deal with degrees of relationship within the range of the possibilities. If in plotting paired scores, they tend to line up from the lower left to the upper right, it means that the variables are positively related. If they line up from the lower right to the upper left, they are negatively related. If they are all over the graph, then it is likely the scores are occurring as random events in relation to each other.

There are formulas that can be used to calculate correlation coefficients either from a rank ordering of the position of subjects or from the numerical

Teaching: Art and Science

> *"Validity* may be defined as the degree to which a test measures what it was designed to measure."

values of their scores on each variable. Such procedures, like those for central tendency and variability, are presented in any introductory statistics book.

The interpretation of a correlation coefficient is dependent upon the number of subjects involved in the analysis as well as the nature of the phenomena being studied. Hence, few generalizations can be made about how a particular correlation coefficient value is interpreted.

Criteria Used to Evaluate Measurement

There are four criteria used to evaluate measurement: **validity, reliability, objectivity,** and **efficiency.** These criteria are appropriate to use in the evaluation of tests used in schools as well as tests in general. While all of these criteria are interrelated, it is validity that is of primary concern in measurement.

Validity may be defined as the degree to which a test measures what it was designed to measure. There are three important kinds of validity related to teaching: **content, concurrent,** and **predictive.**

Validity

    Content validity refers to the degree to which a test adequately samples the subject matter area of concern. Sampling may refer to the subject matter content or, more specifically, to the instructional objectives of the content. In the case of the content, a test has content validity if it samples from the various parts of the content (e.g., chapters) in a reasonable, usually predesignated, manner. In the case of instructional objectives, a test has content validity if it samples the content and process of the objectives rather than some other set of objectives. It is becoming a more common practice for teachers to set up a table of specifications of test items. An illustration of a table of specifications is given in table 16.2. From such a table, the degree of content validity of a test can be relatively easily analyzed. Whether or not a test is a valid measure of a particular content domain is dependent to some extent on the conditions under which the specific objectives were learned. Content validity is a logical inspection activity rather than a statistical one.

    Concurrent and predictive validities are similar concepts. **Concurrent validity** refers to the degree to which performance on one variable is related to performance on another variable at approximately the same point in time. For example, the degree of relationship between performances on a class-

Table 16.2   Table of Specifications

Process	Content			
	Chapter 1	Chapter 2	Chapter 3	Total
Knowledge	5	8	8	21
Comprehension	4	7	4	15
Application	1	3	4	8
Analysis	1	2	3	6
Synthesis	0	1	4	5
Evaluation	0	1	2	3
Total	11	22	25	58

List of Objectives—1 through 58.

room test and performances on a standardized test over the same capability might represent concurrent validity for the classroom test.

Predictive validity (or **criteria-related validity**) refers to the degree to which one variable (**predictor variable**) at a point in time is related to another variable at a future point in time (**criterion variable**). For example, performance on an intelligence test can be used to predict future achievement in school, college, or on the job, based on studies of similar performances of persons on the intelligence test from previous years. In addition, multiple predictor variables (e.g., past achievement and intelligence test scores) can be used to predict future achievement.

Whereas content validity is determined by logical analysis, concurrent and predictive validities are determined through statistical analysis, that is, correlational procedures. Content validity is based on a definition of content, while concurrent or predictive validity is based on a relationship between variables.

Reliability   While validity is the primary concern in measurement, it is, in turn, directly dependent upon the *reliability* of a test. Reliability may be defined as the degree to which a test measures something consistently. While a test may appear to measure a capability or characteristic validly on the surface, inconsistent responses from item to item on the part of test takers would indicate that the characteristic or capability is not being measured by the test. That is, there would be little or no validity for the existence of the characteristic or capability as measured by the test. Since tests rarely measure anything in a totally reliable manner, reliability is as critical a facet in testing as validity. The degree of reliability of a test is analyzed by correlational procedures.

Given its importance, let us take a look at reliability. There is a formula

> "*Reliability* may be defined as the degree to which a test measures something consistently."

for estimating reliability of a test that tells us a great deal about the concept (Ebel, 1972). The formula is as follows:

$$\text{Estim. of Reliability} = \frac{\text{number of items}}{\text{number of items minus one (1)}} \left[1 - \frac{\text{mean} \times (\text{number of items} - \text{mean})}{\text{number of items} \times \text{variance}} \right]$$

From this formula, you can see that there are three factors that determine the reliability of a test: number of items, mean difficulty of the items, and the amount of variability in the distribution of scores. The longer the test, the closer the mean difficulty is to 50%, and the greater the variance, the higher the reliability of a test will be. We'll try a couple of examples. Let us say that one test has forty items, with a mean of 30 and a standard deviation of 5; a second test has eighty items, with a mean of 45 and a standard deviation of 15. Now, let us estimate what the reliabilities of these tests are:

$$\text{Test 1} \quad \text{rel.} = \frac{40}{39} \left[1 - \frac{30(40 - 30)}{40(25)} \right] = 1.03 \left[1 - \frac{300}{1000} \right] = .72$$

$$\text{Test 2} \quad \text{rel.} = \frac{80}{79} \left[1 - \frac{45(80 - 45)}{80(225)} \right] = 1.01 \left[1 - \frac{1575}{18000} \right] = .92$$

The second test, with each characteristic being more desirable, has a higher reliability than the first test. The estimated coefficient resulting from this formula is the lower limit of the actual reliability of the test as determined by correlational analysis. You might want to make up some problems of your own by varying one characteristic at a time to see what effect the change has on the reliability coefficient.

The potential reliability of a test can be broken down into the component parts of reliability: **content sampling error, time sampling error, interrater agreement error,** and **random error** (Anastasi, 1976). That is, reliability = 1.00 minus error. We cannot do much about error for which we do not know the source. The goal, then, is to take as much of the potential 1.00 correlation coefficient into the reliability column as we can from the other three error sources. Content sampling is based on the **internal consistency** of the measure. The more diverse the content domain is, the greater will be the error. Time sampling refers to the stability of performances of the subjects. The more inconsistent the performances are over time, the greater will be the error.

While there is nothing wrong with unreliability of test scores, if that's the best we can do, it is important that we know how reliable the test actually is. We can then take the degree of reliability of the test into consideration when making decisions based on results from it. In addition, we can use more reliable tests in the future, based on our understanding of the factors that affect reliability.

The formula we used to estimate reliability only takes into consideration content sampling; it does not deal with time sampling. While time sampling is usually reported for standardized tests, teachers do not usually give equivalent forms of a classroom test to account for error in time sampling. However, they often do give more than one test before evaluating performances of students. If several tests are given during a course, then time sampling is taken into consideration in the composite test upon which an evaluation may be based. Insofar as content sampling is concerned, a test can have less reliability (if several tests are given) than if only one test was given. If several tests of modest reliabilities are used, the reliability for the composite test will be considerably higher than that of any one test, that is, lengthened tests.

The importance of the degree of reliability of a test depends upon the nature of the decision that one wishes to make. If the decision involves a group of people, then it can be lower than if the decision involves an individual. For example, one might use a test with a reliability of .50 for the purpose of monitoring learning for a group of students. Yet, a test with a reliability of .90 might be used for selection, placement, or terminal assessment of an individual student.

The higher the reliability of a test, the less likely we are to make mistakes in our evaluations, for example, giving wrong grades to nearly all the students in the class. Giving students the wrong grades can also be a validity problem. That is, you can measure something reliably and yet have little or no validity. If we don't know what the criterion is, all the reliability in the world (1.00) won't help.

Some Comments about Reliability and Validity of Tests

As we indicated earlier in our discussion of correlation, the interpretation of correlation coefficients is dependent upon the size of the sample, the nature of the phenomena of interest, and what we have learned from previous studies about the expected values of a coefficient between certain variables.

We will consider a few examples to give you some idea of what correlation coefficient might be expected for a few variables. At the same time, we will illustrate the relationship between predictive (and concurrent) validity and reliability of a test.

> "The interpretation of correlation coefficients is dependent upon the size of the sample, the nature of the phenomena of interest, and what we have learned from previous studies about the expected values of a coefficient between certain variables."

Standardized intelligence and achievement tests often have reliability coefficients for total scores in the high .80s and low .90s. Classroom achievement tests often have **reliability coefficients** for total scores in the .50s and .60s. In addition, subtest scores from standardized intelligence and achievement tests often have reliability coefficients in the .40s, .50s, and .60s. Hence, total scores for the intelligence test might be correlated .80 with total scores for the standardized achievement test and .40 with scores for the classroom achievement test. Likewise, a score on a subtest of an intelligence test might correlate .40 with a standardized achievement test score and .20 with the classroom test score.

Predictive (and concurrent) validity, like content validity, then, depends upon reliability. Since these kinds of validity are based on the relationship between two variables, the reliability of each test will affect the validity coefficients.

Knowledge of reliability and validity is important in selection of a test for decision making. One might discard an intelligence test in which the correlation between equivalent forms of the instrument was .80 and use a self-concept test in which the coefficient was the same between equivalent forms of the instrument. Likewise, one might discard an intelligence test that correlated .50 with school achievement and retain a self-concept test that had the same correlation with school achievement. In general, the test with the most desirable validity coefficients in relation to the purpose of a decision will be selected from those available.

Objectivity may be defined in terms of both test scoring (i.e., reliability) and test sampling (i.e., validity). It may be defined as the degree to which responses to items on a test are scored consistently. For example, if two people respond in the same way to the same test item, objectivity would be absent if the responses were scored differently; for example, one response scored correctly and the other incorrectly. The establishment of criteria for judging performance is critical in gaining objectivity in the scoring of tests. Lack of objectivity in scoring will lower test reliability. It is on the basis of scoring that **free-response** tests (essay, completion, short answer) and **forced-choice** tests (multiple-choice, true-false, matching) are often referred to as subjective and objective tests, respectively.

Objectivity may also be defined as the degree to which content sampling

Objectivity

of a test is free from personal bias on the part of the test constructor in relation to particular content or objectives. For example, if a teacher wrote an essay question based on one objective and not on another objective or used five multiple-choice items on one objective and none on another objective of equal importance, then the test has lost some degree of content validity.

Efficiency *Efficiency* may be defined in terms of the time that it takes both test taker and test user to obtain a measurement. A student can usually make a choice between two alternatives faster than he or she can between four alternatives. Likewise, a student can usually respond to a multiple-choice item more rapidly than he or she can to an essay question. Efficiency of student time, then, is based on the complexity of the decision in terms of such factors as reading, thinking, and writing. A test that is inefficient for its purpose in terms of the amount of time a student has available to demonstrate a capability will have an effect on its content validity, that is, the test will not sample the content adequately.

Efficiency may also be defined as the amount of time required for the teacher to construct a test and score the results. The initial construction of a free-response instrument is usually more efficient than a forced-choice instrument. Likewise, a two-choice instrument is usually more efficient to construct than a four-choice instrument. A forced-choice test can be scored more efficiently than a free-response one. Forced-choice tests can be reused by the teacher, while student answers to free-response tests cannot be reused for subsequent classes. If a teacher has had insufficient time to construct a forced-choice test or insufficient time to read a free-response test, the test's reliability will be affected.

In view of the importance of time for students and teachers, it is critical that an efficient test be selected. The criterion used for selection, however, should be that the test will serve its purpose rather than serve expediency. For example, if our concern was to sample students' knowledge of content within a forty-minute class period, a true-false or matching test would likely be a sound choice, both in terms of student and teacher time. It would also likely yield the most desirable measurement characteristics.

If our concern was to sample students' comprehension, application, and analysis of knowledge in forty minutes, a multiple-choice test would likely be a sound choice on the basis of efficiency and desirable measurement characteristics. If we were interested in sampling the students' capabilities to synthesize and evaluate ideas in the same time frame, an essay test would likely be a sound choice on the basis of efficiency and desirable measurement characteristics.

One final point must be made about efficiency. The response mode of the student is an important consideration in measurement. One learns to write by writing, one learns to speak by speaking, one learns to read by reading, one learns to hit free throws by shooting free throws, and one learns to make decisions by decision making. Knowledge can help to improve such skills, but a free-response or a forced-choice test will not substitute for an oral test if the validity of the test is dependent on one's speaking. Hence, the response mode of the student is an important consideration in measurement. The same criteria are used to evaluate a test, of course, regardless of the response mode required.

Construction, Interpretation, and Uses of Classroom Tests

From this discussion of the foundations of measurement and evaluation, we will now consider the role of testing in classroom decision making. We will focus on classroom tests since most of the teacher's time in formal evaluation involves such instruments.

If the functions of selection (e.g., special education) and placement (e.g., ability grouping) are used in a school, it is likely that someone other than the teacher will have made these decisions. For instance, when a teacher meets a class on the first day, the students will already have been through any selection and placement procedures the school might have. Monitoring and terminal assessment are the evaluation functions for which a teacher has primary responsibility. Thus, it is important that we consider aspects of classroom test construction, interpretation, and uses.

How Can Classroom Tests Be Used Effectively in Teaching?

Let's assume that you are a young teacher and that you have just left a teacher's meeting during the week prior to the opening of school. Mr. MacKenzie, the principal, said at the meeting, "Grades have lost their meaning in recent years. In fact," he said, "last year, the distribution of grades for the entire school was 80% A's, 15% B's and 5% C's. Furthermore," Mr. MacKenzie continued, "the students in this building have slightly above average IQs, and yet on the standardized achievement test administered last January, our kids were below average in knowledge and skills. Consequently," he said, "I think our kids are getting ripped off. Let's make grades mean something, but most of all, let's teach something to the students." Mr. MacKenzie had concluded with the usual reminder to secure a copy of the new teacher's handbook before leaving for the day.

Having nothing else to do this particular evening, you decide to see what the grading policies are to be at U.S. Grant School this year. Under the heading *Marking System* in the teacher's handbook, you find the information concerning the meaning of grades (figure 16.6).

Figure 16.6

A. Competence	B. Effort	C. Progress

1. Criteria
   A—Competent, needs a new placement
   B—More than minimally competent
   C—Minimally competent
   D—Less than minimally competent
   F—Incompetent, needs a new placement

2. Curve
   A—Top 15%
   B—Next 15%
   C—Next 40%
   D—Next 15%
   F—Bottom 15%

3. Standards
   A—90—100%
   B—75— 89%
   C—60— 74%
   D—46— 59%
   F— 0— 45%

4. Self-Reports
   A—Student reports that he or she attained full benefit from experience
   C—Student reports that he or she thought it was a worthwhile experience
   F—Student reports that he or she attain absolutely no benefit from the experience and that it definitely was not worthwhile
   *Use B and D at your discretion

Revision: Please do not use No. 4 this year. This was used on an experimental basis last year. We are still studying the results.

Select one from each group and turn in your choice at the time of your first submission of grades. You cannot change your mind on a marking system during this school year. Of course, you may select a new procedure with the first submission of grades each subsequent year.

Take your pick!

A. ......
B. ......
C. ......

1. ......
2. ......
3. ......
4. Cancel

"Take your pick of the marking systems, the handbook says! Wow! This is just like Mr. Wheeler, my supervisor of practice teaching, said it would be," you are thinking. "What does a grade mean? How is a grade related to monitoring? How is a grade related to terminal assessment?

*"It seems as if effort might be important to monitoring. But it would be meaningless as an outcome. Wouldn't effort result in progress? If it didn't, how could it be called effort? In addition, **progress** would seem to be an important factor in sustained effort. It would appear that finding ways to enable the student to make progress would be the critical aspect of monitoring. If I can point out to the student how well he or she is doing on the objectives, that should be meaningful feedback. In addition, I can use this information for making decisions in my teaching.*

*"**Competence** sounds like the degree to which the student has achieved the objectives of the curriculum. That's a function of terminal assessment. But, competence based on what criterion—standards, a curve, or maybe*

both? Standards seem so arbitrary. If the standards are too high, then everyone may be failing. If they are too low, then everyone may be excellent. How could you establish standards without knowing how students can perform on the measurement underlying them?

"A curve could be a disaster for some of the kids. Someone has to get those F's. Wouldn't that interfere with progress? How can I tell a student that he or she is making progress and then give him or her an F? There seems to be a connection between progress and standards, and between competence and a curve. But, I'm not sure what it is. Oh, well, I have a few weeks to think about the meaning of grades. In the meantime, I will just try to help each student learn, and hope for the best. If I can't find any differences in the performances of the students, then I will just give everyone a C."

To learn the answers to the questions you may have as a young teacher, let's join Ms. Larue's educational psychology class. She's teaching measurement and evaluation, and that's what we are discussing. First, Ms. Larue has decided that if you are to be a student in her class you need to know what the objectives of a particular unit are. Study display 16.1 to learn these objectives.

Next, Ms. Larue would like to learn something about you and your standing in the class. So she gives you a pretest of your entry behavior. The results of the pretest follow:

Student	Score	Student	Score
A	14	M	20
B	20	N	22
C	20	O	21
D	19	P	25
E	24	Q	13
F	18	R	12
G	21	S	30
H	18	T	26
I	21	U	16
J	19	V	22
K	17	W	19
L	20		

From these pretest results, select the letter that has a score beside it that you believe best illustrates your entry behavior. How did you do? Certainly S did fine, considering that this was a thirty-item true-false test. Ms. Larue wanted to get some idea of your basic knowledge of the content, and she wanted to do this very efficiently—in about twenty minutes. While she did as good a job as she could in constructing the test, she was not very concerned about the test having a high reliability. That is, she did not wish to make decisions about

1. Define measurement and evaluation.
2. Distinguish between measurement and evaluation.
3. Identify the reasons for using a table of specifications in test construction.
4. Define efficiency, objectivity, reliability, and validity of a test.
5. Describe conditions which may affect the efficiency, objectivity, reliability and validity of a test.
6. Define difficulty level and discrimination index.
7. Identify factors involved in determining a suitable grading system.
8. Define three measures of central tendency.
9. Define two measures of variability.
10. Describe the relationships among efficiency, objectivity, reliability, and validity.

11. Identify the differences in the purposes of educational and psychological testing.
12. Draw pictures of left skewed, right skewed, and normal curves.
13. Distinguish between a classroom test and a standardized test.
14. Identify the functions of evaluation.
15. Illustrate the use of a mean, median, and mode for a given distribution of scores.
16. Illustrate the use of item analysis in improving given test items.
17. Translate test scores from one standard score unit to another from a given set of data.
18. Interpret the meaning of different values of correlation coefficients.
19. Describe the differences between an intelligence and an achievement test.
20. Identify the usefulness of different kinds of test items.

individuals, but rather she wanted to find out about the characteristics of the group of students. Recall that selection and/or placement tests may have already been given. If not, it is more than likely that the students in your class are going to be with Ms. Larue throughout the school year anyway.

It is difficult to make much sense out of these scores, so we will put them into a frequency distribution:

Score	Frequency	Score	Frequency
30	1	19	3
26	1	18	2
25	1	17	1
24	1	16	1
22	2	14	1
21	3	13	1
20	4	12	1

For Ms. Larue's purposes, a mode would be adequate as an indication of central tendency for the scores. What is the mode for the distribution? The mode will give Ms. Larue some information about the prior achievement of the students in the class. Likewise, a range would be an adequate indication of variability. What is the range of the scores? A chance score on a true-false test of thirty items is 15, that is, a fifty–fifty chance on each item. Three members of the class scored lower than chance. One student attained a perfect score. Fourteen of the students were approximately at the modal score, which made Ms. Larue's job a little easier than if the students were more dispersed. Last year, Ms. Larue recalled that the mode was 20 and the range was 6 on the pretest.

Oh, yes. Unbeknownst to you, Ms. Larue is going to give this test again as a posttest. She wants to see how much you progress so she will only give you your score as feedback. She won't tell you any of the answers. If she did, you would probably remember them and score perfectly on the posttest, but you might not know how, what, or why you answered them that way. By learning only your score rather than the answers, you probably will not even remember having taken the pretest.

Ms. Larue is going to arrange some learning situations for you so that you can have an opportunity to attain the objectives for the unit. You are encouraged to use the objectives, design your own quizzes, and complete the projects designed by Mrs. Larue. She uses the projects as a basis for supplying you feedback related to your attainment of the objectives. Finally, Ms. Larue gives you an accumulated report of your performance on the projects.

The results for the class, based on a total of 20, are as follows:

Student	Score	Student	Score
A	16	M	18
B	19	N	18
C	17	O	19
D	17	P	20
E	18	Q	18
F	18	R	17
G	18	S	19
H	17	T	16
I	19	U	18
J	18	V	19
K	18	W	17
L	20		

L and P seem to have learned a great deal. What happened to S? Let's take a look at the distribution of scores:

Score	Frequency	Score	Frequency
20	2	17	5
19	5	16	2
18	9		

These scores were on clearly defined projects that gave students an opportunity to acquire and use knowledge and skills related to the objectives. Based on the students' informal comments, Ms. Larue concluded that the projects were meaningful to them. Certainly, nearly everyone completed the projects for twenty objectives.

Now comes the moment when Ms. Larue reminds you that your test over how well you have acquired and can transfer knowledge and skills will be coming up in two days. The results are as follows:

Student	Score	Student	Score
A	12	M	27
B	28	N	29
C	13	O	27
D	21	P	29
E	30	Q	14
F	23	R	19
G	26	S	31
H	20	T	28
I	30	U	34
J	21	V	23
K	24	W	22
L	33		

This test was based on the objectives that Ms. Larue and the class had been studying. She selected a four-alternative, multiple-choice test for the fifty-minute period. She included some items that she thought would be easy, some she thought would be difficult, and many that she thought would be challenging to the students. In all, there were forty items. Her primary goal was to find out if there were differences in degrees of competency among the members of the class for the objectives of the unit. She thought there might be individual differences in outcomes, of course. But, she wanted to find out whether she was right and also just what these differences were. The distribution of scores were as follows:

Score	Frequency	Score	Frequency
34	1	23	2
33	1	22	1
31	1	21	2
30	2	20	1
29	2	19	1
28	2	14	1
27	2	13	1
26	1	12	1
24	1		

Note that in the distribution of scores there were no students who scored at chance or below. For a four-alternative test of forty items, a chance score would be 10. A good test for Ms. Larue's purposes here would be one in which the mean is about one-half of the way between the chance score and the total possible. Thus, the mean of the test should be one-half of the distance between 10 to 40, or 25. How did she do? You might want to analyze the results of this test thoroughly in terms of central tendency, variability, and reliability to see if Ms. Larue designed a "good" test.

It would also be helpful for Ms. Larue to look at the characteristics of the items that make up such a test as a great deal can be learned about good teaching (and poor teaching), faulty test items, and for what objectives the students are competent as a group.

Ms. Larue decided to do some reteaching on the basis of the item analysis of the test. She then administered the thirty-item, true-false test two days later. The results were as follows:

Student	Score	Student	Score
A	17	M	29
B	27	N	30
C	25	O	24
D	22	P	29
E	26	Q	22
F	23	R	25
G	23	S	27
H	20	T	25
I	24	U	26
J	23	V	24
K	23	W	21
L	23		

Any progress? The mode is 23. In fact, there is only one student under the pretest mode of 20. No one had less than a chance score. N attained a score of 30; S did worse on the posttest than the pretest. The results look positive for the group as a whole, but maybe a few students are worse off than when we started. Let's see what the change scores look like.

Pre	Post	Change	Pre	Post	Change	Pre	Post	Change
30	27	−3	20	29	+9	18	23	+5
26	25	−1	20	27	+7	18	20	+2
25	29	+4	20	25	+5	17	23	+6
24	26	+2	20	23	+3	16	26	+10
22	30	+8	19	23	+4	14	17	+3
22	24	+2	19	22	+3	13	22	+9
21	24	+3	19	21	+2	12	25	+13
21	24	+3						
21	23	+2						
Mean $= \frac{20}{9} = 2.2$			Mean $= \frac{33}{7} = 4.7$			Mean $= \frac{45}{7} = 6.4$		

Only two students had negative change scores. Curiously, these two students obtained the highest pretest scores. The means show the average change scores for each third of the distribution. Note that the lower third gained the most, the upper third gained the least. Is Ms. Larue a more effective teacher for the lower third of the class than for the upper third? Well, maybe; but we can't tell from this information. What is characteristic of the test is a ceiling effect. The test was not difficult enough to detect as much change in the upper third as the lower two-thirds of the class. S, who had the pretest score of 30, had nowhere to go but down. When you consider that a test score (regardless of the kind of test item) is in part due to luck as well as knowledge and skill, it does not seem surprising that S lost three points.

The test was difficult enough to allow the lower third of the class to demonstrate progress. On this extreme, R may have been lucky on the posttest, or perhaps unlucky on the pretest. At any rate, the pretest was helpful to Ms. Larue, and the posttest does demonstrate some progress was made by the class as a group.

Now comes the time in which Ms. Larue is required to submit a grade for your achievement. The information she has about each member of the class is given in table 16.3. What grade would *you* give to each student?

Ms. Larue considered six possibilities. The first column of grades is based on prepost change scores and personal growth. The second column is based on projects and standards. Column three represents grades based on the discrimination test and the curve. Column four contains grades based on the posttest and standards. Grades in the fifth column are based on combined scores from the discrimination test and posttest and the curve. Finally, column six represents combined results from the discrimination test and posttest, with grades being awarded on the basis of both the curve and standards. Let's see how these possibilities work out.

There are two kinds of criteria that Ms. Larue is trying to take into consideration. First, what criterion is the grade based on? That is, what is the validity of the grade? Is it progress or competency? Second, what is the reference point from which the progress or competency is to be judged? Is it to be judged on interindividual differences (group norm), intraindividual differences (individual norm), or mastery of content (standard norm), or some combination of these criteria?

Some of these concepts have meaning across both kinds of criteria. The following diagram represents the interrelationships of measurement and evaluation criteria:

		Criterion of Evaluation		
		Group Norm	Individual Norm	Standard Norm
Criterion of Measurement	Progress	X	Personal	X
	Competency	Status	X	Mastery
	X-empty			

Table 16.3   Cumulative Results of Measurements/Possible Evaluations of Performances

Student	Pretest	Posttest	Change	Projects	Test D	Posttest	Grade?					
A	14	17	+3	16	12	17	C	B	F	D	F	D
B	20	27	+7	19	28	27	B	A	C	A	C	C
C	20	25	+5	17	13	25	C	B	F	B	F	C
D	19	22	+3	17	21	22	C	B	D	C	D	C
E	24	26	+2	18	30	26	D	A	B	B	B	B
F	18	23	+5	18	23	23	C	A	C	B	C	C
G	21	23	+2	18	26	23	D	A	C	B	C	C
H	18	20	+2	17	20	20	D	B	D	C	D	C
I	21	24	+3	19	30	24	C	A	B	B	C	C
J	19	23	+4	18	21	23	C	A	D	B	D	C
K	17	23	+6	18	24	23	B	A	C	B	C	C
L	20	23	+3	20	33	23	C	A	A	B	B	B
M	20	29	+9	18	27	29	A	A	C	A	B	B
N	22	30	+8	18	29	30	B	A	B	A	A	A
O	21	24	+3	19	27	24	C	A	C	B	C	C
P	25	29	+4	20	29	29	C	A	B	A	A	A
Q	13	22	+9	18	14	22	A	A	F	C	F	C
R	12	25	+13	17	19	25	A	B	D	B	D	C
S	30	27	−3	19	31	27	F	A	A	A	A	A
T	26	25	−1	16	28	25	F	B	C	B	C	C
U	16	26	+10	18	34	26	A	A	A	B	A	A
V	22	24	+2	19	23	24	D	A	C	B	C	C
W	19	21	+2	17	22	21	D	B	C	C	D	C
M	19.9	24.3	4.3	18.0	24.5	24.3						
SD	4.2	3.0	—	1.0	5.9	3.0						
k	30	30	—	20	40	30						
r_t	.64	.51	—	.00	.75	.51						

M = Mean   k = number of items
SD = Standard Deviation r_t = reliability of test

Psychologists have long advocated progress and intraindividual differences while educators have long advocated mastery learning (White, 1965).
Hence, educational psychologists have long had the task of mediating between the art and the science of education. The most commonly adopted
reference point in educational psychology is that of interindividual differences
in competencies. There has been considerable rethinking of these issues under
the auspices of **criteria-** and **norm-referenced testing** (Glaser, 1963; Anderson & Messick, 1974; Kohlberg & Mayer, 1972; Popham, 1976; White,
1965).

Debates related to **mastery learning, competency-based education,** and
behavioral objectives earlier in this decade were all a part of the issues of "how

we can effectively combine criteria- and norm-referenced measurement and evaluation" (Cronbach, 1971; Ebel, 1971). This is the issue that Mr. MacKenzie, the principal, gave up on and that Ms. Larue is trying to resolve.

In Ms. Larue's case, she is interested in finding meaningful individual differences in the progress and competency of students for terminal assessment purposes. It was on this basis that she used different criteria for measurement and evaluation.

We concluded in our earlier discussion that pre-posttest changes were not reliable enough for making decisions about individual differences in progress. Her attempt to grade individual progress would turn out to be a disaster when all the information is considered about each student. Consider the grades in column one.

The pretest was helpful to Ms. Larue for monitoring purposes, and the change scores do indicate progress for the class. If she was serious about attempting to grade on the basis of progress as indicated by this grading system, she would need to design a harder test.

We also concluded that the results from the projects are not reliable enough (.00) for making decisions about individual differences in the competency of students. The projects (column two) were helpful in enabling the students to make progress toward the objectives of the unit. If Ms. Larue had wanted to use the results of the projects for discrimination purposes, she would have monitored the students' learning much more carefully or designed more difficult projects. That is, these projects were designed to provide feedback to the students in the monitoring of learning activities.

The grades based on the discrimination test (column three) would be the most defensible one for assigning grades of any single measure used. But Ms. Larue is also interested in progress. This test was designed to measure degree of competency.

In a sense, the scores on the posttest represent progress (column four). We know there has been a pre-posttest change for the group. The posttest, therefore, is measuring the outcomes of the progress, with a ceiling to conform to the arbitrary standard that was used as criteria to assess it. The only problem here is that the test was not designed to measure degree of competency.

Grades were also determined for a combined score from the discrimination test and the posttest (column five). These scores were added together for each student. For example, student A has a score of 29 (12 + 17). These scores are as reliable as or more so than those from the discrimination test alone. In addition, the total score represents both degree of competency and progress.

Finally, the results of grades based on the discrimination test and the posttest (column six) were used in a different manner than they were in column five. Here, the posttest is used as a measure of minimal competency based on the standards for a C, that is, 60%. Hence, no matter how well a student might do beyond the minimal competency level, he or she would receive only a C on the basis of the posttest. The results from the discrimination test would then be used to assign grades based on the curve to assess degree of competence. Unless a student received a higher grade on the basis of degree of competency, he or she received the grade earned on the minimal competency test. In a sense, each test was used appropriately, according to its purpose. Ms. Larue has a decision to make. Which of the plans would you use if you were in her situation?

The foundation of evaluation is measurement. The foundation of measurement is a test. The foundation of a test is an item. Hence, the place to improve evaluation is at the item level. While a teacher will not likely spend much of his or her time analyzing test items, it is critical to be able to interpret such information in the course of evaluating learning and teaching. In addition, it is a useful skill to be able to do item analysis when a test turns out to be less than desirable in relation to its purpose.

Item Analysis

One of the reasons Ms. Larue chose a multiple-choice test in our illustration was that it would enable us to discuss the test item. Multiple-choice items, such as the one that follows, are particularly good for a discussion of test items.

Stem (question or statement preceding the alternatives)

. . . .

A. Foil (incorrect alternative)

B. Foil (incorrect alternative)

C. Foil (incorrect alternative)

*D. Correct Alternative (or keyed alternative)

This terminology is used in describing multiple-choice tests. Sometimes, *response* is substituted for *alternative*. *Choice, decision,* or *guess* may also be substituted for *alternative*. Let us do an analysis of this multiple-choice item for illustrative purposes.

Ms. Larue has already scored the test of which this item was a part. We will arrange all of the test performances in order, from the highest to the lowest score. Next, we will select the answer sheets of two groups of students. We will select the answer sheets for the upper 27% and lower 27% of the class. Twenty-seven percent is an arbitrary cut-off point we chose for this example because, among possible extreme group cut-off points such as 25%, 33%, or 50%, 27% has turned out to be the most useful for item analysis purposes. These percentages can be approximate for a small group such as twenty-three students. In Ms. Larue's case, we will take the highest and lowest six scorers. Now, we will tally the alternatives chosen by members of each group separately. For item #1, the choices are as follows:

Highest Scorers	Lowest Scorers	Alternative
0	0	A
6	6	*B
0	0	C
0	0	D

We are initially interested in the **difficulty level** and the **discrimination index** of an item. After these are determined, we can then consider the incorrect choices of students and what they may mean. The percentage of students who answer an item correctly is referred to as the difficulty level of the item. In this example, twelve out of twelve students selected the correct alternative. Therefore, the difficulty level of the item is 100%. If you subtract the number of low scorers from the number of high scorers who answered the item correctly and then divide by one-half the total number of students, you will find what is called the discrimination index for an item. In this case, it is $\frac{6-6}{6} = .00$. Level of difficulty (1-mean) and discrimination index (degree of systematic variability) across all the items on a test will accumulate into the reliability of the test. In addition, the discrimination index represents the content validity of a test item in relation to the domain of which it is a part.

Perhaps, these formulas will be helpful to you for finding difficulty level and discrimination index for an item:

$$\text{Difficulty Level} = \frac{\text{number of students who correctly anwered item}}{\text{total number of students}}$$

$$\text{Discrimination Index} = \frac{\text{total number of correct answers in upper group minus total number of correct answers in lower group}}{\text{one-half the total number of students in both groups}}$$

Teaching: Art and Science

The students did fine on this item. This turned out to be an item that was mastered by all the students.

Now, we will consider a multiple-choice item, which we will call item #12. We'll change our format now that you understand the procedure:

	A	B	*C	D	Diff.	Disc.
Upper	0	0	6	0	75%	.50
Lower	1	1	3	1		

This is a format that is often used to set up a test file for forced-choice items. From a card with the item on it, one can select or revise an item easily. Subsequent item analysis information can be added to the card later.

Item #12 would be called an easy item. The format we used for item #12 is particularly helpful in discriminating among students in the lower group. This is a good point at which to consider the meaning of difficulty level. What is the difficulty level of this item for the high scorers? Six of six answered it correctly, or 100%. What is the difficulty level of this item for the low scorers? Three of six answered it correctly, or 50%. While we could find out what the difficulty level of the middle scorers was by retrieving their answer sheets, a sound guess would be about 75%. That is, the average difficulty level for the upper and lower groups is a good estimate of what the difficulty level is for the middle group.

When an item is referred to as easy, moderately difficult, or hard, the reference point is the middle group. Item #12 was mastered by the high group; it was easy for the middle group; and it was moderately difficult for the low group.

Item #7 has some interesting characteristics, too. This item is referred to as moderately difficult.

	A	B	C	*D	Diff.	Disc.
Upper	0	0	0	6	50%	1.00
Lower	2	3	1	0		

A moderately difficult item can make discriminations among all three groups. That is, it was moderately difficult for the middle group.

The results for another item, #37, were as follows:

	*A	B	C	D	Diff.	Disc.
Upper	3	0	1	2	25%	.50
Lower	0	1	3	2		

This item was moderately difficult for the upper group. Thus, it is particularly helpful in discriminating among students in this group. It is referred to as a hard or difficult item.

Finally, the results for item #25 were as follows:

	A	*B	C	D	Diff.	Disc.
Upper	3	0	2	1	0%	.00
Lower	1	0	2	3		

This item was impossible for everyone. Perhaps it was not a part of the unit. Perhaps, it was beyond the capabilities of any of the students. Perhaps, it was mis-keyed.

As was the case for the item that everyone answered correctly, Ms. Larue didn't learn anything about the differences among students in outcomes.

Item difficulty ranges from 0% to 100%. Item discrimination ranges from −1.00 through zero to 1.00. Once the decision is made about what difficult level is desired, items are selected on the basis of the highest positive discrimination indices available. This generalization, of course, is appropriate only after the items available have been considered in relation to content validity. That is, a less desirable item (e.g., difficulty level = 75%, discrimination index = .30) would be selected rather than a more desirable item (e.g., difficulty level = 75%, discrimination index = .50) if the latter was not related to the objective in question.

A left skewed curve indicates that the set of items was relatively easy for the students; a right skewed curve indicates that the set of items was relatively hard for the students; and a normal curve indicates that the set of items was moderately difficult for the students. For an easy test, items might range from a difficulty level of about 50% to 90%, with the majority around 70%. For a difficult test, items might range from a difficulty level of 10% to 50%, with the majority around 30%. For a moderately difficult test, items might range from a difficulty level of about 25% to 75%, with the majority around 50%. Of course, setting a difficulty level for an item or for a test is easy; it is not easy to attain the goal, even with practice.

All of the items illustrated from Ms. Larue's test had the maximum discrimination indices possible for the difficulty levels of the respective items. Therefore, they were excellent items for making decisions related to their respective purposes.

What purposes can item analysis serve in addition to better understanding the test, group performances on particular items, or individual performances across all the items? First, one can identify faulty test items. Second, one can identify objectives that must be learned or relearned.

Faulty items are those that have negative discrimination indices. Such items should be discarded unless the item is a very easy one. Perhaps there is a suitable explanation for such an occurrence, such as a student in a higher score level who searched for a more complex answer or who was ill on the day the objective was considered in class.

Moderately difficult items are designed to make discriminations within the entire group. If they make merely slight discriminations among high and low scorers, then they need to be revised to increase the discrimination indices. Perhaps, the keyed alternative is somewhat incorrect; one or more of the foils are somewhat correct; or both. At any rate, the item requires careful revision.

Items are also faulty if they are too easy or too difficult for their intended purposes. An item can be adjusted by making the correct alternative more or less obvious or by making the foils more or less tenable.

Good test items, like good scoring, result from experiences in teaching, learning, and testing. Constructing tests, analyzing them, interpreting them, and using them contribute to one's measurement and evaluation skills. These experiences also can enable one to understand better whom and what we teach. Some test guidelines are presented in display 16.2.

Earlier in this chapter, we mentioned standard scores with respect to standardized tests. We have also used from time to time the expressions that a student was performing at grade level, below grade level, or above grade level. We have also discussed the normal curve model. In addition, Ms. Larue was interested in combining scores from two tests of dissimilar score scales. Finally, we discussed the formula used at one time to define IQ. All of these ideas can be placed into a better perspective through your understanding of **standard score scales.**

First, we will consider Ms. Larue's idea of combining scores from two (or more) tests. If Ms. Larue had used option five in grading, three of the twenty-three students would have received a grade one letter below what they earned if her intent was to weigh progress and competency equally. The reason that this would have happened is that the two tests have different score scales. If the means and standard deviations were nearly identical, then it would be quite appropriate to combine the scores. That is, converting the raw scores to standard scale scores wouldn't make any difference in the meaning of the scores.

A commonly used standard score scale is a z-score. A **z-score scale** has a mean of 0.00 and a standard deviation of 1.00. The formula for finding a z-score is as follows:

$$\text{z-score} = \frac{\text{one's score} - \text{mean}}{\text{standard deviation}}$$

For example, student B had a score of 28 in test D and a score of 27 on the posttest. The 28 would become $\frac{28 - 24.5}{5.9} = \frac{3.5}{5.9} = .59$. The score of 27 would become $\frac{27 - 24.3}{3.0} = \frac{2.7}{3.0} = .90$. Hence, student B did relatively better on the posttest than he or she did on the discrimination test. These scores can be averaged. Student B would have an average z-score of .75 on the two tests.

1. *Free-Response Test*

   Write a question so that it can be answered.

   Give the students the relative importance of each question and the suggested amount of time to spend on it.

   Have all students answer the same questions.

   Establish criteria for scoring each question before reading any student's answers.

   Read the answer to a question for all students before proceeding to the next question.

   Read the answers without knowledge of the student's identity.

2. *Forced-Choice Test*

   Write a clear question or incomplete statement as a stem.

   Make all of the alternatives of approximately the same length.

   An alternative that is of a different length than the others is often a specific determiner.

   Avoid specific determiners such as always, never, and sometimes for a true-false item or for an isolated alternative.

   Use no more than five alternatives on a multiple-choice item.

   Limit a matching item to 10 stimuli and 15 associative responses.

3. *Speeded Test*

   Allow enough time for nearly everyone to finish a test unless the essence of the test is speed, e.g., some aspects of clerical skills, reading comprehension, short-cuts in arithmetical computation, and use of references.

   The former tests are sometimes referred to as power or accuracy tests.

4. *Open Book Tests*

   For any test other than factual or comprehen-
sion of knowledge, the student should have accessibility to materials used in studies and class for reference purposes. For analysis, synthesis, and evaluation, it is imperative that the materials are available.

5. *Take-Home Tests*

   These experiences are equivalent to practice exercises. If they have been helpful in learning the objectives of an instructional unit or course, one's performance on a test administered under controlled conditions will reflect the meaningfulness of the experience.

6. *Reporting System*

   If a school for which one teaches uses standards as the basis for a marking system, find out what the norm-reference group is on which the standards are based.

   If a school for which one teaches uses a curve as the basis for a marking system, find out on what criteria-reference performance the curve is based.

   For conferences with students and/or parents, be prepared to discuss progress and competence of student in relation to criteria- and norm-referenced performances in educational outcomes as well as psychological factors that may be of importance in relation to them, i.e., characteristics of the learner and the learning situation.

   Collect and revise criteria- and norm-referenced information related to performances of students as a group.

7. *Standardized Test*

   Read the manual carefully for a test. If possible, take the test yourself before administering it to the students.

Of course if Ms. Larue did not want to weigh the results of the two tests equally, then she would not convert them to a standard score scale.

Another commonly used standard score scale is a **T-score.** A T-score may be found by the following formula:

$$\text{T-score} = 50 + 10 \text{ (z-score)}$$

That is, a T-score scale has a mean of 50 and a standard deviation of 10. For example, Student B would have a T-score of $50 + 10 \ (.59)$ or 56 on Test D and $50 + 10 \ (.90)$ or 59 on the posttest. The advantage of a T-score over a z-score is that an interpreter does not have to deal with negative scores.

From the basic formula, you can use any mean and standard deviation you wish. For example, raw **IQ** scores from an intelligence test are usually converted to a standard score scale with a mean of 100. The standard deviation may be 15, 16, or 20, depending upon the particular test. Raw scores from achievement tests may be converted to a standard score scale, with a mean **equivalent** to the **grade** and time of year the test was administered to the students (e.g., 5.5 with a standard deviation of 1.0). Hence, a student in the fifth month of the fifth grade performing at 4.5, would be a grade below level. IQ and grade equivalent scales have historical meaning with respect to developmental concepts connected with them.

Other standard score scales have no particular meaning. For example, the Scholastic Aptitude Test has a mean of 500 and a standard deviation of 100, while the American College Test has a mean of 20 and a standard deviation of 5. Nevertheless, such standard score scales are soon readily understood with respect to the users of them.

Finally, there is a standard score scale that is commonly used in interpreting tests, i.e., **percentile rank.** A percentile rank can be found from the following formula:

$$\text{Percentile Rank} = \frac{\text{number of scores below a particular score plus one-half of the scores at that particular score}}{\text{total number of scores}} \times 100$$

For example, student B obtained a score of 28 on test D. Fourteen students scored lower, and one other student scored 28. Hence, student B's percentile rank was $\frac{14 + 1}{23} = 65$. That is, 65% of the students obtained a score less than student B. If we wanted to, we could compare his percentile rank on the posttest to his performance on test D. However, we cannot find a meaningful average for them as we can with a z-score (or T-score).

Standard score scales, then, can be very helpful at times in interpreting scores from tests of dissimilar raw score scales. The three most common standard score scales are illustrated in relation to the normal curve model in figure 16.7.

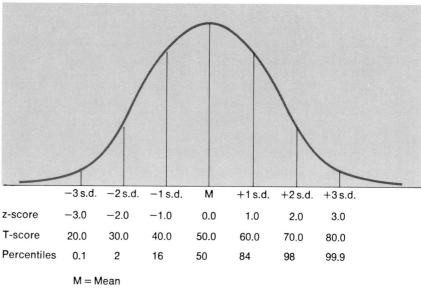

	−3 s.d.	−2 s.d.	−1 s.d.	M	+1 s.d.	+2 s.d.	+3 s.d.
z-score	−3.0	−2.0	−1.0	0.0	1.0	2.0	3.0
T-score	20.0	30.0	40.0	50.0	60.0	70.0	80.0
Percentiles	0.1	2	16	50	84	98	99.9

M = Mean
s.d. = Standard deviation

Summary

In this chapter, we have focused on a number of important principles of measurement and evaluation. There are many issues in this area, and we did not try to resolve them here. However, we have tried to demonstrate some of the factors involved in evaluating learning and teaching. The foundation of evaluation is measurement. If a measurement is judged to be satisfactory, then evaluation can proceed.

The nature of the measurement depends upon the nature of the decision to be made. Tests can be improved through analyzing the items they include and the procedures used to score them. Ultimately, we must be able to understand the meaning of the object to be evaluated. Norm-referenced and criteria-referenced performances are complimentary aspects of testing for the purpose of understanding the meaning of the capability or characteristic to be measured and evaluated.

Psychological and educational testing are both important in the various functions of evaluation in schools. The purpose of psychological testing is primarily related to selection and placement. The primary purpose of educational testing is related to monitoring and terminal assessment. However, the functions of both kinds of testing often cross these lines. Formal testing is an integral part of the art and science of teaching.

Teaching: Art and Science

Suggested Additional Readings

Short-Cut Statistics for Teacher-Made Tests, Second Edition, by Educational Testing Service, 1964 (*Princeton, N.J., 1964*)

This pamphlet presents practical ways of analyzing tests and test results.

All of these short-cuts have passed two basic tests. First, they were all applied to actual data by the writer's son. . . . Second, they have all been discussed with competent statisticians who winced slightly. . . .

from *Short-Cut Statistics for Teacher-Made Tests*

Making the Classroom Test: A Guide for Teachers, Second Edition, by Educational Testing Service, 1961 (*Princeton, N.J., 1961*)

This pamphlet presents practical suggestions related to decision-making in constructing classroom tests.

All teachers have to make tests. But making good tests is not easy. The purpose of this pamphlet is to offer practical suggestions which may help you to make better tests.

from *Making the Classroom Test: A Guide for Teachers*

Handbook in Research and Evaluation by Stephen Isaac and William B. Michael (*San Diego, Calif.: Robert R. Knapp, 1971*)

This handbook presents guidelines for evaluation of instrumental objectives and tests as well as research design and statistics.

Research and evaluation is most relevant when it builds upon and involves the people directly affected. . . . The classroom teacher and the guidance consultant, along with the director or administrator, should have the opportunity to identify problems, set goals, formulate plans, gather data, analyze outcomes, and reach conclusions.

from *Handbook in Research and Evaluation*

acceptance   A quality of an effective teacher; the ability to accept other's feelings.

accommodation   The phase of adaptation in which a person changes internal cognitive structures in order to "take in" new environmental information (see **adaptation**).

acculturation   The process whereby an individual assimilates into a culture; a changing of values and behaviors to conform to the culture in which one lives.

acquired characteristics   A person's traits acquired through life experiences rather than by heredity.

acquisition   Learning of a new capability or behavior (see **learning**).

adaptation   The internal processes involved in learning and using knowledge from one's experiences. Adaptation involves two circular processes: accommodation and assimilation.

adolescence   The period in human development between childhood and adulthood; characterized by accelerated physical and psychological growth.

affective learning   Development in understanding one's self and being responsive to others.

anal stage   The second of Freud's psychosexual stages, named after the primary erogenous zone during this period—the anal region.

animism   Attributing human characteristics to inanimate objects.

approach-approach   A type of conflict in which the person is faced with two equally desirable choices.

approach-avoidance   A type of conflict in which the individual is faced with a choice that involves some desirable and some undesirable elements.

aptitude   Natural or acquired readiness to learn particular skills or knowledge efficiently.

assimilation   The phase of adaptation in which one readily "adds" new environmental information to existing cognitive structures (see **adaptation**).

attachment   A term used to describe the special bond between an infant and its mother, or caretaker.

attention   The learner's state of readiness to "take in" and to learn.

audiovisual method   An instructional method that utilizes auditory and visual input concomitantly (e.g., television).

auditory ability   One's proficiency in using hearing in learning and performance.

autism   A congenital disorder characterized by withdrawal from reality and inability to relate to others.

autonomous morality   According to Piaget, the type of advanced moral reasoning that does not depend on the authority figures around us.

autonomy   Ability to function independently.

auxiliary   In linguistics, a set of morphemes that always contains a tense (*-ed* or other tense ending).

avoidance-avoidance   A type of conflict in which the person is faced with two equally undesirable choices.

basic trust   According to Erikson, the quality of trusting others developed during the first year of life.

battered-child syndrome   A pattern of child abuse that tends to recur within families.

behavioral perspective   The point of view that the person is primarily a product of conditioning and that most psychological phenomena can be explained through learning theory.

behaviorism   School of thought that emphasizes observable events in learning (see **conditioning**).

bilingual child   A child who learns two languages simultaneously; a child who speaks two languages.

bilingualism   Being exposed to more than one language from childhood.

blastocyst   A hollow ball of cells produced by repeated division of the fertilized ovum.

branching program   An instructional program based on the principle of branching. Such a program contains alternative subroutines so that a student can receive instruction in accordance with one's capabilities.

CAI   Computer-assisted instruction.

career choice   The processes leading up to the selection of a desired occupation.

castration anxiety   The young boy's fear, according to Freud, of losing his penis.

causality   The relationship between cause and effect (used by Piaget).

central tendency   Typical (average) performance.

character development   The process whereby an individual's intelligence and personality are brought under the jurisdiction of moral principles; the development of value-laden thinking.

characterization (by a value)   The level of the taxonomy of the affective domain in which the person's values are organized into some type of consistent system.

childhood sexuality   According to Freud, the child's progression from an oral, to an anal, to a genital creature; the principle that children are strongly motivated by sexual impulses.

chromosome   Rod-shaped bodies in the cell nucleus that carry the genes that determine hereditary characteristics.

classical conditioning   A type of learning in which an antecedent stimulus (unconditional stimulus) is the reinforcer that produces the response (see **respondent conditioning**).

classification   The grouping of things that share a common property into classes.

classroom test   Teacher-made test.

client-centered therapy   Developed by Carl Rogers, this therapy sees the client as essentially good and in the process of growth and the counselor as a person who gives genuine feelings to the client in order to help him overcome obstacles to growth.

cognition   A term used in psychology to include such processes as perception, concept formation, understanding, reasoning, judging, and problem solving.

cognitive-developmental   A school of thought that concentrates on the interactive roles of maturation and learning in cognitive development (see **cognitivism**).

cognitive-field theory   A school of thought that stresses the importance of one's perception of a learning situation (see **cognitivism**).

cognitive growth   The process by which the individual becomes rational, logical, and reflective in his thought.

cognitivism   General name of theory family that includes cognitive-developmental, cognitive-field, and information-processing theories of learning.

competence   Able to perform a skill or knowledge adequately to fulfill a criterion (standard) of proficiency.

competency-based education   Approach to schooling based on a criterion (standard) of proficiency.

competency-based instruction   Instruction in which specific outcomes are stated and the learner's progress is evaluated along the way to mastery.

computer-assisted instruction   Use a computer system to perform instructional functions for a student.

conception   The uniting of the male and female reproductive cells.

concept learning   Acquiring the meaning of a class of persons, events, or objects that are related on the basis of common attributes.

concrete operations   A stage of cognitive development in which a person can effectively learn environmental information represented in a concrete mode of reality.

concurrent validity   Degree of relationship between two variables at the same point in time (see **validity**).

conditioning   A type of learning in which a new association is formed between a stimulus and a response, between stimuli, or between responses.

conditions of learning   Circumstances under which a person attempts to learn and perform.

conflict   A situation that arises from or causes frustration or anxiety.

confluence model   The theory that intelligence of siblings tends to decrease in larger families.

conform   To adapt to or to accept customs, tradition, or prevailing opinion; to behave in a way that is acceptable and conventional.

congenital   Present from birth, but not resulting from genetic factors.

conscious mind   The part of our mind of which we are immediately aware.

conservation   The principle that if nothing is added or taken away from an amount, it remains the same.

content   Body of knowledge or set of skills.

content sampling   Degree of relationship between the same subjects' performances on equivalent forms of a test (see **reliability**).

contingency   Consequences for a person's actions depends upon one's fulfillment of a particular condition.

conventional level   According to L. Kohlberg, the level of moral reasoning at which the individual conforms to the rules of conduct and expectations of the family, group, or nation.

convergent thinking   The process involved in one's deriving a solution to a problem that has a known solution to the learner.

correlation   Reciprocal relationship between two variables.

correlation coefficient   Measure of the interdependence between two variables.

courage   According to B. Russell, the realistic ability to face new challenges; an important quality in character development.

covert response   An internal, unobservable response.

creative thinking   The process involved in a person's recombining known elements into a new element such as a product or solution.

criteria-referenced testing   Approach to testing that is based on a criterion (standard) of proficiency (see **norm-referenced testing**).

criteria-related validity   Degree to which test performance forecasts performance on some criterion (see **predictive validity**).

criterion variable   Outcome variable in a prediction equation (see **predictor variable**).

critical thinking   Use of knowledge and logical processes to find illogical relationships among assumptions, premises, and solutions to a problem.

crystallization According to E. Ginzberg, part of the "realistic" stage of adolescence; the period during which the adolescent makes a general choice (see also **realistic period**).

culturally deprived A term used to describe those individuals who are members of a subculture that is significantly different from the cultural mainstream.

culturally different A preferred, nonjudgmental term used to describe those individuals who are members of a subculture that is significantly different from the cultural mainstream.

culturally different child A term used to describe a child who grows up in a subculture that differs from the larger culture in which he or she lives.

culturally disadvantaged A term that implies that any individual who is part of a subculture that is significantly different from the cultural mainstream is disadvantaged.

curiosity According to B. Russell, the child's natural interest in the things around him, necessary for good character development.

cybernetics The study of interrelationships between information-processing systems; the technology of interaction between people and machines.

Deaner (Deanol acetamidobenzoate) A drug often prescribed in the treatment of hyperkinesis.

deductive problem solving The process of using a given general principle to solve a specific problem.

defense mechanisms Psychological processes designed to protect the ego from unacceptable feelings and impulses.

denial A defense mechanism in which the conscious mind denies a feeling or a situation.

deoxyribonucleic acid See **DNA.**

dependent variable The outcome variable in a study—i.e., the effect variable in a cause-effect relationship.

determinism The principle that by an early age the individual's future is determined—either by psychological determinants or by genetic determinants.

diagnostic evaluation Assessment for the purpose of monitoring learning (see **formative evaluation**).

dialectical method The teaching method of questions and answers, in which each question leads not only to an answer but to many new questions as well.

difficulty level Measure of the degree of difficulty of a test item.

diploid A cell containing twice the number of chromosomes, 46, as a mature germ cell. A diploid cell contains a full set from each parent.

discovery method   Learning condition in which a student must use inductive problem solving procedures in an attempt to achieve the instructional objective.

discrimination   A type of learning in which one responds differently to similar stimuli.

discrimination index   Measure of the degree of difference in the performances of subjects (based on overall test performances) on a test item.

discussion method   Learning condition in which a student must use verbal communications with others in an attempt to achieve the instructional objective.

displacement   A defense mechanism in which the person directs an impulse or action toward an object other than that for which it was originally intended.

distributive justice   The idea that rewards and punishments can be distributed appropriately, according to different actions and intentions. (Used by Piaget in his discussions of moral development.)

divergent thinking   The process involved in one's generating possible solutions to a problem that has no known solution to the learner.

dizygotic twins   Twins that develop from two different eggs (ova); as opposed to monozygotic.

DMT   An hallucinogenic drug.

DNA (deoxyribonucleic acid)   The chemically coded molecule in all genes. The basic structure of all living matter.

dominant gene   The gene that will prevail over recessive genes.

double approach-avoidance   A type of conflict situation in which the person is faced with two choices, both of which have equally strong desirable and undesirable elements.

Down's syndrome (mongolism)   A congenital defect characterized by mental retardation and gross physical abnormalities.

drug abuse   Misuse or overuse of a drug to the point where it becomes a necessity to face the ordinary problems of living.

DZ twins (dizygotic twins)   Twins that develop from separate ova; fraternal twins.

early childhood   The first of three maturational levels of childhood, extending from infancy until the child reaches school age.

eclecticism   Practice of attempting to create unity among different learning theories.

ectoderm   The embryo's outer layer of cells from which the skin and nervous system develop.

efficiency   Unit of time required to attain a measurement.

ego   According to Freud, the region of the mind that is the psychic bridge between the instincts and the real world; also, a person's sense of self-worth and importance.

egocentrism   The belief that nothing exists outside of oneself, and that "I am the cause of all actions."

ego integrity   The individual's acceptance of his life as his own responsibility; the fruition of Erikson's eight psychosexual stages of development.

elicitor   Something that elicits a response.

embryo   The developing organism, from conception to about the end of the third month in the uterus.

embryonic period   The period of prenatal growth that follows the germinal period and lasts for about six weeks.

emotion   The psychological equivalent of certain specific biological responses; feelings.

enactive   Mode of representation of reality based on the actions one performs on it.

endoderm   The embryo's inner layer of cells from which develop the digestive tract, liver, lungs, and other organs.

entry behavior   Readiness characteristics of a learner in relation to the instructional objectives and instructional procedures of an educational experience.

environment   All external conditions affecting an organism.

environmentalism   The position that the environment (as opposed to heredity) is primarily responsible for most human traits.

equilibration   The process involved in a person's attempt to "balance" the discrepancy between internal representation of reality and his/her present perception of environmental information (see **equilibrium**).

equilibrium   The state of "balance" in terms of a person's internal representation of reality and his/her present perception of environmental information (see **equilibration**).

erogenous zone   A region of the body that produces intense states of sexual (or physical) excitation.

exceptional child   A broad term used to describe children who fall at either extreme of the normal distribution on some important trait.

existentialism   A philosophy and psychology that emphasizes human freedom and commitment.

experimental test   "Tryout" or pilot test.

expiatory punishment   According to Piaget, this is the punishment that emphasizes retribution for wrongdoing, and is measured solely by the severity of the misdeed.

exploration   According to E. Ginzberg, this is the final stage of the realistic period of adolescence, during which the adolescent investigates job opportunities.

extinction   The effect on a person's behavior resulting from the termination of positive reinforcement.

fantasy period   According to E. Ginzberg, the first stage of adolescence during which the person translates his needs and impulses into occupational fantasies and expectations without regard to a realistic assessment of capabilities and opportunities.

feedback loop   A diagram that illustrates the movement of information from one system, or part of a system, to another.

fetal period   The final period of prenatal growth, from about eight weeks until birth.

fetus   The developing organism from about the third month after conception until birth.

figure   In Gestalt psychology, the main point in a perception; the thing most noticed.

fixation   Remaining fixed at an earlier psychosexual stage.

forced-response   Subject must choose among a fixed set of responses.

formal operations   Stage of cognitive development in which a person can effectively learn environmental information represented in an abstract mode of reality.

formative evaluation   Assessment for the purpose of monitoring learning (see **diagnostic evaluation**).

free-response   Subject must construct his/her own response.

frustration   A feeling produced by the delay of gratification, the thwarting of gratification, or other factors that result in the defeat of one's efforts.

frustration by delay   Frustration caused by the delay of anticipated gratification.

frustration by thwarting   Frustration caused by the inability to reach one's goal.

fully functioning person   One who has mastered the environment within his/her capabilities and has positive feelings about one's self and the environment mastered.

functionalism   Practice of attempting to weigh evidence of the relationship among phenomena.

gamete   A male or female reproductive cell; a sperm or ovum.

gene   Any of the small chemical message units within each chromosome.

generalization   A type of learning in which one responds the same to similar stimuli.

general transfer   Capability of using knowledge or skill learned in one situation in a novel situation (e.g., transfer of skills across subject matter areas).

genital stage   According to Freud, the final stage of psychosexual development. It is during this stage that the individual matures into a fully functioning heterosexual person.

genotype   An organism's hereditary makeup, not always visible on the surface.

germinal period   The period of prenatal growth covering the first two weeks after fertilization.

Gestalt theory   Historical school of thought that emphasized the "wholeness" as opposed to "fragmentation" of spatial and temporal aspects of one's experiences (see **cognitivism**).

"good boy-good girl" stage   Used by L. Kohlberg to describe the stage in moral development in which good behavior is viewed as that which pleases others and gains their approval.

grade equivalent   Standard score scale used to indicate achievement level of students.

grammar   A description of the way in which language is used by native speakers.

ground   In Gestalt psychology, the background of perception.

guilt   A feeling that one has done something wrong.

haploid   A cell containing half the chromosomes of other body cells; in humans, 23 chromosomes; one from each pair.

heredity   Transmission of physical and psychological characteristics from parents to offspring.

heritability   The capability of a trait being inherited, or transmitted through the genes.

heterogeneous grouping   Grouping together people with different qualities (such as good and poor math students).

heteronomous morality   According to Piaget, the type of early moral reasoning in which the child acts according to moral principles given to him or her by the parents and other authority figures.

heteronomy   According to Piaget, the stage in which a person functions under moral constraint, and moral reasoning is dictated by external authority.

hierarchy   Arrangement of things on a continuum based on a criterion such as degree of priority or complexity.

hierarchy of needs   An ordering of needs, from most basic (necessary for survival) to most self-actualizing (including emotional and intellectual growth).

homogeneous grouping   Grouping together people with similar qualities (such as all students with a high or low IQ).

humanism   School of thought that stresses the freedom of an individual as opposed to his/her being controlled.

humanistic perspective   The point of view that the person is always in the process of growth and self-actualization.

human therapeutic experience   According to Boy and Pine, positive interpersonal experiences with others.

hyperactive   Overly active; often used to describe hyperkinetic children.

hyperkinetic   Unable to control physical activity to the degree deemed "normal." Hyperkinetic children suffer from a shortened attention span, spurts of manic behavior, temper tantrums, and high levels of excitability.

hypothesis   A guess or hunch about a possible relationship between variables.

hypothetico-deductive reasoning   Abstract, hypothetical reasoning; according to Piaget, this reasoning comes into existence during the period of formal operations.

iconic   Mode of representation of reality by a person based on one's internal images of it.

id   According to Freud, the instinctual basis of personality; the fount of instinctual energy.

identification   A defense mechanism in which we identify a part of ourself with another person.

immanent justice   According to Piaget, the belief that justice is inherent in the order of the world.

immediate objective   Short-term goal.

imprinting   A learning mechanism by which a particular stimulus is applied at an early age, establishing an irreversible behavior pattern or response whenever that same stimulus is presented in the future.

independent variable   A factor in a study that is manipulated, i.e., the cause variable in a cause-effect relationship.

individualized instruction   Condition under which the learner is allowed to progress at his/her own rate.

individuation   The psychological process of establishing an individual identity, and recognizing clearly the boundaries of self and nonself.

inductive problem solving   The process of using a general principle to solve a specific problem when the general principle is not known to the learner.

infancy   The first period of life after birth; generally, from birth to about one-year-old.

inferiority feelings   According to Adler, inherent feelings of inferiority that prompt behaviors designed to help the individual strive for superiority.

instruction   Communication of information to a student.

instructional method   A vehicle by which information is communicated to the student, such as a lecture, discussion, or television.

instructional objective   Specified goal that the student is expected to achieve from an educational experience.

instructional procedure   Specified conditions under which a student is expected to learn in an educational experience.

instructional psychology   Application of psychology to instructional practices.

instructional theory   School of thought in which the theories of learning are translated into a theory of instruction (and teaching).

instrumental conditioning   A type of learning in which a response must be produced prior to obtaining a reward. There is no specific identifiable antecedent stimulus (see **operant conditioning**).

integrated personality   According to Freud, the healthy personality, in which all of the psychic structures (id, ego, and superego) can function together harmoniously.

intelligence   The capability to meet (or learn to meet) novel situations by new adaptive responses.

interest   A quality of the learner in which he or she has curiosity about the subject matter or another motivation to learn material.

interindividual difference   Differences between persons in one or more characteristics.

internal consistency   Degree of relationship between items on a test administered at a point in time (see **reliability**).

internalization   Incorporating in one's own mind something from without.

interrater agreement   Degree of relationship between independent judges' ratings of subjects' performances (see **reliability**).

intervening variable   A factor that must be either controlled or systematically varied in order to explain the relationship between an independent and a dependent variable.

intraindividual difference   Differences in two or more characteristics within a person.

intuitive   Knowing or learning without the direct intervention of reasoning or logical processes.

IQ   Intelligence quotient that is defined as $\dfrac{\text{mental age}}{\text{chronological age}} \times 100$. May also indicate unit of a standard score scale.

justice   One of the three basic principles used by Piaget to develop his theory of moral reasoning; it is through this principle that morality based on constraint changes to morality based on mutual cooperation.

kernal sentence   A basic sentence that contains a noun phrase and a verb phrase. More complex sentences are derived from the kernal sentence.

kinesthetic ability   Degree of sensivity to bodily position, presence, or movement.

koan   In Zen philosophy, a short anecdote that stimulates thought.

k-terminal string   In linguistics, the series of elements that appear at the base of a tree of derivation. The k-terminal string contains the elements from which more complex sentences are derived.

late childhood   The third, and final, period of childhood, directly preceding puberty; about nine to eleven years old.

latency stage   The period between the Oedipal conflict and puberty, during which (according to Freud) the sexual strivings lie dormant.

law-and-order stage   According to Kohlberg, a period of moral development during which the person is oriented toward fixed rules and a strong tendency to maintain the social order.

learning   Change in a behavior resulting from experience.

learning disabled child   A child whose learning abilities are below his or her general expectations—particularly in one area (such as speech, reading, perception, etc.).

learning style   Characteristics of a student that affect positively or negatively some learning outcome under certain conditions.

learning theory   A systematic explanation of a set of empirical relationships among variables.

lecture method   Verbal presentation of content by a teacher.

left skewed curve   Asymmetrical curve in which the end is on the left side of the distribution of scores.

linear program   Presentation of information in step-by-step progressions.

LSD (lysergic acid diethylamide)   An hallucinogenic drug.

marasmus   Progressive emaciation or wasting away; often used to describe the results of severe maternal deprivation during infancy.

mastery learning   Approach to instruction based on principles of criterion-referenced testing and competency-based education.

maternal deprivation   A condition resulting from the mother's failure to provide sufficient physical and emotional nourishment to the child.

maturation   Change in psychological or physical characteristics resulting from heredity and environment.

mean   Measure of central tendency (arithmetical average) that is defined by summing the scores and dividing by the number of cases.

meaningful learning   A situation in which the readiness of a person is matched with an appropriate learning experience.

meaningful verbal learning   Knowledge acquired in such a way that the learner comprehends its meaning.

measurement   Means of selecting, gathering, and analyzing information.

median   Measure of central tendency that is defined as the middle-most score.

memory faculty   A general ability that can be strengthened through practice.

menarche   The female's first menstrual period, signalling entrance into puberty.

mental discipline   A mental structure that can be taught in one subject and that subsequently affects learning in all other subjects.

mental retardation   A term used to describe subnormal levels of intelligence, based on IQ scores.

mescaline   An hallucinogenic drug.

mesoderm   The embryo's middle layer of cells, between the ectoderm and endoderm.

middle adolescence   Following puberty, including the ages of about thirteen to about seventeen.

middle childhood   The second developmental stage of childhood, usually from about five to nine years of age.

mitosis   The process of cell division.

mode   Measure of central tendency that is defined as the most frequent score.

model   To imitate one's behavior after the behavior of another.

modeling   The behavioral process in which an individual models his behavior after the behavior of another (the model).

mongolism   See **Down's syndrome.**

monitoring   Supervision of the learning process.

monozygotic twins (MZ)   Refers to twins that develop from a single fertilized cell; opposed to dizygotic. Identical twins.

morality of constraint   According to Piaget, the principle of moral development that describes the child's obedience to rules out of fear and respect for authority; opposed to morality of cooperation.

morality of cooperation   According to Piaget, the principle of moral development that describes the child's voluntary agreement to accept and obey rules, with the recognition that rules can be changed by mutual consent; opposed to morality of constraint.

moral realism   According to Piaget, the child's moral belief that regards the objective consequences of an act more important than the subjective, extenuating circumstances surrounding it.

moral relativism   According to Piaget, the idea that moral judgments take into account different circumstances.

moro reflex   The reflex response of an infant who, if startled, will spread its arms and legs apart and then bring them together again.

morpheme   The smallest unit of meaning in speech.

mothering one   The person primarily responsible for the care of the infant.

motivation   Level of arousal of a person in learning or performance situation.

motor   A covert, neurophysical response.

movement   An overt, physical response.

MZ twins (monozygotic twins)   Twins that develop from a single ovum (egg cell); identical twins.

nativism   The position that most important human traits are the result of heredity.

nature-nurture issue   The controversy surrounding the relative importance of environment and heredity in development.

negative correlation   Simultaneous increase in the value of one variable and decrease in the value of another variable.

negative reinforcement   The effect resulting from avoidance or termination of an aversive stimulus.

negative reinforcer   A negative stimulus, the avoidance of which produces a positive response.

negative transfer   An effect in which previous learning interferes with present learning.

negativism   An attitude characterized by resistance, opposition, and doubt.

needs   A feeling of deficit that causes a striving for satisfaction; a basic condition for survival or success.

neobehaviorism   School of thought that attempts to explain the covert processes of the learner in the learning of associations of stimuli and responses (see **conditioning**).

neonate   A newborn child.

normal curve   Symmetrical distribution of scores about the central tendency.

norm-referenced testing   Approach to testing that is based on the comparative performances of subjects (see **criterion-referenced testing**).

objectivity   Degree to which observations of subjects' performances are unbiased.

operant conditioning   A type of learning in which a response must be produced prior to obtaining a reward. There is no specific identifiable antecedent stimulus (see **instrumental conditioning**).

oral stage   The first of Freud's psychosexual stages, named for the mouth—the primary erogenous zone.

ordinal position   Refers to the child's position in the family, with respect to other siblings (oldest, middle, youngest, only).

organization (of values)   In the taxonomy of the affective domain, the learner's internalization of relevant values.

overt response   An observable response.

ovum   Female reproductive cell (egg).

paradigm   A model; a representation of a situation.

peer group   A group of one's contemporaries; the group that one associates most closely with.

peer group pressure   The influence exerted on the individual by the peer group; often, the influence to conform to the values of the peer group.

penis envy   According to Freud, the idea that females have an innate desire for a penis, and envy males for having one.

percentile rank   Percent of cases falling below the value of a given obtained score.

perception   Process of recognizing or identifying a stimulus through one of the senses.

perceptual-motor skill   Proficiency in the coordination of central nervous system and physical movement (see **psychomotor**).

performance   Observable behavior.

performance assessment   Evaluation of change in performance (and learning).

personality   The individual's unique, consistent psychological profile, having both internal and external manifestations.

phallic stage   According to Freud, the third psychosexual stage, named after the genital region, which is the primary erogenous zone.

phenomenal self   The physical and existential self that includes a myriad of self-perceptions.

phenomenological field   The subjective field of awareness to which an individual responds.

phenotype   The expression, or outward appearance, of inherited characteristics.

phenylketonuria (PKU)   A congenital metabolic disorder, resulting in mental retardation.

phoneme The smallest unit of sound in a spoken language.

physiological needs The needs that relate to survival: need for food, sleep, etc.

pica A disorder characterized by an appetite for inappropriate substances, such as dirt, paint chippings, hair from blankets, etc.

placement Arrangement of a student at a particular starting point for instruction.

positive correlation Simultaneous increase or decrease in the values of two variables.

positive transfer An effect in which previous learning facilitates present learning.

post conventional According to Kohlberg, the highest level of moral reasoning, characterized by the person's commitment to principles and beliefs apart from the authorities who hold them.

preconventional level According to Kohlberg, the first level of moral reasoning, characterized by simple, non-abstract reasoning about moral problems.

predictive validity Degree to which test performance forecasts performance on some criterion (see **criteria-related validity**).

predictor variable The forecast variable in a prediction equation (see **criterion variable**).

prenatal period The period of development in the uterus from conception to birth; usually averaging 280 days for humans.

preoperational Stage of development that precedes operational thought.

preoperational period According to Piaget, the period of pre-logical thought from about two to seven years of age.

principled level According to Kohlberg, the period of moral development when the person is oriented toward decisions of conscience in accordance with ethical principles.

principle learning Acquiring the meaning of the relationship between general concepts.

problem-solving skill Learning to learn skill of a general transfer nature.

progress Positive change in performance.

projection A defense mechanism in which the person sees his thoughts and feelings as if they were another's.

project method A teaching method in which students work cooperatively on a project in order to learn.

psilocybin An hallucinogenic drug.

psychodynamic perspective The point of view that the person is primarily a product of unconscious impulses and has learned, in varying degrees, to control these impulses.

psychomotor Coordination of the central nervous system and physical movement (see **perceptual-motor skill**).

psychopathology Literally, a disease of the mind; used for any abnormal psychological condition.

psychosexual conflict According to Freud, repressed conflicts from childhood.

psychosexual stages According to Freud, the stages of personality development, each of which is characterized by and named after the primary erogenous zone: oral, anal, phallic, and genital.

puberty The earliest stage of adolescence, characterized by marked bodily changes including the appearance of the secondary sex characteristics.

punishment The effect of aversive stimulus on a person.

punishment by reciprocity Emphasized punishment that is logically related to the offense; making the punishment fit the crime.

random error Unreliability of a test that cannot be attributed to content sampling, time sampling, or interrater agreement errors (see **reliability**).

range Measure of variability that is defined as the difference between the highest and lowest score.

rationalization A defense mechanism in which the person attributes different motives to his actions, or justifies something he has done that he cannot accept.

reaction formation A defense mechanism in which the person acts in a way that is the opposite of how he unconsciously feels.

readiness Psychological or physical "ripeness" to benefit from a learning experience.

realism According to Piaget, the child's belief that moral decisions are made solely in terms of duty and obligation.

realistic period According to E. Ginzberg, the final stages of adolescent reasoning, in which career choices are arrived at realistically and then critically examined.

reality therapy Developed by William Glasser, reality therapy views the person as having two basic needs: the need to love and be loved, and the need to feel worthwhile.

receiving (attending) A level of the affective taxonomy in which the learner is simply aware of the world and of others around him.

recessive gene A less powerful gene than a dominant one.

recreational therapeutic experience According to Boy and Pine, pleasant social interactions through play-like situations.

regression A "return" to an earlier stage of development; a defense mechanism dealing with situations as one did earlier in life.

reinforcement An effect on a person that increases the probability of a response reoccurring. The effect results from a reinforcer.

reliability The consistency (accuracy) with which a test measures the performances of subjects.

reliability coefficient Measure of the consistency (accuracy) of performances of subjects on a test.

religious therapeutic experience According to Boy and Pine, the person's relationship to that which is regarded as holy.

repression A defense mechanism in which thoughts and feelings are made unconscious; forgetting.

respondent A response elicited by stimulation.

respondent conditioning Any situation in which a response is systematically elicited by a stimulus (see **classical conditioning**).

responding A level of the affective taxonomy in which the learner is able to initiate actions in the world.

response An observable behavior.

retention Relatively permanent change in performance due to practice.

reward A positive reinforcer.

right skewed curve Asymmetrical curve in which the end is on the right side of the distribution of scores.

Ritalin (methylphenidate hydrochloride) A stimulant drug that has been shown effective in the treatment of hyperkinesis and minimal brain dysfunction in children. Recommended for use as an adjunct to therapy and remediative efforts—not a cure!

rote Acquisition of knowledge in such a way that the learner does not comprehend its meaning.

rules According to Piaget, one of the principles used to describe the child's development of moral reasoning. At an early age, the child blindly obeys rules because they exist; later, he learns that rules can be changed through mutual agreement.

rules of the game According to Piaget, the child's early moral belief that rules are fixed and not changeable.

safety needs According to Maslow, a low level of basic needs that are self-protective.

schizophrenia A psychosis marked by defects in logical thinking, inappropriate affect, and other symptoms.

secondary sex characteristic Any of the physical characteristics that differentiate males from females, but are not directly related to the reproductive process, such as pubic hair, facial hair, deepening of the voice, enlargement of the breasts, etc.

selection   Chosen collection of persons based on some criterion of discrimination.

self   A person's continuing identity, cohering all elements of perception.

self-actualization   The process of emotional, social, and intellectual growth whereby the individual comes to fully maximize his or her potential.

self-actualizing needs   The highest level of needs, through which growth is attained.

self-concept   A person's evaluation of one's self.

self-perception   Self-concept; one's feelings and subjective perceptions of oneself.

sensitiveness   According to B. Russell, an integral element in character development.

sensorimotor stage   According to Piaget, the earliest stage of cognitive development, during which the child learns how to direct and control his motor activities while learning how to use sensory information from birth to about two years old.

seriation   The arrangement of elements according to increasing or decreasing size (or some other quality).

sex role   The male or female role an individual is taught to confrom to, usually according to social and familial stereotypes.

sex-role identification   An individual's total identification as a male or female; the identification with a same-sex figure, after whom the individual models him- or herself.

shaping   A learning process in which closer approximations to the desired goal are rewarded.

sibling   A brother or sister.

simulated environment   An environment that represents a larger, more complex environment, used for learning to master the more complex environment.

sincerity   A quality of an effective teacher; the willingness to share his or her true feelings, without deceit.

situational conditions   External (environmental) factors that may affect a person's learning and performance.

skewed   Asymmetrical distribution of scores.

socialization   The process whereby a person learns the prescribed social behaviors and integrates him- or herself into the social structure.

specification   According to E. Ginzberg, part of the final stage of adolescence, during which the person makes a final career choice that is specific to his or her needs and abilities.

specific transfer   Capability of using knowledge and skills learned in one situation to similar situations (e.g., transfer within a subject-matter area).

spermatozoon (Sperm cell)   the male reproductive cell.

standard deviation   Measure of variability that is defined as the square root of the averages of the squared deviations from the mean of the distribution of scores.

standardized test   A test administered under the same conditions to a representative sample of a particular population of interest.

standard score scale   Transformed score scale of raw scores from a test.

stimulus   An environmental event or object that stimulates an organism.

successive approximation   A learning process in which a complex task is broken down into smaller parts.

summative evaluation   Evaluation of students' performances at the end of a segment of schooling (see **terminal assessment**).

superego   According to Freud, the part of the mind that acts as a conscience.

superiority feelings   According to Adler, feelings that compensate for the inherent inferiority feelings.

symbolic   Representation of reality through symbols such as words.

tactile ability   Proficiency in the use of touch in learning and performance.

tactile eroticism   Excitement produced by touching the skin surface.

task   The nature of a learning experience—its goal and processes required to achieve the outcome.

task analysis   Breaking down learning into specific tasks (as from simple to complex).

taxonomy   A classification scheme.

teaching   All of the factors involved in one person's attempt to induce learning in another person.

teaching-learning process   The interrelationship between the role of the teacher and the students in a learning situation.

teaching style   Characteristics of a teacher that affect positively or negatively some learning outcome under certain conditions.

tentative period   According to E. Ginzberg, the period between eleven and seventeen years of age when interests and capacities become relevant factors in selecting an occupation, even though these interests and capacities are not yet fully formulated.

terminal assessment   Evaluation of students' performances at the end of a segment of schooling (see **summative evaluation**).

testing   Measurement and evaluation of subjects' characteristics.

theory   An explanation of the empirical evidence related to a phenomena.

time sampling   Degree of relationship between the same subjects' performances on the same test (test-retest) given on two different occasions (see **reliability**).

total person   The concept that each person is made up of complex emotional, social, and intellectual dimensions, each of which is the result of numerous interactions between genetic and environmental factors.

traditional orientation   The teaching orientation that emphasizes the authoritarian role of the teacher.

trait-treatment interaction   A cross-over effect of student characteristics and instructional methods in learning outcomes.

transfer   Influence of previous learning on one's performance in a novel situation.

transformation   The processes through which any sentence of a language can be derived from a kernal sentence.

transformational grammar   A system of grammar in which all of the sentences of the language are derived, through transformations, from kernal sentences.

tree of derivation   A diagram used in transformational grammar that shows how the sentence is derived from its different branches.

trophoblast   The outer layer of cells in the blastocyst.

trust   A quality of the effective teacher in which the teacher is able to deal with the students without guile or suspiciousness.

T-score scale   Standard score scale with a mean of 50 and a standard deviation of 10 (see **standard score scale**).

ultimate objective   Long-range goal.

unconscious mind   According to Freud, the part of our mind that is not readily accessible to consciousness; the part of our mind where many repressed thoughts remain buried.

validity   Degree to which a test measures what it was designed to measure.

valuing   A level of the affective taxonomy in which definite values are attached to actions and beliefs.

variability   Amount of dispersion of scores from test performances.

variance   Measure of variability that is defined as the mean of the squares of the variations from the mean of a distribution of scores.

venereal disease   A disease transmitted by sexual contact with an infected partner.

verbal   Part of a sentence consisting of a verb form.

visual ability   One's proficiency in using sight in learning and performance.

vitality According to B. Russell, that dimension of physical and spiritual health that is necessary to good character development.

vocational therapeutic experience According to Boy and Pine, the pleasures derived from the work experience.

word recognition The ability to separate certain sounds from others, and to relate these sounds to objects or actions with which they are associated.

zero correlation Absence of relationship between the values of two variables.

z-score scale Standard score scale in which the mean is zero and the standard deviation is one (see **standard score scale**).

zygote The cell formed from the union of two reproductive cells, or gametes.

Abrahams, R. D. *Positively black*. Englewood Cliffs, N.J.: Prentice-Hall, 1970.

Abrams, J. C. Minimal brain dysfunction and dyslexia. *Reading World*, 1975, *14(3)*, 219–227.

Adams, G. R. Classroom aggression: Determinants, controlling mechanisms, and guidelines for the implementation of a behavior modification program. *Psychology in the Schools*, 1973, *10*, 155–168.

Adams, J. F. (Ed.). *Understanding adolescence: Current developments in adolescent psychology*. (3rd ed.). Boston: Allyn & Bacon, 1976.

Addison, R. M. & Homme, L. E. The reinforcing event (RE) menu. *National Society for Programmed Instruction Journal*, 1966, *5(1)*, 8–9.

Alabiso, F. Inhibiting functions of attention in reducing hyperactive behavior. *American Journal of Mental Deficiency*, 1974, *77(3)*, 259–282.

Alexander, T. *Children and adolescents: A biocultural approach to psychological development*. New York: Atherton, 1969.

Alland, A., Jr. Intelligence in black and white. In C. L. Brace, G. R. Gamble, & J. T. Bonds (Eds.), *Race and Intelligence*. Washington, D.C.: American Anthropological Association, 1971, pp. 32–36.

Allport, G. W. *Becoming*. New Haven: Yale University Press, 1955.

Almy, M. Spontaneous play: An avenue for intellectual development. *Bulletin of the Institute of Child Study*, 1966, *28(2)*, 2–15.

Alpert, J. L. Teacher behavior and pupil performance: Reconsideration of the mediation of Pygmalion effects. *Journal of Educational Research*, 1975, *5*, 53–57.

American Council on Education. *A design for general education*. Washington, D.C.: American Council on Education, 1944.

American School Board Journal. Beating school children: A practice that doesn't improve their behavior or their learning. *The American School Board Journal*, 1973, *160*, 19–21.

Amos, W. E. & Grambs, J. D. *Counseling the disadvantaged youth*. Englewood Cliffs, N.J.: Prentice-Hall, 1968.

Anandalakshmy, S., & Grinder, R. E. Conceptual emphasis in the history of developmental psychology: Evolutionary theory, teleology, and the nature-nurture issue. In W. R. Looft (Ed.), *Developmental psychology: A book of readings*. Hinsdale, Ill.: Dryden Press, 1972, pp. 24–34.

Anastasi, A. *Psychological Testing* (4th ed.). New York: Macmillan, 1976.

Anastasi, A., & Cordova, F. Some effects of bilingualism upon the intelligence test performance of Puerto Rican children in New York City. *Journal of Educational Psychology*, 1953, *44*, 1–9.

Anderson, O. R. *Structure in teaching*. New York: Teachers College Press, 1969.

Anderson, O. R. *Quantitative analysis of structure in teaching*. New York: Teachers College Press, 1971.

Anderson, R. Learning in discussions: A resume of the authoritarian–democratic studies. *Harvard Educational Review*, 1959, *29*, 201–215.

Anderson, S., & Messick, S. Social competency in young children. *Developmental Psychology*, 1974, *10(2)*, 283–293.

Arsenian, S. *Bilingualism and mental development*. New York: Teachers College Press, 1937.

Aspy, D. N. The effects of teacher-offered conditions upon student achievement. *Florida Journal of Educational Research*, 1968, *11(1)*, 39–48.

References

Aspy, D. N. Reaction to Carkhuff's articles. *Counseling Psychologist,* 1972, *3(3),* 35–41.

Aubrey, R. T. *Experimenting with living: Pros and cons.* Columbus: Charles E. Merrill, 1975.

Ausubel, D. P. *Theory and problems of adolescent development.* New York: Grune & Stratton, 1954.

Ausubel, D. P. In defense of verbal learning. *Educational Theory,* 1961, *11,* 15–25.

Ausubel, D. P. *Educational psychology: A cognitive view.* New York: Holt, Rinehart and Winston, 1968.

Azrin, N. H. Punishment and recovery during fixed-ratio performance. *Journal of Experimental Analysis of Behavior,* 1959, *2,* 301–305.

Azrin, N. H. Sequential effects of punishment. *Science,* 1960, *131,* 605–606.

Azrin, N. H. & Holz, W. C. Punishment in W. K. Honig (Ed.). *Operant behavior.* New York: Appleton-Century-Crofts, 1966.

Baker, S. L., et al. Impact of father absence on personality factors of boys. Paper presented at American Orthopsychiatric Association meeting, Washington, D.C., March, 1967.

Bakwin, H., & Bakwin, R. *Clinical management of behavioral disorders in children.* Philadelphia: W. B. Saunders, 1967.

Bakwin, H., & Bakwin, R. *Behavior disorders in children* (4th ed.). Philadelphia: W. B. Saunders, 1972.

Baldwin, W. K. The social portion of the educable mentally retarded child in the regular grades in the public schools. *Exceptional Children,* 1958, *25,* 106–112.

Bandura, A. *Principles of behavior modification.* New York: Holt, Rinehart and Winston, 1969.

Bandura, A. *Aggression: A social learning analysis.* Englewood Cliffs, N.J.: Prentice-Hall, 1973.

Bandura, A., & McDonald, F. J. The influence of social reinforcement and the behavior of models in shaping children's moral judgments. *Journal of Abnormal and Social Psychology,* 1963, *67,* 274–281.

Bandura, A., Ross, A., & Ross, S. A. Transmission of aggression through imitation of aggressive models. *Journal of Abnormal and Social Psychology,* 1961, *63,* 575–582.

Banks, J. A. Racial prejudice and black self-concept. In J. A. Banks & J. D. Grambs (Eds.), *Black self-concept: Implications for education and social science.* New York: McGraw-Hill, 1972, pp. 5–36.

Bantock, G. H. *Education and values.* London: Faber & Faber, 1965.

Barrett, W. Introduction. In W. Barrett (Ed.), *Zen Buddhism: Selected writings of D. T. Suyuki.* New York: Doubleday Anchor, 1956.

Barron, F. *Creativity and personal freedom.* New York: D. Van Nostrand, 1968.

Barten, S., Birns, B., & Ronch, J. Individual differences in the visual pursuit behaviors of neonates. *Child Development,* 1971, *42,* 313–319.

Baumrind, D. An exploratory study of socialization effects on black children: Some black-white comparisons. *Child Development,* 1972, *43,* 261–267.

Becker, W. C., Englemann, S., & Thomas, D. R. *Teaching: A course in applied psychology.* Chicago: Science Research Associates, 1971.

Beechhold, H. F. *The creative classroom.* New York: Charles Scribner's Sons, 1971.

Belkin, G. S. *Practical counseling in the schools.* Dubuque, Iowa: Wm. C. Brown, 1975.

Belkin, G. S. Communion in teaching. *Educational Theory,* 1974, *24,* 170–182.

Belkin, G. S. *Psychodynamic dimensions in the teacher-student interaction: A Freudian interpretation.* (Doctoral dissertation, Columbia University, 1974). Ann Arbor, Mich.: University Microfilms.

Bellak, A. A., Kliebard, H. M., Hyman, R. T., & Smith, F. L. *The language of the classroom.* New York: Teachers College Press, 1966.

Benoit, R. B., & Mayer, G. R. Extinction: Guidelines for its selection and use. *Personnel and Guidance Journal,* 1974, *52,* 290–295.

Benoit, R. B., & Mayer, G. R. Extinction and timeout: Guidelines for their selection and use. In G. S. Belkin (Ed.). *Counseling: Directions in Theory and Practice,* Dubuque, Iowa: Kendall/Hunt, 1976.

Benson, G. C. S., & Forcinelli, J. Teaching ethics in high school. *National Association of Secondary School Principals Bulletin,* 1975, *59,* 80–89.

Berelson, B., & Steiner, G. A. *Human behavior: An inventory of scientific findings.* New York: Harcourt, Brace & World, 1964.

Bieber, I. *Homosexuality: A psychoanlytical study of male homosexuals.* New York: Vintage Books, 1969.

Bigge, M. *Learning theories for teachers.* New York: Harper & Row, 1976.

Bigge, M. *Learning theories for teachers* (2nd ed.). New York: Harper & Row, 1971.

Bigge, M. *Learning theories for teachers* (3rd ed.). New York: Harper & Row, 1976.

Bijou, S. W., & Baer, D. M. *Child development* (Vols. 1 and 2). New York: Appleton-Century-Crofts, 1965.

Birns, B. Piaget's contribution to an understanding of intellectual development. Newsletter, *Society of Medical Psychoanalysts,* December 1967.

Birns, B., & Golden, M. Prediction of intellectual performance at three years from infant tests and personality measures. *Merrill-Palmer Quarterly of Behavior and Development,* 1972, *18(1),* 53–58.

Black, K. N. Working mother: What effect is she having? *Forecast of Home Economics, 19,* F50–2 F'74.

Bloom, B., et al. *Taxonomy of educational objectives: The classification of educational goals.* Handbook I: Cognitive Domain. New York: David McKay, 1956.

Bloom, B., Hastings, T., & Madaus, G. *Handbook on formative and summative evaluation of student learning.* New York: McGraw-Hill, 1971.

Bloom, L. A reappraisal of Piaget's theory of moral judgment. *Journal of Genetic Psychology,* 1959, *95,* 3–12.

Bloom, L. *Language development: Form and function in emerging grammars.* Cambridge, Mass.: Massachusetts Institute of Technology Press, 1970.

Blos, P. Second individuation process in adolescence. *Psychoanalytic Study of the Child,* 1967, 22.

Blum, G. S. *Psychoanalytic theories of personality.* New York: McGraw-Hill, 1953.

Bossome, R. M. What is classroom discipline? *Clearing House,* 1964, *39,* 218–221.

Bowlby, J. The nature of the child's tie to his mother. *International Journal of Psychoanalysis,* 1958, *39,* 350–373.

Bowlby, J. Separation anxiety. *International Journal of Psychoanalysis,* 1960, *41,* 69–113.

Bowlby, J. *Attachment and loss* (Vol. 1). New York: Basic Books, 1969.

Boy, A. V., & Pine, G. J. *Expanding the self: Personal growth for teachers.* Dubuque, Iowa: Wm. C. Brown, 1971.

Boyer, J. L., & Boyer, J. B. Needed: Curriculum diversity for urban economically disadvantaged. *Educational Leadership,* 1974, *31,* 624–626.

Brace, C. L., Gamble, G. R., & Bond, J. T. (Eds.). *Race and Intelligence.* Washington, D.C.: American Anthropological Association, 1971.

Bracht, G. Experimental factors related to aptitude treatment interactions. *Review of Educational Research,* 1970, *40(5),* 627–646.

Bradfield, R. H. (Ed.). *Behavior modification of learning disabilities.* San Rafael, Calif.: Academic Therapy Publications, 1971.

Bradley, R. W. Birth order and school-related behavior: A heuristic review. *Psychological Bulletin,* 1968, *70(1),* 45–57.

Bragg, B. W., & Allen, V. L. Ordinal position and conformity. *Sociometry,* 1970, *33,* 371–381.

Bremer, A., & Bremer, J. *Open education: A beginning.* New York: Holt, Rinehart and Winston, 1972.

Briskin, A. S., & Anderson, D. M. Students as contingency managers. *Elementary School Guidance and Counseling,* 1973, *7,* 262–268.

Brown, C. *Manchild in the promised land.* New York: Signet, 1971.

Brumbaugh, R. S., & Lawrence, N. M. *Philosophers on education: Six essays on the foundations of western thought.* Boston: Houghton Mifflin, 1963.

Bruner, J. Learning and thinking. *Harvard Educational Review,* 1959, *29,* 184–192.

Bruner, J. *The process of education.* New York: Vintage Books, 1960.

Bruner, J. *Toward a theory of instruction.* Cambridge, Mass.: Harvard University Press, 1966.

Bruner, J. The functions of teaching. In W. C. Morse & G. M. Wingo (Eds.), *Classroom psychology: Readings in educational psychology.* Glenview, Ill.: Scott, Foresman, 1971, pp. 148–154.

Bruner, J. The process of education revisited. *Phi Delta Kappan,* 1971, *53(1),* 18–21.

Buchanan, J. P. Quantitative methodology to examine the development of moral judgment. *Child Development,* 1973, *44,* 186–189.

Bugelski, B. *The psychology of learning applied to teaching* (1st ed.). New York: Bobbs-Merrill, 1964.

Bugelski, B. *The psychology of learning applied to teaching* (2nd ed.). New York: Bobbs-Merrill, 1971.

Bugental, J. F. T. (Ed.). *Challenges of humanistic psychology.* New York: McGraw-Hill, 1967.

Burland, J. A., Andrews, R. G., & Headsten, S. J. Child abuse: One tree in the forest. *Child Welfare,* 1973, *52(9),* 585–592.

Buros, O. *Mental Measurement Yearbook.* Highland Park, N.J.: Gryphon, 1938.

Buros, O. *Second Mental Measurement Yearbook.* Highland Park, N.J.: Gryphon, 1941.

Buros, O. *Third Mental Measurement Yearbook*. Highland Park, N.J.: Gryphon, 1949.

Buros, O. *Fourth Mental Measurement Yearbook*. Highland Park, N.J.: Gryphon, 1953.

Buros, O. *Fifth Mental Measurement Yearbook*. Highland Park, N.J.: Gryphon, 1959.

Buros, O. *Sixth Mental Measurement Yearbook*. Highland Park, N.J.: Gryphon, 1965.

Buros, O. *Seventh Mental Measurement Yearbook*. Highland Park, N.J.: Gryphon, 1972.

Burton, W. Basic principles in a good teaching-learning situation. *Phi Delta Kappan*, 1958, *39*, 242–248.

Byrne, R. *The school counselor*. Boston: Houghton Mifflin, 1963.

Cancro, R. (Ed.). *Intelligence: Genetic and environmental influences*. New York: Grune & Stratton, 1971.

Cangemi, J. P., & Khan, K. H. The psychology or punishment and the potential school dropout. *Education*, 1973, *94(2)*, 117–119.

Cantor, N. *Dynamics of learning*. New York: Schochen Books, 1972.

Cantwell, D. P. Diagnostic evaluation of the hyperactive child. In D. P. Cantwell (Ed.), *The hyperactive child: Diagnosis, management, current research*. New York: Halsted Press, 1975, pp. 17–50.

Carkhuff, R. *The development of human resources*. New York: Holt, Rinehart and Winston, 1971.

Carkhuff, R., & Berenson, B. G. *Beyond counseling and therapy*. New York: Holt, Rinehart and Winston, 1967.

Carmical, L. & Calvin, L. Functions selected by school counselors. *The School Counselor*, 1970, *17*, 280–285.

Carnot, J. B. Dynamic and effective school discipline. *The Clearing House*, 1973, *48*, 150, 153.

Carroll, J. B. Language and cognition: Current perspectives from linguistics and psychology. Presented April 19, 1971 at IRA Pre-Convention Institute on Reading. (Reprinted in J. F. Rosenblith, W. Allinsmith & J. P. Williams [Eds.], *Readings in child development*. Boston: Allyn & Bacon, 1973.)

Case, R. Piaget's theory of child development and its implications. *Phi Delta Kappan*, September 1973, pp. 20–25.

Cattell, R. B. The structure of intelligence in relation to the nature-nurture controversy. In R. Cancro (Ed.), *Intelligence: Genetic and environmental influences*. New York: Grune & Stratton, 1971.

Chafetz, J. S. *Masculine/feminine or human?* Itasca, Ill.: F. E. Peacock, 1974.

Charlesworth, W. R. Development psychology: Does it offer anything distinctive? In W. R. Looft (Ed.), *Developmental psychology: A book of readings*. Hinsdale, Ill.: Dryden Press, 1972, pp. 3–23.

Child, J., Davidson, H. H., Gerra, J., & Greenberg, J. W. Attitudes of children from a deprived environment toward achievement related concepts. *Journal of Educational Research*, 1965, *59*, 57–61.

Children's Defense Fund. School discipline and its exclusionary impact on students. In *Children out of school in America*. Washington, D.C.: A report by the Children's Defense Fund of the Washington Research Project, 1974, 117–150.

Chomsky, N. A review of B. F. Skinner's *Verbal Behavior. Language*, 1959, *35(1)*, 26–58.

Cohen, S. *The Drug Dilemma*. New York: McGraw-Hill, 1969.

Coleman, J. S. The adolescent subculture and academic achievement. In W. H. MacGintie & S. Ball (Eds.), *Readings in psychological foundations of education*. New York: McGraw-Hill, 1968, 283–296.

Coleman, J. S. *Adolescent society*. New York: Free Press, 1971.

Coleman, J. S., et al. *Equality of educational opportunity*. Washington, D.C.: U.S. Department of Health, Education, and Welfare, Office of Education, Government Printing Office, 1966.

Collard, R. R. Social and play responses of first born and later-born infants in an unfamiliar situation. *Child Development*, 1968, *39(1)*, 325–334.

Combs, A. W., & Snygg, D. *Individual Behavior: A perceptual approach to behavior*. New York: Harper & Bros., 1959.

Committee for the White House Conference on Education. *A Report to the President*. Washington, D.C.: Government Printing Office, 1955.

Conners, C. K. A teacher rating scale for use in drug studies with children. *American Journal of Psychiatry*, 1969, *126*, 152–156.

Conners, C. K. Symptom patterns in hyperkinetic, neurotic, and normal children. *Child Development*, 1970, *41*, 667–682.

Conners, C. K. Deanol and behavior disorders in children: A critical review of the literature and recommended future studies for determining efficacy. *Psychopharmacology Bulletin*, 1973, Department of Health, Education and Welfare, 188–195.

Cooper, J. J. A world they never knew: The family and social change. *Daedalus*, 1971, *100*, 1105–1138.

Cooper, J. J., & Blair, M. A. Parental evaluation as a determiner of ideology. *Journal of Genetic Psychology*, 1959, *94*, 93–100.

Corter, C. Infant attachments. In B. Foss (Ed.), *New perspective in child development*. Sussex, England: Penguin, 1974, 164–183.

Costanzo, P. R., & Shaw, M. E. Conformity as a function of age level. *Child Development*, 1966, *37*, 967–975.

Craig, R. Lawrence Kohlberg and moral development: Some reflections. *Educational Theory*, 1974, *24*, 121–129.

Cronbach, L. The two disciplines of scientific psychology. *American Psychologist*, 1957, *12*, 671–684.

Cronbach, L. *Essentials of psychological testing* (3rd ed.). New York: Harper & Row, 1970.

Cronbach, L. Comments on mastery learning and its implications for curriculum development. E. W. Eisner (Ed.), *Confronting curriculum reform*. Boston: Little, Brown, 1971.

Cronbach, L. Beyond the two disciplines of scientific psychology. *American Psychologist*, 1975, *30(2)*, 116–127.

Cruchon, G. *The transformations of childhood* (F. O'Sullivan, trans.). Dayton, Ohio: Pflaum Press, 1969.

Dale, E. *Building a learning environment.* Bloomington, Ind.: Phi Delta Kappa Educational Foundation, 1972.

Darwin, C. *The origin of species.* (Originally published, 1859.)

Day Care Council of New York, Inc. *Children at risk: The growing problem of child abuse.* 114 East 32 Street, New York City, N.Y. 10010. January, 1972.

de Beauvoir, S. *Le sang des autres.* New York: French and European Publications, 1946.

DeGenaro, J. J. Informal diagnostic procedures: "What can I do before the psychometrist arrives?" *Journal of Learning Disabilities,* 1975, *8(9),* 24–30.

Demos, G. D. Drug abuse and the new generation. *Phi Delta Kappan,* 1968, *50,* 214–221.

Dennis, W. A description and classification of the responses of the newborn infant. *Psychological Bulletin,* 1934, *31,* 5–22.

Dewey, J. *Experience and education.* New York: Macmillan, 1938.

Dewey, J. *The child and the curriculum.* Chicago: University of Chicago Press, 1956. (Originally published, 1902.)

Dewey, J. *Freedom and culture.* New York: Capricorn, 1963.

Dollard, J., & Miller, N. E. *Personality and Psychotherapy.* New York: McGraw-Hill, 1950.

Drever, J. *A dictionary of psychology.* Baltimore: Penguin Books, 1969.

Duchastel, P., & Merrill, P. The effects of behavioral objectives on learning: A review of empirical studies. *Review of Educational Research,* 1973, *43(1),* 53–70.

Duffey, R. V. Moral education and the study of current events. *Social Education,* 1975, *39,* 33–35.

Durkin, D. Children's concept of justice: A comparison with the Piaget data. *Child Development,* 1959, *30,* 289–296.

Durkin, D. The specificity of children's moral judgments. *Child Development,* 1960, *32,* 551–560.

Ebel, R. Criterion-referenced measurements: Limitations. *School Review,* 1971, *79(2),* 282–288.

Ebel, R. *Essentials of educational measurement* (2nd ed.). Englewood Cliffs, N.J.: Prentice-Hall, 1972.

Ebel, R. What are schools for? *Phi Delta Kappan,* 1972, *54(1),* 3–7.

Ediger, M. Discipline and learning. *Education,* 1973, *93(3),* 282–284.

Educational Policies Commission. *The purpose of education in American democracy.* Washington, D.C.: National Education Association and American Association of School Administrators, 1938.

Educational Policies Commission. *The central purpose of American education.* Washington, D.C.: National Education Association and American Association of School Administrators, 1961.

Edwards, A. J. *Individual mental testing: Part I History and theories.* Scranton, Pa.: In text, 1971.

Edwards, J. B. Developmental study of the acquisition of some moral concepts in children aged seven to fifteen. *Educational Research,* 1974, *16,* 83–93.

Elkind, D. *Children and adolescents.* New York: Oxford University Press, 1970.

Elkonin, D. B. Development of speech. In A. V. Zaporozhets & D. B. Elkonin (Eds.), *The psychology of preschool children*, tr. by J. Skybut & S. Simon. Cambridge Mass.: MIT Press, 1971, 111–185.

Ellingson, C. *The shadow children*. Chicago: Topaz Books, 1967.

Ellingson, C. *Speaking of children: Their learning abilities and disabilities*. New York: Harper & Row, 1975.

Endler, N. S., & Marino, C. J. The effects of source and type of prior experience on subsequent conforming behavior. *Journal of Social Psychology*, 1972, *88*, 21–29.

Erikson, E. H. *Childhood and society* (2nd ed.). New York: W. W. Norton, 1963. (Originally published 1950.)

Erikson, E. H. *Identity, youth and crisis*. New York: W. W. Norton, 1968.

Fantz, R. L. Pattern vision in young children. *Psychological Record*, 1958, *8*, 43–47.

Fantz, R. L. Pattern vision in newborn infants. *Science*, 1963, *140*, 296–297.

Fantz, R. L., & Miranda, S. B. Newborn infant attention to form of contour. *Child Development*, 1975, *46*, 224–228.

Fargo, G. A., Behrus, C., & Nolen, P. (Eds.). *Behavior modification in the classroom*. Belmont, Calif.: Wadsworth, 1970.

Farnham-Diggory, S. *Cognitive processes in education*. New York: Harper & Row, 1972.

Fawcus, M. Speech disorders and therapy in mental subnormality. In A. M. Clarke & A. B. D. Clarke (Eds.), *Mental deficiency: The changing outlook*. New York: Free Press, 1965.

Ferenczi, S. *The selected papers of Sander Ferenczi* (Vol. 2). New York: Basic Books, 1966.

Ferguson, L. R. *Personality development*. Belmont, Calif.: Brooks/Cole, 1970.

Fitts, P. Factors in complex skill training. In R. Glaser (Ed.), *Training research and education*. University of Pittsburgh Press, 1962.

Flanders, N. Diagnosing and utilizing social structures in classroom learning. *Fifty-ninth Yearbook of the National Society for the Study of Education*, Part 2, The dynamics of instructional groups. Chicago: University of Chicago Press, 1960, 187–217.

Flanders, N. The Flanders system of interaction analysis. In A. Simon & E. G. Boyer, *Mirrors of behavior*. Philadelphia: Research for Better Schools, 1967.

Flapan, D. *Children's understanding of social interaction*. New York: Teachers College Press, 1968.

Flavell, J. H. *The developmental psychology of Jean Piaget*. New York: D. Van Nostrand, 1963.

Fleischman, E. The description and prediction of perceptual-motor-skill learning. Glaser, R. (Ed.), *Training research and education*. University of Pittsburgh Press, 1962.

Ford, C. S. Self-stimulation. In M. F. DeMartino (Ed.), *Sexual behavior and personality characteristics*. New York: Grove Press, 1966.

Forness, S. R. Educational approaches with hyperactive children. In D. P. Cantwell (Ed.), *The hyperactive child: Diagnosis, management and current research*. New York: Halsted Press, 1975.

References

Forness, S. R., & Esveldt, K. C. Classroom observations of children with learning and behavior problems. *Journal of Learning Disabilities*, 1975, *8(6)*, 382–385.

Forrer, S. E. Battered children and counselor responsibility. *The school counselor*, 1975, *22(3)*, 161–165.

Frankl, V. *Man's search for meaning: An introduction to logotherapy*. Boston: Beacon Press, 1962.

Frankl, V. *The doctor and the soul: From psychotherapy to logotherapy*. New York: Random House, 1967.

Freeberg, N. E., & Payne, D. T. Parental influence on cognitive development in early childhood: A review. *Society for research in child development*. Princeton, N.J.: ETS, 1967.

French, J., & Michael, W. *Standards for educational and psychological tests and manuals*. (Rev. ed.). Washington, D.C.: American Psychological Association, 1974.

French, W., et al. *Behavioral goals of general education in the high school*. New York: Russell Sage Foundation, 1957.

Freud, A. *Psychoanalysis for teachers and parents*. New York: Emerson Books, 1947.

Freud, S. Development of libido and sexual organization. (Originally published, 1935.) Lecture 21, *Complete introductory lectures on psychoanalysis*.

Friedenberg, E. Z. *Coming of age in America*. New York: Vintage, 1965.

Fromm, E. *The sane society*. New York: Holt, Rinehart and Winston, 1955. Paperback editions in quoted. Greenwich, Conn.: Fawcett, 1967.

Frostig, M., & Maslow, P. *Learning problems in the classroom*. New York: Grune & Stratton, 1973.

Gage, N. Theories of teaching. In *Sixty-third Yearbook of the National Society for the Study of Education*. Chicago: University of Chicago Press, 1964, pp. 268–285.

Gage, N. Teaching methods. In R. Ebel (Ed.), *Encyclopedia of educational research*. New York: Macmillan, 1969, pp. 1450–1452.

Gage, N., & Unruh, W. Theoretical formulations for research on teaching. *Review of Educational Research*, 1967, *37*, 358–370.

Gagne, R. *The conditions of learning* (2nd ed.). New York: Holt, Rinehart and Winston, 1965, 1970.

Gagne, R. *Essentials of learning and instruction*. Hinsdale, Ill.: Dryden, 1974.

Gagne, R., & Brown, L. Some factors in the programming of conceptual learning. *Journal of Experimental Psychology*, 1961, *62*, 313–321.

Galbraith, R. E., & Jones, T. M. Teaching strategies for moral dilemmas. *Social Education*, January 1975, 16–22.

Galdston, R. Preventing the abuse of little children: The Parents' Center Project for the study and prevention of child abuse. *American Journal of Orthopsychiatry*, 1975, *45(3)*, 372–381.

Garfinkle, M., Massey, R., & Mendel, E. Adlerian guidelines for counseling. In G. S. Belkin (Ed.), *Counseling: Directions in theory and practice*. Dubuque, Iowa: Kendall/Hunt, 1976, pp. 145–150.

Garry, R., & Kingsley, H. *The nature and conditions of learning* (3rd ed.). Englewood Cliffs, N.J.: Prentice-Hall, 1970.

Gazda, G. M. *Human relations development: A manual for educators.* Boston: Allyn & Bacon, 1973.

Gazda, G. M. *Theories and methods of group counseling in the schools.* Springfield, Ill.: Charles C Thomas, 1972.

Gelles, R. J. Child abuse as psychopathology: A sociological critique and reformulation. *American Journal of Orthopsychiatry,* 1973, *43,* 611–621.

George, P. S. Good discipline through contingency management. *The Clearing House,* 1973, *48,* 145–149.

Gergen, K. J. *The concept of self.* New York: Holt, Rinehart and Winston, 1971.

Getzels, J. W., & Jackson, P. W. The meaning of "giftedness"—an examination of an expanding concept. *Phi Delta Kappan,* 1958, *40,* 75–77.

Getzels, J. W., & Jackson, P. W. The teacher's personality and characteristics. In N. Gage (Ed.), *Handbook of research on teaching.* Chicago: Rand McNally, 1963, pp. 506–582.

Gewirtz, J. L. A learning analysis of the effects of normal stimulation, privation, and deprivation on the acquisition of social motivation and attachment. In B. M. Foss (Ed.), *Determinants of infant behavior.* London: Metheuen, 1961.

Gibson, D., et al. Dimensions of mongolism: II, Interaction of clinical indices. American Journal of Mental Deficiencies, 1964, *118,* 503–510.

Ginott, H. G. *Teacher and child.* New York: Avon, 1975.

Ginzberg, E. Toward a theory of occupational choice. *Personnel and Guidance Journal,* 1952, *30,* 491–494.

Ginzberg, E. Toward a theory of occupational choice. *Vocational Guidance Quarterly,* 1972, *20,* 169–175.

Giorgi, A. *Psychology as a human science.* New York: Harper & Row, 1970.

Glanz, E. C., & Hayes, R. W. *Groups in guidance* (2nd ed.). Boston: Allyn & Bacon, 1967.

Glaser, R. Instructional technology and the measurement of learning outcomes. *American Psychologist,* 1963, *18,* 519–521.

Glaser, R. The design and programming of instruction. In Committee for Economic Development (Ed.), *The schools and the challenge of innovation.* New York: McGraw-Hill, 1969.

Glaser, R. Individuals and learning: The new aptitudes. *Educational Researcher,* 1972, *1(6),* 5–13.

Glaser, R. Components of a psychology of instruction. *Review of Educational Research,* 1976, *46(1),* 1–24.

Glasser, W. Reality therapy and counseling. In C. Beck (Ed.), *Philosophical guidelines in counseling* (2nd ed.). Dubuque, Iowa: Wm. C. Brown, 1971.

Globetti, G. Problem and non-problem drinking among high school students in abstinence communities. *International Journal of the Addictions,* 1972, *7(3),* 511–523.

Goble, F. *The third force.* New York: Grossman, 1970.

Goffman, E. *The presentation of self in everyday life.* Garden City, N.Y.: Anchor Society, 1959.

Goldberg, G. Breaking the communication barrier: The initial interview with an abusing parent. *Child Welfare,* 1975, *54(4),* 274–281.

Golden, M., & Birns, B. Social class and cognitive development in infancy. *Merrill-Palmer Quarterly of Behavior and Development,* 1968, *14(2),* 139–149.

Golden, M., & Birns, B. Social class, intelligence, and cognitive style in infancy. *Child Development*, 1971, *42*, 2114–2116.

Good, T. L., & Brophy, J. E. Changing teacher and student behavior: An empirical investigation. *Journal of Educational Psychology*, 1974, *66*, 390–405.

Gorman, A. H. *Teachers and learners: The interactive process of education.* Boston: Allyn & Bacon, 1969.

Gottlieb, D., & Heinsohn, A. L. (Eds.). "Introduction" in *America's other youth: Growing up poor.* Englewood Cliffs, N.J.: Prentice-Hall, 1971.

Gottlieb, J. Attitudes toward retarded children: Effects of labeling and behavioral aggressiveness. *Journal of Educational Psychology*, 1975, *67*, 581–585.

Gottlieb, J., Gampel, D., & Budoff, M. Classroom behavior of retarded children before and after integration into regular classes. *Journal of Special Education*, 1975, *9*, 143–151.

Graham, R. Moral education: A child's right to a just community. *Elementary School Guidance and Counseling*, 1975, *9*, 299–308.

Grambs, J. D. *Black image: Education copes with color.* Dubuque, Iowa: Wm. C. Brown, 1972.

Gray, S. W., & Noble, F. C. The school counselor and the school psychologist. In J. F. Adams (Ed.), *Counseling and guidance: A summary view.* New York: Macmillan, 1965.

Greene, M. *Teacher as stranger.* Belmont, Calif.: Wadsworth, 1973.

Grinder, R. Parental child-rearing practices, conscience, and resistance to temptation of sixth-grade children. *Child Development*, 1962, *33*, 802–820.

Grinspoon, L. & Singer, S. B. Amphetamines in the treatment of hyperkinetic children. *Harvard Educational Review*, 1973, *43(4)*, 515–555.

Gronlund, N. *Stating behavioral objectives for classroom instruction.* New York: Macmillan, 1970.

Gronlund, N. *Measurement and evaluation in teaching.* New York: Macmillan, 1976.

Groth, N. J. Achievement of autonomy and other developmental tasks in bright and average adolescents. *The Gifted Child Quarterly*, 1973, *17*, 64–67.

Guilbaud, G. T. *What is cybernetics?* New York: Criterion Books, 1959.

Guilford, J. P. Three faces of intellect. *American Psychologist*, 1959, *14*, 469–479.

Guthrie, R. V. *Being black.* San Francisco: Canfield Press, 1970.

Haley, J. *Uncommon therapy.* New York: W. W. Norton, 1973.

Hall, G. S. *Adolescence* (2 vols). (Originally published, 1922.)

Hamburg, B. A. Early adolescence: A specific and stressful stage of the life cycle. In G. V. Coelho, D. A. Hamburg & J. E. Adams (Eds.), *Coping and adaptation.* New York: Basic Books, 1974, pp. 101–124.

Harlem Youth Opportunities Unlimited (HARYOU). *Youth in the ghetto.* New York: HARYOU, 1964.

Harnack, R. S. *The teacher: Decision maker and curriculum planner.* Scranton, Pa.: International Textbook, 1968.

Harrow, A. *A taxonomy of the psychomotor domain.* New York: David McKay, 1972.

Hawley, R. C. *Value exploration through role playing.* New York: Hart, 1975.

Hebb, D. *A textbook of psychology* (2nd ed.). Philadelphia: W. B. Saunders, 1966.

Heidegger, M. [*Being and time.*] (J. Macquarrie & E. Robinson, trans.). London: SCM Press, 1962.

Helfer, R. E., & Kempe, C. H. (Eds.). *The battered child.* Chicago: University of Chicago Press, 1968.

Hellman, I. Psychoanalysis and the teacher. In J. M. Sutherland (Ed.), *Psychoanalysis and contemporary thought.* Chicago: Rand McNally, 1958, pp.135–146.

Helmreich, R. Birth order effects. In J. F. Rosenblith, W. Allinsmith & J. P. Williams (Eds.), *Readings in child development.* Boston: Allyn & Bacon, 1973. (Originally published, 1968.)

Herzog, E., & Sudia, C. E. Children in fatherless families. In B. H. Caldwell & H. N. Riciuti (Eds.), *Review of child development research.* Chicago: University of Chicago Press, 1973, pp. 141–232.

Hetherington, E. M. Effects of father absence on child development. *Young Children,* 1971, *26,* 233–242.

Hewett, F. M. Educational engineering with emotionally disturbed children. In H. F. Clarizio (Ed.), *Mental health and the educative process.* Chicago: Rand McNally, 1969.

Hildreth, G. *Introduction to the gifted.* New York: McGraw-Hill, 1966.

Hilgard, E. R., & Bower, G. H. *Theories of learning* (3rd ed.). New York: Appleton-Century-Crofts, 1966 (4th ed.). Englewood Cliffs, N.J.: Prentice-Hall, 1975.

Hill, J. C. *Teaching and the unconscious mind.* New York: International Universities Press, 1965.

Hirsh, J. Behavior-genetic analysis and its biosocial consequences. (originally presented 1970). In W. R. Looft (Ed.), *Developmental psychology: A book of readings.* Hinsdale, Ill.: Dryden Press, 1972.

Hoffman, L. W. Effects of maternal employment on the child. *Child Development,* 1961, *32,* 187–197.

Holland, J. *The psychology of vocational choice.* Waltham, Mass.: Blaisdall, 1966.

Holland, J. G., & Skinner, B. F. *The analysis of behavior.* New York: McGraw-Hill, 1961.

Hollenberg, E., & Sperry, M. Some antecedents of aggression and effects of frustration in doll play. *Personality,* 1951, *1,* 32–43.

Hollingworth, L. S. The child of very superior intelligence as a special problem in social adjustment. In C. S. Hollingworth (Ed.), *Children above 180 I.Q.* New York: World, 1942.

Holt, F. D., & Kicklighter, R. H. (Eds.). *Psychological services in the schools.* Dubuque, Iowa: Wm. C. Brown, 1971.

Holt, J. Quackery. *New York Review of Books,* August 13, 1970.

Holt, J., Ginott, H., Salk, L., & Barr, D. Discipline: The most perplexing subject of all (a panel discussion). *Teacher,* 1972, *90,* 54–56.

Homme, L., Csanyi, A. P., Gonzales, M. A., & Rechs, J. R. *How to use contingency contracting in the classroom.* Champaign, Ill.: Research Press, 1969.

Horrocks, J. E. *The psychology of adolescence.* Boston: Houghton Mifflin, 1976.

Hunt, J. McV. Probable nature of the deficit from cultural deprivation. Paper presented at the Arden House conference on School Environment for Socially Disadvantaged Children. Harriman, N.Y. December 1962.

Hutchins, R. Are we educating our children for the wrong future? *Saturday Review*, September 11, 1965.

Iowa Department of Public Instruction Dispatch. *Resolution adopted by the National Association of School Boards of Education*, 1976, April–May, *5(6), 2.*

Irion, A. A brief history of research on the acquisition of skill. In E. H. Belodeau (Ed.), *Acquisition of skill*. New York: Academic Press, 1966.

Jackson, R. M., Cleveland, J. C., & Merenda, P. F. The longitudinal effects of early identification and counseling of underachievers. *Journal of School Psychology*, 1975, *13(2)*, 119–128.

James, W. *Talks to teachers*. New York: W. W. Norton, 1958. (Originally published, 1892.)

Janov, A. *The feeling child*. New York: Simon & Schuster, 1973.

Jantz, R. K., & Fulda, T. A. The role of moral education in the public elementary school. *Social Education*, January 1975, 24–35.

Jensen, A. R. Varieties of individual differences in learning. In R. M. Gagne (Ed.), *Learning and individual differences*. Columbus, Ohio: Charles E. Merrill, 1967.

Jensen, A. R. How much can we boost IQ and scholastic achievement? *Harvard Educational Review,* 1969, *39*, 1–123.

Jensen, A. R. Can we and should we study race differences? In C. L. Brace, G. R. Gamble & J. T. Bonds (Eds.), *Race and intelligence*. Washington, D.C.: American Anthropological Association, 1971.

Jensen, A. R. *Educability and group differences*. New York: Harper & Row, 1973.

Jensen, A. R. *Genetics and education*. New York: Harper & Row, 1973.

Jersild, A. T. The voice of the self. *NEA Journal*, 1965, *54*, 23–25.

Johnson, D. J. Treatment approaches to dyslexia. In S. E. Kirk & F. E. Lord (Eds.), *Exceptional children: Educational resources and perspectives*. Boston: Houghton Mifflin, 1974. (Originally published 1969.)

Johnson, G. O. Special education for the mentally handicapped—a paradox. *Exceptional Children*, 1962, *29*, 62–69.

Johnson, W., Stefflre, B., & Edelfelt, R. *Pupil personnel and guidance services*. New York: McGraw-Hill, 1961.

Jones, C. R. *Homosexuality and counseling*. Philadelphia: Fortress, 1974.

Josselyn, I. M. *Psychosocial development of children*. New York: Family Service Association of America, 1948.

Josselyn, I. M. *The adolescent and his world*. New York: Family Service Association of America, 1969.

Joyce, B., & Weil, M. *Models of teaching*. Englewood Cliffs, N.J.: Prentice-Hall, 1972.

Kagan, J. A conversation with Jerome Kagan. *Saturday Review of Education*, March 1973, p. 41–43.

Kahn, R. The delinquent's ability to use information to modify his goals. *British Journal of Criminology*, 1971, *2(1)*, 63–72.

Kant, I. *Critique of pure reason* (F. M. Müller, trans.). (Originally published, 1781.)

Kaplan, B. L. Classroom discipline is more than technique. *The Elementary School Journal*, 1973, *73*, 244–250.

Katz, R. L. The meaning of religion in healthy people. In O. H. Mowrer (Ed.), *Morality and mental health*. Chicago: Rand McNally, 1967, pp. 324–327. (Originally published, 1960.)

Kauffman, J. M., & Hallahan, D. P. Control of rough physical behavior using novel contingencies and directive teaching. *Perceptual and Motor Skills*, 1973, *36(3)*, 1225–1226.

Kay, W. *Moral education: A sociological study of the influence of society, home, and school*. Hamden, Conn.: Shoe String Press, 1975.

Kearney, N. *Elementary school objectives*. New York: Russell Sage Foundation, 1953.

Kelly, H. Adolescents: A suppressed minority group. *Personnel and Guidance Journal*, 1969, *47*, 634–640.

Kempe, C. H., et al. The battered-child syndrome. *Journal of American Medical Association*, 1962, *181*, 17–24.

Kephart, N. *The slower learner in the classroom*. Columbus, Ohio: Charles E. Merrill, 1960.

Kibler, R., Barker, L., & Miles, D. *Behavioral objectives and instruction*. Boston: Allyn & Bacon, 1970.

Kimball, B. Case studies in educational failure during adolescence. *American Journal of Orthopsychiatry*, 1953, *23*, 405–415.

Kinsey, A. C., Pomeroy, W. B., & Martin, C. E. *Sexual behavior in the human male*. Philadelphia: W. B. Saunders, 1948.

Kirman, W. J. Emotional education in the classroom: A modern psychoanalytic approach. In G. S. Belkin (Ed.), *Counseling: Directions in theory and practice*. Dubuque, Iowa: Kendall/Hunt, 1976.

Klatskin, E., Jackson, E., & Wilkin, C. The influence of degree of flexibility in maternal child care practices on early childhood behavior. *American Journal of Orthopsychiatry*, 1956, *26*, 79–93.

Kohlberg, L. Moral education in the schools: A developmental view. *School Review*, 1966, *74*, 1–30.

Kohlberg, L. Early education: A cognitive-developmental view. *Child Development*, 1968, *39*, 1013–1062.

Kohlberg, L., & Kramer, R. B. Continuities and discontinuities in childhood and adult moral development. *Human Development*, 1969, *12*, 93–120.

Kohlberg, L., & Mayer, R. Development as the aim of education. *Harvard Educational Review*, 1972, *42(4)*, 449–496.

Kohlberg, L., & Turiel, E. (Eds.). *Recent research in moral development*. New York: Holt, Rinehart and Winston, 1969.

Kohler, A. D. *MOPPET: An elementary (K-6) humanities program devoted to the development of a lesson process promoting creativity in children*. Doctoral dissertation, Teachers College, Columbia University, 1975.

Konopka, G. *The adolescent girl in conflict*. Englewood Cliffs, N.J.: Prentice-Hall, 1966.

Koppel, D. Mishandling of discipline problems. *Education*, 1972, *93*, 183–193.

Kounin, J. S., & Gump, P. V. The comparative influence of punitive and nonpunitive teachers upon children's concepts of school misconduct. *Journal of Educational Psychology*, 1961, *52*, 44–49.

Krathwohl, D. R. The taxonomy of educational objectives. In M. D. Glock (Ed.). *Guiding learning: Readings in educational psychology.* New York: John Wiley, 1971. (Originally published, 1964.)

Krathwohl, D. R., Bloom, B. S., & Masia, B. B. *Taxonomy of educational objectives: The classification of educational goals—Handbook II: Affective Domain.* New York: David McKay, 1964.

Kraus, P. E. *Yesterday's children: A longitudinal study of children from kindergarten into adult years.* New York: John Wiley, 1973.

Krumboltz, J. D., & Krumboltz, H. B. *Changing children's behavior.* Englewood Cliffs, N.J.: Prentice-Hall, 1972.

Krumboltz, J. D., & Thoresen, C. E. *Behavioral counselling: Cases and techniques.* New York: Holt, Rinehart and Winston, 1969.

Kubie, L. S. Educating for maturity. In M. D. Glock (Ed.), *Guiding learning: Readings in educational psychology.* New York: John Wiley, 1971. (Originally published 1959.)

Kuethe, J. L. *The teaching-learning process.* Glenview, Ill.: Scott, Foresman, 1968.

L'Abate, L., & Curtis, L. T. *Teaching the exceptional child.* Philadelphia: W. B. Saunders, 1975.

Laing, R. D. *Divided self.* New York: Pantheon, 1967.

Lamb, P. *Guiding children's language learning.* Dubuque, Iowa: Wm. C. Brown, 1967.

Lambert, W. E., & Peal, E. The relation of bilingualism to intelligence. In A. S. Dil (Ed.), *Language, psychology and culture.* Stanford, Calif.: Stanford University Press, 1972.

Langer, M. F. New Year's resolution: No more corporal punishment. *Teachers,* 1973, *90*, 12–15.

Lauer, B., Ten Broek, E., & Grossman, M. Battered-child syndrome review of 130 patients with controls. *Pediatrics,* 1974, *54(1),* 67–70.

Lee, G., et a! The classroom. Distributed by New York City, Board of Education. (110 Livingston Street, Brooklyn, N.Y. 11201), 1976.

LeFrancois, G. R. Jean Piaget's developmental model: Equilibration through adaptation. In W. R. Looft (Ed.), *Developmental psychology: A book of readings.* Hinsdale, Ill.: Dryden Press, 1972, 297–308.

Leonard, G. B. *Education & Ecstasy.* New York: Dell, 1968.

Leopold, W. F. *Speech development of a bilingual child* (4 vols.). Evanston, Ill.: Northwestern University Press, 1947

Lewis, M. M. *How children learn to speak.* London: Harrap, 1957.

Lidz, T. *The person.* New York: Basic Books, 1968.

Lifton, W. M. *Working with groups: Group process and individual growth* (2nd ed.). New York: John Wiley, 1966.

Light, R., & Smith, P. Accumulating evidence: Procedures for resolving contradictions among different research studies. *Harvard Educational Review.* 1971, *41(4),* 429–471.

Lincoln, E. A. Effective methods for teaching the inner-city child. *Urban Education*, 1974, *9*, 82–86.

Lindquist, E. F. *Educational measurement*. Washington: American Council on Education, 1951.

Lindsley, O. R. An experiment with parents: Branding behavior at home. In G. A. Fargo, C. Behrus, & P. Nolen (Eds.), *Behavior modification in the classroom*. Belmont, Calif.: Wadsworth, 1970, 310–316.

Lipsett, S. M. Introduction: The mood of American youth. Reston, Va.: National Education Association, 1974.

Locke, J. An essay concerning human understanding. In *The empiricists*. (abr. by R. Taylor). Garden City, N.Y.: Doubleday-Anchor, 1961.

Love, J. M., & Parker-Robinson, C. Children's imitation of grammatical and ungrammatical sentences. *Child Development*, 1972, 311–318.

Lundin, R. W. *Personality: A behavior analysis* (2nd ed.). New York: Macmillan, 1974.

Macmillan, D. L., Forness, S. R., & Trumbull, B. M. The role of punishment in the classroom. *Exceptional Children*, 1973, *40*, 85–96.

Macomber, F. G. The role of educational institutions in adolescent development. In J. F. Adams (Ed.), *Understanding adolescence: Current developments in adolescent psychology*. Boston: Allyn & Bacon, 1968, pp. 232–248.

Mager, R. F. *Preparing instructional objectives*. Belmont, Calif.: Fearon, 1962, 1975. (Previously published as *Preparing objectives for programmed instruction*.)

Mahan, D. J., & Moeller, G. *Faculty team: Organization for results*. Chicago: Science Research Associates, 1971.

Mahler, M. S. Thoughts about development and individuation. *The Psychoanalytic Study of the Child*, 1963, *18*, 307–324.

Mahler, M. S., Pine, F., & Bergman, A. *The psychological birth of the human infant: Symbiosis and individuation*. New York: Basic Books, 1975.

Maier, I., & Hogg, J. Operant conditioning of sustained visual fixation in hyperactive severely retarded children. *American Journal of Mental Deficiencies*, 1974, *79(3)*, 297–304.

Mann, J. H. *Learning to be: The education of human potential*. New York: Free Press, 1972.

Mann, R. D. A review of the relationship between personality and performance in small groups. *Psychological Bulletin*, 1959, *56*, 241–270.

Maritain, J. *Education at the crossroads*. New Haven: Yale University Press, 1943.

Marsico, A. Control without punishment. *High Points*, 1965, *47*, 9–19.

Martin, D. L. The growing horror of child abuse and the undeniable role of the schools in putting an end to it. *American School Board Journal*, 1973, *160*, 51–55.

Maslow, A. H. A theory of human motivation. *Psychological Review*, 1943, *50*, 370–396.

Maslow, A. H. *Toward a psychology of being*. New York: Van Nostrand Reinhold, 1954.

Maslow, A. H. Self-actualization and beyond. In J. F. T. Bugental (Ed.), *Challenges of humanistic psychology*. New York: McGraw-Hill, 1967, pp. 279–286.

Maslow, A. H. What is a taoistic teacher? In L. J. Rubin (Ed.), *Facts and feelings in the classroom.* New York: Walker, 1973.

Mathewson, R. H. *Guidance: Policy and practice* (3rd ed.). New York: Harper & Row, 1962.

May, R. *Psychology and the human dilemma.* New York: Van Nostrand Reinhold, 1967.

McAvoy, R. Measurable outcome with systematic observations. *Journal of Research and Development in Education,* 1970, *4(1),* 10–13.

McBride, A. Moral education and the Kohlberg thesis. *Momentum,* 1973, *4,* 22–27.

McCary, J. L. *Human sexuality.* New York: Van Nostrand Reinhold, 1967. 2nd ed., 1974.

McConnell, T. R., Cronwell, R. L., Bialer, I., & Son, C. D. Studies in activity level: VII effects of amphetamine drug administration on the activity level of retarded children. *American Journal of Mental Deficiency,* 1964, *68,* 647–651.

McCoy, L. Braille: a language for severe dyslexia. *Journal of Learning Disabilities,* 1975, *8(5),* 288–292.

McGurk, H., & Lewis, M. Achievement motivation and ordinal position of birth. *Developmental Psychology,* 1972, *7(3),* 364–367.

McKenzie, H. S., et al. Behavior modification of children with learning disabilities using grades as tokens and allowances as backup reinforcers. In R. H. Bradfield (Ed.), *Behavior modification of learning disabilities.* San Rafael, Calif.: Academic Therapy Publications, 1971, 115–126.

Mead, M. Can the socialization of children lead to greater acceptance of diversity? *Young Children,* 1973, *28,* 322–332.

Mehrens, W., & Lehmann, I. *Measurement and evaluation in education and psychology.* New York: Holt, Rinehart and Winston, 1973.

Metcalf, L. E. (Ed.). *Values education: Rationale, strategies, and procedures.* Washington, D.C.: National Council for the Social Studies. (Forty-first yearbook), 1971.

Meyer, J. B., & Meyer, J. K. *Counseling psychology: Theories and case studies.* Boston: Allyn & Bacon, 1975.

Michael, W., Metfessel, N., & Kersner, D. Instrumentation of Bloom's and Krathwohl's taxonomies for the writing of instructional objectives. *Psychology in the Schools.* 1969, *41(3),* 227–231.

Millar, W. S. Conditioning and learning in early infancy. In B. Foss (Ed.), *New perspectives in child development.* Suffolk, England: Penguin, 1974, 53–84.

Miller, R. V. Social status and socioempathic differences among mentally superior, mentally typical and mentally retarded children. In J. L. French (Ed.), *Educating the gifted.* New York: Henry Holt, 1959.

Miller, W., & Ervin, S. *The development of grammar in child language.* In U. Bellugi & R. Brown (Eds.). *The acquisition of language.* Cambridge, Mass.: Society for Research in Child Development, 1964.

Minuchin, P., Biber, B., Shapiro, E., & Zimiles, H. *The psychological impact of school experience.* New York: Basic Books, 1969.

Mischel, W. Toward a cognitive social learning: Reconceptualization of personality. *Psychological Review,* 1973, *80(4),* 252–283.

Mitchell, D. W., & Crowell, P. J. Modifying inappropriate behavior in an elementary art class. *Elementary School Guidance and Counseling,* 1973, *8(1),* 34–42.

Montessori, M. *The absorbent mind* (C. A. Claremont, trans.). New York: Dell, 1967.

Morris, V. C. *Existentialism in education.* New York: Harper & Row, 1966.

Mosston, M. *Teaching: From command to discovery.* Belmont, Calif.: Brooks-Cole, 1972.

Muller, P. *The tasks of childhood* (A. Mason, trans.). New York: McGraw-Hill, 1969.

Munns, M. The values of adolescents compared with parents and peers. *Adolescence,* 1972, *7,* 519–524.

Murphy, G. *Historical Introduction to Modern Psychology.* New York: Harcourt Brace Jovanovich, 1949.

Nadelman, L. Sex identity in American children. *Developmental Psychology,* 1974, *10(3),* 413–417.

Nagel, T. S., & Richman, P. T. *Competency-based instruction: A strategy to eliminate failure.* Columbus, Ohio: Charles E. Merrill, 1972.

Nagi, S. Z. Child abuse and neglect programs: A national overview. *Children Today,* 1975, *4(3),* 13–17.

Nass, D. R., & Nass, S. Counseling the fatherless child. In G. S. Belkin (Ed.), *Counseling: Directions in theory and practice.* Dubuque, Iowa: Kendall/Hunt, 1976.

National Educational Association, *Report of the task force on corporal punishment.* National Educational Association: Washington, D. C., 1972.

National Educational Association Commission, *Cardinal principles of secondary education.* Unitel States Office of Education Bulletin, No. 35, 1918.

National Society for the Study of Education, *The dynamics of instructional groups* (N. B. Henry, ed). Chicago: National Society for the Study of Education, 1960.

National Society for the Study of Education of the Gifted. 57th yearbook, 1958.

Nation's Schools. It's time to hang up the hickory stick. *Nation's Schools,* 1972, *90,* 8–9.

Neale, R. E. *In praise of play.* New York: Harper & Row, 1969.

Nelson, M. C., et al. *Roles and paradigms in psychotherapy.* New York: Grune & Stratton, 1968.

Niensted, S. Talking with learning disabilities teachers. *Reading Teacher,* 1975, *28(7),* 662–665.

Nordstrom, J. L. Child abuse: A school district's response to its responsibility. *Child Welfare,* 1974, *53(4),* 257–260.

Nurse, S. M. Familial patterns of parents who abuse their children. *Smith College Studies in Social Work,* 1964.

Offer, D. Sexual behavior of a group of normal adolescents. *Medical Aspects of Human Sexuality,* 1971, *5,* 40–49.

O'Keefe, M., & Smaby, M. Seven methods and techniques for solving classroom discipline problems. *High School Journal,* 1973, *56(4),* 190–199.

Page, J. G., et al. Pemoline (Cylert®) in the treatment of childhood hyperkinesis. *Journal of Learning Disabilities,* 1974, *7(8),* 498–503.

Palardy, M. J. Classroom management is more than conditioning. *The Elementary School Journal*, 1970, *70*, 162–165.

Palardy, J. M., & Mudrey, J. E. Discipline: Four approaches. *The Elementary School Journal*, 1973, *73*, 297–305.

Parke, R. D. The role of punishment in the socialization process. In R. A. Hoppe, G. A. Milton, & E. Simmel (Eds.), *Early experiences in the processes of socialization*. New York: Academic Press, 1970.

Parks, J. C. Group guidance   a perspective. In D. Brown & D. J. Srebalus (Eds.), *Selected readings in contemporary guidance*. Dubuque, Iowa: Wm. C. Brown, 1973.

Patterson, C. H. *Counseling and guidance in the schools*. New York: Harper & Row, 1962.

Patterson, C. H. *Theories of counseling and psychotherapy* (2nd ed.). New York: Harper & Row, 1973.

Peck, R. F., & Mitchell, J. V., Jr. The mental health of the teacher. In H. F. Clarizio (Ed.), *Mental health and the educative process*. Chicago: Rand McNally, 1969, 273–278.

Perella, V. C., & Bogan, F. A. Out of school youth—part I. In A. E. Winder & D. L. Angus (Eds.), *Adolescence: Contemporary studies*. New York: American Book Company, 1968, pp. 243–255.

Perkins, K. J. School psychology: From identification to identity. *Journal of School Psychology*, 1964, *2(1)*, 7–16.

Perrone, P. A., Ryan, T. A., & Zeran, F. R. *Guidance and the emerging adolescent*. Scranton, Pa.: International Textbook, 1970.

Persons, R. W. The Mosher Guilt Scale: Theoretical formulation, research review and normative data. *Journal of Projective Techniques and Personality Assessment*, 1970, *34(4)*, 266–270.

Phillips, J. L., Jr. *The origins of intellect: Piaget's theory*. San Francisco: W. H. Freeman, 1975.

Physicians Desk Reference (PDR) (30th ed.). Oradell, N.J.: Medical Economics, 1976.

Piaget, J. *The moral judgment of the child*. London: Kegan Paul, 1932.

Piaget, J. *Six psychological studies*. New York: Vintage, 1967.

Piaget, J. *Genetic epistemology* (Eleanor Duckworth, trans.). New York: Columbia University Press, 1970.

Piaget, J., & Inhelder, B. *Psychology of the child* (Helen Weaver, trans.). London: Routledge & Kegan Paul, 1969. (New York: Basic Books, 1969.)

Piaget, J., & Inhelder, B. *The growth of logical thinking: From childhood to adolescence*. New York: Basic Books, 1958.

Pickering, C. T. Discipline and freedom in childhood and education. *Intellect*, November 1972, 114–116.

Pine, G. J., & Horne, P. J. Principles and conditions for learning in adult education. In A. V. Boy & G. J. Pine, *Expanding the self: Personal growth for teachers*. Dubuque, Iowa: Wm. C. Brown, 1971. (Originally published 1969.)

Piper, T., McKinney, V., & Wick, T. A token reinforcement in a third grade inner city classroom. *Education*, 1972, *93*, 118–122.

Pittel, S. M., et al. Developmental factors in adolescent drug use. *Journal of Humanistic Psychology*, 1971, *11(2)*, 109–128.

Popham, W. J. Normative data for criterion-referenced tests. *Phi Delta Kappan*, 1976, *57(9)*, 593–594.

Porter, A. *Cybernetics simplified*. New York: Barnes & Noble, 1969.

Premack, D. Reinforcement theory. In M. R. Jones (Ed.), *Nebraska symposium on motivation*. Lincoln, Neb.: University of Nebraska Press, 1965.

Price, R. H. *Abnormal behavior: Perspectives in conflict*. New York: Holt, Rinehart & Winston, 1972.

Pulaski, M. A. *Understanding Piaget*. New York: Harper & Row, 1971.

Purkey, W. W., & Avila, R. Classroom discipline: a new approach. *The Elementary School Journal, 1971, 71,* 325–328.

Quay, H. C., Werry, J. S., McQueen, M., & Sprague, R. L. Remediation of the conduct problem child in the special class setting. *Exceptional Children,* April 1966, 509–514.

Rachman, S., & Teasdale, J. *Aversion therapy and behavior disorders: An analysis*. London: Routledge & Kegan Paul, 1969.

Ragsdale, C. How children learn motor types of activities. *49th Yearbook of the National Society for the Study of Education, 1950,* 69–91.

Rainwater, L. *Behind ghetto walls*. Chicago: Aldine, 1970.

Raths, L., Harmin, M., & Simon, S. *Values and teaching: Working with values in the classroom*. Columbus, Ohio: Charles E. Merrill, 1966.

Redl, F. R. Intervention techniques available to the teacher. Paper presented at the conferences of American Orthopsychiatric Association, 1967.

Redl, F. R., & Wineman, D. *Children who hate*. Glencoe, Ill.: Free Press, 1951.

Reichart, S. *Change and the teacher*. New York: Thomas Y. Crowell, 1969.

Reinert, H. R. *Children in conflict*. St. Louis: C. V. Mosby, 1976.

Riessman, F. *Culturally deprived child*. New York: Harper & Row, 1962.

Roback, A. A. *History of American psychology*. New York: Library Publishers, 1952.

Robison, L. E. *Human growth and development*. Columbus, Ohio: Charles E. Merrill, 1968.

Roe, A. *The psychology of occupations*. New York: John Wiley, 1956.

Roe, A. Early determinants of vocational choice. *Journal of Counseling Psychology, 1957, 4,* 212–217.

Rogers, C. R. *Carl Rogers on encounter groups*. New York: Harper & Row, 1970.

Rogers, C. R. *Client-centered therapy*. Boston: Houghton Mifflin, 1951.

Rogers, C. R. *Freedom to learn*. Columbus, Ohio: Charles E. Merrill, 1969.

Rogers, C. R. Learning to be free. In C. R. Rogers & B. Stevens (Eds.), *Person to person: The problem of being human*. New York: Pocket Books, 1971.

Rogers, C. R. The necessary and sufficient conditions of therapeutic personality change. *Journal of Consulting Psychology, 1957, 21,* 95–103.

Rogers, C. R. *On becoming a person*. Boston: Houghton Mifflin, 1961.

Rogers, C. R. A theory of therapy, personality, and interpersonal relationships, as developed in the client-centered framework. In S. Kock (Ed.), *Psychology: A study of a science* (Vol. 3). New York: McGraw-Hill, 1958.

Rosenberg, M. The biological basis for sex-role stereotypes. *Contemporary Psychoanalysis, 1973, 9,* 374–388.

Rosenthal, D. *Genetics of psychopathology*. New York: McGraw-Hill, 1971.

Rothney, J. W. *Adaptive counseling in the schools.* Englewood Cliffs, N.J.: Prentice-Hall, 1972.

Rubin, L. J. School and life. In *Facts and feelings in the classroom.* New York: Walker, 1973.

Ruma, E. H. Counseling the single parent. In G. S. Belkin (Ed.), *Counseling: Directions in theory and practice.* Dubuque, Iowa: Kendall/Hunt, 1976.

Ruppenthal, G. C., et al. Development of peer interaction of monkeys reared in a nuclear-family environment. *Child Development,* 1974, *45,* 670–682.

Russell, B. *Education and the good life.* New York: Boni & Liveright, 1926.

Russell, B. *Education and the modern world.* New York: W. W. Norton, 1932.

Russell, B. Mental health and the school. In N. A. Crawford & K. A. Menninger (Eds.), *The healthy-minded child.* New York: Coward McCann, 1930.

Russell, B. The training of young children. *Harpers Magazine,* August 1927, 313–319.

Russell, B. What shall we educate for? *Harpers Magazine,* April 1926, 586–597.

Sabine, G. *When you listen, this is what you can hear. . . .* Iowa City: American College Testing Program, 1971.

Sanders, L., Kibby, R. W., Creaghan, S., & Tyrrel, E. Child abuse: Detection and prevention. *Young Children,* 1975, *30(5),* 332–337.

Scarth, P. Implications of individual psychology for the school psychologist. *Journal of Individual Psychology,* 1969, *25,* 146–154.

Schachter, S. *The psychology of affiliation.* Stanford: Stanford University Press, 1959.

Scheffler, I. *Conditions of knowledge.* Glenview, Ill.: Scott, Foresman, 1965.

Schlossberg, N. K., & Pietrofesa, J. J. Perspectives on counseling bias. *Counseling Psychologist,* 1973, *4,* 44–54.

Schmuck, R. A., & Schmuck, P. A. *Group processes in the classroom* (2nd ed.). Dubuque, Iowa: Wm. C. Brown, 1975.

Schulz, D. A. *Coming up black: Patterns of ghetto socialization.* Englewood Cliffs, N.J.: Prentice-Hall, 1969.

Sebald, H. *Adolescence: A sociological analysis.* New York: Appleton-Century-Crofts, 1968.

Seeman, M. On the meaning of alienation. *American Sociological Review,* 1959, *24,* 783–791.

Sexton, P. *Education and income.* New York: Viking Press, 1961.

Shane, H. A future-oriented assessment of crucial educational issues. *Phi Delta Kappan,* 1973, *54(5),* 326–337.

Shaw, M. C. Need achievement scales as predictors of academic success. *Journal of Educational Psychology,* 1961, *52,* 282–285.

Shaw, M. C., Edson, K., & Bell, H. The self-concepts of bright underachieving high school students as revealed by an objective check list. *Personnel and Guidance Journal,* 1960, *30,* 193–196.

Siegel, E. *Special education in the regular classroom.* New York: John Day, 1969.

Silberman, C. *Crisis in the classroom.* New York: Random House, 1970.

Silverman, R. E. *Psychology* (2nd ed.). New York: Appleton-Century-Crofts, 1974.

Simon, S. B. Value clarification—a tool for counselors. *Personnel and Guidance Journal,* 1973, *51,* 586–590.

Simon, S. B., Howe, L., & Kirschenbaum, H. *Values clarification: A practical handbook of strategies for teachers and students.* New York: Hart, 1972.

Skinner, B. F. *Verbal behavior.* New York: Appleton-Century-Crofts, 1953.

Skinner, B. F. The science of learning and the art of teaching. *Harvard Educational Review,* 1954, *24,* 86–97.

Skinner, B. F. Teaching machines. In W. H. MacGinitie & S. Ball, *Readings in psychological foundations of education.* New York: McGraw-Hill, 1968, pp. 5–19.

Skinner, B. F. *The technology of teaching.* New York: Appleton-Century-Crofts, 1968.

Skinner, B. F. The free and happy student. *New York University Quarterly,* Winter, 1973, 2–6.

Smart, M. S., & Smart, R. C. *Preschool children: Development and relationships.* New York: Macmillan, 1973.

Smith, B. O. A concept of teaching. In B. O. Smith & R. H. Ennis (Eds.), *Language and concepts in education.* Chicago: Rand McNally, 1961, pp. 86–101.

Smith, K. V., & Smith, M. F. *Cybernetic principles of learning and educational design.* New York: Holt, Rinehart and Winston, 1966.

Sommers, K. M. When children run riot. *Grade Teacher,* 1972, *89,* 55–56.

Spence, K. The relation of learning theory to the technology of education. *Harvard Educational Review,* 1959, *29,* 84–95.

Spinetti, J. J., & Rigler, D. The child-abusing parent: A psychological review. *Psychological Bulletin,* 1972.

Spotnitz, H. *The couch and the circle.* New York: Alfred A. Knopf, 1961.

Spotnitz, H. The toxoid response. *The Psychoanalytic Review,* 1963, *50(4),* 81–94.

Spotnitz, H. *Modern psychoanalysis of the schizophrenic patient.* New York: Grune & Stratton, 1968.

Spotnitz, H. *Psychotherapy of the pre-Oedipal conditions.* New York: Jason Aronson, 1976.

Staines, J. W. The self-picture as a factor in the classroom. In M. D. Glock (Ed.), *Guiding learning: Readings in educational psychology.* New York: John Wiley, 1971, pp. 391–441.

Stallings, L. *Motor skills: Development and learning.* Dubuque, Iowa: Wm. C. Brown, 1973.

Stanley, G., & Hall, R. Short-term visual information processing in dyslexia. *Child Development,* 1973, *44,* 841–844.

Stanton, M. Discrimination by children in moral judgments. *Educational Research,* 1974, *26,* 114–123.

Stephens, J. M. *The process of schooling: A psychological examination.* New York: Holt, Rinehart and Winston, 1967.

Stiller, R. (Ed.). *Illustrated sex dictionary.* New York: Health Publications, 1966.

Stolz, L. M. Effects of maternal employment on children: Evidence from child research. *Child Development,* 1960, *31,* 749–782.

Stolurow, L. M. Computer-assisted instruction. In Committee for Economic Development (Ed.), *The school and the challenge of innovation.* New York: McGraw-Hill, 1969.

Strang, R. Mental hygiene of gifted children. In P. Witty (Ed.), *The gifted child*. Boston: D. C. Heath, 1951.

Strang, R., & Hocker, M. E. First-grade children's language patterns. In M. S. Auleta (Ed.), *Foundations of early childhood education: Readings*. New York: Random House, 1969, pp. 249–254. (Originally published, 1965.)

Stroud, J. B. *Psychology in education* (2nd ed.). New York: David McKay, 1956.

Sutton-Smith, B. The role of play in cognitive development. *Young Children*, 1967, *22(6)*, 361–370.

Suzuki, D. T. *An introduction to Zen Buddhism*. London: Rider & Co., 1949.

Tanner, L. M. Socializing the unsocialized: An interview with Laurel N. Tanner. *Teachers*, 1972, *90*, 32–34.

Templeton, I. Class size. *Educational Management Review Series*. 1972, *8*, 1–7.

Teper-Singer, L. The many faces of role playing. *Health Education*, November–December 1975, 34–35.

Terman, L. M., & Oden, M. H. The Stanford studies of the gifted. In P. Witty (Ed.), *The gifted child*. Boston: D. C. Heath, 1951.

Thom, D. A., & Newell, N. L. Hazards of the high IQ. In I. L. French (Ed.), *Educating the gifted*. New York: Henry Holt, 1959.

Thompson, G. *Child psychology: Growth trends in psychological adjustment* (2nd ed.). Boston: Houghton Mifflin, 1962.

Thompson, T. *Richie*. New York: Saturday Review Press, 1973.

Thorndike, E. *The principles of teaching*. New York: A. G. Seiler, 1906.

Thorndike, R. *Educational Measurement* (2nd ed.). Washington, D.C.: American Council on Education, 1971.

Thorndike, R., & Hagen, E. *Measurement and evaluation in psychology and education* (4th ed.). New York: John Wiley, 1977.

Tinsley, D. G., & Ora, J. P. Catch the child being good. *Today's Education*, 1970, *59(1)*, 24–25.

Todd, V. E., & Heffernan, H. *The years before school: Guiding preschool children* (2nd ed.). New York: Macmillan, 1970.

Tolman, E. There is more than one kind of learning. *Psychological Review*, 1949, *56*, 144–155.

Torrance, E. P. *Education and the creative potential*. Minneapolis: University of Minnesota Press, 1963.

Trager, H. G., & Yarrow, M. R. *They learn what they live*. New York: Harper and Bros., 1952.

Travers, R. M. F. *Essentials of learning* (2nd ed.). New York: Macmillan, 1967.

Travers, R. M. F. *Essentials of learning* (3rd ed.). New York: Macmillan, 1972.

Truax, C. B., & Tatum, C. An extension from the effective psychotherapeutic model to constructive personality change in pre-school children. *Childhood Education*, 1966, *42*, 456–462.

Truax, C. B., Wargo, D., & Volksdorf, N. R. Antecedents to outcome in group counseling with institutionalized juvenile delinquents. *Journal of Abnormal Psychology*, 1970, *76*, 235–242.

Turiel, E. An experimental test of the sequentiality of developmental stages in the child's moral judgments. *Journal of Personality and Social Psychology*, 1966, *3*, 611–618.

Tyler, R. Some findings from studies in the field of college biology. *Science Education,* 1934, *18,* 133–143.

United States Commission on Civil Rights. *A time to listen . . . a time to act.* Washington, D.C.: United States Commission on Civil Rights, 1967.

Viel, P. J., & Galloway, C. G. What's an effective reinforcer? Ask the children! *Elementary School Journal,* 1973, *73,* 315–322.

Vontress, Clemmont E. Counseling Negro students for college. *Journal of Negro Education,* 1968, *37(1),* 37–44.

Vontress, C. E. Cultural barriers in the counseling relationship. *Personnel and Guidance Journal,* 1969, 11–17.

Vontress, C. E. Counseling the racial and ethnic minorities. *Focus on Guidance,* 1973, *5(6),* 1–10.

Wallen, N., & Travers, R. M. F. Analysis and investigation of teaching methods. In N. L. Gage, (Ed.), *Handbook of research on teaching.* Chicago: Rand McNally and Company, 1963, 448–505.

Wasik, B. H. Application of Premack's generalization on reinforcement to the management of classroom behavior. *Journal of Experimental Child Psychology,* 1970, *10,* 33–43.

Watson, J. B. *Behaviorism.* New York: W. W. Norton, 1930, 1970. (Originally published, 1924.)

Weber, C. A. Do teachers understand learning theory? *Phi Delta Kappan,* 1965, *46,* 433–435.

Weil, A. P. Children with minimal brain dysfunction: Diagnostic, dynamic, and therapeutic considerations. In S. G. Sapir & A. C. Nitzburg (Eds.), *Children with learning problems.* New York: Brunner/Mazel, 1973.

Weitzman, L. J., & Rizzo, D. Sex bias in textbooks. *Today's Education,* 1975, *64,* 49–57.

White, M. Little red schoolhouse and little white clinic. *Teachers College Record,* 1965, *66,* 188–200.

White, R. W. Motivation reconsidered: The concept of competence. *Psychological Review,* 1959, *66,* 297–333.

White, W. F. *Psychological principles applied to classroom teaching.* New York: McGraw-Hill, 1969.

Whitehead, A. *The aims of education.* New York: Macmillan, 1929.

Whitley, J. M., Sprinthall, N., Mosher, R., & Donaghy, R. Selection and evaluation of counselor effectiveness. *Journal of Counseling Psychology,* 1967, *14,* 226–231.

Whorf, B. L. Linguistics as an exact science. In J. B. Carroll (Ed.), *Language, thought and reality.* New York: John Wiley, 1956. (Originally published 1952.)

Widseth, J. C. Reported dependent behaviors towards mothers and use of alcohol in delinquent girls. *Dissertation Abstracts International,* October 1972. *33* (4–B), No. 1833.

Wiener, N. *The human use of human beings: Cybernetics and society.* Garden City, N.Y.: Doubleday Anchor, 1954.

Williamson, S. Z. The effects of maternal employment on the scholastic performance of children. *Journal of Home Economics,* 1970, *62(8),* 609–613.

Wilson, C. *Introduction to the new existentialism.* Boston: Houghton Mifflin, 1966.

Wohlwill, J. F. The teaching machine: Psychology's new hobbyhorse. In W. H. MacGinitie & S. Ball, *Readings in psychology foundations in education.* New York: McGraw-Hill, 1968, 22–30.

Wolpe, J. *The practice of behavior therapy.* New York: Pergamon Press, 1969.

Woods, P. A taxonomy of instrumental conditioning. *American Psychologist,* 1974, *29(8),* 584–597.

Wrightsman, L. S., & Brigham, J. C. *Contemporary issues in social psychology.* Belmont, Calif.: Brooks/Cole, 1973.

Yendovitskaya, T. V., Zinchenko, V. P., & Rizskaya, A. G. Development of sensation and perception. In A. V. Zaporozhets, & D. B. Elkouin (Eds.), *The psychology of preschool children* (J. Shybut & S. Simon, trans.). Cambridge, Mass.: MIT Press, 1971, pp. 1–64.

Zinberg, N. E., & Weil, A. T. The effects of marijuana on human beings. *The New York Times Magazine,* May 11, 1969, 89.

Zukow, A. H. Helping the hyperkinetic child. *Today's Education NEA Journal,* November–December 1975, *64(4),* 39–41.

Cover photo: Bob Coyle
Dubuque, Iowa

3

Cohen, S., 193
Coleman, J., 123, 363
Collard, R.R., 141
Collins, B.E., 588
Combs, A.W., 266-269
Commission for the White House
    Conference on Education, 304
Conners, C.K., 535
Cooper, J.J., 172-173
Cordova, F., 152
Corter, C., 99
Costanzo, P.R., 106, 156
Craig, R., 294
Creaghan, S., 135
Cronbach, L., 363, 594, 622
Cronwell, R.L., 535
Crowell, P.J., 538
Cruchon, G., 120-122
Curtis, L.T., 46

Dale, E., 319
Darwin, C., 38
Davids, A., 159
Davidson, H.H., 153
de Beauvoir, S., 586
De Genaro, J.J., 528
de Mare, P.B., 588
Demos, G.D., 192
Dennis, W., 344, 347
Dewey, J., 305, 312, 499
Dobzhansky, T., 70
Dollard, J., 447
Dorow, L.G., 473
Drever, J., 5, 266
Duffey, R.V., 294
Dunn, 382
Durkin, D., 287
Duschatal, P., 363

Ebel, R., 309, 594, 609, 622
Ediger, M., 468
Educational Policies Commission, 304,
    309
Educational Testing Service, 631
Edwards, A.J., 17
Edwards, J.B., 294
Egan, G., 405, 589
Elkind, D., 183
Elkonin, D.B., 87
Ellingson, C., 532-533
Ellis, H.C., 338
Endler, N.S., 172
Engelhardt, 553
Engelmann, S., 414, 418, 480
Erikson, E.H., 54-55, 71, 96-98, 104,
    122-123, 199
Ervin, S., 87
Esveldt, K.C., 528

Fantz, R.L., 76
Fargo, G.A., 457

Farnham-Diggory, S., 594
Fawcus, M., 85
Ferenczi, S., 430
Ferguson, L.R., 92
Fernald, G., 541
Field, J., 202
Fitts, P., 350
Flanders, N., 364, 498
Flapan, D., 149
Flavell, J.H., 77, 233, 281
Fleischman, E., 343
Forcinelli, J., 294
Ford, C.S., 178
Forness, S.R., 450-451, 528, 537
Forrer, S.E., 135
Frankl, V., 373, 434
Frazier, H.H., 131
Freeberg, N.E., 83
Freud, A., 96, 430
Freud, S., 51-52, 55, 92-95, 198-199,
    274-275, 369, 426
Friedenberg, E.Z., 172
Fromm, E., 375, 377
Frostig, M., 90, 414-417
Fulda, T.A., 281-282, 293

Gaddis, W., 158
Gage, N.L., 362-364
Gagné, R., 314, 326-327, 331-335, 350,
    364
Galbraith, R.E., 294-295
Galloway, C.G., 460
Gampel, D., 518-519
Gardner, R.A., 558
Garfinkle, M., 140
Garry, R., 213, 225
Gazda, G.M., 182, 382-383, 397
Gelles, R.J., 133-134
George, P.S., 452
Gergen, K.J., 266, 299
Gerra, J., 153
Getzels, J.W., 363, 521-522
Gewirtz, J.L., 99
Gibb, 573
Gibson, D., 46
Ginott, H.G., 385, 443, 466
Ginzberg, E., 194-195
Giorgi, A., 23
Glanz, E.C., 579
Glaser, R., 230-231, 234, 480-481, 621
Glasser, W., 396
Globetti, G., 190
Goble, F., 60
Goethe, 360
Goffman, E., 389, 406
Golden, M., 82
Golubchick, L., 27
Gordon, E.W., 47-48
Gorman, A.H., 569-571
Gottlieb, D., 192
Gottlieb, J., 518-519
Graham, R., 283, 294

Grambs, J.D., 153-154, 159
Gray, S.W., 11
Greenberg, D., 202
Greenberg, J.W., 153
Greene, M., 62, 368, 405, 436-437
Greer, R.D., 473
Grinder, R.E., 41
Grinspoon, L., 536-537
Gronlund, N., 318, 594
Grossman, M., 130
Groth, N.J., 522
Guetzkow, H., 588
Guilbaud, G.T., 482
Guilford, J.P., 314, 326-327
Gump, P.V., 451
Guthrie, R.V., 174, 176

Hagen, E., 594
Haley, J., 175
Hall, G.S., 198
Hall, R., 530
Hallahan, D.P., 539
Hamburg, B.A., 166
Harlow, H.F., 102
Harmin, M., 295-296, 298
Harnack, R.S., 487
Harrow, A., 232, 343-345, 349-350, 352,
    359
Hartup, W., 106
Hastings, T., 594, 603
Hawley, R.C., 297
Hayes, R.W., 579
Headsten, S.J., 130
Hebb, D.O., 221
Heffernan, H., 100-101, 109
Heidegger, M., 435
Heinsohn, A.L., 192
Helfer, R.E., 129
Hellman, I., 430
Hellmuth, J., 542
Helmreich, R., 144
Henry, N.B., 352
Herzog, E., 136
Hetherington, E.M., 106
Hildreth, G., 521
Hilgard, E.R., 213, 222, 319, 362
Hill, J.C., 430
Hill, W.F., 339
Hirsch, J., 47
Hocker, M.E., 121
Hoffman, H., 533
Hoffman, L.W., 138
Hogg, J., 538
Holland, J., 194
Holland, J.G., 329
Hollenberg, E., 451
Hollingsworth, L.S., 522-523
Holmes, D., 202
Holmes, M., 202
Holt, F.D., 10
Holt, J., 405, 466, 536
Holz, W.C., 452-454

White, M., 621
White, R.W., 123
White, W.F., 574-575
Whitehead, A., 305
Whitely, J.M., 387
Whorf, B.L., 124
Widseth, J.C., 190
Wilkin, C., 101
Williamson, S.Z., 138
Wilson, C., 377
Woods, P., 220
Wrightsman, L.S., 288

Yarrow, M.R., 110
Yendovitskaya, T.V., 75-76
Young, J.D., 508

Zajonc, R., 142-143
Zeran, F.R., 195
Zimiles, H., 145
Zinchenki, V.P., 75-76
Zukow, A.H., 534

Subject Index

DMT, 187
DNA. *See* Deoxyribonucleic acid
Dominance, 389-390
Dominant genes, 42-43
Double approach-avoidance conflict, 262-263
Down's syndrome, 45-46
Drug abuse, 184-193
Drug treatment for hyperactivity, 511, 535, 536, 537, 539
  opponents of, 536, 537
Dyscalculia, 532
Dysgraphic, 532
Dyslexia, 511, 529-531
  auditory, 530, 531
  definition of, 529
  developmental, 529
  diagnosis of, 530
  treatment of, 530-531
  visual, 530
Dyssynchronous, 532

Early childhood, 120
  psychomotor development in, 350
Eclecticism, 215, 230
Educable mentally retarded (EMR), the, 517, 518
  educational approaches for, 517, 518
  in the regular classroom, 519
  social position of, 517, 518, 519
  and teacher attitude, 518
  as underachievers, 527
Educating for maturity, 260
Education
  definition of, 4
  existentialism and, 62-63
  goals of, 304-308
  of preschool child, 98
  and psychotherapy, 425-441
Education and the Good Life, 245, 274
Education at the Crossroads, 378
Educational goals, problems with, 318-319
Educational objectives, 232-234, 305-306
Educational outcomes, 595-596
Educational Policies Commission, 309
Educational psychologist, the, 12, 19
  role of, 30-31
Educational psychology
  definition of, 4-6
  history of, 12-18
  perspectives of, 21-25
  premises of, 18-25
Educational testing versus psychological testing, 595-597
Effectance, 123
Effective teacher, the, characteristics of, 382-397
Efficiency and testing, 612-613
Egg cell, 41

Ego, 52, 93, 104, 274, 369
Ego functioning, and minimal brain dysfunction, 531
"Eight Ages of Man," 54-55, 96-98, 122-123
Elementary school
  influence on development, 144-157
  intellectual growth of, 123-129
  moral education in, 293-295
Elementary school years, role of, 119-157 passim
Elicitor, 480
Emitted behaviors, 219
Emotional conflicts, 261-264
Emotional development, 49-64
Emotional education, 425-441
Emotional growth, 157, 254-264
  in the classroom, 260-261
Emotionally disturbed, the
  anxiety and, 542
  characteristics of, 549-552
  in the classroom, 512, 516, 542-557
  poor impulse control, and, 543
Emotions, 254-258
Empathy, 228, 385-386, 420
Empiricism, 14-15
Enactive content, 333
Enrichment, 83
Enrichment programs, for the gifted, 519, 523, 525
Entry behavior, 233, 235-236
Environment, 61, 63
  internal versus external, 56
  versus heredity, 37-49
Environmental education, 337
Environmental reorganization, 420
Environmentalism, 39-40, 41
Epistemology, 13-16
Equilibration, 124, 127, 223
Equilibrium, 66
Erikson's theory of personality, 54
Erogenous zone, 92-95
Essay Concerning Human Understanding, 14-15
Estimate of reliability, 609
Ethnic awareness, 109-110
Ethnic differences, 174-175
Evaluation, 232, 235-239, 326
  criteria of, 620-623
  functions of, 601-602
  of the learner, 513
  of learning and teaching, 591-630
  of moral development theories, 287-288
  versus measurement, 594-595
Evolution, theory of, 38
Examples, use of, 155
Exceptional learner, 511-558
Executive Action, 289
"Existence precedes essence," 62
Existential theory of personality, 62-64

Existentialism, 59, 62, 63, 224, 368, 434-437
Expanding the Self, 269-273
Experience, 15
  as part of lesson, 501-505
Experimental psychology, 16, 22
Explanation, 215
Expressive behavior, 413
Extinction, 59, 324, 447-449, 457
Extraversion, 122
Eye color, 42

Faculty team, 580-581
Family, influences of, 128-129, 133, 135-139, 144, 154-155
Fantasy period, 194
Father-absence, 135-139
Feedback loop, 222-223, 483-485, 595
Feelings, and teaching methods, 488-489
Fifth-graders, 277-278
Figure-ground, 65, 249
Firstborn, 140, 141-144 passim
Fixation, 93
Flexibility, 172
Forced-choice tests, 611, 613
Formal operational thought, 183-184, 233, 238
Formal operations, period of, 67
Formative evaluation, 602, 603
Forms, Platonic, 13
Fourth-graders, 145-146
Fraternal twins, 44
Freedom, 62-63, 171, 436, 437
  loss of, 376-379
Freedom and Culture, 499
Freedom-from, 377, 379
Freedom-to, 377, 379
Free-response tests, 611, 613
French-Canadian learners, 152
Frustration, 262
Functionalism, 215, 230

Gamete, 41
Generation gap, 173
Genes, 41-43
Genetic epistemology, 124
Genetics, 32, 37-49, 127
Genotype, 42-43, 48
Genuineness, 388-389
Gestalt psychology, 65
Gestalt theory, 222-223
Gifted learners, 148
Giftedness, standards of, 521
Ginzberg's theory, 194-196
Glue, abuse of, 188
"Good boy–good girl" stage, 284
Grading, 613-634 passim
Grammar, development of, 87-91
Gratification, and personality development, 93

Stanford-Binet test, 82, 515, 520
Stasis, 370
Statistics, 602-607
Stimulant drugs, to treat hyperactivity, 535, 536, 537
Stimulus, conditioned versus unconditioned, 57
Stimulus, 56, 57, 65, 216, 219-221, 328-330, 414, 418, 419
Stinginess, 93
Striving for superiority, 123
Structure in Teaching, 494
Subject matter, presentation of, 490-496
Sublimation, 369
Successive approximation, 219
Suicide, 185
Summative evaluation, 602, 603
Superego, 52, 275, 369
Superiority feelings, 53
Surrogate mother, 102
Survival of the fittest, 38
Symbolic content, 333
Synectics model, 424
Syntax, learning of, 88-91
Synthesis, 232, 314-318, 326
Systematic observation, as a screening technique, 528

T-score, 629
Tactile abilities, 345, 349
Tactile eroticism, 93
Tactile sensitivity, 76
Taoistic teacher, 370, 397
Taste, sense of, 76
Tautology, 126
Taxonomy, definition of, 247
Taxonomy of educational objectives, 232, 247-254, 314
Teacher, the
  attitudes of, 154-155
  behavioral position on, 371-372
  and classroom interventions, 470
  communications of, 391-394
  as diagnostician, 534, 540
  and drug abuser, 192-193
  effective characteristics of, 382-397, 432-433
  and evaluation of exceptionality, 513, 527, 528, 529, 531, 533
  and genetics, 44-45, 48
  humanistic perspective of, 369-370
  of the hyperactive child, 538, 540
  information on early development of, 107-114
  insecure feelings of, 395-396
  and the intellectually gifted, 525
  mental health of, 387
  personality of, 363, 369-372, 432-433
  and preschool development of, 112, 113
  problems of, 372-379
  psychoanalytic perspective of, 369

qualities of, 171-172, 228
role of, 8, 45, 368, 489-490
and role in psychomotor learning, 349-351
self-knowledge of, 394-397
as stranger, 437
training of, 382-383
using CAI, 226
Teachers, home visits, 157
Teaching, 362-364
  applied psychological models of, 414
  and behavioral theory, 446-472 passim
  client-centered approach to, 431-433
  the culturally disadvantaged, 152-155
  definition of, 412-413
  effectiveness of, 363
  evaluation of, 591-630 passim
  existential view of, 434-437
  goals of, 20
  helping model of, 419-422
  humanistic perspective of, 431, 437-440
  methods of, 487-496
  models of, 413-425
  personal satisfaction in, 381-382
  Piaget's theory and, 68-69
  of preschool children, 107-114
  principles of, 471-472
  process of, 20-21
  psychoanalytic view of, 426-430
  the pubescent, 164-167
  rewards of, 380-382
  Rogerian perspective of, 385-386
  Rogerian view of, 396-397
  setting of, 21
  Skinner's view of, 371-372
  structure in, 494-496
  styles of, 230-231
  subject matter in, 490-496
  theories of, 362-364, 410-440
  variables of, 21, 24
  versus instruction, 479-480
  as vocational choice, 193-196
Teaching approaches, for the exceptional learner, 540-543
"Teaching is learning," 380-381
Teacher-learner interaction, 513
Teaching-learning process, 225-227, 303-304
Teaching machines, 492-494
Teaching method, 226-227, 487-488
  definition of, 487-488
  versus instructional method, 488
Teaching methods, 234, 235-239
  comparison of, 494
Teaching: From Command to Discovery, 497
Teaching games, 492
Teaching group, 574-577
Teaching process, theory of, 413-425
Teaching team, 6-12
Team approach, 6-12
Team cooperation, 389

Technology of Teaching, 372
Television, influence of, 123
Temper tantrums, 93
Tentative period, 194
Terminal assessment, 601-602
Testing
  assumptions underlying, 597-599
  educational versus psychological, 595-597
  history of, 17-18
  intelligence, 601
  norm-referenced, 621-622
  pretesting and posttesting, 613-631 passim
  role of, 594-595
Test results, grouping, 615-623
Tests, 594-630 passim
  classroom, 599-601
  construction of, 613-633
  efficiency of, 612-613
  error estimates in, 609
  forced-choice, 611, 613
  free-response, 611, 613
  objectivity of, 611-612
  reliability of, 608-613
  standardized, 599-601
  validity of, 607-608
Textbooks, sex biases in, 107
Theory, definition of, 214-216
Therapeutic experiences, 269-273
Third force, 59, 224
Three-step process model, 414-415, 418
Time-sampling error, 609
Toilet training, 93
Total person, 24-25, 48, 465-466
Touch, and personality development, 102
Traditionalism, 216-218, 229
Trait-treatment interactions, 234
Traits, 42-43, 47
Transcendental epistemology, 15-16
Transfer, 212, 213, 216, 223, 303, 313, 325, 335
Transference, 428-430
Trust, 228, 396-397
Turner's syndrome, 46
Twelve-year-olds, 149
Twin studies, 44, 47

Ultimate objectives, 305-306
Unconditioned stimulus, 446
Unconscious, 23, 52
Unconscious mind, 424-430 passim
Underachievement, 526, 527
  contributing factors to, 526
  remediation of, 527
Underachiever, 526, 527
  and IQ, 526

Validity, 607-608
Value clarification, 291-298